The Occult :
Church of Rome

Michael Hoffman

Independent History and Research

Coeur d'Alene • Idaho

THE OCCULT RENAISSANCE CHURCH OF ROME

Printed in the United States of America

First Edition

ISBN: 978-0-9909547-2-9

Independent History and Research, Post Office Box 849, Coeur d'Alene, Idaho 83816

RevisionistHistory.org
rarebooks14@imac.com

TABLE OF CONTENTS

"Depuis la Renaissance l'on tend á travailler de plus en plus passionnément pour l'avénement du Royaume des Sciences et du Robot social." [i]

Louis-Ferdinand Céline

---

[i] "Since the Renaissance there's been a tendency to work more and more passionately for the coming of the Kingdom of the Sciences and of the social Robot."

"You know that among the pagans the rulers lord it over them and their great men make their authority felt. This is not to happen among you."

Matthew 20:25-26

"Bastardo sodomita! Per i tuoi peccati Roma sarà distrutta." [ii]

Brandano da Petroio to Pope Clement VII

Dedicated to
Gordon Pratt

Introduction

This is a book consisting of neglected sources pertaining to the Neoplatonic syncretism of the Renaissance pontiffs, as well as their Hermetic-Kabbalistic theology, their usury and institutionalized subterfuge, which formed a *hidden concordance* within what had once been Jesus Christ's Catholic Church, but which had, by the early sixteenth century, been transformed into the Church of Rome, in the course of a little over one hundred years. We should not marvel at the speed with which the revolution was accomplished, in view of the fact that centuries later the *public emergence* of the usurper Church was made manifest in something approximating half the time (1965-2015).

Charity and justice necessitate stating from the outset this writer's observation that it would seem that the Holy Spirit guided many thousands of parish priests and many more laity throughout the Renaissance and post-Renaissance era, and that this guidance was also reflected in the lives of some bishops and cardinals. We cannot account for this supernatural mystery in terms of theology, except in the realm of the miraculous. We acknowledge that the Church of Rome in America in the nineteenth and twentieth centuries continued to produce Christians of exemplary character, such as Fr. Pierre De Smet and Fr. Joseph Cataldo in their work defending the American Indian; Providence nun Mother Joseph of the Sacred Heart, who founded twenty-nine charity hospitals, schools and orphanages; Fr. Charles Coughlin, Dorothy Day, Flannery O'Connor, and many more Catholic servants of God like them, who managed through grace, to preserve and personify the essence of the root Church of Jesus Christ that had been the Catholicism of old. Moreover, the mostly Irish-American and Italian-American Catholics with whom we were raised in the 1950s and early 1960s, had their faults certainly, but in the main were decent, honest and upright people with whom as a child and adolescent, we were fortunate to associate, and who to this day we recall fondly. In view of their kindness and dedication to God, some were surely saints, if known only to Him.

In the United States, in terms of Protestant adherence to the Natural Law, America became great as a result of that adherence, and much of the persecuting spirit of post-Renaissance Catholicism was vitiated by Catholicism's American sojourn (we note that even before they arrived on these shores, Irish-Catholics had little of the inquisitorial spirit, having been for centuries the object of inquisition by the British Crown). The unique situation of the Church in America having planted roots in a Protestant nation in the nineteenth century, is marked by the freedom of worship which Catholics enjoyed; and more than mere tolerance, the American experience was also unique for the freedom of opportunity it afforded. In 1831, President Andrew Jackson appointed a Roman Catholic, Roger B. Taney, as Attorney General of the United States. One does not shrink from terming it miraculous that five years later Taney became the fifth Chief Justice of the United States Supreme Court: the highest justice presiding over the nation's highest court was a member of a minority religion who decided the law in a majority Protestant land. [1]

It seems miraculous too that at the parish level so much that one can describe as the good spirit of immemorial Catholicism remained present in the pews, up to the 1960s, and in some cases even beyond that notorious decade. The Church of Rome being a hierarchical organization, it would be understandable to believe that it was the hierarchy of the Church that was responsible for the fine moral character of many Catholics, *prior* to the "post-Conciliar era," which became, in the wake of Vatican Council II in the pontificates of Paul VI and John-Paul II, the penultimate revolutionary dissolution (after five centuries of spasmodic moral and ethical subversion and degeneration at the top). It is at this juncture that we encounter yet another apparent miracle: the faith of the people somehow preserved many of them from complicity in the depravity to which the post-Renaissance hierarchy had sunk over hundreds of years, not the least of which was the secret and widespread, *systematic* molestation of children, enabled by bishops, cardinals and pontiffs.

The United States of America's premier campaigner for social justice and peace between nations in the years from 1932

---

[1]   Cf. Hoffman, "Chief Justice Roger Taney, A Profile in Courage," in *Revisionist History* no. 44.

through the early 1940s, was a Catholic priest who had a radio audience of nearly one-third of the entire country (a listenership estimated at 50 million, at a time when the population of the United States was some 132 million). This was the aforementioned Fr. Coughlin, who was eventually silenced and nearly completely suppressed by order of Pope Pius XII; a subversive diktat to which Coughlin subserviently submitted, to the detriment of the cause of world peace. This is merely one instance of the obstruction of the implementation of Christ's Gospel which obedience to the disaster-producing clique of popes has wrought.

The vast majority of the Catholic people and their parish priests, along with a tiny handful of prelates such as Cardinal McIntyre in Los Angeles, would never have dreamed of trading the Mass of the Council of Trent, itself only a slight revision of the Mass of the High Middle Ages and hence of European civilization at its zenith, for the New Order of Mass of Pope Paul VI of 1969, subject as it was to novelties and revisions of phenomenal mediocrity. Yet they did so out of "obedience." Of King George III, Thomas Paine wrote in 1776, "The sovereignty of a despotic monarch assumes the power of making wrong right, or right wrong, as he pleases or as it suits him." It would be a blasphemous lie to assert that Jesus Christ come to earth to enable a ministry of totalitarianism by "infallible" dictators, such as Paul VI. The very notion of such power being invested in one man bearing the title, "Supreme Pontiff," in connection with the Gospel of our Lord, is a mockery.

Much of the usury, deceit and occult ideology inflicted on the Church of Christ, beginning mainly in Italy in the fifteenth century, was due to the failings, incompetence or outright betrayal by various, nearly all-powerful human beings leading the Church and usurping the Petrine ministry. When in the nineteenth century Lord Acton departed the Church of Rome in the wake of the declaration of papal infallibility at Vatican Council I, he did so having pronounced a fundamental truth with regard to the fallen nature of *every* human being: "Power corrupts and absolute power corrupts absolutely." This book is a chronicle of that corruption.

Jesus promised never to abandon His *ecclesia* ("assembly of the ones who have heard the call"), so that the "gates of hell shall not prevail against it." The perception, however, that His *ecclesia* is directed by the cabal of Pharisaic-occult usurers and

Judases who have occupied Rome for more than five hundred years, is among the queerest we can imagine.

One need not be in Holy Orders in order to be qualified to opine that believers who endeavor to uphold Scripture, and the Tradition of the Early Church, and those examples directly and unwaveringly conforming to those twin sources of divine direction, with faith in Jesus Christ as our Savior, and hope in His promise of eternal life, *will never be abandoned or disappointed.*

His will is done on earth as it is in heaven, even at the beginning of this third millennium. *Jesus is the very spirit of Truth, and where there is Truth there He is.* Consequently, the true Christian welcomes and embraces the truth without fear. It is in the camp of the Adversary where dwell those who are fact-averse, and who call a man-made cult of Renaissance provenance, "The Faith."

What this book is not

Alexander Hislop was a Scottish Presbyterian minister who had very little (that we can locate) to say about the recrudescence of the religion of ancient Babylon within the creed of Orthodox Judaism. While the charge of Judaizing is generally a blanket condemnation falsely laid at the door of Martin Luther, it can be stated with accuracy that among the later Protestant fundamentalist sects of the eighteenth and following centuries, this Judaizing was a common feature. Hislop penned a pamphlet in 1853, *The Two Babylons: Their identity and the Present Antichrist Also the Last.*[2] In 1858 he enlarged it into a volume of more than 300 pages, bearing the title *The Two Babylons; or the Papal Worship Proved to be the Worship of Nimrod and His Wife,* which sold many tens of thousands of copies and has never been out of print. Between 1862 and 2015 *The Two Babylons* was reprinted at least forty-three times. Its thesis is common to the Protestant Fundamentalist sects and those that deny the divinity of Jesus, such as Jehovah's Witnesses: that the Catholic Church from the time of Emperor Constantine in the fourth century onward, became the Antichrist, and rapidly degenerated into a form of propitiation of pagan deities. The Church that fought the

---

[2] Edinburgh: W. Whyte & Co.

usurious Money Power to a standstill, the Church of Pope Gregory the Great, St. Augustine and St. Thomas Aquinas; the Church of Saxon England and King St. Edward the Confessor, is alleged to have been a sinkhole of heathen sorcery. Lest we imagine that such dementia was limited only to Protestant Fundamentalists of the most marginal sort, it was also reflected in the theology of the Rev. Charles Spurgeon, among the most influential of the English Victorian preachers of London, whose voluminous writings are revered by numerous schools of contemporary, conservative Protestant-Reformed thought.

Like Hislop, who not only paid no attention to rabbinic blasphemy and Kabbalistic paganism, but incorporated some of Judaism's occult traditions into his book, [3] Spurgeon believed that Judaism was superior to Catholicism, repeating the old chestnut that no Jew could be blamed for shrinking from horror at converting to Christ when confronted by the "superstitions of Rome." It seems that Rev. Spurgeon was somehow abysmally ignorant of Judaism, even though Dr. Alexander McCaul, the eminent Anglican Professor of Hebrew and Rabbinic Literature at King's College London, had penned an extensive treatise, *The Old Paths/Talmud Tested,* which had been prominently published in England in several printings, demonstrating that rabbinic Judaism was a system of magic and delusion founded not upon the Old Testament, which it nullified, but upon the Babylonian Talmud.

Spurgeon's folklore concerning Orthodox Judaism is so far off the mark as to be humorous, were it not for the fact that the conversion of precious Judaic persons is of signal importance for the salvation of souls. Indeed, the greatest liberator of Judaics in the Church age was the Roman Catholic itinerant preacher St. Vincent Ferrer. Spurgeon would have us believe that the many thousands of Judaic persons who Ferrer brought to Christ were worse off than when they bowed their knees to the "sages" of the Talmud, and the cadavers of rabbis in Judaic cemeteries every bit as relic-ridden as any Renaissance-

---

[3] Cf. Ralph Woodrow, *The Babylon Connection?* (2004), pp. 26-27. Woodrow errs when, in considering the significance of the incorporation of the pagan symbolism represented by obelisks, he dismisses it as a mere peccadillo. His mistake however, does not reduce the credibility of much of the rest of his refutation of Hislop's falsehoods and non-sequiturs.

Catholic basilica. We quote from a sermon by Spurgeon which is reprinted in his *Works*:

"The blood of Israel hangs in great clots upon the skirts of Rome and will bring down upon that thrice-accursed system the everlasting wrath of the Most High! Did they not grievously oppress the Jews in Spain and every other Catholic country— remorselessly hunting them down as if they were unfit to live— torturing them in ways that it were impossible for us to describe, lest your cheeks should blanch as you heard the horrible story? The men that were of the same race as the Christ of God were so hated by the professed followers of Jesus that no indignities were thought to be great enough, and no severities to be fierce enough for execution..."

Notice the carnal emphasis in Rev. Spurgeon's talk on the significance of the victims being (supposedly) members of ethnic Israel: "...*the same race as the Christ of God...*" Here is the special prerogative of race-obsessed Judaism from a race-obsessed Protestant "Reformer." If these victims had *not* been of the same race as Christ, would the Inquisition have been somehow less criminal? It is a lacuna of history that the Inquisition was to some extent, in lands such as Spain, in the hands of crypto-Judaics and their gentile Romanist agents, who employed it to crush conservative Catholics who sought to restore the Church to its pre-Renaissance mission, which included bearing witness to the evils of the occult, and the rabbinic counterfeit of the Old Testament.

The Protestant Isis

What does Spurgeon have to say about the atrocities Jews instigated against the Catholic Christians in the early centuries A.D., and of the "remorseless hunting" and "torturing" of English recusant Catholics in the reign of Protestant Queen Elizabeth I? The Queen's Torturer was the sadistic psychopath Richard Topcliffe:

"It was over the next decade (1578-1588) that he (Topcliffe), built the reputation that lasts to this day, both as an exponent of inquisition, and more generally as a hunter, snuffling out Catholic(s)... When we think of torture under Elizabeth it is the rack that first comes to mind, and there is no doubt that

Topcliffe was a master of its tensions and pressures. He was inventive in his cruelties, too, with all the thoughtful ingenuity of an artist perfecting his technique: the impact of a session on the rack could be magnified by placing a stone beneath the victim's spine, for example...

"Who authorized Topcliffe's work? Most obviously the Privy Council and, in particular Lord Burghley – and later his son Sir Robert Cecil. But there is no avoiding Elizabeth's complicity in such matters either, and she seems to have retained faith in his services until the end of her reign, despite the vicissitudes in his reputation....As for Topcliffe, he certainly felt confident enough to address at least one letter to Elizabeth as his 'goddess.' This was, of course, the routine iconography of the court and there are many examples of such rhetoric from Hatton, Raleigh and others. But for Topcliffe to be drawn into such a circle, a man whose sole political worth derived from his apparent talent and enthusiasm for torturing those considered enemies of the state, tells us something about Elizabeth's relationship with him..." [4]

In comparison to "Bloody Mary," her half-sister and predecessor on the throne, it was Elizabeth who deserved the stigma of "Bloody." Mary ought to more accurately be known as "Fiery," since her crime was the burning of Protestant dissidents, not butchering dissidents, as Elizabeth did. If these distinctions appear trivial, consider that a whole universe of information-warfare turns on them. In The Myth, Tudor Queen Mary I becomes the cruelest sort of prototypical Roman Catholic fiend, while Queen Elizabeth I is showcased as a paragon of humane liberalism, as historian Paul Johnson has the *chutzpah* to proclaim on p. 341 of his book *Elizabeth I* (1974): "For the first twenty years of her reign (1559-1579) Elizabeth refrained from virtually any form of state action against those who declined to accept the form of religion laid down by parliament. Even those who made no secret of their religious beliefs, and felt unable to take the oath to the Queen, were left unmolested, provided they expressed no ostensible disloyalty to the regime...She 'would not have any of the

---

[4] Matthew Lyons, "Richard Topcliffe: The Queen's Torturer," June 25, 2013. https://mathewlyons.wordpress.com/2012/06/25/richard-topcliffe-the-queens-torturer/

consciences unnecessarily sifted, to know what affection they held for the old religion."

This stance, *if it were an accurate appraisal*, would reflect a policy light years ahead of the attitude of the Catholic "Bloody" Mary. Johnson makes it look as though a hapless Elizabeth was forced into acting against Catholics due to their treason and disloyalty, otherwise she respected the sovereignty of their consciences. This is the universal virus of deception that attends the account of the reign of "Good Queen Bess." Queen Mary I is made the hideous Catholic foil to the liberated Protestant Elizabeth I. This fraud is repeated in virtually every Hollywood movie produced about Elizabeth up to the year 2016, as well as most of the leading biographies and histories published in English. The truth is very different, however. In 1559, *in the first year* of her ascension, Elizabeth enacted The Act of Uniformity, which massively violated the conscience of every Catholic in her realm, i.e. a slight majority of the English people at that time. Here was a law that was not only despotic, it was also undemocratic in the extreme. It directs that the Catholic Mass, which had existed in England for eleven hundred years, will be immediately outlawed. Only Church services based on the state-mandated, Protestant *Book of Common Prayer* were to be permitted:

"And further be it enacted by the queen's highness, with the assent of the Lords and Commons in this present Parliament assembled, and by authority of the same, that all and singular ministers in any cathedral or parish church, or other place within this realm of England, Wales...or other the queen's dominions, shall...be bounden to say and use the Matins, Evensong, celebration of the Lord's Supper and administration of each of the sacraments, and all their common and open prayer, in such order and form as is mentioned in the said book (the *Book of Common Prayer*)."

The penalty for the failure of a clergyman to conform to the *Book of Common Prayer,* or to adhere to the liturgical services in England as they had existed for eleven centuries and offer the Mass, rather than the official Anglican service, was the loss of office and income, and imprisonment for six months (for a second offense one year imprisonment was stipulated; for a third offense the penalty was imprisonment for life). If any

English man or woman were to speak against the *Book of Common Prayer* or in favor of the Catholic Mass, for a third offense the penalty was also life in prison. Anyone who sought to stay at home on Sunday and "having no lawful or reasonable excuse to be absent," refuse to attend the Protestant-Anglican service on Sunday, was subject to a fine. [5]

Life imprisonment for speaking against the *Book of Common Prayer* was "moderation"? This coercion of the consciences of her subjects was enacted by the authority of Queen Elizabeth, that reputed Protestant free-spirit so vastly superior to the repressive Catholic Queen Mary. What a farce. When the chasm between fact and fiction is as gaping as this, one wonders how the historians who peddle the legend of Elizabeth's religious tolerance can live with themselves. Twenty-fours years after Johnson, the agit-prop was maintained by another author of consequence, Alison Weir, in *Elizabeth the Queen* (1998; p. 335), who writes that in 1581, "Both Parliament and the Council had repeatedly urged the Queen to take stern punitive measures against the Catholic recusants...Although...she had hitherto preferred to act with moderation...she now recognized...that harsher sanctions were called for."

Elizabeth's murder of the Jesuit poet Rev. Fr. Edmund Campion, who had not at any time engaged in any conspiracy against her, is an indelible proof of her harrowing inquisitorial cruelty. [6] Campion was no Jew however, and does not seem to have elicited the sympathy and indignation toward his plight from Spurgeon and reformers like him, concerning the horrible

---

[5] Cf. Elizabeth's Act of Uniformity (1559), 1 Eliz. Cap. 2 in Henry Gee and William J. Hardy, *Documents Illustrative of English Church History* (1896), pp. 458-467.

[6] Cf. Michael Hoffman,"Edmund Campion's Jesuit Challenge to Bad Queen Bess," in *Revisionist History*, April-May, 2016. Pleas to the queen to spare Campion came from surprising quarters, including at least one principled Protestant. John Foxe possessed a humanity and decency like that of Campion. He was the author of the *Acts and Monuments of the Latter and Perilous Days*, known popularly as *Foxe's Book of Martyrs,* an encyclopedic account of — among other acts of persecution —the episodic Catholic killing of Protestants. Foxe was the leading Protestant martyrologist in the English-speaking world and it was Foxe who interceded for Campion. The noble Foxe believed that 'When men of false doctrine are killed, their error is not killed; nay it is all the more strengthened, the more constantly they die." It has taken Christendom many centuries to apprehend that wisdom.

abuse Campion suffered under a Protestant English government which, with the poet Edmund Spenser, viewed Queen Elizabeth I as the "New Isis."

Where, pray tell, came this Protestant-Elizabethan identification of the female head of the Church of England with Isis? Papists will imagine it came from some Protestant source. The cult of Isis was in fact transmitted into Christendom by the Neoplatonic-Hermetic papacy which, from Pope Alexander VI onward, adored the "cunning one," she "who tricked Ra by sending a serpent." [7] What was this serpent? At the time that Pope Alexander established the cult of Isis in his private papal apartment, the Catholic school of nominalism was replacing the warrant of Scripture with the *aggiornomento* of equity.

The troubadour of the cult of Queen Elizabeth I was Spenser. In his *Faerie Queen* he associated Elizabeth's cultus with Isis, and in particular with a certain attribute of the cunning one:

"His wife was Isis, whom they likewise made
A goddess of great power and sovereignty,
And in her person cunningly did shade
That part of justice which is equity." [8]

Equity is situation ethics by another name. By equity law, God's Word is "made of none effect" through the circumstances of the particular era in which man finds himself in history. Convoluted pretexts are put forth to justify this nullification. Equity has always bedeviled the Church, but it came boldly into its own with the rise of the Catholic nominalist school of

---

[7] Patricia Turner and Charles Russell Coulter, *Dictionary of Ancient Deities* (2000), p. 243.

[8] "The Faerie Queen" *in The Poetical Works of Edmund Spenser*, vol. III (Little Brown, 1842), Canto VII, p. 321.

theology. [9] Before John Calvin became a Protestant he was a precocious Catholic youth at the papist Collége de Montaigu, where he came under "the influence of the celebrated nominalist theologian, John Mair, regent at Montaigu from 1525-31." [10] After his father's death in 1528, Calvin was admitted to the Catholic law school at Orléans: "Calvin came to embrace the humanist approach to legal studies at Orléans. His circle of friends remained those sympathetic to humanism."[11] He subsequently transferred to the Collége Fortet, where he studied under the Catholic nominalists Francois Vatable and Pierre Danés, and encountered the leading law tome of French jurisprudence, the *Annotationes in quattuor et viginti Pandectarum libros* (1508) of Guillaume Budé, who: "deals with equity in *Annotationes in Pandectarum libros*. The fundamental principle of legal interpretation is that equity...is that which remits from the law." [12]

"The function of Equity is the correction of the (civil or common) law where it is deficient by reason of its...tendency to establish rules without exceptions."[13] Equity may be applicable and desirable in those cases entailing upon the laws of man; when applied to the laws of God however, equity is rebellion.

Calvin never repudiated the *epikeia* he imbibed from the Church of Rome's lawyers and theologians in France. After Protestants had been schooled in Catholic nominalist equity, some of them established their own version of it, supposedly

---

[9] "Ockham and Scotus in the Middle Ages...postulated the view that any 'good' is *nominal*, i.e., it is what it is only because God regards it as good. This was opposed to the 'realist' view that God wills a thing because it is good....Situation ethics, at the level of human value judgments, is likewise nominalistic...The whole mindset of modern man, *our* mindset, is on the nominalists' side...(the) flat assertion that there are no intrinsic values and that value exists only 'in reference to persons.' Martin Buber is...plain about it; he says that 'value is always value for a person rather than something with an absolute, independent existence." Joseph Fletcher, *Situation Ethics: The New Morality* (1966), pp. 57-58. On the Catholic nominalist school that adopted the equity of usury in the fifteenth century, cf. Hoffman, *Usury in Christendom*, pp. 162-173.

[10] Guenther H. Haas, *The Concept of Equity in Calvin's Ethics* (Paternoster Press, 1997), p. 7.

[11] Ibid., pp. 8-9.

[12] Ibid., pp. 36-37.

[13] Howard L. Oleck, "Historical Nature of Equity Jurisprudence," *Fordham Law Review*, vol. 20, no. 1 (1951), p. 23.

"independent of popery," after which equity could be openly embraced by Protestants while concealing its papist roots, just as Isis had been imported from Rome to London. When Spurgeon and Hislop and their innumerable followers hold aloft their "Reformed faith," derived from Calvinism, as the preeminent godly antidote and polar opposite to Rome's theology, they are perpetrating a fraud on the public, which is only exceeded in the depths of its brazen disregard for the facts of history, by the Right-wing Catholic campaign to brand equity-nominalism's situation ethics as a uniquely Protestant abomination, free of any Catholic origin or culpability.

The application of equity in both papal and Protestant theology arose mainly from the devil's desire to *unchain the Money Power,* previously bound in law and *practice* by the Catholic Church. This diabolic objective succeeded, as we shall see in a subsequent chapter, first by its rise within the papacy, over the strenuous protests of Martin Luther at a time when John Calvin was a child — and then, following suit, within the Reformed Church itself in so far as it heeded Calvin (and since he was not a pontiff, many Calvinists ignored or defied his nullification of the Biblical law against usury). Calvin had grudgingly permitted usury on grounds similar to those of the nominalist Catholic Johann Eck, Luther's theological nemesis, who had justified it on behalf of the Catholic usury bank of Fugger, although Calvin did not admit of this antecedent.

It may come as a shock to conservative Reformed Christians that Calvin, the celebrated champion of *sola Scriptura,* is: "not a Biblical literalist...Calvin's response is that the prohibitions against usury in the Old Testament are part of the civil legislation of the Jews. These laws were binding on the Jews in their society, but they are not for us today...(Calvin wrote), 'it follows that usury is not unlawful, except in so far as it contravenes equity...I therefore conclude that *usury must be judged, not by any particular passage of Scripture, but simply by the rules of equity.*" [14]

What bragging rights do Protestants possess over papist Catholics when the former resort to John Calvin as a faithful guide in the application of God's Biblical commands and standards on usury, when he permits lawyers' rules of equity to trump the statutes and commands in the Word of God? Some conservative pastors of Reformed churches have derogated the exigent question of how the love of money has come to be weaponized in Christendom, on the basis that the provenance of the weaponization is not clear, or that the law of God in the matter of profit on loans is a source of some confusion. What is confusing about Luke 6:30-36? Since the Word of God proclaims that the love of money is the root of all evil (I Timothy 6:10), should there not be a greater sense of urgency among the Reformed in resolving this alleged "confusion"?

It is important to make note of the fact that Calvin's statements on his permission for usury were put forth unadorned by duplicity, however. His equity was a fact he stated plainly and without circumlocution. He wrote of his preference for *epikeia* above the Logos, though not in those terms. His candor is found in all of his writings which we have reviewed, public and private. He had nothing to hide because

---

[14] Haas, op. cit., p. 120; emphasis supplied. Haas neglects to take notice of the extent to which Calvin hounded usurers and regarded them as unworthy of membership in the Christian congregation. When he was pastor in Geneva all profits on loans were banned and many capitalist businesses which we take for granted nowadays as supposedly benign and ethical, were severely restricted. Calvin regarded usury as a sometimes necessary but generally (with some exceptions), moral evil. Cf. this writer's *Usury in Christendom: The Mortal Sin that Was and Now is Not* (2012), pp. 186-187, 207-208 and 259-261. The Renaissance Church of Rome and its latter-day pontiffs maintained an elaborate pretense with regard to the dogma on usury, while redefining it in accordance with nominalism and equity, and then claiming that nothing had changed. A Conservative Catholic former professor at Notre Dame University contested our statements about the popes and usury by contending that the papist laws contra usury are still on the books. Actually they are not, having been removed from canon law, but even if the assertion were true, what exactly would that signify? The Communist Party's laws guaranteeing freedom of speech were never formally removed from the Soviet Constitution, yet the significance of those laws for the Russian and other captive peoples, was near zero. In fact, the disparity between what is on paper and what is actually forbidden or permitted in real life, compounds the corruption.

he was so steeped in the Church of Rome's modernizing legal philosophy that he could not see the Scriptural nullification at the heart of it (we are not excusing his faith in Catholic nominalist economic theory). Truly he was blind in this matter. But since he concealed nothing, then the case, pro or contra his position, can be argued on its merits and demerits without begging the question.

With Rome the obstinacy of its true believers seriously impedes clarity on the subject of *papal usury*, in that the denial of the fact of papal permission for profit from loans curtails an analysis of the consequences of that permission. Usurious Catholic banking is wrapped in dissimulation and sly euphemism; notably when profit gained from loans was explained away with the *lucrum cessans* escape clause, rather than terming it what it was: interest on loans. The papacy profited from the maintenance of dishonest, veiled forms of usury as early as the beginning of the sixteenth century, for instance in the traffic between Catholic bankers in the French city of Lyons, and the Vatican:

"The ability of the bankers to play with the exchange rates allowed them to loan money...and thus make a profit. Naturally each transaction necessitated two bills exchange: one that transferred the money to Lyons and the other that from Lyons transferred the money back to a beneficiary in Rome. These operations, moreover, allowed the bankers to avoid running afoul of the anti-usury laws, because the eventual profit was not a fixed sum as a percentage, but rather a recompense for risk, which varied from day to day. The interest rate was by this time an accepted part of financial dealings (and was attached to all the loans conceded to the Apostolic Chamber), but it was always specified that it was due to *lucri cessantis*." [15]

There is no evidence that John Calvin earned a dime from any form of usury operation. All evidence is that he forbade it in Geneva, Switzerland and drove usurers from the congregations in which he exercised oversight. Pope Pius IV: "The strength of that heretic (Calvin) consisted in this, that money never had the slightest charm for him." [16]

---

[15] Francesco Guidi Bruscoli, *Papal Banking in Renaissance Rome: Benvenuto Olivieri and Paul III* (2007) p. 183.

[16] Cf. Francois Guizot, "Calvin," in *Museé des protestants célébrés* (1822).

Spurgeon on "the Jews":

"Israel would never worship images, saints and virgins! Blessed were they as a nation for this thing, at least, that they utterly rejected the idolatry of which Rome is shamelessly guilty! It were far better to not be a Christian than to think Popery to be Christianity, for it is one of the vilest forms of idolatry that ever came from the polluted heart of man!"

Where is this racial Israel of which Rev. Spurgeon writes, which would "never worship images" and "utterly rejected...idolatry"? Has he heard of a book called the Old Testament, which contains a rather extensive record of Israel's episodic idolatry of every conceivable type? When, pray tell, did this cease? At the time in which Israel demanded of the Roman government the crucifixion of their Messiah? In the centuries afterward, when their religious masters residing in Babylon committed the spurious "Oral Law of Moses" to writing, comprising the Talmud and Kabbalah?

Of that "glorious Israel" that "utterly rejected...idolatry," it is said in the Old Testament, at Ezekiel 16:23-25: "To crown your wickedness...declares the Lord God...At the entry to every alley...you opened your legs to all comers in countless acts of fornication. You have also fornicated with your big-membered neighbors, the Egyptians...you do not act like a proper prostitute because you disdain to take a fee...you bribe them to fornicate with you."

What is the supposed righteousness of the race-obsessed Rev. Spurgeon's Christ-less Jews and Judaism, but the rags and tatters of perdition?

Rev. Spurgeon said of Jews: "Some are devout—devout men with some of whom it has been our privilege to have hearty fellowship in matters of common interest touching the things of God. When we have spoken together of the Providence of God and of faith in the Divine Mercy, we have been much of the same mind...we were able, in comparing notes, to feel the same zeal for the value of the Old Testament and for the Glory of the ever-blessed God!...I marvel not that Jews are not Christians when I know what sort of Christianity, for the most part, they have seen. When I have walked through Rome and countries under Rome's sway—and have seen thousands bow before the image of a woman carried through the streets—when I have seen the churches crammed with people bowing down before pieces of bone, hair and teeth of dead saints, and such like things—I have said to myself, 'If I were a worshipper of the One true God, I would look with scorn upon those who bow before these cast clouts, moldy rags, pieces of rotten timber and I know not what besides!' No, no, good Jew! Join not with this idolatrous rabble! Remain a Jew rather than degrade yourself with this superstition!" [17]

These so-called "Jews" (we are not sure how Mr. Spurgeon has ascertained for certain they are indeed the direct descendants of Abraham, Isaac and Jacob), congregate in graveyards and hold in awe and as material generators of spiritual power, the bodies of their deceased rabbis. Amulets are crafted by Orthodox rabbis for a fee of money (we possess a two volume set of a magic amulet-making manual recently published by Israeli rabbis). Either curses or protection are to be dispensed to those who wear those amulets.

What is sorriest about the macabre comedy that comprises Rev. Spurgeon's homily, is *his ignorance of the role of Judaic agents in transforming the Catholic Church from that of Christ to that of the occult, by embracing the superstitious doctrines of the very Judaism which he extols and imagines is entirely separate from post-Renaissance Catholicism.* In this regard he is as bamboozled as the Right-wing Catholics who are gulled by the Renaissance Church's outbursts against certain Jews, most of which were theatrical. Both the New Age occultist, the Protestant Fundamentalist, and the "conservative" Catholic believe that the Church of Rome in the Renaissance period under study, was the nemesis of all that Judaism represented, when in truth it was *the vessel into which Judaism poured its Talmudic and Kabbalistic sorceries and iniquities. After these had been fully absorbed into the corpus of the Church at the highest levels, only then did the Renaissance and post-Renaissance pontiffs mount their theatre of ostentatious "persecution" of Judaics*, which was still so much of a charade that when Pope Leo XIII issued his encyclical contra Freemasonry (*Humanum Genus*, 1884), he scrupulously

---

[17] "The Vine Of Israel: A Sermon Delivered by C. H. Spurgeon at the Metropolitan Tabernacle, Newington." (May 9, 1878).

omitted all mention of the Brotherhood's most virulent source of inspiration and direction, the rabbinic Kabbalah.[18]

Returning to Rev. Hislop and his *Two Babylons*, we note the degree to which Hislop was in revolt against the original classical Protestantism of the sixteenth and seventeenth century which identified the Roman Constantine as a Biblical hero, and the Church prior to the Renaissance as not generally stricken by corruption and defection.

In his acclaimed 1685 *Annotation Upon the Holy Bible*, the English Calvinist Matthew Pool (also spelled Poole), in his commentary on Revelation 13:6, wrote: "..for 'till the year 1260, when the Inquisition was set up, (the Doctrine of Transubstantiation having been about that time decreed by Innocent the Third, and confirmed by the Council of Lateran), the persecution was not great...the Doctrine of Transubstantiation, though it might be broached one hundred years before, yet was made no doctrine of their Church of Six Hundred Years after the first beginning of the papacy, and therefore cannot well be reckoned among Antichrist's first blasphemies."

In his introduction to Revelation 13, Pool places the rise of Antichrist in Rome three centuries *after* Constantine: "...we must distinguish between the rise and reign of Antichrist. It doth not seem to me reasonable to make his reign to commence higher (sooner) than 600 or 606, when he (the bishop of Rome) arrogated to himself the Primacy..."

Targeted toward lay consumption and commissioned by the Puritan Parliament of England at the time in which the Westminster Assembly sat (1643-1649), another Protestant commentary, the monumental *Annotations Upon All the Books*

---

[18] The Kabbalah consists of several books, the most notable being the *Zohar*, which was written, like the Babylonian Talmud, mainly in Aramaic. According to academic consensus, it was compiled in the thirteenth century by the Spanish Sephardic Rabbi Moses de León (1250-1305). But de León himself attributed it to a second century A.D. rabbi, Shimon ben Yohai, whose signature statement was "Even the best of the gentiles should all be killed," and who is a principal figure in the *Zohar,* which is a work of sorcery, extravagant superstition and depraved glosses on the Old Testament, though the Establishment press will have none of it, describing it as having a "playful appeal," and an "endearing mixture of whimsy and sanctity,"as well as a theology of the "universal supremacy of love." (Jeremy Adler, "Book of Splendour," *Times Literary Supplement*, November 4, 2016, p. 29).

of the Old and New Testaments,[19] had a heroic view of
Constantine, free of Hislop's frenzies and in keeping with the
early Christian perspective on this renowned protector of
Christ's people. In the annotations upon Revelation 12,
"Constantine and his successors" are referred to as "God's
deputies." His troops are equated with "Michael and his
angels," and as subduers of paganism. [20]

Hislop's other contention is that the Blessed Virgin Mary,
who, according to Catholic theology, was conceived without sin
(since Jesus was the New Adam who could incarnate only in
the uncontaminated "soil" of another Eden), and who is
sometimes referred to as the "Queen of Heaven," is actually a
barely concealed personification of a pagan goddess.

Who else should be Queen of Heaven other than the Mother
of God? Who would dare depose this humble ever-Virgin
Israelite who is the most blessed woman in all creation, having
been chosen to bear the veritable flesh of God Himself? It is a
tragedy that the radical Protestant reaction to her
disproportionate status within the papist cult of mariolatry, is
to depose her of the *rightful* and *proportionate* honor due her.
There is nothing occult about such appropriate honor. In fact, it
is the occult that dethrones Mary, and where she is dethroned,
into the vacuum rushes either a New Age or Judaic
("Shekhinah") goddess, or its polar opposite, the sterile, empty
quarter of a Protestantism that is often, in some churches,

---

[19]   London: John Legatt and John Raworth, 1645; reprinted in 1651, 1657,
and 1658. The annotations were by a team of scholar-theologians led by
Thomas Gataker, John Ley, William Gouge, Meric Casaubon, Francis Taylor,
Daniel Featley and John Reading. Their work came to be known as "The
Assembly's Annotations" and "The English Annotations."

[20]   Elizabeth Clarke notes with regard to Protestant annotations
(commentary) upon the Bible, that whereas Calvin commenced his religious
reform with the idea that the Bible text itself enabled "readers to discern God
more clearly," by the next century Calvinists were of the opinion that, in view
of the heresies that had arisen among the Bible readers, good English
scholarship was available to prevent the heresies and "fond fantasies" that
might result from the reading of an unannotated Bible. "Origen, it is
suggested, would not have castrated himself if he had read 'a Marginal Note
upon Matt. 19:12.' (The note in the Geneva Bible might well have deterred
any would-be self-mutilator, insisting that castration is only a metaphor for
'the gift of continence,' and that in any case, this gift is very rare: after all,
none 'may rashly abstain from' that Protestant institution of marriage)."
Clarke, *Politics Religion and the Song of Songs in Seventeenth Century
England* (2011) p. 108.

nearly blind to the most blessed woman in all creation, has no
female figure of abiding holiness in its art or liturgy, and often
only grudgingly acknowledges her in the most niggardly terms
of recognition.

It is true that in the minds of some followers of the Church
of Rome, Mary has been ascribed goddess-like qualities as the
so-called "Co-Redemptrix of the Universe." There is indeed
such a phenomenon as mariolatry, and it exists among some
percentage of the followers of Rome.

In our study of the incursion of paganism into Renaissance
Catholicism and the concealed veneration of the witch-goddess
Isis, we acknowledge that the witch-goddess cult existed in the
Church in the Renaissance and to give but one example, in the
papal apartment itself. This was *not*, however, "Mary disguised
as Isis."

The Papal Isis

Regarding the papal apartment in the Vatican, art historian
Anja Grebe writes, "Although the pope had "his bed chamber,
living quarters and treasure chamber there, the front areas in
particular...were used for official occasions such as diplomatic
receptions, audiences...consistories (meetings with cardinals),
the signing of treaties and even parties. In his diaries, the
pope's master of ceremonies, Johannes Burchardus (1440-1506)
distinguishes between the more public areas and the 'secret
rooms' (*camere secrete*) accessible as a rule only to a small
number of religious and secular dignitaries. The pope also
provided high-ranking visitors with guest rooms...Among his
first guests were King Frederick I of Naples and Marquis
Gianfresco II Gonzaga of Mantua, as well as the latter's
adversary, Charles VIII of France, in January, 1495. In
response to the newly completed frescoes, the French king is
reported to have declared that in no other palace had he seen
'decoration of this kind.'" [21]

The papal apartment in question comprises six rooms and
side-rooms located on the first floor of the papal palace. It was
constructed by order of Nicholas V, who reigned from
1447-1455. The papal apartment of the late fifteenth century
was designed by members of the Curia, including Annio da

---

[21] Grebe, *The Vatican: All the Paintings* (2013), p. 160.

Viterbo and Bartolomeo Platina, and painted by "Pintoricchio" (Bernardino di Benedetto di Bagio; 1453-1513). In those environs, Mary's image is entirely separate from the pagan images and depicted correctly, chastely and reverently, without occult symbolism. In that space, Isis is never equated with the Mother of Jesus: "...in the Vatican itself...there is a mural by the master Pintoricchio that shows Isis, seated on a Renaissance throne, instructing Hermes Trismegistus at her right hand and Moses at her left—which surely suggests...that the wisdom shared by the pagan and Hebrew sages was originally revealed neither by Yahweh nor by Jove, but by the consort of the dead-and-resurrected Egyptian Savior Osiris." [22]

This is depraved in and of itself. Because it did not defame Mary by incorporating her into the cult of Isis, does not exculpate this Renaissance papal devotion to pagan Hermetic syncretism. In this realm the Christian treads the razor's edge between the extremes of papalolatrous credulity and Protestant denial of Mary's significance. It is a minefield where precision, attention to context and respect for details that contradict one's thesis, are essential if an accurate account is to be rendered.

The Isis iconography in the papal apartment was no mere artwork, or whimsical elucidation of the follies of mythology. Its expression was pedagogical and worshipful—an evocation of the Neoplatonic-Hermetic theology *which had been alien to the Church until the Renaissance*. This fact is critically important if we are to maintain fidelity to the facts, rather than pursuing the highly partisan agenda of the nineteenth century researcher Hislop and an extremist faction within the Left-wing of seventeenth century Calvinism.

Pool, in his influential *Annotations*, while superior to Hislop, would nonetheless have us believe that the Church defected after six hundred years. He says this occurred because he opines that a literal belief in the words of Jesus Christ in John 6:53-57 is a sign of the Antichrist: "Verily, verily, I say unto you, Except ye eat the flesh of the Son of man, and drink his blood, ye have no life in you. Whoso eateth my flesh, and drinketh my blood, hath eternal life; and I will raise him up at the last day. For my flesh is meat indeed, and my blood is drink

---

[22] Joseph Campbell, *Mythic Worlds, Modern Worlds* (2003), p. 153.

indeed. He that eateth my flesh, and drinketh my blood, dwelleth in me, and I in him." Why are Catholics acolytes of the Antichrist if they believe the preceding words of the Gospel of St. John as the Church interpreted them from Justin Martyr onward?

Some Protestants forget what a struggle it was to win and hold formerly pagan lands for Christianity and its civilization. The very formation of what it means to be English occurred in the century Matthew Pool decreed to be the century when Rome lost the Faith. It was Arthur, his Catholic son Edward and equally Catholic grandson Athelstan, who laid the foundation for taking Wessex and Mercia from the savage Viking hordes, and uniting them under Athelstan, who was the first to rightfully bear the title *Rex totius Britanniae*. These Catholic kings fashioned the Anglo-Saxon nation. There is something repellant about an armchair Fundamentalist from the comfort of his study, dismissing this titanic Christian struggle and subsequent victory, as smacking of Antichrist because Catholics took Jesus at His word in John 6:53-57. Retroactive criminalization of the past is often a signpost of revolutionary dictatorship.

The Renaissance popes lacked the candor to publicly declare any such criminalization. Rather, they resorted to skullduggery as reflected in the papal apartment that paid *latria* to goddess Isis and her putative disciple Hermes Trismegistus—the infernal patron of the Catholic popes and theologians of that era (with honorable exceptions, among them Savonarola).

"It may seem astonishing that in the apartment of the pope, Christ's representative on earth, and moreover in a room dedicated to the lives of the saints, a number of whom sacrificed their lives in the fight against paganism, the ceiling is decorated with...Isis...the traverse arch depicts...a beautiful woman assuming her throne as the Egyptian queen Isis....Despite the fact that the legend takes place in ancient Egypt, Pintoricchio *depicts the figures in fifteenth-century dress.*" [23]

The papal worship of Isis in the late fifteenth century is apart from the *dulia* (veneration, as distinct from *latria*, i.e. worship), which the orthodox theology of the pre-Renaissance

---

[23] Anja Grebe, op. cit., p. 181; emphasis supplied.

ecclesia accorded to Blessed Mary. The Renaissance popes were conveying by means of the high art of the Italian masters (more seductive because of their incomparable aesthetic), *a symbolic continuity between the Egyptian religion and the papal religion* —a culmination of the Humanism which was derived from Neoplatonic-Hermeticism. Renaissance Rome's occultism was an Egyptianizing religion for which Isis was "Mistress of the Word in the Beginning." After the sorcery had taken sufficient and deep root, the Inquisition was revived to maintain a stage play for the non-initiated who needed to believe that the post-Renaissance Church was the same bastion of anti-occultism as the pre-Renaissance *ecclesia* had been. This hoax depended as much upon the psychology of self-deception among conservative Catholics, as the elaborate inquisitorial theatricals themselves, wherein expendable small fry were sacrificed for the sake of a *public image of reaction* that prevailed over the *covert reality of revolutionary occultism* installed in the depths of the Church.

Our sleuthing mission is concerned with the conspiracies of the sons of Belial (בְלִיַעַל) boring into the bowels of the Church of Jesus Christ. Yet in this process of detecting the Judas theology and its agents, one must exercise caution so that all is in proportion, and we do not commit the reverse error and strain at gnats (Matthew 23:24), becoming like "Zeal-of-the-Land-Busy," the character in Ben Jonson's *Bartholomew Fair*: a Protestant fanatic who mistook a basket of gingerbread-men pastries for "popish idols."

The Puritan concern for a living faith in conformity with the Gospel and an end to criminal politics was admirable. But much good will was squandered because a "Zeal-of-the-Land-Busy," such as Oliver Cromwell, suppressed the English Christian people's day of rest at Christmas, which paid honor to a date said to commemorate the glad tidings of great joy over the incarnation of Israel's Messiah. Zeal-of-the-Land-Busy condemned it as pagan. Protestant scholar Ralph Woodrow writes:

"But wasn't December 25th an evil day? Did not pagans honor this day as the birthday of the sun-god? Without attempting to go into details, let's assume December 25th was indeed an ancient, popular, pagan celebration in honor of the sun-god. Assume, also, that church leaders, seeking to do away with this pagan celebration, gradually replaced it with a celebration to honor the birth of the Sun of righteousness, Jesus Christ—on the same day. Was this substitution a dangerous compromise? Or an opportunity to "overcome evil with good" Romans 12:21? This could all be debated, I'm sure. But regardless of how this came right or wrong, Christmas became an established day on our calendar. The result has been that every year in many parts of the world, and in millions of cases, the story of Jesus Christ, his birth and life, is told. The Sun of righteousness (Mal. 4:2) has so far out-shined any former supposed sun-gods, Sol, Osiris, Horus, or Mithra do not even cross our minds...I have known people who would rather argue (even with unconverted people) that Christ was not born on December 25, than to put emphasis on the fact that *He was born*—regardless of when—and what He can do in our lives *now*!" [24]

The Church-period predating the Renaissance was not perfect and some seeds of the occult—principally Neoplatonism —had been planted well before the Quattrocento. There were also terrible errors committed during the Crusades, including the Sack of Constantinople in 1204, which fatally sapped Christendom's eastern Byzantine outpost and contributed to its long decline, and eventual catastrophic fall to the Ottoman Muslims in 1453.

Long before Vatican Council I, the idea of the infallibility of the pope had metastasized in the medieval period, as witnessed in the canonizations of saints, in which it was held that the judgment of the pontiff was infallible. We can trace this development to the period 1050-1150 when the Bishop of Rome and his Curia began to usurp from local bishops the one thousand-year-old subsidiary function of proclaiming the sainthood of a deceased local Christian, i.e. the certainty that the person was in heaven. Papal claims to absolute, supreme authority were enlarged by the demise of subsidiarity.

Circa 1040, Pope Benedict IX issued the first decree of canonization. His language was unprecedented in Christ's ecclesia: *"Statueremus et decenemus"* (We establish and decree"). His establishment and decree was to the whole Church by apostolic authority, asserting, in this instance, the

---

[24] Woodrow, *Christmas Reconsidered* (2006), pp. 20-21 and 41.

sainthood of the late Simeon of Syracuse, an itinerant monk. This represented the marginalization of the local church and its bishop, in favor of the bishop of the diocese of Rome. Immemorial Christian practice had granted the right of proclaiming a Christian a saint to the local bishop. It was a species of modernist innovation to take that right away. Over a long and arduous period of evolution, the *gradual process* of papal monopoly over sainthood culminated in the declaration by Urban VIII in 1634, of the reservation of that right exclusively to the pontiff.

Our concern is for the study of the development of absolute obedience to the Bishop of Rome without which the Tridentine Latin Mass could not have been suppressed (some prefer the term "derogated"), in 1969 and thereafter, throughout nearly the whole Church. The success of the suppression depended upon the loss of memory among the laity and priests, of the Tridentine Mass and its subsequent replacement by a liturgy of the reigning pope (Paul VI). If rights of local bishops in such matters had not been gradually extinguished, prelates such as Cardinal James McIntyre in Los Angeles and an estimated half dozen other bishops and cardinals in favor of the Tridentine Latin Mass in America, would have created comparatively large havens of liturgical preservation. These very likely would have saved generations of Catholics from imposed amnesia with regard to the suppressed rite.

The Middle Ages also saw the rise of a disconcerting obsession with making contact with the physical remains of the corpses of those declared to be saints. This focus on dead matter and anatomical parts of saintly cadavers ("relics") both real and fake, resulted not only in a lucrative traffic that would become a grievance of the Reformers, it did, under certain (not all) circumstances, come to dominate medieval conceptions of the Gospel, lessening emphasis on the paramount value of a *personal spiritual relationship with the living God*, adherence to faith in Him and the obedience to His commandments which arises from that faith, and which contributes to the Kingship of Christ. It would be wrong to dismiss relics altogether, or the pilgrimages that grew up around them, but it seems equally wrong that such customs would be allowed to become rife with superstition and an unbalanced emphasis that detracted from the daily struggle to live according to a Biblical standard.

Nonetheless, the medieval Church for all its faults, was still the Church of Jesus Christ, the scourge of usurers, evangelizer of millions of pagans, and the source of laws of liberty by which a free people are governed (such as the Magna Carta, in large part the result of efforts by the Catholic Archbishop of Canterbury, Stephen Langton). The rule in Britain of King Arthur (sixth century), King Alfred the Great and St. Edmund of East Anglia (ninth century), and St. Edward the Confessor (eleventh century), are among the most exemplary templates of Christian government in the history of our civilization. As Eleanor Parker observes, "AElfric's description of St. Edmund is a portrait of an ideal Anglo-Saxon king: wise, humble, virtuous and kind to the poor and weak." AElfric of Eynsham:

"Edmund the blessed, King of the East Angles, was wise and honorable, and always honored Almighty God in noble conduct. He was humble and virtuous and endured so resolutely that he would never submit to shameful vices, nor on either side deviate from his virtuous practices, but was always mindful of the true teaching: 'Have you been appointed as ruler? Do not exalt yourself, but be among men as if you are one of them,' (Ecclesiasticus 32:1). He was generous to the poor and like a father to widows, and with benevolence always guided his people to righteousness, and restrained the violent, and blessedly lived in the true faith." [25]

By their fruits ye shall know them. The fruits of the Church prior to the Renaissance were spectacular. Of course, God preserved His people in both the Renaissance and post-Renaissance, as we noted at the outset, and as we discover in the lives of saints such as Joseph of Cupertino, Father Damien of Molokai, Brother André and other post-Renaissance Catholics; preserved by grace miraculous. Surely there are saints today in the surviving traces of the immemorial Church, gripped as it is in a crisis which is not new. Crisis is the condition of the Church. It was in crisis when St. John wrote the Book of Revelation.

---

[25] W. W. Skeat, *Passio Sancti Eadmundi* (cf. *Ælfric's Lives of Saints*, EETS 94 and 114, vol. II, pp. 314-334); translated from medieval English by Eleanor Parker (http://aclerkofoxford.blogspot.co.uk/2014/11/eadmund-se-eadiga-eastengla-cynincg.html).

Acknowledgment

As an independent scholar without institutional affiliation, the completion of this book was dependent on benefactors who generously contributed to support our research and writing. Unfortunately, the notion that "error" has no rights has gained a foothold in the United States of late, a fact which would have appalled the Founding Fathers, who considered the doctrine one of the most pernicious aspects of the fratricidal wars of religion in the Old World. Because of this circumstance, we will not name our benefactors in these pages, lest they become a target for loss of reputation, career, or worse. They are known to God and this writer, and our prayer is that their reward will be great, and that tolerance and respect for Christians who radically dissent from the reigning consensus in matters of history and religion, will be restored.

Chapter I

More Catholic than the Pope

The Catholic-Kabbalist Giles of Viterbo gave the inaugural address at the Fifth Lateran Council, where he urged Julius II to crush the aggression of the Islamic Turks. In many cases one can take incidents like that in the lives of the various Catholic players who people our Renaissance chronicle, and extrapolate from those acts the conclusion that they were, for all their "imperfections," stalwarts of the Faith, who may have "flirted with" or "dabbled in" the occult, or occasionally "went astray" within it, but for the most part they accomplished much good for the true Church in spite of these peccadilloes. That sort of reasoning is like saying that on his way to return the thirty pieces of silver, Judas gave an inspirational, impromptu talk to a gathering of Jews, admonishing them to defend elderly women when they are beset by robbers, and thus we must not be too harsh on him.

Some of the evil-doers profiled in this book did some good things, in addition to some very bad ones, and they may have uttered pious and orthodox statements from time to time. In San Francisco, at his People's Temple, Jim Jones funded a soup kitchen that served one and all, no questions asked. Those who would modify the judgment of history on Jim Jones of Jonestown because he distributed free food to an impoverished community, are probably not the ideal audience for this book. The scoundrels we study remain even to this day some of the most accomplished master deceivers in western history. The fraud and masquerade we encounter in these pages is not only a product of a particular conspiracy or cabal, it is older than the pyramids and of an institutional character. One essential element of these diabolists is their doubling: they are two-faced operators for whom double-thinking, double-dealing and double-talk are second nature. The extent of their Janus character would seem to be of an immensity greater than we can imagine. We are in the presence of the servants of an intelligence almost without limit; and second only to God. It is a distant second, but it is nonetheless of a vastness in terms of the extent of its craftiness, guile, deviousness and subterfuge, as to dwarf the ratiocinative powers of mere human beings.

The epistemological problem an investigator and historian of the actions and impact of this intelligence faces, is in the matter of intention. Much of what the force behind Cryptocracy achieves is so fantastic that humans have difficulty embracing the reality of it, and as a defense-mechanism they dismiss aspects of it which they may occasionally glimpse in their otherwise quotidian world, as "coincidence."

Therefore, one hesitates to present what one believes to be true because it is in the nature of mankind to refuse to believe it. The scholar of secret societies takes the risk of damaging his credibility in the eyes of the average reader or listener, by divulging the darkest corners of his research, and hence, there is the temptation to suppress the most freakish and eerie data, and limit oneself to less threatening information and conclusions. If we were to succumb to this temptation, however, then the writing of this book would be pointless. We will risk our credibility in order to convey what we believe to be the whole truth, as we can grasp and articulate it.

In occult lore the patron of the Vatican is not St. Peter but his double, the deity Janus, who in legend also bears a key. The Vatican, together with the district of London known as "the City," and Jerusalem, are citadels of occult corruption. The Vatican seems to have had that destiny imposed on it intentionally, from antiquity. The capital of the Church of Rome's double-talk, double-mind and double-dealing, has as its tutelary deity the Roman god Janus; the god of beginnings, and of doors and passageways. He who held the key of Janus had tremendous authority. The status of Janus was not minor. He was of cosmic significance: *"divum deus"* (god of gods). [1] These facts were not lost on the Neoplatonic-Hermeticists:

"According to Aulus Gellius, the word (Vatican) derived from the ancient custom of seeking prophecies (*vaticinii*) from the guardian deity of the site, and Festus Pompeius [2] similarly connected it to seers (*vates*)...No student of the Vatican's pre-Christian importance for occult Rome was more ardent than

[1] Simon Hornblower and Antony Spawforth (eds.), *The Oxford Classical Dictionary* (2003), p. 793.

[2] A circa second century A.D. Roman lexicographer.

Giles of Viterbo. Keenly interested in the ancient Etruscans, especially their reputation for esoteric religious lore, Giles points out in his *Historia XX saecolorum* that Janus, the founder of the Etruscan religion, had been the patron deity... Hence, the ancient cult of Janus in the Vatican meant that from the earliest times this Roman site had been consecrated for the true religion...A further confirmation of this, Giles suggests, appears in the parallel of Janus and St. Peter as key-bearers...the *Mons Vaticanus* (w)as the true holy mountain, and from this particular locus of sanctifying grace the whole world came to be governed." [3]

Hermeticism was an elitist occult philosophy which flourished within the papacy and Neoplatonic Vatican networks from the Renaissance onward. It claims privileged possession of a secret knowledge from antiquity which betokened the potential to revolutionize the believer's understanding of existence. Access to this knowledge is reserved for the highest levels of the Church of Rome and its agents.

The occult Church of Rome revealed itself in the art and architecture which it sponsored. In many cases ecclesiastical art and architecture of the Renaissance era is a hieroglyphic representation of theological innovation — the new religion publicly presented in a visual language.

Here we encounter Humanism opposed to Divinism. As categories, Humanism together with Neoplatonism represent pagan subjectivism advertised as the free spirit's liberation, just as recourse to the rabbinic texts was presented in the Renaissance in the same terms, as humanity being free at last to access the limitless availability of all knowledge, as a first step in the escape from Catholic bigotry to Catholic liberalism, and from a Scripturally-faithful Catholicism to a pagan gnosis. At the close of the Middle Ages, the early Humanists cultivated the ground for the coming re-entry of Neoplatonic-Hermetic-Kabbalism, a rebirth of the sorcery and heathenism against which the God of Israel had warred in the Old Testament: "It was the fourteenth century crisis of faith in institutions and human virtue that brought into being the first phase of the

---

[3] Charles L. Stinger, *The Renaissance in Rome* (1998), pp. 184-185.

humanist movement. The hope of Petrarch, his followers Boccaccio and Salutati, and later generations of humanists, was that the sufferings of the present world could be remedied by recovering the virtue of the ancient world they admired so much, and principally the ancient pagan world...

"As in other humanist works of the fifteenth century...Ficino had a vision of what Christianity could be that is higher and finer than the historical Christianity practiced in his time. The vision was most famously captured in the religious practices depicted in Thomas More's *Utopia*, written thirty-two years after (Rev. Fr. Marsilio) Ficino's apologetic tract (*De christiana religione*) and...in dependence on Ficino's theology. Ficino in 1474 is calling for Christians to reform their own theology and praxis along lines similar to those advocated by Pico della Mirandola twelve years later." [4]

In the course of this pilgrimage, the Humanists picked up, from the Midrash on Noah and Ham, racism, the rabbinic disease, along with the rabbinic theory of Black African subhumanity (Maimonides, *Guide of the Perplexed,* in the uncensored Shlomo Pines translation). It is an irony of history that rabbinic racism entered the West in earnest through the popularization, among the ecclesiastical and cultural intelligentsia, of Kabbalistic, Midrashic and Maimonidean texts and traditions.

In the name of the expansion of knowledge the Renaissance contracted it. God's light is all expansive, never ending and unlimited. The Renaissance spirit is the embodiment of fraud: the exploration of the bogus "freedom" the serpent offered in the Garden. The "freedom" of the serpent is not a limitless universe, but a hermetically sealed prison, the claustrophobia and blindness of human subjectivity, the theater of our mirrored ego mistaken for the cosmos. The enemies of this gnosis were Augustine and Aquinas, orthodox Catholic guides to the cosmic mind of God, and God's unfettered Creation. "We see the things you created because they exist. But they exist only because you created them" (*The Confessions of St. Augustine,* XII). Reality exists within and is generated by the mind of God, the limitless expanse. During and after the Renaissance this reality was eclipsed and falsified by the

---

[4] Jens Zimmerman, *Re-Envisioning Christian Humanism* (2016).

doctrine of the Kabbalah: *Man, the Measure of All Things*. This found its expression in Pico della Mirandola's *On The Dignity of Man*, a treatise which Pope "Saint" John Paul II regarded as blessed and seminal. The project of "liberation" was in actuality an occluding, self-referential construct which limited humanity to one severely crippled and warped corner of experience, giving rise to the techno-nihilist hell today, predicated upon, paradoxically, mystical superstitions tempting us to play god. Succumbing to these temptations leads to the death of nature, not its enhancement. The great contest in our time is between medieval-Catholic fidelity to nature and Renaissance neo-Catholic consent for the god-man who will "improve" and "perfect" it.

From the Renaissance onward, the voice of God and the Word of God were diminished, eclipsed by the human will, proceeding from the exalted image of the Catholic-Kabbalistic man-god, to the Protestant utilitarian *epikeia* of John Calvin, the lawyer who "reconciles" the divine law on usury, through to an accommodation with the situation ethics of the Renaissance, doing violence to the Logos in the process.

The vision of humanity as the Creator's image-bearing beings, endowed by that Creator with unalienable rights, is obliterated by the revolt against the Creator's Law—statutes and judgments which were transmitted to men and women for the protection and enhancement of their iconic status as *imago Dei*, with God-given rights that are not to be revoked by man. Any revocation is instituted by rebels against God. The primary motivation for this revocation is the lust for money, which in the Renaissance, for the first time in Christian civilization, began to be formally instituted in the form of ecclesiastical permission for subjecting the human being to exploitation by the renting of money. The image of God would henceforth be commodified: the human endowed by God was lowered to the status of the subhuman, the consumer, degraded by a mechanism for aping creation, the process of money breeding money. Man did not evolve from apes. The ape was once a man and under the spell of the Money Power became the beast we have with us today, in designer jeans and a T-shirt.

Another rabbinic metaphysic: an artificial dichotomy constructed from the promulgation of the illusion of two beings, the *human* and the *hominid*: the humans possessed of the spirit of God, and the hominid representing the clutter of useless eaters, the "supernal refuse" as Rabbi Shneur Zalman of Lyady termed them; the occult teaching that there are people who resemble humans but have no God-spirit. Here is the Jew/*goy* divide, expressed in the western occult in categories such as the secret society dichotomy of "initiate and cowan," or "reality and phenomena":

"At Cambridge University, Lytton Strachey was a member of the Apostles—more properly, the Cambridge Conversazione Society—whose secret proceedings, the reading and discussion of papers behind locked doors...were governed by principles of absolute candor. In the lingo of the (Cambridge) Apostles, other people were mere 'phenomena' while they themselves were 'realities.'"

Since the Renaissance, Rome has been less the Catholic Church and more its own Church, of Rome that is—a Neoplatonic-Hermetic secret society—the *locus classicus* of which is the Kabbalah, repository of "secret and most arcane wisdom," and the legends and texts attached to the mythical figure of Hermes (Mercury) Trismegistus. [5]

The usury, magic and paganism which captured the Vatican in the era under examination is vigorously denied by true believers who simply will not allow themselves to countenance it. They choose delusion over truth and call themselves followers of the world's greatest truth teller. This bipolar mentality is of enormous utility to the dark forces under study. "Traditional" Catholic Bishop Richard Williamson wrote in his column, *Eleison Comments,* of April 5, 2014, titled "Canonizations Unreal":

"The 'canonization' of two Conciliar Popes, John XXIII and John-Paul II, is scheduled for the last Sunday of this month, and many believing Catholics are scared stiff. They know that the Conciliar popes have been (objective) destroyers of the Church. They know that the Church holds canonizations to be infallible. Are they going to be forced to believe that John XXIII and John-Paul II are Saints? It boggles the mind. The

---

[5] In the thirteenth century the rabbi and Kabbalist Moses de Leon wrote concerning the culmination of the theology that was originally an oral transmission of esoteric doctrine which was committed to writing in the early centuries A.D: "This is what is called 'kabbalah' (reception), owing to the fact that it is a reception (traceable back) to Moses from Mount Sinai."

Archbishop (Marcel Lefebvre) said that like the mass of modern men, the Conciliar Popes do not believe in any truth being stable. For instance John-Paul II's formation was based on truth evolving, moving with the times, progressing with the advance of science, etc. Truth never being fixed is the reason why in 1988 John-Paul II condemned the SSPX (Society of St. Pius X) Episcopal Consecrations, because they sprang from a fixed and not living or moving idea of Catholic Tradition. For indeed Catholics hold, for example, every word in the Credo to be unchangeable, because the words have been hammered out over the ages to express as perfectly as possible the unchanging truths of the Faith, and these words have been infallibly defined by the Church's popes and Councils."

Nevertheless, "The vigilance and the pastoral solicitude of the Roman Pontiff...according to the duties of his office, are principally and above all manifested in maintaining and conserving the unity and integrity of the Catholic faith, without which it is impossible to please God..." [6]

The "traditional" Catholic writer dares to use his conscience and private judgment to disclaim the judgment of the Apostolic See which is to be disclaimed by no one. Nor can it be judged.

"Traditional" Catholics quote Vatican Council I and omit a key sentence from its decree. Here it is: "...the See of St. Peter always remains unimpaired by any error..." We know of "traditional" Catholics who revel in this astonishing, "infallible" statement and at one time quoted it often, but now, not quite as often. The late twentieth and twenty-first century popes view these "traditional" and "conservative" Catholics as ignoramuses sadly in need of initiation into the hidden verities of the Church, as understood by the pontiff and the hierarchy, in all secrecy.

Imagine what an inside joke it must be in Rome when the "traditional" Catholics come calling and boldly declare that, when it comes to Judaism, they want the Church returned to the way it was before Vatican II. "Guys," the cardinals and clerics are thinking, "what you wish for *is now, and has been, for five long centuries*. The only difference being that *we went public with it in 1965*."

---

[6] Pope Benedict XIV, Apostolic Constitution Pastoralis Romani Pontificis, March 30, 1741; excerpted in *Papal Teachings: The Church* (St. Paul Editions, [1962], p. 31.

The Second Vatican Council was the culmination of Renaissance popery. The gnosis of *Renaissance* popes is reflected in the theology and actions of *modern* Popes Paul VI, John Paul II, Benedict XVI and Francis. The Roman Church in the Renaissance did not have a "vacant see." All of the pontiffs who reigned (with the exception of the Avignon interregnum), were incontrovertibly popes and some of those popes approved the overthrow of Catholic dogma that had been held by all the Church since the first century A.D. The others who did not overthrow it condoned the revolution by the fact that they did not restore the dogma. Those popes were not just material heretics, they were formal ones.

The "Conservative" and "traditional Catholic" movement as now constituted is doomed to failure because the post-Renaissance popes of Rome and their hierarchies will not be taught doctrine and history by "traditionalist" cowans, dupes and *goyim*. The post-Renaissance popes and their hierarchies possess the key to a mystery of history which the "traditional" Catholics do not: the "traditional Catholic" papacy and its administrative organs and instruments radically *departed from the dogma of the Church, beginning around the last decades of the fifteenth century. The magisterial dogmas that were tossed away were never restored.* For five hundred years the three Traditions of the Renaissance Church of Rome have been: 1. Judaism and the occult; 2. Lying and deceit; and 3. The root of evil itself — the legalization of the love of money.

When "traditional" Catholics appeal for a restoration of tradition, what can be the reaction of the contemporary Vatican's bishops, cardinals and pope, other than mirth and mockery? If one desires 500 years of Catholic tradition, then *look to the Second Vatican Council and you will find the culmination of five hundred years of Renaissance occult Catholic tradition,* contrasted with fifteen hundred years of Catholic Truth as taught by Jesus, the Apostles, the Fathers of the Early Church and most of the theologians of the Middle Ages.

The Vatican II document *Nostra Aetate* was the public acknowledgement of the accommodation and blending of the Roman Church with Pharisaic Judaism which had been underway since the late 1400s. This sub-rosa hybrid process started in the Renaissance era with Judaizing popes such as Alexander VI, Leo X, Sixtus V and Clement VII. This clandestine fact is part of the illumination process of high-level initiates at the Vatican, who are informed sub-rosa that "traditional Catholicism" is hopelessly compromised and double-minded, in that it claims to oppose Pharisaic Judaism and yet it ignorantly pledges allegiance to all popes previous to Vatican II, when in fact some of those pontiffs were as much in league with the Talmudic/Kabbalistic imperium as Popes Paul VI, John Paul II, Benedict XVI or Francis.

One of the reasons why the "traditional" Catholic movement has been outclassed and out-fought by its enemies is that many "traditional Catholics" believe the myth that the Judaizing of the Church commenced with the Second Vatican Council and the popes thereof. Until Catholics confront the *full history* of the panoply of papal treason and alliance with Talmudic Judaism, they will be fighting a Vatican that smirks at their naiveté, and accords to itself the patriarchal task of gradually initiating childish traditionalist leaders into the elder gnosis of post-Renaissance "Catholicism"—the traditions of the Pharisees and the love of money—which Jesus Christ, the Apostles, and the Fathers of the Early Church vigorously challenged and exposed with every fibre of their being.

To win in chess one needs to stay at least three or four moves ahead of one's opponent. In the game at hand, the Vatican Cryptocracy is three or four light years ahead of "traditional" Catholics. The *cri de coeur* should be, we want the Church restored to the way it was *before the Renaissance*— before the de facto legalization of the mortal sin of usury, the crucial clandestine support for the Talmud and Kabbalah, and the permission to lie and deceive (mental reservation and equivocation). Until these three sides of the Renaissance papal pyramid are dismantled, there can be no "restoration" of the True Church.

These are radical truths which many will shun so as to return comfortably to their candy-coated world of make-believe, where they may soothe themselves with corrupt delusions and reassuring myths. But in the combat for Christ's Church there can be no half-strength measures and no compromise with the harsh truth about the ecclesiastical history of the Father of Lies. Either we are for the whole truth or we are nothing. Either we face the facts and struggle on the basis of the demands of revelation, or we will answer for it in this life and the next. One of the best summations of the Process we are studying was put forth by Socrates Scholasticos (380-439 A.D., alternately spelled "Scholasticus"), in his *Ecclesiastical History*. In volume one, chapter 22 he analyzes the infiltration methods of the Manicheans as they sought to subvert the Church with deceptive pseudo-Christian texts as part of their conspiracy: "The contents of these treatises are apparently accordant with Christianity in expression, but thoroughly pagan in sentiment."[7]

Scholasticos' insight into the agents of paganism inside the Church centered on their *"parasitically surviving within Christianity" by using the development of doctrine as their vehicle.* Here is unveiled the neopagan syncretic theology of the Renaissance papacy behind the appearance of orthodoxy; a theology which never lifted its hold over the Church of Rome, not even under Pope Leo XIII, the so-called "Light from Heaven" and supposed scourge of Freemasonry who refused to expose the rabbinic-Kabbalistic foundation of the masonic order in his famed 1884 "anti-masonic" encyclical *Humanum Genus*. Consequently, the encyclical constitutes a colossal act of misdirection. Furthermore, on his watch, Pius X chose the personnel who were the authors of the 1917 Code of Canon Law, which omitted all mention of the mortal sin of charging profit on loans.

These highly esteemed and celebrated "conservative" pontiffs, who are revered as "paladins of pious Catholic orthodoxy," failed to assault the axis of the evils they purported to address. They excoriated symptoms and by so doing they lent to the Church of Rome in that time an undeserved public relations reputation for unmasking and combatting occult subversion. The calculated dissimulation of these popes testifies to the fact that the arcane Neoplatonic-Hermetic-Kabbalist-Renaissance theology is untouchable in papal Rome, no matter which pontiff, Liberal or Conservative, occupies the "Chair of Peter," and no matter how many thundering

---

[7] *The Ecclesiastical History of Socrates Surnamed Scholasticus* (fifth century AD; English translation 1853), vol. 1, p. 57. The Manichaeans, like Kabbalistic Orthodox Judaism (for example Chabad-Lubavitch), promulgated the doctrine of reincarnation (also known as "transmigration of souls"). Socrates Scholasticos/Scholasticus writes, "Manichaeus...distinctly affirmed a transmutation of bodies, a notion which closely approximates to, and was doubtless borrowed from, the opinions of Empedocles, Pythagoras and the Egyptians, respecting the transmigration of souls."

denunciations they directed at the modernist and masonic branches of the Renaissance theology.

One reason the covert pagan movement that came to the fore in the Catholic Renaissance survived was its secret alliance with and submission to papal authority and supremacy. Its leaders who did so (Father Ficino, Giovanni Pico della Mirandola, Johannes Reuchlin and many more), lived to freely pass on their spiritual bacillus, while equally diabolic occultists such as Giordano Bruno, were burned — not for their ideas, but for their defiance of popery. Consequently, the Neoplatonic-Hermetic heretics were usually almost always wearing a highly pious mask, outwardly conforming and deferential to the authority of the Supreme Pontiff.

The special protection afforded the occult virus which Rev. Fr. Marsilio Fincino and the Kabbalah-crazed Count Giovanni Pico della Mirandola [8] and others like them cultivated in the deepest bowels of the Church, has never been expelled. It remains the arcane gnosis of the post-Renaissance papacy. It made the papal permission for usury possible. It institutionalized equivocation, lying and child molestation. (The foundations of the institutionalization extend as far back as the beginnings of clericalism, and secrecy for the sake of the protection of the "higher-souled" clergy and their operations, as exposed by St. Peter Damian in the middle of the eleventh century).

The special protection afforded the occult virus made possible the public emergence of the doctrine of the Second Vatican Council document, *Nostra Aetate*, which denounced "anti-Semitism" (a phrase that can mean almost anything), without warning of the anti-*goyimism* of the sacred rabbinic texts of Talmudic-Kabbalistic Judaism, thus creating an unequal equation, conveying an advantage to the "persecuted" enemies of Christ; while hatred toward the followers of Christ, and gentiles in general, went unmentioned and unlamented by the Second Vatican Council.

Notice we do not say that the occult virus made the doctrine or the ideology itself possible, but rather *the public emergence*

---

[8] Giovanni Pico della Mirandola should not be confused with his nephew, *Gianfrancesco* Pico della Mirandola. They differed in age by only six years. Gianfrancesco attached himself to Fr. Girolamo Savonarola and his reaction against the conspirators, but whether sincerely or as an infiltrator and spy, remains a point of historical contention.

of the doctrine and ideology was made possible, timed to coincide with the *zeitgeist*. The doctrine and the ideology pre-date by centuries Rousseau, Kant and the French Revolution, and by decades Calvin and Luther. Protestantism, occultism and Judaism were propelled into the West by the Renaissance papacy, germinating through the centuries. These actions were screened from public view and from the view of the laity and all those Catholics not initiated into the highest echelons of the hierarchy. The screen was by no means total, and it was in partial public view symbolically and brazenly in accordance with *chutzpah*, from the mid-1400s onward, when the magical doctrine of the sexualization of everything came to the fore in Church-appointed, Church-financed and Church-approved art works and architecture. These embodied and enshrined nudity, paganism, homo-erotic seduction and demonic paradigms and paragons which unambiguously pointed to the substitution of Neoplatonic-Hermetic diabolism, with its ape of God, for the plain Gospel of Jesus Christ, as had been taught and conveyed by the true Catholic Church from the Resurrection of Jesus Christ until the coming of the accursed "Renaissance," which actually signifies a rebirth of forces hitherto chained.

Throughout this work we distinguish between the Catholic Church and the Church of Rome as it metastasized during and after the Renaissance. The distinction is critical. Frederick Meyrick of Oxford University wrote, "The value of truth for truth's sake is a thing apparently unappreciated and inappreciable by the Roman theological mind, *in so far as it is Romish or distinct from Catholic*."

A contributing factor in the rise of the Protestant Reformation was the authority claimed by the pope of Rome, a claim that pre-dates the Renaissance. In the 1599 edition of *The Geneva Bible,* which was the influential English Calvinist translation of the Scriptures in wide use in Elizabethan England, we read at the commentary on Rev. 11:7: "Boniface the Eighth...who lifted himself in so great arrogancy...that he called himself Lord of the whole world."

Protestant Dr. Gary DeMar writes, "Boniface VIII was pope of the Roman Catholic Church from 1294 to 1303. In his special charter, Papal bull *Unam Sanctam* of 1302—considered by the Reformers as one of the most heretical statements of Papal authority ever made—Boniface insisted, 'Furthermore, we declare, we proclaim, we define that it is absolutely necessary for salvation that every human creature be subject to the Roman Pontiff."

"Traditional Catholics" (and even many "conservative" ones) believe that unfettered freedom of the press such as enjoyed by Americans under the Constitution is a Masonic vice. They also condemn "private judgment." Then, relying upon the very vices they condemn, they proceed to publish their critiques of the Church since the 1960s. "Catholic traditional" Bishop Richard Williamson writes:

"...modern Catholics have tended to put too much faith in the pope and too little in the Church, and here is the answer to that reader who asked me why I do not write about infallibility in the same way that the classic Catholic theology manuals do. Those manuals are marvelous in their way, but they were all written before Vatican II, and they tended to attach to the Pope an infallibility which belongs to the Church. For instance, the summit of infallibility is liable to be presented in the manuals as a solemn definition by the pope, or by pope with Council, but in any case by the pope. Modern Catholics have tended to put too much faith in the Pope...in the same way that the classic Catholic theology manuals do."

Were the classic theology manuals modern or "traditional"? Was it only theology manuals that taught this excessive faith in the pope? Absolutely not. *It was the popes themselves who promulgated this faith in themselves and the papacy.* Are their teachings not subject to revision because they were written before Vatican II? Is it not true that "traditional" Catholics claim to cling to the whole Church as it existed prior to the Second Vatican Council? Yet now we see a rejection of theology manuals that are pre-Vatican II as advised by a "traditional" Catholic bishop who seeks to restore the Church as it existed before Vatican II. How do we adequately account for the painful, self-contradictory gymnastics which certain Catholics undertake to try to resolve the dilemma of heretical popes, and which leads them into what can only be described in terms of an oxymoron: madhouse modernist-traditionalism.

This modernist-traditionalist (sic) theology on papal power, which would never have been concocted if today there was a reigning pontiff of the "traditional Catholic" Pius X type on the papal throne, was invented in response to the Neoplatonic gang of pontiffs elected since Pope John XXIII in 1958. Here is a conservative Italian observer, Antonio Socci writing in *Libero*, October 5, 2014:

"...the Church belongs to Christ and not the popes, who are only temporary administrators and not masters.... They are subject to the law of God and the Word of God and must serve the Lord by protecting the *'depositum fidei'* entrusted to them. They cannot take possession of it or change it according to their own personal ideas..."

Protestant readers of Mr. Socci's statement will ask him, what took Catholics like you so long to realize this truth?

The Revelation of the Method of Pope Francis came in many ways, one of which was in connection with his Synod on the Family, which in October 2014, produced Italian Archbishop Bruno Forte's *Relatio post disceptationem,* which states: "Without denying the moral problems connected to homosexual unions it has to be noted that there are cases in which mutual aid to the point of sacrifice constitutes a precious support in the life of the partners." After an uproar, the Vatican, with Hegelian guile, took one public relations step back and announced that the *Relatio post disceptationem* was a preliminary document and not a final pronouncement. This was for image-management. The substance was something else: Archbishop Forte remained in the pope's hand-picked inner circle of top synod advisors on the issue. *Two steps forward.*

The Synod of Bishops on the Family met in further sessions in 2015. *Amoris Laetitia* ("The Joy of Love") is a papal document, technically an apostolic exhortation, written by Francis as the result of the Synod. It was made public April 8, 2016. Cardinal Christoph Schönborn of Vienna stated in an interview with the Jesuit journal *Civilta Cattolica*, that *Amoris Laetitia* is part of the Magisterium.

On September 5, 2016 the bishops of the Buenos Aires region of the pope's native Argentina drafted a set of guidelines intended to assist local priests in putting *Amoris Laetitia* into pastoral practice, particularly chapter eight, which makes reference to "discernment regarding the possible access to the sacraments of some of those who are divorced and in a new union." The guidelines say that some civilly remarried couples who can't adhere to the Church's teaching of celibacy ('living like brothers and sisters'), who have complex circumstances, and who can't obtain a declaration of nullity for their first marriage, might undertake a "journey of discernment," and arrive at the recognition that in their particular case, there are factors that "diminish responsibility and culpability."

For divorced Catholics in these exceptional cases the bishops wrote, "*Amoris Laetitia* opens up the possibility of access to the sacraments of Reconciliation and the Eucharist." The guidelines, dated September 5, reached Pope Francis, who answered on the same day, writing: "The document is very good and completely explains the meaning of chapter VIII of *Amoris Laetitia*. There are no other interpretations. And I am certain that it will do much good. May the Lord reward this effort of pastoral charity." [9]

"More Catholic than the Pope"

On the Internet five months earlier, incensed by *Amoris Laetitia,* the Rorate Caeli Catholic-traditionalist blog, self-advertised as the most popular in the English-speaking world, issued the following statement:

"The Catholic Faith is not something invented anew by each pope according to his own opinions, predilections, understanding, or whims. The pope is only good as a 'yardstick' when he formally teaches in accordance to 'the Faith once delivered unto the saints,' as St. Jude the Apostle wrote. When Pope Liberius assented to the unjust excommunication of St. Athanasius the Great, and signed off on an ambiguous creedal formula that could be accommodated to the Arian or semi-Arian heresies, every faithful Catholic was then 'more Catholic than the pope.'

"When Pope Honorius I uttered false theological opinions and failed to correct and condemn the Monothelite heretics, every faithful Catholic was then 'more Catholic than the pope.' Indeed, they were so much more Catholic than Honorius that the Church posthumously condemned him as a heretic, a decision that Honorius' successor St. Leo II approved. '*We anathematize the inventors of the new error, that is, Theodore, Sergius...and also Honorius, who did not attempt to sanctify this Apostolic Church with the teaching of Apostolic tradition, but by profane treachery permitted its purity to be polluted.*' For

---

9https://cruxnow.com/global-church/2016/09/12/pope-okays-argentine-doc-communion-divorced-remarried/

most of the Church's history, priests praying their Office repeated the *anathema* pronounced against Pope Honorius.

"When Pope Stephen VII desecrated the remains of Pope Formosus during the hideously shameful *Synodus Horrenda* (the 'Cadaver Synod'), every Catholic who strove to practice justice and who respected the sanctity of the human body was then 'more Catholic than the pope.'

"When Pope John XII effectively 'turned the Lateran palace into a brothel,' as contemporary historians so colorfully put it, and when Pope Benedict IX gave himself over to unchastity and bloodshed, every faithful Catholic who strove to cultivate the virtues of chastity, purity, mercy, and peace in their personal conduct was then 'more Catholic than the pope.'

"When Pope John XXII preached in his sermons the error that the faithful departed do not enjoy the Beatific Vision until after Judgment Day at the end of the world, every faithful Catholic was then 'more Catholic than the pope' — and the loud and outraged cry of the faithful against him led him to retract his error, and his successor then infallibly defined John XXII's opinion as heresy.

"Papal infallibility doesn't mean papal impeccability or papal omniscience. The obligations of docility and obedience do not extend so far that one must stand on one's head and cross one's eyes in order to see how a scandalous, erroneous papal utterance is in fact true after all. Most of what a pope says is not infallible, and papal authority has never extended to having the right to introduce teachings and laws that contradict or go counter to the Faith." [10]

"As Rorate has argued since day one of the first Synod— (Pope) Francis is leading the destruction of the family and the defiance of the words of Jesus Christ Himself." [11]

Early in his career, before his final break with Rome, the Augustinian monk Martin Luther made his own correct observations about the popes similar to the preceding "traditional" Catholic discernment, and it does not make them less true because it was Luther who expressed these views. The

---

[10]   http://rorate-caeli.blogspot.com/2016/04/more-catholic-than-pope.html#more

[11] http://rorate-caeli.blogspot.com/2016/09/for-record-pope-francis-confirms-amoris.html

conservative Catholic rejoinder to Luther, prior to the public emergence of the Liberal theology among the 1960s popes and their successors, was that the Pontiff is sovereign. He has no judge on earth. No individual's conscience can refuse the pope's theology, and "it is absolutely necessary for salvation that everyone be subject to the Roman Pontiff," including in the realm of the nullification of the Word of God under the Church of Rome's euphemism for betrayal of divine law, the "development of doctrine." The traditional answer to Luther was that *in practice* the pope's power is indeed unlimited.

Luther's rage against the pope's development of permission for usury (profit on loans) is one of the most tightly suppressed motivating factors of the early Protestant Reformation. He wrote:

"The heathen were able, by the light of reason, to conclude that a usurer is a double-dyed thief and murderer. We Christians, however, hold them in such honor, that we fairly worship them for the sake of their money...Whoever eats up, robs and steals the nourishment of another, that man commits as great a murder...as he who starves a man or utterly undoes him. Such does a usurer, and sits the while safe on his stool, when he ought rather to be hanging on the gallows, and be eaten by as many ravens as he has stolen guilders...

"Meanwhile, we hang the small thieves...Little thieves are put in the stocks, great thieves go flaunting gold and silks...there is, on this earth, no greater enemy of man (after the devil), than a gripe-money and usurer, for he wants to be god over all men...a usurer and money glutton—such a one would have the whole world perish from hunger and thirst, misery and want...so that he may have all to himself and every one may receive from him as from a god, and be his serf forever.

"To wear fine cloaks, golden chains...to be deemed and taken for a worthy, pious man...Usury is a great huge monster, like a werewolf, who lays waste all...and yet decks himself out and would be thought pious..."

In this case, Luther's views were a reaffirmation of the Roman Catholic dogma of almost all of the popes prior to the Renaissance, all of the Fathers of the Early Church, of St. Thomas Aquinas and St. Anthony of Padua. After Neoplatonic-

Hermeticism invaded the hierarchy of the Church of Rome it succumbed to the "development of doctrine," in this instance the early modernist heresy of the neo-Catholic Nominalist school, which made 5% usury respectable and fueled the Catholic Fugger usury empire (the Fuggers were the buccaneer-capitalists who banked the Renaissance papacy's indulgence loot). Catholics denounce John Calvin for supposedly *pioneering* the five percent interest rate in Christendom, but Calvin wasn't even born when Nominalism and the "Five Percent Fuggers" were first in the ascendant; and Calvin was a child when Medici Pope Leo X began the gradual derogation of the immutable Catholic law against profit on loans (which was sustained by all of his successors), beginning with his papal bull of May, 1515.

To this day, much of the conservative Catholic world believes the story that Rome stood against the money-gluttons, while it was the early Protestants like Luther who were the first to enable them. In fact, after the Medici established their "*monte*" usury banks on a firm foundation, the Money Power was in a position to buy ecclesiastical offices and choose personnel in the hierarchy of the Church. From the sixteenth century until now the Church of Rome has been under the suzerainty of money.

The popes of the late fifteenth and early sixteenth centuries were Hegelian dialecticians centuries before G.W.F. Hegel. Neoplatonism is anterior to Hegelianism. Both are based in magical thinking: the projection of the inevitability of observations about reality that nullify the permanence of the Word of God in the Scriptures. Here is the slogan of every revolution: "History is on our side." In the theology of this spiritual virus, the insinuation is that the pendulum-swinging god of changing times — not the God of the Bible who does not change (Malachi 3:6) — inevitably favors the revolution. This temporal chauvinism has consistently trumped Biblical dogma in the post-Renaissance Church, although for Machiavellian purposes of dissimulation, it was, up until recently, seldom publicly conceded. *In western civilization, no power on earth could advance this sorcery that puts forth revolutionary change as an invincible historical force, half so well as the papacy.*

After the eclipse of the divine right of kings and the absolute power of those secular monarchs, the papacy alone possessed those pharaonic prerogatives. The Cryptocracy would have us believe that the Freemasons are the hereditary enemies of the papacy. We witness their ritual stabbing of the papal tiara and cursing of the pope. One stands in awe at this virtuoso misdirection and how effectively the image it has produced has been burnished by both the black and white players in this alchemical theatre. We're now in the last act of the theatrical however, and the tragi-comedy is not ending as we have been led to believe it would. We are beginning to detect from the corners of the stage that the papacy is the able servant of the same occult process of which the Freemasons are a part. From Alexander VI to Leo X, from Paul VI, John Paul II, and Benedict XVI to Francis, the *development of the doctrine* on money, liturgy, Pharisaic Judaism, sexuality and the family has been and is underway according to ever-mutating situation ethics.

Pontiffs with a conservative reputation are as culpable as liberals. In 1947, in his encyclical *Mediator Dei,* Pius XII *repudiated a retun to the tradition of the Catholic Church*: "...the desire to restore everything indiscriminately to its ancient condition is neither wise nor praiseworthy. It would be wrong, for example, to want the altar restored to its ancient form..."

With no earthly check on the pontifical power there is no limit to the revolutionary havoc which the bishop of Rome can wreak. This is the surpassing utility of papalolatry to the Cryptocracy.

The "development of doctrine" is not only a 1960s phenomenon. It is the inheritance of the Church since the permission granted for the rise of the Fugger Money Power and, even more contentiously, but as we hope to demonstrate, the resurrection of fealty to the diabolism of Pharaonic Egypt in the aftermath of the Council of Florence.

"...the biggest problem in the Church...is—whatever one wishes to call it—papalolatry, hyper-papalism, that adulation of the pope that is unprecedented in the history of the Church, and the assumption that the power of the Pope has no limits, no boundaries, such that his pronouncements can change doctrine, of course under the guise of development controlled by the Holy Spirit, at will." [12]

---

[12]   Ross Douthat, http://rorate-caeli.blogspot.com/2016/01/op-ed-to-ross-douthat-with-affectionate.html#more • January 15, 2016.

"*...unprecedented in the history of the Church...*" This is what Right-wing Catholics are now asserting: the misapprehension (if not outright amnesia) with which the adversaries of Pope Francis console themselves. The contemporary conservative mind has difficulty entertaining the datum that papal absolutism has been the traditional dogma of the papacy since the late Middle Ages. According to this Roman doctrine, which was an innovation in the medieval era, Catholics must submit to popes like Francis and to his innovations.

To escape the record of subjection which Catholics have permitted to the popes for the past nine hundred years, "traditional" and "conservative" contemporary Catholics have recast a theology of the papacy, of what the non-popes have owed the pope, but they lack the candor to admit this. Instead, they pretend that refusal of obedience to the pontiffs was the case in the Renaissance, in the Baroque era and all subsequent eras up until the supposedly "unprecedented" papalolatry of the present.

Antonio Socci is a surrealist in this vein: "What many (also among believers) ignore are the very rigid limits that the Church has always placed on popes, while at the same time recognizing Petrine 'infallibility' in 'ex-cathedra' proclamations on matters of faith and morality. Specifically in the Dogmatic Constitution *Pastor aeternus*, through which Vatican Council I defined papal infallibility, we find 'For the Holy Spirit was promised to the successors of Peter not so that they might, by His revelation, make known some new doctrine, but that, by His assistance, they might religiously guard and faithfully expound the revelation or deposit of faith transmitted by the apostles."

When he cites what he fantasizes are "the very rigid limits that the Church has always placed on popes," if we charitably resist the urge to pronounce Mr. Socci demented, then we are left with the realization of the obligation of offering to Him and mankind in general, a desperately needed education in the suppressed, authentic history of the Church.

What is the use of this alleged qualifier — "For the Holy Spirit was promised to the successors of Peter not so that they might, by his revelation, make known some new doctrine..."—if there is no mechanism for enforcement when a pontiff indeed does promulgate "new doctrine"? The qualifying statement is toothless. It appears that it was included in *Pastor aeternus*, to assuage the consciences of Catholics rightly disturbed by the prospect of any human being spiritually elevated above the rest of humanity and declared possessed of infallible judgment (whether at certain special times under certain circumstances, or not).

The notion that in halcyon days of the Renaissance and successive ages, "very rigid limits" were "always placed on popes." is a species of Brobdingnagian self-delusion that requires no further comment.

The Word of God forbids gaining profit from loans of money among Christians. This was always the magisterial dogma. The glory of the true Catholic Church was Her law against profit from loans of money as taught by the Magisterium: as a dogma to be definitively held. On this point no further modification or alteration was to be implemented. It was a truth that could not be challenged among believers. Yet it was incrementally overthrown by the tinkering, tampering "infallible" popes of yesteryear. Today, no Catholic lender who makes his living making money breed money is forbidden communion, or made to confess his crime in the Sacrament of Penance. This has been the case since the 1830s and the pontificate of "the infallible" Pope Pius VIII.

The papal innovators of usury were too clever to challenge the divine dogma openly, and have always, in public, spoken eloquently in favor of the dogma and forcefully against avarice, since to do otherwise would reveal them for what they are. Catholic victims of deception point to this sham as their alleged proof that the popes actually changed nothing that was substantially God-ordained. What they managed to overlook prior to the pontificate of Francis was the exceptionally shrewd "pastoral" means that were employed to gradually transform profit on loans from a mortal sin to no sin at all. This *pastoral* tactic for nullification of the Law of God is, in the twenty-first century, not as difficult to perceive as in the past. A mind open to the proposition that devious tactics by revolutionary popes is not, in fact, unprecedented, can grasp the most notable contemporary example of those tactics: Pope Francis, spiritual heir of Giovanni di Lorenzo de' Medici. Roberto de Mattei, writing in *Il Giorno* (Italy): "Francis presents himself as a conservative, he doesn't speak against the dogmas, but his pastoral strategy is, per se, revolutionary, as it subordinates the truth to praxis, moreover on a hot issue like the family. In this way it marks a profound discontinuity in the history of the papacy..." [13]

Catholic dupes impel themselves to believe that Francis is the pontiff who *originated* this chameleon pastoral technique for radical nullification of God's Law by means of rhetoric upholding it and tactics for overthrowing it. The amnesia is appalling. On the contrary, the pastoral strategy of Pope Francis marks a profound *continuity* in the history of the papacy. Revolution inside the Church achieved by pastoral techniques has marked "the history of the papacy" for more than five centuries. The popes of the past sustained usury not by changing the dogma in the sacred books, but by legalizing usury *de facto*, as a form of "pastoral care" and "compassion" (*"pieta"*). When the popes allowed Neoplatonic-Hermeticism into the hierarchy of the Church and with it, esoteric Judaism; and likewise when they removed the immemorial penalties for profiting from loans of money— refusal of Communion and absolution to unrepentant usurers, the requirement to make restitution after the usurer quits his occupation, and a refusal of burial to the impenitent usurer — then they proceeded to establish a precedent for *all the revolutionary papal changes that would follow*: coerced suppression of the Latin Mass, shenanigans in synagogues, prayers with Buddhists, pagans and rabbis at Assisi; Voodoo in Benin, protection for child molestation facilitators, and declarations that "Jews" need not be actively converted to the Gospel because "Jews" don't need Faith in Jesus Christ to be saved. Scapegoating Pope Francis as an unprecedented phenomenon of papal revolution is willful ignorance. Francis is a terminal, *"Peter Romanus"* fragment of a five hundred year old timeline.

Advancing Satan's kingdom with "a wink and a nod"

Take for example the notorious "Borgia Pope" Alexander VI, who is almost universally denounced by many informed Catholics for his egregious sexual indiscretions. This is often followed however, in the next breath, with the qualifying

---

[13]   March 9, 2015. Translation by Francesca Romana, via http://rorate-caeli.blogspot.com/2015/03/the-popes-impossible-revolution-for.html#more

statement, "But even Alexander left the doctrine of the Church untouched."

What this statement rests upon is the notion that whatever the personal sins, failings and disgusting immorality of a pope, short of his formal declaration against a dogma of the Church, he has not negatively impacted the Faith of Catholics or undermined the teaching of Jesus Christ.

We mention Pope Alexander VI in this vein because he was critical to the growth and success of the Neoplatonic-Hermetic-Kabbalist cancer inside the Church. As we shall see, he protected and patronized the two most influential and flagrant, out-of-the-closet Catholic occultists of the fifteenth century, Ficino and Giovanni Pico, yet he did not, it is true, on any occasion issue an encyclical letter or any kind of edict for the record endorsing demonology, or nullifying the First Commandment of the Decalogue. He merely furthered the career of those who did. The papalolaters insist that Alexander VI did no serious harm to the Faith or the Church itself as a result. These folks remind this writer of the comic movie character Chico Marx who asked, "Who are you going to believe —me or your own eyes?"

Our own eyes indicate that the Church of Jesus Christ is harmed as much by slowly chipping away at its foundations through sub-rosa, papally-enabled subversion and infiltration, as it would be if a pontiff were to issue a document amounting to the same thing. Actually, the clandestine conspiracy is likely to be more lethal to souls than a public testament, because the former preserves the absolute authority of the institution of the papacy, while the latter causes Catholics to question its claims on their submission.

The playboy Borgia pope was never guilty of formally promulgating any papal documents contrary to immutable Biblical dogma. By other means however, he created a safe haven for the forces of Satan. Because he used other means, the cult mentality decrees that for all of his sins of the flesh, he sinned not against the Faith. The fact that Alexander VI is known to history mainly as a playboy pope rather than a pope of occultism, is itself an indication of the success of the conspiracy in suppressing exposure of its capture of the papacy.

Pope Francis did not formally promulgate any papal documents contrary to immutable Biblical dogma. Yet in the second decade of the twenty-first century he was a leader in grinding Biblical statutes and standards into the dust. Catholic writer Matthew Schmitz observed, "Instead of explicitly endorsing communion for the divorced and remarried couples, he has quietly urged them on with a wink and a nod."

Alexander VI was far from being the only Renaissance pontiff guilty of enabling the diabolic. If these types of papal actors constitute the definition of a "Holy Father" then we are prisoners of the lexicon of hell.

Vatican Council I—*Pastor aeternus*: Dogmatic Constitution on the Church (1870)

The "jurisdictional power of the Roman Pontiff is both episcopal and immediate. Both clergy and faithful, of whatever rite and dignity, both singly and collectively, are bound to submit to this power by the duty of hierarchical subordination and true obedience, and this not only in matters concerning faith and morals, but also in those which regard the discipline and government of the Church throughout the world...no one can depart from it without endangering his...salvation...he is the supreme judge of the faithful...The sentence of the Apostolic See (above which there is no higher authority), is not subject to revision by anyone, nor may anyone lawfully pass judgment thereupon.... this See of St. Peter always remains unblemished by any error...So then, should anyone, which God forbid, have the temerity to reject this definition of ours: let him be anathema."

The preceding is a statement worthy of Pharaoh or a Grand Rabbi. Jesus was not crucified so His People would be under bondage to any new chief priest: "Stand fast therefore in the liberty wherewith Christ hath made us free, and be not entangled again with the yoke of bondage" (Galatians 5:1). 'Oh, but that is a Protestant sentiment!,' the papists will assert. No, it is a thoroughly Catholic conviction that those who were bought for a price by the blood of Christ must not return to Egypt again. To submit to the claims over us of a Pharaoh-Pontiff, whose office and powers evolved over the passage of time, constitutes scorn and contempt for Our Lord Jesus Christ. Before Catholics were damaged by the information-warfare which has been at work in the Church of Rome for so many centuries, they would have perceived that Vatican Council I's *Pastor aeternus* was both anti-Catholic and

Antichrist. To reiterate that ancient *sensus Catholicus* now is to be branded a Protestant, or a "fallen-away Catholic." But who is it that has actually deserted the Faith?

When the First Vatican Council of 1870 decreed the pope to be infallible under certain *"ex cathedra"* conditions, the *prestige* of the "Vicar of Christ on earth" rose to such heights that it eclipsed the Ordinary Magisterium and we had the monstrous situation of the near idolatry of a fallen human being possessed of the power and authority to add or subtract, or otherwise alter the Deposit of the Faith, always under cover of Machiavellian cant language that renders black into white by stating that the changes are in conformity with the Deposit of the Faith, and represent an organic "development" as "Blessed" John Henry Cardinal Newman, among other prominent Romanists, taught.

The pope's supreme, commanding authority is certainly not limited to *ex cathedra* statements. According to the official *Denzinger* Catholic Manual of Theology no. 1830: "And since the Roman Pontiff is at the head of the universal Church by the divine right of apostolic primacy, We teach and declare also that he is the supreme judge of the faithful [cf. n. 1500], and that in all cases pertaining to ecclesiastical examination recourse can be had to his judgment [cf. n. 466]; moreover, that the judgment of the Apostolic See, whose authority is not surpassed, is to be disclaimed by no one, nor is anyone permitted to pass judgment on its judgment [cf. n. 330 ff.]."

"No one may pass judgment on the judgment" of a mere man. "Conservative" Catholics under Pope Francis deny that this supreme dictatorship ever existed and refuse to see that without the pope's total power, few of the changes which they decry could have been instituted. Individual bishops could have refused to implement them. The Right-wing's much dreaded *"collegiality,"* (the pontiff sharing power and authority with the bishops) which many "conservative" Catholics fear and shrink from as "liberal poison," is actually a powerful prophylactic against papalolatry.

"...the See of St. Peter always remains unimpaired by any error..."—Vatican Council I, Dogmatic Constitution *Pastor aeternus,* n. 4; and Denz. 1836.

Popes on Papal Authority

• Pope Benedict XIV: "The Holy Apostolic See and the Roman Pontiff have primacy in the entire world. The Roman Pontiff is the Successor of Blessed Peter, the Prince of the Apostles, true Vicar of Christ, Head of the whole Church, Father and Teacher of all Christians." [14]

• Pope Leo XIII: "Thus, it is an absolute necessity for the simple faithful to submit in mind and heart to their own pastors, and for the latter to submit with them to the Head and Supreme Pastor." [15]

• Pope Leo XIII: "...the strong and effective instrument of salvation is none other than the Roman Pontificate." [16]

• Pope Leo XIII: "Union with the Roman See of Peter is...always the public criterion of a Catholic...You are not to be looked upon as holding the true Catholic faith if you do not teach that the faith of Rome is to be held." [17]

• Pope Pius XII: "Nor must it be thought that what is expounded in Encyclical Letters does not of itself demand consent, (or that) in writing such Letters the popes do not exercise the supreme power of their Teaching Authority. For these matters are taught with the ordinary teaching authority, of which it is true to say: 'He who hears you, hears me' (Luke 10:16); and generally what is expounded and inculcated in Encyclical Letters already for other reasons appertains to Catholic doctrine." [18]

Papal statements of absolute command and obedience over humanity, from Pope Boniface VIII onward, represent a papalolatrous theology. What "conservative" and "traditional" Catholics are evading is the fact that it is an innovation that

---

[14] Apostolic Constitution *Etsi Pastoralis*, May 26, 1742; excerpted in *Papal Teachings: The Church*, p. 32.

[15] *Letter Epistola Tua*, June 17, 1885; excerpted in *Papal Teachings: The Church*, p. 263.

[16] Ibid., p. 353.

[17] Encyclical *Satis Cognitum*, n. 13.

[18] Pius XII, Encyclical *Humani Generis*.

has been in force since the 1200s in claiming that the pope is owed the type of obedience decreed above.

Sometimes when these extravagant authoritarian claims are made the pope is not mentioned and the old "trust me" con of the salesman is put forward. St. Robert Bellarmine declares in his catechism, "The Church is the spouse of God and the Holy Spirit her teacher; for that reason there is no danger that she would deceive or would do anything or teach that something must be done that is opposed to the Commandments of God." [19]

Human nature is fallen. The pope is a sinner. Power corrupts. The absolute power conferred immorally, unethically and erroneously on the Bishop of Rome is the source of almost all of the crises in the Church of Rome today, yet Right-wing Catholics in the twenty-first century pretend that the pontiff's absolute power has never manifested or been taught. This will be their line until they witness a "traditional" pope on the throne, another Leo XIII or Pius IX, X or XI. When a *traditional* papal dictator to their liking is elected, they will advocate complete submission, and embrace all the ultramontane claims for the authority of the pope which have existed for almost a millennium. If such a pope were to be elected, popery would be reinstalled in their ranks, just as they were uninstalling it during the pontificate of Francis.

It was situation ethics that permitted profits on loans of money due to "modern realities," and it is situation ethics that has derogated the authority of the pope after Leftist Pope Francis was elected. In praise of an investigative report by Gian Guido Vecchi of the Italian newpaper *Corriere della Serra* of July 16, 2015, Rorate Caeli, the "traditional" Catholic blog on the English-language Internet, stated: "...surely this article should help put an end to the pious myth that the Holy Spirit always chooses the Pope..." [20]

If this statement by Rorate Caeli had been made at any time during the pontificate of a pope pleasing to "traditional" Catholics, they would have denounced it as a species of Protestant blasphemy. When there is a liberal pontiff not to their liking however, they resort to this type of thinking

---

[19]Bellarmine, *Doctrina Christiana: The Timeless Catechism of St. Robert Bellarmine,* transl. Ryan Grant (2016), p. 105.

[20]   http://rorate-caeli.blogspot.com/2015/07/the-original-story-when-jesuit-cardinal.html#more

themselves. Since they claim to know the Faith better than anyone, it would appear that the Holy Spirit is sometimes absent when it comes to selecting the "Vicar of Christ on earth." But if God does not choose the pope, then who does? What happens to more than a thousand years of the claims to authority made for the pontiff, when a pontiff occupies the "Chair of Peter" on the basis of "pious myths"? How many Protestants were impoverished, imprisoned or killed for believing about the papal "Peter" what "Traditional Catholic" Rorate Caeli believes in the twenty-first century?

The pope's *Pastor aeternus* decree of Vatican Council I defined not just the dogma of infallibility, but the full and immediate power of the pope over all the bishops and the entire Church. In addition to the formula *"ideoque eiusmodi Romani Pontificis definitionis esse ex se irreformabilis"* (definitions by the Roman Pontiff are unreformable per se); the ungodly clause *"non autem ex consensu Ecclsiae"* (not with the consensus of the Church) was added. The assent of the people of God ("the Ecclesia") united with priests and bishops of the Catholic Church, is never required when the "Holy Father" makes rulings binding on all humanity. In the theology of popery, the Pontiff alone is sovereign judge, and he himself has no judge on earth. Pope Pius IX promulgated the Apostolic Constitution *Pastor aeternus* as a law of faith. *Pastor aeternus* establishes that the primacy of the pope consists in true and supreme powers of jurisdiction, independent of any other power, over all the pastors and over the entire flock of the faithful on earth. He possesses this supreme power not by delegation on the part of the bishops nor the entire Church, but by Divine Right. This is the foundation of pontifical sovereignty; of the Pope's supreme jurisdiction over the Church—its magisterium and governance. Even when a pope betrays and subverts the deposit of the faith and morals, transmitted for safeguarding by Jesus Christ to the Church, *there is no mechanism for deposing him*, or for refusing his authority or disobeying his commands (although there is a suppressed precedent from the Council of Constance).

The Bishop of Rome comes to own the Church of Jesus Christ and for the sake of that one bishop's power, that Church has suffered disrepute, desertion and revolt. Far better to have made that bishop suffer thus, than the unspotted Bride of Christ, but like all false gods, this idol is a usurper. The depths to which even eminent theologians such as St. Robert

Bellarmine will go to furnish ludicrous pretexts for the maintenance of popery is a strange wonder to behold. Bellarmine declared that even when a pope isn't a Catholic he is still the pope. He could be a devil and he would continue as pope, with all power of the Keys of Peter:

"St. Robert Bellarmine explains that a pope who loses the virtue of faith does not, for that reason alone, cease to be pope. This is evident since Bellarmine held that a pope who is an occult (secret) heretic retains his office; and to be clear, an occult heretic is one who is guilty of formal heresy — the mortal sin of heresy — in the internal forum (the realm of conscience), but which has not become public and notorious in the external forum...In support of this position, Cardinal Bellarmine cites the authority of Melchior Cano, a theologian from the Council of Trent, who explains that since an occult heretic remains united to the Church by an external union, a Pope who is an occult heretic retains his office.

"Bellarmine also notes that this is the unanimous opinion of all the authors he cites in his book, *De Ecclesia*: 'Occult heretics are still of the Church, they are parts and members...therefore the pope who is an occult heretic is still pope...' By referring to a pope as an occult heretic...Bellarmine...is referring to a pope who has committed the sin of heresy in the *internal forum* and thereby lost the faith *entirely*." [21]

The successor of St. Peter need not believe in Jesus Christ in order to qualify as the leader of the Church of Jesus Christ? This is what "traditional" Catholics hold, but this doctrine is not actually traditional; it is a subversion of the tradition of the Church of 100 A.D. "Traditional" Catholics are modernists masquerading as traditional. They maintain a devolutionary peregrination away from the Catholic tradition of the First Century A.D. by subscribing to the dictatorship of the pontiff who possesses the power of an Oriental emperor and, since the Renaissance, the sorcery of the Egyptian *mekashfim*. Papal absolutism was implanted and cultivated by occult forces many centuries after the Church was founded by Our Lord. By this architectonic of absolute monarchy the Cryptocracy knew

---

[21] John Salza and Robert Siscoe, *True or False Pope?* (St. Thomas Aquinas Seminary, 2015), pp. 145-146.

hundreds of years ago that by putting their man on the papal throne they could, through that one fallible sinner, degrade and pervert the authentic Catholic Church and compel the Catholic people to follow their clerical leaders in gradually abandoning the True Faith. This is precisely what has occurred, according to plan.

The bulwark against this wickedness from the powers that be was the laity and their parish priests who were shocked, despondent and inconsolable over betrayals which they did not begin to grasp until the mid-1960s and early 1970s. Had they the right to reject a pope's commands and derogations, the Catholic rank-and-file in 1969 would have never promulgated Pope Paul's New Mass by suppressing the old Mass; they would not have submitted to the papal teaching that the Judaic religion is redeemed by its carnal connection to the patriarchs. They would have never adopted a policy of secrecy that shielded child molestation facilitators, or slyly insinuated two castes of Christians—the highly-souled Brahmins in Holy Orders and the lower-souled unordained—a divide which would have had to exist from the institution of the Eucharist at the Last Supper—signifying the depraved proposition that Christ's chosen apostles had higher souls than His Blessed Mother.

The masterstroke of the Cryptocracy for degrading the Church of Jesus Christ was the slow imposition of the office of sovereign papal dictator, which first split the Church in 1054, when the Russian and Greek Orthodox discerned the pharaonic transformation underway, elevating that sinner, the Bishop of Rome, from his proper place as *primus inter pares* (first among equals), to the status of Oriental potentate over and above all. The priest who consecrates the Host, and the Bishop of Rome who assumes the See of Peter, ought to be the most humble servants of all, and the last to be served, or they are nothing—a mockery of what it means to be a shepherd of God. The Protestant "protest," when it was sincere, arose in the face of this mockery.

If the office of pontiff had been under limits, as it had been in the majority of Christianity's first millennium, then institutionalized diabolism, deceit and secrecy would not have gained the deluding and beguiling power on earth which it possesses in our time.

"...the white which I see, is black, if the Hierarchical Church so decides it."

The founder of the Jesuits, Ignatius Loyola, wrote "Rules for Thinking with the Church." Rule 13, teaches: "That we may be altogether of the same mind and in conformity with the Church herself, we ought always to hold that the white which I see, is black, if the Hierarchical Church so decides it."

Consequently, according to the Jesuit founder, if our God-given reason and our conscience tell us something is good while the Church of Rome decrees that it is bad, Ignatius teaches that we must believe that it is bad. The converse is also true: if our reason and our conscience tell us that something is evil, and the Church of Rome decrees it to be good and holy, then it is, by papal decree. Here is the basis of rabbinism, Stalinism, Hitlerism, Maoism and every tyranny over the mind of man. According to Pope Boniface, everyone in the world must be subject to Pope John Paul II and Pope Francis. According to Pope Pius XII, Pope Francis was to be obeyed not only when he speaks "*ex cathedra*," but also when exercising his "ordinary teaching authority," of which it is said: *He who hears the pope, hears Christ.* Therefore, when Pope Francis stated that Catholics are overly concerned about unborn children murdered in the womb, we are hearing the voice of Christ.

Instead of recognizing that popery produces nullification of the Word of God by the "Vicar of Christ on earth," we get a tortured casuistry consisting of mental gymnastics. "Cardinal Timothy Dolan, America's foremost Catholic prelate, appeared on NBC's 'Meet the Press' on March 9, 2014 and commented as follows on the 'coming out' of a 'gay' college football star: "Good for him...I would have no sense of judgment on him.... God bless ya. I don't think, look, the same Bible that tells us, that teaches us well about the virtues of chastity and the virtue of fidelity and marriage also tells us not to judge people. So I would say, 'Bravo."

This is how a "Prince of Church" in the Year of Our Lord 2014 reacted to a celebrity's announcement that he engages in acts—"men with men, working that which is filthy" (Romans 1:26)— "Bravo." Pandering to a simplistic hippy misreading of the Gospel (Judge not man, like the Good Book says), Dolan synchronizes with the prevailing culture and places himself atop the latest worldly trend. But the gospel is profoundly counter-cultural. The "Good Book," which is filled with the judgments of God and His Divine Son, warns, "Woe unto you when the world speaks well of you."

What we are seeing is the highly visible rotten fruit which papalolatry has wrought in the Church for many hundreds of years —formerly concealed under a mountain of disinformation and misdirection—now visible in this Age of the Making Manifest of All that is Hidden, when Catholics have been sufficiently processed that deceitful masking devices can be dispensed with and the truth about the Neoplatonic and Hermetic popes of usury no longer needs to be concealed in order to maintain the flow of shekels from the pay-pray-and-obey peons in the pews.

Given the early medieval legacy and heritage of the true Catholic Church which existed in the minds and hearts of the common priests and people from the 15th through the mid-twentieth centuries, it was necessary for the papal pupils of Hermes Trismegistus and the Kabbalah to confine their machinations to the hierarchy of their Church of Rome, while maintaining in the common people the illusion that they still dwelled in the sanctum of the medieval Church, contending against Money, Judaism and Freemasonry. The Church of Rome knew that when the processing of humanity reached the correct apex in point of time, the legacy of medieval Catholicism could and would be finally extirpated with a few strokes of the papal pen.

When the time was right, usury emerged in full and the people did nothing because the law of the Church of Rome would not permit them to resist. When the time was right, Pope Paul VI acted as another Church of England Bishop Cranmer and another Church of England Queen Elizabeth I, and outlawed throughout the world (with a few exceptions the better to enforce the general rule)—the suppression of the medieval rite of the Mass which had existed essentially unchanged in its essentials for centuries of Christian history. As a result of this papal despotism, millions of Catholics more or less lost their faith or their sanity, to one degree or another, in the wake of this unconscionable act of theft on the part of the Holy Roman Pontiff and his Robber Church. This writer was a witness to the alcoholism, agony and despair of faithful priests who, in obedience to the Pontiff, submitted to the summary trashing of the Tridentine Latin Mass, which was the only worship they had known. Suddenly it was obsolete. This writer was a witness to devout Catholic laymen and women becoming cynics and agnostics in the face of this robbery. This writer was a witness to the closing of the Capuchin-Franciscan major seminary, wherein the rector of that seminary, perhaps the holiest priest we have ever known, whose devotion at Mass bordered on reverence so profound it was nearly ecstasy, was reduced to a hopelessly confused wreck; a Doubting Thomas who questioned the most basic tenets of the Deposit of Faith.

There has been no significant reparation made and no reckoning on this earth for this horrendous sabotage. War was made by the elite of the Church of Rome, led by the Pope of Rome, against their own faithful priests and people, as Neoplatonic-Hermeticism emerged from five centuries underground to crush the Faith permitted to exist until such time as the prophesied stage of human alchemy had reached a sufficient level of processing.

Anticipating an objection, we assert that yes, even Pope "Saint" Pius X, who despite his repeated famous jeremiads against "the scourge of modernism," *never lifted even one finger against the root of evil*—the love of money—Rome's "decriminalization" of usury—incrementally relaxed and diluted, leading to the abolition of all ecclesiastical penalties by Pope Pius VIII, and the absence of all such penalties in the 1917 and 1983 Codes of Canon Law. Moreover, it is worth noting that the criminally negligent 1917 Code was compiled largely in the pontificate of Pius X, who did not live to see it actually promulgated.

The "Jews" were cleverly branded and scapegoated as the iconic usurers, but as historian Prof. Goldwin Smith writes concerning the Catholic usurers, "The Lombards and Cahorsins...took up the business (of usury)...the money trade...in Italy...was in the hands of native houses, such as the Medici, Bardi, and Peruzzi, while at a later period the Fuggers of Augsburg were the Rothschilds of Germany."

The Fuggers were an anti-Lutheran Church of Rome banking house who had been placed in charge of the receipts from the sale of indulgences. They pioneered the five percent rate of interest on loans, which has been pinned on John Calvin as the miserly originator thereof. Our understanding of the papacy's filthy lucre reached a new order of magnitude in 1832, when the Rothschilds began to finance of the Church of Rome, two years after Pius VIII removed the last penalties and obstacles to "Catholic" usury and those who practiced it.

Employing the draconian power of the papacy, Pope John Paul II, that flak for the Pharisees, declared in a Roman synagogue and to the world's media that the unbelieving mockers of Jesus Christ were the "elder brothers in the Faith" of Catholics, and through Church documents authorized by this pontiff, strongly intimated that evangelization of the "Jews" was no longer a primary objective because "Jews" could gain salvation through their racial heritage, rather than by their Messiah, King Jesus.

The popes of the Renaissance and post-Renaissance stopped Islamic would-be conquerors in their bloody tracks in order to preserve the occult state that was the Church of Rome and her empire. But with regard to Judaic power, despite certain setbacks and pogroms which the Church of Rome engineered to gain temporary negotiating advantage with its rival and sometime partner, and despite the anger and hostility of the Catholic priests and laity at Talmudism, it was the religion of the Talmud and the Money Power which gained strength after strength, and went from victory after victory by the clandestine connivance of the Church of Rome. The Renaissance and post-Renaissance Church successfully ran its operations because those operations ensured that Catholics placed authority above truth—"underestimating truth and overestimating the popes."[22] Catholics concede to the person of the pontiff an infallibility coming from, and belonging to, God alone. This elevation of the Bishop of Rome generates a "creeping infallibility," which leads Catholics further and further astray, submitting to doctrines, disciplines and acts contrary to the Gospel.

Niccoló Machiavelli (1469-1527) of Florence offered the following counsel to the Renaissance princes of Church and State. His teaching became the papal charter:

"Every one admits how praiseworthy it is in a prince to keep faith, and to live with integrity and not with craft. Nevertheless our experience has been that those princes who have done great things have held good faith of little account,

---

[22] *Eleison Comments,* February 15, 2014.

and have known how to circumvent the intellect of men by craft, and in the end have overcome those who have relied on the word of the prince.

"...a wise lord cannot, nor ought he to, keep faith when such observance may be turned against him, and when the reasons that caused him to pledge it exist no longer.

"...it is necessary to know well how to...be a great pretender and dissembler; and men are so simple, and so subject to present necessities, that he who seeks to deceive will always find someone who will allow himself to be deceived.

"One recent example I cannot pass over in silence. (Pope) Alexander VI did nothing else but deceive men, nor ever thought of doing otherwise, and he always found victims; for there never was a man who had greater power in asserting, or who with greater oaths would affirm a thing, yet would observe it less; nevertheless his deceits always succeeded according to his wishes, because he well understood this side of mankind.

"...a prince ought to take care that...he may appear to him who sees and hears him altogether merciful, faithful, humane, upright, and religious. There is nothing more necessary to appear to have than this last quality, inasmuch as men judge generally more by the eye than by the hand, because it belongs to everybody to see you, to few to come in touch with you. Everyone sees what you appear to be, few really know what you are, and those few dare not oppose themselves to the opinion of the many..." [23]

The Renaissance Medici and Guise clans were students of Machiavelli and a template for the Mafia, having engineered one of the great acts of Antichrist treachery in the history of Renaissance Europe, the mass murder of thousands of unarmed Protestants, and women and children in Paris, 1572. This mass murder was praised by the pontiff of the day. Can it be said that he was Catholic? Or was he an anti-Catholic intending to ruin the reputation of the Church?

When the Bishop of Rome does deviate, Christians have the duty to admonish him and expose his *fallibility*, as Christ did to the teachers of falsehood of His day. No obedience or deference is owed to any "spiritual authority" on this earth, be

---

[23]   Machiavelli, *The Prince* (emphasis supplied); circulated in manuscript beginning in 1513; first printing: 1532.

he pontiff or Protestant pastor, who repeatedly and knowingly imparts falsehood. The theology that says otherwise was promulgated by fallible pontiffs enshrining idolatry of "His Holiness." Resistance against the highest religious authority in the Church of Rome is always incumbent on every Christian when that authority betrays the perennial truths of the Gospel as always taught by the true Catholic Church. The ones who are called to challenge the usurpers are those who most profoundly value the safeguarding of the One, Holy, Catholic and Apostolic Church founded by Jesus Christ, against which the gates of hell shall not prevail, because at least some Christians, however few, will always deploy, in obedience to divine fiat, and rally to defend and advance the true Church founded by the Resurrected Christ. This is a challenge mounted against the Left flank to defend against those who seek to use psychological pressure from academia and the mass-media to morally stigmatize those who uphold the Word of God concerning Pharisaic ("Orthodox") Judaism, homosexuality, divorce, contraception and abortion. The defense is mounted against the Right flank where dwell those who believe that the Bishop of Rome is a sovereign authority endowed with the right to nullify God's law against usury, murder Protestants and Anabaptists in Europe, devolve Christ's Ecclesia into a Neoplatonic-Hermetic hierarchical institution for the elevation and protection of clerics whose souls, allegedly enhanced by the mark of ordination, are covertly deemed higher souls (*Neshama HaElyonah* in the words of the rabbis), than those of the laity, and therefore more worthy of protection from criminal prosecution than the children which some of them prey upon. We have made reference heretofore to Catholics among whom we lived in the 1950s and 1960s; to their rectitude and in some cases, sanctity. Thinking on those people from our past, many of whom are now deceased, and visualizing their faces and their way of life from out of the "mystic chords of memory," it is difficult for us to believe that very many of them would have any active connection in the twenty-first century to what passes for the "Catholic Church," in view of the revelations of *systematic* molestations of helpless Catholic children, whose predation was facilitated by numerous bishops and cardinals (many of whom still living are comfortably retired) and at least one "infallibly canonized saint" (John Paul II).

How do we distinguish between the Catholic Church and the usurper Church of Rome? The Catholic Church always taught that profit on loans of money (usury) was a sin that separated man from eternal salvation. The Church of Rome gradually usurped the Catholic Church by seizing the papacy and using a type of "signs of the times" *pilpul* (intellectually dishonest, Talmudic-style casuistry), so as to submit to the Money Power and replace the eternal, unchanging Word of God with situation ethics, justified by allusions to "changing economic realities."

Five centuries later the same trend is in place: "The reasoning of the clerics who advocate for a radical revision of the teaching of the Church on the question of homosexuality takes as a given that the phenomenon of same-sex couples, with their respective children, is one of a considerable size and grows in an irresistible way, as a 'sign of the times' to which the Church cannot deny welcoming and positive recognition anymore" (Sandro Magister, *L'Espresso*).

Revolutionary overthrow by pastoral means

Most of the evils which befell the Church, from the sale of indulgences to the rise of Neoplatonic-Hermeticism within the hierarchy, as well as the alliance with the Rothschild bank from 1832 onward, to the public emergence of Neoplatonic-Hermeticism in the twentieth century Church, all lead back to the Renaissance root of *incremental relaxation* of moral and dogmatic laws against usury which *led to the eventual total nullification* of those divine laws. These facts represent the beginning of the discernment of the true Church and the impostor Church. How was this *gradual* revolution in the Church's attitude toward money achieved? To answer we turn to a replay by Pope Francis of the incrementalism and plausible deniability put into motion by Leo X Medici, and his successors. It works like this:

Pope "Francis would like to liberalize Church doctrine on marriage, the family, and homosexuality, but he knows that he lacks the support and institutional power to do it. So he's decided on a course of stealth reform that involves sowing seeds of future doctrinal change *by undermining the enforcement of doctrine today*. The hope would be that a generation or two from now, the gap between official doctrine and the behavior that's informally accepted in Catholic parishes across the world would grow so vast that a global grassroots movement in favor of liberalizing change would rise up at long last to sweep aside the old, musty, already-ignored rules....It's a brilliant, clever, supremely Machiavellian strategy—one that promises to produce far-reaching reforms down the road while permitting the present pope...to claim plausible deniability ('I haven't changed church doctrine!')." [24]

On October 17, 2014 Cardinal Raymond Burke, who was then the head of the Supreme Tribunal of the Apostolic Signatura (canon law court), stated concerning Francis, "The pope has done a lot of harm...' Burke...went on Catholic television in 2013 to rebut remarks Pope Francis made to an interviewer that the church had become 'obsessed' with abortion and sexuality to the exclusion of other issues.' Burke said, "We can never talk enough about that as long as in our society innocent and defenseless human life is being attacked in the most savage way. The pope, more than anyone else as the pastor of the universal church, is bound to serve the truth,' Burke said. 'The pope is not free to change the church's teachings with regard to the immorality of homosexual acts or the indissolubility of marriage or any other doctrine of the faith."

But Cardinal Burke, surely you are aware that popes have changed the church's teachings on profit from loans of money, and on Judaism; popes violated the First Commandment when they invited the smoke of Satan (pagan and Kabbalistic philosophy) into the hierarchy of the Catholic Church and conveyed it via Catholic universities and seminaries and via hieroglyphic public art. Cardinal Burke has nothing to say about these earlier papal violations of truth and the law of God. Consequently, one wonders if he is sounding an alarm because he is genuinely outraged, or because Francis is giving the papal game away by his blatant embrace of the actual praxis of the Church of Rome since the late fifteenth century? Dante in *The Inferno* connected usury to sodomy. Francis was only being papally consistent when he sought to soften the laws against the latter after his predecessors removed the barriers to the former.

---

[24] Damon Linker, "Pope Francis' Machiavellian strategy to liberalize the Catholic Church," theweek.com, October 15, 2014.

The Vatican philosophy is the occult philosophy of the Renaissance. It is also known as the "post-conciliar orientation" and the "Forte Theology." It can be summarized as follows: "...according to the 'Forte Theology' of the partial Monday *relatio*—all bad things have '*semina Verbi*,' and 'elements of sanctification,' lying, cheating, and destroying are not even 'sins' properly, but just 'steps' on the path to an 'ideal' of truth, faithfulness, and integrity that is nearly impossible to achieve..." This is the Kabbalistic dogma viewed through a "Catholic" lens.

Neo-Catholics would seem to have little or no idea what a true Catholic believes according to the Church founded by Jesus Christ and those who remained faithful to His Ecclesia through the centuries. A vast sea of texts and decrees, doctrines, encyclicals and pious practices and sideshows accumulated by the man-made Churchianity that usurped the true Church, mesmerizes and misdirects its adherents, implanting a false picture of what it means to be Catholic. For them Catholicism consists in veneration of the pontiff and nearly blind faith in the local cleric; in other words in popery and priestcraft. Where is this in the Gospel? And after five hundred years, where has it finally led? Catholics of the first few centuries after Christ would not recognize the Church of Rome as having much of anything to do with the Faith bequeathed to them.

They would never sign on to the ban on human reason and divinely instilled conscience stigmatized by the Church of Rome as "private judgement." Freedom of the press is no more masonic than listening to one's conscience is Protestant (Freemasons have a history of burning the printing presses of their opposition; masonic "freedom of the press" is a hoax). Freedom of inquiry and the sanctity of a Christian conscience are pre-Renaissance Catholic virtues that should never be conceded to detractors as something anti-Catholic. "Traditional" Catholics practice private judgment when they refuse the Mass of Pope Paul VI or pick and choose which pope they shall follow, or declare that certain popes are not popes— the "Vatican II Popes" have been deposed by the declarations of various priests ordained by Archbishop Marcel Lefebvre who later had themselves made "bishops" (all these acts were by private conscience and judgment). Fr. Jürgen Wegner, United States District Superior of Archbishop Lefebvre's Society of St.

Pius X (SSPX) wrote that exposing Catholics to the Novus Ordo Mass of Pope Paul VI is known to be harmful to their faith. The pope's own Mass is harmful to the faith of Catholics? How was this decided by Fr. Wegner and published in a mass mailing of September 2015, devoted to honoring a priest, Msgr. James Byrnes, who, by the light of his private judgment, has refused to offer the Novus Ordo Mass? It was decided by Wegner's conscience and private judgment.

We have seen these same "traditional" Catholics proclaim the need to only read a Catholic Bible that contains "annotations" by Rome's theologians, since it is too dangerous for Catholics to read the words of Christ by themselves without annotations—they might lead to "private judgment." The irony is lost on these tragicomic characters who burlesque Catholicism.

The bishops of Rome when they were humble servants of God and cognizant of their human fallibility, were often true shepherds and guarantors of the unity so sorely lacking in the Protestant world. But as Romanism replaced Catholicism with the passage of centuries, the popes became enveloped in a mystique worthy of an emperor. They had directed the people away from seeing that the supposed "infallible papacy" had become like the "princes of the house of Israel" who "hate the good and love the evil," as written in the Book of Micah, chapter three.

The post-Renaissance papacy is the last significant absolute monarchy on earth. The person who is elected pontiff rules the Roman Church with complete authority. Papists have explained this by means of allusion to an alleged historical miracle: that other than Pope Honorius I who "strayed" doctrinally but (it is alleged) "only briefly" into Arianism, the papacy has otherwise been free of dogmatic error. Catholics grant that the papacy has had rum popes who fell into concupiscent situations involving mistresses, children out of wedlock and similar sexual failings common to human frailty. Other than Honorius however, who is deemed not to have formally pronounced in favor of heresy, legend has it that the papacy has been miraculously preserved from error in theology. "Traditional" Catholics maintain that this was true until the pontificate of Paul VI (some say until John XXIII).

Reading the Russian Orthodox author Fyodor Dostoevsky, we saw the papacy described as being of Antichrist rather than

Christ. This troubled us because we could not find any grounds for impeaching the testimony of Dostoevsky. In studying Talmudic Judaism, we discovered that during the Renaissance the Vatican enabled Talmudism to a startling degree in spite of having a reputation for "antisemitism." In studying the occult, we found that, once again during the Renaissance, the popes embraced Neoplatonic-Hermetic-Kabbalism.

"Traditional" and "Conservative" Catholics often indict early Protestantism for being the occult precursor to Freemasonry. They are willfully ignorant of the occult roots of the Church of Rome commencing with the Renaissance era, and the extent to which occultists united with Rome against early Protestant churches and beliefs. Concerning the conversion of Protestants:

"...there are broader questions involved in (Bishop Juan) Caramuel's Hebrew studies at Prague. One of his principal responsibilities as Ferdinand III's President of the Council of Reformation for four years was the process of conversion and re-Catholicization of the Protestant populations. Yossef Schwartz of Tel Aviv University has suggested that (Cistercian theologian Juan) Caramuel may have seen the Ashkenazi Jews as an asset in this endeavor. Y. Schwartz's thesis is that commentaries on Jewish texts such as the Talmud and the Cabbala—that chronologically postdate the canonical Hebrew Bible—represent a hermeneutic tradition sharing much in common with the Catholic tradition of theological commentary on sacred texts throughout Late Antiquity and on into the Middle Ages. Stemming from similar sources and similar methods, he argues, these two traditions would have shared more in common with each other than either did with the new and heretical doctrines of Protestantism. Rather than studying Cabbalism in order to better refute it, the Cistercian's curiosity may have had the positive purpose of being a key for the conversion of the Jews. In this rather odd sense, the rabbinical community of Prague could be placed, in Caramuel's eyes, on the pro-Catholic side of the ledger in the Counter-Reformation drive to eliminate heresy." [25]

---

[25] Henry W. Sullivan, "Jews of Prague & Jews of Spain: Juan Caramuel's Account of Medieval Sephardic Writings," in *Juan Caramuel Lobowitz: The Last Scholastic Polymath*, p. 158.

The Spanish monk and bishop, Juan Caramuel (1606-1682), aide to Catholic Emperor Ferdinand III and allegedly assigned the mission of the evangelization of the Judaic people, set forth in his "Sephardic Commentary," sustained plaudits for top Iberian-Judaic occultists and Talmudists, among them Abraham ibn Ezra, Shlomo ben Yitzhak, Moses Maimonides, Moses Nahmanides, Solomon ben Gabirol, Rabbi Yehudah of Portugal and Rabbi Judah ha-Levi. Of these individuals he wrote in perfect conformity with the tenets of syncretic Church of Rome modernism, "Let those who have been examined here suffice so envy may realize that Spain (I praise my native land; I do not condemn other regions)—whether she be Jewish, whether she be Mohammedan—has given men to the world who would, singly, be enough for her to be pronounced illustrious and be so indeed." [26]

Caramuel was Abbot-Superior of the Benedictines of Vienna, Grand-Vicar to the Archbishop of Prague, and Bishop of Satrianum, and later of Campagna. He is regarded as a pioneer of the elastic "probabilist" morality that would be expanded by Alphonsus Liguori. Caramuel's probabilism was based in part on the thought of the Polish Rabbi Samuel of Lublin (Rabbi Samuel Eliezer Ben Judah Edels; 1555-1631).[27]

Caramuel's ally, Bishop Joseph Maria Ciantes, had been appointed by Pope Urban VIII in 1626 to convert the Judaic community in Rome. As part of his evangelism of the Judaics, Bishop Ciantes wrote two apologetic works on the Trinity (1667) and the Incarnation (1668). "Both books were based mainly on ideas taken from Jewish Cabalistic sources..." [28]

Bishop Caramuel's thoroughly modern, extremist negation of sin has not yet been surpassed even in our twenty-first century. Inside the Church of Rome he represents one wing of the rigged stringent-lenient "pair," which is a thinly disguised replication of the Talmudic-theological schools of Shammai and Hillel and the *gevurah/chesed* pair. These are lawyer's distinctions. God's law is not subject to casuist categories of rigor and laxity. These categories are artificially imposed upon

---

[26] Caramuel, *Dominicus* (Vienna, 1655).

[27] Cf. Jean-Robert Armogathe, "Caramuel: A Cistercian Casuist," in *Juan Caramuel Lobkowitz : The Last Scholastic Polymath*.

[28] Yossef Schwartz, "On Rabbinic Atheism," pp. 131-132.

the Word of God by those with a mentality of lawyers and Talmudists who describe themselves as theologians. They seek to forge a path above duality; beyond good and evil. Observe the backward premise from which Bishop Caramuel proceeds to nullify God's law:

"Moral obligation, in Caramuel's view, arises from the imposition of law. 'I deny that any moral malice can be understood without (reference to) a precept,' he argues...in the *Benedicti Regulam*. 'As a result, if all laws were to be taken away (whether this is possible or not), there would remain nothing that could be described as morally evil." [29]

"With the protection of (Pope) Alexander VII, Caramuel clearly weathered the initial storm over his controversial work. Blaise Pascal began to publish anonymously a series of short, satirical counterattacks...Pascal did not analyze probabilism's theoretical foundations; instead he simply listed 'the decisions those casuists who had adopted probabilism rendered in particular cases. In the *Provincial Letters*, probabilism appears not merely ridiculous but even sinister in light of the outrageous actions that its principles will justify." [30]

While it is true that Caramuel's book *Apologema* was consigned to the Index of Forbidden Books in January, 1664, the consignment was necessary to temporarily satisfy the concerns of those conservatives who still respected the original Catholic Church. Let us not stop there, however. But rather, observe what occurred afterward, to the supposed "banned" author: Bishop Caramuel subsequently established, with permission of the hierarchy, a printing plant for his supposedly "forbidden" book!

In 1664, he published two additional volumes on moral theology and then joined the brotherhood of the *Academia napoletana degli Investiganti*. Five more books would follow. In 1673, at the behest of the Catholic queen-regent of Austria, Caramuel was appointed bishop of the diocese of Vigevano, a more centrally located and lucrative posting.

---

[29] Julia A. Fleming, *Defending Probabilism: The Moral Theology of Juan Caramuel,* p. 38.

[30] Ibid., p. 14.

As we endeavor to demonstrate in the pages that follow, Caramuel and his Vatican protectors were representative of the situation ethics that would come to replace Catholic dogma.

The revolution within the Church did not commence with the Second Vatican Council. It was nearly three hundred years old by the time the secular-Enlightenment in Europe erupted in the eighteenth century.

Chapter II

Neoplatonic-Hermeticism

In the historical period under examination "Neoplatonic Hermeticism" emerged under the auspices of a "Hermetic" system of belief ascribed to the mythical, eponymous "Hermes Trismegistus," linked to the "Neoplatonic" belief system ascribed to Plato's followers in the period 200-500 A.D. forward. It advanced much farther than the old witchcraft systems that tried to dominate in the Middle Ages. Neoplatonic-Hermeticism commanded the Renaissance Church in part because it was self-advertised as angel light and sweetness: a clean system of occult knowledge that pre-dated Christ and prophesied of Him by means of Egyptian "white" magic, and a rabbinic Kabbalism which was allegedly harnessed to benevolent rather than malevolent forces. [1] A Christian and Biblical veneer was thereby attached to the devil's magical gnosis. To gain entrée to the circles of syncretizing ecumenism and liberalism it was dubbed the *philosophia perennis* (perennial philosophy, i.e. the eternal philosophy), and the *prisca theologia*," (first theology), i.e. the "ancient wisdom narrative," and this make-believe was the "rocket fuel" which helped to propel it into dominion over the Church of Rome (at a time when Martin Luther was a child and John Calvin was not yet born), and helped to establish it as the referential corpus of western esotericism from then until now.

Neoplatonic-Hermeticism is the spiritual force and ideological impetus which "split the Church" before there ever was a Protestant Reformation. The clever agents of Rome's information warfare have managed to lay the blame for this division on "the Protestants." By this device researchers need

---

[1] Judaic Kabbalists of the fifteenth century such as Yohanan Alemanno encouraged the promulgation of the Neoplatonic-Hermetic myth that Platonism resulted from the doctrines of the Biblical patriarchs. Cf. Kocku von Stuckrad, *Location of Knowledge in Medieval and Early Modern Europe: Esoteric Discourse and Western Identities* (2010), p. 38. Alemanno was a mentor and companion of Giovanni Pico della Mirandola and scholar in residence in the home of the Judaic da Pisa family in the 1480s and early 1490s. Decades later, Daniel ben Isaac da Pisa would become a favorite of Pope Clement VII.

not trouble themselves with an authentic investigation into what led to the division of Christendom after the first breakup, between the Orthodox East and the Roman West in 1054. They could satisfy themselves with a cliché: "The Protestants caused it."

While much of the arcane doctrine of which Neoplatonic-Hermetic Catholics taught and advocated is at such a level as to be difficult to grasp without a considerable introduction to the subject matter, many orthodox Christians understand what syncretism and religious indifferentism are, and the threat these pose to the Gospel. "...in the light of Neoplatonism, the humanist discovered in mythology something other and much greater than a concealed morality: they discovered religious teaching—the Christian doctrine itself." [2]

Actually, they discovered nothing of the sort. What they discovered was the right time for putting a false Christ over on the princes and churchmen and other higher-ups. He who said, "I am the Way, the Truth and the Life. No one comes unto the Father except by Me," cannot be absorbed into the eternal pagan psychodrama. Hence, He must be transmogrified. Thus was born *"The Christ"* of symbolism and *"The Christ"* of the New Age. This pseudo-Christ was imparted by means of the arcane Renaissance papist theology which holds that the pre-Christian pagan religions prophesied and foreshadowed Jesus:

"Interpretation by means of symbols, in fact, made it possible not only to discern a lofty wisdom beneath fictions of the most diverse character and the most unedifying appearance: it further led to a grasp of the fundamental relationship between this profane wisdom (variable in its outward but immutable in its teaching) and the wisdom of the Bible. Just as Plato accords with Moses, and Socrates 'confirms' Christ, so Homer's voice is that of a prophet. And the Magi of Persia and Egypt, who in their turn mask sacred maxims under a cloak of Fable, are linked to the sages of Israel. Against this background it was inevitable that the same idea which declining paganism has evolved should occur to the humanists — namely, that all religions have the same worth, and that under varied forms, however puerile and monstrous in

---

2 Jean Seznec, *The Survival of the Pagan Gods* (1981), p. 98.

seeming, is hidden a common truth. Marsilio Ficino leans toward a universal theism, with Platonism as its gospel." [3]

"Contrary to popular assumptions, the Enlightenment was not anti-religious...its roots reached deeply into the soil of Neo-Platonism and Kabbalism...a line may be drawn...to Renaissance Neo-Platonists like Nicholas of Cusa...and Pico della Mirandola, all the way to...the Enlightenment. In his *On the Peace of Faith* (1453), Nicholas of Cusa envisions a conference in heaven where the religions are finally reconciled, recognizing that they are one in their moral and spiritual core..." [4]

The Renaissance project was intended to follow the rabbinic model of transformation, whereby the Israelite religion of the Old Testament was changed into the Talmudic/Kabbalistic religion of pagan Judaism, under a compelling Biblical veneer. Long before the *proposed* synthesis between Plato and Moses, came the *realized* synthesis of the Talmudic Moses (not to be confused with the genuine Moses of the Pentateuch)—and Egyptian and Babylonian paganism. This monstrosity is almost always presented by university professors and the corporate media of our day as a trend toward liberation, human fulfillment, peace and love, and so forth. Actually it led to the acceleration of the enslavement of Black people (about which we will have more to say) and playing god with nature by "perfecting" God's "imperfect" Creation, which resulted in the rise of a "scientific" and "medical" priesthood that subjugates Nature. "Such a stance is also found in Abraham Abulafia's book *Or-ha-Sekhel* and, following him, Moshe Narboni's *Commentary on Avicenna's Intentions of the Philosophers*, where the claim is made that the prophet who can change the course of nature is the highest among all the prophets." [5]

Harvard Professor Gilles Quispel writes, "In 1460 a monk brought a Greek manuscript to Florence. The monk, one of the agents that the city's ruler, Cosimo de' Medici, had been sent to

---

[3] Seznec, p. 98.

[4] Michael Horton, *The Christian Faith: A Systematic Theology* (2011) pp. 59-60.

[5] Moshe Idel, *Kabbalah in Italy: 1280-1510* (2011), p. 311.

scour Europe's monasteries for forgotten writings of the ancients, and what he now brought his patron was a codex containing fourteen treatises attributed to Hermes Trismegistus, an ancient Egyptian sage. This work's arrival caused a great stir, because Hermes, identified with the Ibis god Thoth, was held to be older than Plato and Moses and the underlying inspiration of all philosophy and religion that followed him...This manuscript contained the nucleus of the *Corpus Hermeticum*...Along with some astrological and alchemical works, also named after Hermes, these tracts became the fundamental writings of the Renaissance, together called Hermeticism...Hermetic writings...lived on in secret societies such as the Freemasons and the Rosicrucians." [6]

Marsilio Ficino

Rev. Fr. Marsilio Ficino (1433-1499), a gifted Catholic philologist and magician with a mastery of early Greek, made the first Latin translation from the recently discovered codex at the urgent request of his patron, Cosimo de' Medici, [7] who, in 1462, ordered that Ficino put aside his translation of Plato's complete works (*Opera omnia*) in favor of *Pimander* (a.k.a. the "*Corpus Hermeticum*"), [8] which was alleged to have been authored by Mercury/Hermes in antiquity. Ficino's translation of *Pimander* (*Corpus Hermeticum*) was printed in 1471. His version of Plato's *Opera omnia,* dedicated to Lorenzo de' Medici, would be published in 1484, on a day timed to coincide with the astrological conjunction of Saturn and Jupiter.

The occult Catholic Neoplatonism of Ficino is one of the earliest sources of the ideology of modernism manifested by the Second Vatican Council and in its "post-conciliar" aftermath; and the "spirit of Assisi" as exemplified, beginning in 1986, by Pope "Saint" John Paul II's syncretic parliament of world religions in Assisi, Italy. Ficino's Renaissance Catholic Platonism "was part of the humanist project to embrace non-

---

6 Quispel adds that in Egypt in 1945 "a better version in Coptic of parts of the Hermetic *Asclepius*, preserved in Latin among the work of Apuleius," was discovered near Nag Hammadi.

7 From whom Ficino received a villa in 1463.

8 Named *Pimander* after the "spirit" that legend has it dictated the *Corpus Hermeticum* to Hermes in his sleep.

Christian sources of religious wisdom...Ficino believed that Christianity was in desperate need of reformation...in terms of its theological content. In Ficino's mind, Christian theology had been barbarized by centuries of ill-conceived dependence on Aristotelianism...Ficino understood that in antiquity the best Christian theologians had relied on Platonism...Ficino's goal was to use a revived Platonism to dramatically reshape contemporary Christianity. In particular, his goal was to rethink the relationship between Christianity and the other great world religions, to break down the narrow, dogmatic barriers imposed in late antiquity that separated Christianity from other forms of religious wisdom. This led him to a new kind of Christian apologetics that, unlike the Christian apologetics of the medieval period, did not seek in any straightforward way to demonstrate the falsity of other religions and the truth of Christianity." [9]

The Neoplatonic-Hermetic theology of Marsilio Ficino, Catholic priest, theologian and Cathedral Canon, was transmitted from fifteenth century Catholic Italy to seventeenth century Protestant England and from there to those intellectuals who comprised the early Enlightenment:

"In the case of Platonism, it was a combination of humanistic linguistic skill and philosophical acumen, in the person of Marsilio Ficino, which proved fundamental to its revival in the Renaissance...His own philosophical inclination was towards Plato rather than Aristotle, primarily because, as a priest, he considered Platonism to be more compatible with Christianity. It was Ficino who put Platonism on the philosophical map of the Renaissance...which provided the intellectual framework for his Christianized interpretation of Plato...Much of the literary influence of Ficinian Platonism was channeled through the vernacular tradition...Take the case of Ficino's Latin commentary on (Plato's) *Symposium* (1469). He (Ficino) himself translated it into the vernacular, but it was also transformed by one of his followers, Girolamo Benivieni, into a densely allusive...Italian *canzone*.[10]...The central theme

---

[9] Jens Zimmerman, op. cit.

[10] In Italy, a poem set to music.

of the *Symposium*, Platonic love, as Christianized and purified by Ficino—Plato's homosexual characters are converted into chaste male friends, united by their shared devotion to God...Platonism as a philosophical system, rather than a source of literary themes and motifs, was promoted in the mid-seventeenth century by a group of (Protestant) Cambridge clergymen and professors...(t)he Cambridge Platonists..." [11]

These Platonists in Protestant Britain were on the receiving end of Ficino's two-hundred-year-old legacy.

The "Cambridge Platonists" included Benjamin Whichcote (1609-1683); John Smith (1618-1652); Henry More (1614-1687) and Ralph Cudworth (1617-1688). These were Fr. Ficino's spiritual and ideological heirs and the transmitters of his Catholic-Neoplatonic-Hermeticism to the Enlightenment, having realized its radical ends:

"The acceptance by the Cambridge Platonists of Plato and his disciples under the leadership of Plotinus (204-270 A.D.) —'Divine Plotinus!'— went hand in hand with their bold rejection of the entire Western theological tradition from St. Augustine through the medieval schoolmen to the classic Protestantism of Luther, Calvin and their variegated followers in the seventeenth century...Luther and Calvin and the entire array of Protestant theologians were greeted with the worst possible disapprobation...

"The return of the Cambridge Platonists to 'the ancient and wisest philosophers...was a return to a tradition which included many more philosophers besides Plato, the Neoplatonists, the Greek fathers and the thinkers of fifteenth-century Florence. This tradition was rooted in 'the primitive theology of the Gentiles' [12] which, according to Ficino, had begun with Zoroaster...Hermes Trismegistus...passed thence to Orpheus and Pythagoras...a variant of it appears implicit in Cudworth's *True Intellectual System* and it was once outlined by (Henry) More:

---

[11] Jill Kraye, "Philologists and Philosophers," in *The Cambridge Companion to Renaissance Humanism* (Cambridge University, 1998), pp. 149-151.

[12] Ficino, *De christiana religione*, ch. 22: "*Prisca Gentilium Theologia, in qua Zoroaster, Mercurius, Orpheus, Aglaophemus, Pythagoras consenserunt, tota in Platonis nostri uoluminibus continetur.*"

"Plato's school...well agrees with learned Pythagore,
Egyptian Trismegist, and the antique roll
Of Chaldee wisdom, all which time hath tore
But Plato and deep Plotin do restore." [13]

Father Ficino wrote, "Hermes Trismegistus (Hermes the thrice-greatest) was the first father of Theology, followed by Orpheus, who occupied the second place in the ancient theology. Aglaophemus was initiated into the sacred mysteries by Orpheus, to be succeeded in theology by Pythagoras, who in turn was followed by Philolaus, the teacher of our divine Plato." [14]

Plato was a forerunner of the Gnostics. For Plato the body was mainly the vessel that held the soul captive to materiality. At death, the soul was released from its bodily "prison."

"For Plato, the soul is the non-material aspect of a human being, and is the aspect that really matters. Bodily life is full of delusion and danger; the soul is to be cultivated in the present both for its own sake and because its future happiness will depend upon such cultivation. The soul, being immortal, existed before the body, and will continue to exist after the body is gone. Since for many Greeks 'the immortals' were the gods, there is always the suggestion, at least by implication, that human souls are in some way divine...Death is frequently defined precisely in terms of the separation of soul and body, seen as something to be desired.

"Hades, in other words, is not a place of gloom, but (in principle at least) of delight. It is not terrifying, as so many ordinary people believe, but offers a range of pleasing activities —of which philosophical discourse may be among the chief, not surprisingly since attention to such matters is the best way, during the present time, of preparing the soul for its future. The reason people do not return from Hades is that life is so good there; they want to stay, rather than to return to the world of space, time and matter...What happens to souls in Hades—at least, to souls who go there to begin

---

[13] C. A. Patrides, *The Cambridge Platonists* (1969), pp. 4-6. "Plotin," i.e. Plotinus.

[14] Some accounts have Ficino putting Orpheus or Zoroaster in first place and Hermes second.

with...Judgment is passed according to the person's previous behavior...Plato frequently hints at a future for souls *after* their immediate post-mortem existence; some will return into other bodies.

"...influences that steered Plato towards his view of the soul and life after death...(t)o begin with, it is a natural outworking of his larger ontology: according to the theory of Forms, the world of space, time and matter is of secondary ontological significance, and the unseen world of Forms, or Ideas, is primary.

"...Already in Socrates' time the (occult) mystery religions had begun to flourish, offering (so it seemed) a comparable benefit to philosophical wisdom...Beginning with the Orphic cult, but fanning out much more widely, these religions (if that is indeed the right term for them) offered the initiate access to a world of private spiritual experience in the present time which would continue into the world beyond death...

"A further development, whose origins are obscure and controversial, was gnosticism. Many lines of Platonic thought led straight in this direction. The immortal (and perhaps even divine) soul is imprisoned in the unsuitable body, forgetting its origin in the process. During the present life those with this spark may have the fact revealed to them; as a result, they become possessed of a 'knowledge' *(gnosis)* which sets them apart from other mortals, and are assured of a continuing blissful existence thereafter...

"Plato's ideas on the soul (and much else besides) were, in addition, severely modified by his equally influential pupil Aristotle. He took the view that the soul was the subtance, or the species-form, of the living thing; this represents a turning away from the lively Platonic view of the soul as more or less independent, and superior, entity to the body." [15]

Catholics and others conditioned by the Platonic and Neoplatonic Churchianity that passes for Christianity nowadays, may not find much fault with Plato's soul doctrine. The fault is this: Plato has no place in his theology/philosophy for the dead person's return to his or her body in the Resurrection. Of course, the Catholic Church does make ample

---

[15] N.T. Wright, *The Resurrection of the Son of God* (2003), pp. 49-53.

room for this truth, and numerous councils and papal bulls can be cited which affirm it in no uncertain terms. But in the *practice* of the faith, the emphasis is decidedly not on *our resurrected body, and our entirely new life after Jesus returns*— the future *reality* which radically contradicts Platonic, Gnostic, Manichaean, Neoplatonic and Hermetic mystical occult fantasy.

The Second Coming of Jesus will mark the beginning of a restoration that He will initiate when He returns. Again, this is a Biblical future reality that runs counter to the western occult mirage imprinted on our minds through the Neoplatonic and Hermetic infiltration of the Church. If we are honest with ourselves, many of us will admit that we are infected with this occult virus: we picture our after-life in heaven mainly as eternally experiencing the beatific vision. We have little or no sense of the actual future foretold by God's Word.

How was this ignorance inculcated in us? How have "devout Catholics" and their "learned priests," and "conservative" Protestants and their "scholarly ministers," failed to grasp what our future consists of, according to the Word of God? Is this desideratum the result of an accident, or a conspiracy? The greatest experience of our future existence has been rendered a footnote, when it is referred to at all: *under Christ, we will administer God's kingdom in our restored, resurrection bodies.* This fact from the Book of Revelation undercuts all of the mystical mumbo-jumbo that emanates from the occult, which has migrated into private revelations and apparitions that proliferate in the Church of Rome, aided by clerics and prelates in whose interest it is to furnish these soporifics to the people of God.

What is at stake is the Christian's correct knowledge of reality: that *God's Creation which we inhabit on earth, is basically good*, in spite of the flaw which our first parent's disobedience in the Garden brought into that Creation. Our life on God's earth is precious and wonderful, and God is a God of the living. True Christians will live again in their renewed, physical bodies. Jesus will completely restore the Creation on His return, and we will be in our bodies as part of that restoration.

These Biblical truths are heresy to the occult gnosis of the western secret societies, which finalized their usurpation of the hierarchy of the Church in the Renaissance. Much of

Protestantism inherited some of Neoplatonic-Hermetic Rome's errors, in spite of contending against other aspects of papal theology, while also adding new errors of their own invention.

There is most certainly a disembodied state after death, while we await the Resurrection. But that state is *not the final destiny of Christ's Faithful*, as so many have been led to believe through the influence of paganized agents of error. Our destiny is the "restoration of all things" (Acts 3:21)—the glorified Creation where Heaven will be a transformed earth, which we will experience in our glorified, regenerate, *immortal bodies* (Romans 8:11). The failure to consistently preach and propagate this wondrous future as the overarching reality of life after death, has misled, demoralized and alienated millions of people, causing them to reject a saving faith and hope in Jesus and His Gospel.

The false picture inculcated in our minds of a shabby existence on a wretched planet earth that must be escaped, coupled with the vision of an eternal, disembodied post-mortem fate, is strong evidence of the extent to which Neoplatonism has replaced Christianity in churches where this delusion has been allowed to proliferate.

"The influence of Platonism on the church father Origen (A.D. 185-254) was so thorough that the early Church theologian taught not only that the soul was the immortal part of human beings that preexisted eternally, but also that this soul was often reincarnated in different bodies. For Origen, Christ is primarily the soul's educator, who, by his moral example and teaching, leads us from the transitory realm of material things to the invisible realm that is the soul's true realm..." Origen taught that 'Christ's ascension was 'more an ascent of mind than of body...'" [16]

The disconnection between the soul and the body, transmitted by Catholic Neoplatonists to the Renaissance Church, penetrating its theology and positing a disconnection between the resurrection body and the soul, represents another grave peril for the Christian believer: it tills the soil for a theology which leads to the heresy of modernism, in which Christ's resurrection is denied outright, or at the very least, obscured by cant language.

---

[16] Horton, op.cit., p. 48.

"In *The Education of the Human Race* (1778), rationalist philosopher G.E. Lessing [17] (1729-1781)...said, regardless of whether Christ literally rose from the dead, such facts of contingent history are insufficient to ground or to challenge eternal principles of reason. On the basis of this Platonist prejudice, Lessing asserted that Christianity's supernatural claims are indemonstrable...this trajectory leads to the theologian Rudolf Bultmann (1884-1976), who said, 'The Jesus of history is no concern to me...I am deliberately renouncing any form of encounter with a phenomenon of past history, including an encounter with the Christ after the flesh." [18]

Platonized Catholicism (Neoplatonic occultism) combined Platonism and Gnosticism in propounding an ontological dualism of "realms of the forms" and "appearances." In Neoplatonism the redemption Jesus gained for us in history, in the-here-and-now, is always sublimated to a putative secret gnosis behind that redemption, which is supposed to be an indispensable key to full enhancement of Christ's salvation mission. In actuality, a false Christ is formulated, the Christ of the spirit as opposed to the true Christ who made possible our redemption. In the infernal marriage of Platonism and Manichaeism, the soul is trapped in the flesh. Redemption is found in escape from the body and the world in which the body has incarnated by the will of God, into the immortal spirit world. [19]

Contrasted with these delusions is the truth of the Biblical narrative of reality: a covenant between God and His people unfolding in the history of human life on earth. "In contrast to Plato, biblical religion looks for true knowledge of God in the realm of history, particulars, and flux, rather than in an ostensibly higher realm...transcending these factors." (Michael Horton).

---

[17] "Religious pluralism and relativism lie at the heart of modernity, as is evident in Lessing's clever parable of Nathan the Wise (1778), which is similar to Nicholas of Cusa's *On the Peace of Faith...*" Horton, p. 61.

[18] Horton, op.cit., pp. 60-61.

[19] From which, the Neoplatonist Iambilchus (250-325 A.D.) taught, divine powers could be obtained by way of the precise enactment of ceremonial magic.

Christ's resurrection was spiritualized by the Vatican's Renaissance Catholic occultists in secret, while outwardly the Church of Rome issued bold proclamations of Biblical truth concerning the imperative to believe in the efficacy of Christ's physical resurrection from the dead. This masquerade was maintained in history for as long as it took for the *zeitgeist* to change. Then the time for public statements of the formerly hidden doctrines had arrived. Liberal and Conservative churchmen such as Pope Paul VI on the Left, and Pope Benedict XVI on the Right, undertook this unveiling.

As Matthew Vogan observes, Benedict XVI (the former Cardinal Joseph Ratzinger) "entered office with a formidable reputation as the Vatican's arch-conservative 'enforcer' of doctrine...It is alarming to think of the extent of the heresies held by those who have authority within the bounds of Rome if Ratzinger is to be considered conservative."

During the pontificate of Francis, naive and self-deceived, Janus-minded "Conservatives" and "Traditionalists" in the wolf-pen of the post-Renaissance Church of Rome, bewailed the still-living Benedict XVI's absence from the papacy like sheep bleating for Little Bo Peep. They were pining for the Hermetic heretic who wrote in his book *Einführung in das Christentum* (1968): [20]

"According to the Epistle in Ephesians, Christ's work of salvation consisted precisely in bringing to their knees the forces and powers seen by Origen in his commentary on this passage as the collective powers which encircle man: the power of the milieu, of national tradition; the conventional 'they' or 'one' that oppresses and destroys man. Terms like original sin, resurrection of the flesh, last judgment, and so on, are only to be understood at all from this angle, for the seat of original sin is to be sought precisely in this collective net that precedes the individual existence as a sort of spiritual datum, not in any biological legacy passed on between otherwise separated individuals...Resurrection expresses the idea that the immortality of man can only exist and be thought of in fellowship of men, in man as the creature of fellowship..." [21]

---

[20] Translated and published in English as *Introduction to Christianity* (Herder and Herder, 1971).

[21] Ratzinger, ibid., pp. 186-187.

The future Pope Benedict XVI—the Vatican II theological expert Rev. Fr. Joseph Ratzinger—was inextricably intertwined with the theology of his Renaissance-Catholic predecessors, upholding, in an unbroken chain of transmission, nearly six hundred years of Neoplatonic-Hermetic heterodoxy, when he wrote that the coming of Jesus Christ was prophesied "according to Plato," in the latter's blueprint for deceit and dictatorship, *The Republic*. The future pope wrote that Plato's alleged prophecy "is always bound to move a Christian deeply."[22]

The future Pope Benedict XVI continues: "To our generation, whose critical faculty has been awoken by Bultmann, talk of the ascension, together with that of the descent into hell, conjures that picture of the three-story world which we call mythical...Indeed, since there is no absolute point of reference...basically one cannot any longer speak at all of 'above' and 'below'— or even of 'left' and 'right'; the cosmos no longer exhibits any firm directions. No one today (1968) will seriously contest these discoveries. There is no longer such a thing as a world arranged literally in three storys." [23]

"In *Introduction to Christianity*, Ratzinger explicitly denies the resurrection of the body. 'It now becomes clear that the real heart of faith in the resurrection does not consist at all in the idea of the restoration of bodies, to which we have reduced it in our thinking; such is the case even though this is the pictorial image used throughout the Bible'...one thing at any rate may be fairly clear: both John (6:63) and Paul (1 Corinthians 15:50) state with all possible emphasis that the 'resurrection of the flesh,' the 'resurrection of the body,' is not a 'resurrection of physical bodies.'

"Ratzinger could not be more explicit about his interpretation of 'the biblical pronouncements about the resurrection'. He says that their essential content is not the conception of a restoration of bodies to souls after a long interval; their aim is to tell men that they, they themselves, live on...because they are known and loved by God in a way that they can no longer perish...the essential part of man, the

22 Ibid., pp. 222-223.

23 Ibid., pp. 237-238.

person, remains...it goes on existing because it lives in God's memory.'

"(In) Ratzinger's theology of the resurrection of Christ...he dismisses an 'earthly and material notion of resurrection' and resists defining it as a real historical event. He says that it is 'impossible for the Gospels to describe the encounter with the risen Christ; that is why "they can only stammer when they speak of these meetings and seem to provide contradictory descriptions of them."

"Ratzinger: 'Christ is the one who died on the cross and *to the eye of faith*, rose again from the dead.' How far this is from the biblical truth of passages such as John 20:27: 'Then saith he to Thomas, Reach hither thy finger, and behold my hands; and reach hither thy hand, and thrust it into my side: and be not faithless, but believing'.

"The Fourth Lateran Council has asserted – and Councils are regarded as infallible in Roman Catholic dogma–that all men 'will rise again with their own bodies which they now bear about with them.' Ratzinger was involved in producing the new *Catechism of the Catholic Church*, which was approved with 'Apostolic Authority' by the previous pope ("Saint" John Paul II) in 1992. This document states that 'the resurrection of the flesh' (the literal formulation of the Apostles' Creed) means not only that the immortal soul will live on after death, but that even our 'mortal body' will come to life again'...While this could be more precise it appears reasonably categorical. How then may...Pope (Benedict) continue to deny such a statement of the Church's official teaching? It can be done only by the Jesuitical distinction that he makes between his official and private views (despite the fact that his books are all marketed with 'Pope Benedict XVI' more prominently displayed than his real name).

"Despite the seemingly-binding nature of the new *Catechism*, some point to the fact that it was not prepared by a full Council and are able to take some refuge in Ratzinger's comments that the *Catechism* seeks to leave debated questions as open as possible. Ratzinger also views doctrinal formulations as having an 'infinitely broken nature' in 'man's continual effort to go beyond himself and reach up to God.'

"An explanation closer to the heart of the matter is that it is typical of Roman Catholicism to say both 'yes' and 'no' at the same time to biblical doctrine. It says 'yes' to the authority of

Scripture but simultaneously 'no' by exalting the Church's teaching above it. This is also part of that 'all deceivableness of unrighteousness' (2 Thess. 2:10) with which the system presided over by the man of sin is characterized. It is well able to bring together the incompatible as well as the diverse. There is a deceivability that goes beyond any other..." [24]

The demonic delusion at the heart of the occult "isms" (Platonism, Neoplatonism, Hermeticism and Kabbalism), which is fundamental to the western secret societies, whether in the Latin West or the Greek world, is the principle that man, through his theurgy, is a partner with God in wonder-working in this life, and God, whose existence is linked to the "World Spirit," is in some sense dependent on man. The Biblical truth concerning the reality of God is absolutely separate from the preceding matrix of enchantment:

"What is remarkable is that the triune God—self-existing, perfect and independent—would nevertheless create and enter into covenantal relationships with creatures in freedom and love...God transcends heaven itself, which He has created (I Kings: 8:27); Matthew 24:35). As Paul explained to the Athenian philosophers, this is one of the attributes that highlight the contrast between God and the idols: 'The God who made the world and everything in it, being Lord of heaven and earth, does not live in temples made by man, nor is He served by human hands, as though he needed anything, since He himself gives to all mankind life and breath and everything (Acts 17:24-25).

"...in Isaiah, God's name [25] becomes especially understood as referring to God's eternal and independent existence apart from the creation (e.g. Isaiah 40:28; 41:4; 43:10-20; 44:6; 48:12). God reveals His name in the midst of demonstrating His eternal purpose and immutable nature...Yahweh can be trusted to bring to pass everything that He has promised. His Name can be invoked with total confidence, both because He is

---

[24]   Matthew Vogan, "Does the Pope Believe in the Resurrection?" *Free Presbyterian Magazine*, September, 2010. Vogan's references are to the Ignatius Press edition of *Introduction to Christianity* (2004), pp. 98, 152, 211-212, 240-241, 243 and 256.

[25] YHVH, "Yahweh" — "I Am who I Am."

faithful to His promise and because He is not dependent on creatures for realizing His purposes. Egypt's pantheon is the foil. In contrast to the various nature gods, limited by their specific areas of provenance, Yahweh is the Sovereign God (Deuteronomy 4:34-35). Precisely because God is not dependent on anyone or anything He has created, we are assured that nothing will keep Him from being there for us...the gospel itself is embedded in the very name of Israel's God. The fact that God is incomparable and transcends the world...(e)vil powers never have the last word, because although God enters into the matrix of creaturely powers, He is never simply one player among others. God remains qualitatively and not just quantitatively distinct from creation...

"...according to Platonism, Neoplatonism...(t)he world does not exist as a free choice and act of God but as the necessary emanation or aspect of His being...God...needs the world for the realization of His existence, happiness and perfection: God's being is in His becoming.

"...In Paul's Mars Hill speech, Paul points out that 'in (God) we live and move and have our being' rather than vice versa (Acts 17:28). There is relatedness, but it is that of the world to God rather than of God to the world. Even in the Incarnation, the eternal Son assumed our humanity rather than vice versa. It is precisely in God's independence and freedom from contingency that a hospitable space is opened for the freedom of contingent reality...this 'unbounded, limitless, absolutely undetermined, unqualified' view of God is irreconcilable with pantheism ancient and modern: 'Babylonian, Hellenistic, Neoplatonist, Kabbalistic and Spinozistic." [26]

According to occult fable, Plato was a master of Egyptian magic, deeply immersed in Pharaonic occultism. This is silly stuff but it persisted as Neoplatonic-Catholic legend. In the third century A.D. Diogenes Laertius, in his *Lives of Eminent Philosophers*, wrote that Plato sojourned in Egypt five years while gaining its "wisdom."

It is now generally agreed that the Greek text of the *Corpus Hermeticum* was written around 300 A.D., approximately the same time when it is surmised that the Kabbalah and Babylonian Talmud were beginning to be compiled. Gilles

---

[26] Michael Horton, op. cit., pp. 230-233.

Quispel, in the book *The Way of Hermes*, writes that *Poimandres*, the first of the fourteen Hermetic texts that comprise *Pimander (Corpus Hermeticum)*, "echoes the main theme of esoteric Judaism."

Furthermore, Walter Scott, editor of the four volume Oxford University text, *Hermetica: The Ancient Greek and Latin Writings Which Contain Religious or Philosophic Teachings Ascribed to Hermes Trismegistus* (1924-1936), asserts that Plato and his *Timaeus* were a powerful influence on the writings attributed to Hermes.

The Egypt of Isis, Osiris and Anubis was the master theological image of this process of transformation. This is reflected in several of Ficino's treatises, in particular *De voluptate* and *Di dio et anima*. In the former he describes Hermes Trismegistus as "the wisest of all Egyptians," whose god is the source of all creation. In the latter he writes, "Mercurius Trismegistus, an Egyptian philosopher far more ancient than the Greeks, whom Greeks and Egyptians called a god because of his boundless understanding and knowledge..."

"The other significant development of the Renaissance...was the spreading influence of Kabbalah in European magical thought. The mystical system of Kabbalah...had been percolating into Christian magic before the late fifteenth century, but it was its espousal by another Florentine philosopher and natural magician, Pico della Mirandola (1463-1494), that introduced it to a new readership and led to renewed engagement with its occult promises. Johannes Reuchlin, a German humanist scholar and expert in Greek and Hebrew, further advanced its influence north of the Alps." [27]

The Catholic trio of Ficino, Pico and Reuchlin represented highly placed and connected Neoplatonic Catholic "Humanists" whose Egyptian Hermeticism and rabbinic Kabbalism would give birth to Rosicrucianism and Freemasonry from within the Renaissance Church of Rome itself.

"The importance of the work of Marsilio Ficino of Florence...in the awakening, transmission and dissemination of esoteric knowledge in the West cannot be overestimated...In the Renaissance, this wisdom was assumed to originate with...the Egyptian Hermes Trismegistus, and...passed down

---

[27] Owen Davies, *Grimoires: A History of Magic Books* (2010), p. 46.

via Pythagoras and Orpheus to the 'divine Plato' and his interpreters...Ficino played a major role in the 'rebirth' of classical learning we know as the Renaissance, through his commitment to the renewal of Platonic and Hermetic philosophies and his determination to integrate their metaphysics into Christianity...His ordination as a priest (in 1473) and later as a canon of Florence cathedral enabled him to 'sanctify' the pagan philosophy while confirming the supremacy of the established religion." [28]

"Ficino...translated the *Corpus Hermeticum*, which he saw as containing a core of teachings handed down from very ancient times through Orpheus, Pythagoras, Plato and Hermes himself." [29] "Ficino's pupil, Pico della Mirandola...used Qabalistic [30] and Neoplatonic ideas in an attempt to find common ground between Christianity, Judaism and Islam...Another advocate of Qabalism was the Franciscan (friar) Francesco di Giorgio...whose *De Harmonia Mundi* combined Qabalism with a preoccupation with the ideas of universal harmony..." [31]

"Plato Hermeticised"

"In the geneaology of ancient wisdom, Ficino places Hermes (or his analogue in Roman mythology, Mercurius), at the beginning of theology. Insisting upon the continuous transmission of one and the same doctrine of esoteric thought from Hermes to Pythagoras, and from Pythagoras to Plato, Ficino goes so far to assert that when Plato is treating certain ideas, 'he does not present his own view but that of the Egyptians.'

"...it is fair to say that the Plato...(we) meet...upon reading Ficino's *Theologia Platonica* is Plato significantly Hermeticised. For Ficino, Plato merely reproduces the Greek philosophy that Moses has already established in the Scriptures, and what Hermes has revealed in the *Corpus*

28 Angela Voss, ed., *Marsilio Ficino* (2006), pp. 1 and 3.

29 Christopher McIntosh, *The Rosicrucians: The History, Mythology and Rituals of an Esoteric Order* (1998), p. 7.

30 "Qablistic" and "Qabalah" are alternative spellings of the Kabbalah root word.

31 McIntosh, op. cit., pp. 7-8.

Hermeticum. Believing Hermes to have been contemporary with Moses and to have communicated a parallel wisdom to a line of adepts through the ages, Ficino not only grants Hermes the status of Christian prophet, but wonders whether Hermes Trismegistus *is* in fact Moses. In the *Theologia* he writes, 'Mercurius Trismegistus has expounded this same origin of the world's generation even more plainly. It should not seem surprising to us that Mercurius knew such things if he was the *same man* as Moses.' Reading Christian theology back into Plato, and thence back into the *Hermetica*, Ficino propounds a syncretic philosophy in which Hermes Trismegistus is the one authorial and originating source of all other philosophies....The philosophies of Plato, Plotinus, Pythagoras and Christianity, are all stirred together in an incongruous literary-philosophical mixture...Showing a complete agreement between the teachings of Hermes, Moses, Plato and Christ, Ficino suggests that (the Book of) *Genesis* may be made to yield to the same message as the *Timaeus*, and both to yield to the one philosophy expounded in the *Pimander*. The idea of Hermes as the originating *fons et origo* of a tradition of wisdom which leads to an unbroken chain from Moses to Plato was the dominant genealogy for two centuries." [32]

The reference to the two-century limit of influence is more properly an allusion to a Renaissance time-frame when Hermes was literally believed to have been the actual contemporary of Moses (or to have been Moses himself under another name). This literary hoax was overturned most famously and resoundingly by the French Protestant scholar Isaac Casaubon, over the objections of Cardinal Cesare Baronius, with the appearance, in 1614, of Casaubon's irrefutable critique of the provenance of the *Corpus Hermeticum*, which proved philologically that it could be no older than the first century A.D. This later dating not only disproved the widespread Catholic belief that the texts attributed to Hermes Trismegistus were contemporaneous with Moses, but it also demolished the myth that Trismegistus had been the source of Plato's thought. (Substantial fragments of ancient Egyptian

---

[32] Kiran Toor, *Coleridge's Chrysopoetics* (2011), p. 33-34.

doctrine were indeed present in the writing attributed to Hermes, however).

Baronius was the author of a twelve volume Counter-Reformation history of the Church, *Annales Ecceliastici,* written from 1588 to 1607. He sought to prove the *bona fides* of the Church of Rome against the Protestants, with a long section on alleged "gentile testimony" to the truth of Jesus Christ. Among the sanctified gentiles in his list are "Mercurius Trismegistus" and the Sibyls, according to the lore of Lactanius. By crediting as foundational to the Catholic Church what amounted to the occult genealogy of the Neoplatonic-Hermetic conspiracy itself, Baronius revealed a devastating truth about the Church of Rome since the Renaissance, which made for a rather poor argument against Protestantism.

The *Hermetica* of Trismegistus and the oracles of the Syballines were no kind of corroboration of Christianity. Proceeding from that fact, Casaubon, in his *De rebus sacris et ecclesiasticus exercitationes,* discredited Baronius and the papist Church itself for continuing to promote the Neoplatonic-Hermetic narrative. By relying upon Lactanius as his source, Cardinal Baronius, a Catholic scholar highly favored by the hierarchy, furnished evidence of the fact that the occult theology was still predominant in papal Rome. Baronius was aware that Lactanius' account of gentiles who allegedly heralded the coming of Jesus, was hopelessly tainted with the Neoplatonist claims made for Hermes ("Mercurius") Trismegistus, as a prophet of Catholicism. Casaubon proved that the account of Hermes Trismegistus had been concocted sometime after the coming of Christ, and that this fraudulent prophet and the forged texts attached to his name, had been created by conspirators in the early centuries after Christ and then reintroduced during the Renaissance, which appears to have been the case. What was worse for the Counter-Reformation, was that the other forgeries—the texts said to have been composed by St. Paul's convert, Denys (also known as Dionysius) the Aeropagite—were defended as authentic not only by Cardinal Baronius, but by Rome's principal apologist against the Protestants, Cardinal (later Saint) Robert Bellarmine, who was thus implicated in an imposture.

The cult of Hermes Trismegistus is not limited to the two centuries before Casaubon debunked it. It is alive and well in the present, in part because the point of the hoax that survived into the Renaissance—to disseminate Egyptian paganism under Christian auspices—has of course been dropped, in favor of accessing the traces of Pharaonic-Egyptian magic and theology present in the Hermetic texts, without the need to justify them by asserting they prophesied of Christ. Furthermore, history has yet to adequately account for the possibility of a conspiracy of forgers (if indeed there was an enterprise deserving of such a title), conceivably launched by Neoplatonic-Christian deceivers, who not only tricked the West into accepting the Trismegistus texts as having been written in deep antiquity, but who also successfully assigned the voluminous writings falsely attributed to St. Paul's convert, Dionysius the Areopgite. These pseudoepigrapha may have been produced near in time to one another, and if that is so, they may suggest the existence of a cabal organized for the purpose of propagating the *prisca theologia*. It is also worthwhile to recall that the Old Testament pseudoepigrapha known as the Mishnah and Gemara (comprising the Talmud Bavli), were created in the same approximate time period, the first few centuries A.D.

Rabbinic Judaism represents the infernal marriage of the occultism of ancient Egypt with the Bible. The rabbinic claim for the Talmud and Kabbalah is that they are Bible-rooted books that explain and elaborate God's Scripture. Ficino, Mirandola, Giorgio (1466-1540) and the other members of the Church of Rome's occult coterie were the crypto-rabbis of the Catholic world. When Pope Pius X wrote against the "synthesis of all heresies" here it was, the syncretic claim that Egyptian diabolism, as filtered through its subsequent manifestations in the sorcerers of Babylon and Orphic and Attic Greece, and the heirs of these cumulative traditions— the rabbinic descendants of the Pharisees—proved the truth of Jesus Christ and the Bible. Ficino asserted in his *Concordia Mosis et Platonis* (Basel, 1561) that Plato proved Moses true. The Hermetic philosophy of the *Corpus Hermeticum* was regarded by the Catholic-occultists as an ancient theology, parallel to the revealed wisdom of the Bible, supporting Biblical revelation.

Ficino's *De triplici vita libri tres* ("Three Books on Life"), or simply *De vita*,[33] considered a "classic of Catholic Humanism" is, in its volume three, titled *De vita coelitus comparanda* ("Life matched to the heavens"), a complex amalgam of philosophy, magic and astrology including, in fidelity to Egyptian magic, advocacy of talismans and amulets. Trismegistus is featured in the final chapter of volume three which treats of the man-is-god thesis of the *Asclepius*, wherein Hermes laudes the Pharaonic Egyptian veneration of statues into which spirits had been imbued:

"You must know, O Asclepius, the power and force of man. Just as the Lord and Father is the creator of the gods of heaven, so man is the author of the gods who reside in the temples. Not only does he receive life, but he gives it in his turn. Not only does he progress towards God, but he *makes gods*.

"Do you mean the statues, O Trismegistus?'

"Yes, the statues, Asclepius. They are animated statues full of *sensus* and *spiritus* who can accomplish many things, foretelling the future, giving ills to men and curing them....What we have said about man is already marvelous, but most marvelous of all is that he has been able to discover the nature of the gods and to reproduce it. Our first ancestors invented the art of making gods. They mingled a virtue, drawn from material nature, to the substance of the statues, and since they could not actually create souls, after having evoked the souls of demons or angels, they introduced these into their idols by holy and divine rites, so that, the idols had the power of doing good and evil. These terrestrial or man-made gods result from a composition of herbs, stones, and aromatics which contain in themselves an occult virtue of divine efficacy. And if one tries to please them with numerous sacrifices, hymns, songs of praise, sweet concerts which recall the harmony of heaven, this is in order that the celestial element which has been introduced into the idol by the repeated practice of the celestial rites may joyously support its long dwelling amongst men. That is how man makes gods." [34]

---

[33] Florence: Antonio di Bartolommeo Miscomini, 1489; reprinted in Venice in 1498 and in Bologna in 1501 by Benedetto Faelli.

[34] The *Asclepius* of Hermes Trismegistus according to Ficino. Quoted by Frances A. Yates, *Giordano Bruno and the Hermetic Tradition* (1991), p. 37.

It is not difficult to perceive from what occult motives some manifestations of the *abuse* of the Roman Catholic tradition of statue veneration (*dulia*) degenerated into statue worship (*latria*), which is God's definition of hatred of him: Exodus 20: 4-5, "Thou shalt not make unto thee any graven image...Thou shalt not bow down thyself to them, nor serve them: for I the Lord thy God am a jealous God, visiting the iniquity of the fathers upon the children unto the third and fourth generation of them that hate me." Hermes in *Asclepius* surpasses even this heinous evil with his praise for humans who "invented the art of making gods" by having "evoked the souls of demons or angels."

This is black magic of the deepest dye. It emanates from the doctrine of man-is-god as expressed by Giovanni Pico della Mirandola in his Pope "Saint" John Paul II-certified book, *Oratio de hominis dignitate* ("Oration on the Dignity of Man"), which he borrowed from Ficino's edition of the *Asclepius:* "And so, O Asclepius, man is a *magnum miraculum*, a being worthy of reverence and honor. For he goes into the nature of a god as though he were himself a god; he has familiarity with the race of demons, knowing that he is of the same origin; he despises that part of his nature."

This poison was disseminated throughout the hierarchy of the Roman Church, including the Renaissance papacy. From that starting point, Catholic occultists who had a mysterious near immunity from prosecution by the Inquisition, inseminated it into the elite intellectual current of the West, which gave birth to the man-is-god sects like Rosicrucianism, Freemasonry and Mormonism, to denominate but three of the numerous, major institutional manifestations of the envenomed fruit of Catholic-Hermetic magic and self-worship.

Frances Yates: "The best guide to what Ficino thought of the *Asclepius* is...the (*A)rgumentum* before his translation of the *Corpus Hermeticum*, called by him *Pimander*, where he says that of the many works of Hermes Trismegistus, two are 'divine,' the one the work on the Divine Will, and the other on the Power and Wisdom of God. The first of these is called the *Asclepius*, the second *Pimander*.

"Thus the *Asclepius* is for Ficino, a 'divine' work on the Will of God, intimately associated with other 'divine' work by this most holy and ancient Egyptian, the *Pimander*, on the Power and Wisdom of God...for Ficino and his readers, what they thought to be the Mosaic piety of the Egyptian Genesis, and the Christian piety of Egyptian regeneration, would have rehabilitated in their eyes the Egyptian religion of the *Asclepius*...So it would become a legitimate practice for a (Christian) philosopher, even a devout practice associated with his religion, to 'draw down the life of the heaven' by sympathetic astral magic, as Ficino advised in his work on magic, the *De vita coelitus comparanda*.

"The rehabilitation of the *Asclepius*, through the discovery of the *Corpus Hermeticum*, is, I believe, one of the chief factors in the Renaissance revival of magic." [35]

For Rev. Fr. Ficino, Hermes Trismegistus is more than the personification of magic. He represents the secret gnosis that harmonizes all creeds into one Kabbalistic, Neoplatonic, Hermetic, Catholic unity. In these pages we see Ficino's attraction to sorcery. How to reconcile this with the Gospel? Fr. Ficino concludes that its dangers can be avoided if its study and practice are confined to a select society ("a learned, philosophical circle"), and *kept secret* from "the ignorant *vulgus*, who would distort it into idolatry and superstition." (Presumably only the ignorant have the perspicacity to call a spade a spade).

Renaissance sorcery is concealed under a layer of rhetoric about "good magic":

"The spiritual magic of the Renaissance—Marsilio Ficino being its...most influential representative—is built on the principle of universal pneumatic sympathy. The first corollary of this principle is that man endowed with a hegemonikon

---

[35] Yates, *Giordano Bruno*, op.cit., pp. 40-41. The scholarship of Yates, who died in 1981, has mostly stood the test of time, being esteemed a modern classic in spite of detraction from Wouter J. Hanegraaff. He denies that Renaissance magic was Hermetic or that Ficino was a Hermeticist (cf. *Esotericism and the Academy*, 2012, pp. 332-334). He cites D.P. Walker's *Spiritual and Demonic Magic* (Pennsylvania State University, 2000), as an antidote to Yates. Yet on pp. 40-42 of Walker's book we find the core of Frances Yates' thesis confirmed. Walker describes Hermes as "undoubtedly a capital source for Ficino's general theory of magic..." (Our own bone of contention with Yates is with her naiveté, not her scholarship *per se*. Her estimation of much of the Catholic-Hermetic and Catholic-Kabbalistic theurgy was that it constituted benign "white" magic).

located, generally speaking, in the heart, the organ corresponding to the sun in the cosmos, has the capacity to impart voluntary changes to his own phantasy. These changes, due to the continuity of the pneuma, are transmitted to the objects aimed at by the manipulator. This phenomenon (is based on) links between individuals according to the transcendental information that the pneumatic conveyances of their souls have accumulated during their descent through the planetary heavens. As for the magic proper, it represents knowledge permitting the performer to exploit the pneumatic currents which establish occult relations between the world's parts...Renaissance magic (has its) point of departure in Ficino's treatise *De vita coelitus comparanda* (the third book of Ficino's *De vita*), which specifically states the following principles: just as the soul of the world is concentrated in the sun, whence it radiates to all parts of the universe through the *quinta essentia* (which is the ether or the pneuma), the human soul is concentrated in the heart and enters the body through the spirit...(In *De Vita,* Book 3, Chap. III Ficino writes that) 'the Platonists by adapting our spirit to the spirit of the world by means of the magic and talismans (*ars physica*) and emotions (*affectum*), try to direct our soul and our body towards the blessings of heaven. That causes the strengthening of our spirit by means of the world spirit, through the action of the stellar rays acting beneficently upon our spirit, which is of the same kind as these rays, this lets it attract to itself celestial things." [36]

"As befitting his role as high priest, Hermes' authority extended to the domain of ritual magic. Ficino states in his introduction to the *Corpus Hermeticum* that Hermes was identified with the Egyptian Thoth, the god who invented hieroglyphs, and that his writings are concerned with 'secret mysteries' and 'stupendous oracles." [37]

Ficino was in favor of the use of magical amulets for good luck and protection from harm (whether to the soul or the

---

[36] Ioan Couliano, *Eros and Magic in the Renaissance* (University of Chicago Press, 1987), pp. 127-128.

[37] Angela Voss, op cit. p. 17.

body). But he camouflaged his beliefs behind a smokescreen of doublespeak:

"Although clearly attracted by...the talismanic magic of the theurgists, Ficino had to deny approval of them, affirming Thomas Aquinas's condemnation of artificial images as lures for evil daemons. In his On obtaining life from the heavens he carefully hides behind Iamblichus, Proclus and Synesius in suggesting that 'in materials which are naturally akin to the things above and have been collected from their various places and compounded at the right time and in the proper manner, you can receive forces and effects which are not only celestial, but even daemonic and divine.'

"Much of what previous scholars have referred to as Ficino's 'self-contradiction or 'inconsistent views' ceases to be problematic when we realize how adept he is at using different contexts for different purposes...He keeps his pagan and Christian voices separate, moving effortlessly between them...as a Platonist, he will see through the cosmos to the Divine Mind; as an orthodox Catholic, he will locate God beyond the limits of the stars; as a Hermetic magician, he will use images and invocations to sympathize with the world-soul; as a faithful follower of Aquinas, he will deny the legitimacy of talismanic magic; as a physician, he will claim that the powers sown in the world by the anima mundi are natural, health-giving properties; along with Plotinus, he will suggest that they are gods; and as a true occultist, he will remain silent when necessary." [38]

And as an astrologer he will denounce astrology (in his Disputatio contra iudicium astrologorum), while doing his own version of it. Ficino also concealed the ideological debt he owed to Proclus, among the Platonic authorities. [39]

Truth is not in the occult or occultists. They justify deception by secretly stating that humans need to be tricked into seeing what is real. The tricksters themselves become inured to

---

[38] Angela Voss, op cit. p. 19 and 25-26.

[39] "Proclus was—after Plato, Plotinus and the Aeropagite—the Platonic authority to whom Ficino was most indebted, even though he often concealed the debt..." Michael J.B. Allen, "Marsilio Ficino as a Reader of Proclus," in Essays in Renaissance Thought and Letters (2015), p. 183.

deception in the process, and subsequently have difficulty distinguishing between truth and lies, or in perceiving the hypocrisy and duplicity in a reputed enemy of astrology who in actuality is only exposing a *version* of astrology which is not to his liking.

According to historian D.P. Walker, who adds further insight into Ficino's many-layered duplicity, the god-making passages in the *Asclepius* of Hermes Trismegistus are "undoubtedly a capital source for Ficino's general theory of magically influencing the spirit so it may become receptive to celestial influences. In the summary of this theory, with which *De Triplici Vita* ends, he presents a paraphrase of the... (*Asclepius*) as a source of Plotinus' *Ennead*...which...is the 'liber Plotini' on which the whole *De Vita coelitús comparanda* is supposed to be a commentary.

"This chapter of Plotinus, as Ficino interprets it, states that one can attract into, and retain in, a material object 'something vital from the soul of the world and the souls of the spheres and the stars,' that is, celestial spirit, if the object is of a material and form which reflects the celestial source of spirit in question. This passage and the *Asclepius* one, fit in with, and connect together, Ficino's astrological medicine, music and talismans; and he is plainly using them to reinforce his own theory. He cannot, however, quite pass over the fact that Hermes is talking about pagan idolatry and demons, and therefore goes on to a worried and muddled defense of his own magic. He admits that the Egyptians' magic was 'illicit,' because the demons in the statues were worshipped as gods; but implies that demons are alright if used as means and not worshipped as ends. He then provides an alternative line of defense by citing Thomas Aquinas to show that purely astrological magic could not produce demon-inhabited images; therefore, we are left to imply, his own talismans and Orphic singing have nothing to do with demons.

"...When he is trying to defend his own magic, Ficino frequently cites Thomas Aquinas. Now Thomas' position with regard to magic is, in the genuine works, quite clear. Natural substances, such as herbs and gems, may have certain powers connected with their astrological affinities, and it is legitimate to use these in medicine; but, if letters or characters are engraved on the stones, or invocations and incantations are used with the herbs, any resultant effect is the work of bad demons, and the operator has entered into an express pact with the Devil. Thomas associates the *Asclepius* with magic, and quotes Augustine's emphatic condemnation of the passage on idols. Thomas' view thus plainly condemns both Ficino's talismans and his astrological music, and Ficino makes his defense against the condemnation very weak by quoting the idolatrous *Asclepius* passage and connecting his own magic with it." [40]

St. Augustine in *The City of God Against the Pagans* (the last three words of the title are usually omitted by modernists), attacked Hermes for being "friendly to the tricks of demons" and for mourning the decay of paganism on the eve of the birth of the Christian *Ecclesia.*

The authentic books of the Bible comprise the most unique document on earth, which is as it should be, given its divine authorship. Alone among the religious texts venerated by mankind, it is completely separate from the eternal pagan psychodrama and forbids every form of magic, sorcery and divination in every one of its forms: Lev. 19:26; Ex. 22:18, Deut. 18:9-14; Isa. 47:12-15; Dan. 1:20; 2:2, 4:7, 5:11; Gal. 5: 19-21; Rev. 18:23, 21:8, 22:15. This disenchanting function of the Word of God is execrated by the opponents of the Bible. They preach and convey what is supposed to be a great contrarian secret, that the Bible is actually no different than many other "wisdom" texts of the *prisca theologia*—yet another compilation of secret traditions, written in code, that are part of the long inventory of primordial, pantheistic knowledge that underlies all creeds, from Animism, Shamanism, Buddhism and Hinduism, to Islam, Judaism and Christianity. The "truths" of this "perennial wisdom" are almost always conveyed gradually, to a privileged elite, under secrecy. This is the conceptual foundation of virtually all occult organizations and secret societies in the West, and of the syncretic theology which has clandestinely ruled the papacy with an iron hand inside a velvet glove since the late fifteenth century. The god of what was officially condemned by the sadly compromised Pope Pius X as "modernism" in his 1907 encyclical, *Pascendi Dominici Gregis,* held dominion over his predecessors for 400 years.

---

[40] D.P. Walker, op. cit., pp. 41-43.

About this fact he said nothing. His concealment in itself constituted the crime of misprision.

Many Catholics will register shock at these assertions and dismiss them on the basis of past programming and conditioning. Stereotypes of the popes as the enemies of Freemasonry, witchcraft and Judaism, for which they supposedly endured the enmity of the world, will come to mind. This book does not entertain stereotypes or appearances, however.

What many readers have accepted all of their lives as "Catholic truth" is in some cases founded upon the disingenuous subtleties of confidence tricksters and the mutating virus of deception they have planted under cover of religious mysticism. It is true that some times the popes of the Renaissance burned, banned or seized the Talmud in some manner, or executed occultists like Giordano Bruno, who had become a rebel against the occult system which placed the pontiffs at the head of the esoteric work. These medieval atavisms were undertaken by popes of the Renaissance for purposes of *reculer pour mieux sauter* — to step back (temporarily) in order to jump forward (into the occult program).

We study, in addition to the conspiracies of subversive, heretical popes, the crimes of their agents, without which the papal *magnum opus* could not have succeeded. Among the popes' leading clerical and lay co-conspirators, were Ficino with his talismanic and astral magic, Giovanni Pico and his magical and Kabbalistic theses, Reuchlin with his "Catholic Kabbalah," Giles of Viterbo, Agrippa, Giorgi, Lazzarelli, Patrizi, Steucho, Trithemius, Galatino, Ricius, d'Estaples, Foix de Candale, Benci, Nesi, Benivieni, Di Domenico, Del Nero, and lesser conspirators. This may appear to be a list of mostly obscure Catholic theologians and intellectuals, but everyone of these were giants of the occult imperium who would influence the thinking of the West for centuries. With regard to Reuchlin, against his conservative critics he had the protection of *both* Leo X *and* a proto-Protestant cabal whose secret members authored an influential satire *Epistolae obscurorum virorum* ("Letters of Obscure Men") mocking the opponents of the Catholic Kabbalah as pedantic and grossly ignorant poseurs.

Out of the Neoplatonic-Hermetic Catholic networks would coalesce an early form of Rosicrucianism, an ancestor of

Freemasonry, with roots in the covert alliance of Protestant and Catholic defenders of Reuchlin.[41] During much (though not all) of the period encompassing the controversy over Reuchlin's writings, Pope Leo X was his secret protector.

Rosicrucianism has been misrepresented as an almost exclusively Protestant off-shoot, through the simple but effective ruse of dating its beginnings from after the Protestant Reformation, and identifying its progenitors as proto-Protestants and fellow-travelers. In fact, the leaders of the early Rosicrucian movement were inspired by a *dramatis personae* of papist occultists. What began in Florence under the Medici was transmitted to the early Rosicrucians, who were "deeply imbued with Magia and Cabala, with the works of Henry Cornelius Agrippa and Johannes Reuchlin...the *De Harmonia Mundi* of Francesco Giorgi, and the works of 'Marsilius Ficinus Theologus." [42]

It was Catholic Neoplatonic-Hermeticism that was the seedbed of Rosicrucianism. [43] Henricus Khunrath's 1609 Rosicrucian manifesto, *Amphitheatre of Eternal Wisdom,* was a key text of the Rosicrucian fraternity: "In Khunrath's work we meet with the characteristic phraseology of the manifestos...the stress on Magia, Cabala and Alchymia as in some way combining to form a religious philosophy which promises a new dawn for mankind." [44]

---

[41] Thomas De Quincey argued that after Rosicrucianism arrived in England it evolved into Freemasonry. Cf. "Historico-Critical Inquiry into the Origins of the Rosicrucians and the Freemasons" (1824); reprinted in *De Quincey's Collected Writings* (1890), vol. 13, pp. 384-448: "Toward the end of the sixteenth century, Cabalism, Theosophy, and Alchemy had overspread the whole of Western Europe..." (pp. 440-401). Tobias Churton wrote, "On April 16, 1658, five years after receiving the great secret, (Elias) Ashmole (1617-1692) finished writing the preface to the alchemical text *The Way to Bliss*...The publication included suspected heretic Doctor Everard's transcript and notes. John Everard, D.D. (ca. 1575-ca. 1650), made the first printed English translation of *The Divine Pymander*, published in 1650. The *Pymander* contained the first four books of the *Corpus Hermeticum*, anciently attributed to Hermes Trismegistus...Hermes was an ancient 'patron' of the Freemasons...and a 'star' of Andreae's *Chemical Wedding of Christian Rosenkreuz*..." *The Invisible History of the Rosicrucians* (2009), p. 356. (Ashmole was made a Freemason on Oct. 16, 1646).

[42] Yates, *The Rosicrucian Enlightenment* (1986) p. 96.

[43] Cf. McIntosh, *The Rosicrucians*, op.cit., pp. 11-14.

[44] Yates, *The Rosicrucian Enlightenment,* op. cit., p. 38.

"The authors of the (Rosicrucian manifesto) *Confessio Fraternitatis* agree with the astrologers that their epoch is entering into the sign of Mercury, who is assimilated by Michael Maier [45] with Hermes Trismegistus....Hermes as the mediator *par excellence* between gods and men, (is) a function also ascribed to him by the alchemists and by Heinrich Khunrath...Thus it is normal for astrologers to regard Mercury as 'the lord of the word,' and for the *Confessio Fraternitatis* to proclaim the coming of 'the age of the tongue." [46]

It was important for the Church of Rome, as part of its dialectic process, to control, or at least shape, the inevitable conservative backlash and reaction to the infiltration of the Vatican by Neoplatonic-Hermetic forces. Beginning around the time of the Council of Trent and the "Counter-Reformation," the occult popes planted their men in the ranks of those who were sounding an anti-occult alarm. Take for example the deep cover infiltrator Johann Weyer, the always faithful disciple of the Catholic occultist Cornelius Agrippa, the practicing sorcerer and author of *De occulta philosophia*, deeply implicated in the Hermetic doctrine of gnosis. His head-spinning Jekyll-and-Hyde disciple Weyer has come to be known in popular history as a writer who mercifully modified the witch hunt by suggesting that some accused witches were merely mentally unbalanced. This signature caricature of Weyer's biography omits his pivotal role in the sixteenth century as an explainer of the occult, rather than the supposed leader of the attack on the occult infiltration of the Church. From 1530 to 1534 Weyer had been Agrippa's collaborator in sorcery. Watch for it: in 1563 Weyer's celebrated anti-occult book *De praestigiis daemonum*, was published in the final year of the Council of Trent, intended as a guide for the inquisitors. Parts of it read as though we had written it. In its pages Weyer surgically deconstructs the diabolic lineage of the "idolatrous magic" of the Egyptians, the Babylonians and of Zoroaster, who "transmitted the arts of idolatrous magic on to other peoples, so

---

[45] Michael Maier (1569-1622), Count-Palatine at the court of the Holy Roman Emperor Rudolf II; poet-laureate at the University of Padua, and Rosicrucian leader.

[46] Roland Edighoffer, "Rosicrucianism I," in *Dictionary of Gnosis and Western Esotericism*, (2006), p. 1011.

that the whole world came to be filled with the fumes of impiety as though from a furnace or factory of wickedness."

So far so good; here was rhetorical red meat for churchmen who had been deeply disturbed by the rise of the new order of occultism which they had glimpsed in the hierarchy of the Renaissance Church. Now, at last, it appeared that a cleansing counter-reaction was setting in that would chase the infiltrators out of the Church. That hollow legend has had very durable legs ever since, aided by liberal media and academia which hold to it uncritically.

The truth is, Weyer was one of the Renaissance Vatican's occult agents; a secret member of the "sublime religion" ever since he had been apprenticed as an adolescent to Agrippa. *Weyer was one of several Catholic advisors to the Inquisition who was controlling the anti-occult opposition*: shaping it and directing it:

"Wyer had not...forgotten Agrippa's insistence on differentiating between the sublime religion known as *mageia*[47] among the ancients, and the sacrilegious practices that had come to be confused with it. He...admits that there must be such a thing as natural magic, not least because of the gospel account of the Magi from the East who followed a star...Interestingly, and probably due to the formative influence of Agrippa, Weyer's genealogy of demonic magic...does not include the Florentine platonists or their

---

[47] *Mageia* is a word freighted with significance in the occult text *Corpus Hermeticum,* attributed to Mercury/Hermes. It is part of the famous phrase from that text, *"philosophia men kai mageia,"* which "bears on the quest for gnostic salvation." Cf. Brian P. Copenhaver, *Hermetica: The Greek Corpus Hermeticum* (2000), p. xv.

sympathizers. Moreover, Plato is not given a place of any special prominence." [48]

The pope's foundational sorcerers and theorists of magic are given a pass by Wyer. His intentional myopia remains intact in the twenty-first century. Weyer misdirected Catholic investigators away from "Florentine platonists or their sympathizers." [49] His counsel to the inquisitors misled them and led them away from the chief culprits. In the land of the occult nothing is as it seems.

The Magi: A Cautionary Tale

Furthermore, Weyer's use of the Magi in the Jesus infancy narrative as an alibi for the Christian practice of "natural" or "white magic" in Catholicism is a vexation that is still with us. Close students of the Bible whose integrity is intact can see that the Word of God makes zero distinctions between "good" and "bad" magic: they are all condemned without reserve. The assumption that the Magi were benevolent is not found in the New Testament. It is a widely held assumption which would seem to be at variance with a crucial, overlooked fact: the Magi revealed the existence of the infant Jesus to the murderer

---

[48] Wouter J. Hanegraaff, *Esotericism and the Academy* (2012), pp. 85-86; (emphasis supplied). Hanegraaf is a good source for raw data and we salute his work ethic, but like many liberals he views the investigation of a Neoplatonic conspiracy seeking the destruction of Christianity during the Renaissance as a figment of a "paranoid imagination" (p. 40). He describes the radical religious syncretism posited by the *philosophia perennis* as "a deeply conservative...perspective," contrasted with what he regards as its revolutionary opposite, the *prisca theologia*. We can see no drastic difference between the two; both of them are pagan survivals. Furthermore, though he concedes on p. 71 of *Esotericism* that the revolutionary-syncretist Catholic Bishop Agostino Steuco claimed that the "One Truth" had always been available through Zoroaster and Hermes, Hanegraaff nevertheless describes Steuco as a "conservative intellectual" (p. 70), who "sought to reveal Catholic doctrine as the hidden core of paganism" (p. 73). What is conservative about a Catholic Bishop (which Steucho was), identifying Catholicism as the hidden core of paganism? Steuco's statement is anything but. Hanegraaff further defines Steuco's "conservatism" in terms of his having spurned "a return to the sources of revelation (the Bible and the apostolic community)." Hanegraaff imagines that the rejection was reflective of Steuco's "solid orthodoxy" (p. 70 and 72). Hanegraaff would seem to be part of the "popular trend in Renaissance and Byzantine cultural and social history of rehabilitating all ideological dissenters (heretics) into a vague, all-inclusive Christianity."

[49] On Plato in this context cf. Niketas Siniossoglou, *Radical Platonism in Byzantium* pp. 154-155.

Herod. St. Matthew's description of them, using the Greek word, *magoi,* derived from the Persian word *magus*, denotes a priest of the Persian religion, i.e. Zoroastrianism. The numerous Biblical injunctions against magic, whether of Zoroaster or anyone else, gives pause to the widespread assumption that the Magi were unambiguously virtuous. It seems that they *may perhaps have became so* in the presence of the Christ child, when they bowed to worship Him (Matt. 2:11); although even that may have been a ruse. If they were sincere in their alleged adoration, then their days of practicing the magic of Zoroaster would have come to an end at that moment, yet the Scripture is silent on any such possible conversion. Ficino promulgated the identification of the Persian Magi as Zoroastrians.

One Bible commentary states, under the heading, *The 'Star' Seen by Astrologers after Jesus' birth*:

"The 'astrologers from eastern parts,' hence from the neighborhood of Babylon, whose visit to King Herod after the birth of Jesus resulted in the slaughter of all the male infants in Bethlehem, were obviously not servants or worshipers of the true God. (Matt. 2:1-18) As to the "star" (Gr., *a'Ster'*) seen by them, many suggestions have been given as to its having been a comet, meteor, a supernova, or, more popularly, a conjunction of planets. It is also notable that only these pagan astrologers 'saw' the star. Their condemned practice of astrology and the adverse results of their visit, placing in danger the life of the future Messiah, certainly allow for, and even make advisable, the consideration of their having been directed by a source *adverse* to God's purposes as relating to the promised Messiah. It is certainly reasonable to ask if the one who 'keeps transforming himself into an angel of light,' whose operation is 'with every powerful work and lying signs and portents,' who was able to make a serpent appear to speak, and who was referred to by Jesus as a 'manslayer when he began,' could not also cause astrologers to 'see' a starlike object that guided them first, not to Bethlehem, but to Jerusalem, where resided a mortal enemy of the promised Messiah." [50]

---

[50] Raymond Franz et al., *Aid to Bible Understanding* (1971), p. 1552.

Those who may be offended by a skeptical view of the delightfully quaint, Christmas-themed interpretation of a star which is followed by benevolent Magi, should be aware that this interpretation has been repeatedly cited by occultists and employed as a loophole through which to drive their claim of the existence of "good magic" in the New Testament. On June 23, 1439, during the Council of Florence, in the city which would become the citadel of the Neoplatonic-Hermetic infiltrators of the Catholic Church, *reggimenti* of the city of Florence engaged in an extravagant ritual dressed like the Magi. These *Palleschi* [51] were members of a Florentine secret society, the *Compagnia de' Magi,* which was organized and funded by the Medici.

In 1459, Cosimo de' Medici spent a large sum for an art work executed by Benozzo Gozzoli, *The Journey of the Magi,* a fresco which was displayed at Cosimo's palace. He had another Magi-fresco installed in his monastic quarters in San Marco. The Medicis' obsessive identification with the magicians from the East culminated in Sandro Botticelli's breathtakingly beautiful 1475 painting, *Adoration of the Magi,* which depicts Cosimo as the Magus kneeling in front of the Virgin, and his two sons as the other two Magi. Brigitte Tambrun asserts that Cosimo's Magi fixation was an integral part of his mission for the revival of Neoplatonism in Florence. [52] Time and again in occult literature we find reference to the Magi having used "white magic" in the "Christmas story," with the implication that this lends support to the practice of other forms of "good magic."

Brigitte Tambrun: "Plato makes his return because he is the inheritor at the same time of the *Magi*...and of Hermes...The fresco of Benozzo Gozzoli presents a genealogy of wisdom: the *Magi* — Plato — Christ, doubled by a geographical orientation...Orient—Greece—Florence...while at the same time always recalling and referring to the point of origin: the oriental *Magi* are the originators of the wisdom of the Greeks—

---

[51] Partisans of the Medici in Church and State were known as *Palleschi,* a reference to the red balls (*palle*) of the Medici coat of arms).

[52] Brigitte Tambrun, "Plethon," in *Dictionary of Gnosis & Western Esotericism* (2005).

Pythagoras, [53] Plato, Plotinus, Plethon—are the inheritors, and this wisdom comes to Florence thanks to the Medici who gather it."

The Catholic artist "Hieronymus Bosch" (Joen van Aken; 1450-1516), included in his painting of the visit of the Magi to the Christ child, *The Adoration of Magi* (circa 1494), macabre and foreboding details which haunt the scene and subtly undercut the benevolent aura surrounding the Magi.

As the Magi approach Mary and the infant Jesus, "Staring out from the (doorway of the) crumbling, thatched-roof stable...is a red-faced figure usually associated with the Antichrist...With an unsettling grin; naked, creamy white limbs; glittering jewelry and golden spiked headdress, he suggests not the subject's solemnity but what will become a constant theme in Bosch's paintings—the inescapable dualism in the world of good and evil. Additional details—such as the grim, ghostlike face that peers through the rotting wall at right; an ominous owl in the rafters clutching its prey; and in the distance, a tiny figure pulling a horse ridden by a monkey (the latter a symbol of lust) and approaching a brothel (its flag a giveaway)..." [54]

A project of gargantuan megalomania

The texts attributed to Plato and Hermes, and later the rabbinic Kabbalah were advertised in various guises, as "harbingers of Christ," and "testifying to the divinity of Christ." This pretense of the *prisca theologia* and *philosophia perennis* was embraced by many Renaissance Catholic intellectuals at the highest levels of the Vatican and widely proclaimed by Johannes Reuchlin and many others, in opposition to Judaic converts to Catholicism such as Johann Pfefferkorn, who contested it vigorously. True Catholics however, perceived that Hermetic Neoplatonism and Kabbalism seemed to agree with Christianity only on "a surface level of common signifiers."

---

[53] "One might...define later Pythagoreanism as Platonism with the Socratic...element amputated. In fact, Plato remained the principal source for all later Pythagoreans—Plato's myths, and in particular the *Timaeus*...neo-Pythagoreanism converges, in the philosophical realm, with Neoplatonism." Walter Burkert, *Lore and Science in Ancient Pythagoreanism,* p. 96.

[54] Mary Tompkins Lewis, *Wall Street Journal*, June 8, 2016, p. D5.

The central tenet of the Kabbalah is a project of gargantuan megalomania: making an Absolute of the human intellect. Neoplatonic humanism, expressed by Giovanni Pico della Mirandola in his *Oration on the Dignity of Man*, reflects a similar perverted hubris; the spirit of autonomy which seduced our first parents— that salvation lies in *grasping Being*, not God's grace. The line of "old sages" who "grasped this Being" were dubbed by Barlaam of Calabria, "Enlightened-ones, Illuminati," on the Neoplatonic model of an elite consisting of "true philosophers." [55]

Neoplatonic-Hermeticism infiltrated the Church under an aura of intense Catholic piety and devotion. The conspirators went through the motions and assumed the forms of devotion.

"When Ficino publicly commented upon St. Paul's *Epistle to the Romans* in the Cathedral of Florence, some time at the end of 1497, he was not only echoing a long tradition of ancient and medieval exegesis of the Pauline epistles. He was also reiterating a position that he had started to develop in the 1470s in his treatise on St. Paul's rapture (*De Raptu Pauli*) and in his *Platonic Theology,* regarding the soul's divine powers. At the time he delivered his interpretation of *Romans*, he had completed his commentaries on Plato, Plotinus and other major Neoplatonic philosophers, and he was about to publish his commentary on Dionysius the Aeropagite. These works had a profound impact on Ficino's reading of Romans...Ficino saw Plato and his Neoplatonic successors as theologians rather than philosophers, that is to say, as divinely inspired...In this context, St. Paul perfectly embodied the model of Christianity

---

[55] The earliest formal reference that we have been able to locate to the "Illuminism" from which the Illuminati derived their name, is in reference to the work of the medieval Persian Neoplatonic-Hermeticist Shihab al-Din Yahya Suhrawardi (b. 1154), who was sentenced to death and executed in Aleppo, Syria in 1191. In his principal writing, *Hikmat al-Ishraq* ("The Philosophy of Illumination"), he placed the "science" of the individual's subjective mystical experience, above revealed dogma: "This science is the very intuition of the inspired and illuminated Plato...and of those who came before him from the time of Hermes." The school of theology developed in Suhrawardi's name was termed the "School of Illuminism." Cf. Von Stuckrad, op. cit., p. 28.

as Ficino understood it: a form of mystical spirituality in agreement with Neoplatonic metaphysics..." [56]

Hermetic Renaissance Catholicism is supposed to be a religion purified of negativity and illusion; the higher type of Christianity. But it is not Christianity. It is the gnostic religion of Buddha and Ammon-Re, not of the God of Israel, or the Bible, or Jesus Christ. In this religion the world is a horrible place. "Hermes tells Tat that those who partook in the gift of God regard time spent here as a misfortune. 'Disregarding the gross and the subtle, they hasten to the One alone." [57] In this religion magic talismans are recommended by Catholic clerics like Ficino: "If you obtain these Phoebean stones which we have been talking about, you will have no need to impress images on them. You should hang them, encased in gold, around your neck, on a yellow silk cord, when the Sun passes through Aries or Leo and is ascendant, or when it is mid-sky and facing the Moon." [58] It is this Ficino who, on October 6, 1487, Lorenzo de' Medici recommended be made Bishop of Cortona.[59] Some seventeen years earlier, Cosimo de' Medici had appointed Fr. Ficino head of the Platonic Academy of Florence, which featured research, publications and public lectures by Cristoforo Landino and others for the indoctrination of the Catholic hierarchy and elite laymen into the new religion.[60]

---

[56] Maude Vanhaelen, "Ficino's Commentary," in *The Rebirth of Platonic Theology* (2013), pp. 205-206.

[57] Clement Salaman, "Echoes of Egypt in Hermes and Ficino," in *Marsilio Ficino: His Theology, His Philosophy, His Legacy* (2002) p. 122.

[58] Clement Salaman, op. cit. p. 128.

[59] P.O. Kristeller, "Marsilio Ficino and his Work after Five Hundred Years," in *Marsilio Ficino e il ritorno di Platone* (1986).

[60] Critics say that Ficino's enterprise amounted to nothing more than an "informal intellectual gymnasium." However, Fr. Ficino himself refers to his Platonic Academy in the preface to his translation of Plotinus (ca.1490-1492) and also in a September, 1462 letter to Cosimo de' Medici. The conspiracy-minimizers can quibble about what constitutes an "academy," but the fact is, Ficino was handsomely paid by Medici to "draft translations, and in his lectures, commentaries, treatises and letters, he explained Plato to the Florentine public." He had numerous students and an extensive audience. Cf. Arthur M. Field, *The Origins of the Platonic Academy*.

The Inquisition in Legend and Reality

The magical doctrine of Hermes Trismegistus circulated unimpeded in Spanish universities, monasteries and the Escorial library of the Spanish kings throughout the sixteenth and seventeenth centuries. It is our contention that "notoriously repressive," papally-chartered institutions such as the Spanish Inquisition were not only friendly toward Neoplatonic-Hermeticists such as Ficino — by the time of the Renaissance *the Inquisition had been mostly captured by those intellectual forces.*

The Spanish Inquisition in the Renaissance was tasked with crushing conservative Catholics who were on the trail of executive members of the Church of Rome's occult Cryptocracy. Evidence of the former is provided by the nineteenth century Spanish-Catholic historian Marcelino Menéndez Pelayo in his *Historia de los heterodoxos espanoles,* in which he records that Marsilio Ficino was left untouched by the Inquisition in Spain and his works and the influence of Hermes Trismegistus were allowed to flourish. "If the Sainted Office of the Inquisition can be accused of anything, it would be in not having restricted the circulation of books that well-deserved its rigors." [61]

Catholic libraries in Spain in the sixteenth century were well-stocked with occult books admitted into circulation by the Inquisition. The works of Marsilio Ficino, the magical treatises attributed to Hermes Trismegistus and "Hermetic works in general" enjoyed "orthodox status." [62]

Ficino's magical doctrines were disseminated throughout "Inquisitorial Catholic Spain" by such luminaries of Throne and Altar as Pedro Mexia (1497-1551), secretary to the Spanish Holy Roman Emperor Charles V and an author of books such as *Silva de varia lección.* patronized by Spain's bishops, cardinals and royalty. In his *Silva,* Mexia popularized Father Ficino's treatise on the occult properties of stones, including the use of aetites, which is related to the stone magic of the Babylonian Talmud, in tractate Shabbat 66b. In pagan lore, aetites are reputed to ward off the female demons who cause complications for pregnant women. Superstition of this sort from Ficino pertaining to avoiding a gaze from a menstruating

---

[61] *Historia de los heterodoxos espanoles,* (1992), vol. 2, p. 437.

[62] Susan Byrne, *Ficino in Spain* (2015), p. 27.

woman, evil eye betwitchment and the teachings of Hermes Trismegistus, were published in popular books approved by the Church in Spain. One of the high Spanish officials responsible for circulating the works of Ficino and Hermes in Spain was Charles V's ambassador to London and Venice, Diego Hurtado de Mendoza.

The Spanish government's slow decay into an impenetratable thicket of bureaucracy and regulation can be traced in part to its faith in the pagan model of law that Ficino's followers were free to disseminate under the Holy Inqusition. Hugo de Celso, author of the highly influential 1538 magnum opus, *Las leyes de todos los reynos de Castilla* (*The Laws of All the Kingdoms of Castile*), was one of sixteenth century Spain's most eminent legal authorities. In his book, Celso informed the Church and aristocracy of Spain that their laws were derived, "According to Marsilio Ficino" from "the philosopher Plato" and "Prometheus" who "received the laws that Mercury (Hermes) gave him."

Hector Pinto (1528-1584) [63] Professor of Scripture at the University of Coimbra (Portugal), in his seminal book, *Imagen de la vida cristiana* (*Image of the Christian Life*), which was translated from Portuguese and circulated widely in Spain, elaborated upon Ficino's claims concerning the sources of the law of Catholic nations. Pinto listed these as Osiris, (Egypt's god of magic), Zoroaster and Mercury (Hermes). Pinto adds that "anyone who wishes to see this in detail should read Ficino on Plato..." [64]

The eminent Spanish-Catholic jurist associated with the School of Salamanca, Jerónimo Castillo de Bobadilla, in his legal treatise, *Política para Corregidores y Señores de vasallos, en tiempo de paz y de guerra y para prelados en lo espiritual y temporal* ("Policy of Magistrates and Lords of Vassals in Peacetime and in War, and of Prelates Spiritual and Temporal"), which formed the administrative foundation of the law in the reign of the arch-papist, King Philip II, specifies that

---

[63] Cf. http://www.prdl.org/author_view.php?a_id=3703

[64] There is a reference to "falsehood" in Pinto's litany of the occult agents who he says, following Ficino, had formed the basis of the law of Catholic nations. When he says "falsehood" Pinto is alluding to the Islamic claim of Muhammed to law-giving inspiration from the Angel Gabriel.

the laws of Spain are derived from Hermes Trismegistus, Zoroaster and Plato.

An extraordinary case of Renaissance-Catholic powers importing Judaizing ideas into Christendom is found in the account of the compilation and circulation of the Plantin *Polyglot Bible*. A Catholic exegete and translator of ancient Hebrew into Latin, who interpreted the Bible in conformity with rabbinic lies and malice, was the erudite Italian-Dominican, Sanctes Pagninus (1470-1536), a one-time student of Savonarola, who had led Pagninus on the path to the *authentic* Catholic Hebrew Republic of *true* Israel. Pagninus turned his coat however, and joined the Talmudic/Kabbalistic counterfeit, where he used the rabbinic glosses of David Kimchi and other neo-Pharisees to interpret theological concepts in Old Testament Hebrew. The French scholar Fr. Richard Simon (1638-1712) described Pagninus as "neglecting the ancient interpreters of Scripture to rely upon the opinion of the rabbis." Pagninus' Hebrew-to-Latin Old Testament translation was published as the famous *Royal Polyglot Bible* ("Biblia Regia"), from the distinguished publishing House of Plantin, in Antwerp, under the patronage of King Philip II of Spain. Philip dispatched his own undeniably brilliant Hebrew scholar, his chaplain Fr. Benito Arias Montano (1527-1598; usually referred to as only Arias Montano), to supervise the project. Montano, after having mastered Hebrew under the guidance of Renaissance-Catholic scholars, allied with the Neoplatonic-Hermetic conspiracy. Montano included in the multi-volume *Royal Polyglot Bible* both Pagninus' rabbinic-influenced Old Testament, as well as outright Talmudic commentary on the Bible compiled by Franciscus Raphaelengius, and his (Montano's) own degenerate Kabbalistic theses.

Readers of this writer's *Judaism Discovered* (pp. 236 and 766-768), are aware that the main introductory levels of rabbinic exegesis of the Bible are as follows: the literal meaning, or *Peshat*, followed by *Remez* (allegorical meaning), *Derush* (legal and Midrashic meaning) and *Sod* (the secret magical meaning). When rabbinic interpretation was first introduced in the conservative early Middle Ages, it had to present its Biblical theology to Christians solely in terms of *peshat*. By the time of the Renaissance however, rabbinic power and prestige had grown to such an extent that it was bold enough to teach Christians to parse the Bible according to the most distorted and diabolical of all of its levels of falsification, the level of *sod*. This foothold was achieved by putting forth among Christians the hoax that by mastering the occult interpretive methods of the Kabbalah, the divinity of Christ could be proved at the highest level of intellectual and spiritual understanding. One of the agents of this fraud was Philip II's Arias Montano, sometime advisor to Spain's sadistic military officer, the Duke of Alba, whose scorched earth polices in the Netherlands weakened Catholicism's hold on the Dutch people.

Montano's neo-Platonic treatise, *De arcano sermone* appears in the *Apparatus* volume of the *Royal Polyglot* Bible: "*De arcano sermone*...refers to the symbolic sense of the Hebrew Scriptures...This arcane meaning is not as accessible to everyone as is the literal; it embraces a whole range of nuances...oneiric (oracular), mystical and secret or Kabbalistic senses...Arias Montano envisaged several levels of comprehension and he mentioned both arcane and even more arcane (*magis arcanum*) significances, reserving the latter, more secret and profound, for the events and types of the Old Testament which point to the person of Jesus or the mysteries of the New Testament." [65]

"Inquisitorial Renaissance Catholic Spain" was riddled with this type of corrupt occult tradition. Montano's teacher had been Fr. Cipriano de la Huerga (1509-1560), rector of the Cistercian College at Alcalá and Professor of Biblical studies: "Cipriano de la Huerga believed that there were secret traditions handed down from God to Moses on Sinai and which were subsequently passed on by oral tradition to an unbroken chain of chosen men..." [66] Simple-minded New Age enthusiasts and "conservative and traditional Catholics" alike are in for a rude awakening: high level occult conspirators enjoyed immunity from the Spanish Inquisition because in many instances they were in charge of it. (Montano, for example, was the official papal expurgator of books in Spain).

---

[65]   Magne Saebo (ed.), *Hebrew Bible Old Testament: The History of Its Interpretation from the Renaissance to the Enlightenment* (2008), p. 244.

[66] Ibid., p. 237.

Spirited conservative Catholic resistance to the publication of the *Royal Polyglot Bible* was mounted by Leon de Castro, Dean of the Faculty of Theology and Professor of Ancient Languages at the University of Salamanca, who declared that any Bibles compiled in conjunction with rabbinic advisors were a work of "Judaizing heresy."

"It is...important to note that in spite of the declaration of the Council of Trent in favor of the Vulgate as the 'authentic' version of the Bible, the Church of Rome neither condemned these independent translations (such as the *Royal Polyglot)* out of hand nor tried to prevent its adherents from consulting them...They (the independent translations) succeeded in demonstrating the value of Jewish commentaries for a better understanding of the Old Testament...This, in theory, was the standpoint of the Roman Catholic Church during the second half of the sixteenth century, but in fact the violent opposition of Leon de Castro to the Antwerp *(Royal) Polyglot* would suggest that such broadmindedness towards versions other than the Vulgate was by no means general." [67]

In a pattern that will repeat itself for centuries inside the Catholic Church, when courageous churchmen sought to repel rabbinic infiltration and the recondite ecumenical tradition it spawned, they were often overruled by forces at the top of the "obelisk." In the case at hand, the warnings of the faithful Prof. De Castro were rejected by Spain's Grand Inquisitor, as well as Pope Gregory XIII (under the malignant influence of the Spanish Jesuit Juan de Mariana). It is an irony of ecclesiastical history that the Antwerp *Royal Polyglot Bible* came to be renowned as the Counter-Reformation's answer to Protestant

---

[67] G. Lloyd Jones, *The Discovery of Hebrew in Tudor England: A Third Language* (Manchester University, 1983), pp. 52-53. Prof. G. Lloyd Jones wants us to believe that the rabbis, in the person of Saaida Gaon, through "scientific study of the Scriptures and of the Hebrew language...gave Rabbinic Judaism superiority in the special province of Karaism" (p. 3). There you have it, the rabbinic deceivers and Scripture twisters immersed in the traditions of Babylon and the Pharisees, have bested the *sola Scriptura* Karaites. How do we know this? By professorial proclamation: the *ipse dixit* of G. Lloyd Jones. Saaida Gaon (882-942 A.D.) specialized for purposes of polemics against the Christians and the Karaites (Judaics who rejected both the Talmud and the New Testament), in arguing from the *peshat,* or literal meaning of the Bible (even though the secret rabbinic teaching decrees that the literal meaning is the most inaccurate of all possible readings). Saadia is said to be the founder of Hebrew philology, producing a Hebrew dictionary and a Hebrew grammar.

Bible studies, *when it actually served to infuse rabbinic and neo-Platonic Kabbalistic ideas into Protestant England*, where it became a reference work for Anglican Old Testament exegetes in the reigns of the Protestant monarchs Elizabeth I and James I, and was an influence on the translation of the King James Bible of 1611.

The relentless stereotype of "Judaizing Protestants" that was seeded into the Catholic grassroots, particularly in the Right-wing, functions as a means of obscuring *the Judaizing Catholic precursor of Protestantism*. The Renaissance-Catholic responsibility for transmitting rabbinic ideas into Protestantism is seldom acknowledged by Catholics who often resort to monotonously parroting the "Judaizing Protestant" cliché.

In certain respects, Anglicanism was a project of the *Corpus Hermeticum* of the Catholic neo-Platonists of Florence and Rome. Protestant Hebrew translators such as Leo Jud (1482-1542) and Immanuel Tremellius (1510-1580) both of whom transmitted rabbinic glosses to Reformation linguists, were acting under the inspiration of their occult Catholic predecessors and contemporaries. The Cryptocracy has arranged it so Protestants alone are made to bear the stigma of "Judaizing," while few allude to "Judaizing Renaissance Catholicism."

Judaizing: Distinctions and Definitions

Konrad Pellican of Zurich was a Christian Hebrew scholar who picked the brains of rabbis and riffled through their books of Hebrew grammar, but eschewed their traditions and interpretations. His star pupil, Sebastian Münster, Professor of Hebrew at the University of Basle, turned his back on Pellican and succumbed to the pull of Talmudic lore, as did many non-Judaic Renaissance Hebraists. Richard Simon wrote that Münster "would have done better to have followed the method of Konrad Pellican, his Hebrew master, who was in the right in thinking we ought *only* to borrow the grammar from the rabbis, not the sense (of the text)."

This too was Martin Luther's position, that it was permissible to take the grammar from Judaics but not their interpretation of the meaning of the Hebrew scriptures. It was Luther's objective to publish Bibles in the vernacular based on the most accurate translation of the Hebrew. By 1519, Luther was seriously studying Hebrew and beginning to revive the Hebrew scholarship of medieval Catholic exegetes, largely free of rabbinic falsification. By 1530, he was fluent in Hebrew despite a modest disclaimer in his *Table Talk* concerning his struggles with Hebrew grammar and his reliance on Christian Hebraists for assistance.

During the twelve years he translated the Bible into German (1522-1534) Luther received assistance from a circle of linguists who were Christians and not Judaizers: the Leipzig-based Hebraist Bernard Ziegler; Matthew Aurogallus, professor of Hebrew at the University of Wittenberg and a compiler of Hebrew dictionaries and grammars; Caspar Cruciger the Elder; the Hebrew prodigy Andreas Osiander, also of Wittenberg, and Johann Förster. In the case of Förster, Osiander and Aurogallus, they surpassed the most learned rabbis of their time. They laid the groundwork for what would become an early modern Lutheran heritage of Christian scholarship in Hebrew and Aramaic *defiantly independent of rabbinic tradition.*

Johann Förster's 1543 Hebrew dictionary carried a disclaimer on its title page explicitly denying any dependence on rabbinic commentaries: *"Dictionarium Hebraicum Novum, non ex Rabbinorum commentis."* In his preface, Förster warned that "Among Christians the rabbinic commentaries are controlling the work of translation and explanation." He decried the "feeblemindedness of those Christians who have embraced without discernment the commentaries of the Jews, in which there is no light, no knowledge of God and not even a proper understanding of Hebrew." According to Förster, rabbinic commentaries were riddled with deception, bringing into Christ's church "more obscurity and error than light and truth."

Luther's estimation of rabbinic Hebraism was more severe than even Förster's. Luther rejected and ridiculed the rabbinic exegesis of the Hebrew Scriptures. In *Lectures on the Book of Genesis,* he denounced the rabbinic traditions about the first book of the Bible. Luther said that the rabbis erred miserably in their exposition of the Old Testament because of their obsession with showing off their supposed grammatical and intellectual prowess. In their eagerness to defame Christ they unscrupulously twisted the text of the Bible and distorted its meaning. Luther's views on Judaism were nearly a verbatim transmission of the medieval Roman Catholic view. In his 1543 *Treatise on the Last Words of David*, Luther advised Christians to pay no attention to the grandiose claims of the rabbis to scholarship: "...the words in many a (Scripture) passage are incomprehensible to them. They are far from having one harmonious, perfect and flawless Hebrew Bible, even from the point of view of grammar, to say nothing of theology, where they are so very incompetent...We Christians have the meaning and import of the Bible because we have the New Testament, that is Jesus Christ."

Given a choice between the rabbi's interpretation of Scripture and that of St. Augustine, Luther thundered, "I would let the Jews with their interpretation and their letters go to the devil, and I would ascend into heaven with St. Augustine's interpretation, without their letters." For Luther, parsing the Old Testament was only possible when undertaken "in the direction of the New Testament, in opposition to the interpretation of the rabbis." Christians must be aware, said Luther, of the "usual habit of perverting the Scriptures to which the Jews everywhere adhere."

We are not endorsing Lutheran theology, its statist political theory, or its persecution of Anabaptists. Luther was culpable for sinful error, large and small, beginning with the fact that he disobeyed Christ's command to love one's enemies, as evinced by the disgusting imprecations he hurled at Catholics, Muslims, Judaics and Anabaptists. There was also his gullible and somewhat egotistical belief that his brand of Christianity would convert the "Jews" of his time in droves, when Catholicism was failing to do so. He admitted at the end of his life that this had been a chimera and that his mission to convert Judaics had been a nearly complete failure.

Compared with St. Vincent Ferrer (1350-1419), Luther is not in the same league. Since the days of the early Church, no Christian in the Latin West can compare with Vincent when it comes to converting Judaics. Almost none of St. Vincent's writings and sermons have been published and translated in modern editions. The two significant biographical studies in English have been allowed to go out of print for more than 55 years.

The *true record* of his life is neglected and obscured by the Catholic establishment, for a reason: Pope John Paul II repudiated St. Vincent Ferrer when he issued a blanket condemnation, echoing the Second Vatican Council. Addressing the whole sweep of Catholic history, the pope defiantly attacked exposure of Judaism *by anyone*. By this enormity he could only mean that not even Church Fathers and canonized saints are exempted from his unprecedented papal condemnation, in the course of which he named the religion of Judaism which is the Jesus-denying religion of the Talmud, "intrinsic" to Catholicism:

"Once again, through myself, the Church, in the words of the well-known declaration *Nostra Aetate*, deplores the hatred, persecutions and displays of anti-Semitism directed against the Jews at any time and by anyone. I repeat, by anyone...

"The Jewish religion is not 'extrinsic' to us, but in a certain way is 'intrinsic' to our own religion. With Judaism therefore we have a relationship which we do not have with any other religion. You are our dearly beloved brothers and, in a certain way, it could be said that you are our elder brothers...

"Notwithstanding the Church's awareness of her own identity, it is not lawful to say that the Jews are 'repudiated or cursed,' as if this were taught or could be deduced from the Sacred Scriptures of the Old or the New Testament." (Rome: Synagogue Discourse, April 13, 1986).

As we study the work of Pico, Reuchlin and the fifteenth and sixteenth century pontiffs in the following pages, we will be equipped to grasp the fact that John Paul's bold elocution in the Roman Synagogue was the triumphant public endorsement of the theology of the occult Renaissance Church.

St. Vincent Ferrer's heroic, twenty year mission to the Judaics of Europe, wherein he reminded them of their religion's black evil, of their desperate need to convert, that their elder brother was Satan, and that all who are spiritual heirs of the Pharisees are cursed, is now denounced by the Church of Rome. This denunciation is Hermetic-Kabbalistic to its core, but it took five hundred years for it to be *publicly* asserted by a pope.

In Luther's case it should be observed that he had no intention early in his career to split from the Catholic Church. There are no signs of any such desire other than internal reform, especially of simony and usury. The powers that ruled Rome at the time goaded Luther into breaking away. This was the mission of the conspirators who ran the pontificate of Pope Leo X. These operatives deliberately instigated Protestantism in Europe, as we will observe when we track the tangled web of perfidy surrounding the protection which the Church of Rome accorded to the celebrated Catholic-Kabbalist Reuchlin. [68]

The Church was surfeited with undercover Judaizers; this was the belief of the peasantry as expressed by William Langland in his classic medieval work, *Piers the Plowman*. St. Vincent Ferrer was born just after Langland died. Ferrer began to clean up the inquity that the common folk had decried. If Luther had been another Ferrer, the world would be a very different place today, because Luther's anti-rabbinic, Gutenberg-era printed tracts would have indelibly marked the Church. Instead, he was driven out, as many Catholics are driven out today. Luther then succumbed to the temptation to create a new church, in the course of which he published radical truths about rabbinic Judaism's demonic incarnation of deception and verbal subterfuge, which he hammered home with a fearless candor. Until the ascendance of the religion of Holocaustianity in the 1970s, Luther's defiant legacy of adherence to Jesus Christ's side in His clash with the Pharisee schools of Shammai and Hillel in first century Palestine, ensured a vital tradition of centuries of conservative Lutheran skepticism toward Judaism in German-speaking nations and Scandinavia,[69] and in America as well, wherever conservative Lutherans settled. Luther revived the Christian truth that the Bible, from Genesis to Revelation, is the rightful inheritance *only* of the followers of Jesus Christ.

---

[68] Luther, though opposed to the Kabbalah (he formally denounced it in his treatise, *Vom Schem Hamphoras und vom Geschlecht Christi*), supported the Catholic Reuchlin mainly out of spite—he accepted at face value the Cryptocracy's cover story (in play even now), that Reuchlin was being "rigorously persecuted" by the Catholic hierarchy. The reverse was true: on almost every occasion in which a Dominican inquisitor attempted to expose Reuchlin in a church court, and sought Reuchlin's condemnation as a heretic, it was the inquisitor who was stymied, harassed and libeled by the ecclesiastical mafia operating under Leo X.

[69] Most notably by the University of Heidelberg's Lutheran philologist, Prof. Johann Andreas Eisenmenger, in his magisterial *Entdecktes Judenthum* (two volumes, 1700), which represented the inaugural and nonpareil forensic demolition of rabbinic Judaism in western letters, unsurpassed even in our time (the volumes was seized and banned by the Holy Roman Emperor).

"Luther's German Bible cannot be regarded as a primary channel of Jewish exegesis in the way that the versions of his three contemporaries, Pagninus, Münster and Leo Jud were. Although, as a vernacular Bible it ranks above these Latin translations, those using it would not often find rabbinic explanations of difficult words being preferred to the renderings of the Septuagint...Furthermore, his Biblical commentaries, as we have seen, were not calculated to encourage his fellow Christians to look for the elucidation of problematic passages in the works of the rabbis or to turn to the local Jewish community for help with the text of the Old Testament. Yet throughout his career his attitude toward the Hebrew language was positive. He was obviously convinced that a thorough knowledge of it was an essential part of the training of (a Christian)... In 1523 he told the Bohemian Brethren, '...learn Latin, Greek and Hebrew well...St. Augustine was obliged to confess, as he does in *Christian Instruction,* that a Christian teacher who is to expound the Scriptures must know Greek and Hebrew in addition to Latin.' Luther was uncompromising in his insistence on the importance of Hebrew." [70]

Catholic priests are free to refer to Martin Luther as "accursed," and we have heard them do so with vehemence, but these same priests are forbidden to accost a rabbi by name, or pronounce any jeremiad against servile papal pilgrimages to synagogues. St. Vincent Ferrer entered many synagogues—in order to tell the assembled congregation in no uncertain terms that they were slaves to sin, delusion and the devil.

John Calvin and Judaizing

With regard to Jean Cauvin, the French lawyer known to history as "John Calvin," some of his followers are numbered among the foremost witnesses against rabbinic perfidy in history. Among these the most illustrious is the 17th century English Puritan scholar William Prynne, a man of immense learning and the author of more than 200 books:

"Even in a century of intellectual omnivores he was acknowledged a prodigy...The journalist Marchamont Needham

---

[70] G. Lloyd Jones, *The Discovery of Hebrew*, op.cit., pp. 64-65.

described him as 'one of the greatest paper worms that ever crept into a library..." (Hugh Trevor-Roper).

Despite the ceaseless recitation of the myth that "Oliver Cromwell readmitted the Jews into England," the fact is that Parliament rebuffed Cromwell's *attempt* at readmitting them, largely due to the widespread circulation of a book by the Puritan Prynne, which he compiled expressly to support the ancient Catholic laws which forbade their presence in England:

"During the Protectorate, an address was presented on behalf of the Jews, soliciting the free exercise of their religion; a measure which Prynne opposed in his laborious tract, *Short Demurrer to the Jews Long Discontinued Remitter into England*...the Jews failed to obtain a legal establishment under Cromwell...their return occurred in the reign of Charles II." [71]

"The indefatigable and resolute Mr. Prynne published a very zealous remonstrance against it (the readmission of the Judaics to England), the aim of which was to show that permitting the Jews to reside in England, according to the foregoing proposals (by Cromwell), was highly criminal, being the greatest affront offered to the Son of God that any Christian government could be guilty of." [72]

Calvin's *An Answer to a Certain Jew's Questions and Objections* affirms medieval teaching on Judaism and carnal Israel, although with none of Luther's energy and sustained deconstruction. Calvin was theoretically and philosophically critical of rabbinic tradition in general. Calvin criticized Rabbi Isaac Abravanel for departing from the clear meaning of passages in Scripture. At one point Calvin terms Abravanel, a "twister," and a "trifler" brazenly "babbling about matters utterly beyond his knowledge." Calvin frequently condemned rabbis for seeking "new and subtle interpretations" and being "actuated by pure malice." Yet, a significant portion of Calvinists today, like contemporary Catholics, can be said to be in the camp of the rabbis or, at the very least, indifferent to the evil of the religion of Orthodox Judaism.

---

[71] *The English Reports* Volume XXXVI, Chancery XVI (Edinburgh, 1904), p. 718).

[72] *The Parliamentary or Constitutional History of England* Vol. XX [London, 1757], pp. 476-477).

The Kabbalists inside the Catholic Church emphasized learning the Hebrew language, not for the better understanding of the Bible, but rather to pervert it for occult rites involving a specially reserved pronunciation of the word *Yahweh,* the Hebrew name for God, as part of the Hermetic belief that Hebrew is a "wonder-working" magical language. Use of the sacred name *Yahweh* was forbidden by the Mishnah, except by the high priest. (Pope Benedict XVI also ordered it suppressed during his reign.) Early English-vernacular Protestant and Catholic Bible translations adhere to this superstition.

There were two schools of Hebraism in Christendom: the original one, which mastered Hebrew as the patrimony of Christian Israel, and the Neoplatonic-Hermetic-Kabbalistic variety which learned it for use in magical ceremonies and for raising the prestige of the rabbis and their books. To the glee of the occultists, certain Christian opponents of Judaism equated Hebrew study with Judaizing. This foolish equation allowed the Neoplatonic-Hermeticists to mock their conservative opponents as illiterates and ignoramuses, and led to activists who campaigned against Judaizing within the Church, to be proud of their ignorance of Hebrew, thereby conceding to the rabbis exactly what the rabbis' claimed to be their exclusive property, the language of the Old Testament.

Certain individual Roman Catholic scholars put up a noble fight against Rome's Renaissance Kabbalism, but their obedience to Rome was used to silence and obstruct them. "In a Lenten sermon, Jean Catilinet, provincial superior of the Franciscans in Burgundy, accused him (Cornelius Agrippa, Johann Reuchlin's disciple), of being a Judaizing heretic who had introduced into Christian schools the criminal, condemned and prohibited art of Kabbalah. Despising the Fathers and Catholic doctors he had made it clear that he preferred the Jewish rabbis, and had bent sacred (Hebrew) letters to heretical arts and to the Talmud. Although Agrippa freely admitted that he did not disparage the Hebraic tradition and that he had frequent recourse to Talmudic works, he strenuously denied the charge of heresy; it was the ignorance of the Kabbalah among his opponents that led to such a monstrous accusation." [73]

Agrippa's deceitful suggestion that the contents of the Kabbalah would not be offensive to Hebrew-literate Catholics is testimony to the crying need for Christians to have greater knowledge of the rabbinic texts, and not just a few lines of pornographic insults against Jesus and Mary contained in the Talmud of Babylon. The objective of our book *Judaism Discovered* was to provide an advanced study of the religion of the Talmud and Kabbalah. Imagine a future in which, in our Christian colleges and seminaries, the dark corners of the Mishnah, Gemara, Midrash and Zohar are as fully exposed as much as the errors of Karl Marx and Saul Alinsky.

The danger of rabbinic texts like the Kabbalah is more than just a generalized trend toward "Judaization." Occult Hermeticists have viewed the old Catholic Mass as a magical rite and the priest as a type of magician. This was Agrippa's thesis in *De occulta philosophia* — enthusiasm for what he claimed were the magical dimensions of highly ritualistic religion, where the emphasis is on objects and form. The New Age theosophist C.W. Leadbeater (1854-1934) honored the Catholic rites in his classic 1920 occult text, *The Science of the Sacraments*.

The papist alliance with occultists and reliance upon their texts has been the history of the Church of Rome since the Renaissance. This esoteric tradition created a precedent. If the Catholic martyr and saint, John Fisher, Bishop of Rochester, could make use of the rabbis to craft his polemical points against Luther, why not traditional Catholics today? How much more "traditional" can you get than St. John Fisher? It was this rabbinic epistemology that shaped the methodology of Karl Rahner, Yves Congar, Josef Ratzinger (Pope Benedict XVI) and other avant-garde theologians of the Left and the Right. The clandestine legacy of the Catholic hierarchy's entanglement with the occult has inspired modernist conspirators to build on this centuries-old Neoplatonic and Hermetic precedent. This is their inner tradition.

---

[73] G. Lloyd Jones, p. 91.

In his 1525 rejoinder to Luther, *Defense of the Sacred Priesthood*, John Fisher, who was fluent in Hebrew, consulted rabbis to gain what he imagined would be a true comprehension of the Biblical texts related to his subject:

"In his *Defense of the Sacred Priesthood* he discusses at length the nature of Melchizedek's sacrifice in Genesis 14:8 and quotes several rabbinic authorities in support of his explanation. He refers to Moses Ha-Darshan, an early 11th century French exegete and haggadist, to Pinchas ben Jair and Simeon ben Johai, [74] two second-century rabbis, to Rashi, Kimchi and the Targums as affirming that the sacrifice of the Messiah will be of the same substance as that of Melchiedek..."[75]

Some of the enthusiasm for Hebrew in Christian Europe and Britain was not rabbinic in orientation. It was inspired in part by the Christian intuition that Europeans were descended from the ten lost tribes of Israel, who had traveled north and settled on the continent in the Atlantic sea which they would one day transform into Europe.

The Christian practice of making laws for governing human society based on the Bible is exceedingly controversial in the Church. Christian philosophers have argued that Old Testament laws were a curse on Israel until such time as the Messiah would arrive. According to this thinking, in the post-Messianic age, *only* liberty must guide the Christian ship of state in the formulation of its laws. From this antinomianism arose the novel concept of prisons as places of punishing confinement, which Pennsylvania Quakers took one step further, inventing solitary confinement for an entire prison population, a practice which appalled Charles Dickens when he witnessed it on his tour of America, and which is in place at present at the Federal prison at Florence, Colorado, where prisoners are deliberately made to "rot." [76] The assumption that all Old Testament practices were accursed ones and that novelties spun from the minds of modern Christians are always

---

[74] "Simeon ben Johai" is Rabbi Shimon ben Yohai, reputed founder of the Kabbalah who decreed, "Even the best of the gentiles should all be killed."

[75] G. Lloyd Jones, p. 96.

[76] Cf. "Slow Rot at Supermax, *Los Angeles Times,* May 5, 2006.

more salubrious, overlooks the havoc that the mind of man can play, as in the wastrel and inhuman modern prison system, which would be strictly illegal under Old Testament statute. It was in the interest of discovering what, among God's old covenant laws, should be preserved for the better ordering of human society, that the dream of the Hebrew Republic came to the fore in Savonarola's Florence and the Puritan Commonwealth of New England. For Catholics, the latter two have been models of how not to govern, and in the case of New England specifically, a synonym for trivial, killjoy, blue laws and a fanaticism so preposterous that it outlawed the celebration of Christmas. Compared with legions of men stored in prison-warehouses for years, away from their wives and families, in what are in fact schools for crime and homosexuality, the "horror" of Sunday blue laws or a five shilling fine for keeping Christmas, as absurd as it was, would seem to pale in comparison.

In early 16th century Italy the papacy licensed the publication of the Talmud and other virulent Judaic polemical writings against Christianity. It is repeatedly stated in books and movies that the "antisemitic" popes "always hated and burned the Talmud"; therefore Christians believe this lie. The mesmerists have seen to it that the "proper" beliefs should be induced and we believe properly. A movement comprised of hypnotics cannot wage a battle independent of the direction of the Cryptocracy, however much they cloak themselves in the trappings of religion.

The information we present on the popes and the Talmud and Kabbalah is not an indictment of the Catholic Church, the root of which is Jesus Christ; any more than an exposé of Judas indicts the Gospel. We are indicting those *betrayers of the Church* who periodically have held high office or, indeed, the highest office. Naive persons imagine that these betrayers occupied the Chair of Peter beginning in the 1960s. A share of the Vatican's long-hidden Machiavellian tactics for the overthrow of the Gospel are being revealed in our time.

"The *Relatio post disceptationem* presented on the 13th of October, despite the rehashing it underwent, didn't obtain the expected majority of two-thirds (of the vote at the synod on the family), on two crucial points: the admittance of the divorced and remarried to Communion and the opening up to homosexual couples, attesting 104 in favor, 74 not in favor on the first point, and 118 for, 62 against, on the second. In spite of the evident débâcle, Cardinal Reinhard Marx, Archbishop of Munich, one of the most passionate exponents on the 'progressive' wing, said he was satisfied, *since revolutionary processes are done in successive stages*. On some themes, he explained, *'we took two steps forwards and then one backwards."* [77]

Where did Cardinal Marx learn this clever tactic? In part from the record of the popes who derogated, in stages, God's Law against profit on loans: first, from 1515 to 1830, and then with the two Codes of Canon Law promulgated in the twentieth century. There is a Roman proverb, *"Ma ciò che la dottrina non ammette viene ammesso dalla prassi, in attesa di essere sancito"* ("What doctrine does not admit is admitted in praxis, waiting for sanction").

One of the basic tenets learned in Thomistic philosophy is *first principles:* one must not proceed from false premises, from the idea that the revolution began with Kant or Rousseau, or the Enlightenment, or the French Revolution of 1789. Actually it started in the Garden of Eden with the serpent, 6000 years before Vatican II. Later, Jesus said, "Did I not choose you twelve and one of you hath a devil?"

One-out-of-twelve was an enemy agent *in His very presence*, yet Catholics are incredulous when we proffer a higher statistic for the papacy (every pope from 1515 onward). As with usury, the occult infiltration of the Church did not begin with the Enlightenment, much less with "the Council." It commenced in the late 1400s with its Neoplatonism and Hermeticism. In an important address to the Brussels *Société de philosopie* in 1958, Francois Masai argued that the *'caractére libertine, incrédule, anti-chrétien du platonisme byzantin'* was due not only to historical contingencies, but to the very principles of Platonic philosophy..." [78]

The "traditional" Catholic fairy-tale in sum: 1. They cannot give their allegiance to the Second Vatican Council because it represents a radical departure from the unbroken, unchanging teaching and doctrine of the Church from the time of Christ.

---

[77] Roberto de Mattei, *Corrispondenza Romana*, October 22, 2014.

[78] Niketas Siniossoglou, op. cit., p. 53.

2. They trace the seeds of subversion in the Church to the eighteenth century, to Rousseau in France and Kant in Prussia. 3. They teach that the modern departure from truth has its roots in the Reformation and Enlightenment, and the overthrow of the Bourbon dynasty in the French Revolution.

We reply: Kant is a symptom. Furthermore he is not wholly favored by the Cryptocracy, however much his radical epistemology seems to synchronize with modern theories of perception concerning dogma. Kant's philosophy cuts both ways: it not only opened the Church to scrutiny, it represented a substantial setback to the prestige of Orthodox Judaism among the intelligentsia. Catholic Neoplatonism burnished the reputation of Judaism among the intellectuals of the West. How can Kant be worse than the Catholic-Kabbalists and how is it that they escape the main burden of culpability among "conservative" and "traditional" Catholics?

Kant was contra-Judaism. We have never known of any philosophy that was contra-Judaism in the essence of its core precepts that was embraced for any significant length of time by the Cryptocracy. A Kantian would never have been allowed to teach at the Catholic Society of St. Pius X Winona, Minnesota seminary. A Neoplatonic-Hermeticist was, however, given the right to lecture at the seminary and lead seminarians on field trips to historic sites in the U.S. where he "explained" to them the "poisonous roots" of the Founding Fathers' anti-monarchial republican revolt. His writing was published by the Society's Angelus Press. This "traditional Catholic" occultist was made a papal knight by Pope John Paul II. He continues to direct "traditional Catholics" through his writing, speeches and interviews.

The Zionist historian Jonathan M. Hess explains what is objectionable to Zionists in the philosophy of Kant:

"Kant's *Religion within the Limits of Reason Alone*...dedicated an inordinate amount of time and energy denigrating Judaism and denying that it had any substantive link to the pure religion of reason introduced by Jesus...Kant's *Religion within the Limits of Reason Alone*...presented Judaism as a 'collection of mere statutory laws' that did not deserve to be called a religion, and that was incompatible with the Kantian ideal of moral autonomy. As a worldly political commonwealth that 'excluded from its communion the entire human race,' and 'which showed enmity toward all other people and which, therefore, evoked the enmity of all,' Judaism for Kant was an historical faith utterly devoid of ethical impulse and virtually 'irreconcilable with humanity itself.' Jesus, in contrast, figures in *Religion within the Limits of Reason Alone* as...the 'living archetype of the moral disposition in all its purity...' [79]

What Kant sought to achieve in the dawn of the modern age was an end to Judaism's immunity from criticism. It is true that Kant's imperative consisted of universal criticism of all ideologies. Yet Kant was one of the few modern philosophers of integrity for this reason: he did not exclude Judaism from his withering critique of institutionalized dogma. Why make an equal opportunity skeptic like Kant the poster boy for the modern devaluation of truth, while giving a pass to Ficino, Mirandola, Reuchlin and the Renaissance popes? Kant did not peddle deceit. He advocated the skepticism his conscience demanded of him.

At this juncture questions are bound to arise: if the papacy was part of the Cryptocracy from the late fifteenth century onward, why did the conspirators trouble to found and maintain Freemasonry, with its aim of destroying tiara and crown? Why did the Freemason Giuseppe Garibaldi destroy the papal state if the pope was a fellow-traveler?

This is like asking, why bother to start General Motors with its aim of building automobiles when there is already a Ford Motor Company that builds automobiles? Or, why did the Gambino crime family make war on the Colombo crime family? Have we not the wit to comprehend that institutions can have similar goals and serve the same devil, and still be vicious rivals, savagely competing for money, power and the fealty of the people? Why did the troops of Holy Roman Emperor Charles V nearly destroy Rome in 1527? Why did Pope Innocent XI support the Protestant army of Prince William of Orange? When that army defeated Irish and French Catholic troops at the Battle of the Boyne, why did Innocent's successor,

---

[79] *Germans, Jews and the Claims of Modernity* (2002), pp. 140-144; 148.

Alexander VIII, order a *Te Deum* sung in honor of the Protestant victory? [80]

Rome represents one wing of an enormous executive. Rivalry with the Anglo-Saxons was intense before the Reformation, and even prior to the Cryptocracy gaining a hold over the Vatican. Intense rivalry between the Catholic monarchs of France and Spain was episodic and sometimes lethal. Secret alliances with Freemasons, Protestants and non-Christian bankers were made, broken and re-constituted. This is not the history of the Boy Scouts, yet Catholics suspend their suspicions of the papacy and are as jejune as boy scouts when they encounter the dealings of the popes prior to the modern era.

Why did the pope have Savonarola executed? Though he made mistakes, Savonarola was, in general, part of the true Catholic resistance to the Church of Rome's Cryptocracy, in this case as it existed in Florence. Years after Savonarola was burned, Clement VII used his own army to put Florence under siege, as part of a mopping up operation to pacify the troublesome population who were in revolt against their Neoplatonic masters a quarter-century after Savonarola's death. Where did Clement VII acquire the gold to undertake the costly expense which the siege of Florence entailed? The source of the funds was supposed to be disclosed in the records

---

[80] Catholic Stuart King James II who had fled England for Ireland, was a creature (like his late brother, the English King Charles II), of the king of France, which made James despised in his native land, including among English Catholics, as well as at the court of Pope Innocent XI, who was an enemy of the Gallicanist French King Louis XIV, the butcher of the Huguenots. The Battle of the Boyne was a defeat for French interests and for James, who proceeded to flee Ireland. For a pioneering account of the calamitous French and French-Jesuit influence on James II, and revisionist data on Catholic-Protestant relations in England, including Innocent XI's amity toward King William of Orange, cf. "Gallicanism, Innocent XI and Catholic Opposition," in *Shaping the Stuart World, 1603-1714*. [Some researchers have suggested that the Protestant William of Orange was financed by the Catholic usury banking house of Odescalchi, operated by Pope Innocent XI's family. Cf. "The Pope and the Sun King," *The Scotsman*, September 5, 2009].

of the papal camera. The record-keeping was circumvented, however. *Who were Clement's bankers?* [81]

Freemasonic mobs and armies were (and are) part of the Hegelian dialectic, although since this predates Hegel we may rightly call it the dialectic of the Zohar. The Masons were killing the Catholics in the name of being rid of "priestcraft," while in the masonic Lodge they dubbed each other "High Priest, "Grand Hierophant" and other bombastic, priestly titles. The Freemasons represented the rabbinic pillar of *chesed* — literally, mercy — but more accurately, an outward show of hippie-type liberation from "dogma," extending back to Rabelais' Abbey of Theleme, and revived in Sir Francis Dashwood's "Hellfire Club." The Masons pretended that they wanted Freedom of speech for the nations, and for every lodge brother to live in freedom. But in fact theirs was a very circumscribed *church*, even more strict than that of their papist rivals.

We don't see evidence that Masonry actually wanted to destroy the Tiara; that was a cover story to deflect attention from the covert objective—*to capture it*—and with each successive capture, sow more poison by means of the neo-Catholic sin against the First Commandment, *papalolatry*, so that even a pope like Pope "Saint" Pius X cooperated with the usury-Money Power, and failed miserably, and indeed with gross negligence, to extirpate these toxins from the bowels of the papal edifice and curial office when he had the authority to do so.

The history of the Church of Rome in the age of the Renaissance is akin to Tim Finnegan's legendary ladder—one false step after another. It is an irony that both Ultramontane

---

[81] "Clement VII (1523-34), whom Joseph ben David Yehaf, in his commentary on the *Five Megillot* (p. 41b, Bologna, 1538), calls 'the favorer of Israel,' displayed particular interest in the internal affairs of the Jewish community, which had been divided into contending parties. Within the community there existed no authority that could settle these quarrels, and an invitation to go to Rome was therefore issued to Daniel ben Isaac of Pisa, who was highly esteemed by the pope...When David Reubeni and his follower Solomon Molko came to Rome, Clement VII not only offered them protection, but provided them with letters of recommendation. While in Rome Reubeni lived in the houses of Cardinal Ægidius (Giles of Viterbo), R. Joseph Ashkenazi and R. Raphael, Joseph Zarfati, the physician Moses Abudarham, and Isaac Abudarham." Cf. Joseph Jacobs and Schulim Ochser, "The Community Organized," in the *Jewish Encyclopedia* (1906), topic, "Rome." http://jewishencyclopedia.com/articles/12816-rome

Catholics and flaming New Age hippies are loath to abandon their mutually cherished belief that Rome in any era other than the modern one, was the implacable enemy of occult forces.

Any historian expecting to find a document signed by one or more popes of the Renaissance stating, "I am a Satanist," will be disappointed. There are true believers who will not accept the occult nature of the Church of Rome unless we produce such a document. The Renaissance and post-Renaissance papacy did not operate with the guileless candor of Jesus Christ. It shaded its true nature with a hundred different forms of camouflage and misdirection. It is easy to become lost in the thicket of these illusions.

Chapter III

The Serpent in the Garden of the Quattrocento

Much of what we are about to recount concerning the occult incubator that was the Catholic republic of Florence would not have occurred to the extent that it did, had it not been for the Medici family, whose members are today known mainly as patrons of fabulous Renaissance art works, and progenitors of two pontiffs, Giovanni di Lorenzo de' Medici (Leo X), and Giulio di Giuliano de' Medici (Clement VII). While Medici diabolism and usury are comparatively little known, their criminal politics are difficult to conceal.

"After the banishment of the main representatives of the Albizzi faction in 1434, Cosimo de' Medici worked aggressively to consolidate his power. By directly controlling the officials in charge of voting procedures (the *accoppiatori*), he made sure that only his supporters were appointed to the key positions of the city government...In addition, Cosimo and his descendants further strengthened their rule by creating special executive commissions (*balìe*) whenever their power seemed to be at risk. The *balìe* passed laws and made crucial decisions regarding the fiscal system, the commune's foreign politics, and the administration of the law. The establishment of new councils controlled by members of the ruling party diminished the republican character of the Florentine government and intensified discontent among the opponents of the Medici. Modern scholars have rightly described the Council of Seventy as a sort of life senate. It was created by Lorenzo the Magnificent (Cosimo's grandson) in 1480 and held Florentine politics in check until Piero de' Medici's fall in 1494. But this pattern of Mediciean interference in the government of Florence helps explain why in his dialogue *On Liberty*, composed shortly after the Pazzi's attempt to overthrow the Medici, Alamanno Rinuccini commends the conspiracy as a glorious act. He believed that the conspirators deserved the highest praise, for they had tried to restore the citizens' liberty, which Lorenzo, 'the tyrant of Florence,' had usurped. "...Self-promoting intellectuals in the Medici court had celebrated Lorenzo's government as the culmination of early quattrocento humanist civic ideals; yet Florentines perceived that behind the republican facade held up by official propaganda, their liberty had been severely restricted by the Medicean regime. It need not surprise us that within a city disappointed by the betrayal of long-shared ideals, Savonarola's movement met with enormous success. During the last decade of the quattrocento, many citizens followed Savonarola's call not only in response to its religious appeal, but also in the hope of seeing their political aspirations as a free city realized at last." [1]

Magic, paganism and the proto-modernist pseudo-Christian religion of syncretism did not simply arise out of nowhere and manifest overnight during the Catholic Renaissance. It had been a seed awaiting germination, even in the thirteenth century of the Catalan Ramon Lull (now deemed "Blessed" by the Vatican and regarded as a figure of wisdom by "traditional" and conservative Catholics), who was a would-be germinator. From Lull the virus moved to the University of Padua in the fifteenth century, where the "rigid" Aristotelian tradition was challenged by humanists. In the years 1417-1423, Nicholas of Cusa rejected scholasticism and took up Lull's ideas in Padua, where he "encountered Lull's new vision of human dignity." By 1430, Cusa was germinating the alien "New Philosophy" under the pious cloak of proving the doctrine of the Trinity. In his treatise, *De Trinitate*, St. Augustine had asserted that the Holy Trinity had left its mark on every part of creation. Augustinian Trinitarianism was exploited by occult-Catholics to provide cover for their magic and paganism: it was "of great importance to the Platonic theology of the Renaissance because it sanctioned the peculiar zeal with which Ficino, Pico della Mirandola and other humanists searched for rudimentary trinities among the pagans...with special reference to the foreknowledge of the Trinity supposedly shown by Orpheus, Plato and Zoroaster...Ficino...fully exercised the gentle art of piloting these thoughts into a Christian haven...Strange to say, this foible...was shared by so intransigent a Dominican as St. Antoninus of Florence, who not only accepted the doctrine of the 'vestiges of the Trinity' in its theological aspects...but went

---

out of his way to quote pagan witnesses, in *testimonia Trinitatis in doctrinis ethnicorum*, among them Hermes Trismegistus, the Sibyls and Plato..." [2]

Almost always these syncretic bridges to the pagan realm were "piloted into a Christian haven" with a great show of Catholic rhetoric and ostentatious declarations of devout faith in Jesus and His Church. There was no limit to the far-fetched fantasies the Neoplatonists would mount so as to convince the Catholic world that pagan magicians and diabolic beings of antiquity were heralds of Christian truth. "As a Christian Platonist, Cusanus (Nicholas of Cusa) was not frightened by polymorphic views of the deity; he had learned from Proclus to accept them as preparatory stages of initiation...In their enthusiasm for mystical triads, Renaissance Platonists accepted Iamblichus's view, *De vita pythagorica* xxviii, that the tripod of Apollo was a trinitarian symbol...that (the goddess Diana) shared in the same mystery seemed indicated by her name Trivia, and by the 'three faces' attributed to her in *Aeneid IV*...

"The *Ovide Moralisé* [3] blandly called her a trinitarian goddess, and she still appeared as such, with the inscription *Theologia*, on the Tomb of (Pope) Sixtus IV, looking up toward the Christian heaven where three heads are surrounded by-sun rays. As pagan goddess of the moon she foreshadows the triple glory of the Christian sun." [4]

In "the light of Neoplatonism, the humanists discovered in mythology something other and much greater than a concealed morality: they discovered religious teaching—the Christian doctrine itself...Against this background, it was inevitable that the same idea which declining paganism had evolved should occur to the humanists—namely, that all religions have the same worth, and that under their varied forms, however puerile and monstrous in seeming, is hidden a common truth.

---

[2] Edgar Wind, *Pagan Mysteries in the Renaissance* (1968), p. 241-243.

[3] The *"Ovide Moralisé* ("Moralized Ovid") is perhaps the most important work of the later French Middle Ages...written by an anonymous Franciscan. The *Ovide Moralisé* played a pivotal role in transmitting descriptions of the pagan gods, of mythological figures like Orpheus...and over 60,000 lines of philosophical and theological commentary to future authors and artists of the Western tradition." https://moralizingovid.wordpress.com/

[4] Wind, op. cit., pp. 248-249; 251.

Marsilio Ficino leans toward a sort of universal theism, with Platonism as its gospel." [5]

"In the earliest of his works—a Christmas sermon preached at Coblenz in 1430—Nicholas (of Cusa) brought together the most diverse types of material...sources which presage the beginning of a new epoch: the Bible and the Talmud, the *Sibylline Oracles* and *Hermetica*...The change was the consequence both of Nicholas' ever-deepening commitment to the...idea of man's dignity and of the ever-increasing range of sources on which he drew. During the period of his engagement at the Council of Basle (1432-1437), he had broadened immensely his knowledge of the philosophical traditions of late antiquity...He learned the differences between the Platonic tradition and the 'Aristotelian sect' which was entrenched in many universities.

"Whereas in his earliest sermons he had drawn on Macrobius for Platonic opinions, he now began to make use of Plato himself—especially the *Timaeus*—of Philo, Proclus, Pseudo-Dionysius...Nicholas'...synthesis represents a high-water mark in the evolution of the new understanding of reality which appeared in Western Europe...With respect to the creator, man is a 'human god' or a 'second god' (*De coniecturis* 2:14)...This new tradition, although forced for a time underground by medieval Aristotelianism...found representatives..." [6]

This "new understanding of reality," which was destined to become the motif of the much-celebrated Church-sponsored "Renaissance Art epoch," represents a radical departure from the ancient Biblical-Christian understanding of human beings as damaged by original sin and ineluctably subordinate to their Creator. The revolutionary anthropomorphic teleology of the Catholic Renaissance gave rise to a counter-reaction from Martin Luther and John Calvin, who demanded a return to fidelity to the hierarchical Biblical ordering of God and man, and the consciousness of man's fundamental *deformitas naturae* upon which the true Church had been founded.

---

[5] Seznec, op. cit., p. 98.

[6] Charles H. Lohr, "Metaphysics," in *The Cambridge History of Renaissance Philosophy* (1992), pp. 548, 550, 553 & 556.

"Luther's concept of man was in sharp contrast to this exalted picture of human potentiality, for he centered his view on the fall...Luther...insisted that human nature was wholly corrupted by original sin...Man's high opinion of himself, according to Calvin, had to be deflated, and he had to be convinced of his own corruption and debility." [7]

This is not to deny the *imago Dei,* the image of God belonging to our first parents at their creation, and intrinsic to it (*imago Dei intrinseca*). This is acknowledged. As a result of the Original Sin of Adam and Eve however, there was henceforth an alteration of the *forma substantialis* of humanity toward an acquired *inclinatio ad malum acquisita* (inclination to do evil). This too must be acknowledged. The Soviet Communist and Hitlerian National Socialist utopian schemas, like all utopian arrangements both religious and secular from the early modern era onward, are essentially rooted in the Renaissance-Kabbalistic theology of the perfectibility of man who, it is insinuated, is like unto God.

"This discovery authorizes the utopian to project man's actual capacities into a hypothetical future and to describe the biological and historical processes at the end of which a different man—or, rather mankind—will emerge in full possession of the desired attributes. Instead of refining the idea of God, as the religious utopian claims he does, it would be more accurate to say that the above schematized process naturally oversimplifies it and makes it grossly anthropomorphic...Such a new science is supposed to explore the conditions of emergence of man-become-God." [8]

The Renaissance theology is the mother of the modernist heresy, not only in terms of syncretism but in modernism's utopian futurism and faith in inevitability of human progress. "This Renaissance Platonist vision stressed man's position as a terrestrial god and combined it with a transformed Gnosticism

---

[7] Jill Kraye, "Moral Philosophy," in *The Cambridge History of Renaissance Philosophy* (1992), p. 314. In this particular case concerning "the depravity of post-lapsarian man," the reformers were restoring the original theology of the Catholic Church prior to the rise of the occult Church of Rome.

[8] Thomas Molnar, *Utopia: The Perennial Heresy,* p. 112. Prof. Molnar was a conservative Catholic philosopher.

holding that by the powers of the intellect man will create an earthly paradise." [9]

Man's dignity and unalienable rights (among them equality before the law), derive from his pre-lapsarian creation, which became congenitally depraved after the Fall and which finds conditional restoration by the grace of Christ in the covenant between believer and Redeemer. We say conditional because this sanctification is dependent on continuing faith in Jesus. "If you are an unbeliever when you die, then Christ did not die for you." (St. Ambrose).

Plethon's Illuminati

As we excavate the next step in the progression of the Neoplatonic-Hermetic-Kabbalistic conspiracy within the Church we discover that the ideas of Cusa and his personal colleague Georgios Gemistos (see below), coincide with the rise of secret societies inside the Church. Chief among them in terms of imposing a curtain of secrecy, was the Roman Curia. The Vatican bureaucracy as we know it was extensively developed and enlarged in this time period, and it was at the Council in Ferrara and Florence 1438-1439, that an itinerant Byzantine Neoplatonist, Georgios Gemistos, who was taught by a Judaic "intermediary"—i.e. his handler, "Elissaios, a Jew of Zororastrian background and polytheist inclinations"— commenced his campaign in the West against Aristotle and orthodox Catholicism.

Gemistos (ca. 1360-1452), was called by his cognomen, "Plethon" (sometimes spelled "Pletho"). His lectures in 1439 were published under the title, *On the Differences between Plato and Aristotle (De Differentiis)*. Some of these addresses, a milestone in the overthrow of Aristotle and Aquinas, were sponsored by Cardinal Giuliano Cesarini the Elder and hosted at the latter's palace, in the presence of Cosimo de' Medici. Here was the acceleration of the theological and cultural transmission of Neoplatonic paganism into the leading circles of the Catholic Church in Florence.[10]   In these addresses, Plethon held that there was a profound link between the Chaldeans and the Persian Magi. "The call for a new reading of

[9] Clark Trinkaus, *The Sixteenth Century Journal* (no. 4, 1990), p. 709.

[10] Cf. Ficino's preface to his 1492 translation of Plotinus Neri; as well as the research of Johannes Irmscher (1994).

Plato and the attack on Aristotle in the *Differences* initiated a lively and long-standing debate regarding the relation between Plato's and Aristotle's philosophy that has been seen as announcing the end of the medieval theologico-philosophical epoch and the rise of a new way to do philosophy." [11]

Plethon helped to dissolve the traditional theology of the Catholic Church and initiate the rise of paganism in Catholic habiliments; first as a substratum and later as the command ideology of the Renaissance and post-Renaissance papacy.

Antedating the ascendance of what came to be known as the Florentine Platonic Academy, the Eastern Church was dealing with the phenomenon of Byzantine humanism manifested within the Neoplatonic-Hellenist conspiracy as early as the ninth century, emanating from the School of Philosophy of Magnaura, headed by "John the Grammarian" and "Leon the Mathematician," circa 855 A.D. Leon was the author of a cunning work which foreshadowed the *modus operandi* of the "pious" Neoplatonist popes and prelates of the Renaissance. Leon's book, the *Thousand Line Theology* (*Chiliostichos theologia*), seemingly denounced Hellenism and paganism. On closer examination however, we discover the Neoplatonic mysticism of Pseudo-Dionysius ("Denys") the Aeropagite. Orthodox Christian dogma on the Original Sin of Adam and Eve and Christ's incarnation were derogated by Leon. He hinted that salvation is found outside the Church by means of "deciphering the secret language of God." Leon's followers included, in the fourteenth century, Petrarch's teacher, the Pythagorean monk Barlaam of Calabria, and in the fifteenth century, Plethon.

Another slick "conservative Christian" who had promoted occult Neoplatonism under a veil of anti-occult polemics, was the medieval Eastern Orthodox monk Michael Psellos (1018-1078), author of the *Chronographia,* and compiler of the *Magic Oracles of the Magi,* which he renamed the *Chaldean Chronicles.* Psellos added a spurious Christian gloss to its Pythagorean, Zoroasterian and Neoplatonic contents and these were embraced by Plethon nearly three centuries later; inspiring him to circulate the doctrine at the Council of Florence, as an affirmation of gnostic beliefs "mistakenly" rejected by the early Church. Plethon suffered no repression

---

[11] Niketas Siniossoglou, *Radical Platonism in Byzantium* (2011), p. 6.

whatsoever from papal Rome as a result of his bold, public, pagan-occult evangelism.

Niketas Siniossoglou, in his notable book, *Radical Platonism in Byzantium,* elucidates the camouflage by which Psellos, by "explicitly condemning Hellenism in the form of occult divinatory practices, allowed Hellenism to slip in by the back door in the form of speculative philosophical theology." [12] creating a foothold for the occult philosophy within the Catholic Church, which was the objective of his proselytizing mission.

We know we are confronting the principles of diabolic hermeneutics when these tools of doubletalk and concealment are employed. Four hundred years after Plethon, two of Pope Leo XIII's most renowned encyclicals were promulgated with similar shrewd misdirection: *Humanum Genus* and *Rerum Novarum.* Both are held aloft by supposed "conservative" and "traditional" Catholics as superb examples of the exposition of unalloyed dogmatic certainty and militant rebuke of evil. Look closer however, and we catch sight of the spirit of Michael Psellos hovering over *Humanum Genus,* the pope's statement on the occult and Freemasonry which scrupulously avoids the *very foundation* of the Freemasonic plague, *Kabbalistic* Judaism. By means of this staggering omission, for generations millions of Catholics have been misdirected away from knowledge of the true root of the masonic order.

Furthermore, Leo XIII's encyclical on social justice and the rights of workers to be free of oppression, *Rerum Novarum,* omits any restoration—or even a suggestion of a groundwork for a reinstatement of a restoration—of the Church's immutable ban on taking profits from loans. It is upon usury that the backs of the workers are broken and the Money Power made ruler over Church and State. The alibi for this development of the doctrine on money stems from that other

---

[12] Because "Platonism is made the measure for interpreting Christian doctrine." Siniossoglou, op. cit., pp. 77 and 109. It is highly instructive to read Siniossoglou's entire section on the smokescreen mounted by Psellos (pp. 71-85). Siniossoglou affords his readers an education in how outward-appearing advocates of conservative Christian orthodoxy can be the opposite of what they appear. He explains well the intricate mechanism of their doublespeak, which has considerable relevance to Renaissance and post-Renaissance papal documents.

principle of Neoplatonism, situation ethics: that which was beneficial in the past may be harmful in the present.[13]

Out of the doublespeak in Florence supported by the wealth and political authority of Cosimo de' Medici, came the movement which would convince Renaissance Rome that Neoplatonic-Kabbalistic-Hermeticism was a benefit to the Church and a divinely-ordained development of ecclesiastical doctrine, while reassuring the Catholic people, parish priests and laity, that the Church continued to be an ultra-inquisitorial bastion of vigilance against paganism and heresy, a legend widely accepted even in our twenty-first century.

Plethon founded a pagan brotherhood and his principal text, *Nomoi*, was a blueprint for a pagan utopia. [14] His specific model for realizing this dream was infiltration by Plethon's secret society of initiates, of which the Greek Catholic Cardinal Basilios Bessarion was a member.[15] Plethon's "philosophical-religious brotherhood" anticipated "European secret orders such as the Illuminati." [16] Plethon named his camarilla *"Phratria,"* after the old hereditary brotherhood that had practiced the sorcerous "Attic arts" associated with Attica, the birthplace of the Eleusinian mysteries in Greece, where the festival of the *Phratria* had been known as the *Apaturia*. It took place yearly, over a seventy-two hour period, in the autumn, marked by sacrifices to the gods, mostly animal, but on rare occasions, human beings were ritually sacrificed by the *Phratrians*. Plethon's group had chapters in Italy as well as Greece. He wrote his Neoplatonic, Zoroasterian *Book of Laws* exclusively for his revival of this brotherhood.

A conservative Catholic truly deserving of the name, George of Trebizond, was present in Cardinal Cesarini's palace for a lecture by Plethon, in the course of which he put a question to the Greek magus. Trebizond recounted his confrontation with Plethon in his book, *Comparatio philosophorum Platonis et*

---

[13] Siniossoglou, p. 83.

[14] Cf. Francois Masai, *Plethon et le Platonisme de Mistra* (1956).

[15] Masai, pp. 300-314: Plethon's secret society had first formed in Mistra, in southern Greece.

[16] Masai, p. 300; Igor P. Medvedev, *Neue philosophische Ansätze im späten Byanz* (1981), pp. 547-548.

Aristotelis: "I myself heard him (Plethon) at Florence asserting that in a few more years the whole world would accept the same religion with one mind, one intelligence, one teaching.

"And when I asked him, 'Christ's or Muhammad's?,' he said: 'Neither. But it will not differ much from paganism.'" [17]

Trebizond was outraged by Plethon's brazen response and by the fact that he was free to offer it under the roof of the cardinal and the protection of the Medici. [18] Trebizond did his best to warn of the "devastating effect that the Platonic contagion...would have on 'religion and politics,' as a 'great apocalyptic drama' unfolded a real 'neopagan conspiracy." [19]

Then as now however, Catholic conservatives were obstructed and suppressed by liberal prelates. Trebizond became a victim of an early form of selective, though de facto, censorship, and he was denounced by Plethon's disciple, Cardinal Bessarion, in the latter's book, *Calumniatorem Platonis* (1469). Bessarion was at the head of a large network of influential members of the ecclesiastical elite. They facilitated the wide dissemination of *Calumniatorem Platonis,* and did all they could to limit the circulation of Trebizond's book:

"Bessarion's famous treatise, a reply to his adversary George of Trebizond's *Comparatio philosophorum Platonis et Aristotelis,* became one of the most important texts of the Renaissance. It had been written in Greek in the late 1450s and the 1469 first edition was based on Perotti's rephrasing of Bessarion's own translation into Latin, with substantial additions by other protégés of Bessarion's. The first Aldine edition (based on a copy of the 1469 edition with emendations by a member of Bessarion's household), was published in 1503...Despite George of Trebizond's superior Latinity and force of argument, Bessarion's treatise was widely distributed and became well-known; George's treatise was only

---

[17] George of Trebizond, *Comparatio Platonis et Aristotelis*, folio V63.

[18] Later, long after the horse was out of the barn, for public consumption Rome had some of Plethon's books burned. This pacified conservatives, even as Plethon's ideas continued to be adapted and espoused by the Catholic hierarchy.

[19] Patrick Nold and Alison Frazier, "Introduction," in *Essays in Renaissance Thought and Letters* (2015), p. xxxiii.

published once, in 1523, in a garbled edition caused by the earlier mis-binding of the manuscript exemplar." [20]

Trebizond, defender of the Catholic theology of all time, was opposed by Pope Nicholas V, who had him dismissed from his position in the Vatican bureaucracy. "He was made secretary to Nicholas V, but lost the favor of the pope by his fierce advocacy of Aristotle against Bessarion, Pletho, and other learned Greeks." [21]

Trebizond was, however, championed by conservative elements in the leadership of the Greek Orthodox Church, including no less a figure than Georgios-Gennadios Scholarios, the future patriarch of Constantinople, who had written a polemic, *Against Plethon*.[22] Scholarios was no Orthodox bigot or rustic. He was a sophisticated theologian with a life-long admiration for St. Thomas Aquinas, the Roman Catholic theologian who wrote after the schism between the Latin and Greek churches. "There has been a tendency to describe the clash between Scholarios and Plethon as a conflict between a reactionary theocrat and a visionary reformer, but a serious examination of their work reveals that Scholarios was capable of foresight and pastoral sensitivity...while Plethon was known to advocate ideological repression far greater than any he himself ever suffered, as in his suggestion that all dissenters...

---

[20] Cf. J. Monfasani, "A tale of two books: Bessarion's *In Calumniatorem Platonis* and George of Trebizond's *Comparatio Philosophorum Platonis et Aristotelis*," in *Renaissance Studies 22*, pp. 1-15. Also cf. Sotheby's auction catalog: http://www.sothebys.com/en/auctions/ecatalogue/lot.8.html/2008/continental-and-russian-books-and-manuscripts-including-science-and-medicine-l08409

[21] "George of Trebizond" in *The Cyclopedia of Biblical, Theological, and Ecclesiastical Literature* (1880).

[22] Cf. M.H Blanchet, *Georges-Gennadios Scholarios* [Vers 1400-Vers 1472]: *Un Intellectuel Orthodoxe Face a la Disparition de L'Empire Byzantin* (2008).

'found teaching against our doctrine shall be burned alive." [23] Fourteen years after Plethon's death, around 1464, Patriarch Scholarios alerted his flock to the menace of rabbinic Judaism in his *Refutatio erroris Judaeorum*.

The coming struggle over the Neoplatonic-Hermetic takeover of the Church of Rome was presaged by the arrival of Plethon, the Christ-denying heretic, who was advanced and defended by Cardinals Cesarini and Bessarion, as well as Pope Nicholas V. After Nicholas of Cusa, Plethon was the most high profile, public purveyor of the occult toxin inside the bowels of the Church in the fifteenth century, when we qualify his profile as being that of an infiltrator whose theology was *completely undisguised*. [24]

The devious legion of Church infiltrators who followed Plethon would, contrary to him, paint themselves in pious hues, as devoutly *Christian*-Platonists, *Christian*-Hermeticists and *Christian*-Kabbalists, in defiance of the fact that their Neoplatonic, Hermetic and Kabbalistic dogma represented

---

[23] Christopher Livanos, "The Conflict Between Scholarios and Plethon," in *Modern Greek Literature: Critical Essays* (Routledge, 2003), p. 25. Plethon's murderous, would-be dictatorship screened by a facade of enlightened liberalism, is the pattern of the western secret societies, from the Medici to the Masons. For example, those who swallow the masonic propaganda that "freedom of speech for all citizens of the Republic," is a right sincerely promulgated by Freemasonry, do not know its real history, wherein David C. Miller's anti-masonic printing plant was burned by Freemasons in Batavia, New York (cf. Thurlow Weed and Harriet A. Weed, *Autobiography of Thurlow Weed* [1884], pp. 218-219). Eighteen years afterward, in 1844, the *Nauvoo Expositor*, an Illinois newspaper opposing masonic leader Joseph Smith, founder of the Mormons, was destroyed by his order (cf. Hoffman, "Masonic America," in *Revisionist History*, June-July, 2014, p. 5). Masonic "freedom of speech" is propounded in a nation to obtain that right for the initiates of the Lodge, and not necessarily for the mass of humanity, the non-masonic "cowans," from whom any and all rights may be withdrawn at will by the pyramid-and-obelisk men. This is the true essence of that "Abbey of Thelema" which is the template of the secret societies that are derived from the Neoplatonic-Hermetic fish-hook: a big front proffering hippie-bait— freedom, bliss and enlightenment. Once hooked, the processed initiates encounter an even bigger back: an occult church with rules far more rigid and draconian than in the maligned, "repressive" medieval church.

[24] Siniossoglou, demonstrates in *Radical Platonism in Byzantium: Illumination and Utopia in Gemistos Plethon*, the fact that Plethon clearly rejected Christ and that Plethon's "pagan Platonic paradigm" brought to fulfillment latent tendencies among Catholic humanists toward a distinctive anti-Christian and pagan outlook."

demonic forces that are, patently, spiritually irreconcilable with the Gospel, and profoundly hostile to it.

Plethon's influence over the Council of Florence and in the Catholic salons of that city helped to spread the Neoplatonic contagion to the patricians of the Church of Rome. Let us track Plethon's anti-Christian ideology. In Plato's *Timaeus,* the philosopher's intellect alone guides him to knowledge of ultimate reality. From this rationalism, disconnected from Biblical revelation, proceeds the conceit of man's *tikkun olam,* according to Plotinus (ca. 204-270 A.D.), one of the founders of Neoplatonism: "It is...announced in Plotinus according to whom the descent of the soul in this world occurs for the sake of the perfection of the universe...Plethon's revival of this model acquires a revolutionary dimension...a metaphysical *mundus inversus...*" [25]

In this inverted world, in the imagination of philosophers, humans are placed above the hierarchy of divine creation as revealed in the Scriptures (God and the angels above, and man below)—*to become co-redeemers of the universe.* This notion of co-redemption of God's creation by a human being is a tenet of both the Kabbalah and Neoplatonism and finds overt expression in post-Renaissance Church of Rome theology, in

---

[25] Siniossoglou, ibid., p. 187.

the form of a de facto belief in the Blessed Virgin Mary as "Co-Redemptrix of the Universe." [26]

Plethon was the Saul Alinsky of his day, using religion as a vehicle for social engineering. In *Nomoi*, Plethon's main text, he relates that revolutionary change requires religion as its vehicle. His "...ideological and political reforms presuppose religious reformism, the shift from Christianity to paganism."[27] As we observed earlier, according to Plethon, to enforce the occult "reform" those who object to it must be executed.

Cosimo de' Medici considered Gemistos Plethon a second Plato, and dedicated himself to founding a Neoplatonic academy in Florence to perpetuate the legacy of this serpent in the Quattrocento. The Roman Catholic Church would never be the same.

---

[26] "Co-redemptrix" and "Co-redeemer" denote an impossible human equality with the divine which is classic Neoplatonism. Cf. in Church of Rome theology, Acts of the Fifth International Symposium on Marian Coredemption, *Mary at the Foot of the Cross-V: Redemption and Coredemption under the Sign of the Immaculate Conception* (Franciscans of the Immaculate, 2005). Also: "Mary is the intermediary through whom is distributed unto us this immense treasure of mercies gathered by God, for mercy and truth were created by Jesus Christ. Thus as no man goeth to the Father but by the Son, so no man goeth to Christ but by His Mother."— *Octobri Mense*, Encyclical of Leo XIII, Sept. 22, 1891. Here Pope Leo taught falsehood, "For there is one God and one mediator between God and mankind, the man Christ Jesus." (I Timothy 2:5). Giving Mary a higher place than God's Word allows is a slippery tactic for dismissing her altogether by causing the *appropriate veneration of her* to be falsely equated with "Mariolatry." Terming Mary, who is indeed the *Theotokos*, as Mary the "Co-redemptrix" of the Universe (and consequently the alleged co-Redeemer of herself), is not *appropriate veneration*, but *inordinate adoration,* amounting to the idolatry of a human being. Jesus Christ is our only Redeemer. Mary is without doubt the greatest human who ever lived, conceived without sin (because Jesus, the new Adam, could only incarnate inside an uncontaminated "Eden"). It is exceedingly sad that many Protestants have a higher opinion (and esteem) for Sarah, Ruth, Judith and Deborah, than for the woman who said to the angelic messenger of YHVH, "Be it done unto me according to thy word" (Luke 1:38), thus making possible the Incarnation; the woman who William Wordsworth rightly described as "our tainted nature's solitary boast." The papal occultists nearly always exalt Marian devotions, and often practice them personally and publicly, for they know that by showing themselves to be her supposedly earnest acolytes, they are sure to gain faith in their rule, in the eyes of some "Marian" Catholics. (This tactic was Pope "Saint" John Paul II's specialty).

[27] Siniossoglou, op.cit., p. 386 and 409.

Chapter IV

The Priest and the Platonists

"I am a real Christian, that is to say a disciple of the doctrines of Jesus, very different from the Platonists, who call me infidel and themselves Christians and preachers of the gospel, while they draw all their characteristic dogmas from what its author never said nor saw. They have compounded from the heathen mysteries a system beyond the comprehension of man, of which the great reformer of the vicious ethics and deism of the Jews, were he to return to earth, would not recognize one feature."

Thomas Jefferson

The founding of the occult movement inside the Catholic Church in the fifteenth and early sixteenth centuries was the work of three seminal Catholic thinkers: Ficino, Giovanni Pico and Reuchlin, supported by a network of collaborators. Keep in mind as we follow the trail of their conspiracy that other than farcical token punishment for public consumption, as for example the brief, theatrical incarceration of Pico, *no significant repression was ever directed against this trio of diabolic occultists by the Pope of Rome or the Inquisition.* On the contrary, the record shows that to the extent that the Renaissance pontiffs could do so without exposing their own complicity, these three pivotal founding members of the occult infiltration of the Church of Rome, were generally shielded by the highest elements in that Church.

While there were many hoaxes embedded in the Hermetic mythos, the two principal ones were the contention that the main Hermetic texts, the *Asclepius* and Ficino's translation of the *Corpus Hermeticum*, were written in remote antiquity by an all-wise Egyptian priest. The second principal hoax associated with the advancement of Hermeticism in an overwhelmingly Christian society and culture such as existed in the fifteenth century in Italy, was the insistence by the leading Neoplatonic-Hermetic "Catholics" that Hermes Trismegistus testified of Christ.

No serious scholar any longer believes that Hermes Trismegistus lived in close proximity to the time of Moses, as the Florentine occult theologian and priest Marsilio Ficino asserted in his dedication ("Argumentum") of *Pimander* to Cosimo de' Medici. Frances Yates asks, "How was a Christian magus to get round Augustine?' She answers her own question: "Marsilio Ficino did it by quoting Augustine's condemnation and then ignoring it..." [1]

A Judaic scholar writes, "First and foremost, Kabbalah was studied, translated, and amalgamated into Christian speculation in a very specific intellectual circle, which emerged two decades earlier as part of the efforts of Marsilio Ficino. Ficino was not only instrumental in rendering into Latin the huge Platonic, Neoplatonic, and Hermetic *corpora*; he was also a thinker who offered a synthesis between the various forms of thought he translated, and Christian theology." [2]

As Rev. Fr. Ficino progressed deeper into sorcery, some Renaissance Catholics began to ask questions concerning how it was that a priest at the top of the pecking order in Medici Florence, was involved with magic and astrology?

"What has a Christian to do with magic and images? Ficino counters by pointing out that in ancient times priests always did medicine, mentioning Chaldean, Persian and Egyptian priests; that medicine is impossible without astrology; that Christ Himself was a healer. But above all he emphasizes that there are two kinds of magic, one demonic magic which is illicit and wicked, the other natural magic, which is useful and necessary. The only kind of magic which he has (allegedly) practiced or advised is the 'good and useful kind'—*magica naturalis*. He writes: "How elegant, how artistic and refined is this modern natural magic!"

"...Ficino's magic was a religious magic, a revival of the religion of the world. How could a pious Christian reconcile such a revival with his Christianity? No doubt the Renaissance religious syncretism, by which the Neoplatonic triad was connected with the Trinity, would account for regarding sun-worship theoretically and historically as a religion having

---

[1] Yates, *Giordano Bruno and the Hermetic Tradition*, p. 11.

[2] Moshe Idel, "Jewish Kabbalah in Christian Garb," in *Kabbalah in Italy: 1280 to 1510* (2011), p. 234.

affinities with Christianity, but this would hardly account for the revival of it as a religious cult. The moving force behind this revival was...Ficino's deep interest in the Egyptian magical religion described in the *Asclepius*...When Hermes Trismegistus entered the Church, the history of magic became involved with the history of religion in the Renaissance." [3]

The Italian-Catholic Renaissance, pioneered by the Florentine Medici agent Rev. Fr. Marsilio Ficino, summoned from the bowels of the secret occult orders, the understanding of Plato [4] as a theologian from the *classical past* who had channeled the wisdom tradition of the universal religion of the *deep past*, the "perennial philosophy," [5] and *"prisca theologia"* of Hermes Trismegistus, Zoroaster ("Chaldean Oracles") Orpheus ("Orphic Hymns") and the "sages" of the Kabbalah.[6] Marsilio Ficino leaned toward a universal theism, with Neoplatonism as its gospel." [7]

Egypt was the master theological symbol/image of this process of transformation. This is reflected in several of Fr. Ficino's treatises, in particular *De voluptate* and *Di dio et anima*. In the former, he describes Hermes Trismegistus as

---

[3] Yates, *Giordano Bruno,* pp. 80, 82-83.

[4] Along with Plato's four major theological successors: Neoplatonism's founder, Plotinus (see pp. 85-86), his pupil Porphyry (234-305); as well as Iamblichus (see p. 90), author of *On the Egyptian Mysteries* (translated by Ficino); and the Neoplatonist systematizer, Proclus (412-485).

[5] The perennial philosophy has exponents on the Left and the Right. The former are more familiar in popular culture: the comparative religious studies departments of colleges and universities, the New Age movement, and writers such as Frithjof Schuon, Huston Smith and Aldous Huxley. On the Right, in addition to the Renaissance "Catholics" who pioneered it and made it their specialty, such as the curator of the Vatican library, Agostino Steucho (1496-1549), the perennial philosophy is a fixture of the movement centered around René Guenon, and further to the Right, Julius Evola.

[6] This is the *universalism* of the Neoplatonic-Hermetic theology. It is a *solvent*—the universal *distillation* of all of the gods of the pagans into one syncretic religion of demons (I Corinthians 10:20-21). To the contrary, the true Roman Catholic Church's self-description as *universal* (catholic) is a reference 1. to the offer of God's grace to all mankind; and 2. the theology of the Eucharist as described by the Apostle Paul, "Because there is one bread, we who are many are one body, for we all partake of the one bread." The attempt to conflate occult universalism with the universal *ecclesia* of Jesus Christ is a fool's errand.

[7] Jean Seznec, p. 98.

"the wisest of all Egyptians," whose god is the source of all creation. In the latter he writes, "Mercurius Trismegistus, an Egyptian philosopher far more ancient than the Greeks, whom Greeks and Egyptians called a god because of his boundless understanding and knowledge..." With regard to the late fifteenth century Church, James Stevens Curl points to *the increasing Egyptianisation of the Bishop of Rome himself.*" [8]

He notes that in Catholicism at this time, "It must be remembered that the notion that all magic, all knowledge, all skills, and all basic architectural wisdom came from Egypt, was powerful..." [9]

While the Neoplatonists had already gained a foothold in the Vatican, it fell to the Medici-subsidized Ficino to produce and "baptize" the first accessible translation in print of the central canonical text of pagan Hermeticism:

"The *Corpus Hermeticum* were a group of Greek religious and philosophical texts written in the first few centuries after Christ. Although clearly influenced by Greek philosophy, they were thought to encapsulate the far more ancient thoughts of Hermes Trismegistus...Hermetic writings were known in medieval Europe, but their intellectual relevance was boosted massively when, in 1460, a Byzantine monk brought a version of the *Corpus* to Florence, where it was translated into Latin by Marsilio Ficino (1433‾99) and published in 1471. As a consequence, Ficino became a central figure in the world of intellectual occultism. His conception of magic was hugely influential, and the lynchpin of the intellectual magic traditions of the early modern period...

"The other significant development of the Renaissance, which would have more of an influence on the development of future grimoires than Hermeticism, was the spreading influence of Kabbalah in European magical thought. The mystical system of Kabbalah that developed in medieval Spain had been percolating into Christian magic before the late fifteenth century, but it was its espousal by another Florentine philosopher and natural magician, (Giovanni) Pico della Mirandola (1463-94), that introduced it to a new readership

---

[8] Curl, *The Egyptian Revival* (2005), p. 90. Ibid.

[9] Ibid.

and led to renewed engagement with its occult promises. Johannes Reuchlin, a German humanist scholar and expert in Greek and Hebrew, further advanced its influence north of the Alps. In 1490 he travelled south and visited Pico—a sign of the developing European network of occult philosophers." [10]

In 1463, the highly placed papal agent Cosimo de' Medici gave the gifted Roman Catholic linguist and polymath Marsilio Ficino the lifetime use of the palatial "Villa Medici di Careggi," but before he did so he set him to work urgently translating a recently discovered copy of the treasured *Corpus Hermeticum,* the key occult text attributed to Hermes Trismegistus. The aforementioned Latin translation produced by Ficino was renamed by him, *Pimander.*

"...word came to Ficino from Cosimo that he must translate Hermes first, at once, and go on afterwards to Plato...Ficino made the translation in a few months...It is an extraordinary situation. There are the complete works of Plato, waiting, and they must wait while Ficino quickly translates Hermes...What a testimony this is to the mysterious reputation of the Thrice Great One! Cosimo and Ficino knew from the Fathers that Hermes Trismegistus was much earlier than Plato...Egypt was before Greece; Hermes was earlier than Plato. Renaissance respect for the old, the primary, the far-away, as nearest to divine truth, demanded that the *Corpus Hermeticum* should be translated before Plato's *Republic* or *Symposium*, and so this was in fact the first translation that Ficino made." [11]

And thus begins the peregrination to gnosis, the marriage of Neoplatonism and Hermeticism as part of the grand occult architecture of the esoteric *Prisca Theologia*, the syncretic religion of the Renaissance Catholic Church, intoxicated with Plato's concept of a world spirit and a world soul, as well as Egyptian and Zoroasterian influences on Plato (*Phaedrus* and *I Alcibiades* respectively). The pantheon of gods, deities and demigod-sages becomes as inclusive as the term polytheism connotes. Orpheus, Pythagoras, Hermes and Zoroaster all had a hallowed pride of place in the pagan firmament which was invading the Latin Church, to a lesser or greater degree,

---

[10] Owen Davies, *Gimoires: A History of Magical Books*, p. 46.

[11] Yates, *Giordano Bruno op. cit.,,* pp. 13-14.

depending on whether it is Plethon, Ficino or Giovanni Pico who is influencing the direction of this infernal hierarchy. For Ficino, Hermes and Zoroaster trumped Orpheus and Pythagoras. Indeed, like the Medici, Father Ficino was fixated on the primary archetype of the Three Chaldean Magi at the Epiphany of Christ who were there, as he perceived it, to proclaim Jesus as the new Zoroaster.

It was Zoroaster who was reputed to be the originator of the star-centered astrological magic by means of which the Magi had located the Christ child. In this context, Jesus was viewed as the incarnation of the occult *priscus theologus*, the reconciler of the Abrahamic faith with the ancient pagan wisdom of Egypt and Greece, as expressed in Platonic and Neoplatonic Catholicism, a syncretism ascribed by Ficino to the Athenian convert Dionysius whose conversion by St. Paul at Areopagus is mentioned in the Book of Acts. A series of treatises attributed to this Pauline Christian "Dionysius the Areopagite," reflect Plato's philosophy in his *Parmenides*.

Historians now know that the Christian Dionysius who was the contemporary of the Apostle is guilty of none of the fraudulent writings said to be his. In actuality, many of these were actually penned by Pseudo-Dionysius (also called Pseudo-Denys) in the fifth century A.D. It was Martin Luther who said of him, "Dionysius is most pernicious; he platonizes more than he Christianizes." Pseudo-Denys/Dionysius is a saintly figure in the eyes of Right-wing Catholics and the subject of a panegyric by William Riordan, Professor of Theology at the "conservative-Catholic" Ave Maria University in Florida, in his Jesuit-published book, *Divine Light: The Theology of Denys the Areopagite* (Ignatius Press, 2008). The author attempts to uphold Catholic Neoplatonism while reproving pagan Neoplatonism. The result is a farrago of contradictory claims and arguments. He is aggrieved, for example, that Jaroslav Pelikan judges Pseudo-Denys/Dionysius to have been a heretic. Riordan alludes to "Denys' use of certain Neo-Platonic formulations for the purposes of his own properly Christian theological enterprise...in Denys, this transforming assumption of the Platonic intuition into the Christian view, reaches a new, more developed form. His original and specifically Christian contributions gave Neo-Platonism an extended life when its death was very imminent." [12]

John M. Dillon writes of the post-first century hoaxer who posed as the Aeropagite who was the contemporary of St. Paul:

"At some time around the fifth century CE, an enterprising Christian controversialist...highly educated in the intricacies of contemporary Platonism...published a series of remarkable works, under the pseudonym of 'Dionysius the Aeropagite' [13] — thus seeking boldly to upstage the whole late Platonist system by implying that this first-century Athenian convert of St. Paul had anticipated every aspect of it. In a series of works of great theoretical and linguistic complexity...'Dionysius' sets before us a conspectus of his (lightly) Christianized version of Procline Neoplatonism...The works of Dionysius first come to notice at a conference held in Constantinople in 532 between a group of Orthodox followers of the Council of Chalcedon, led by Bishop Hypatius of Ephesus, and a group of partisans of Severus (a Monophysite theologian and statesman), where the Severians adduce 'Dionysius' as an authority, and Hypatius expresses some skepticism as to the provenance of the works cited. However, Dionysius survived this first test, and a commentary composed on the corpus shortly afterwards by John of Scythopolis seems to have confirmed his credentials....

"...adaptation of a very distinctive Syrianic-Proclean system of triads occurs in Dionysius' account of the structure of the angelic world in the *Celestial Hierarchy*. In that work... Dionysius sets out the succession, or *hierarchia* (a term which he seems to have invented), of the divine orders of beings in a series of triads, interestingly reminiscent of that proposed for the intelligible realm by Syrianus and faithfully adopted by Proclus. For Syrianus and Proclus, we may recall, the intelligible realm comes to be divided into a sequence of three levels: an intelligible triad of entities, an intelligible-intellective triad (each element of these subdivided into further triads), and an intellective hebdomad, consisting of two triads and a seventh entity, the so-called 'membrane.' However, what we basically have is a sequence of triads...Such a triadic

---

[12] *Divine Light,* pp. 71; 74 and 75.

[13] In other words, Pseudo-Dionysius.

system as this for the heavenly realm has really no warrant in Scripture, and it is remarkable that Dionysius should have felt moved to propound it.

"A salient feature of later Neoplatonism, from Iamblichus onwards, was the elevation of theurgy, the performance of rituals to attract the favor of the gods...With this theurgic tradition Dionysius appears to set off the divine activity from the human, and to denominate the former *theourgia*, thus subtly altering the connotation of the compound 'god-work' to cause it to mean 'work of *the gods*'...The latter human component he renames *hierourgia*...for Dionysius the 'hierurgic rites' are the sacraments, but they fulfill the same role and possess the same rationale as the rights of the Iamblichean or Procline theurgist." [14]

It was Fr. Ficino who breathed an extended life into "Denys," though here it must be conceded that prior to the time of the Florentine priest, even medieval Catholicism suffered to a degree from the influence of Platonism and Neoplatonism, and nowhere more so than in the development of a theology of the soul which exists in the Kabbalah but not the Bible.

The study of the theology of Plato and Neoplatonism has been subject to so much mystification that it has become a murky and baffling enterprise that has defied comprehension by the average Christian. The reason there can be no such thing as "Christian Platonism" or "Christian Neoplatonism" is the huge disconnect between the Platonic cosmology and the Biblical. There is no ecumenical bridge between the two and that fact violates a fundamental tenet of the syncretic occult religion, which insists on the supposed truth that all contemporary creeds have a common derivation. In order to put forward this fraud they must resort to their most common tactic, lying and deception.

According to Plato and Platonism, material creation is a prison from which "the soul" blessedly escapes at death. There is no resurrection of the body in Plato or Platonism, or the whole of pagan Greek thought, for that matter. Pagan Platonism posits a disembodied immortality which has been freed at last from sordid physical Creation. As far back as the

---

14 John M. Dillon, "Dionysius the Aeropagite," in *Interpreting Proclus: From Antiquity to the Renaissance* (2014), pp. 111-112; 118-119; 121.

first century A.D. and "the Jew, Philo of Alexandria," this pagan belief that the body is the "prison house of the soul" began to circulate among Christians. Philo venerated Plato as "most holy Plato." Eusebius (263-339), "the father of Church history" promoted the fable that Philo had met St. Peter in Rome. St. Jerome even includes Philo among the Church Fathers.

Philo personified the early Platonism that supported the emerging Gnostic view that matter itself is evil. For the true Christian however, "sin entered as an alien force into the universe" (Romans 5:12). The fact that creation was subjected to the bondage of corruption...implies that its original state was otherwise (Romans 8:20)...it is not intrinsic to the creation per se...For Philo, the ultimate goal is to escape and cast off the material: that takes the form of...an immortality of the soul after death. For (St.) Paul, the ultimate resolution comes through resurrection and new creation...Believers will receive glorified bodies like Christ's...Likewise, all of creation will be set free from its bondage and participate in redemption (Romans 8:21). [15]

Another aspect of Plato's philosophy which is irreconcilable with the gospel of Jesus Christ is the Platonic demiurgic construct, which posits that one force created the universe, and another, the "Demiurge," operates it (*Timaeus*, pt. II).

"...some thinkers have synthesized Christian theism with Plato's god, the Demiurge. Certain points must be noted before an alleged correspondence can be confirmed...Taking Plato's philosophy as a whole, I believe that all such demonstrations would be forced. One would have to isolate abstractly certain attributes or characteristics of Plato's god, change their meaning as they appear in the holistic structure of Plato's philosophy, then synthesize these attributes or characteristics with Christian theism. Not only does such a procedure destroy the distinctiveness of Christian theism...(s)uch an adventure is an injustice to Christian thought...We must underline, therefore, that Plato's formulation of god is not a faithful

---

[15] Charles A. Anderson, *Philo of Alexandria's Views of the Physical World* (2011), p. 191.

response to the revelation of the Christian God, but rather a rejection of Him." [16]

It is this "injustice to Christian thought" which is the duplicitous objective of the syncretists, beginning with Philo and extending to the pontificates of the late twentieth and early twenty-first century. It is not a "conspiracy theory" to perceive this unmistakable chain of transmission.

In traversing the numerous texts of "Christian" Neoplatonism, one will travel far before encountering an unambiguously egregious transgression of the First Commandment. Instead, in seemingly interminable books of this canon, one is met by a gradual conditioning process, in the form of a seemingly harmless metaphysic, which in reality takes us further away from the clarity and truth that comes with immersion in the Word of God as the highest and ultimate source of wisdom. In "Christian" Neoplatonism, the lucidity of the gospel of Jesus Christ is subsumed in a welter of mystical speculation—an extended make-believe excursion into the spirit realm, where phantasmagoric conjecture is presented as a higher reality. This was the peril of "Christian" Neoplatonism for the Church and the believer. The deeper the engagement with its conjectures, the deeper is the inculcation of extra-Biblical doctrines and notions which generate an enchanted pagan mentality in the mind of the Christian. Take for instance this seemingly innocuous excursus on the "geometrical images in Christian Neoplatonism":

"Christian Neoplatonists are as readily prepared as their pagan predecessors to conceive the cyclic process of causation in terms of geometrical images, and much of the earlier doctrine is repeated without significant alteration...Christian writers are no longer concerned with a set of schemata which apply primarily to the sensible world and are transferred thence by analogy to the realm of intelligible essences, but with geometrical shapes which apply with varying degrees of precision to created things...The second geometrical illustration used by the pagan philosophers is much more common in Christian texts...In the first place it is applied to

---

16   William A. Dennison, *Paul's Two-Age Construction and Apologetics* (University Press of America, 1985), pp. 9-10.

God through analogy to created things, and Ps.-Dionysius (Pseudo-Dionysius) argues as follows:

"...it is possible to speak of him (God) in a manner fitting the divine. In this sense the rectilinear signifies the emanation of his potencies toward created things, the circular indicates his self-identity, and the spiral represents the combination of emanation and stability.'

"Secondly, it is applied to created things and especially the angelic and human intellects, in which case the pagan Neoplatonic theory that the three shapes relate to different faculties or modes of cognition is revived. This theory is applied by Maximus (the Confessor) in both a physical and epistemological context, for during his argument about the end of each creature's motion which is God, he stresses that created things move either in a rectilinear, circular, or spiral manner, while elsewhere he equates the faculties of sense, intellect and discursive reason with these three types of motion." [17]

Another Platonic doctrine contrary to Scripture is a teaching about the soul utterly disconnected from the body. In the Nicene Creed, Christians recite the affirmation of the dogma that "we look for the resurrection of the dead, and the life of the world to come." The Platonists and Neoplatonists cannot honestly subscribe to the Biblical belief that it is the body, not just the "soul," or the *nous* (mind), that is the Lord's Holy Temple. The concept of a soul completely divorced from the body is something we find in Plato, not the Bible.

Psyche represents the *whole* of that creature into which God breathed life; (in Hebrew, *nishmath hayyim)*, thereby creating the living human being, *nephesh hayyah*. The body-soul Manichaean duality is a delusion of Platonism, not of the Scriptures or Christ's true Church.

The *pneuma* is the divine force of YHVH that will give life to the glorified, immortal resurrection body. This is the Christian believer's victory over death, not the state of disembodied immortality of the *supersapientialis scientia platonica,* which is mistaken for eternity by the minions of Churchianity. This latter belief is a Satanic lie of occult origin, advanced under

---

[17] Stephen Gersh, *From Iamblichus to Eriugena: An Investigation of the Prehistory and Evolution of the Pseudo-Dionysian Tradition* (1978), pp. 251-253.

Platonic and Neoplatonic auspices and infiltrated into the Church long before the Renaissance. The continuing dubiety surrounding the truth about the reality and nature of the afterlife is the contaminated legacy of the occult philosophy. As Neoplatonism spread through the Church prior even to the Middle Ages, its chief characteristic was the propagation of confusion through the dissemination of a multiplicity of allegorical and mystical traditions and cosmologies put forth as complimenting and enlarging Christianity, but in fact at radical variance with the Word of God.

No single person is more responsible for the advancement of Neoplatonism within the Catholic Church and Christendom at large than Rev. Fr. Marsilio Ficino, translator of the first complete Platonic oeuvre (*Platonis Opera Omnia*), which became a bestseller after Ficino's death, having been reprinted in at least thirty separate editions in the sixteenth century alone. Ficino in his commentaries on Plato's writings fitted them into a systematic theology of neo-Catholic syncretic origin, embellished with the addition of translations of Proclus, Plotinus and Iamblichus, and the teachings of Hermes, Zoroaster and Pseudo-Dionysius. This foul melting pot was perpetuated by the pope of Rome, who subsequently endowed university chairs in Platonic philosophy for occult heretics such as Francesco Piccolomini in Padua and Francesco Patrizi in the Vatican itself. They in turn imparted to the Church the idea that the ancient pagan sapience representative of Hermes Trismegistus and Plato, had heralded and prepared the way for Jesus Christ and His Church.

Reincarnation

Isaac Abarbanel was a prominent Spanish rabbi who emigrated to Italy in 1492, after the expulsion of the Judaics from Spain. Abarbanel authored his major theological treatise, *Mif'a lot Elohim,* on reincarnation (also called "metempsychosis" or the "transmigration of souls"), in Catholic Italy, circa 1500. Abarbanel drew on the Iberian Kabbalistic theology he inherited from the school of the medieval Spanish Rabbi Moses Nahmanides,[18] as well as Catholic-Neoplatonism:

---

[18] Sometimes known by his acronym the "Ramba*n*," (not to be confused with Moses Maimonides referred by the acronym "Ramba*m*").

"...in regard to Abarbanel's thought concerning the transmigration of souls...Abarbanel expresses an inclination toward a Neoplatonically 'rationalized' Kabbalah, characteristic of the Italian Renaissance milieu in which he wrote the bulk of his works on this topic, while maintaining a sense of esteem for and even deference to the more arcane Nahmanidean Kabbalah of his prior Iberian environs. Within this one illustrious thinker, the 'exoteric' and the 'esoteric' trends meet in a synthetic attempt to safeguard and to expound upon the kabbalistic notion of *gilgul neshamot* (the reincarnation of souls).[19]

"Though he exhibits an inclination toward philosophical speculation, as a proponent of the Kabbalah, Abarbanel takes strong issue with 'Aristotle and the interpreters of his books... (who) sought ways to deny' the real possibility of transmigration. According to Abarbanel, such attempts at denial are fundamentally mistaken. 'Those who deny it,' he writes, 'they are the people who walk in darkness.' Not only is the idea philosophically possible despite the false claims of Aristotle and his interpreters...among the Christians, as a received tradition [20] from the mouths of the prophets who saw the light of Torah, it is Truth and must be accepted. As a direct tenet of the Jewish kabbalistic tradition, Abarbanel has no need to be careful or to conceal his support for Transmigration, and can argue forcefully in its favor. This, in fact, is what he does, attempting to moor the doctrine as expressed within the writings of Plato and other ancient thinkers in his own understanding of the *prisca theologia* tradition as based upon the Jewish Kabbalah. Abarbanel's longest and most definitive treatment of transmigration which specifically deals with the idea of human reincarnation, lies within his commentary on Deuteronomy 25:5-6. This is the commandment appertaining to the institution of levirate marriage, and there the Torah states (in Deuteronomy 25:5-6):

"When brothers dwell together and one of them dies and leaves no son, the wife of the deceased shall not be married to a stranger, outside the family. Her husband's brother shall unite

---

[19] Other mystical terms in the context of *ma'asei merkava* (the "doctrine of the soul and the economy of justice"), include *sod ha'ibur* (the secret of passing from body to body), and *ituk* (soul relocation).

[20] *Kabbalat ha-nevi'im*, i.e. the traditions of Kabbalah.

with her: take her as his wife and perform the levir's duty. The first son that she bears shall be accounted to the dead brother, that his name may not be blotted out in Israel." [21]

In this misreading of the Torah we are offered a glimpse into Orthodox Judaism's profound, intimate and irrefutable Kabbalah connection, which has been long denied by deceivers and apologists. As the revival of the superstition of ancient Egypt, Sumer and Babylon (Sumer was located in what would become Babylon), Orthodox Judaism is surfeited with occult practices and doctrines which for centuries were successfully hidden from public view, partly in order to encourage the rise of the hoax that rabbinic Judaism is a religion faithful to the Old Testament, which forms one-half of the synthesis popularly referred to as "the Judeo-Christian heritage." Actually, every time this bastard hybrid is pronounced as a given fact it blasphemously yokes the Gospel of Jesus Christ with the squirming serpents of occult Egypt and Babylon, as represented by Judaism and its Babylonian Talmud and Kabbalah.

The Orthodox Judaism of which the Renaissance popes and their successors were smitten, teaches multiple levels of secret Biblical meanings (sod)—meanings which were unseen by Jesus Christ or his apostles—and which are brought to the surface (rasu lemor) by the mediation of rabbinic "sages." For the rabbis, the esoteric decoding of the Bible's concept of Levirate marriage is contained within sod ha-'ibbur, the secret of impregnation, which they link to gilgul, metempsychosis, i.e. reincarnation. In Deuteronomy, when there are two brothers and one dies without having produced a child, it is the duty of the living brother to have sexual congress with the wife of the deceased brother and to have children with her, out of respect for the deceased brother. Orthodox Judaism adds to Deuteronomy the man-made teaching that the newborn infant produced by the union of the surviving brother and his brother's widow, is the reincarnation of the soul of the dead brother.

This belief of Orthodox Judaism is evidence of the degree to which Kabbalistic occult fantasy has been embraced by the

---

[21] Brian Ogren, *Renaissance and Rebirth: Reincarnation in Early Modern Italian Kabbalah*, p. 103.

rabbis. Here hangs our indictment of Moses Nahmanides, the "Ramban," portrayed as the "anti-idolatry rabbinic paradigm of Biblical probity," who, it is supposed, defeated the Dominican "Friar Paul," a Judaic convert to Catholicism, in the "Barcelona Disputation" of 1262, arranged by King James I of Aragon, wherein the Ramban is reputed by the Judaics to have succeeded in refuting the friar's charges and presenting himself as an opponent of occult superstition. [22]   The record shows however, that Nahmanides did indubitably traffic in Kabbalistic dogma. Like Rabbi Ezekiel Landau, another *halakhic* authority promoted as being renowned for his opposition to pagan mysticism, Rabbi Nahmanides' sterling reputation in this regard is a hoax. The black magic mendacity of Nahmanides ("Ramban") was permitted publication in Catholic Venice by Pope Leo X in 1517:

"To unlock the ultimate secret of Job, not unlike his method throughout his commentary to the Torah, Ramban tells us he relies on his own insights and what God reveals to him. He will meditate upon the Scriptures to unlock the mystery of Job. Yet, he cannot allow himself to reveal the secret of the climax explicitly to us. The Kabbalistic secret in a word is 'reincarnation.' Kabbalistic traditions, he stresses, are part of an oral tradition passed down from Moses to Prophets to Sages...Ramban dwells on the secret of Job in ch. 33 of his commentary to Job...Ramban's *Commentary on the Book of Job* appeared only in the first *Mikra'ot Gedolot* edition in Venice in 1517...Kabbalists explain God was kind enough to allow redemption for past sins in a past life...Ramban's key to Job, *viz* reincarnation, was adopted by all subsequent Kabbalists.

"...*Shalshelet haKabballah* 13a claims that Uts died without children and Buz, his   brother (Genesis 22:21) married Uts'

---

[22] Unfortunately, Friar Paul presented arguments in line with Ramon Marti's defective anti-Judaic polemic, *Pugio fidei*; among these was Marti's assertion that the Talmud—and similar rabbinic sacred texts—prove the Messianic identity of Jesus, including Marti's absurd contention that Talmud tractate Sanhedrin 43a gives evidence of Jesus's royal descent from King David, when it does no such thing. 43a actually testifies to the fact that the Roman government in Palestine (in other words Pontius Pilate), sought to acquit Jesus of the capital charge against him, which had been insisted upon by the Jewish leaders. Cf. Ursula Ragacs, "Reconstructing Medieval Jewish-Christian Disputations," in *Medieval Exegesis and Religious Difference* (2015), p. 107.

wife. Job came from this levirate union. Ramban alludes to transmigration of souls in regards to the law of levirate marriage in his comments on Genesis 38:8." [23]

The fidelity of "Ramban" (Nahmanides) is to the Kabbalistic pagan doctrine, not the Biblical doctrine. This can be seen in his commentary on the Book of Job reflecting the Kabbalistic Zohar (1:180 a-b), which teaches that Job was a reincarnated soul from a Levirate marriage. As demonstrated, Rabbi Nahmanides regurgitates this unscriptural delusion.

Genesis 38, involving the obligations of levirate marriage, is also a vessel of Kabbalistic reincarnation falsification, as noted in connection with the Renaissance's Rabbi Abarbanel, yet the "proof-texts" for this delusion are in the *Chumash* and *Midrash*, non-Kabbalistic rabbinic texts of mainstream Orthodox Judaism.

In the Old Testament Jews and Israelites are constantly sinning and portrayed as evil doers. Genesis 38 concerns a proud Jewish leader, Judah, who, in the denouement, declares that Tamar, a (presumed) Canaanite, is "more righteous than I!" (Genesis 38:26).

In Genesis 38, Judah has taken up residence in the Canaanite territory of Adullam, southwest of Jerusalem. The woman Tamar,[24] who is of unspecified ethnicity, marries Er, the thoroughly wicked eldest son of Judah and Judah's Canaanite wife.[25] We do not learn Judah's wife's name, only the name of her father; consequently she is called merely "Shua's daughter." The Talmud cannot stomach the fact that the Bible identifies Judah's wife as a Canaanite, so the rabbis transform Judah's wife into the daughter—not of a Canaanite—but of a "merchant" (cf. BT Pesachim 50a which considers it impossible that Judah would marry a Canaanite woman).

---

[23] Cf. Herbert W. Basser, "Kabbalistic Teaching in the Commentary on Job," in *Biblical Interpretation in Judaism and Christianity*, pp. 97-98.

[24] The name Tamar denotes "date palm."

[25] "Judah saw there (in Adullam) the daughter of a Canaanite man, whose name was Shuah. And he took her and entered into her and she conceived and bore a son and called his name Er. And she conceived and bore a son still again and she called his name Onan. And again she bore a son and called his name Shelah." Genesis 38: 2-5.

God kills Er. While God had killed masses of people in the Flood and in Sodom and Gomorrah, Er is the first person in the Bible that He *singles out* for death. In the Biblical account given in Genesis 38, as it concerns Judah and Tamar and the sons of Judah, the focus is on levirate marriage: the obligation of the brother of a deceased husband to marry his brother's widow. Orthodox Judaism in its sacred texts, the Babylonian Talmud and the *Midrash,* teaches the doctrine of reincarnation in explaining the supposed "secret" (*sod*) layer of meaning of Genesis 38, beneath the literal (*pshat*). This is the spiritual disease of the rabbis, and of the occult in general, the conceit that the plain meaning of Scripture almost always conceals a deeper esoteric significance which only the cognoscenti can plumb.

In the *rabbinic exegesis* of Genesis 38 we are at the level of *sod*, which, though it appears in Talmudic texts, is suffused with delusions from the Kabbalah: "They knew the secret significance of levirate marriage: how it enables the soul of the deceased brother to be reincarnated." [26] In rabbinic Judaism levirate marriage [27] is known as *yibum*, which has come to signal, over millennia of accumulated traditions, the process by which the *gilgul* (reincarnation) of the deceased brother is reborn through the child conceived by his surviving brother and his surviving widow.

In the Word of God, Onan, the *yabam* (brother-in-law) of Tamar, had the right to decline the obligation to serve as a *levir*, but he would be subject to ritual public humiliation (the widow would remove his shoe and spit in his face). Onan committed several transgressions: 1. He attempted to deceive God by appearing to accept the levirate duty and then faked it. 2. His means of faking was *coitus interruptus,* taking his pleasure of Tamar in the sex act and then practicing contraception by spilling his seed on the ground rather than inseminating her. 3. He compounded the latter sin by committing it repeatedly ("*whenever* he went into his brother's wife he spilled his seed upon the ground;" 38:9). The syntax shows that this happened more than once. 4. All of these

---

[26] *The Zohar Volume Three* (Stanford University, 2006), p. 144.

[27]   The union between Ruth and Boaz was levirate and levirate unions survived into the time of Christ (Matthew 22: 23-24).

offenses were committed out of lust, obviously, but also from jealousy and greed, so that Onan will inherit his deceased brother's estate, rather than his brother's male or female offspring who would inherit had Onan caused Tamar to conceive. God kills Onan for these transgressions. After the death of Onan, the only surviving son of Judah is the youthful Shelah, who Judah promises to Tamar after Shelah reaches adulthood.

This was a ruse on Judah's part. Judah feared that Tamar was a jinx who would inexplicably also cause the death of Shelah. He thereby deceived her into thinking Shelah would come to her when he matured. Fearing for Shelah's life if he became intimate with Tamar, Judah unjustly withholds the adult Shelah from fulfilling the promise of levirate union with Tamar (38: 11; 14). The deceiver, Judah, becomes the deceived however, when, after the death of Judah's Canaanite wife, Tamar disguises herself as a prostitute and seduces Judah, who offers to pay for her services with livestock from his flock. Because he does not have the payment in his possession, he offers her three promissory pledges in the form of his *staff,* and his *seal,* which is presumably worn on a *cord.* Tamar's possession of his seal, cord and staff is tantamount to possessing Judah's I.D. card. She will produce these months later when her pregnancy becomes apparent and she is about to be executed on Judah's order. These identifiers lead to Judah's exposure as the client of a presumed prostitute and his subsequent contrition for his sin.

For the rabbis, the sin committed by Onan in Genesis 38 is not chiefly what the text demonstrates it to be, the *coitus interruptus* practiced by Onan, i.e. "Onanism" (analogous to the sin of masturbation in historic Christianity). In Judaism, Onan's primary transgression was his refusal to assist the soul of Er, his elder brother, in reincarnating on earth:

"Onan knew that the child...born of his union with Tamar would be a reincarnation of Er's soul, and he was too selfish to let this happen..." [28]

The preceding commentary from the *Chumash* is one of numerous editions that constitute a standard work in Orthodox Judaism. The *Chumash* is not by any stretch of the

---

[28] *The Chumash* (Brooklyn, New York: Mesorah Publications, 2009), p. 209.

imagination a Kabbalistic work. The *Chumash* commentary incorporates the famous, authoritative exegesis of Rashi and other high rabbinic authorities and *gedolim*. Without resorting to the text of the Kabbalah itself, Orthodox Judaism presents its reincarnation teaching concerning Genesis 38, as promulgated not in the Kabbalah but in Judaism's exegesis of the Pentateuch ("*Chumash*") found in many, if not most, Orthodox Judaic households, having the status of a revered, standard reference work. Judaism's belief in reincarnation is taught in this commentary on the *Chumash*. The persistent propaganda story—that one encounters magic and superstition only when one crosses over the chasm that separates Kabbalah from Orthodox Judaism — is shown to be a falsehood in consideration of the rabbinic *gilgul* (reincarnation) doctrine as manifested in non-Kabbalistic texts like the *Chumash*.

The humbling Biblical account of Israelites in Genesis 38, is overturned in the prideful, racial-nationalist Babylonian Talmud, as well as in rabbinic commentary on the *Chumash* and the *Midrash,* which all insist that Tamar was certainly not a Canaanite. With the usual Midrashic resort to fantasy, the rabbis stoop to fabricating a tale of Tamar being the daughter of Noah's son, Shem (cf. Bereishis Rabbah 85:10). The rabbinic commentary on the *Chumash* states: "As someone who was to play such a significant role in the destiny of Israel, it is inconceivable that she was of Canaanite descent."

The Word of God imparts the humbling fact that the Biblical patriarch Judah was ashamed that he had lusted after Tamar, and that he repented of his fornication with her. He is held to be even more culpable because he lusted after her and succumbed to his lust while she was disguised as a sacred prostitute of the fertility religion of the neighboring pagans, in this case, the Canaanites (the term used to describe Tamar in Genesis 38:21-22 is *q'desah,* a word for temple prostitute; earlier in Genesis 38 she had been referred to only as a *zonah*, a common prostitute). Sex with such a prostitute was an act of propitiation to the goddess of the local pagan cult, a condemned act (cf. Hosea 4:14). In the moving turnabout, after seeking to have Tamar, his daughter-in-law, burned to death for having been a whore (38:24), Judah subsequently recognizes his own guilt and bears witness against himself, self-effacingly and contritely asserting her righteousness above his.

What does the rabbinic mentality do with this noble Biblical lesson in humility? It overthrows it, and in doing so absolves Judah, who is too racially significant in the race-obsessed religion of Judaism to be allowed to bear such guilt, therefore the blame must be transferred. Who do the rabbis blame for Judah's act of lust with a woman he thought was a pagan temple prostitute? In the occult philosophy where man has equalled or exceeded His Creator, the rabbis blame God:

"Rabbi Yochanan said, 'Judah sought to pass by Tamar. The Holy One, blessed is He, dispatched the angel of lust to trap him. The angel said to Judah, 'Where are you going? From where will kings arise? From where will great men arise? Only then Judah detoured to her by the side of the road. He was coerced, against his good sense." (*B'reshith Rabbah* 85:8).

One of occult-Renaissance Catholicism's most esteemed rabbis, Rashi, quotes approvingly the following passage from the Midrash, "...a *tzaddik* (saint) of his status would not lower himself to consort with a harlot. Against Judah's will, however, G-d's angel drew him to her...A heavenly voice came forth and proclaimed, 'It was by me that these events were thus directed." [29]

Orthodox Rabbi Rabbi Nosson Scherman: "Of his own free will, Judah would never have united with her, so an angel forced him into the path of a 'harlot' to begin the creation of the Davidic dynasty." [30]

Here we have a Biblical patriarch exonerated rather than denigrated by the tradition of the rabbis, but the one being denigrated is God Almighty Himself! The rabbis have no shame and they certainly have no fear of their subordinate, Yahweh. Sins of the ancient Jews are palliated, denied or absolved through Talmudic and Midrashic fantasy scenarios such as the one put forth for Judah.

Talmudic and Kabbalistic Judaism is suffused with ego-rebellion against the Logos. This revolutionary egoism was infiltrated into the arcane theology of the papacy and the *crème de la crème* of its theological elite. It is a foundation of tyranny over mankind. For this tyranny to operate successfully, the

---

[29] *The Midrash Says: The Book of Beraishis* (Brooklyn, NY: Bnay Yakov Publications, 1999), pp. 364-365; 367.

[30] *The Chumash* op. cit.,, p. 211.

true Biblical-Hebrew teaching, which is completely separate from the pagan psychodrama which rabbinic Judaism absorbed from the occult lore of Babylon and Pharaonic Egypt, must be cast off. Ellen Myers, commenting on Thomas Molnar's essay, "The Gnostic Tradition and Renaissance Occultism," writes:

"Molnar shows that 'the Hebrew-Christian concept of separating God and man as Creator and created, of not confusing their natures, their persons, their powers,' stands apart from 'practically all other religious and para-religious doctrines and systems [which] identify God and self.' Molnar believes that 'Christianity is hard to bear,' because it requires of man 'insertion in the hierarchy of creation, acceptance of a role assigned by the Creator above the rest of other creatures, yet definitively and distinctly not divine.'

"Here Molnar rightly shows that biblical creation *ex nihilo* is the root and ground of Christianity, as well as of the enmity of almost all other religions and thought systems...What non-believers really desire and attempt to bring about is the overthrow of the reality created by the God of Christianity, and to become divine creators of a different reality of their own making...Humanist utopians have perennially written about their ideal 'city' as 'the final symbol for man's divinization'..." [31]

Authentic conservative Christian philosophers such as Thomas Molnar and Aleksandr Solzhenitsyn have observed the trail of destruction of the utopian Renaissance heresy, from the opening salvo of its revolutionary proclamations to the last corpse exhumed from its gulags. The Catholic monk Francois Rabelais's Renaissance "Abbey of Thelema" was a philosophical utopia where, supposedly, the only rule was, "*Fais ce que voudras*" (Do what you will). Humanity casts off the God of the Bible and they proceed on their own way, guided by men and women of the past who trod the same, putative "path of liberation," and who happen to be Neoplatonists and Kabbalists. The occult being mostly lies, this maxim, "Do what you will," does not denote what it purports to state. It actually signifies, in practice, total freedom only for *elite members* of the institution, and bondage for "lesser beings." In this context, "utopia" consists of "Thelemic freedom" for occult tyranny,

---

[31] Ellen Myers, "Thomas Molnar: A Christian Scholar for our Time," in *Creation Social Science & Humanities Society Quarterly Journal,* (vol. 9, no. 4, 1987).

which is a plausible description of the Renaissance and post-Renaissance Roman Church.

Returning to the doctrine of the Renaissance Rabbi Abarbanel, he believed that the levirate marriage ordered in the Torah was devised by God to facilitate the reincarnation of souls. This theology is sustained by the Neoplatonic-Kabbalistic belief that the soul is completely independent of the body, and that it is a separate essence that does not come into being with the body.

"For Abarbanel, who follows here in the Neoplatonic tradition, the separate soul of the individual is able to move through the cosmos, from its place in the supernal realm to the sublunar realm and back again, only by means of the soul vehicle; a *minori ad maius*, its movement as a non-corporeal entity between two human beings must depend upon that vehicle.

"Abarbanel's exposition of the theory of the soul vehicle comes in his *Mif'alot Elohim,* written in 1499...Within *Mif'alot Elohim*, he establishes the essential separateness of the human soul from the body, thereby allowing for its separate movement within the cosmos and the possibility of its entrance into a new body upon its circulation out of a previous body. Basing himself on the *prisci theologi*, who in his interpretation had the Torah as their foundation, he asserts:

"The Torah Truth is that all of the human souls were created before the existence of bodies, at the beginning of creation. And indeed, this was the opinion of the great ancient philosophers like Hermes Trismegistus who is called Hanoch, and Pythagoras, and Plato, and others beside them. And indeed, we have not found anything [of favor] concerning this within Aristotle.

"For the soul to be able to transmigrate, it must be a separate entity from the body that, from time to time, enters into a relation with the body. For this to be the case, Aristotle's theory of the fundamental connection between soul and body must be incorrect. According to Aristotle, 'we can dismiss as unnecessary the question whether the soul and the body are one: it is as though we were to ask whether the wax and its shape are one, or generally the matter of a thing and that of which it is the matter.' The soul is the form of the body and only has any real relevance or substance in a state of unity.

"Abarbanel rejects this idea off hand; for him, as confirmed by the same precedent sources that would be important to the likes of Ficino yet with the 'Torah Truth' as the ultimate base, the soul must be prior to the body and ontologically superior to it...Unlike Aristotle, the 'true' *prisci theologi,* who received their ideas in accordance with this true Torah view, support and give credence to the idea of a soul that can transmigrate, both through the spheres and among bodies. The soul is separate and prior to the body, and therefore can logically cycle through the cosmos, and in and out of different bodies.

"...Through the notions of the world-soul and its emanated astral bodies...Abarbanel...tries to give the idea of the astral body direct Kabbalistic legitimacy by attributing the idea to his Kabbalistic predecessor, Nahmanides. According to Nahmanides in his *Sha'ar ha-Gemul,* the sinning soul will be punished in purgatory by being burned with a thin fire. [32]If this is the case, reasons Abarbanel, then the 'thin fire' must be burning the soul through the medium of the thin material that is the astral body; otherwise it would have no effect upon the fundamentally immaterial soul. Nahmanides, then, according to Abarbanel, hints here at the existence of the ethereal, astral body.

"Notwithstanding Abarbanel's attempt to frame everything under a Kabbalistic rubric by invoking the *sefirot* by utilizing the imagery of the emanated spark, and by citing precedence in the Kabbalistic figure of Nahmanides, it is important to note that his language concerning the soul vehicle is much closer to the Neoplatonism of Iamblicus, Synesius and Ficino...Abarbanel uses the term 'spirit' for his conception of the astral body, links it directly to Plato, and understands it to move in a naturally circular motion.

"The human spirit, he writes, 'is of the nature of the heavens and from the sphere of the upper things, and it always moves in a circular motion from itself, like the movers of the heavens and the stars. And it is according to this that the wise Plato said that the soul moves by itself in a circular motion, while it

---

[32] Nahamanides, *The Writings of Rabbi Moses ben Nahman*, vol. 2, p. 265.

is in the body and also when it is outside of the body, before it enters it and also after it is separated from it." [33]

Since the Renaissance has done its work of subversion of Catholic theology, many Catholics have difficulty finding very much that was in error in the soul-doctrine of Ramban (Rabbi Nahmanides), and while these suppositions have been largely absorbed by Catholic intellectuals without much comment or analysis, almost sub-consciously, they have created an enchanted mentality in Catholics who fancy themselves paragons of anti-occult convictions, yet nevertheless somehow believe that wearing an amulet-like piece of cloth known as the "scapular," [34] saves them "from the fires of hell;" or that "Jacinta," a ten-year-old female visionary, had the rabbinic-like power to alter the dogma of the Bible concerning the deadliest sin, by proclaiming that most people are eternally damned *not* due to the most egregious evil cited by the Word of God (*the love of money*: I Timothy 6:10), but rather due to *sexual lust*: "More souls go to hell because of sins of the flesh than for any other reason"—Jacinta Marto. [35] As this child's reputed saying was promoted throughout the Church of Rome after 1920, eventually becoming the folk belief of the Catholic masses, the practice of usury ascended to new levels of ubiquity. Twenty-two years afterward, in 1942, Pope Pius XII established the Vatican usury bank, *Instituto per le Opere di Religione* ("Institute for the Works of Religion"), without significant opposition.

If it is assumed that neo-pagan choreographies are confined to the Catholic lower classes, we note that in the intellectual class, under the influence of minds conditioned by Neoplatonic

---

[33] Ogren, op. cit., pp.115-116;121-122.

[34] Numerous Catholics wear the scapular without magical intent: solely as an outward sign of their inward commitment to the Biblical virtues which Mary embodied. In those cases the scapular functions as a symbol of Christian faith and not as an amulet.

[35] John De Marchi, *Fatima From the Beginning*, transl. I.M. Kingsbury (Edicoes Missoes Consolata, 2006) p. 198. No accusation of wrong-doing is directed against this child for how her alleged statement was exploited by the Church of Rome. At the end of her brief life she stoically endured the torments of botched medical care for the influenza which killed her. She had been a witness to extraordinary events at the *Cova da Iria* ("Cove of Irene") in Fatima, Portugal in 1917, for which science has no explanation.

mysticism, we encounter "educated Catholics" just as susceptible to priestcraft (men's unscriptural inventions added to the gospel under pretense of divine authority), and subject to institutions and traditions ordained not by the laws of God's Word, but metaphysical addenda.

In terms of our personal experience, it was not long ago that we were observers at a well-attended lecture by a "traditional" Catholic university professor who had no qualms about offering encomiums for Plato as a guide to the sapience from which Catholics would profit. We know of an international "traditional" Catholic school-system for women in which formation in "Catholic wisdom foreshadowed by Plato," is a staple. Popery is inherently Neoplatonic to such an extent that awareness of it among papists is virtually nil. There is almost no vigilance in these matters in the quotidian world of Right-wing Catholics, who otherwise pride themselves on ferreting out the influence of "Protestants and Freemasons."

Rev. Fr. Ficino was a chameleon and the intensity of his occult teachings waxed and waned with the response to them. When informed conservative Catholics with influence, like Antonio degli Agli [36] and Bartolomeo Scala, began to warn against Ficino in terms of "fools who philosophize with the pagans," [37] Ficino would, in the aftermath of this cumulative and mounting criticism, late in life in *private* letters to Martinus Uranius and Zanobi Acciaiuoli, regret what he claimed were his youthful indiscretions. These private remarks of his have been recycled to allegedly prove that Ficino was a good and pious Catholic after all. This claim overlooks the fact that a "good and pious Catholic" would have repudiated his heretical books *in public* and *showed where they were defective and ordered them withdrawn*. The public Ficino refrained from any evidence of true repentance, however. We are expected to accept that his ruse in a few letters to correspondents

---

[36] Antonio degli Agli, *De mystica statera* (Naples, circa 1456), quoted in Field, *The Origins of the Platonic Academy of Florence,* pp. 173-174.

[37] Scala, *Epistola de nobilioribus philosophorum sectis.* Scala's work affords us the opportunity to second his judicious approach toward the admirable qualities of ancient thinkers such as Aristotle and Cicero *where they reflected the Natural Law,* while rejecting syncretism and the occult. For Scala contra Ficino cf. Alison Brown, *Bartolomeo Scala, 1430-1497, Chancellor of Florence* (1979), p. 219; and Hanegraaff, *Esotericism,* p. 44.

represented a sincere change of heart. If sincere, a change of heart, in Catholic theology, requires an attempt at reparation and restitution, by undoing damage that has been done. Instead, Ficino enjoyed the privilege of having his occult works seep into the Church over five centuries: "After Marsilio Ficino published it in 1489, his *Three Books of Life* (*De vita libri tres*) enjoyed great success. Almost thirty editions by 1647, made it the most influential account of magic of its day, perhaps of all Western history." [38]

Ficino's template of occult belief and covert action by elite insiders of the Church, coupled with the spectacle of outwardly pious, ceremonial orthodoxy maintained for the masses of Catholic laity, was rigorously adhered to by the papacy from the Renaissance to the mid-twentieth century, until those same masses had been sufficiently conditioned over time by a control system of unconditional obedience to the pontiff, and gradual exposure to a soft version of the Neoplatonic-Hermetic theology. By 1965 they were prepared to reluctantly submit, however grudgingly at first, to the early stages of the radical public alterations of the Faith which the occult ideologues of the hierarchy now projected in the open. Consequently, by the pontificate of Pope Francis, the people had been for decades deeply immersed in the later stages of the foreordained "*solve et coagula*" crucible of *human* alchemy.

The demonic magic of the *Asclepius* distinguishes it as among the most Satanic of the texts attributed to Hermes Trismegistus. "Magic comes closest to philosophy...in the famous 'god-making' passages of the *Asclepius* which show that material objects can be manipulated to draw a god down into a statue and thus ensoul it."[39]

As part of this "drawing down," the magician, according to the *Asclepius* of Hermes, obtains the power to "ensoul" dead matter. Because there was no analogy with digital AI (Artificial Intelligence) or robots in that bygone era, the power of the

---

[38] Brian P. Copenhaver, "How to do Magic, and Why: Philosophic Prescriptions," in *The Cambridge Companion to Renaissance Philosophy* (2007), p. 137. The first edition of Ficino's *De vita libri tres* was published in Florence by Antonio di Bartolommeo Miscomini. It was reprinted in Venice in 1498; then in Bologna in 1501 by (Benedetto Faelli); with 27 additional editions up to the early modern period.

[39] Copenhaver, *Hermetica*, p. xv.

sorcery was described as having the capability of "bringing statues to life."

In his *Summa Contra the Gentiles,* St. Thomas Aquinas put forth a refutation of the alibis and specious justifications which apostate Christians offered for their conceited involvement with the occult. In this regard, the saint chastises Hermes by name, reiterating the condemnation of St. Augustine:

"The position of Hermes is disposed of by these considerations, for he spoke as follows, as Augustine reports it in the *City of God*: "Just as God is the maker of the celestial gods, so man is the maker of the gods who are in the temples, content in their nearness to man. I mean the animated statues, endowed with sense and spirit, that do such great and unusual things; statues that foresee future events, predicting them from dreams and from many other things, that cause weaknesses in men and also cure them, that give sorrow and joy, in accord with one's merits.

'This view is also refuted by divine authority, for it is said in the Psalm (134:15-17): 'The idols of the Gentiles are silver and gold, the works of men's hands. They have a mouth and they speak not...neither is there any breath in their mouths." [40]

In the third volume of his *De vita trilogy,* the *De vita coelitus comparanda* ("On obtaining life in the heavens"), Fr. Ficino impresses upon the minds of his Catholic readership his "lofty spiritual teaching" concerning what he regards as the benevolent utility of the Egyptian magic of Hermes, notwithstanding Aquinas:

"When any (piece of) matter is exposed to superior things...immediately it suffers a supernal influence through that most powerful agent, of marvelous force and life, which is everywhere present...as a mirror reflects a face, or Echo the sound of a voice. Of this Plotinus gives an example when, imitating Mercurius, he says that the ancient priests, or Magi, used to introduce something divine and wonderful into their

---

[40] St. Thomas Aquinas, *Summa Contra Gentiles,* vol. 3, ch. 104, p. 93 (1956 Image Books edition translated by Vernon J. Bourke and reprinted by the University of Notre Dame in 1975). Also see chapters 105 ("Where the Performance of the Magicians Get their Efficacy"), and 106: "That the Intellectual Substance which Provides the Efficacy for Magic Works is not Morally Good."

statues and sacrifices. He (Plotinus) holds, together with Trismegistus, that they did not introduce through these things spirits separated from matter (that is demons), but *mundana numina*...Mercurius himself, whom Plotinus follows, says that he composed through aerial demons, not through celestial or higher demons, statues from herbs, trees, stones, aromatics having within them a natural divine power (as he says)....

"There were skillful Egyptian priests who, when they could not persuade men by reason that there are gods, that is some spirit above men, invented that illicit magic which by enticing demons into statues made these appear to be gods....

"I at first thought, following the opinion of the Blessed Thomas Aquinas, that if they made statues which could speak, this could not have been only through stellar influence but through demons...But now let us return to Mercurius and to Plotinus. Mercurius says that the priests drew suitable virtues from the nature of the world and mixed these together. Plotinus follows him, and thinks that all can be easily conciliated in the soul of the world for it generates and moves the forms of natural things through certain seminal reasons infused with its divinity. Which reasons he calls gods for they are not separated from the Ideas in the supreme mind.'

"An interpretation of this passage is that Ficino used to agree with Thomas Aquinas, who explicitly condemns as demonic the magic in the *Asclepius*, but since he has read Plotinus' commentary he (Ficino) understands that, though there may have been bad Egyptian priests who used demonic magic, Hermes Trismegistus was not one of them. His power came only from the world, from his insight into the nature of the All as a hierarchy in which the influence of the Ideas descends from the Intellect of the World, through the 'seminal reasons' in the Soul of the World, to the material forms in the Body of the World. Hence, celestial images would have their power from the 'world' not from demons, being something in the nature of shadows of Ideas, intermediaries in the middle place between Intellect and Body, links in the chains by which the Neoplatonic Magus operates his magic and marries higher things to lower things.

"Thus the magic of the *Asclepius*, reinterpreted through Plotinus, enters with Ficino's *De vita coelitus comparanda* into the Neoplatonic philosophy of the Renaissance, and, moreover, into Ficino's *Christian* Neoplatonism. The latter feat necessitated, as we have seen, much ingenious evasion of authoritative Christian pronouncements." [41]

Man, the occult Catholics tell us, has been endowed with special powers of creation—not the least of which is bringing dead matter such as the building blocks of sculpture, marble and clay—to life, a feat consonant with the legendary creation of the *golem* by the sixteenth century rabbinic Kabbalist, Judah Loew of Prague.

What have these works of darkness and megalomania to do with Jesus Christ? Catholic Renaissance magicians like Ficino and Giovanni Pico were the apotheosis of Satanic pride and they spread that spiritual contagion throughout the Church, by means of *much ingenious evasion of authoritative Christian pronouncements*.

Ficino's published volumes were public texts and the sorcery and syncretism he advocated were little different from what Giordano Bruno would put forth in the next century, but Fr. Ficino was subservient to the papacy and Bruno was not, and there rests the difference. When a curial investigation of Ficino was proposed in 1489, it was quashed. Bruno meanwhile, was burned for advocating what Ficino's books had taught him, whereas Ficinio did not experience a single hour in any prison or before any Catholic court or tribunal. His heresy was notorious and it was perpetrated for decades in Florence, 170 miles north of the Vatican. Yet throughout his life and career he was completely immune from interdiction or repression of any kind. This immunity was not unique to Marsilio Ficino.

---

[41] Yates, *Giordano Bruno*, op.cit., pp. 66-68.

Chapter V

Pope Alexander's Wizard

"Pico's vision of the dignity of man, of man's transformative power as magus, owes a profound debt to his fellow Florentine Marsilio Ficino's recuperation of the ancient *hermetica* and of the reputation of its alleged author, Hermes Trismegistus. Together, Ficino and the younger Pico resurrected earlier traditions, some of them highly unorthodox, to give birth to a vigorous progeny, Renaissance magic." [1]

"Not until Pico della Mirandola did a Christian attempt to use cabalistic doctrines in a distinctly positive way, in support of Christian truth for Christians." [2]

Giovanni Pico, the young Count of Mirandola, was profoundly influenced by a declaration in the *Asclepius,* which he subsequently fashioned into an escutcheon of the Catholic Renaissance and its new magical understanding of the "dignity" of man. The *Asclepius* had proclaimed to the immense satisfaction of Pico and the popes and prelates who followed and shielded him: "*Magnum miraculum est homo, animal adorandum et honorandum*" ("Man is a great miracle, a living being to be adored and honored").

Humans are indeed a miracle of God and as images of the divine they are due the dignity conferred upon them by their Creator. Our attention is drawn to the self-worship principle being established by this maxim of which Giovanni Pico was so enamored, which is also a principle evinced in the dogma and practice of Orthodox rabbinic Judaism. Here again we identify a primary characteristic of the occult mentality: the narcissism of devils.

---

[1] James J. Bono, *The Word of God and the Languages of Man: Interpreting Nature in Early Modern Science and Medicine — Volume 1: From Ficino to Descartes*, pp. 26-27.

[2] Werner L. Gundersheimer, *Journal of the Warburg and Courtauld Institutes*, Vol. 26, No. 1/2 (1963), p. 38.

The Pharisees criticized Jesus for teaching and conveying the secrets of the universe, how it functioned and the meaning of life, directly to the peasants of Israel (the *am ha'aretz*), who were castigated by the Jewish religious elite for their "ignorance" of the Oral Law that would be, a few centuries later, committed to writing as the Mishnah and later, the Gemara, forming the Babylonian Talmud. Jesus Christ was engaging in the anti-occult act par excellence: freely teaching everyone, of whatever rank or status, both high and low; rich and poor alike. Those who had ears to hear and eyes to see were not excluded from knowledge by an Egyptian, Chaldean or Babylonian caste system or hierarchy. He violated the two-tier system of law and justice which is the mark of any despotism: one law for the "insiders" and another for the masses. The test of the justice of any code of law or legal system is its universality: does it apply to everyone?

In the supposedly vastly superior, enlightened, benevolent occult world, in comparison to which the true Catholic Church before the Renaissance is contrasted to ill effect, there is no such equality before the law. There is no right to access all the truth which the Son of God related while on earth. As noted, Pico expressed this elitism in his *Oratio De Hominis Dignitate*, more commonly known as *The Oration on the Dignity of Man*. But to what man is Pico referring, concerning this dignity? It is not Humanity. It is not the People. Rather, it is the "perfect" ones:

"...to disclose to the people the more secret mysteries, things hidden under the bark of the law and the rough covering of words, the secrets of the highest divinity, what was that other than to give what is holy to dogs and to cast pearls among swine? Consequently, it was not human prudence but divine command to keep these things secret from the people, and to communicate them to the perfect..." [3]

Here in a few lines is the encapsulation of the ideology which had thrust itself up from what had been only cracks in the cement of the medieval ecclesiastical edifice, to become the full-blown arcana of the Renaissance Church of Rome, empowering its systematic child molestation, lying ("mental reservation"), usury banking and "white" magic which has

---

[3] Giovanni Pico della Mirandola, *On the Dignity of Man*, (transl. C.G. Wallace), p. 30.

enveloped the hierarchy of the Church of Rome from then until now, no matter which "saintly" pontiff was at the helm. It is actuated by keeping the reality of these mortal sins and crimes, which flourish *sub rosa*, hidden from the people, i.e. the parish priests and the laity.

Pico cites Christ's words in Matthew 7:6 concerning dogs and swine, so as to maintain the legitimacy of the secrets-keeping occult ideology in a Christian milieu. Our Lord, however, is most certainly not referring exclusively to the peasants and the poor or, for that matter, the wealthy and the officials, when he warned us not to give that which is sacred and holy to dogs and swine. As St. Peter declared, "God is no respecter of persons" (Acts 10:34). This is a truth that the Neoplatonic-Hermetic cabal cannot countenance, since that movement is based on division, while laying claim to the pluralist title of unifier and reconciler. The human being who behaves like a dog or a swine according to Jesus, who turns and rends the man or woman who conveys great truths, is *any person,* from PhD. to peasant, who lacks the vision to perceive that a profound truth has been freely and openly related, and lacks the gratitude to appreciate the magnitude of the gift. Contrary to Pico, Matthew 7:6 is not a mandate to exclude the common people, the *am ha'aretz*, from realities which the "perfect" may savor at will. To accuse the people of being pigs and dogs *in toto,* holds them up to contempt and constitutes an abominable derogation of their dignity as human beings. If we comprehend the depravity of the mind chained to occult idolatry, then we should not be surprised at the double-standard and *chutzpah* of Pico in undermining the supposed objective of his own homily.

"Ficino's pupil, Pico della Mirandola...used Qabalistic and Neoplatonic ideas in an attempt to find common ground between Christianity, Judaism and Islam (which) brought accusations of heresy against him...Pope Alexander VI absolved him of heresy in 1493. Another advocate of Qabalism was the Franciscan (friar) Francesco di Giorgio...whose *De Harmonia Mundi* combined Qabalism with a preoccupation with the ideas of universal harmony..." [4]

---

[4] McIntosh, op. cit., pp. 7-8.

Pico was not Father Ficino's student alone. He studied canon law at the University of Bologna (1477-78), and theology at the University of Ferrara (1479), Padua (1480-1482), Pavia (1483-1484) and Paris (1485-1486). He studied with Ficino from 1484-1485. Pico taught that there was a great secret underlying the world's significant religions, an *occulta concatenatio* ("hidden connection") between them indicating their common root and heritage.

"Much of what Giovanni Pico della Mirandola has to say about the Tetragrammaton is found in the 900 *Conclusiones*, or *Theses*, which he planned to debate in Rome in 1486. This extraordinarily daring and innovative program blended Classical, Late Antique and medieval philosophy; Christian Kabbalah; the Hermetic tradition; and Pythagorean mathematics into a syncretic system designed to expose the unity and power of Ancient Truth and its ability to work both reformation and miracles...The antecedents of this bold project may lie in the highly syncretistic Neoplatonic systems developed in Late Antiquity after Plotinus—as in Proclus's *Platonic Theology*, for example...

"The openness of Medici Florence to the generous integration of these diverse traditions no doubt provided a sympathetic context for the development of Christian Kabbalah...the extraordinary effervescence in European culture in Florence was also stimulated by the first major synthesis of Renaissance thought and Kabbalah...Pico without ambiguity declares that Kabbalah 'is the key to understanding the marvelous power of Christ's name...' Pico's use of Gematria, manipulation of numerical values of Hebrew words, is enthusiastic and prepares us for the later work of Reuchlin. Pico himself compares his *Scientiam alphabetariae revolutionis* with the *Ars combinadi* of Ramon Lull (c. 1235-1316)...." [5]

Pico described his agenda in these terms, "The following nine hundred dialectical, moral, physical, mathematical, metaphysical, theological, magical, and kabbalistic opinions, including his own and those of the wise Chaldaeans, Arabs, Hebrews, Greeks, Egyptians, and Latins, will be argued

---

[5]   Robert Wilkinson, *Tetragrammaton: Western Christians and the Hebrew Name of God* (2005), p. 317.

publicly by Giovanni Pico della Mirandola, the Count of Concord... The doctrines to be debated are proposed separately but in respect to the parts of philosophy they are intermingled as in a medley, everything mixed together."

His *Nine Hundred Theses* (also known as *Nine Hundred Conclusions*), was published in Rome on December 7, 1486 by Eucharius Silber. Copies were dispatched to Catholic universities and posted throughout the "Eternal City." Pico was not seriously expecting to actually be debated by the hierarchy of the Church. His announcement was a public relations device to garner attention for his *Theses* which would win admirers throughout the West, thanks in part to the notoriety of the "proposed debate" concerning their merits and validity.

The see-no-evil academic Establishment takes at face value Pope Innocent VIII's pro forma condemnation of thirteen of the *900 Theses*. This narrative sets up the caricatured, set-piece psychodrama of Liberated Lover of Learning vs. Benighted, "Burn 'em at the Stake!" conservative Catholic authority figures. The pope could not publicly do otherwise than what he did when a large number of Pico's *Theses* centered on the rehabilitation of rabbinic theology, specifically the demonic Kabbalah. In 1487, no pontiff, no matter how much he might have been in secret sympathy with Pico, could have accepted with even neutrality the conclusion that a Judaic manual of black magic (Kabbalah) "testified of Christ" and was in fact a Christian text, as Pico had boldly proclaimed.

It was the outré aspect of the alleged proposed debate that electrified the Catholic intelligentsia and burnished Pico's reputation in what would soon become, in the sixteenth century, an above ground movement. Apologists may point to Innocent VIII's *rhetoric* against Pico's *Theses* all the like. It does not alter the fact that Pico, and most of his followers after his death, were virtually invulnerable to papal repression or inquisition. Eventually his followers were promoted to the highest levels of the Church, including popes who took Pico's counsels to heart.

Those who approach the subject of the papacy in the Renaissance who trust in surface appearances are going to be duped. To consider Innocent VIII an anti-occult pontiff is a sad jest. He did what was required of him in *the particular time-period when the advancement of the occult virus depended upon gestures that appeared to retard it.* Consequently, in the superficial legend, Innocent VIII is the anti-occult pope who interdicted Giovanni Pico della Mirandola. Actually, Innocent made the necessary gestures for appearance sake of impeding Pico, and with those gestures he mollified conservatives. The record shows that the pope's token and brief obstruction of Pico actually served to shield the Kabbalistic-heretic from demands from conservatives for stronger measures against him. By slapping Pico's wrist, Pico's enemies were pacified. To take this papal ruse at face value is wishful thinking on the part of those seeking grounds for their own confirmation-bias concerning the "staunchly conservative" Innocent VIII. False beliefs like this are founded upon ignorance. It was Cardinal Lorenzo Cibo, the "staunchly conservative" future Pope Innocent VIII, who was the earliest patron of Flavius Mithridates, the Kabbalistic Judaic who, thanks to future Pope Innocent, became preacher to the papal household of Sixtus IV, Pico's handler, initiator and a homosexual suitor for Pico's affections, as well as a Professor at a papally-chartered college. By bringing Mithridates to Rome and sponsoring his rise inside the Church, Innocent VIII while a cardinal made possible the Kabbalism of Pico.

Pico's books survived to proceed to shape the intellectual life of the Catholic world long after Pico and Innocent VIII were in their graves.[6] In remarkably short order a reprint of the first edition appeared the next year (1487) in Ingolstadt, home to the University of Ingolstadt where Reuchlin, and much later Adam Weishaupt, would be members of the faculty. Its remarkable immediate re-publication in what would become, in the late eighteenth century, the capital of the Bavarian Illuminati (a city which, in 1487 was entirely in the orbit of the Church of Rome), is seldom mentioned. Behind the curtain of received opinion and consensus reality, Pico's magnum opus was circulating without hindrance, issued by a German Catholic printing press. It was in high demand in record time. It was reprinted without interdiction in Catholic France (Paris) in 1532, in Catholic Italy (Venice) in 1557, and again in Paris in 1601. The genie was out of the bottle.

---

6 The Vatican preserved copies of the first edition of the *Nine Hundred Theses* and the Vatican Library in the twenty-first century continues to retain the *editio princeps*, as does the British Library. A hand-written facsimile of the 1486 printing is in Vienna at the *Osterreichische Nationalbibliothek* in Vienna.

Whole sections of the *Nine Hundred Theses* contain propositions undermining or contradicting St. Thomas Aquinas. Yet modern Catholic writers frequently misrepresent Pico as a Thomist. Only because the details of what constitutes the Kabbalah are largely unknown or obscured can Pico, for whom the doctrines of the Kabbalah are at the heart of his *philosophia nova*, be presented by "Catholic scholars" as supposedly in agreement with St. Thomas Aquinas. The depth of deception and misdirection is instructive.

"Pico's historians have been especially insistent on an impossible agreement between himself and the writer he planned to attack most violently at Rome, St. Thomas Aquinas. In part, at least, systematic reasons lay behind this conflict, since Thomas's system regularly violated the cosmic symmetries critical to Pico's 'new philosophy'...

"Pico's supposed agreement with Thomas has been especially emphasized by Catholic historians including (Avery) Dulles (1941) and DiNapoli (1965); also cf. the French theologians De Lubac (1974) and Roulier (1989). Renaissance antecedents for this reading were provided by Gianfrancesco Pico (his nephew), who in his (posthumous) spiritualized biography of his uncle (*Opera*, fol. 5v), claimed that whatever differences Pico had with Thomas early in life...Pico...disagreed with the Dominican theologian on only 'three or four out of ten thousand propositions...'

"The extreme violence of Pico's early polemics with the Dominicans is suggested in Pico's defense of his first examined thesis in (his) *Apology*, [7] in *Opera*, 125-150...Gianfrancesco also quotes Pico's passing praise for Thomas in the *Heptaplus,* which was written while Pico was actively attempting to repair his differences with the Dominicans..." [8]

Later in the *Theses*, Pico favorably quotes "the Arab...Moses the Egyptian." This is reference to Rabbi Moses Maimonides

---

[7] Within his *Apology*, his harshest criticism of Aquinas and the Dominicans will be found in Pico's section on the descent of Christ into "hell." (Actually Jesus descended into *sheol* (שְׁ[אֹל) i.e. the grave, not the fiery pit of hell (*Gehenna*-γέεννα, from גהנום/גהנם).

[8] Stephen A. Farmer, *Syncretism in the West: Pico's 900 Theses* (1998), pp. 47-48.

who was no Arab though he was influential among the family of the Kurdish Islamic King (and conqueror of Jerusalem), Saladin. In his *Avodah Zarah* laws, in *Avodat Kochavim* chapter 10, Maimonides, a legal authority of great repute in Ashkenazi Judaism, issued binding admonitions for killing Christians. Of Jesus Christ he wrote, "May the name of the wicked rot." [9]

In spite of this hate-speech, Maimonides is included in Pico's synthesis and here it is apropos to observe the shape-shifting quality of syncretists like Pico and the extent to which theological and spiritual identities are manipulated and fused. For example, we can point to the very real, fundamental differences between Plato and Aristotle but by the time of the emergence of the first wave of Neoplatonists in Rome, Athens, Alexandria and Apamea in the 3rd to the 5th centuries after Christ, the differences between Platonists and Aristotelians were being blurred and for a time a symbiosis was crafted. There is not a strict respect for objective truth in syncretic systems, as for example in the massive syncretic tome by Proclus, *Platonic Theology*, which is featured in Pico's *Theses*. The Church of Rome from the Renaissance onward is a shape-shifting enterprise deeply committed to relativism and situation ethics concealed beneath a stern dogmatic veneer. The Catholic Pico, and before him Proclus, are personifications of this "modernist heresy" which is anything but modern. "Proclus's goal was to demonstrate that every line of Platonic Scriptures was in total harmony with every other —with the supreme syncretic principle that 'all things exist in all things in their own mode,' ensuring that in times of special exegetical need, any god, mythopoeic image, or abstract concept could stand in for any other...Pico planned to correlate this material further with the ten Kabbalistic *sefirot*, with Pseudo-Dionysius's hierarchies of angels, and related syncretic constructs...that Pico found in the 'Chaldean Theologians,' Pythagoras, Mercury (Hermes) Trisemegistus, Zoroaster, Orpheus etc." [10]

The final destination of this syncretic peregrination is the lie that God and Satan are one. Pico in his *Nine Hundred Theses*

---

[9] Hoffman, *Judaism Discovered* (2008), p. 483.

[10] Farmer, op.cit., pp. 314-315.

insinuates this as follows: *"Eaedem sunt litterae nominis cacodemonis qui est princeps mundi huius et nominis dei Triagrammaton, et qui sciuerit ordinare transpositionem deducet unum ex alio"* ("The letters of the name of the evil spirit who is the prince of this world and of the three-letter name of God are the same, and whoever knows how to order the transposition can deduce one from another").

In his *Conclusiones Magicae* of his *Theses,* Pico distinguishes between black magic and good magic. The former he terms *potestatum harum tenebrarum* ("powers of darkness"), and the latter he designates as "natural magic," and asserts that the Church permits it and does not prohibit it: *"Magia naturalis licita est et non prohibita."* From there he proceeds to state the most grievous heresy of his *Theses,* which eventually infiltrated elements of the hierarchy of the Church of Rome, never to be completely eradicated: *"Nulla est scientia quae nos magis certificet de diuinitate Christi quam magia et cabala"* ("There is no science that assures us more of the divinity of Christ than magic and kabbalah").

He further alludes to the word magic and gematria incumbent on his version of supposed "angelic" sorcery: *"Ex secretioris philosophiae principiis necesse est confiteri plus posse caracteres et figuras in opere Magico, quam possit quaecunque qualitas materialis"* ("Out of the principles of the more secret philosophy it is necessary to acknowledge that characters and figures are more powerful in a magical work than any material quality"). Thomas Aquinas explicitly condemned as demonic the use of words and numbers in magical rites.

In his section of the *Theses* on "Conclusions Cabalisticae," Pico proceeds to put forth delirium for occult suckers and the self-deceived, i.e. that every follower of the Kabbalah is a believer in Jesus: "Every Hebrew Kabbalist, following the principles and sayings of the science of Kabbalah, is inevitably forced to concede, without addition, omission or variation, precisely what the Catholic faith of Christians maintains concerning the Trinity and the divine Person, Father, Son and Holy Ghost...No Hebrew Kabbalist can deny that the name of Jesus, if we interpret it following the method and principles of the Kabbalah, signifies precisely all this and nothing else, that is: God the Son and the Wisdom of the Father, united to human nature in the unity of assumption through the third Person of God, who is the most ardent fire of love."

There is no denying that Pico, with Italian Medici backing, forged the symbiosis of Judaism and Catholicism by founding the tradition of "Christian Kabbalah," an oxymoron if ever there was one. He did so under the direction of his handler, the aforementioned Guglielmo Raimondo de Moncada, the enigmatic Judaic "convert to Catholicism" who was known by his alias, "Flavius Mithridates." With papal patronage Moncada/Mithridates was appointed Professor of Oriental Languages at the Studium Urbis in Rome in 1482. He was an early teacher of Pico.[11]

"...there are reasons to suspect a sinister role for Flavius Mithradites, whose reputation in the Renaissance as something of a con man was apparently well-deserved. Pico's involvement with this colorful figure—who liked to style himself as Pico's scorned lover—constitutes one of the strangest personal stories of the period..." [12]

There can be no question of Pico's esteem for Judaism's Oral traditions which formed the Talmud, and its black magic textbooks classified under the heading, Kabbalah ("cabala"). Referring to the Oral Law traditions in his *Oration on the Dignity of Man*, Pico wrote:

"Esdras, then governor of the church, after he corrected the book of Moses, clearly knew that the custom instituted by the forefathers of passing the doctrine on by hand could not be preserved through the exiles, slaughters, flights, and captivity of the people of Israel, and that the secrets of heavenly doctrine, granted to him by God, would henceforth perish, as they could not remain long in memory without the mediation of writings."

Pico moves from the Oral Law tradition in general to an elucidation of the origin of the Kabbalah specifically: "Consequently, he decreed that all the wise men who were then left should be called together, and each of them should bring together what he remembered about the mysteries of the law.

---

[11] Pico's other Judaic "mentor" was Elia del Medigo.

[12] Farmer, op.cit, p. 14.

After scribes were summoned, it should then be written down in seventy volumes, for there were about that many wise men in the Sanhedrin. Do not take my word only for this, fathers, but listen to Esdras himself speaking:

"...you will save the last seventy books so that you may pass them on to the wise among your people. For in them is the heart of understanding and the fountain of wisdom and the river of knowledge. And so have I done.'

"These are the words of Esdras. These are the books of the knowledge of Cabala. Esdras proclaimed at the beginning in a clear voice that in these books was rightly the heart of understanding, that is, an ineffable theology of supersubstantial deity, the fountain of wisdom, that is, an exact metaphysics of intelligible angels and forms, and the river of knowledge, that is, a most sure philosophy of natural things. Pope Sixtus IV, who preceded Innocent VIII under whom we happily live, provided with the greatest care and zeal, that these books should be translated into Latin for the public advantage of our faith. [13]

"Moses on the mountain received from God not only the law which, as written down in five books, he left to posterity, but also a more secret and true interpretation of the law. But God commanded him to publish the law indeed to the people, yet not to pass on in writing the interpretation of the law..." [14]

Pico's buncombe is a classic restatement directly from the rabbinic storehouse of fairy tales which they have woven outside the Bible and which Jesus Christ denounced in solemn warnings in Mark 7 and Matthew 15 as the "traditions of men." Here these fantasies of rabbis are proposed by Pico as the basis for the clandestine theology of the Renaissance Church of Rome. To justify this Judaizing, the scoundrel Pico della Mirandola will drag Jesus down into this stew of mendacity, but first he sought to rehabilitate the Hermetic magicians of Egypt, Persia, Babylon and Attic Greece by stating that to the extent to which those sorcerers accepted the notion of an extra-Biblical Mosaic revelation, they were not idolaters, but members of the perennially true religion. This led to the

---

[13] Pico della Mirandola, *On the Dignity of Man,* (op.cit.), pp. 31-32.

[14] Hanegraaff, *Esotericism* (op.cit.), p. 56.

formation of the legend, revived by the New Age Theosophists in the late nineteenth century and accepted as true by the Nazis, that Moses himself was a magician.

Pico then proceeds to mount an outlandish hoax concerning the contents of the satanic Kabbalah, claiming that these rabbinic texts contain a refutation of those who argue that Jesus was not the Messiah. He adds that the Kabbalah affirms the Trinity, the divinity of Jesus, Christ's atoning sacrifice and, to top it all off, the same theology "which we read daily in Paul and Dionysius, in Jerome and Augustine"! [15]

What a disgraceful farce from a shameless liar. The misfortune for the Catholic Church is that, along with Fr. Ficino, Pico was among the most influential of papist writers for Catholic intellectuals in the sixteenth and seventeenth centuries. His brazen deceit helped to convert numerous Catholic leaders into Kabbalists and Talmudists, who nonetheless remained inside the Church, burrowing ever deeper.

These were not democratic levelers. Infiltrators in this era were in favor of a gloriously elaborate liturgy, cappa magna gowns, an aristocratic Church and an elected papal monarch who was sovereign above all laws, just as *Chazal* (the collective authors of the Babylonian Talmud) were sovereign above all laws, having overruled God Himself, and having convinced God to confess their superiority over Him (Bava Metzia 59b). Meanwhile, the demands of the Dialectic are such that contemporary disinformation takes the form of "conjecture" which posits the likelihood that Pico only praised and promoted the Kabbalah as part of an "apologetic attempt" to use it as "an anti-Jewish tool of conversion." [16]

Christ, the Trinity, the saints *and* ceremonial magic; imagine that; and in rabbinic texts that are actually Christian texts, only the rabbis don't know it yet. This is Catholic?

Pico himself assures us that this is the case. After restating his belief that "the traditions of Egypt" and "the philosophy of Plato" agree with "Catholic truth," he writes concerning the

---

[15] Pico della Mirandola, *On the Dignity of Man*, (op.cit.), p. 32.

[16] Pier Cesare Bori, "The Historical and Biographical Background of the Oration," in *Pico della Mirandola Oration on the Dignity of Man: A New Translation and Commentary* (2012), p. 104.

rabbis of the Renaissance, "If they agree with us anywhere, we shall order the Hebrews to stand by the ancient traditions of their fathers; if anywhere they disagree, then drawn up in Catholic legions we shall make an attack upon them. In short, whatever we detect foreign to the truth of the Gospels we shall refute to the extent of our power, while whatever we find holy and true we shall bear off from the synagogue, as from a wrongful possessor..." [17]

Academics insist that it is so — that Pico's project was a fully Catholic, "apologetic and polemical" conversion mission to the Jews, and that he honestly believed that the Kabbalah was a Christian series of volumes which, once the Jews understood the true nature of their own rabbinic writings, as revealed to them by Pico, they would be converted to Catholicism. These claims are completely divorced from reality.

To paraphrase C. Wright Mills, *here we are approaching a curious juncture in the history of human insanity.* There is nothing in the text of the Kabbalah that even remotely testifies of Jesus Christ or the Gospel. The nine volumes of Daniel Matt's complete English translation of the Zohar (*Sefer ha-Zohar*, "Book of Radiance"), which comprise the major corpus of the Kabbalistic books, as well as Nathan Wolski's tenth volume in the series, *Midrash ha-Ne'lam*, representing the earliest edition of the Zoharic texts (published by Stanford University), all testify to the fact that the Kabbalah consists of a pottage of magic, superstition, demonology, hallucinatory fantasy, and relentless falsification of the Bible. The light of Jesus Christ is entirely absent from the Kabbalah, while the goddess, denominated *"Binah"* and *"Shekhinah"* and symbolized by the moon, is omni-present (cf. Zohar 3:19b). The Kabbalah offers a catalogue of pipe-dreams about Biblical patriarchs and matriarchs. A few examples:

---

[17]Mirandola, Giovanni Pico, "Proem to the Third Book, Third Exposition: Of the Angelic and Invisible World" in *On the Dignity of Man, On Being and the One, Heptaplus* (dedicated to Lorenzo de' Medici 1489), transl. by Douglas Carmichael et al. (1965).

•Adam engendered female demons from his spilled semen. Eve copulated with Satan and conceived Cain (Zohar 1:55a).[18]

•The nocturnal emissions of males are caused by *Na'amah*, the mother of the king of demons who titillates men in their sleep (Tishby, *Zohar*, 3:1365-66; pp. 309-310).

•The patriarchs Amram, Levi and Benjamin were conceived without sin (Zohar, 1:57b).

•The manner in which Abraham attempted to sacrifice Isaac was wrong and God holds a grudge against Abraham for this wrong (Zohar 2:33a).

•Moses used a speculum-like device (akin to a crystal ball) to view invisible beings (Zohar 2:23b).

The Kabbalah spans the gamut from pornographic and nonsensical to profoundly Satanic:

•Israel must make sacrifices to Satan so that he will leave Israel unmolested (Zohar 2:33a.)

•The evil impulse is good, and without the evil impulse Israel cannot prevail in the world (*Zohar* 1:61a).

There is much more like this, enough to fill many dozens of pages. Pico was either a deliberate deceiver concerning the contents of the Kabbalah, or he was a fraud who had scant knowledge of the Aramaic language,[19] taking the word of Flavius Mithradites and other Judaics concerning its contents.

One of the objectives of the Cryptocracy during the Renaissance was to raise the status and prestige of rabbinic Judaism by absolving it of traditional Catholic charges of diabolism, counterfeiting the Bible and exhibiting an antichrist hatred. Whether or not Pico was a conscious conspirator or a useful idiot in misrepresenting the Kabbalah and achieving this objective, the mission was indeed accomplished. The Kabbalistic theology which crept into the Roman Catholic Church stoked the trend toward Renaissance paganism in papal Italy:

---

[18] In *Pirqei de-Rabbi Eli'ezer*: 21, Rabbi Yehudah and Rabbi Shimon teach that even Abel was contaminated with the slime which the serpent injected into Eve during their alleged sexual intercourse. (*Pirqei de-Rabbi Eli'ezer* is an influential text in the writings of Rabbis Amram Gaon, Rashi and his grandson Jacob ben Meir ["Rabbeinu Tam"], and Moses Maimonides).

[19] Pico often refers to the Judaics of his time as "Hebrews," but the major Kabbalistic and Talmudic texts were written in Aramaic, not Hebrew.

"Pico set out to prove the Christian truth by means of Jewish Kabbalah...In the attempt to apply midrashic techniques such as *gematria, temurah* and *notarikon* which had formerly been restricted to Jewish circles...unheard-of new possibilities seemed to open up for scriptural exegesis and metaphysical speculation. Not only did the biblical text reveal hidden levels of meaning never suspected before, but the correspondences that could be established with pagan mythology and philosophy seemed simply stupefying...The dialectics of concealment and revelation are central to Jewish kabbalah...not only did kabbalah become an integral part of the Renaissance discourse of ancient wisdom, but this innovation resulted in a very strong emphasis on 'esotericism' in the specific sense of a concern with hidden or concealed secrets...such concerns were already implied by the very concept that Christian truths lay concealed under the surface of ancient pagan myths and philosophies, but could be uncovered by means of allegorical or symbolic exegesis.

"This potential came to full development under the influence of a tradition, Jewish kabbalah, which had always been esoteric to its very core. It lies entirely in the line of this development that—to give only one famous example—Heinrich Cornelius Agrippa published his great compendium of ancient wisdom in 1533, he called it *De occulta philosophia*...His well-known dedicatory letter to Johannes Trithemius confirms that he saw his work as an attempt to revive the science of the Magi and other sages of antiquity, and its third and final book was dominated by the kabbalah." [20]

"Pico's other esoteric methods were equally extreme. Following the fact that numbers were represented by letters in Semitic languages and Greek, various techniques commonly known as *gematria* were developed in antiquity for transforming words and texts through their numerical values...These methods were employed widely in antiquity in dream analysis, mystical and prophetic exegesis, apocalyptic composition, as well as for syncretic ends, and following predictable patterns became progressively more complex and systematic in the Middle Ages. Thus (Gershom) Scholem notes

---

[20] Hanegraaff, *Esotericism* (op.cit.), pp. 63 and 65-67.

one kabbalistic manuscript that lists seventy-two methods of
gematriot, presumably one for each of the characters in God's
secret name of seventy-two letters...

"In one thesis he (Pico) claimed that unspecified *gematria*-
like techniques were the key to his syncretic fusion of natural
magic and Cabala. Pico employed related esoteric methods that
involved anagrammatic manipulation of Scriptures, drawn
mainly from the thirteenth and fourteenth century writings of
the Spanish kabbalist Abraham Abulafia and his
commentators. In the *Apology*, Pico compared this 'science of
the revolution of the alphabet' (*scientia alphabetariae
revolutionis*) or 'art of combination' (*ars combinandi*), as he
variously called it, to the method known to the Latins as the
ars Raymundi—that is, to the anagrammatic methods of the
Christian Spaniard Raymond Lull...Pico syncretically fused
gematria with other numerological techniques in his 'way of
numbers' (*via numerorum*)...His goal here was to unite the
numerological symbolism of the Pythagoreans—syncretically
fused with Neo-Paltonic metaphysics in deep antiquity—with
gematria and less formal types of number symbolism in
Scriptures, in the Greek and Roman church fathers, and in
various scholastic and esoteric sources, in order to unveil secret
harmonies buried there...

"The origins of the gnostic *aeons*, Christian, Buddhist and
Hindu trinities, Neo-Platonic *henads*, kabbalistic *sefirot*, and
countless analogous constructs can all be traced to
compilational processes like these...Correlations like this were
not systematically 'neutral.' They were a powerful force in the
progressive movement towards transcendentalism, ethical and
religious universality...(t)ransformed by repeated syncretic
fusions..." [21]

This is the theological basis for Pope John Paul II's 1986
Assisi prayer assembly of the world's religions, including
leaders of Talmudic-rabbinic, Buddhist, and animist (pagan)
religions in Italy, nearly 500 years after Pico published his
Nine Hundred Theses in Italy in 1486. Father Marsilio Ficino's
pagan magic expressed in his *De vita coelitus comparanda*
became the synthesis of the magical theology (*magia naturalis*)

---

[21] Farmer, op.cit., pp. 63-65; 75-77.

of Pico, and both derived direction from Ficino's 1463 translation of the *Corpus Hermeticum*, which was presented to the Church and the West as benevolent Renaissance white magic.

The Neoplatonic-Hermetic objective of penetrating the Church sufficiently to derogate its faithful witness to the Biblical proscription against all forms of magic and sorcery, by concocting a category of "natural" or "white" magic, was achieved by the new "enlightened" attitude toward rabbinic texts. Pico wrote: "I have proposed theorems about magic, too, wherein I have signified that magic is two-fold. The first sort is put together by the work and authorship of demons, and is a thing, as God is true, execrable and monstrous. The other sort is, when well explored, nothing but the absolute consummation of the philosophy of nature...Zoroaster's magic is nothing but that knowledge of divine things wherein the kings of Persia educated their sons...the magic of Xalmosis is medicine of the soul...When we shall have well explored these wonders by means of this natural magic we are speaking of, we shall be inspired more ardently to the worship and love of the maker..."[22]

More often spelled "Zalmoxis," in Greek legends of Thrace, the magician Xalmosis/Zalmoxis is a Pythagorean trickster who fakes his own death and resurrection.[23] Pico invokes his name as a signal to his fellow initiates, conveying the occult doctrine that prevarication and duplicity are necessary tools and truth cannot be revealed to non-initiates. As we have already noted, in the argot of the Pharisees and the Talmud of Babylon, Judaic peasants who preferred the written Torah (Old Testament) and scorned the man-made Oral traditions, were derided as peasant ignoramuses. About them, the Talmud states in BT Pesahim 49: a-b: "Our Rabbis taught: Six things were said about the ignoramuses: We do not commit testimony to them; we do not accept testimony from them; we do not reveal a secret to them; we do nothing for their orphans; we do not appoint them stewards over money; and we must not join their company on the road. If an *am ha'arertz* loses something,

---

[22] *Pico della Mirandola: Oration on the Dignity of Man* (1998), pp. 26-27 and 29.

[23] Cf. Burkert, *Lore and Science*, op. cit.,, p. 157.

the scholar is not required to notify him; the *am ha'arertz* should not benefit from any physical good in this world!" [24]

"We do not reveal a secret to them." This is the two-tiered law system of an anti-Biblical ideology. Jesus was hounded by the Pharisees for speaking freely and openly to the peasants of Israel. Why would he not? They were "the people" who loved Him and John the Baptist. But the insider/outsider, lord/peasant dual-standard, is ever present in the organizations of the occult. It is one of the most telling signifiers of the western secret societies.

To adhere to Biblical doctrine faithfully without adding to it or subtracting from it is an anti-occult action. The western occult movement historically has sought to tar Moses, the Bible and Jesus Himself as heirs to a "secret tradition." There are scores of books claiming Jesus was schooled in the forerunner of the Talmudic tradition; that he did not come to found "Christianity" and that he was observant of the occult customs of the rabbis. Occult agents occupying teaching positions in universities, and executive positions in publishing houses and media outlets, repeat these lies and gain credibility from the repetition.

The New Testament bears witness to the fact that Jesus was not the heir of any "perennial" theology consonant with the beliefs of the Pharaohs, Plato, Zoroaster or the rabbinic Oral Law system. Jesus Christ is completely outside the pagan *weltanschauung*. It has nevertheless been the task of mountebanks such as Giovanni Pico della Mirandola to drag Him down into that swamp. The effort is futile.

Scripture scholar John F. MacArthur summarizes the profoundly disenchanting, anti-occult nature of Our Lord and Redeemer, Jesus Christ: "On one occasion a group of Scribes and Pharisees from Jerusalem chided Jesus for allowing His disciples to 'transgress the tradition of the elders' by not (ritually) washing their hands before they ate. Jesus countered by asking, 'And why do you yourselves transgress the

---

[24] Cf. the *am ha'aretz* section of *Judaism Discovered* (2008), pp. 29-30. Modern Orthodox Judaism interprets BT Pesahim 49b as stating that "Jewish ignoramuses are greater antisemites than Gentiles." The Kabbalah (Zohar: Exodus 7b) teaches that at the "end of days" the *am ha'arertz*, these "wicked Jews," will become the allies of the enemies of Klal Yisroel" (the "Jewish" people).

commandment of God for the sake of your tradition? (Matt. 15:1-6; Mark 7)...After Jesus' first cleansing of the temple, 'the chief priests, and scribes, and elders came to him, and began saying to Him, 'By what authority are you doing these things?' (Mark 11:27-28). 'These things' referred to not only his driving out the moneychangers from the temple (vv. 15-16) but also to His authoritative teaching (vv. 17-18). Those leaders knew that Jesus had not been educated in a scribal school or personally tutored by a leading rabbi. Nor did He ever credit venerated scribes or rabbis as the source of His teaching...Jesus' authority did not come from ecclesiastical title, scribal training or sacerdotal position, none of which He possessed. Nor did it come from popular Jewish beliefs of His time, many of which were based on myths, legends, and racial and religious prejudice (cf. Titus 1:14). It clearly did not come from rabbinical tradition....Jesus, the sinless and perfect Son of God, limited Himself to speaking nothing during His incarnation except the truth He received from His Father." [25]

Pico and his fellow Gnostic-papists professed to possess secret knowledge which placed them on a higher level than mere common Catholics. He and his cohort thought they knew God better than others, but in fact they knew Him not at all. Their deeds show them to be detestable, disobedient antichrists. "Nothing unclean and no one who practices abomination and lying shall ever come into the holy place..." (Rev. 21:27). Occultists proceed "according to the course of this world, according to the prince of the power of the air, of the spirit that is now working in the sons of disobedience...They attempt to deceive with empty words and because of these things the wrath of God comes upon the sons of disobedience." (Ephesians 2:2 and 5:6).

Observe Pico the serpent at work as he quotes approvingly the tradition of secrets-keeping occultism: "It was the opinion of the ancient theologians that divine subjects and the secret Mysteries must not be rashly divulged...the Egyptians had sculpted sphinxes in all their temples, for no other reason than to indicate that divine things, even when they are committed to

---

25 John F. MacArthur, *The MacArthur New Testament Commentary: Titus* (1996), pp. 126-127.

writing, must be covered with enigmatic veils and dissimulation." [26]

Pico is dropping more than a hint about the methods that are being used when he writes that "divine things...must be covered with...dissimulation." The definition of *dissimulation* is "concealment of what really is, under a feigned semblance of something different." This is how Satan's work in the world advances—under another name—such as "Christian Kabbalah" and "Vatican II ecumenism."

The Church hierarchy was becoming more and more enigmatically veiled during the Renaissance. To unmask child molestation or conspiracy and infiltration inside the Church became ever more difficult as a consequence of this veiling, which violates the Word of God. Jesus declared, "I spoke openly to the world...and in secret I have said nothing" (John 18:20). This is the simple, clean, pure and gloriously straight path to God. It overcomes paganism, Gnosticism, Neoplatonic-Hermeticism, Freemasonry, Talmudic and Kabbalistic Judaism and Rome's Renaissance usurper Church. This is the test of any institution or organization: is it completely open or does it keep secrets? Concealment became in-grained in the framework of Rome's hierarchical popery as it cast off the last vestiges of the true Catholic Church. This was its Neoplatonic-Hermetic inheritance which continues in the twenty-first century.

"Whenever 'the mysteries of the ancients' were invoked by...Ficino or Pico della Mirandola...they saw the early mystery cults through the eyes of Platonic philosophers who had already interlarded them with *mystéres littéraires*. Thus Plato appeared to them...as the heir of an ancient wisdom for which a ritual disguise had been invented by the founders of the mysteries themselves. And the philosophical cunning thus imputed to those early sages was ascribed also to the Neoplatonic magicians..." [27]

Pico merges Pharaonic Egypt, Plato and the Kabbalah in the belief they contain at least some of the waters of the rivers of Catholic truth. His papally-protected disciple, Lodovico Lazzarelli, was more specific. In his *Crater Hermetis*, Lazzarelli

---

[26] Pico della Mirandola, *Commento* (1486).

[27] Edgar Wind, op. cit., p. 7.

quotes approvingly Porphyry's statement that with regard to occult tradition ("wisdom"), "The first of those who began to pass on the tradition drank the clear waters of the Nile" and "it was by way of him (Hermes), that wisdom reached the Hebrews."

When Pope Pius X wrote against the "synthesis of all heresies" here it was, the perverted syncretic claim that Egyptian diabolism, as filtered through its subsequent manifestations in the sorcerers of Babylon, Orphic and Attic Greece, Persia and the heirs of these cumulative traditions—the rabbinic descendants of the Pharisees—proved the truth of Jesus Christ and the Bible.

If we limit ourselves to a study of Neoplatonic-Hermetic and Kabbalistic usurpation of the Church solely in terms of the decay of divine dogma and the infiltration of the hierarchy, then we will fail to see the result of this revolution within the Church of Rome. One cannot adopt the theology of Judaism in its Talmudic and Kabbalistic forms, and the Babylonian and Egyptian paganism from which it derives its gnosis, without aspiring to be that 'god' in the Garden of Eden which was the destiny promised to Adam and Eve if they would disobey their Creator. The first disaster was brought about by pride; by man-playing-God. The Church *prior* to the Renaissance and the post-Renaissance eras, had labored ceaselessly to teach man his place in the universe. He could advance by the talents of his God-given reason within the bounds of Revealed Truth and Natural Law. But he could not aspire to be himself a god by manipulating creation, whether through nuclear power, genetic modification of crops or cloning humans. The way forward for these civic forms of black magic was paved by the Renaissance ideology as birthed in Catholic Italy by Cusa, Plethon, Ficino and Ficino's pupil, Pico.

Giovanni Pico della Mirandola died in Florence on November 17, 1494 at the age of thirty-one. He would not live to see his ideology ascendant in the Church of Rome but he would not die until he had made that ascendancy certain. Agrippa, Erasmus and Johannes Reuchlin were his intellectual heirs, students and admirers. By the time Reuchlin's career was at its nadir we have indisputable evidence of the role that the Church of Rome played in providing cover to Reuchlin, who was an alter-Pico. Pico had suffered no lingering negative consequences for his diabolism. His philosophy was so lightly (though with much theatrical fanfare) interdicted by Pope Innocent VIII [28] that it gained posthumous circulation throughout Europe and Britain, becoming the Reuchlin movement, and branching out into many other sectors of the papist vineyard, through Steuco, Lazzarelli and numerous neo-Catholic conspirators and infiltrators.

"Despite his papal troubles, Pico found time in these years for intense textual studies, most of them conducted in Florence or in the villa at Fiesole that Lorenzo de' Medici gave to Pico...In this period Pico composed the *Heptaplus, Commentary on the Psalms, On Being and the One, Disputations against Divinitory Astrology*, and a number of other works." [29]

His text with the title that refers to an opposition to astrology is not what its name implies. "...the text's main arguments...are in total harmony with the cosmological ideas that Pico introduced eight years earlier in the *Nine Hundred Theses*. Pico never doubted that (astrological) influences of some sort flowed from the heavens to earth. The question was how those influences operated." [30]

Pico disputed horoscope astrology and predictions related to individual destinies. He did not deny what he termed "true astrology," which he said consisted of astrological magic as it related to the cosmos—magical power derived from the stars. This star-cult is the mandate of the state religion of Pharaonic Egypt. [31] In addition to citing its core stellar theology in his *Disputations,* he simultaneously denounces Egyptian black magic and declares vehemently that he is "no magician" of that tradition. By the time Pico wrote the *Disputations* he was seeking cover for his diabolic Kabbalism in the *Nine Hundred*

---

[28] Relatively few historians have sought to investigate the extent to which Pope Innocent VIII's relatively mild strictures imposed on Pico were colored by the fact that in political and legal battles for control of the duchy of Mirandola fought between factions of the Mirandola family, Pope Innocent was allied with Pico's brother (and heir) Antonmaria, who resided for a time at the papal court, against the faction led by Galeotto della Mirandola (Gianfrancesco's father), who were backed by the imperial court.

[29] Farmer, op. cit., p. 138.

[30] Ibid., p. 139.

[31] Cf. Richard H. Wilkinson, *The Complete Temples of Ancient Egypt* (2000), pp. 37 and 173; R.A. Schwaller de Lubicz, *Sacred Science* (1982), pp. 26-28 and 174-179; Rosalie David, *Religion and Magic in Ancient Egypt* (2002), p. 90.

Theses, and his Neoplatonism in his *Concord of Plato and Aristotle.* Consequently, in the pages of his *Disputations* one finds denunciations of the evil emanations of Chaldeans, Egyptians and even "Hebrew *magistri.*" Beware of this dissimulation.

"Anyone doubting that Pico was capable of intentional duplicity of this sort only needs to recall the subtle debating traps planted on every page of the nine hundred theses...Pico (had) an obvious motive for seeking whatever intellectual cover the *Disputations Against Divinitory Astrology* might provide."[32]

Indeed, in the first sentence of his *Nine Hundred Theses* he refers to the "*Theologicis, Magicis, Cabalisticis, cum suis tum sapientum Chaldeorum...Aegyptiorum...*" ("Theological, Magical, Cabalistic opinions, including his own and those of the wise Chaldeans and...Egyptians...").

The study of the lives of these occult initiates is akin to the vigilance necessary in approaching Talmudic, Kabbalistic and other rabbinic sacred volumes where unscrupulous techniques for subterfuge and duplicity, found under technical exegetical terms such as *Gezara shava* and *pilpul,* are rampant and institutionalized.[33] Pico, as a close student of the Kabbalah and other sacred rabbinic texts, adopted these crooked and disingenuous methods for his own. His nephew, Gianfrancesco, seems to have followed suit.

Though Gianfrancesco Pico della Mirandola was disinherited by his Uncle Pico, in favor of his enemy inside the family, Giovanni's brother, Antonmaria Pico, Gianfrancesco nonetheless gained control of some of his uncle's posthumous manuscripts, which were eventually sold to Cardinal Domenico Grimani and deposited in Rome. For the remaining four decades of his life Gianfrancesco spinned his uncle's views into a pious conservative, Catholic-Orthodox milieu and painted an equally cosmetic and distorted picture of him in his 1495 biography, the *Vita Ioannis Pici Mirandulae* (published in 1496 along with the collected works [*Opera*] of Giovanni Pico della Mirandola; Gianfrancesco's biography was subsequently translated and published in England by Thomas More).

---

[32] Farmer, op. cit., p. 149.

[33] These techniques are examined in *Judaism Discovered,* pp. 169-174; 229-236.

Gianfrancesco is often identified as a zealous follower of Savonarola and this allegation is "proof" to some people that Gianfrancesco was indeed a true Catholic. Yet we must ask, what true Catholic would falsify the life and work of his uncle to the extent that Gianfrancesco did in his *Vita Ioannis Pici?* We also note that in the pivotal battle between the Neoplatonists and the Thomists over the ethical validity of the views of Aristotle, Gianfrancesco sided with Plato against Dante and Aristotle. Gianfrancesco was not an unambiguously orthodox Roman Catholic. It seems he may have been tasked with ensuring that his Uncle Giovanni Pico was presented to the uninitiated Catholic posterity as an eccentric thinker who was nonetheless within the bounds of what constitutes a good Catholic. That "good Catholicism" would however, soon bear fruit named Reuchlin. Moreover, before his decease, Pico gained a papal ally, Alexander VI. There were more to come.

The conservative Protestant scholar Casuabon saw in the philosophers of the Church of Rome, the heresy of syncretism. Casaubon, in his *De rebus sacris et ecclesiasticis,* eloquently denounced Rome's syncretic attempts to link Hermes and Christ, stating that they "are without value, seeing as how not even the apostle uses profane sources when discussing the faith...Shall we be of such little faith as to defend Christian truth by means of pagan evidence?...I resolutely condemn and detest this project with all my heart. For he offends the truth with his assumption that it required a defense of lies, that is, the support of the devil."

Pico's syncretism, which views superstition-steeped rabbinic antichrists as a bridge to a profound understanding of the Old Testament—and therefore the roots of the Church itself—is also the theology of Cardinal De Lubac, the Second Vatican Council, and Popes John Paul II, Benedict XVI, Francis, and many other "princes of the Church." De Lubac was to such an extent an epitome of dissimulation that he manages the thaumaturgic balancing act of lauding Pico, the personification of the spirit of the Renaissance, while reproving the Renaissance. [34]

It is not the case that Pico was condemned in the sixteenth century and only revived by the modernist enablers of the Judaizing delusions of the twentieth. We should be mindful that "traditional" popes and "Catholic saints" are numbered among Pico's followers, including Thomas More, one of the favorite saints of contemporary conservative Catholic intellectuals. [35]

Pico himself thanks Pope Sixtus IV for publishing "with the greatest care and zeal" the satanic Kabbalah into Latin "for the public advantage of our faith," and causing "delight among the Hebrews" who "cherish" these books with "religious awe." [36]

When the usurper Church of Rome synthesized these pagan traditions in the name of the authentic Roman Catholic Church, the Protestant Reformation was given invaluable ammunition against it, provided by Rome itself. Many Catholics became Protestants after witnessing the desecrating synthesis. The Huguenot philologist Casaubon rightly demolished the papist Hermes Trismegistus hoax and when he did so before the literate elite of Europe, with that demolition went much of the credibility of the Church of Rome itself, which had failed to thoroughly cleanse itself *internally* (as opposed to rhetorically) of the spiritual infection of the Hermetic occultism it had fostered and extended.

Martin Muslow: "The thesis of concordance held that ancient wisdom, Christian doctrine and contemporary natural

---

[34] "...the movement of the Renaissance, even without considering its most serious excesses, ended in denying the ideal of Christianity, the whole life of men in society being thenceforth uprooted from the maxims of the Gospel..."—Cardinal Henri de Lubac, *"Explication chrétien de notre temps,"* transl. Anne Englund Nash, in *Theology in History* (1996), p. 444. "Toward the end of his career he wrote a very favorable monograph on the Renaissance Platonist Giovanni Pico della Mirandola..." (David Grumett, *De Lubac*, 2007, p. ix). We have published for the first time in English translation an extract from De Lubac's "monograph" (in chapter fourteen).

[35] On Thomas More, Pico, Henry VIII and Thomas Cromwell, cf. this writer's "Truth Devoured by a Wolf," in *Revisionist History* no. 78. In his *Life of John Picus* (1510), More translates into English the biography of Pico della Mirandola which had been penned in Latin by Gianfrancesco. More adds his own ideas and deletes some parts of Gianfrancesco's original text, making it almost as much More's book as that of Pico's propagandistic nephew.

[36] *On the Dignity of Man,* (op.cit.), pp. 31-32.

philosophies were principally in accord. Especially after the Council of Trent the thesis seemed well-suited for combining a reformed orientation with a reflection on origins...often linked with a certain Egyptophilia as well as a conception of Hermeticism as the oldest form of human wisdom."

Casaubon was a formidable Protestant Hebraist and according to the script of the papists this should make him a Judaizer in sympathy with the Talmud and cognate texts. This was not so, however. He was a dedicated student of the writing of the Swiss Protestant Talmud expert Johannes Buxtorf (1564-1629), Professor of Hebrew and Rabbinic Literature at the Protestant University of Basel. Authors Anthony Grafton and Joanna Weinberg are incredulous at the fact that Buxtorf, in spite of his scholarly knowledge of Hebrew, Aramiac and Judaism, opposed the religion of the rabbis. "Casaubon had found a way to focus on what still seems the strangest feature of Buxtorf's work: the unremitting hostility he showed toward the people whose languages, beliefs and rituals he had studied more intensively than any Christian before him." [37]

It is inconceivable to Grafton and Weinberg that a deep knowledge of the inner doctrines of Judaism such as, in Buxtorf's case, the *Shulchan Aruch* and its didactic section, *Orah Hayyim*, would lead to hostility toward Judaism (it seems they have never heard the name Johann Andreas Eisenmenger). Contrary to Romanist claims, Casaubon had no objection to Buxtorf's loathing for the rabbinic system: "Casaubon noted Buxtorf's prejudices, but did not make clear the extent to which he shared or qualified them. The nature of his ethnographic interest—like so much of his method as a Judaist—remained steeped in ambiguity." [38] This is a sly way of sneaking past the reader the fact that *there is no evidence* that Casaubon had any sympathy for Judaism.

"Buxtorf explained that his primary goal in revealing the true religion of the Jews to his fellow Germans had been religious and polemical: 'that we may be admonished to set before ourselves as the object of meditation the incredulity of

---

[37] Grafton and Weinberg, *I Have Always Loved the Holy Tongue* (2001), p. 149. This duo is asserting that Buxtorf has greater knowledge of Judaism than the apostles Peter and Paul and all of the Church Fathers, a tissue of absurdity which Buxtorf would have confuted.

[38] Ibid., p. 149.

the Jews, and the hardening of God and his equally terrible wrath and severity toward them'...Buxtorf noted that Judaism no longer rested on Moses and the prophets, but instead on the false laws and rules introduced by scribes and rabbis..." [39]

"Hoc etiam de ceremoniis, quibus Judaei in feriis et festis inter eos receptis superstitiosam ipsorum fidem exercentes utuntur, dictum adeo sufficit, ut indequilibet satis perspicere possit, quod religio ipsorum non amplius super Mose et prophetis, sed supermendaciis meris, falsique Rabbinorum et Scribarum (id quod ab initio libri huius mihi demonstrandum proposui) constitutionibus fundata sit. Sequitur iam praeterea de consuetudinibus nonnullis aliis, secundum quas in vita ipsorum privata se gerunt." [40]

The Church of the Renaissance introduced into the schools and monasteries of Catholicism the philosophy of the *concordia philosophorum* which teaches that there is a concord between paganism and Christianity.

"...*concordia philosophorum*, the idea that there is one basic, common kernel of truth in all philosophical systems, no matter how different they might be at first sight. This conviction culminated in Giovanni Pico della Mirandola's huge and unfinished project to bring to light the common truth of all philosophical and esoteric traditions...This idea was closely interrelated with the notion of a 'perennial philosophy,' the conviction that there was one, largely secret tradition of esoteric wisdom, dating back to the first beginnings of creation...This philosophical-esoteric *sapientia* (wisdom) or 'secret doctrine' was passed on from one 'sage' or 'magus' to the other, thus constituting a tradition that was thought to include figures like Zoroaster, Moses, Hermes Trismegistus, Orpheus, the Pythagoreans and Plato. The most important, though not the first, representative of this mode of thought was Marsilio Ficino, who affirmed that long before the Scriptures were revealed to man, there was a tradition of *prisca theologia*

---

[39] Ibid., p. 147.

[40] Johannes Buxtorf, *Synagoga Judaica*, (1604), chapter 25.

(ancient theology) or *prisca philosophia* that foreshadowed Christian truth..." [41]

To achieve the objective of the subversion of the Church, the pillars of authentic Roman Catholicism had to be derogated. "We find that (Francesco) Patrizi had already in 1571 deployed the esoteric/exoteric distinction in order to wipe out Aristotle by maintaining that all of Aristotle's esoteric and substantial assets were merely appropriated from Platonic thinking." [42]
However, as in the belt of transmission for relaxation of the laws against taking a profit for loaning money, which began inside Catholic circles and then spread to Calvinist ones, the Neoplatonic-Hermetic poison of Ficino, Pico and Francesco Patrizi of Cherso, (the pope's professor), was spread by Padua University graduate Johannes Jessenius (also called "Jessen") into Lutheran Wittenberg in 1593, and by Eilhard Lubin in Lutheran Rostock in 1598. Raphael Elgin disseminated it in Calvinist Zurich in 1595 and Marburg in 1609.
Jessenius had been a student of the Catholic Neoplatonic-Hermetic conspirator and Professor at Padua University, Francesco Piccolomini. Prof. Piccolhomini was a disciple of Pico and a colleague of Patrizi. [43] In 1593, Jessenius published excerpts from Patrizi's *Nova de universis philosophia* in his own volume, *Zoroaster, Nova, brevis, veraque de universo philosophia*. "Jessenius follows Piccolomini's plan of reconciling Plato and Aristotle with the help of Hermetic texts, which was in accord with the dimensions of Pico della Mirandola's idea of philosophical concord."[44]

---

[41] Cees Leijenhorst, "Francesco Patrizi's Hermetic Philosophy," in *Gnosis and Hermeticism from Antiquity to Modern Times* (1998), pp. 127-128.

[42] Cf. Maria Muccillo, *"La vita e le opere di Aristotle nelie Discussions peripateticae di* Fancesco Patrizi da Cherso," *Rinascimento II*.s. 21 (1981), pp. 53-119, and M.J. Wilmot, *"Aristotles exotericus, acromaticus, mysticus*: Two Interpretations of the Typological Classifications of the *Corpus aristotleicum* by Francesco Patrizi da Cherso," N*ovelles de la République des Lettres* (1985), pp. 67-95.

[43] Cf. Sandra Plastina, *"Concordia discors: Aristotleismus und Platonismus in der Philosophie des Francesco Piccolomini,"* in Martin Mulsow ed., *Das Ende des Hermetismus.*

[44] Tomás Nejeschleba, "Johannes Jessenius," p. 367, in *Francesco Patrizi: Philosopher of the Renaissance.*

Let us consider this "secret doctrine" which is the hallmark of Gnostic and masonic sects and offshoots. The maintenance of this secrecy takes precedence over *all other duties and obligations to God and man*, as George W. Bush showed forth when asked on national television by NBC News host Tim Russert on February 8, 2004 about his membership in the "Skull and Bones" brotherhood: "It's so secret we can't talk about it." [45]

The conspirators behind the "Gnostic Gospels" hoax insist that Jesus taught a secret doctrine. The occult imperium operates by this swindle: "Join with us and obtain the secret wisdom." The Gnostic Gospels we are told, were suppressed by fanatical, uptight Christians because they presented Christ's revolutionary secret gnosis for freedom and happiness. Like the Talmud and Kabbalah, the Gnostic "scriptures" directly contradict the written Word of Jesus Christ, *who established no aristocracy of secrets administered by a priestly caste.* The literal meaning of the Bible is anathema to all demonic brotherhoods and sisterhoods. "I speak with him face to face, even plainly, and not in dark sayings" (Numbers 12:8).

"All the words of my mouth are with righteousness. Nothing crooked or perverse is in them. They are all plain to him who understands, and right to those who find knowledge" (Proverbs 8:8-9). The Prophet Isaiah declared, "When a King (i.e. Christ) shall reign in righteousness, the eyes of them that see shall not be dim. The heart of the rash will understand knowledge, and the tongue of the stammerers will be ready to speak plainly" (32: 1, 3-5)." Here is liberation.

In addition to the promise of a "secret doctrine," the gods of the pagans and gnostic sects impart, as noted, the teaching that all religions have the same root. This belief existed in a state of dormancy as the Catholic Faith, in the first millennia of its existence, gained adherents and faithfully taught that Jesus Christ was the one and only door to heaven and the Father. It was masonic popery, the abomination developed in Rome during the Renaissance, which awakened those dormant occult forces. One may quote Leo XIII in *Humanum Genus* against Freemasonry incessantly, yet when Leo refrained from identifying the root of the masonic conspiracy in Rome's own

---

[45] The interview is online: https://www.youtube.com/watch?v=gwJDs1cg9Eo

Renaissance Hermeticism and the rabbinic Kabbalah which had been empowered by the Renaissance papacy, his *Humanum Genus* only served to fulfill the same cunning masterstroke of misdirection as did Benedict XIV with his encyclical *Vix Pervenit*—"against usury"—which provided a gaping loophole on *behalf of usury*. In the aftermath of *Vix Pervenit*, "the great papal bulwark against usury," profit on loans continued to metastasize in the Catholic world virtually unimpeded. Toothless rhetoric had prevailed over the restoration of God's law, as it has done time and again from the pens of "wonderfully orthodox pontiffs" of the post-Renaissance age.

History testifies that the leading Neoplatonic-Hermetic-Kabbalist conspirators inside the Church of Rome (not the low level patsies consigned to the flames, along with those who failed to submit to papal supremacy, like Bruno), were largely immune to *serious and enduring* interdiction and punishment. In spite of whatever slap on the wrist had to be administered to tranquilize and outfox the remnant of outraged true Catholics, the top conspirators went to their graves secure in their persons and positions—their influence growing exoterically and then waxing and waning esoterically, as circumstances and situations required, finally emerging under Pope Paul VI at the Second Vatican Council. Here was the fruition of five hundred years of Renaissance and post-Renaissance conspiracy. Here was manifested within the Church of Rome the spirit of Ficino, Pico, Reuchlin and the rest of the Vatican's Renaissance gang. Masonic ideology had manifested in Neoplatonic-Hermetic Rome long before "Freemasonry" arrived in the garments of the neo-Protestant world as a sometime rival of the masonic popery of the neo-Catholic world. "Continuity...was assured...by the continued progress and popularity of Hermetic doctrine, which issued in Rosicrucianism, Freemasonry, and varieties of alchemical and astrological arts." [46]

Let us not call ourselves followers of Jesus Christ and then be seduced by artful deception: usury was not first revived in Christendom by John Calvin but by the Church of Rome while Calvin was a child; Masonic ideology was not born out of the Reformation or the Enlightenment (though certain forces in

---

[46] Thomas Molnar, *The Pagan Temptation* (1987), p. 76.

both those camps most certainly served as its booster rocket). Masonic ideology was born inside the papist, ecclesiastical magisterium's Neoplatonic-Hermetic imperium. For elite Catholics, *the Renaissance papacy nurtured and harbored a supra-religious, supra-national philosophic universalism that would serve as the cornerstone upon which its supposed deadly enemy, the Masonic Lodge, would be constructed.* [47]

The diabolic genius of this rarefied two-tiered process consisted in the fact that among the lower tier of common people and parish priests, Rome maintained a milieu of inquisitorial antipathy for the occult, just as it instilled an anti-usurious social gospel among the same peasants and priests which gained for the Robber Church of the Great Usurpation, a permanent, undeserved aura of militance on behalf of the poor and against "the bankers and the Masons."

Thus was the double-mind institutionalized. Double-minded Catholics have a cavernous black hole at the center of their minds that allows them to maintain two mutually contradictory ideas simultaneously and fail to detect that fact. They run to false shepherds for a remedy. Pope St. Pius X is a hero of theirs, yet they do not ask themselves why his famous encyclical *Pascendi Domini Gregis* (1907) failed utterly in its alleged intention of interdicting modernism. How could any honest prelate who is not mentally feeble warn of religious syncretism making its way inside the Church, while refusing to unmask the *progenitors* of this spiritual infection?

In similar fashion, Pope Pius IX denounced, in his *Syllabus of Errors*, as one of the deceptions of Satan: "Every man is free to embrace and profess that religion which, guided by the light of reason, he shall consider true. Man may, in the observance of any religion whatever, find the way of eternal salvation, and arrive at eternal salvation." Pope St. Pius X enlarged the indictment put forth by Pius IX: "Here it is well to note at once that, given this doctrine of experience united with that of symbolism, every religion, even that of paganism, must be held to be true. What is to prevent such experiences from being found in any religion? In fact, that they are so is maintained by not a few. On what grounds can Modernists deny the truth of an experience affirmed by a follower of Islam? Will they claim a

---

[47] See the appendix, "The Influence of Neoplatonic Thought on Freemasonry: Pico della Mirandola and his *Oratio de Hominis Dignitate.*"

monopoly of true experiences for Catholics alone? Indeed, Modernists do not deny, but actually maintain, some confusedly, others frankly, that all religions are true. That they cannot feel otherwise is obvious. For on what ground, according to their theories, could falsity be predicated of any religion whatsoever?"

Where in either statement by these "great traditional" popes is a single indictment of the Renaissance "Catholic" fathers of modernism? *Why is not one of the conspirators who started it all named and unmasked?* Nowhere in the renowned encyclicals of the two popes will we find this vital information. It has been omitted. Pius IX and Pius X did not cite them. Citation would have fatally undermined the pillar of the occult conspiracy: the inculcation of blind obedience to the "ecclesiastical magisterium" (notwithstanding the fact that the papist conspirators deny that the obedience they require is blind). Modernism and syncretism were produced by *the ecclesiastical magisterium itself* after 1450. The two "anti-modernist" popes cannot admit this. They rail against the modernist idol while they make an idol out of obedience to the heads of the Church. This is bipolar. As long as obedience to the heads of the Church takes precedence over the Word of God, modernism and diabolism will flourish. Like usury after *Vix Pervenit*, modernism grew after the *Syllabus* and *Pascendi Domini Gregis*. These are double-minded papal documents. Observe what Pope St. Pius X teaches about the doctrine of St. Thomas Aquinas:

"And let it be clearly understood above all things that when We prescribe scholastic philosophy We understand chiefly that which the Angelic Doctor (Thomas Aquinas) has bequeathed to us...We admonish professors to bear well in mind that they cannot set aside St. Thomas, especially in metaphysical questions, without grave disadvantage."

On the contrary, Your Holiness, your Church of Rome began to "set aside" Aquinas' doctrine against profit on loans of money 392 years before you penned your encyclical! Isn't 392 years sufficient time for one of the subsequent members of the august fraternity of those who are called the "Vicar of Christ on earth" to name names, indict the guilty and reinstate the immemorial dogmatic and Thomistic prohibition against all profit from loans of money?

To the contrary, while it is true that Pope St. Pius X died before the 1917 Code of Canon Law could be promulgated, the Code had been compiled largely on his watch, by *periti* selected by him. This Code of Canon Law removed all prohibitions against profiting from loans of money. *"They cannot set aside St. Thomas...without grave disadvantage."* Yet this is precisely what this double-minded pope, who is lionized by "conservative" and "traditional" Catholics as the paragon of what it means to be a pontiff, perpetrated in the 1917 Code, against the same St. Thomas Aquinas who he counsels others not to abandon.

Does one imagine that this blatant contradiction is lost on the Cryptocracy? Does one imagine that they will fail to exploit it by making their subordinates and initiates cognizant of how even the pontiff with a reputation as the supreme opponent of modernism, had succumbed to situation ethics? Patrician gnostics do not pride themselves on believing as do the plebes. They take pride in being an elite above humanity who perceive that which is veiled. One such not-so-arcane secret which they detected is the tragic case of Pope Pius X who, in allegedly thundering against the evils that had infiltrated the Church, managed to steer clear of any direct threat to the *root and branch* of the conspiracy, though during his relatively brief pontificate he did indeed vex sundry low and mid-level flunkeys and patsies regarded as expendable by their elite masters.

Pius X concludes his encyclical *Pascendi* with an admonition to Catholics to obey *"the ecclesiastical authority in any of its depositories."* This is a message of conformity well-pleasing to the post-Renaissance Cryptocracy which, since the late fifteenth century, has maintained control over the Church of Rome no matter who occupies the Chair of Peter. The Pyramid and Obelisk Men prevail.

The blind alleys and dead ends into which those who have earnestly sought to contend for the Gospel of Jesus Christ have instead been repeatedly dispatched and neutralized, is a powerful contributing factor in the success of the diabolic process. We have engendered a tradition of defeat and grown accustomed to it. We wear our defeat like a comfortable leather coat of long usage. We have God on our side and yet we continue to abandon Him to follow the well-tread path of hypnotic bondage to the Pyramid-and-Obelisk. Is this dark fate what Jesus Christ intended for His people?

Giovanni Pico told the hierarchy of the Church that by using the ancient Egyptian magical gnosis with which Pharaoh's sorcerers confronted Israel and Moses (Exodus 7:11), and which later became the Kabbalah, we can teach the world to know the divinity of Christ. As we have seen, this lunacy infiltrated not only the Church of Rome. By means of Catholic agents, it slithered into Protestant denominations as well.

Occultists are consummate hoaxers. They convinced the western world that their fraudulent pagan superhero Hermes Trismegistus, was a factual historical personage. It took considerable intellectual effort, most effectively undertaken initially by Casaubon, to prove that Hermes was an elaborately concocted myth. Giovanni Pico's fraud corresponds to the sly syncretism which the "Catholic" Kabbalists employed to gain acceptance for the black magic texts of the rabbis, on whose behalf Pico della Mirandola employed an energetic apologetic apparatus, arguing that the major religions, including Catholicism, were all reflections of the primordial religion "of Adam." The true Adam of Scripture was not Pico's focus, however. For the occult Renaissance, Adam is the *"Adam Kadmon"* of the Kabbalah, not the Book of Genesis. The Neoplatonic-Hermetic gnosis teaches that pure wisdom from deep antiquity emanated from the Kabbalistic Adam who preceded the Adam of Genesis. "The concept likely evolved from the older idea—prominent in Philo's writings—of a heavenly man who was created at the same time, or prior to, the earthly Adam...While Adam Kadmon is said to take the shape of a human, it may well be that this is intended in much the same way various constellations of stars are identified in astrology. Thus Adam Kadmon could be understood as a constellation of stars in the shape of a man...Above all, Adam Kadmon is part of the complex Kabbalistic theory of God's emanations of the world, containing the ten *sefirot*." [48]

This "Adam Kadmon" is a symbol of counterfeit reality: Satan as the ape of God. All of Satan's spiritual and intellectual systems reflect this characteristic. Like Hermes

---

[48] Howard Schwartz, *Tree of Souls* (2004), pp. 15-16. *"Sefirot"* is also spelled *"sephirot."* Concerning the "ten *sephirot*," see chapter 18, "Occult Miscellany."

himself, the essence of this Kabbalistic-Gnostic-Neoplatonic entity serves to represent an idea: that Satan is worthy of a worship which bestows upon the worshipper secret knowledge of the universe withheld from others. The account of Adam Kadmon in the rabbinic *Midrash* relates that when "he was created...he was so awesome the angels mistook him for God and began to worship him." Since he was an androgyne, most Christians would be appalled to encounter Adam Kadmon in the flesh in view of the fact that he possessed a bosom like a woman and the genitalia of both male and female. This creature would be stylized in the nineteenth century by the "Catholic" mystic Eliphas Lévi, as "Baphomet," the infamous sigil of modern devil worship. Renaissance-Catholic conspirators endeavored to drag Jesus Christ into this cauldron by claiming that the New Testament links Jesus to Adam Kadmon in I Corinthians 15:45-50. The passage from Corinthians reads: "Thus it is written, 'The first man Adam became a living being; the last Adam became a life-giving spirit. But it is not the spiritual that is first but the natural, and then the spiritual. The first man was from the earth, a man of dust; the second man is from heaven. As was the man of dust, so also are those who are of the dust, and as is the man of heaven, so also are those who are of heaven. Just as we have borne the image of the man of dust, we shall also bear the image of the man of heaven. I tell you this, brothers: flesh and blood cannot inherit the kingdom of God, nor does the perishable inherit the imperishable."

There is no hidden meaning in the preceding Scripture passage. The opening line refutes the Kabbalistic absurdity that is being foisted upon us. Contrary to the Kabbalistic "Adam Kadmon" buncombe, the *first Adam* was a flesh and blood living being. It is the *last Adam* who is the spiritual Adam—Jesus Christ. The reference to His "spiritual body" is an allusion to His imperishable, post-Resurrection body, animated by the Third Person of the Trinity, the Holy Spirit.

To non-initiates, the Renaissance conspirators used the Adam of the Bible as the primordial reference point of their appeal to divine cosmic knowledge preserved from antiquity. Among initiated insiders it was understood that the "Kadmon" Adam of the Kabbalah is the one regarded as the source of this knowledge which, when fully rediscovered in the future, will reanimate the image of Adam. It would appear that the

Neoplatonic-Hermetic future is here, as versions of Kadmon's androgyny are being created through the powers of surgery, as well as the *pharmakos* (φάρμακος, οῦ, ὁ), warned of in the Book of Revelation, which gave notice in Revelation 18:23 and 22:15, of the forthcoming employment of pharmaceutical agents to sustain Satan's illusion—his disfigured mimic of God's natural creation. Writing in 1487 in *Heptaplus*,[49] Pico stated: "Because what is said by the Hebrews is new to the Latins, it could not be easily understood by our people unless, hatched from a twin egg, I explained a great part or almost the totality of ancient teachings of the Hebrew dogmas...showing how much these ideas agree with Egyptian wisdom, how much with Platonic philosophy and how much with Catholic truth."

Rabbinic Judaism's root is in the sorcery of Pharaonic Egypt, which is also represents a treasured repository of theology and symbolism for Freemasonry. Pico candidly links his twisted version of "Catholic truth" to Judaism through "Egyptian wisdom."

Pope Alexander Adopts Pico's Theology

"In the last years of his life, Pico's situation was greatly eased by the advent to office in 1492 of a new pope. In that year, Innocent VIII was succeeded as the spiritual head of Christendom by Alexander VI, the Borgia pope, one of the most publicized and colorful characters of the Renaissance...the Borgia pope was not at all averse to astrology and magic, but, on the contrary, was deeply interested in those subjects, and he came most impressively to the rescue of Pico's orthodoxy. The bulls for Pico's absolution which Lorenzo de Medici had failed to obtain...were promulgated by Alexander VI on June 18th, 1493, less than a year after his elevation to the Holy See.

"Not only that, the pope wrote a personal letter to Pico himself, beginning *'Dilecte fili Salute & apostolicam benedictionem.'* In this letter, Alexander rehearses the whole history of Pico's case, mentioning the nine hundred theses, the *Apologia*, the commission which had accused Pico of heresy, his flight to France, and ends by completely absolving both him and his works from all taint of heresy. Pico is described as illuminated by a *'divina largitas'* and as a faithful son of the

---

[49] English translation: New York, 1977, introduction to pt. III, pp. 51-52.

Church. This letter was printed in all the editions of Pico's works, thus encouraging readers to accept, on the highest authority, the writer's views as of unimpeachable orthodoxy. And this would include the view which was the chief cause of the outcry against Pico, and of the commission which Alexander quashed, that *Magia* and *Cabala* are valuable aids to Christianity.

"It was in this changed atmosphere that Pico wrote, about 1493-4, his *Disputationes adversus astrologiam divinatricem.* This work against astrology used to be taken as proof that Pico was free from astrological superstition. But its title alone shows that the kind of astrology which Pico is against is divinatory astrology, the normal astrology based on belief in the determination of man's fate by the stars and using calculations based on horoscopes to foretell the predestined future. And it has recently been pointed out that Pico repeats in this book what is practically Ficino's theory of astral influences borne on a 'celestial spirit.' Further, Pico actually cites 'our Marsilius' as one of those who have written against astrologers 'following in the traces of Plotinus, in the interpretation and exposition of whom he has much aided Platonic studies, amplifying and enlarging them.' This could be an allusion to that commentary on Plotinus, the *De vita coelitus comparanda* and its *Magia naturalis* (including Plotinised talismans) as a work indirectly defended through being drawn in amongst those against astrology.

"In short, Pico is really defending the Fincinian 'astral magic' (he does not use this expression) which...is quite a different thing from astrology proper, being a way of escape from astrological determinism by teaching how to control and use the stellar influences. Written about 1493-4, which is about the time that the Pope had exonerated Pico from all blame, the book against astrology is really a vindication of *Magia naturalis.*

"It is into the context of the controversy about Pico, in which Alexander VI came out so strongly on the side of the Magus, that one should put the extraordinary 'Egyptianism' in the frescoes painted by Pinturicchio for Alexander in the Appartamento Borgia in the Vatican....very strange are the Egyptian scenes in the Room of the Saints. The emblem of the Borgia family was the bull, and the Borgia bull becomes identified in this series with Apis, the bull worshipped by the

218   Pope Alexander's Wizard

Egyptians as the image of Osiris, the sun god. It is by a series of allusive shifts in meaning as the frescoes tell their story that the Egyptian Apis bull, or the sun, becomes identified with the Borgia bull, or the pope as the sun.

"The Egyptian series begins with the story of Io, turned into a cow by Juno, who set Argus to watch her. Argus was killed by Mercury, a scene shown in one of the paintings where Mercury, with drawn sword, is dispatching Argus. Having been rescued by Mercury from Argus, Io escaped into Egypt where she became the goddess Isis. After the scene with Mercury and Argus, there follows in the frescoes, a scene where Io-Isis is seated on a throne, with a figure on her left identified by Saxl as Moses. The figure on her right is obviously the same person as the one shown with the zodiac in the Room of the Sibyls. He is, I suggest, again Hermes Trismegistus...The Mercury who killed Argus was, according to Cicero, Hermes Trismegistus who afterwards went into Egypt and gave the Egyptians their laws and letters. This is mentioned by Ficino in the *argumentum* before his *Pimander* text: *Hunc (i.e. Trismegistus) asserunt occidisse Argum, Aegyptiis praefuisse, eisque leges, ac litteras tradidisse.*'

"Hence, the Mercury in the fresco who kills Argus would be Hermes Trismegistus, and the next scene would show him in Egypt, as the lawgiver of the Egyptians, with, beside him, the law-giver of the Hebrews, Moses. This would be the usual Hermes- Moses comparison with which we have become so familiar in our study of *Magia* and *Cabala*.

"Why did the pope have such a program painted early in his reign, a program which glorifies the Egyptian religion...associates Hermes Trismegistus with Moses? The answer to this question is, I believe, that the Pope wished to proclaim his reversal of the policy of his predecessor by adopting Pico della Mirandola's program of using *Magia* and *Cabala* as aids to religion. [50]

"The most startling manifestation of Roman 'Egyptology' appears in the decorative scheme of the 'Room of the Saints' in the Appartamento Borgia, the series of residential and

---

[50] Yates, *Bruno*, op. cit., pp. 113-116.

ceremonial rooms in the Vatican Palace that Pinturicchio [51] frescoed for Alexander VI in the early years of the second Borgia pontificate...In the Pinturicchio ceiling, Io-Isis sits enthroned, teaching the Egyptians, with Moses and Hermes Trismegistus at her side. The next scene shows her marriage to Osiris...then Osiris was murdered by his evil brother, and the pieces of his body scattered over all Egypt. Isis manages at length to gather the bodily parts of her former consort, and erects a pyramid over his tomb. There he appears as Apis, the bull, and is worshipped by the Egyptians as the living image of the resurrected god. In the last scene, the bull, elevated by his priests, is borne triumphantly before the faithful, before the beginning of sacred rites. At the head of the procession appears a child blowing a horn decorated with another Borgia heraldic emblem, the double crown of the royal house of Aragon. These elements suggest a final metamorphosis of Apis-Osiris into the Borgia pope himself and have a parallel in the pope's own ceremonial appearance raised aloft on his *sedia gestatoria* (ritual throne)...in the Pinturicchio ceiling, Io-Isis, the link between Hellenic and Egyptian civilization, and Osiris-Apis, the image of the slain and resurrected divine king, are the sacred progenitors of the Borgia pontificate..." [52]

In the papal apartment we observe an exquisite illustration by Pinturicchio of the transmigration of a repeatedly reincarnated soul who begins as Io, becomes Isis and

---

[51]Bernardino di Betto (1454-1513), known as Pinturicchio (also spelled Pintoricchio).

[52] Charles L. Stinger, *The Renaissance in Rome,* pp. 304-306. In 1503 Julius II (Giuliano della Rovere), succeeded Alexander VI (after the brief interregnum of Pius III's pontificate). "It was during Julius's pontificate, moreover, that Giles of Viterbo, so often an articulator for the Della Rovere pontiff of the papacy's sacred mission and destiny, developed a deepening interest in Hebraic studies...Giles devoted attention to Talmudic literature, but above all he cultivated the cabala...which he and other Renaissance cabalists believed contained the hidden wisdom revealed to Adam...Roman interest in the cabala did not originate with Giles...(a)s Pico points out (concerning) Julius II's uncle, Sixtus IV...(to whose) pontificate...belongs the Good Friday, 1481 sermon of Flavius Mithridates. This converted Sicilian Jew, who had come to Rome through the patronage of (Giovanni Battista) Cibo, the future Innocent VIII, dazzled his Vatican audience in the course of a two-hour oration with citations from...the Hebrew '*arcana*'...(Stinger, pp. 306-307). Establishment historians declare that Innocent VIII was opposed to the occult, yet here he was, while still a cardinal, bringing Pico's Judaic handler inside the Vatican and facilitating this Kabbalist's position as preacher to the papal household.

eventually reincarnates as Alexander VI, Pope of Rome! The occult-Renaissance Church is thus established symbolically inside the Vatican itself. Our Borgia pope has been well camouflaged by the Church of Rome. To historians both Catholic and secular, Alexander VI is notorious for having fathered eight children by three different women, and that among these offspring were the murderous Cesare and his amorous sister, Lucrezia; and that Alexander sold on occasions too numerous to number, the rank of cardinal to the highest bidder, and in general put the Roman Church up for auction (less remarked upon is his judicial murder of Savonarola).

This is essentially "Borgia Pope" Alexander VI's profile in pop history. In our post-modern world these details are not particularly galvanizing, being mainly fodder for cynicism and a demoralizing, shoulder-shrugging retort, along the lines of, so what else is new? The Vatican can absorb cynics. In some respects it has turned cynicism back upon its critics by painting them as holier-than-thou Puritan bibliomaniacs who make no allowance for human flaws and failings. The point would be well taken were it not for the suppressed fact that Pope Alexander's theology was Neoplatonic-Hermetic-Kabbalism. Rome cannot so readily dismiss or spin (at least not yet), transgressions against the First Commandment committed by a pontiff. Popular history does not report the singular marvel of Alexander VI's papacy, which has nothing to do with simony or fathering children out of wedlock. This prodigy is something that remains "too hot to handle" for the spin-doctors. Even at this late date, it is an occult success so spectacular and damaging that even Rome's confidence tricksters would have difficulty explaining it to the marks in the pews. Consequently, Alexander's major crime isn't written about to any appreciable extent in most papal biographies or mainstream histories.

This pontiff opened a Pandora's Box that has never been closed. He safeguarded, cultivated and unleashed upon the world none other than the master architect of the occult Trojan Horse inside the Church, Giovanni Pico della Mirandola. Even with the lapse of more than five hundred years, for having secured this world-historic objective of the dark forces, Alexander VI receives scant acknowledgement. His secret remains potentially explosive and for that reason it is still being kept.

As Frances Yates wrote, "The profound significance of Pico della Mirandola in the history of humanity can hardly be overestimated. He it was who first boldly formulated a new position for European man, man as Magus using both *Magia* and *Cabala* to act upon the world, to control his destiny by science. And in Pico, the organic link with religion of the emergence of the Magus can be studied at its source." [53]

What exactly is the connection between Pico's *Magia* and our era's science? "It is one of the more profound ironies of the history of thought that the growth of mechanical science, through which arose the idea of mechanism as a possible philosophy of nature, was itself an outcome of the Renaissance magical tradition." [54]

Mechanism divested of the appearance of magic would by deception appear in the modern era to represent the triumph of materialism over Renaissance mysticism, the apparent overthrow of *Magia* and *Cabala* by rules of evidence and the scientific method, and the replacement of the magus with the scientist. In truth however, the materialistic scientist who creates artificial intelligence, clones living beings, modifies DNA, tampers with embryos, and engineers plant genetics, *fulfills the role of the magus* envisioned by Giovanni Pico and Cornelius Agrippa; their Protestant disciple John Dee, and a legion of epigones. Certain scientists harness the power of the material world to the eons-old objective of the sorcerers of antiquity, and the god they serve. To do so, the scientist in the modern age, no less than the Renaissance magus who is his progenitor, rejects the *Logos* (John 1:1-5) and revolts against the Order of Creation divinely ordained by the Word. This infernal network entered history by means of the imprimatur which Pope Alexander VI first granted to Giovanni Pico della Mirandola.

---

[53] Yates, *Bruno*, op. cit., p. 116.

[54] Yates, *The Rosicrucian Enlightenment*, op. cit., p. 113.

Chapter VI

Bonfire of the Verities

Omnes nefas vicitis, victoribus omnia sancta.[1]

There were many honorable Catholics in the Renaissance era who stepped forth to voice concern, protest or active opposition to the Neoplatonic-Hermetic conspiracy. One of the earliest was George of Trebizond, the enemy of Gemistos Plethon at the Council of Florence and the author, in 1458, of *Comparatio philosophorum Platonis et Aristotelis* (which was tightly suppressed and not published until 1523 and then only in a handful of copies). Trebizond detected the true nature of the Neoplatonic-Hermetic conspiracy, but was excessive in his assessment of Plato, attributing to him sexual sins for which there is no evidence.

Girolamo Savonarola, though there are certainly problems with some of his views and approaches to rulership, was the outstanding and implacable, counter-revolutionary defender of the true Roman Catholic Church in the early Renaissance, and as such there was no way he could escape the flames of the papal Inquisition, barring a miracle.

He was the scion of a respected Italian family: his paternal grandfather Michele Savonarola was the author of learned scientific treatises, professor of medicine at the University of Padua and physician to the princely court of Ferrara. Michele's brother had been a canon lawyer; his father a wool merchant. Girolamo's mother was descended from the House of Bonacolsi, the one-time lords of Mantua. When Girolamo Savonarola was born in September 1452, his godfather was of the House of the Duke Borso d'Este.

Tutored first by his grandfather, Savonarola matriculated at the University of Ferrara, where he received an advanced degree. At the age of twenty he penned the poem, *De ruina mundi*. He discovers that the world "esteems those who are the

---

[1]   "To the conquered all crimes, to the victors all holiness." This "victor's justice" apothegm is attributed to the Medici. Cf. *Fire in the City: Savonarola and the Struggle for the Soul of Renaissance Florence* (2006), p. 285.

enemies of God and Rome is in the hands of pirates (captained by Pope Sixtus IV)":

"Ah, look at that catamite and at the pimp,
Dressed in purple, frauds looked up to
By the common people and adored by a blind world.

"Earth is so pulled down by every vice
That it will never stand again.
And Rome, the capital, slips into the muck,
Never more to rise again.

"Avoid all those who put on the purple.
Flee from palaces and ostentatious loggias,
Speaking to the few alone,
For you will be the enemy of all the world."

Shortly after he joined the Preaching Order of St. Dominic (Dominicans) he was making distinctions between the Church as the pure bride of Christ and the harlot in Rome, from his monastery in San Domenico where he took his final vows. In 1479 he was named Novice Master at the monastery of Santa Maria degli Angeli in Ferrara. In 1482 Savonarola was dispatched to the San Marco monastery in the city of the princely Medici, Florence where he served as professor of sacred Scripture and theology and where Lorenzo the Magnificent was the boss of all bosses. He journeyed there on foot, carrying only his Bible and breviary. In 1484 Sixtus IV died and was replaced by Innocent VIII toward whom Savonarola was also dismissive as evidenced by his poem, *Oratio pro ecclesia*. In 1487 he returned to San Domenico and the University of Bologna, having made little impression on the Florence of the 1480s.

Savonarola returned to Florence for good in the spring of 1490, at the invitation of Lorenzo, but the honeymoon was short-lived. He preached that men in holy orders were wrong to seek out *gran maestri* (great lords) because of the opportunities for being compromised by the relationship. In his Advent sermons of 1490 (which spilled over into the Christmas season through January 1491), he tore into fraudulent financial transactions and the greedy rich. An embassy by five leading citizens of Florence descended on Savonarola urging him to preach in a more traditional and flattering manner. Savonarola answered with fifty Lenten sermons, beginning Ash Wednesday, February 16, 1491.

"The opening sermon stresses the idea that ceremonial externals in religion may betoken an inner void: a people without true faith and commitment...The succeeding sermons introduced a wealth of themes...the doctrinal ignorance of the laity, thieving priests and their cupidity for lucrative posts (benefices), the purchase and sale of Church offices (simony), the lechery of clerics, sodomy and the oppression of the poor, such as by unjust taxation. The last of these claims is strongly enunciated in the Sunday sermon of 27 February when the friar also remembered that the rich in Florence expect to collect interest on their taxes—a customary Florentine practice. God's justice will come down on this, he declared." [2]

His fiftieth sermon on the Wednesday after Easter (April 6) turned from the clergy and admonished the ruling class for their pride, tyranny, greed and oppression.

"The Savonarolan struggle...provoked venomous resistance, and this reminds us of the vital links between Church and society, clerics and patrons. Owing to the enormous scale of ecclesiastical rights and properties, of profitable office and income-paying benefices, local families and politicians had, as it were, too much invested in neighboring religious houses to keep politics out of the Church, or the Church out of politics. Ambitious clerics with the right connections routinely borrowed money from bankers in order to buy lucrative Church offices... and bishoprics were sometimes passed on, if not indeed willed, to family members." [3]

The "Carnival" season in Florence was a scandal to Savonarola as it would be to any Christian. "...to him these were pagan antics and the quintessence of the Medici's poisonous legacy. By substituting acts of piety, charity and reverence Florentines would transform Carnival into a fitting prelude to holy Lent." [4]

---

[2] Lauro Martines, *Fire in the City: Savonarola and the Struggle for the Soul of Renaissance Florence*, p. 25.

[3] Ibid., p. 32.

[4] Donald Weinstein, *Savonarola: The Rise and Fall of a Renaissance Prophet* (2011) p. 217.

In 1496 during the vile pagan Carnival revels which featured obscene antics and bonfires, Savonarola's youth auxiliary, the *fanciulli, and* Savonarola's lieutenant, Fra Domenico da Pescia purged the city of all "dirty and vain paintings" and blasphemy. The boys reversed the carnival: where there had been rock fights they erected barriers for collecting alms for the "shame-faced poor." They erected altars with crucifixes with candles burning before them and they made the bonfires into the most famous conflagration of the age, the "Bonfire of the Vanities," wherein people were encouraged to toss objects of evil or luxury. A mountain of cosmetics, pornographic books, statuettes of naked women, dice and other gambling paraphernalia were tossed into the flames. These ceremonies were marked by processions of young people, estimated to number upwards of eight thousand in a city of 40,000, marching behind giant crucifixes and images of the Blessed Mother and shouting, "Long live Christ!"

"...in the last year of Savonarola's life, as his Florentine enemies, with the backing of Rome and the cardinal clergy, increased in the city's governing councils and intensified their attacks...Now the marching and scouting boys' groups confronted a growing resistance, including abuse, threats and outright assaults. Gamblers might reach for knives or even swords if San Marco's children (named after Savonarola's monastery) happened to come on the scene..." [5]

Now came Savonarola's contest with Pope Alexander VI (Rodrigo Borgia). "Savonarola's leading Florentine enemies... needed all the help they could summon to get the Florence they longed for...so as to bring back carnival, gambling, horse races and—the Piagnoni alleged—untroubled anal sex...Alexander was the natural and obvious prince to turn to for help...." [6]

Savonarola was threatened by the pope's agent with "excommunication *latae sententiae*," i.e. automatic excommunication for disobedience. The effectiveness of the harbinger of excommunication was vitiated somewhat by the fact that Pope Alexander had last used this threat on one of his mistresses, Giulia Farnese, after she had returned to her husband. If she did not come back to the papal bedchamber she

---

[5] Martines, op. cit., p. 118.

[6] Ibid., p. 126.

was informed that she would incur *latae sententiae*. Nonetheless, a papal order silencing Savonarola was observed by the monk from October 1495 to February 17, 1496 when he launched his Lenten sermons with more warnings and admonishment of usurers, blasphemers and sodomites, and the aristocrats of the Roman Curia who were "happily ensconced" in a city with "10,000 whores."

Pope Alexander was determined to crush Savonarola but on many occasions he was thwarted by the influential Neopolitian Cardinal Oliveriero Carafa, who was in sympathy with Savonarola. Finally, it has been alleged by historian Lauro Martines[7] that it was "even likely...that in the summer of 1496, the General Procuator of the Dominicans, Ludovico da Ferrara, in Florence on a mission for the pope, sought to tempt Savonarola with the secret offer of a red hat, a cardinalate, on the understanding that he accept certain conditions. This alone makes sense of one of Savonarola's asservations, uttered in a sermon of 20 August 1496 in the Hall of the Great Council and cast directly at the Signory (the ruling body of Florence): 'My Lord God I want only you. It is not my habit to seek human glory. Away with that! I seek no glory but in you, my Lord. I want no hats, no mitres large or small. I want nothing, unless it be what you have given to your saints: death. A red hat of blood: this I desire." [8]

In November 1496 Pope Alexander announced a reorganization of the Dominican monasteries of Italy aimed at placing new superiors over Savonarola. Cardinal Carafa had by this time caved in, and yet another attack, this one bureaucratic, had been tailored to nullify and depose the Dominican friar.

---

[7] Unfortunately Prof. Martines has fallen for the standard tale that Giovanni Pico della Mirandola and Marsilio Ficino were sympathetic to Savonarola. It is true that they had the wit to pay lip service to him, as did Niccolo Machiavelli. However, these three men were polar opposites of all that for which Savonarola stood, which included his strong animus toward the occult as evidenced by his support for George of Trebizond's attack on Neoplatonism (cf. Hanegraaff, *Esotericism*, p. 79). Savonarola's guide was the Bible, against which he measured everything. No one has doubted his sincerity and no sincere conservative Bible interpreter could endorse Pico's occult synthesis of Christ and Kabbalah, or Ficino's amalgamation of magic and the doctrine of the Church.

[8] Martines, p. 137.

On May 12 (1497)...the pope (Alexander VI) issued his long-gestating breve of excommunication. His Holiness complained that a 'certain friar' Girolamo Savonarola of Ferrara of the Order of Preachers and at present so-called vicar of San Marco of Florence had continued to disseminate 'pernicious dogma' to the detriment of the Florentine people...On June 18, 1497, the order of excommunication arrived and was read out, with bell, book and candle, in five Florentine churches...Savonarola responded...'It is unreasonable to believe that we are obligated to obey our superiors in everything; rather we ought to be obedient to a superior only insofar as he represents God, but he who commands what is contrary to God does not represent God and is not our superior. So, it is not only just but necessary that he disobey the papal order...Marshaling opinions of theologians, jurists, papal decretals and decisions of church councils he demonstrates the limits of papal power, 'the power of the keys,' to impose an unjust sentence. When such a sentence is null, as in the present case, it is his duty to proclaim this publicly, come what may." [9]

The "most serious attacks on Savonarola and his supporters came from the pulpit and the pens of other friars." These included Franciscan Fr. Domenico da Ponzo, an agent of the Duke of Milan (Ludovico Sforza), and the monk Angelo de Vallombrosa who offered to strangle Savonarola with his bare hands. "In a letter to the friars of San Marco (11 July 1497), Vallombrosa denounces him as "the most bitter enemy and detractor of the clergy, prelates and the Roman See." Vallombrosa is "outraged by the heretical claim that the excommunication should not be obeyed because Alexander VI is alleged to be a simonist, not the true pope..." This Borgia pontiff was indeed a simonist: he had purchased his papal office. Furthermore, "Under Pope Alexander, cardinalships were sold for a minimum of 15,000 gold ducats; a few years later, the Medici Pope, Leo X, sold them for not less than 25,000 ducats..." [10]

Papist allegations against Savonarola ran the gamut from the laughable (that he had dared to advocate radical monastic poverty), to formidable, as issued by Girolamo Porcari, Bishop

---

[9] Weinstein, op. cit., p. 230.

[10] Martines, op. cit., pp. p. 161 and 286.

of Andria, governor in papal territory, and one of the twelve judges of the *Rota*, (the papal court). In his *Dialogus Tusci et Remi adversus Savonarolam*, Porcari asserted that to refuse to obey the pope results in damnation.

The machinery of papal usury, simony, sex depravity and corrupt bureaucracy was now engaged in arranging for the torture and execution of the Dominican friar who had interfered to so great an extent with the traditional rackets and occultism of the Florentine and Roman Catholic ruling class. In February, 1497, Pope Alexander admonished the priors in Florence to send Savonarola to Rome in chains. They demurred and merely demoted him from preaching in the huge Cathedral of Florence to the confines of the church of San Marco. At this time the reverence for Savonarola among the people of Florence was undiminished. His problems were entirely with the hierarchy of the Church and armed gangs dispatched by the entrenched gangsters, aristocrats, occultists and sodomites. For years it was necessary that Savonarola be accompanied by bodyguards to protect against the gangs. One such gang, the Compagnacci ("rowdy companions"), led by the Florentine nobleman [11] Doffo Spini, when they could not assault Savonarola's person, smeared excrement on the altar and pulpit of the Cathedral of Florence when he was regularly preaching and offering Mass. Spini was a frontman. Behind him were the Medici.

It is a testimony to the esteem of the grassroots for Savonarola that even under enormous pressure, both religious and political, from the pope and the elites, the Republican leaders of Florence withstood, as late as March 1497, the calls for his arrest. One motive for their loyalty to the Dominican reformer was their fear of civil war should he be seized. Another view, among the priors, was that Savonarola had not committed any heresy and was guilty of nothing more that fighting for a renewal of fidelity to Jesus Christ and His Gospel against entrenched pockets of corruption that led all the way to the Vatican.

Savonarola was not Luther. He held to the Mass and all Catholic dogma, but he believed that the papacy as it had devolved in the Renaissance, was predicated on blind faith in a

---

[11] Florentine noblemen had their own anti-Savonarola confederacy, loosely organized as the *Arrabbiati*.

mere man who happened to hold the Petrine office. If that man was leading souls to hell, did he have to be obeyed? What was the highest law of the Church, if not the salvation of souls?

"Savonarola had intensified his assault on Rome and the Curia in late February and March, not only by scorning the validity of the excommunication, but also by proposing and insisting that the men behind it were 'heretics'...He also hit out at Pope Alexander by introducing the example of a notorious earlier pontiff, the 'wicked pope' Boniface VIII (1294-1303), 'who began as a fox and died like a dog." [12] Boniface is noted for having reversed the safe haven Pope Celestine V had granted to the most faithful followers of St. Francis of Assisi, the so-called "*Fraticelli*" or "Spirituals." (*Fraticelli* later became a catch-all term for any far-out Catholic fraternity suspected of rigorist tendencies).

The papists see in Savonarola's defiance of the Borgia pope an unpardonable transgression that merited, or at least understandably led to, the fires to which he was eventually consigned. We define papism as the heresy of the ultramontane who place a man on a throne above the salvation of souls or the preaching of the truth. If Savonarola was justifiably killed for embracing the latter over the former there is no hope for anyone who seeks to live and act as Jesus did and who was killed for defying the "legitimate" religious authority of his time. The Protestant Reformation was a revolt that began in defiance of papalolatry and which might have been dampened had Savonarola been accorded a Gospel-standard and treated fairly.

Getting nowhere doctrinally, the pope and the curia now threatened the Signory of Florence with an interdiction on the goods of Florence which would obstruct their sale in Europe. The interdict would be tantamount to classifying the Republican leaders of Florence as outlaws, signifying that any force could pillage the city or kill them with impunity.

Not everything was perfect about Savonarola or his doctrines; he could be as fallible as the Borgia pope, or any man. His most grievous error was having accepted the Renaissance "Monte" system of gradual permission for low interest usury "on behalf of the poor," which had yet to gain

---

[12] Martines op. cit., p. 206.

papal approval (that would come in 1515), but which was in practice in banking redoubts like Florence. Because of this, among his staunchest supporters were the directors of this alleged "charity" bank, led by Lorenzo Lenzi.

Savonarola also allowed himself to be drawn into a theatrical tempting of God through "ordeal by fire," which he did not undergo and which turned the Florentine mob against him after four years of strong support from the people. The enemies of Savonarola were formidable politicians and intriguers. They appear to have persuaded Savonarola to engage in a primitive trial-by-fire initiated by the Franciscan friar Francesco di Puglia who offered to prove that Savonarola deserved to be excommunicated by walking through fire. He demanded that Savonarola walk with him to determine who would be burned and who would be spared. Savonarola would have none of it. Surely the devil, as well as God, had power to preserve his servants from flames.

But the prospect of such a fiery test was a spectacle too great for the pagan-minded of Florence and it became a highly anticipated contest and one the masses felt that Savonarola was certain to win. Because he would not participate, a proxy was appointed who would walk through the flames on his behalf. Savonarola should not have allowed this representation. It only instigated the large crowd massed in the Piazza della Signoria to a frenzy of impatience and near riot in the expectation of the vending of a miracle on demand.When heavy rain fell with lightning, and the fiery trial was canceled, the proceedings had approached the level of farce. Somehow the day's activities were spun so that Savonarola would take the blame for allegedly not allowing his proxy to walk into the non-existent flames (due to the rain, the fire had not been lit). The crazed masses had been cheated of their entertainment and through some still opaque process, Savonarola was charged with responsibility for the debacle and made the scapegoat. This was the first point at which his popularity began to wane. A mob formed and rampaged through the sectors filled with supporters of Savonarola. Some were killed. The aristocrat-led gangs besieged his San Marco monastery without fear of reprisal from the Republican government. Savonarola was taken on April 8, 1498.

The original transcripts of the trials of Savonarola in Florence were all "lost," even though Florentine and Roman officials and curia members were obsessive record-keepers. Years later an account was furnished by the Vatican without the transcripts. The account read like a Stalinist show trial and has little credibility. Savonarola's "confession" was patently scripted and out of character from his entire previous life, his sermons, writings and his speech patterns. "I did all for vain reasons" is a one-sentence distillation of the tenor of the doctored testimony. He was doomed and his verdict was decided ahead of time. Moreover, he was tortured, which was the way of many "Christians" in that age. Henceforth the propaganda machine of Rome and Florence would have its way with him. Florence has betrayed Dante. It was doing the same to Savonarola.[13]

Savonarola was imprisoned under harsh conditions in April and May, while Pope Alexander demanded he be taken to Rome. The city fathers of Florence offered a compromise, if they could control the public trial and confine the monk's execution to their own backyard they would give the pope a twenty percent cut of the new tax, the *Decima*, which they planned to impose on the clergy. The pope demanded twenty-five percent and then agreed to leave Savonarola in Florence. The torture of Savonarola proceeded through the third week in May. It had gone on for weeks and it appears that he lost his mind in the course of the prolonged and savage torment, including some types of homosexual molestation as performed on him by the Inquisitor Giovanni Manetti.[14]

On May 22, 1498 the now defrocked Girolamo Savonarola, together with his two friends, the defrocked monks Silvestro Maruffi and Domenico da Pescia, were hanged on a high gibbett in the government square. Their bodies were burned to ashes on the spot, to preclude the possibility of any relics being gathered, and the ashes were then thrown into the Arno River. Dozens of Savonarola's monks were exiled. Painted sheets falsely depicting Savonarola sodomizing children were circulated in the streets. The *Compagnacci* hung the fetid corpse of a donkey on the doors of Savonarola's Church of San Marco. The carnival float for St. John's Day (June 24) featured

---

[13] Martines, op. cit., p. 248.

[14] Ibid., p. 265. Martines undertakes an analysis of Savonarola's reported testimony which undercuts the credibility of his trials (Martines, pp. 266-273).

a pig as a stand-in for "that pig of a friar," Savonarola. His leading followers were beaten, fined or both.

One of the chief heresiarchs of the Neoplatonic-Hermetic fraternity gloated over Savonarola's death. The Medici's creature, Rev. Fr. "Marsilio Ficino explained that it was no ordinary human hypocrite who had deceived the Florentines, but an astute demon, servant of malicious astral forces— Antichrist himself," [15] —i.e. "*ab Antichristo Hieronymo Ferrariense hypocritarum.*"

The trial of Galileo and the burning of Giordano Bruno have been seared into the collective historical memory of the world, while Girolamo Savonarola's memory has been reduced to a tawdry cartoon: a bigoted friar inciting the masses to an irrational puritanical frenzy which left the pope no choice other than to take punitive action against him. It's like a slogan from Orwell's *Animal Farm*: repression of Savonarola good; repression of Bruno bad. Martin Luther was fifteen-years-of-age when Savonarola was burned. John Calvin would not be born for another eleven years. Together they would take Savonarola's rage at the occupant of the papal institution to another level. Savonarola had believed that French King Charles VIII's invasion of Italy was a heaven-sent scourge of a corrupt land. One wonders whether he would have regarded the rise of the *Protesting* Catholics in a similar light.

Papists will say that Luther and Calvin went too far and in certain respects that is true. They threw the proverbial baby out with the bathwater. But consider this: after Savonarola was deposed, degraded, libeled, show-tried, tortured and hanged, and his "heresy" with him, sodomy returned to Florence after having been throughly suppressed for the four years the monk held sway over the city. There was nowhere near any campaign against sodomy in Florence by the pope and his minions to match in energy or ferocity the campaign against Savonarola. Obviously, he was judged the greater threat by far. "Savonarola's fight against the practice of anal intercourse was directed against compliant women as well. He knew that this vice was honored in marriage as well as in female prostitution. Homosexual males held no monopoly. Florence's reputation for sodomy was so widespread in the Germany of that day, that to sodomize 'was popularly dubbed

---

florenzen, and a sodomite a *Florenzer.* Savonarola reacted by insisting, in a number of his sermons, that sodomites deserved to be stoned or burned alive in public. He was a Biblicist, determined to keep the strict letter of the Bible, and his inspiration was the Old Testament's horror of sodomy. The act in question, in seeking sexual pleasure as a thing frankly divorced from the will to procreate, seemed to sum up carnal debauchery." [16]

Savonarola regarded "sacred scripture as the sole, exclusive and absolutely infallible source of true knowledge: the certainty given to absolute faith in the Bible...See the opening sentences of Savonarola's treatise against astrology: [17]

"The foundation of Christian religion is the sacred Scripture of the New and Old Testament, which we are obliged to believe down to the smallest iota, and we must approve all that it approves, and disapprove of all that it disapproves of, since it is made by God, who cannot err." [18]

Some Catholics will aver that Savonarola was skating dangerously close to the thin ice of the Protestant tenet of *sola Scriptura* (the Bible only). In fact, he was on the solid ground of Catholic theology from Apostolic times onward: no church doctrine, canon, pronouncement or practice can contradict the Bible.

One legacy of the suppression of the Church's most indefatigable foe of anal intercourse is the fact that permission for rectal sex entered the official theology of the Catholic Church. One of its leading theologians, Rev. Dr. Father Heribert Jone, O.F.M, Cap., J.C.D., in his 1929 manual, *Moral Theology*, which was reprinted seventeen times in German and English, ruled directly contrary to Savonarola concerning a husband sodomizing his wife: "...it is neither sodomy nor a grave sin if intercourse is begun in a rectal manner with the

---

[16] Martines. op. cit., p. 284.

[17] *Trattato contra li astrologi I, I,* in *Savonarola, Scritti filosofici,* vol. 1, p. 278.

[18] Hanegraaff, *Esotericism* (op.cit.), p. 81.

intention of consummating it naturally, or if some sodomitical action is posited without danger of pollution." [19]

Aftermath

"Some preachers stirred the apocalyptic cauldron, claiming a share of Savonarola's prophetic and charismatic gifts. Martino di Brozzi, ragged, self-styled holy madman, appeared in Florence at the end of 1500 to declare that the killing of Savonarola proved that Florence and Rome were about to be scourged...He was imprisoned....To possess Savonarola's writings was a criminal offense. His books were to be surrendered, confiscated, destroyed...San Marco and its allied houses were enjoined from conducting services and ceremonies in honor of the three martyrs or from singing *Ecce Quam Bonus* (which was) Fra Girolamo's favorite psalm."

In the city-state of Florence, still a Republic in keeping with Savonarola's reform, his surviving "devotees resumed their campaigns for moral and political renewal...(and) their determination to prevent the return of the Medici...To achieve these objectives as well as to protect it against the continuing hostility of the papacy and the Holy League, Florence needed political unity, and this favored the continuation of the *governo civile* and Great Council with its indelible Savonarolan imprint...In 1502 the Great Council voted to make the Gonfaloniere of Justice a lifetime office and elected Piero Soderini, brother of Paolantonio, Savornarola's old political ally and mentor. Piero...promoted many Savonarolan goals.

"...Florence regained Pisa through its own initiative. Backed by (Savonarolan) Gonfaloniere Soderini, Niccoló Machiavelli, secretary of the Ten, was able to create a citizen militia and reduce the city's dependence on foreign *condottieri* of uncertain loyalty. The new model army was part of the force that laid siege to Pisa and took its surrender in June 1509.

"...In August of 1512 soldiers of the Spanish viceroy in the service of Pope Julius and Cardinal Giovanni de' Medici seized

---

[19] Heribert Jone, *Moral Theology* (Tan Books and Publishers, 1993), p. 539. This pervert goes on to decree that a husband having intercourse while his wife is menstruating, while not recommended, is not morally objectionable (p. 535). Catholics enslaved to a hierarchy that pushes this sewage rather than the Word of God will suffer in body, mind and soul. Jone's highly touted *Moral Theology* bears imprimaturs and was published in nine languages by Catholic publishers over many decades.

the town of Prato, a few miles from Florence, sacked it and killed hundreds of its (Catholic) inhabitants. When the Florentines learned that six thousand Spanish troops were on their way to the city, they abandoned all thought of resistance. Soderini fled. Cardinal Giovanni de' Medici and other members of his family returned to the city as conquerors. They enlisted the support of leading citizens (many former republicans now becoming good Mediceans); convened a *Parlamento,* which appointed a *balia,* or civic commission, and proceeded to demolish the key (Republican) institutions of the intervening two decades. Great Council and Council of Eighty were no more. They dissolved the militia (for his involvement in the Soderini government Machiavelli was imprisoned and tortured) and trashed the Great Hall of Five Hundred, symbol of the Savonarolan *governo civile.* Florence would now be ruled from Rome by ministers of Cardinal Giovanni, soon to be elected Pope Leo X (1513-1521).

"While Soderini and his allies had been trying to save the popular republic, (the) Piagnoni (group) kept Savonarola's apocalyptic teachings alive. San Marco friars spread the word locally and their exiled brothers were making fresh converts in outlying Dominican houses and lay circles in Tuscany and beyond. Those teachings were received and interpreted in various ways. Some grasped the essential unity of Savonarola's prophetic apostolate in which he fused Christian living *(il ben vivere)*...republican government and civic apotheosis in a single glorious vision." [20]

Florence would lurch back and forth between a Savonarola-like republic and a Medici tyranny until another Medici Pope, Clement VII, imprisoned or killed the last of the Piagnoni friars and Medici rule was definitively imposed over Florence.

Pico

It is necessary that we return to the *vita* of Giovanni Pico della Mirandola, to address tall tales about his "persecution" by the Church and the papacy, his "imprisonment" and his "friendship" with Savonarola. These tales are shot through with the thick veils of misdirection which accompany the accounts of the lives of many of the Neoplatonic-Hermetic

---

[20] Weinstein, op. cit., pp. 298-302.

conspirators. The story *behind* the story of poor, pitiful Pico's imprisonment by the "Inqusition" due to "his writings" is one such case of occult propaganda. In May, 1486 in Arezzo, Pico made off with the wife of a low ranking Medici official, the tax collector Giuliano Mariotto de' Medici, who pursued his bride and Pico to the border with Siena. A fight ensued and men in Pico's large contingent of bodyguards were injured and slain. Pico was locked up in the Arezzo prison and the woman was restored to her husband. None of this had anything to do with heresy, the Church or the Inquisition, and as usual Pico had a golden parachute. Lorenzo de' Medici, putting Pico's interests ahead of his kinsman Giuliano, obtained Pico's release.

Then in January, 1488, near Lyons, France, to placate conservative Catholics, a charade was arranged for their benefit: Pico underwent a farcical arrest and imprisonment in Vincennes, "by order of the pope." Upholders of the notion that the Church of Rome was hot on the heels of the heretic Pico conclude the narrative at this point. They omit the following fact concerning his quick release: "Influential admirers and supporters set diplomatic wheels in motion and won his release. Among them was Lorenzo de' Medici," in whose villa at Fieole, Pico took up residence, allegedly in great piety and observing strictest continence (but actually in the company of his concubine). [21]

Tales of Giovanni Pico's supposed "friendship" with the anti-Medici Savonarola, of his collaboration with Savonarola on anti-astrological treatises, and alleged desire to take the Dominican habit shortly before his death from natural causes, [22] mostly emanate from Pico's nephew Ginafrancesco, the enigmatic mover and shaker who attached himself to Savonarola as a disciple, but who was likely a spy charged with keeping an eye on the reformer while cleansing his Uncle Pico's legacy of its more extreme occult associations.

After Giovanni Pico's death, Savonarola prayed for the soul of Pico and mercifully opined that he was in purgatory rather than hell. The notion that Pico the sexual libertine and Kabbalist who made no public recantation or repentance for either of these transgressions, was a devout and sincere

---

[21] Ibid., pp. 70-71.

[22] Ibid., pp. 141-142.

convert to Savonarola's Catholic orthodoxy, is untenable. Giovanni Sinibaldi, one of the inner circle at Savonarola's San Marco monastery, wrote that Pico was deceiving Savonarola. Sinibaldi claimed that while volunteering to submit to Savonarola's regimen of severe ascesticism, Pico was keeping a prostitute on the sly. [23]

What we know for certain about Savonarola undercuts all the legends of him lending support to Pico's views. The monk's relentless "disparagement of humanist intellectuals who were more Platonic than Christian" [24] puts paid to the myth that there was some sort of alliance between the two. Fraternal relations, such as they were, could be maintained only through the pagan Pico's occult traits of shameless hypocrisy and masquerade: "From the humanist Crinito we have the idyllic story that when Pico smiled indulgently at Savonarola's denunciation of the pagan philosophers, the *Frate* (Savonarola) embraced and saluted him as the most learned philosopher and expert on Christianity of the age." [25]

"The portraits of the later Pico drawn even by avid *piagnoni* (friends of Savonarola)...more often remind us of the bold magician-priest of the nine hundred theses who was literally prepared to marry the world,' than of the self-effacing Christian of his nephew's *Vita*, where we find the humble (and even self-flagellating) Pico vowing to wander barefoot preaching the simple word of Christ once his current literary projects were complete. Suggestions, in fact, exist of serious conflict between Pico and Savonarola..." [26]

---

[23] Ibid., p. 143.

[24] Ibid., p. 144.

[25] Ibid., p. 142.

[26] Farmer, op.cit., pp. 150-151.

Chapter VII

The Sorcerer Abbott

The Catholic occultist, cryptographer and Benedictine Abbot Johannes Trithemius (1462-1516) was born Johann Heidenberg in Trittenheim, Germany on the banks of the river Mosel, near Trier. In the early 1480s he met his first handler, "an unnamed Jew" he had worked under while studying at the University of Heidelberg. Soon afterward he joined the Benedictine order and from the precocious age of twenty-one he headed the Benedictine monastery of Sponheim in the Palatinate for the succeeding twenty-three years, and became renowned throughout Europe. Was he named abbot at such a young age solely due to his merit, or was his career being guided by the Cryptocracy, thanks to his handler? Sponheim was a wealthy monastery with a fabulous library of some 2,000 volumes of arcana, almost too perfectly suited to the requirements of Trithemius to have been a coincidence.

In 1499 his occult Catholicism was discovered and controversy erupted among the Carmelites of Ghent over his book of black magic and cryptography, *Steganographia*. (The title refers to his favored technique of composing secret messages delivered by demonic spirits). Later the French Catholic scholar Carolus Bovillus joined the fray on the side of orthodox Catholicism and in correspondence termed Abbot Trithemius a demonic magician.

In 1505 Trithemius departed Sponheim and its extraordinary library. In 1506 he assumed the leadership of the monastery of St. Jacob of Würzburg. Besides *Steganographia* he authored three other cardinal occult works: *De daemonibus*; *Antipalus maleficiorum;* and *De septem secundeis*; and at least one exclusively devoted to cryptography, *Polygraphia*.

"Trithemius was at one with the circle of literary figures he had befriended at Heidelberg before his arrival at Sponheim, a number of whom, headed up by the gifted poet Conrad Celtis, later formed themselves, with the departed Trithemius included, into a kind of academy modeled after the Florentine Platonist circle of Marsilio Ficino and Pico della Mirandola. The humanists comprising this so-called *sodalitas literaria*

Rhenana generally met on an informal basis in the house of the Heidelberg jurist Johannes Vigilius (Wacker), and in addition to Celtis included such foremost luminaries of the German renaissance as Rudolf Agricola (before his premature death in 1486), Johannes de Dalberg (the Bishop of Worms), Johannes Reuchlin and Johannes Wimpheling.

"...We are able to pinpoint the exact year in which the legend of Trithemius the magician began because, by Trithemius' own account, we can specify the precise event which put this legend into motion. The responsible party, as it happened, was not some hostile antagonist anxious to malign his good name with rumors of demon-conjuration and the like, but Trithemius himself, who in 1499 addressed a letter to his good friend Arnold Bostius, a Carmelite monk of Ghent in modern Belgium, summarizing the contents of a handbook the abbot had recently commenced and was furiously attempting to complete as quickly as possible. The subject of the handbook was steganography, that is, the art of writing secret messages and communicating them long distances by occult means.

"...Regardless of whether Trithemius' readers were in basic sympathy with the abbot's audacious extension of the concept *artes liberales* to include occult subjects like that of steganography, they could not but marvel at the great impact Trithemius was having upon the learned and powerful of Europe simultaneously with the proliferation of his magical legend." [1]

Among these "learned and powerful" Catholics were Rutger Sicamber de Venray of the Augustinian monastery of Heyna; the Carmelite Johannes Evriponus, Robert Gaguin, Superior-General of the Order of Trinitarians; Dietrich von Bülow, the Bishop of Lebus; Count Philip, the Duke of Bavaria; Matthäus Herbenus, Rector of St. Servatius in Maastricht; Werner von Themar; Dietrich Gresemund the Younger; the Margrave Christopher of Baden; the Margrave-Elector Joachim of Brandenburg; the Dutch Canon Cornelius Aurelius, along with other assorted "princes, prelates, nobles and magistrates" and, in 1512, one Holy Roman Emperor — Maximilian — who studied under Trithemius when the latter became the Abbot of the monastery in Würzburg.

---

[1] Noël L. Brann, *The Abbot Trithemius (1462-1516): The Renaissance of Monastic Humanism* (1981), pp.15, 18-19.

During "Margrave Christopher of Baden's visit in the same year...it is made plain that the principal cause of his attraction to Sponheim was the abbot's specialized knowledge in the occult studies...the Margrave entered Trithemius' cloistered walls ostensibly with the purpose of 'seeing the library,' but at the same time as he was perusing the abbot's books 'added to his knowledge and cognition certain arcana in the pursuit of which he had summoned Trithemius to his castle at Lutzenburg the year before'...within two years he returned 'to see and speak with the abbot Trithemius, with whom he discussed and shared certain secrets in the hidden mysteries of nature (*in abditis naturae mysteriis quaedam secreta*)." [2]

Trithemius swung between two poles of neo-Catholic Renaissance magic: the white or "natural" magic of Ficino and Pico, and black magic which Trithemius utilized in an exceedingly circumspect manner, as for example in his *Synusiastes Melanii Triandrici ad Yaymielem,* a private treatise he prepared for his wealthy but impotent client, "Joachim," which advised the invocation of demons. The *Synusiastes,* printed posthumously in the *Paralipomena,* eventually was acquired by Heinrich Khunrath [3] (1560-1605). *Synusiastes* was censored in parts by Busaeus, and uncensored editions are very scarce but can be found in the *Antipalus* manuscript in the archives of Cornell University. [4]

---

[2] Ibid., pp. 27-28.

[3] Heinrich Kunrath of Leipzig, author of *The Amphitheatre of Eternal Wisdom*. He is described "as 'one of the most remarkable theosophists and alchemists of the late sixteenth century,' and 'one of the greatest Hermetic philosophers...'" (Forshaw, p. 108). Kunrath was another heir of the Ficino-Pico-Reuchlin contagion by way of Paracelsus. His critic, the Lutheran physician and chemist Dr. Andreas Libavius of the University of Jena, correctly identified the ideology of Paracelsus and followers like Kunrath, as being predicated on "the search for power by summoning of evil spirits" (Allen G. Debus, *The French Paracelsians,* [1991], p. 61). Libavius was that rare breed: a practitioner of alchemy who "objected strongly to the introduction of mysticism and the occult into the sciences," and to the opposite extreme: inquisitorial mentalities such as Jean Riolan the Elder (1539-1605); Censor of the Parisian Medical Faculty and a leading physician and anatomist, who suspected most any science, however thoroughly rational, of being infected by the black arts. Jean Riolan the Younger was court physician to the Queen Mother of France, Marie de' Medici, and an opponent of William Harvey. Riolan *pere* and *fils* were Galenists.

[4] Stuttgart, Staats-und Stadbibliothek, Codex in Folio 212 (Peutinger), ff. 118r-130v, 236r-245r, codex M 61. ff. n.n.

Trithemius was defended by his Catholic confrére, the monk Johannes Butzbach, who compared him to St. Albertus Magnus, Dominican Prior of Teutonia (1254-1257) and the teacher of Aquinas. Butzbach deceptively described Trithemius in terms of a benevolent, Catholic white magic, which excluded demonic black magic. This, as we have seen, was not true:

"...in this book he (Trithemius) deals with natural magic; he teaches with extreme elegance with the strongest arguments and a multitude of testimonies as did recently the erudite Pico that this magic is different and has to be distinguished from the magic which is impious and criminal. Indeed, no person who has read Pico's *Apologia* could be in doubt that 'magic is twofold;' as the author says, the one is concerned with the entire work and authority of the demons, a practice most certainly abominable and unnatural. The other is, when correctly examined, nothing but the absolute perfection of natural philosophy.

"...Agrippa (Trithemius' disciple), then in his early twenties, showed in 1510 the first manuscript draft of his *De occulta philosophia* to Trithemius. Both were attached to Johannes Reuchlin and they had a frank discussion...in regard to a good many secrets and the 'two ways' of magic. The abbot urged him not to stop at the mere natural magic...but to probe under the veil of initiation into the prodigies of magical practice." [5]

It is seldom that we have a clear admission from one of the significant infiltrators inside the Church concerning the two-faced strategy of deception which was one of their tools for duping the public. "...what interests us in this document is Trithemius's instigation to double-dealing; he revealed this attitude only to the few disciples who had arrived at the final initiation. Certainly also, Trithemius's game with magic and witchcraft amounts to double-dealing. In his form of magic, the aspect of ceremonial magic is present; indeed it is prevalent. In the *Steganographia*...there is to be found, apart from a strange cryptography, spiritual magic of the cabalistic type. His letters to Joachim von Brandenburg, beside the one to Agrippa...leave little room for doubt; and yet Trithemius wrote three works against witches who engage in the same practices.

---

[5] Paola Zambelli, *White Magic, Black Magic* (2007), pp. 53-54.

"(Trithemius) advised (Cornelius) Agrippa over his decision whether to present his work *De occulta philosophia* (and the hermetic tradition that lay behind it) openly, or in secret, i.e. through a circle of initiates. It is very remarkable in this context that Trithemius, a prelate, advised Agrippa, a layman, to keep an initiatic attitude.

"...All this leads me to believe that in his maturity Trithemius had not forsworn that *'Reformatio hermetica'* which Noël L. Brann, his recent biographer, has read into his letter of 1499 to Arnold Bost ('Bostius')...I cannot...trace a change in Trithemius's attitude toward the Hermetic conception..." [6]

One of his chief areas of study and expertise was cryptography, and more than mere codes and ciphers, masked language understood only by the initiated. This was a practice of Plethon, Ficino, Giovanni Pico, and Reuchlin as well. (The latter personage Bishop Trithemius had met on more than one occasion.) It took the form of hypocritical double-talk laden with Catholic pieties, along with an esoteric language for communicating actual arcana to insiders. It should be noted that when time and place were auspicious, concealment was abandoned and the occult doctrine was communicated in public with revelatory potency, most often in the form of Catholic works of art executed by initiates. Trithemius has the distinction of having combined the occult orientation toward extreme secrecy with an intermittent inclination toward a stratagem of the Cryptocracy in the 20th century, dispensing with the customary dissimulation in favor of the Revelation of the Method (making manifest of what is concealed by the one who initially concealed it).[7] These episodes of conceal-and-then-reveal (the "cryonic freeze-thaw process" denoted by James Shelby Downard), are a mark of the magical praxis of Trithemius. He was preoccupied both with secrecy and with making proclamations of secrets. There is a mocking trickster aspect to this phenomenon.

"Trithemius was a notorious follower of the magical sciences. He had unashamedly maintained that ceremonial practices were indispensable in magic and had criticized those

---

[6] Paola Zambelli, ibid., pp. 60-61; 69; 74.

[7] As analyzed in this writer's *Secret Societies and Psychological Warfare* (2001).

who, following Ficino and Pico, claimed not to go beyond 'natural' magic. He kept in manuscript form most of his magical works, sharing them only with a close circle of initiates; some of these writings were published many decades after his death, others are to this day unpublished..." [8]

Abbot Trithemius, like nearly every Catholic occultist examined in these pages, was a liar and extraordinarily dishonest. He was known to produce occult forgeries and imaginary sages ("Pelagius of Majorca") and colleagues ("Libanius Gallus"). Among contemporary Orthodox Catholics he had a reputation for presenting fables as history (*"Ego non pro historico, sed fabulatore omnium falsissimo reputo"*). Among "experts" of our time he is however, reputed to be an eminent humanist. Though today most Establishment historians and academics imagine that "Pelagius of Majorca" was an actual historical figure, in the time of Trithemius the name was tangentially associated, at least among those "in the know," with fraud: Francesco Zambeccari's 1504 translation of a version of the letters of the early Church heretic Pelagius [9] compiled by a certain "Libanius,"[10] was somewhat notorious for containing more than a hundred of the epistles attributed to Pelagius that had been faked by the translator. In terms of cryptography, which too often we associate with numbers rather than conjuring misdirection by means of written words and patter, the mission to deceive is assisted by a sophisticated process of intentional signaling to the percipient that he or she is being deceived, within a context of a macabre joke at their expense. Cryptography like this constitutes psychological warfare. The conjuration by Trithemius of "Pelagius of Majorca" and "Libanius" may have been toward that objective. If so, it affords us insight into the methods—born from a

---

[8] Zambelli, p. 75.

[9] The original Pelagius was an actual person and originator of what has come to be known as the "Pelagian heresy" through his commentary on St. Paul. Cf. Thomas P. Scheck, "Pelagius's Interpretation of Romans" in *A Companion to St. Paul in the Middle Ages* (2013); and Dominic Keech, *The Anti-Pelagian Christology of Augustine of Hippo, 396-430* (2012).

[10] "From Cracow in Poland we get as early as 1504 a Libanius: *Epistolae* translated from the Greek by the Italian humanist Francesco Zambeccari...This Libanius is printed for the Cracow publisher Jo. Haller by one Joannes Clymes, who is never heard of again..." (E.P. Goldschmidt, *The First Cambridge Press in its European Setting* [1955], p. 45).

mentality steeped in profound deception—by which the "Catholic" Neoplatonists, Hermeticists and Kabbalists plied their infiltration of the Church.

The historical record is replete with the chicanery of these scoundrels. Giovanni Pico's Judaic handler, Guglielmo Raimondo Moncada (alias "Flavius Mithridates"), took the anti-Christian Kabbalistic teaching that declared that the passage in Deuteronomy 31:16 about "playing the harlot" alludes to the Blessed Virgin Mary, and turned this Kabbalistic statement completely around, boldly misrepresenting it as "a Kabbalistic confirmation of Christianity...Mithridates' skillful presentation of what he wanted Pico to believe, was the input for Pico's original 'experiment with the principles' and stands at the origin of the Christian Kabbalah. This unique constellation was going to have far-reaching consequences...for the standard argument used later by Christian Kabbalists in order to defend the legitimacy and the usefulness of their 'discovery' for a Christian readership... " [11]

Shameless liars like Moncada/Mithridates and his theological heirs, such as Johannes Reuchlin and other Renaissance-Catholic intellectuals, are the rule, not the exception in the occult Church of Rome. Non-conspirators among the Christian public not privy to initiation in the conspiracy were viewed as cattle, beasts of burden and wicked persons. This was how the Pharisees of Christ's time viewed the common Israelites who flocked to His message: deadbeats and evil-doers.

Students of this subject who take at face value statements of popes, "pope-saints," and other "Lord Bishops" and high churchmen are going to get quickly lost in coils of delusion, because any underhanded deception, no matter how low or unscrupulous, is justified in the eyes of the occultists, due to their view of the nearly sub-human status of the common people. In a longer preface to *Steganographia* printed posthumously, Abbot-Bishop Trithemius wrote, "Ancient philosophers, masters in art as well as in nature, when they discovered secrets, concealed them in various ways and figures, to avoid that they might become known to the wicked."

---

[11] Cf. Saverio Campanini, "Talmud, Philosophy and Kabbalah: A Passage from Pico della Mirandola's *Apologia* and its Source," in *The Words of a Wise Man's Mouth are Gracious*, Mauro Perani, ed. (2005), pp. 444 and 447.

The "wicked" to whom Abbot-Bishop Trithemius is pointing are the parishioners and parish priests; that is to say, the vast majority of the people known as Roman Catholics. "*Ineffabilium mysteriorum secreta*" and the "steganographic" craft must be concealed from the "evil" public according to the occult rationale which itself stems from Kabbalistic-Talmudic Judaism.

Inside the Church, secrets are to be guarded by distraction, coded language and doubletalk, of which Trithemius was the professor. Almost nothing about the occult is to be stated in a straight-forward manner. "Magic and all its ceremonies could not fail to attract a man like Trithemius, with his love of prophecies and propaganda, games and forgeries, who put his vast culture at their service. The authenticity or pseudoepigraphy of magical treatises are thus a key which Trithemius used purely and simply to confer prestige and authority on the doctrines they contained and which he simply attributed or denied to their reputed authors. This too was a game that the great humanist played, to the detriment of less cultured or more naive men, like Joachim of Brandenburg. If Trithemius forged the genealogy of the Hapsburgs, if he did not hesitate to write pseudoepigraphic sources, this was all the more reason why he felt entitled to do the same with magical treatises and the sacred figures of their authors. We need not be surprised at this if we remember that even a great philologist like Erasmus did not hesitate to forge and put into circulation a treatise on martyrdom which he attributed to one of the Fathers of the Church in order to send out a metaphorical religious message." [12]

Very ignorant "students of the occult," as it manifested in the "inquisitorial" Church of Rome have been given the opportunity, by Trithemius himself, of claiming him as a witch-hunter who was a conservative defender of the genuine doctrine of the Church. It doesn't occur to them that his writings that buttressed the belief that witch-hunts were justified were a smokescreen for advancing his principal objective, the reconciliation of sorcery and magic with Catholic theology. Behind the front of a witch-hunter was a witch-advocate; this is too much for some people to countenance.

---

[12] Zambelli, op. cit., p. 100.

Nonetheless, the evidence demonstrates that he penned for public consumption *Antipalus maleficiorum* and *Liber octo quaestionum*, as well as *De morbo caduco et maleficiis*—all of these being works *against witchcraft*, while clandestinely, for the Neoplatonic-Hermetic brotherhood inside the Church, he wrote *apologetics for magic*—*Nepiachus, Polygraphia* and in particular his *De Septem secundeis,* which entailed Kabbalistic magic.

Shakespeare deals with this phenomenon in Macbeth: "What, can the devil speak true?...'tis strange, and oftentimes to win us to our harm the instruments of darkness tell us truths, win us with honest trifles—to betray us in deepest consequence." [13]

In the summer of 2016, one of the leaders of Britain's "traditional" Catholics, who is at the same time an apologist for the Talmud, became the spokesman [14] for a group of prominent Church of Rome conservative laity and religious, who signed a theological critique [15] of the "apostolic exhortation" *Amoris laetitia* of Pope Francis, requesting that the pope condemn certain liberal propositions contained within it and warning of its "dangers to the faith."

The notion that the occult is always on the Left is disinformation emanating from the Cryptocracy. We have found in virtually every history of the Renaissance Vatican by an author or authors who can accurately be described as Leftist or New Age, a remarkably conforming insistence that the Vatican and the popes were nearly always a reactionary bulwark against all magic, Kabbalism and Neoplatonic Hermeticism. These Leftist and New Age writers often parrot, nearly verbatim, pre-1960s Right wing papal and Vatican statements to the effect that the Church of Rome has always stood against, and restricted and severely repressed, the occult. On the Right, the conservatives and traditionalists are nearly totally blind to Talmudic and occult infiltration of their ranks. They can't seem to process Shakespeare's explanation of occult

---

[13] Banquo in dialogue with Macbeth, Act 1, Scene, 3: 105 and 120-124.

[14] http://rorate-caeli.blogspot.com/2016/07/appeal-to-cardinals-text-revealed.html

[15] http://2n613ar7ekr056c3upq2s15c.wpengine.netdna-cdn.com/wp-content/uploads/2016/07/45-theologians-censure-AL.pdf

methodology. It doesn't occur to them that "Catholics" who go about promoting Mary, the Rosary and the Latin Mass, and who organize against the liberalization of marriage and family law put forth by Pope Francis ("*Amoris laetitia*"), could be part of the occult imperium.

After the death of Abbot Trithemius, his occult works (*Nepiachus, Polygraphia* and *De Septem secundeis*), began to circulate more widely inside the hierarchy of the Church of Rome as the program they put forth became ever more secretly influential: a Catholic rationale for occultism rooted in the insistence that magic was a divinely sanctified—if necessarily covert—branch of Catholic theology. This arcane doctrine held that the world's most accomplished magician was the priest at Mass, and the foremost magical act in all of the occult was the transformation of ordinary bread and wine into the literal flesh and blood of God Himself, as effectuated by the priest-magician, who was to be esoterically revered as such.

Abbot Trithemius and virtually every other Church of Rome occultist cited in these pages established the priest as magician to draw the faithful away from Scriptural standards of behavior without which the the Kingdom of Yahweh on earth (Matthew 6:10) cannot come about. At the center of the "magical" Catholicism of the Neoplatonic-Hermetic conspirators is the depiction of Jesus as a practitioner of "white" magic, which is precipitously close to the rabbinic disparagement of Him as someone who learned sorcery in Egypt and led Israel astray by means of it. The Neoplatonic-Hermetic theology presents a series of "good" magicians who used "benevolent magic": Hermes, Pythagoras and Jesus. In the third century A.D. Porphyry the Neoplatonist put forth the notion, rejected by St. Augustine, that to successfully create "white magic" the magician had to be a holy person. Neoplatonic-Hermetic Catholics teach that non-Judaics can share in Jewish magical power through the Catholic priesthood:

"While recently visiting in Rome, Reuchlin reported in his Cabalistically inspired *De verbo mirifico*, Pico had proposed to him 'that no names in magical and lawful enterprises possess a virtue equal to that residing in the Hebrew tongue or languages most nearly derived from it.' The reason, Pico instructed Reuchlin, is that at the beginning of creation all the names given to existent entities 'were formed from the Voice of God; therefore that in which nature exercises its most potent magic is the Voice of God.' This was not to say, however, Pico further apprised Reuchlin, the Jews were granted an exclusive monopoly in this regard. Also granted access to the secrets of Cabala were certain specially prepared gentiles. Admittedly, the case for this contention was made harder by the appearance of magical counterfeiters in the ranks of the gentiles; when these pretend to effect miracles, Reuchlin agreed, 'it proves to be an illusion (*praestgium*) rather than a true miracle, and takes place not with the help of God, but by a pact with demons." [16]

So what was the true miracle in the eyes of these occultists? The Catholic Mass. Conservative and traditional Catholics ought to be on high alert against this misuse of the Mass, but mostly they are not. They have been indoctrinated to believe that threats come only from the Left, as well as from "Protestant-leveling and reductionism." Much of the occult is Right-wing, however: addicted to the courtly theatre of showmanship, elaborate ceremony and costume. Trithemius personified those prelates who were steeped in the occult and engaged in hunting those persons *who would not submit to them and were labeled witches and heretics*, while reserving to themselves and their court the practice of magic, which was conflated with divine miracles, thus expunging the dividing line between miracle and magic which had existed since the days of Moses and Aaron's battle with the priests of Egypt, and which had been precisely and solemnly demarcated by Augustine and Aquinas.

"Trithemius's demonology throws valuable light on what he was about in his own magic. For while expressly rejecting demonic magic out-of-hand, even showing a willingness to send its perpetrators to the stake, he implied at the same time that angels, with whom pious Christians seek both approximation and similarity, can legitimately be invoked to produce results foreclosed to demons." [17]

---

[16] Noel L. Brann, *Trithemius and Magical Demonology*, p. 30.

[17] Ibid., p. 83.

"Echoing the noble sentiments of another great magician of his age who had played a part, if indirectly, in Trithemius's occult education, Pico della Mirandola, Agrippa passionately proclaimed in his *De triplici ratione cognoscendi Dei*: 'O what a great miracle is man, especially he who is a Christian' (*O magnum miraculum homo, praecipue autem Christianus*). Expanding on the Christianized reworking of a Hermetic theme, Agrippa characterized the said *miraculum Christianum* as he 'who has been established in the world, dominates over the world and effects operations resembling those of the world's creator.' The marvelous operations (*opera*) performed by such Christians, declared Agrippa, 'are popularly termed miracles, of which the root and foundation is faith in Jesus Christ." [18]

The proclamation of a "Jesus-the-Magician" trope is the culmination of the Neoplatonic-Hermetic conspiracy inside the Church of Rome.

Abbot Trithemius largely escaped interdiction during his lifetime by his Catholic superiors or any sort of "inquisition." He was largely free to rule over monasteries and write and publish books of "Catholic magic." After his death, "on the heels of a generally favorable treatment of the abbot's monastic career, Bellarmine felt compelled at last to give fair warning against two of his writings, the *De septem secundeis* and *Steganographia*, which he correctly perceived to be related through their sharing of an angelic-planetary overview." Bellarmine's criticism was comparatively mild and he salvaged Trithemius' reputation by means of a lie: "Bellarmine claimed, with not an iota of evidence to back up his contention, that their author Trithemius had already started the process for a return to the protective arms of the church by having realized the error of his ways." [19]

Numerous Catholic Neoplatonist-Hermeticists would build upon Trithemius, just as he had constructed his theology upon Ficino, Giovanni Pico and Reuchlin. Among these would be Francesco Giorgi, a Venetian Franciscan theologian who "pointed the way to this conciliating potential of magic, by calling on a mix of Neoplatonism, Hermeticism, Cabala, and orthodox Catholic doctrine to produce what he termed, in his

---

[18] Ibid., p. 155.

[19] Ibid., p. 173.

De harmonia mundi, 'a man well-harmonized with God' (*homo bene chordatus cum Deo*).

"With the same conciliatory function of magic in mind...Francesco Patrizi da Cherso (1529-1597) declared: 'The first and most excellent part of magic is nothing else but theology and religion, and if it is not completely true, as the truth subsequently has been revealed by Christ, it nevertheless approaches more closely to that truth than all other studies.' Patrizi's aspiration in this writing was to enlist the *Hermetica,* together with other surviving texts of the so-called *prisca theologi,* in support of universalist-minded Catholic reform movement...In making his appeal to a *reformatio magica,* Patrizi recommended to Pope Gregory XIV, in the dedicatory preface to his *Nova de universis philosophia* (1591), that the hierarchical church vest the program of magical renewal in the Society of Jesus (Jesuits) as its most suitable vehicle." [20]

In 1608 a former member of the Jesuit order, Johann Cambilhon, charged the Jesuits with promoting the occult. His charge was given currency by the fact that numerous books of "Catholic magic" remained in print in Catholic countries and not listed on the Vatican's Index of Prohibited Books. Cambilhon's accusation led to the papacy placing Trithemius' book *Steganographia* on the Index the next year. Trithemius had been dead for 94 years during which time his *Steganographia* had circulated freely. Protestants amplified Cambilhon's testimony and the Church scrambled to impose damage control, and thus a wave of anti-Trithemius declarations were issued. The sincerity of these can be judged in light of the fact that in 1614, at the Jesuit headquarters at Ingolstadt in Bavaria, Adam Tanner S.J., chairman of the theology faculty at the University of Ingolstadt, established a Jesuit forum for the rehabilitation of the posthumous reputation of Abbot Trithemius. His oration pro-Trithemius was published by the Jesuit Order itself. It was followed by a vindication of the Catholicism of Trithemius' magical doctrines by the Benedictine Abbot Sigismund of Seeon.

"Instances of demonic magic, Tanner held in his Ingolstadt oration of 1614, no more entail the rejection of magic in principle

---

[20] Ibid., p. 175.

than instances of heresy entail the rejection of theology in principle. The same rule applies to magic as to religion with which it is fundamentally bound up: the winnow must be separated from the chaff. Taking up the question of Trithemian magic in particular to illustrate his point...as evidenced by large tomes of his historical and spiritual writings recently coming to light, exhorted Tanner, Trithemius proved himself to be not only a piously faithful Christian and reform-minded monk but an illustrious paradigm of Christian erudition sought out for counsel by the foremost princes and ecclesiastical dignitaries of his age...Moreover, by conjoining to this understanding a further appreciation of the abbot's exceptional contributions to the literature of Christian piety...he will allay his suspicions even further, seeing him for what he really is, 'a man very learned and orthodox in his Catholicism, in which capacity he served not only as a monk but as a high priest of monks...Tanner's Ingolstadt appeal was to find significant resonance...among his fellow Catholics, including other Jesuits..." [21]

"The great Trithemius stands readied with illustrious weapons, and by their use will vindicate his own reputation.' In this way a Benedictine abbot following the example of Trithemius in more than the conventionally monastic manner, Sigismund of Seeon (d. 1634), signaled his intent, in an introductory ode of his *Trithemius sui-ipsius vindex* (1616), not so much to defend his subject's cryptographical brand of magic, as to have him articulate his own defense. Expressing puzzlement as to how the esteem for 'so great a man, one who had been so aptly commended by the Catholic Church for his letters and learnedness, had fallen to its present nadir...

"Posing the question of whether, by his choice of the suspicious language in which the writing was cast, Trithemius played at least some part in bringing his troubles upon himself, Sigismund replied that this decision was made for good reason. 'Trithemius was warranted in employing numbers, signs, and strange names belonging to spirits and other entities,' the writer explained following the usual esoterist guideline, 'so that he might so fully envelop his art in mysteries that it would not be easily penetrated by anyone who was not first, in

---

[21] Ibid., pp. 192 and 194.

honesty and piety, initiated into its precepts.' In adopting this esoterist expedient, continued Sigismund, Trithemius was but following the example of the ancient sages, who likewise, 'if they discovered any arcana, either of nature or of art, lest they came to the notice of depraved men, concealed them by various modes and figures.' And if that were not enough to prove the legitimacy of this practice, we have the testimony of holy scripture itself, with examples like that of Moses, who found it necessary to explain 'the arcane and ineffable mysteries of the creation of heaven and earth' in the language of riddle and enigma...In like manner 'the Greeks and Egyptians always used figures and obscurities for the concealment of sacred and divine things.' In parallel fashion the jurists, mathematicians, musicians, rhetoricians, poets, alchemists, and even strategists of the military art have long recognized the need to hide their ideas under the mask of cryptic enigmas—this to make them inaccessible to those for whom they were unintended.

"...Trithemius was 'a lover of a more secret philosophy' (*secretioris philosophiae amator*) who, far from enlisting demons in his steganographical operations, was always careful to employ only 'licit and natural means.' In further fulfillment of his promise to have Trithemius act as his own vindicator, Sigismund appended the expressly demonological fifth, sixth and seventh books of the *Octo quaestiones*, the effect of which, Sigismund agreed with their author, was to establish a clear-cut boundary between Trithemian magic and that of wicked sorcerers." [22]

Other Catholic support for Trithemius came from the eminent Catholic Bishop and casuist-probabilist Juan

---

[22] Ibid., pp. 201-203.

Caramuel y Lobkowitz. [23] He was called to the occult citadel of Prague to head the Benedictine monastery of Montserrat, known for its conservative Counter-Reformation mission. For four years of his Prague station he served on a body charged with the extirpation of heresy. Also during his time in the heavily occultic and Judaic city of Prague he collaborated with several rabbis of the Prague Jewish community. "Caramuel notes that the pope has far less to fear from the Jews than the emperor does from Swedish mercenaries." [24]

He was the author of influential works of theology including his *Rationalis et realis philosophia* (1642), and *Theologia moralis fundamentalis* (1652). Caramuel y Lobkowitz left Prague for Rome in 1655, the year his old friend Chigi was elected to the papacy as Alexander VII. [25] He was named Bishop of Vigevano in Lombardy in 1673. His theology is outwardly impressive in its erudition and inwardly thoroughly distorted as befits a high member of the Neoplatonic-Hermetic conspiracy who enjoyed the protection and promotion of popes and Catholic kings in the seventeenth century, and who wrote in his *Pax Licita,* "There are no such things as sins in themselves."

In 1635 Caramuel reprinted Trithemius' *Steganographia.* He inveighed against its detractors and he urged the Inquisition to pursue the critics of Trithemius, not his defenders. Concerning demonology in Trithemius, "Caramuel indicates that demonic 'incantations' are only encoded texts

---

[23] Cf. pp.77-78 herein. Caramuel is a Spanish-version of the name Cramer. His father was of Luxemburgh; his mother was a De Vries, which is Flemish, but her mother, Caramuel's maternal grandmother Regina, was the daughter of Jan Popel von Lobkowitz. Bishop Caramuel was educated at the University of Salamanca in Spain and among his teachers were leading Catholic theologians: Benito Sanchez Herrera, Juan Martinez de Prado, Angel Manrique, and the Jesuit Pedro Hurtado de Mendoza. In 1638 he was awarded a doctorate in theology from the University of Louvain and through the intervention of Philip IV, King of Spain, and Fabio Chigi, the papal nuncio in Cologne, he was named abbot of a monastery in Germany. In 1646 he was appointed Spanish Counselor at the Imperial Court, where he was a confidant of the Jesuit-educated Holy Roman Emperor Ferdinand III. Cf. below, Fleming, *Defending Probabilism.*

[24] Julia A. Fleming, op. cit., p. 62.

[25] Caramuel and Chigi sometimes clashed after the latter was elevated to the papacy, but never to such a degree as to impede his consistent promotion in the hierarchy.

whereas the names of demons represent the code of messages."[26] Caramuel never suffered for his occult views. He enjoyed consistent promotion in Catholic royal and religious ranks under popes and Catholic kings.

Trithemius attracted additional posthumous support from the Dean of Münster Cathedral, Bernhard von Mallinckrodt, as well as the theologian and Benedictine Prior, Jean d'Espieres.

"Believing magic to be just as deserving as any other 'handmaiden' to theology in the traditional *artes liberales,* Trithemeius considered it to be an adjunct to sound Catholic doctrine." His own Benedictine Order regarded his views on Catholic magic as a "minor digression of the abbot in light of the larger picture of his eminently pious way of life and unrelenting commitment to his monastic vows" and the Benedictines proceeded to distinguish "Trithemius's good, natural and Cabalistic magic from the wicked magic of the demonically inspired sorcerers." [27]

Abbot Trithemius, like Catholic Fr. Ficino, Catholic Giovanni Pico and Catholic Reuchlin, was a Catholic theological bridge to the very Rosicrucian, masonic, theosophist and modernist trends that Leo XIII and Pius IX, Pius X and Pius XI would make declamatory expostulations upon, to "warn the faithful." But any genuine warning would include a revelation of the origin of the toxic thought, and that origin was a Renaissance papacy which consistently shielded, covertly protected and in those instances where orthodox Catholics became too vigorous in opposition, imposed token "punishments" which today are cited by dupes to "prove" that the papacy combatted the Neoplatonic-Hermetic Kabbalists. The documentary record gives evidence that in each generation occult Catholics went from strength to strength, giving form and content to the very conspiracy which Right wing Catholics imagine they are battling by their loyalty to "conservative" and "traditional" Catholicism.

Paraphrasing Trithemius' biographer Noel L. Brann, we observe that "in the culminating Rosicrucian and theosophical stages of the Catholic magical movement, what heretofore were

---

[26] Ioan P. Coulianu, *Eros and Magic in the Renaissance*, p. 169.

[27] Brann, op. cit., pp. 240-241.

relatively minor subterranean streamlets of Catholic thought—astrology, Pythagorean numerology and Hermetic and Cabalistic magic—became expanded into major streams and rivers." [28]

How the Catholic Church became famous for fighting against these "streams and rivers" which it permitted to arise and flourish within its bosom, is among the most neglected lacunae in the chronicle of Christendom. It testifies to a dual Church, the one visible for the benefit of the well-intentioned but sadly ignorant and bamboozled priests and parishioners who tend toward conservatism; and the other diabolic, led by numerous popes who were either active conspirators or mute accomplices to the covert escalation of magic, homosexual predation upon children, usurious money power, and lying and deceit advanced by a hierarchical "magisterium" shrouded in the blackest folds of an institutionalized secrecy which is the *sine qua non* of most of the western occult camarilla.

---

[28] Ibid., p. 253.

Chapter VIII

Reuchlin's Revolution

"...of the Christian cabalists who may be considered 'humanists'—i.e. who came to *cabala* as to an ancient fountain of wisdom...Johannes Reuchlin, by far the most important and productive, was Pico's disciple." [1]

Before we take up Johannes Reuchlin, the foremost contemporary heir to the legacy of Giovanni Pico della Mirandola, we will return to the Catholic-Kabbalist and Fifth Lateran Council luminary, Giles of Viterbo (1469-1532), who is a link to other popes of the occult Renaissance: Julius II (Giuliano della Rovere), who was the patron of Michelangelo and whose papacy had been made possible by Sixtus IV (Francesco della Rovere). Julius was the immediate predecessor of Leo X (Giovanni di Lorenzo de' Medici).

"It was during Julius' pontificate, moreover, that Giles of Viterbo, so often an articulator for the Della Rovere pontiff of the papacy's sacred mission and destiny, developed a deepening interest in Hebraic studies. Earlier, following Annio da Viterbo's lead, Giles had pursued Egyptian lore. But around 1507 he returned to the serious study of Hebrew and Aramaic he had begun a dozen years earlier in Florence. Giles devoted attention to Talmudic literature, but above all he cultivated the cabala, the esoteric medieval Jewish theosophy, which he and other Renaissance cabalists believed contained the hidden divine wisdom revealed to Adam, Moses and the other patriarchs, and from them descended in oral transmission down the centuries.

"Roman interest in the cabala did not originate with Giles....Julius II's uncle Sixtus IV (who had made Julius a cardinal), sought to have a Latin translation made of it. To Sixtus's pontificate also belongs the Good Friday 1481 sermon of Flavius Mithridates. This converted Sicilian Jew, who had

---

[1] Werner L. Gundersheimer, "Erasmus, Humanism and the Christian Cabala," *Journal of the Warburg and Courtauld Institutes*, Vol. 26, No. 1/2 (1963).

come to Rome through the patronage of Cardinal Cibo, the future Innocent VIII, dazzled his Vatican audience in the course of his two-hour oration with citations from Latin, Greek, the Hebrew 'arcana,' and 'Chaldean'...In 1486, at Perugia, this same Mithridates undertook to teach Pico the rudiments of Hebrew and initiated him into the profundities of esoteric Jewish lore....Most important, Mithridates made accessible to Pico the cabala, translating for him the basic texts. Pico, who eventually returned to Florence...became the pivotal figure in advocating cabalistic exegesis of the Old Testament as the key to finding a hidden concordance between Neoplatonist metaphysics and Christian revelation. Foremost among those taking inspiration from Pico's efforts was Giles of Viterbo. Like Pico, the Roman Augustinian was drawn to the esoteric richness of the cabalistic method. By means of metaphor, number mysticism and the riddles of acrostics, hidden depths in the Scriptural text could be revealed...Cabalistic studies preoccupied Giles for the remainder of his life...the cabala determined the basic structure of his *Historia XX saecolorum*, the universal history he composed for Leo X in the years 1513-18." [2]

Ficino and Pico's theology was transmitted to many leading Catholic prelates and laymen in Europe in the decades ahead. One of the earliest and most influential of these was Johannes Reuchlin (1455-1522), the celebrated German-Catholic Renaissance humanist from Pforzheim, [3] which at the time of his birth was administered by the Margrave of Baden. Reuchlin studied at the Pforzheim Latin School, the University of Freiburg in Breisgau, and the University of Paris under Robert Gaguin (a translator of Pico's works into French), and at Basle University. Reuchlin's handler in Rome, who personally directed his path up the ladder of the occult Catholic Brotherhood, was Rabbi Obadiah Sforno.

"He (Reuchlin) returned to his native country and obtained an appointment as personal advisor to Count Eberhard im Bart

---

[2] Stinger, op. cit., pp. 307-308.

[3] In Pforzheim in 1267, Judaics were alleged to have been guilty of the ritual murder of the Catholic child, Margaret of Pforzheim; Pforzheim became a regional cultural center. It was intentionally incinerated in heavy fire-bombing by the British during World War II.

of Würtemberg...The following year, 1483, he went on the first of his visits to Italy as one of the group of advisors who accompanied the Count. He appeared before Pope Sixtus IV in his capacity as Count Eberhard's Latin interpreter and his legal negotiator concerning Tübingen University which had been founded in 1477 by Count Eberhard to provide qualified staff for his court. [4] Pope Sixtus IV presented the Count with the 'Golden Rose'...the granting of such a symbol to Eberhard indicated he was a person who the Pope could rely on for his loyalty. Thus Reuchlin in his role as private secretary was known for his scholarly ability at a very early stage to the most powerful person in the Church. While in Italy they were also introduced to Lorenzo de Medici...and to several other scholars, among them Giovanni Pico della Mirandola..." [5]

After receiving his doctorate in law from Tübingen University, Reuchlin proceeded to advance to the top of the German-Catholic ruling circles: as a justice on an appellate court, a judge at the Imperial Chamber Court at Speyer; one of the three judges of the Swabian League, and as an emissary to the Holy Roman Emperor Maximilian I. Often times the cases he judged were derived from Catholic Canon Law. Reuchlin used his position as a powerful Catholic jurist to advance the legal status of Judaics to the level of citizen, which contradicted the *via antiqua* of the Church as embodied by Aquinas and medieval Popes Innocent III and Gregory IX, and other pontiffs, as well as councils and theologians.

From 1482 onward, his patrons were the Florentine Medici dynasts among whom was the Medici Pope Leo X. Reuchlin took Giovanni Pico della Mirandola's Catholic Kabbalah to the next level of progression with his seminal works of rabbinic mysticism, *De virbo mirifico* of 1494 (which argued that all religions including Judaic Kabbalism and the paganism of Hermes share with Christianity fundamental, sublime truths), and *De arte cabalistica* (1517), his heinous book of black magic

---

[4] Tübingen would soon become a hotbed of Catholic nominalism from which sprang the first substantive Catholic theological justification for taking profit on loans of money. Cf. this writer's *Usury in Christendom: The Mortal Sin that Was and Now is Not*, pp. 163-168; 171-172 and 176.

[5] Daniel O'Callaghan, *The Preservation of Jewish Religious Books in Sixteenth Century Germany: Johannes Reuchlin's Augenspiegel* (2012,)p. 26.

which he *dedicated to Leo X,* and which the pope accepted without disapproval of any kind.

Canonized as "St. Johannes Reuchlin" by Erasmus, Reuchlin is among the most important inheritors of the legacy pioneered by Ficino and Pico, as this legacy began to further reveal itself, as the Renaissance in Italy and Germany devolved further into the depths of Neoplatonic-Hermetic Kabbalism. All three men were Judaizing enemies of the ancient Catholic faith. Yet they had powerful patrons within the hierarchy of the Church of Rome. Reuchlin was a prime mover in the campaign for the improvement of the political and legal status of Judaic persons. [6]He regarded the Scholastic/Thomistic inheritance as a "barbarous and uncultivated philosophy." In Pico's immediate wake, he further advanced the Kabbalah within the papacy and among practicing sorcerers: "Reuchlin...introduced the Kabbalah, which became very important in ceremonial magic."[7]

In 1490 Reuchlin met for a second time in Italy with Giovanni Pico della Mirandola. Pico "confirmed for him that the study of Jewish Cabbala and Christian beliefs were directly related and could be integrated to an orthodox Christian philosophy." [8]

Reuchlin's handlers consisted of Rabbi Joel of Rosheim, who referred to him as "one of the scholars of the nations who had helped to restore the (Oral) Torah to its proper place," and Catholic Bishop Johannes von Dalberg, who brought him rare Kabbalistic manuscripts and encouraged his Judaizing mission, in return for which, in 1494, Reuchlin dedicated his inaugural Kabbalistic book, *De verbo mirifico,* to Bishop Dalberg.

At the behest of Rabbi Rosheim, in 1492 Catholic Holy Roman Emperor Friedrich III conferred the title of "Count Palatine" on Reuchlin. In 1498 Reuchlin represented Elector Philip of Palatine before the papal court, where he successfully had a papal edict against Philip withdrawn. In a letter to Leo X in 1517, he wrote:

---

[6] On Reuchlin's philo-Judaism cf. Max Brod, *Johannes Reuchlin und sein Kampf: Eine historische Monographie* (1965).

[7] Paola Zambelli, *White Magic, Black Magic,* op. cit., p. 15.

[8] O'Callaghan, op.cit., p. 40.

"I was the first to bring Greek studies back to Germany and the first to present and teach the art and study of the Hebrew language to the universal church." Wilhelm Maurer asserts that Reuchlin's sympathy for Judaism was intensified by his study of Pythagoras and Kabbalah. For Reuchlin the synthesis of Pythagoreanism, Platonism and Kabbalism reflected an integral Christian legacy.[9]

One of Reuchlin's well-placed protectors was the German Catholic Jacob Questenberg, who was papal secretary in 1504 and head of the Secretariat for the College of Cardinals in 1514. Emperor Friedrich meanwhile, had been guided by Rabbi Jacob ben Jehiel Loans (1440-1493), who served as Reuchlin's guide as well, in the last year of the life of the rabbi. Reuchlin addressed Rabbi Loans as "My lord, dear master Jacob...with deep longing I wish to see your blessed face to delight in the radiance of your bright countenance by hearing your most pure doctrine."

Reuchlin "believed that the evangelical purity of faith that he sought was hidden in the Scriptures and Jewish Cabalistic philosophy...He never considered his research to be a deviation from orthodox belief, but a legitimate correction...he also believed they ("Jews") possessed a secret wisdom, the esoteric philosophy of the Cabala. If they could be prevailed upon to divulge these teachings to Christians, it would benefit the initiated, and lead them to a deeper insight into the mysteries of their beliefs...He believed that by the publication of the *Augenspiegel*, he would generate sufficient support for his views among scholars and educated lay people that they would cause the (Catholic) authorities to reconsider their coercive measures. The publication...led to a moratorium on the destruction of Jewish books." [10]

Reuchlin's *Augenspiegel* ("Eye Mirror"), submitted to the Imperial Council, consisted of four parts: two are related to preventing rabbinic books from being confiscated or destroyed. The third and fourth sections are attempts to refute Thomistic scholastics and the eminent and much-maligned (by modern "historians") Judaic convert to Catholicism, Johann Pfefferkorn

---

[9]   Wilhelm Maurer, "Reuchlin und das Judenthum," in *Theologische Literaurzeitung*, pp. 535-544.

[10] O'Callaghan, op.cit., pp. 2-3.

(ca. 1468-1522), author of *Handt Spiegel* ("Hand Mirror"). At considerable expense, according to Reuchlin himself (in his *Defensio*), one thousand copies were published by the renowned printer Thomas Anselm of Tübingen, and "could have been sold rather than given away, had it not been for interference in Frankfurt from a common priest" ("*plebius sacerdos*").

The Cryptocracy was greatly inconvenienced by the monkey wrench that Pfefferkorn had tossed into the machinery of Judaization, which Catholics like Ficino, Pico and now Reuchlin were constructing inside the Church's theological and philosophical superstructure. *Augenspiegel* was written to specifically counter Pfefferkorn. The opening paragraph reads:

"Doctor Johannes Reuchlin's *Augenspiegel*. Judge of Civil Law of the Swabian League for His Imperial Majesty, the Archduke of Austria and the Electors and Princes; his truthful apologia against and contrary to the untruthful slanderous pamphlet previously published and distributed by a baptized Jew named Pfefferkorn."

Thanks to scholarly and sincere Judaic converts like Pfefferkorn the usual dumbshow concerning the contents of the texts of the Babylonian Talmud and ancillary sacred rabbinic books could not so easily be misrepresented as benign. Consequently, in Reuchlin's defense of the religion of Judaism's holiest books, he was forced to begin by accepting the undeniable fact that they contain imprecations against, for example, Jesus and Mary. One would think that fact would be sufficient to ensure a heavy embargo on the Talmud, for example, but Reuchlin was a lawyer and court official with powerful backing from Uriel von Gemmingen, the Bishop of Mainz, and other Catholic prelates and princes, and it fell to him to undertake the absurd two-fold task of approving the *distribution* of blasphemy while disapproving of its *contents*. Reuchlin wrote:

"In this pamphlet you will find: a description of the case including an appropriate preface, declarations, and demands; advice on whether the Jewish books are to be burned; to the point brought up regarding sundry Jewish books and writings, you will find an answer to every point without exception in the counsel that follows. Throughout the counsel, at the outset, in the middle and at the end, all parts are evaluated concerning the underlying question of whether a book that intentionally sets out to mock, slander and blaspheme Our Lord Jesus, His holy mother, the saints, or our Christian doctrine, should be seized and burned, if it is willfully possessed by a Jewish individual. This is to be undertaken, however, with the understanding that if such writings are found blasphemous or heretical and are consequently forbidden to Jewish people, according to Christian doctrine, they therefore should be confiscated and burned.

"Concerning the peculiarity of the Talmud; that it is compiled from various and sundry books into one and is categorized into different sections; in which books of the Talmud, cited above, are blasphemy or heresy that are forbidden to Jews, according to Christian principles or laws, should be burned as advised hereafter...Apart from these writings, other books that are not officially condemned or forbidden by Christian doctrine, without regard to whether their contents are found useful or useless, good or bad, frivolous or foolish, should be permitted to remain and left untouched as with the other extant erroneous texts; all of their other books to be treated similarly....Lastly, a truthful repudiation of the false claims by the baptized Jew made in the pamphlet cited as follows. To all and sundry in whichever most esteemed, honorable stand or degree they may be, who are seekers of truth and enemies of lies, disseminated verbally or in writing, which ought to be despised according to God's laws, I, Johannes Reuchlin, doctor of imperial laws, beg you to give heed to the libelous act in which falsehood was poured out in secret schemes in a published, libelous and execrable pamphlet entitled *Hand Mirror*, by a baptized Jew named Pfefferkorn...and publicized by way of numerous copies at the last Frankfurt Spring Fair."

Reuchlin was outraged that a "converted Jew," someone he regarded as little better than a peasant, had dared to challenge his lofty intellectual and legal credentials as a member of the Catholic ruling class in the Holy Roman Empire. According to Reuchlin, Pfefferkorn personally paid a call on him at his home in Stuttgart in the late summer of 1509, thinking Reuchlin would aid him in his campaign and seeking to enlist him in it. Reuchlin supposedly gave Pfefferkorn a sheet of paper listing the "scholarly reasons" why he would not join with Pfefferkorn. These reasons were rejected and therein lies one root of their conflict.

Pfefferkorn and Reuchlin would also clash in April, 1511 at the imperial court of the Catholic Holy Roman Emperor Maximilian in Würtemberg. There the Emperor's Catholic "experts" criticized and attacked Pfefferkorn, not Reuchlin. This was a departure from the favor Pfefferkorn had initially received in 1509 from Maximilian, who at that time conferred upon him the right to confiscate books throughout the Holy Roman Empire that blasphemed Jesus Christ or contradicted the Law of Moses in the Torah. The latter was a particularly enlightened mandate. Pfefferkorn's license from the emperor to ensure the integrity of the Old Testament stood in contrast to the anti-Old Testament heresy of Marcion which was popular in Catholic circles in Europe in the early 16th century; even Erasmus was tainted by it. [11] But as we shall see, with the exception of the local Dominican Order in Germany, and some local Franciscans, the Church of Rome and Catholic rulers such as Emperor Maximilian, would toss Pfefferkorn to the wolves of Talmudic-Kabbalism.

Reuchlin is presented by Establishment historians as a fount of Renaissance humanist progressivism, yet in the pages of his *Augenspiegel*, Reuchlin's venom was unlimited: he suggested that Pfefferkorn should be executed for disclosing official secrets, and insinuates that Pfefferkorn's wife is a prostitute.[12]

Proceeding further in the introduction to his *Augenspiegel*, Reuchlin again raises the specter of executing Pfefferkorn for publishing a different pamphlet, "which calls on the subjects of the empire to create an insurrection against the authorities which is forbidden by imperial law and punished by hanging." This pamphlet was Pfefferkorn's 1509 jeremiad against usury, *In diesem buchlein vindet yr ein entlichen furtrag wie die blinden Juden yr Ostern halten*. The only "insurrection" Pfefferkorn was advocating was against Judaic bankers and shylocks, yet Reuchlin misrepresented his writing as stirring up a treasonous revolt against the Catholic kingdom itself.

After several pages of self-justification and accusations contra Pfefferkorn, Reuchlin proceeds to his lawyer's brief for

---

[11] "And would that the church of the Christians did not give so much preference to the Old Testament." Desiderius Erasmus in a letter to Wolfgang Koepfel, March 13, 1518.

[12] O'Callaghan, op.cit., p. 114, footnotes 31 (second paragraph) and 34.

the Talmud under the title, "Counsel on Whether to Confiscate Suppress and Burn All the Books of the Jews," which in itself is a con, since no one was advocating confiscating or burning the Old Testament.

He begins his argument with an unintentionally risible ecumenical statement that would not be out of place in the Catholic Church of the late 20th century: "Every person should be allowed to retain his old, inherited traditions, customs and possessions, even if he is a robber. Consequently Jews should be permitted to retain their synagogues, called 'schools' in peace and tranquility and should not be obstructed."

The synagogue of robbers should be permitted, on the grounds that they are "old, inherited traditions"! Concerning the non-Biblical canonical rabbinic texts of Judaism, Reuchlin is equally phantasmagoric: "...only a very few (passages) will be found to contain mockery, slander or blasphemy against Our Lord God Jesus and His Venerable mother and against apostles and saints." In indicating where these offensive statements will be found he uses a clever tactic and misdirects attention away from the Talmud by indicting the obscure *Nizzahon* and the non-rabbinic book, *The Toledet Jesu*. The latter, though among the most vicious of anti-Christian works, is not part of the rabbinic canon and therefore cannot be definitively laid at their door. What Reuchlin terms the *Nizzahon* is the *Nizzahon Vetus*, ("Old Book of Polemic") a medieval (probably late 13th century) German-Ashkenazic repository of anti-Christian arguments for polemical purposes, which contains slurs typical of the Talmudic mentality, including the oft-stated one that the Blessed Virgin Mary was a "promiscuous woman." However, unlike the Talmud or the *Mishneh Torah* of Maimonides, the *Nizzahon Vetus* is not a source of rabbinic *halacha* (law) and does not have canonical status in rabbinic Judaism.[13] This datum affords Reuchlin the opportunity to discount these texts and the hatred behind them as apocryphal, and to continue with his sideshow by lending support to the comical Judaic claim that "Jews" themselves were in the habit of destroying the *Nizzahon* and *Toledet Jesu*: "I heard quite often from Jews with whom I had many discussions some time ago at the court of Frederick III...that such books were appropriated and

---

[13] An English translation of the text of the *Nizzahon Vetus* is included in *The Jewish-Christian Debate in the High Middle Ages* by David Berger (1996).

destroyed by the Jews themselves and it has been forbidden to write these kinds of books..."

Reuchlin proceeds to the Talmud, a very different kettle of fish in his view: "I will commence by addressing the Talmud, a compilation of all of God's laws. It was compiled 400 years after Christ's birth...the nobly born and most learned Count Giovanni Pico della Mirandola writes in the *Apologia* that the Talmud was compiled 150 years after Christ...Now it is likely that after the death of Our Lord Jesus the Jewish leaders saw that the Christians wanted to 'keep a tight rein'...and in consequence these leaders came together in that time to preserve the old doctrines and confute the disputations of the heathens and converted Jews. Thus they collected in book form the opinions and expositions of their old masters and of their most gifted, profound, and erudite scholars. And, so as to preserve these great efforts and labors, which they and their forefathers had in composing and writing them, *a work in which God Himself would take pleasure*, they have commanded their own people to hold this book in great reverence. It is reasonable and understandable, consequently, that so as to keep their writings from being treated with contempt by their descendants, they were committed to writing down all that was applicable. This was done so that they could be better at defending themselves against the Gentiles and apostate Jews."

Reuchlin gives himself away when he opines that "God himself would take pleasure" in the Talmud; this is consonant with the inordinate pride and self-praise which is common in the Babylonian Talmud, from which Reuchlin seems to have drunk deeply. We continue with his writing in the *Augenspiegel*: "I say that the Talmud must not be burned or repressed...It is common knowledge that there has to be superstition and error and that human reason cannot stop it, as St. Paul says in I Corinthians 11...And we do not term superstitious those who erroneously comment on the Sacred Scripture and maintain their view contrary to the Holy Ghost. It is said correctly that the Jews cannot be heretics since they never were believers in the Christian religion. Hence they cannot be classified as heretics and their disagreement termed heretical. Consequently, it is valuable to us to preserve the Talmud and maintain it."

The Rabbinic Curse on Christians

In his *Augenspiegel*, "the esteemed Renaissance savant" Reuchlin lies flagrantly concerning the existence of the rabbinic curse on Christians which is contained in the *Birkat Haminim Amidah* prayer. Pfefferkorn had unmasked it in his 1509 pamphlet with the satirical title, *Ich bin ain Buchlinn, der Juden veindt is mein namen* ("I'm a little book, the Jew's enemy is my name"). Reuchlin attempts to debunk Pfefferkorn's accusation in that pompous tone of indignant sanctimony which then (and now) is employed against those who are branded "anti-Semitic." He produces this boldface lie about the *Amidah*: "...far from praying for the demise of Christianity, (rabbis) pray for its peace and harmony" (Reuchlin, *Defensio*, 1513).[14] This denial is an insult to the intelligence of his readers.

We will quote Reuchlin's falsified version of the rabbinic curse. Then we will explore at length the evidence for its existence and implementation in Judaism. We ask for your forbearance as we do so. Reuchlin is so considerable an icon of Renaissance humanism, that anything less than a comprehensive marshaling of the evidence would be insufficient to document the extent to which he was an unscrupulous liar and faker. We intend to leave no stone unturned in demonstrating the willingness of unscrupulous deceivers of the prestige and caliber of Johannes Reuchlin to perpetrate a hoax for the sake of upholding the reputation of Pharisaic Judiasm.

Reuchlin writes contra Pfefferkorn: "Recently a pamphlet was published hostile to the Jews, where reference was made to a prayer said to be incorporated in their prayer books which they are supposed to repeat against Christians...As a result grave charges have been brought against them, that they curse the Apostles, the whole Church and the Holy Roman Empire. In this way one could readily instigate so much hatred against the Jews on the part of the ignorant that they suffer the loss of

---

[14] Years before, Reuchlin had written a pamphlet, *Why the Jews Have Been in Exile So Long*, attesting to the anti-Christian content of the *Amidah* prayer. Pfefferkorn believed Reuchlin's *volte face* was due to him being on the rabbis' payroll. This would not be unusual, as we have seen concerning financial arrangements for Archbishop Uriel and Emperor Maximilian himself.

life and limb. If, however, one examines it in the correct light one finds nothing against the baptized or the Apostles, Church or Empire."

Reuchlin advances his falsification by engaging in the old rabbinic game of pretending the word *minim* in the *Birkat Haminim* is not a reference to Christians. He employs similar tactics to deny the truth that as a *part of the religion of Judaism, its adherents are obligated to ritually pray for disaster to befall the followers of Christ.*

The eminent *halachic* authority "Rambam," (Moses Maimonides) wrote: "In the days of Rabban Gamaliel, the *minim* became numerous in Israel and they caused trouble for the Jews, seducing them to turn away from God. When they saw that this was more significant than any other human need, Rabban Gamaliel and his court acted and established an additional blessing that would include a petition before God to make the *minim* perish. He established it in the *amidah* so that it would be set in everyone's mouths. Consequently, the number of blessings in the *amidah* is nineteen." [15]

By way of excursus, we are explicating one of the so-called *Amidah* "prayers of benediction," the *Birkat Haminim*, which contains the murderous, ritual curse on the Christians (the "*minim*"), a curse which has echoed perpetually down the corridors of time since at least the days of Rabbi Gamaliel, when it was enacted at the rabbinic academy of Yavneh (known in Greek as "Jamnia"), in the late first century A.D.[16]

J. Louis Martyn in his essential text, *History and Theology of the Fourth Gospel,*[17] sees a reference to the *Birkat Haminim* curse in John 9:22, "His parents said these things because they feared the Jews, for the Jews had already agreed that if anyone

---

[15]   Mishneh Torah, Hilkhot Tefillah Unesi'at Kapayyim 2:1. For an elucidation of the *amidah*, cf. footnote 272 on p. 279 of *Judaism Discovered.*

[16] This is a reference to Gamaliel II who survived the destruction of the Temple in 70 A.D.

[17] Westminster John Knox Press (2003), pp. 47-66. David Instone-Brewer extended Martyn's thesis by tracing the *Birkat's* origin to the time of Gamaliel I. Cf. *Journal of Theological Studies 54*, no. 1 (2003), pp. 25-44. Support for Martyn's thesis has been subjected to excision. *The Catholic Study Bible* (Oxford University) edited by Donald Senior, in its 1990 edition supported Martyn. The 2011 edition removed the support. Raymond E. Brown endorsed Martyn's thesis in 1979 in *The Community of the Beloved Disciple,* but omits it in his 1997 *An Introduction to the New Testament.*

should confess Jesus to be Christ, he was to be put out of the synagogue" (also cf. John 12:42, and in particular John 16:2, for the homicidal aspect). Justin Martyr, the second century A.D. Christian Father who was raised in Samaria, in his *Dialogue with Trypho,* repeatedly stated that Jews ceremonially curse Christians, "For in your synagogues you curse all those who through Him are called Christians." [18]

In the Babylonian Talmud (hereafter "BT"), we read in Berakhot 28b-29a: "Rabban Gamaliel said to the sages: 'Is there anyone who knows how to enact the *birkat haminim*? Shmuel HaQaton (Samuel the Little) stood up and enacted it." In BT Megillah 17b it is stated: "Once judgment was passed on the wicked, the *minim* perished..and once the *minim* perished, the horns of the righteous are elevated."

The rabbis have hotly denied that *minim* refers to Christians. [19] From the time of Reuchlin forward they deployed a massive p.r. corps and thought police to ensure that no respectable scholar ventured to state the truth that the *Birkat Haminim* is a curse on the followers of Jesus Christ, which has never been rescinded by the theological heirs of the rabbis who authored the original enabling *taqqanah* (legislation).

Birkat Haminim also serves as a litmus test for heresy. Any Judaic in the synagogue who stumbles or hesitates in pronouncing the curse is suspected of being a crypto-Christian; a determination that, if confirmed, would lead to the imposition of another curse, the *cherem* (curse of expulsion), upon any secret Judaic-Christian. BT Berakhot 29b states concerning the "blessings" that comprise the *Amidah* and of the unique nature of one of them in particular: "If one errs in (reciting) any one of the blessings we do not remove him, but in the *birkat haminim*, we do remove him."

Let us consider the evidence of the Geniza texts which come from the Ben Ezra Synagogue of Old Cairo, Egypt, circa 1000 to 1300 A.D. These were obtained by Solomon Schechter who began to publish them in 1898; among these was the *Birkat*

---

[18] *St. Justin Martyr, Dialogue with Trypho,* ch. 96:2. In ch. 137:2 Justin shows he is not deceived by the claim of the rabbis to being Israel: "Do not scorn the King of Israel as the chiefs of your synagogue instruct you to do after prayers."

[19] Cf. for example, Joseph Hertz (Chief Rabbi of England), *The Authorized Daily Prayer Book*, p. 143.

Haminim. Every *Birkat Haminim prayer* in the geniza manuscripts begins, "May there be no hope for *meshummadim.*" [20] The *meshummadim* are Jewish converts to Christianity. Among the most illustrious in the Middle Ages who assisted the Church in discovering the truth about the Talmud were Nicholas Donin, Peter Alfonsi, Peter Galatin and Paulus Cristiani. The latter debated Rabbi Nachman (Nachmanides) in Barcelona in 1263, with King James I of Aragon in attendance. [21] During the Renaissance, the former rabbi Victor von Carben, Johannes Pfefferkorn and Anthonius Margaritha, [22] were all sincere converts to Christianity.

From Christ's earliest apostles to all Jews who would later convert to belief in Jesus as Savior, Judaism prayed that there would be no hope for the physical or spiritual salvation of these converts. *Meshummad (*also called *mumar)* signifies those who are worthy of extermination, from the Hebrew root *sh-m-d,* which connoted the Old Testament capital penalty for engaging in idolatry. [23]   The "idolatrous crime" of these converts is described by Dr. Ruth Langer of Hebrew Union College: "Throughout the High Middle Ages and beyond, apostates often do provide less than friendly information to Christian authorities about the inner workings of the Jewish community."

The legal text *Sefer Ha'Eshkol* was authored by Rabbi Abraham ben Yitzhak (1085-1158) who ruled the Judaics of the Provencal region of medieval France as *rosh yeshiva* and head of the rabbinic court. Such was his prestige that he was referred to by posterity simply as "the Rav, Av Bet Din." In the authenticated edition of his *Sefer Ha'Eshkol* published by

---

[20] Ruth Langer, *Cursing the Christians?* (Oxford University Press), p. 45.

[21] Nachmanides was treated courteously and paid for his trouble. King James observed that no one so wrong had ever argued so well.

[22] Margaritha stayed loyal to the Catholic Faith early in his career and then wandered into Neoplatonic Hermeticism later. His father was Rabbi Samuel Margoles. Anthonius's brother was Rabbi Moses Mordechai of Cracow. In his book *Der gantz Jüdisch glaub* Margaritha described how some Judaics offered a *groshen* (coin) to Christians so the Christian would become the scapegoat into which the Judaic's sins were allegedly transferred, rather than the usual *kapporoth (*"sin chicken").

[23]   Brown, Driver and Briggs, *A Hebrew and English Lexicon of the Old Testament*, p. 1029.

Shalom Albeck in 1910, (pp. 26-27), he defines *minim* as "the followers of the crucified Jesus."

The rabbinic texts possessed of the force of law containing the curse on the *meshummadim* and/or *minim*, were closely guarded and retained as a secret teaching far from the prying eyes of inquisitive Christian scholars. Rabbi Jacob ben Asher (1269-1340), who was known as the "Tur" after his magnum opus legal text of the same name, referred to the *Birkat Haminim* as *qelalat haminim,* "the curse of the *minim.*" To confuse Christian investigators, *qelalat haminim* was deliberately misprinted in rabbinic texts as *qelalat hamalshinim;* and the curse on the *meshummadim* was erased from printed rabbinic liturgical texts of what otherwise would have constituted a very troubling rabbinic penumbra.[24] Then as now, this censorship enabled Judaism's legion of liars (both Judaic and gentile) to repeatedly and brazenly deny that there was any such curse; *many continue to deny it to this day.*

Another subterfuge is to claim that the *meshummad* "deny the Torah" and deserve their punishment. Two exceedingly influential *halachic* authorities, Rabbi Jacob ben Asher (the "Tur") and his father, Rabbi Asher ben Yehiel ("the Rosh"), indict the *meshummad* for denying the "two forms of Torah," the written *and* the oral; the latter being the source of the Talmud and Kabbalah.[25] This was one of the supposedly "idolatrous" transgressions of converts to Christianity in the eyes of their persecutors. Actually, the *meshummad* uphold the written Torah and deny the ersatz oral "Torah" of rabbinic Judaism.

In the *Sefer Ha-Chinukh,* the medieval work describing and explaining the rabbis' commandments, Commandment 93 stipulates that it is a requirement to kill all Jews who participate in "idolatry," like the Christians (*minim*) do, "because they trouble Israel." Commandment 34 states that

---

[24] This type of erasure, and cognate forms of concealment and misdirection, are not put into place ad hoc, but as a traditional tactic implemented as a function of the formal rabbinic principle of *Halakha Ve'Ain Morin Kain* ("It is the *Halakha* but we do not instruct it to the public," i.e. *am ha'aretz* and *goyim*). Cf. Shitah Mekubetzet and BT Menachot 36b.

[25] p. 64. Cf. *Teshuvot HaRosh,* 4:20. *Tur,* OH 118.

there is no restriction on killing these people because the lives of such people have no value.[26]

Meshummadim are Judaic converts to Christ who Talmudic-observant Jews have an obligation to allow to "fall into a pit" (Bava Metzia 2:33; Avodah Zarah 26:B). This also applies to the *minim*:

"The Hebrew and Aramaic root of the word '*minim*' simply means 'kind' or 'type.'...this usage corresponds with that of the term's cognate in Christian Aramaic dialects, where it is a common translation of the Greek *ethnos,* the Septuagint's translation of the Hebrew *goyim* (other nations), and the New Testament's term for gentiles. This expansion of meaning to include gentiles creates a trajectory that enables rabbis in Christian Europe to understand the *minim* to be (or include) 'the students of Jesus of Nazareth,' i.e. gentile Christians...In the medieval European context, the *birkat haminim,* is fully a curse of Christians. Every single European Jewish community adopts the basic form of the *birkat haminim* found in the *Seder Rav 'Amram Gaon*...every single medieval community continues to introduce the prayer with a curse of *meshummadim*...(and) by curses of *minim*..." [27]

Rashi (the acronym of Rabbi Shlomo Yitzhak, 1040-1105), was a renowned exegete who glossed the Bible and the Talmud. His commentary is published with the Babylonian Talmud itself. Rashi defined *minim* as "the students of Jesus of Nazareth" or more specifically, as the *galahim* (the "tonsured ones," i.e. Catholic priests), as did one of the top tier *Gadol ha-Dor* rabbis, the Rhinelander Rabbi Eliezer ben Yoel HaLevi

---

[26] A decoy text cited to claim that this teaching was not in force is *Hilkhot Mamrim* 3:3 from Maimonides' *Mishneh Torah*: "Do not lower the *minim* into the pit too quickly." This is not much of a defense for Maimonides, who does not prohibit enabling the deaths of Christians, but only cautions against an impetuous "lowering." Maimonides' more candid teaching on *minim* is found in his "Iggeret Teiman" (*Epistle to Yemen*, circa 1173). Cf. the Abraham Halkin edition, American Academy for Jewish Research, 1952.

[27] Langer, op. cit., pp. 59 and 66. "*Nozerim*," supposed to be derived from the word Nazareth, was regarded with the passage of time as synonymous with *minim*. Karaites (Jews who rejected the Talmud and adhered only to the Old Testament), were sometimes grouped by the rabbis in the *minim* category and subject to execution. Cf. Marina Rustow, *Heresy and the Politics of Community: The Jews of the Fatamid Caliphate* , pp. 350-351.

(1140-1220),[28] as well as many others (such as Rabbis Shmuel ben Meir and Yehuda ben Barzilai).

The accurate definition is also found in Judaism's bigoted, anti-Christian texts of the era, such as the *Sefer Yosef HaMeqane*, and the aforementioned *Nizzahon Vetus*. The latter argued that the New Testament was filled with absurdities and contradictions. We are aware of no establishment-approved scholar who denounces *Nizzahon Vetus* for having made that claim, [29] though hundreds of them denounce scholars who venture to write criticisms of the Talmud. Albert Ehrman, in his 1974 New York University dissertation, styles the hate-filled *Nizzahon* text a "defense of Judaism." Any defense of Christianity that entails an attack on the Talmud is almost automatically stigmatized as "hate literature." This tactic is a recrudescence of the rabbinic practice of classifying someone as a *min* just for being, in the words of Rabbi Elazar of Worms, "irreverent about the Talmud" (*Perushei Siddur Ha Tefillah LaRoqe-ah*, p. 342).

As Christians in medieval Europe began to become aware of these curses, their hostility toward the rabbis in their midst understandably increased. In 826, Agobard (769-840), the Christ-like Archbishop of Lyon who opposed the worship of carved statues, wrote *De Insolentia Judaeorum,* an informed protest to the Carolognian monarch Louis the Pious, against rabbinic curses.

Establishment historians omit the ritual and perpetual curses and blasphemies uttered by the adherents of the rabbis, and focus exclusively on the defensive Christian reaction to the hate speech of the synagogue, and then portray the defense as irrational Christian bigotry; just as, with regard to Catholic Spain, they minimize accounts of the Judeo-Muslim murder and enslavement of Catholics, and focus instead on demonizing

---

[28] For Rashi cf. BT Shabat 139a, s.v. *bitulei 'amgoshei*; BT Sanhedrin 100b s.v. *minim*; BT Avodah Zarah 26b s.v. *minim*; and Judah Rosenthal,"Anti-Christian Polemics in the Biblical Commentaries of Rashi," in *Studies and Texts in Jewish History* (Jerusalem, 1967), pp.101-116. For Halevi cf. *Teshuvot UVi'urei Sugiyot* (no. 1051).

[29] Actually the *Nizzahon Vetus* says far worse. It is so hateful of Jesus that it claims God created the Tree of Good and Evil in the Garden just to kill Him: mankind would know death and this would be the means by which the "wicked" Jesus could be killed and all the world would know that He was not God. Cf. David Berger's edition of the *Nizzahon Vetus*, p. 46.

the Catholic defense against the slavery and murder. When this tactic is applied to medieval Catholic Europe as a whole, Judaics are portrayed as innocent lambs victimized by monstrous Christians for no rationally valid reason. For this cartoon equation to be persuasive, the fact that the rabbis and their followers were petitioning God to destroy Christians is denied or concealed.

Documented Christian reports on the *Birkhat Haminim* curse began in earnest with the converted Judaic Nicholas Donin, around the year 1230. The heroic Donin sent to Pope Gregory IX a list of thirty-five Talmud passages that constituted hatred of God and Christians. In June, 1240 in Paris, Donin single-handedly debated four eminent rabbis. The charges against the Talmudic rabbis which Donin raised were specifically targeted against the *Birkat Haminim*.[30] Only the most rabid partisans attempt to disparage Donin's scholarship. He had his facts in order, putting forth citations from relevant Talmudic texts, including a note that the *amidah* prayer of eighteen "benedictions" is really nineteen, referencing BT Berakhot 28b. Donin correctly tracked the origin of *Birkat Haminim* to the rabbinic academy of Yavneh and a gloss of Rashi, as well as the connection between BT Rosh Hashanah 17a and Rashi's gloss that defines *minim* as "the followers of Jesus of Nazareth." One of Donin's debating opponents, Rabbi Yehiel, lied constantly and denied almost everything, asserting that the Jesus in the Talmud was not the same as Jesus of Nazareth, and that Jews do not pray for the downfall of Christian nations.

Yehiel appears to have been as sophisticated and shrewd as any twenty-first century rabbi: denying everything and pledging allegiance to the French king and queen before whom the debate was held. He only "lost his cool" in the presence of Donin personally, against whom he spewed venom, terming him a traitor who would never be forgiven. While the French monarchs were gracious toward Yehiel, Donin's well-documented points were hugely influential and resonated among Christians for centuries, in the writings of medieval

---

[30] "The Talmud on Trial: The Disputation at Paris in the Year 1240," in *Jewish Quarterly Review*, no. 47 [1956]; and *The Church Versus Talmudic and Midrashic Literature* [Jerusalem, 1970]. The Latin text of Donin's exposé of the *birkat haminim* may be found in "*La Controverse de 1240 sur le Talmud*," ms. Paris Bibliotheque National Latin 16558.

popes such as Clement IV (*Damnabili Perfidia Judaeorum*, July, 1267) and Honorius IV (letter to the Archbishop of Canterbury, November 30, 1286); in the Provencal breviary of Matfre Ermengaud (1290); in the homilies of the Dominican preacher Giordano da Rivalto (1304), in the Dominican Bernard Gui's *Practica officii inquisitionis heretice pravitatis* (1323; cf. section V:4, "About the intolerable blasphemies of the Jews against Christ, our faith and the Christian people in the *birkat haminim*"); and in the writings of the Judaic convert Abner of Burgo (a.k.a. Alfonso of Valladolid), in his *Libro de las Batallas de Dios* (1336) and *Libro de las malliciones de los Judios*.

On February 25, 1336 the King of Castille, Alfonso XI, decreed that the *Birkat Haminim* was forbidden throughout his kingdom. Echoing Nicholas Donin's learned indictment, the King declared to the rabbis: "You curse Christians and converts to the Christian faith, judging them to be heretics and even mortal enemies, and you entreat God to ruin and destroy them." In 1380 King Juan I reinstated King Alfonso's prohibition. The Judaic convert Bishop Paul de Santa Maria of Burgos (1351-1435) wrote in his *Scrutinium scriptarum* concerning the contents of the *Birkat Haminim,* that the Jews, "not only do not pray for gentiles, but they pray for the destruction of the Church of Christ and of his disciples, as is evident of a certain prayer of theirs which is said by them in their synagogues. In this prayer, they clearly say, 'Let all heretics perish quickly,' which words Rabbi Solomon and Rabbi Moses explain thus, 'These heretics are the disciples of the Nazarene." [31]

Privately, in their own clandestine writings, the rabbis acknowledged that the *Birkat Haminim* cursing of Christians was a contributing factor in their expulsion from Spain by Catholic Queen Isabella. [32] In 2012, Ruth Langer of Hebrew Union College-Jewish Institute of Religion, made a

---

[31] *Incipit dyalogus qui vocatur Scrutinium scripturarum* (Johann Mentelin, 1474), distinction 5, chapter 7, p. 83.

[32] Cf. Shlomo ibn Verga, *Sefer Shevet Yehuda* (Bialik Institute reprint, Jerusalem, 1947).

monumental admission: "Most of the Christian accusations about the *birkat haminim* were not wrong." [33]

Johannes Reuchlin was lying about the *Birkat Haminim* curse. He lied repeatedly and knowingly. Reuchlin's *Augenspiegel*, for all its bluster and self-advertised remarkable scholarship is not a particularly impressive polemical work in that it is in some places preposterous[34] and in many other parts demonstrably false. Nonetheless, Reuchlin succeeded because the Hermetic-Kabbalistic Cryptocracy created on his behalf a celebrity victim image, like that of Galileo, which has proved difficult to correct factually.

Occult conspirators defended Reuchlin in their satirical book, *Epistolae obscurorum vivorum*,[35] which excited intense avant-garde interest by successfully branding those who opposed Reuchlin as benighted laughing-stocks. The *Epistolae obscurorum vivorum* was written from the point of view of a reactionary Jew hater and in a kind of pigdin Latin, to mock Pfefferkorn and his allies as low-bred dolts. In large part thanks to the *Epistolae obscurorum vivorum*, Reuchlin emerged

---

[33] Langer, op. cit., p. 93. As the Renaissance era approached, Talmudic infiltrators were strategically placed in the hierarchy of the Church. Here we glimpse the authentic root of the Second Vatican Council, as Langer observes (p. 106): "...under the influence of Renaissance humanism...these discussions of the *birkat haminim* now find a new context...growing from a more academic interest in it and not solely from a polemic against it or a desire to convert Jews." Cognizant of the need for a new *modus operandi,* in the Renaissance period the Cryptocracy seeded the impression that "the Talmud and the Kabbalah confirm the truth of the Christian faith when interpreted correctly." No one in their right mind subscribes to so fanciful a hypothesis today, but even Anthonius Margaritha was seduced by it. He subsequently endorsed subverters such as Pico and Reuchlin.

[34] In addition to the preceding examples, we bring to your attention this statement by Reuchlin (which could have been written by John Paul II or Benedict XVI), "Our Apostle Paul studied the complete Jewish wisdom and attended a rabbinical school. What became of him? The greatest of the Apostles!" Reuchlin omits the datum that Paul bitterly regretted his past membership in the religion of the Pharisees, grounded as it was in anti-Biblical traditions of men, which included *violence* against Christians: "You have heard of my former life in Judaism, how I persecuted the Church of God violently and tried to destroy it. And I was advancing in Judaism beyond many of my own age among my people, so extremely zealous was I for the traditions of my fathers." (Galatians 1:13-14).

[35] *"Letters of Obscure Men,"* first published in Cologne in 1515, and reprinted with additional matter in 1517.

from the controversy as "an exemplar of Renaissance erudition and progressive, humanist ideals on the path to the advancement of humanity from darkness to light."

Reuchlin's *Augenspiegel* is a tissue of lies and misrepresentation, but it mattered not. The Cryptocracy saw to it that an enduring image prevailed over a fleeting reality. The "reactionary" Judaic-convert Pfefferkorn, and his allies among the Dominican theologians of Cologne, were painted in the booklet *Epistolae obscurorum vivorum* as bigoted, block-headed louts. There matters have stood these past five centuries.

Some truth concerning Pfefferkorn's authentic character is beginning to come to light. Ruth I. Cape, Pfefferkorn's English translator, who cannot be described as his admirer, nonetheless concedes that his writing contains a "vast array of images and powerful metaphors." These are so eloquent they "contribute to a better understanding of the Early New High German language and its use at the beginning the sixteenth century." Cape states further that the work for which Pfefferkorn is best known, *Der Juden Spiegel* (published in German and Latin in 1507 and 1508), "is a carefully structured pamphlet...a mirror of the struggle and obstacles faced by every person who tries to find a new identity, and symbolizes what a society in transition might experience. In that respect *Der Juden Spiegel* is a timeless document that speaks to readers of all centuries." [36]

In other words it is a classic, and not as the secret society adepts portrayed it: a poorly written hack job by an ignorant scribbler. It was this jaundiced view that the occult Brotherhood hoped to paint—and succeeded in unfairly painting—Pfefferkorn with in the eyes of the intelligentsia of Europe, one of whom was Erasmus, who was infuriated that Pfefferkorn was obstructing the rehabilitation of rabbinic writings.

Pfefferkorn's numerous *Catholic* critics dismissed him as a "half-Jew." [37] Erasmus amended and compounded the racial insult by terming Pfefferkorn a "Jew-and-a-half." [38] It was perversely ironic that anti-Judaic racial prejudice was wielded

---

[36] Ruth I. Cape, *The Jews' Mirror* (2011), pp. ix and xii.

[37] This was untrue; he was Judaic on both his mother and father's side.

[38] Letter to Willibald Pirckheimer, November 2, 1517.

by promoters of Talmudic and Kabbalistic ideology, in order to discredit a Christian convert who obstructed their campaign to persuade Christendom of the benevolence of the rabbinic texts. False witness against Pfefferkorn on the part of "enlightened" Renaissance Catholic humanists was relentless. In 1514 malicious false witness was circulated claiming that this devoutly orthodox, converted Catholic missionary had posed as the messiah, desecrated the Communion wafer and ritually murdered a Christian infant. [39]

While Pfefferkorn struggled against a deluge of libel, his adversary was rising high. Reuchlin candidly averred that the popes were behind both his Talmud project and his Kabbalah promotion:

"That is enough said about the Talmud and why it should not be suppressed or burned. Now to the third section of the Jewish books concerning the divine secrets, utterances and words of God, called the Kabblaah. I could say a lot both for and against it, for our Holy Father Pope Innocent VIII had the Kabbalistic volumes carefully examined and evaluated twenty years ago by eminent bishops and doctors in the course of a case against that nobly born, erudite Count, Giovanni Pico Della Mirandola, of blessed memory. At that time he (Pico) announced publicly that he was willing to go to Rome to dispute on themes and conclusions, among them namely the thesis: 'There is no other science that provides us with greater certainty of Christ's divinity than magic and the Kabbalah'. The theologians of the Holy Scriptures wrote and said many things contrary to this affirmation, in spite of the fact that they were completely ignorant as to what kind of creature the Kabbalah was. Nevertheless, the aforementioned Count refuted their assertions with conviction.

"...Following Innocent's death, his successor, Pope Alexander VI, commissioned many learned cardinals, bishops and officials of the Holy Office of the Inquisition to thoroughly assess the merits and demerits of the books and speeches...Following these deliberations, His Holiness decided that the Count had rightly studied and written appropriately on the Kabbalah, and therefore his book entitled *Apologia,* was approved by a papal

---

[39] Cf. *Die geschicht und bekantnüß des getaufften Juden genannt Johannes Pfefferkorn* (1514).

ruling in 1493. The decision was reached that Pico had studied thoroughly the books of the Kabbalah, and correctly stated that those same books of the Kabbalah, of which there must be approximately 70, demonstrate not only the spirituality of Moses, but the truth of our Christian faith as well...

"It is quite obvious from Count Mirandola's *Apologia*, a book that has been approved by Pope Alexander, that the books of the Kabbalah are not only not malignant, but are also exceedingly helpful to our Christian faith. Pope Sixtus IV ordered them to be translated into our Latin for the use of us Christians. Hence, there is an adequate basis for me to conclude that such Kabbalistic books should not, nor can they be legally suppressed or burned."

The papacy and the top echelon of the hierarchy of the Church of Rome supported Reuchlin's defense of Pico and the Talmud and Kabbalah, while Pfefferkorn was forced to struggle for support. This fact of history shatters the stereotype of the Renaissance Church put forth by the Establishment. According to their fables, the papacy would destroy someone like Reuchlin, while Pfefferkorn would enjoy considerable ecclesiastic support.

Initially, Pfefferkorn had the ear of educated Catholics within and outside the Church, the Catholic aristocracy and the Dominican order in Cologne. It was not until he confronted and frustrated Reuchlin's mission of extending the theology of Giovanni Pico della Mirandola that his troubles began in earnest. Having dared to attempt to halt the progress of the Neoplatonic-Hermetic-Kabbalistic conspiracy he would be falsely accused by the Church of Rome and its allies, of heresy, incompetence and fraud.

Johann Pfefferkorn converted to Catholicism together with his wife and one of his children when he was thirty-seven years of age (circa 1505). During the years 1507-1521 he had the distinction of having penned more publications on Jews and Judaism than any other Christian in the West. For one extended period during his writing career he had no other source of income than in a shelter for the poor (alms house), and as a *salzmeister* (distributor of salt).

Pfefferkorn's *Der Juden Spiegel* in particular was everything Catholic Christianity could hope for from a Judaic convert:

"In the first part of the book Pfefferkorn addresses himself to the Jews, asking them to leave 'the path of darkness' and to finally understand the truth of the Christian faith. He then lists and comments on ten tenets of the Jewish faith, as they had been fairly common in debates between Jews and Christians for centuries. By quoting the Pentateuch and the prophets, he tries to demonstrate to the Jews that the New Testament is foreshadowed in the Old Testament, that Jesus was indeed the Messiah and highest prophet, that Mary has a special status as virgin and mother of God, that there are proofs of the trinity, that the use of images and the adoration of the cross have a valid place in Christian religion, and that Jesus did indeed rise from the dead. Pfefferkorn adds two points of his own. He explains that some Jews would be inclined to accept the Christian faith, yet hesitate to convert when they see the bad examples some Christians set...He also deplores the unremitting reluctance of his former co-religionists to assume the Christian faith. Yet Pfefferkorn shows himself determined to think of ways that could lead these 'blind and obstinate' Jews to 'the light of eternal salvation.' The first part ends with Pfefferkorn's excitement about having found the 'true Messiah,' grace and forgiveness of his sins, and 'eternal glory and salvation.' The official first part of the pamphlet comprises one-half of the whole book. Its length is clearly an indication of the importance of this specific topic in the context of the mission to the Jews.

"In the second part, Pfefferkorn addresses himself to the secular rulers and Christians in general, and describes how they have contributed to the problems in the mission to the Jews. He accuses the Christian authorities of protecting (unconverted) Jews for their own selfish financial benefit by granting them houses and by allowing them to take usury. He criticizes them for not forcing the Jews to listen to sermons, and for not confiscating their non-biblical books (Talmud and Kabbalah) that are full of lies. Pfefferkorn appeals to the Christian authorities' sense of moral responsibility, and demands that Jews should not be permitted to practice usury and that they should work for their living. In order to learn about the word of God, they should also be forced to attend Christian sermons. Their Talmudic books should be confiscated, because he considers them not only misleading but also a major contributor to their obstinacy, and thus an obstacle to Jewish conversion. This last demand is significant, since in the following two years, Pfefferkorn received a mandate from the Emperor Maximilian I, which enabled him personally to confiscate Jewish books throughout the empire."[40]

This mandate would prove to be fleeting.

Pfefferkorn posed a substantial threat to the conspirators. His work had the potential to undo nearly a century of plotting to gain acceptance for the Talmudic and Kabbalistic theology within the Church. To be certain that Pfefferkorn would be obstructed, Maximilian I was offered a substantial bribe from the rabbis to rein in Pfefferkorn, which is precisely what the Emperor of the Holy Roman Empire did, once his pockets were filled:

"Following a well-established line in polemical reasoning that goes back to the thirteenth century when the anti-rabbinical charges brought forward by the (Judaic) convert Nicholas Donin had led to the burning of the Talmud in Paris in 1242, Pfefferkorn argued that the Talmud...was the main reason for the Jewish unwillingness to accept the Christian faith...

"Pfefferkorn was introduced...to Kunigunde of Bavaria, the sister of Emperor Maximilian I, who had retired after the death of her husband to a monastery in Munich. She wrote a favorable letter of introduction for Pfefferkorn, who met the emperor in Padua and received permission to examine the contents of the Talmud. The emperor issued this mandate in August 1509 and confirmed that the Jews should hand over their books to Pfefferkorn for examination when asked by him, and that Pfefferkorn was entitled to confiscate all books considered anti-Christian and contradicting the laws of Moses and the prophets.

"Returning from Italy, Pfefferkorn traveled to Frankfurt am Main, a town with a major Jewish community, and confiscated a number of books (some fifteen hundred). The Jewish community turned to the Archbishop of Mainz, Uriel von Gemmingen, who, apparently offended by what he regarded as an illegitimate intervention by the emperor, protested and

---

[40] Cape, op. cit., pp. x and xi.

wrote to the emperor that Pfefferkorn did not have the expertise to judge Jewish books. The Jews of Frankfurt, legally subjects of the emperor, also sent him a delegation to protest this interference in their internal religious affairs.

"Maximilian I retracted, and in November 1509 issued a new mandate authorizing Uriel von Gemmingen to arrange an inquiry in which a number of experts were to be asked for their opinions. These experts included representatives of the universities of Cologne, Mainz, Erfurt, and Heidelberg; the prior of the Dominicans in Cologne and inquisitor, Dr. Jacobus Hoogstraeten; the convert and priest Victor von Carben; and the Hebraist scholar and lawyer Johannes Reuchlin. The emperor intended to judge the case according to the recommendations of these experts. This did not prevent Pfefferkorn from continuing to confiscate Jewish books in a number of communities, among them again in Frankfurt. Alarmed by this, *the Jews of Frankfurt entered into secret negotiations with the emperor and reached a financial agreement with him.* In May 1510, the emperor ordered that all confiscated books should be restored to the Jews. Pfefferkorn tried in vain to persuade the emperor to revoke this mandate and was told to wait for the final decision.

"...Johannes Reuchlin was the only one explicitly to oppose the confiscation of the Talmud, giving both legal and theological reasons. His report, *Ratschlag*, argues that Jews, as *concives* or fellow-citizens of the empire, had the same legal rights as Christians, including the right of protection against seizure of property by force or without due process of law. In Reuchlin's eyes it was illegal to confiscate and burn Jewish books since the Talmud contained proofs for the truth of Christianity." [41]

This is further evidence of the extent and scope of the charade set in motion by the occult conspirators in the Church, fronted by Reuchlin. They alleged that the Talmud (like the Kabbalah), "contained proofs for the truth of Christianity." At this point in time, under Pope Leo X, anyone of any stature who foiled the agents behind this subversive nonsense would be

---

[41] Maria Diemling, "Conversion, Anti-Judaism, Controversy: The Rise and Fall of Johannes Pfefferkorn," in *The Jews' Mirror,* op. cit., pp. 23-25 (emphasis supplied).

rendered infamous and reduced to impotent ignominy, which was to be the the the fate of Pfefferkorn. Judaic historian William Popper writes:

"Pfefferkorn began his work in Frankfort and immediately a violent protest was raised by Jews, supported by some friendly Christians...the Elector Mainz and the Archbishop Uriel of Gemmingen...On November 10, 1509, Pfefferkorn went to the Emperor at Tyrol, and secured a decree from him that confiscation should be carried out. The Archbishop Uriel of Gemmingen however, was appointed to decide the issue in regard to the Talmud...the Jews again sent friendly Christians as delegates to the Emperor, to carry before him letters recommending leniency; among them was one from the Archbishop Uriel, who seems to have played a double role in the affair, but to have been more a friend than an enemy of the Jews.

"These delegates declared that Pfefferkorn's charges were false, and the Emperor was persuaded to issue a new decree ordering the return to the Jews of their confiscated books. Pfefferkorn answered with a letter printed in Latin and...broadcast throughout Germany; in it he reviewed the whole case and roused the German people to agitate against the Jews...

"A long controversy between Reuchlin and Pfefferkorn followed...Reuchlin was accused of heresy and a commission, appointed to investigate, determined to give its decision not only against him, but naturally against the Talmud and the whole of Jewish literature. But there was still a spirit of justice and broad-mindedness even in parts of Germany, and while the students of Mainz objected to the proceedings as illegal, men of influence likewise interfered. Even though preparations had been made for the audo-de-fé (of the rabbinic texts) and men were ready on the appointed days to light the fires, a hasty message from Archbishop Uriel postponed the carrying out of the sentence for one month; he ordered the commission to reopen the case after one month and threatened, if it refused, to nullify all its previous work and to deprive it of all power to act in the future. The case reopened, dragged along slowly and was carried to Rome. In November, 1513, Pope Leo X, beloved of the Jews in Italy, persuaded by his Jewish physician Bonet de Lates, ordered all former verdicts to be set aside...the Bishop of Speier himself decided that Reuchlin's writings were not heretical or false...A humanist party arose throughout Europe in support of Reuchlin..." [42]

The preceding history, while readily accessible, is largely unknown, in part, perhaps, because it constitutes one more nail in the coffin of the caricature of the early and middle-Renaissance papacy as a hammer "against the Jews." What Pfefferkorn endured under Archbishop Uriel and Pope Leo X is not very different from what Bishop Richard Williamson endured from Cardinal Roger Mahony and Pope Benedict XVI in 2009. [43]

Throughout the campaign against Pfefferkorn, snobbery was invoked to paint him as deficient in scholarship and intellect, while his opponents, as personified by Reuchlin, were puffed as paragons of genius, learning and decency. This snob appeal was played up by the Neoplatonic-Hermetic operatives behind the writing and circulation of the *Epistolae obscurorum vivorum*, which rapidly acquired a reputation as a daring and intellectually brilliant act of defiance of the established order. As Europe's intelligentsia processed further into Renaissance humanism, and scholasticism began to fall into disrepute, Pfefferkorn was successfully caricatured as an obtuse ultra-conservative who had no right to contradict the views of Christian humanists of the calibre of Reuchlin.

The merits of Pfefferkorn's expert inside knowledge of Judaism's canonical books was not directly contested in the *Epistolae obscurorum vivorum*. The authors were too astute for that. We know now that one of the co-authors of this anonymous pamphlet was a Catholic-Lutheran double-agent, one "Crotus Rubeanus," who, in 1517, was a doctor of Catholic theology at the University of Bologna and a humanist; then a convert to Lutheranism and one of the first Lutheran

---

[42] William Popper, *The Censorship of Hebrew Books*, pp. 21-25.

[43] In the course of an interview with a Swedish television news crew in Germany, Bishop Williamson stated that it was his opinion that approximately 200,000 to 300,000 Judaics had died in the "holocaust" during World War II, and not six million. The child-molestation facilitator Mahony then banned him "from entering any Catholic church, school or facility of the Archdiocese of Los Angeles" until he retracted his statement ("Cardinal Mahony bans Bishop Williamson from L.A. archdiocese," Catholic News Agency, March 5, 2009).

"missionaries to Prussia." Then, in 1530 "Rubeanus" reverted to Catholicism. Another author of the *Epistolae* is said to have been Ulrich von Hutten, the man Emperor Maximilian crowned poet-laureate in 1517.

The behind-the-scenes maneuvering within the Roman Catholic Church and the Royal Court against the Judaic-Catholic convert Pfefferkorn and in favor of the rabbis and Reuchlin, is labyrinth. There is the treachery of the Prince Archbishop Uriel of Mainz (designated a prince because he was one of the seven "Electors" who chose the Emperor). As Pfefferkorn was working for the Gospel and exposing the Talmud in Frankfurt am Main, the Judaic community sent the son of Simon Weissenau, the wealthiest Judaic in Frankfurt, to "appeal" to the Prince Archbishop Uriel in Aschaffenburg. It didn't hurt the cause of the Judaics that Uriel was in debt for a substantial sum of money (fifteen hundred gulden) to Weissenau. Consequently, Uriel defended the Talmud against the confiscations by Pfefferkorn. Placing his priests under a threat of harsh punishment, the Prince Archbishop commanded all clerics under his jurisdiction to refuse to cooperate with Pfefferkorn's seizure of the Talmud.[44]

The record also shows that Emperor Maximilian, who was supposed to be an ally of Pfefferkorn in Germany (in part, so the story goes, due to appeals from Maximilian's devout Catholic sister, Kunigunde von Bayern), nonetheless employed Henricus Cornelius Agrippa, one of the leading Satanic Kabbalists inside the circles of the Church of Rome, as a spy in Spain, and later in an important military capacity. [45]

Maximilian accepted bribes from Jonathan Levi Zion, one of the leaders of the Frankfurt Talmudists. [46] Maximilian's military ally, Duke Erich of Braunschweig, was in heavy debt (fifty-four hundred gulden) to Itzing Bopfingen, a Judaic loanshark in Frankfurt. In return for Maximilian halting the confiscation of the Talmud, in May, 1511, Bopfingen promised to lift the interest on the duke's debt for three years.

---

[44] In the early years Uriel had supported Pfefferkorn's confiscations of the Talmud.

[45] Cf. Albert Rabil Jr. (ed.), *Declamation on the Nobility and Preeminence of the Female Sex* by Henricus Cornelius Agrippa, (1996) pp. 4 and 6.

[46] Erika Rummel, *The Case Against Johann Reuchlin* (2002), pp. 11-12.

Defenders of the papacy of Leo X will point out that he eventually "silenced" Reuchlin. Taken out of context it seems that this datum settles the matter. When considered as part of Leo's papacy as a whole however, one comprehends that Pope Leo had permitted Reuchlin to spread his occult virus far and wide, until the conservative counter-reaction grew so intense that Leo went *on record* "silencing" Reuchlin. This was a farce; a token gesture intended for consumption by pious believers in the integrity of the pope and his word. The fact of the matter is that Reuchlin was certainly not "silenced." In the last years of his life Reuchlin was a very vocal and high profile professor at the Catholic University of Tübingen. More significantly, he and his occult-Catholic cabal were victorious. A "Golden Age" of Talmud publishing commenced in Catholic Europe thanks to their efforts. While the Vatican launched a draconian crackdown on Protestant books, an edition of the complete Talmud was published by the printing house of Bomberg, with *papal sanction*:

"The natural liberality of Pope Leo X and the many influences friendly to Jews that surrounded him prompted his interest in Jewish literature and not only moved him to grant permission for a Jewish press at Rome but resulted in his open advocacy of the Talmud...Toward the beginning of the sixteenth century Joseph Pfefferkorn, a Moravian Jew, finding himself in straitened circumstances...embraced Christianity and, as a violent and bloodthirsty Jew hater, seems to have flourished for many years thereafter. We are not so much concerned with his successful method of earning a living as with the fact that his attacks on the Talmud, encouraged by the Dominicans of Germany, the most illiterate and stupid of all the monastic brethren, led to the conflict between the Humanists and Obscurantists, which brought out the noble Reuchlin's temperate and well-considered defense of the Jews and their literature. The charge of heresy brought against Reuchlin by the Dominicans raised the issue of the relation of the Talmud and rabbinical writings towards Christianity. The trial of the case dragged from Mainz to Speyer, and thence to Rome, but long before the final decision was rendered, Pope Leo X gave unmistakable indication of his position in the controversy between culture and ignorance. This noble son of Lorenzo di Medici, whose plastic intellect had been moulded by the master hand of Poliziano of Florence, who had been initiated into the mysteries of the Hebrew tongue and its literature, was deaf to the importunities of ignorant monks and overzealous apostates. To the great consternation of the faithful, he followed the suggestion of his friend, Cardinal Egidio of Viterbo, to permit the establishment of a Hebrew press at Rome and he officially endorsed Daniel Bomberg's project to print a complete edition of the Talmud...whereupon Messer Daniel, within five years, completed this magnificent work, sparing no expense...to the delight of Jews and Christian scholars and to the chagrin and despair of the pious multitude." [47]

Feeling the heavy hand of papal tyrants to *"the great consternation of the faithful...and to the chagrin and despair of the pious multitude,"* is an old story in the Church of Rome. These Renaissance and post-Renaissance dictators are supposed to be Christ's shepherds, yet with impunity they suppressed the *birthright* Christ bequeathed unto His people by right of their redemption by His blood. This spectacle shows that these travesties are transpiring not in His Church but in another organization altogether, administered by Antichrist "Holinesses" and "Eminences."

"Traditional" Catholics rejoin that it is because modernist prelates are not traditional that they are tyrants. It is this fantastic Janus-mind of the "traditionalists" that consigns them to a fantasy world where they cannot be effective because they are proceeding from specious premises. One cannot get more "traditional" or more tyrannical than Pope Leo X or Archbishop Uriel of Mainz, who are role models for the Vatican modernists of the twentieth and twenty-first centuries.

The destiny of Catholic lay people, friars and parish priests, from the Renaissance to the present, is to be placed under the heel of occult tyrants in the Vatican who are grand masters of masquerade. It was said of even the leaders of the pagan Roman Republic that they fulfilled their sacred duty of protecting the commons from the aristocracy. This has too often been the reverse of the case in the Church of Rome since the Renaissance. The bishops and cardinals failed to protect the common Catholic people from the aristocracy of the popes and

---

[47] David Amram, *The Makers of Hebrew Books in Italy* (1963), pp. 160-162.

in most cases, colluded with them. Was this Christ's plan for the members of His Church for whom He shed His life's blood, a two-tier system in which specially privileged, costumed gangsters lord it over the Faithful?

"Daniel Bomberg established his famous printing house in Venice and even received the blessing and approval of Leo X. In subsequent years Bomberg printed two editions of the (Babylonian) Talmud (and an edition of the Palestinian Talmud), based on the explicit approval of the pope." [48]

The full ramifications of what the Pope of Rome wrought when he granted permission for the publication of the "Talmud Bavli" (Babylonian Talmud) are nearly incalculable. Sincere Judaic converts such as Johann Pfefferkorn had related to the hierarchy of the Church the fact that rabbinic Judaism effectively could not exist without recourse to the Talmud of Babylon, which served to increase their "obstinancy." The Talmud was the sustenance of the religion which institutionalized not only the denial that Jesus was the Christ, but idolatry, nullification of the Word of God in the Bible,[49] and the robbery, murder and financial oppression of non-Jews. Without an authoritative printed edition of the Talmud Bavli at hand, Judaics and their rabbis were more susceptible to Catholic evangelism, and what is more, they might begin to enjoy a life free of the curse of tyrannical micromanagement of their lives by Talmudic bureaucracy and its regulatory minutiae. Before Leo X, the legacy of the faithfulness and vigilance of the popes and Councils of the Middle Ages had produced a crisis for the Talmud in Europe and Britain. By the dawn of the early Renaissance the Talmud was nearing extinction—existing mainly in fading and crumbling manuscripts of widely varying textual reliability and authority.

---

[48] Amnon Raz-Krakotzkin, *The Censor, the Editor, and the Text: The Catholic Church and the Shaping of the Jewish Canon in the Sixteenth Century* (2007), p. 40. Pope Leo's printing permit for the House of Bomberg is cited as a precedent by Pope Clement VII, in his letter to Bomberg of July 26, 1532.

[49] "...in some instances violation of the law may be the only appropriate means to fulfill it, an idea expressed in Talmudic literature in the saying attributed to Reish Laqish, '*Pe'amim she-bittulah shel torah zehu yesodah*: 'There are occasions when the nullification of the Torah is its foundation." Cf. Elliot Wolfson, "Messianism in the Christian Kabbalah," in *Jewish Messianism in the Early Modern World* (2001), p. 152.

Pope Leo X rescued the Babylonian Talmud from eradication, a circumstance largely unknown, even today. The Cryptocracy has seen to it that the Church of Rome has been made notorious as a Talmud-burner, not a Talmud-preserver.

The Van Bombergens had been a wealthy Catholic merchant dynasty in Antwerp. The scion, Daniel van Bombergen (1483–ca. 1550), later known as "Daniel Bomberg," emigrated to Italy, where his master-craftsman printing facility was established with a reputation for superior quality paper and binding, and meticulous attention to detail. Bomberg partnered with the Judaic pseudo-convert to Catholicism, Felix Pratensis, an Augustinian monk known in Catholicism as Fra Felice de Prato, to found, under the initial aegis of Pope Leo X, a publishing enterprise which printed *many thousands of volumes of sacred rabbinic books* over the course of twenty-three years of operation.

The fact that Felix had been the handler of the youthful Giles of Viterbo, squares the circle of conspiracy. Bomberg was a gentile. "It was Felix who initially persuaded Bomberg to found a printing press in Venice. The first (Catholic printing) privilege was granted Bomberg in 1515. Between then and 1538 Bomberg had produced 186 Hebrew texts," including "the first complete Babylonian Talmud 1519-1523." [50]

In fact, the astute businessman Bomberg obtained that privilege through his partnership with Felix "Fra Felice" Pratensis, for it was Felix who had first "been granted a ten-year papal *approbatio* and a comparable *privilegio* by Pope Leo X in Rome..." [51]

Bomberg petitioned for a similar privilege for his operations in Venice. Through Felix Pratensis' connections inside the papal curia, he managed to assist his Catholic partner Bomberg in excluding all other rivals, including the Catholic Aldus Manutius, who was at the time the leading printer in Venice. "When his petition was granted, Bomberg had effectively won for himself a monopoly of all Hebrew printing in Venice...he had the support and imprimatur of Pope Leo X, who had openly vouched for the value of Hebrew works for the

---

[50] Robert J. Wilkinson, *Orientalism, Aramaic and Kabbalah in the Catholic Reformation* (2007), pp. 45-46.

[51] David Stern, *The Hebrew Book in Early Modern Italy*, Joseph R. Hacker and Adam Shear, eds., (2011) p. 79.

Christian religion....The importance of Pope Leo's approbation for the success of Bomberg and Pratensis's publishing project should not be underestimated..." [52]

The deluge of conspiracies against the Church of Jesus Christ on the part of the Renaissance popes and their hierarchies is often of such a depth that one almost needs wings to stay above it and not drown. Bomberg obtained his printing monopoly largely due to having been selected for that bonanza by Giles of Viterbo, [53] who had been placed on his Kabbalistic path in his youth by his Judaic Augustinian-monk "tutor," Bomberg's future partner, Felix "Fra Felice Prato" Pratensis. Viterbo, who we introduced earlier, was a second generation Catholic-Kabbalist of power and influence.[54]

During the negotiations over the printing rights for the Talmud, Giles was Superior-General of the Augustinian Order. His monk, Martin Luther, reported to him in Rome in the winter of 1510-1511. Leo X made Giles a Cardinal in 1517. He was a serious contender for the papacy in the conclave that ended in the election of the Dutchman Adrian VI. His influence continued in the curia under the pontificate of Clement VII. He initiated hundreds of future leaders of the Church—Catholic scholars, prelates, monks and priests—in the Satanism of the Kabbalah. As we shall see, he was responsible for inspiring the publication after his death of an *overt* and *blatant* herald of the Kabbalistic expropriation of the Catholic Church, included as an illustration in the first-ever "Catholic" publication of the Syriac New Testament.

With Giles in Bomberg's corner, it was no wonder that the Catholic merchant from Antwerp was transformed into the Talmudic printer of the age, issuing large print runs of high quality, multi-volume folio sets. The Bomberg Talmud itself became one of the great ornaments of typographic achievement

---

[52] Ibid., pp. 79-80.

[53] Some scholars like Robert J. Wilkinson allude to him almost solely by his patrynomic, "Egidio da Viterbo," while others, such as John W. O'Malley, use the name Giles of Viterbo.

[54] Giles of Viterbo's magnum opus was *Libellus de Litteris sanctis*, taken from the Kabbalah tractate *Sefer ha-temunah*. He was in bondage to the Kabbalistic mysticism surrounding the female and male deities, and the delusion that the letters of the ancient Hebrew and Syriac alphabet revealed supernatural secrets. (Syriac is a form of Aramaic).

and book production of the sixteenth century. It is not an exaggeration to say that it was the finest edition of the Babylonian Talmud in western history up to the time of its publication, and it ensured the continuation and expansion of rabbinic Judaism over the next two hundred years. Through Bomberg, *the Renaissance Pope of Rome served as the father of a new birth of Talmudic Judaism.*

Bomberg's editorial staff consisted, in addition to Felix, Jacob ben Hayyim ibn Adoniyahu, a Judaic scholar who "was a full fledged Kabbalist."[55] Bomberg published Kabbalistic books, such as the *Zror ha-mor*, in addition to the Talmud. Bomberg's rabbinic texts issued under the supervision of Ibn Adoniyahu were invaluable for the success and continuation of Judaism. Writing in the nineteenth century of Ibn Adoniyahu's work for the pope's printer more than three hundred years earlier, C.D. Ginsburg stated that the Bomberg volumes overseen by Ibn Adoniyahu were so authoritative that no textual redactor of modern times should dare to deviate from them without giving a conclusive reason for doing so.

Other rabbinic and Judaic scholars on Bomberg's payroll were: the leader of the Venetian Judaics, Rabbi Hiya Meir ben David, as well as Rabbi Meir Katzenellenbogen, the chief rabbi of Padua and judge of the Judaic court of the Republic of Venice; his son, Rabbi Shmuel Katzenellenbogen, and Chaim ben R. Moshe Alton, Avraham de Balmes and David ben-Eliezer Halevi Pizzighettone.

The latter Judaic scholar (Pizzighettone) was responsible for the textual integrity of the heretofore hand-printed *Mishneh Torah*, the huge twelfth century anti-Christian polemic and legal treatise of the famous Moses Maimonides, which was published by Bomberg in 1524. Like his Talmud, the publication of Bomberg's *Mishneh Torah* with the blessing of the Church of Rome, helped to perpetuate within Judaism Maimonides' blasphemy against Christ and his appeals to

---

[55] Stern, op. cit., p. 83.

violence against Christians, by institutionalizing it in the form of a printed multivolume series of high quality.[56]

After Bomberg's death, more Catholic printers took his place, building on his foundational Talmud text, which remained unsurpassed and largely intact, even though subsequent editions would bear the name of the printer who undertook the work. With regard to one of Bomberg's Catholic successors, Marc Antonio Giustiniani, who published the Talmud in Venice from 1546-1551, the eminent Polish Rabbi Moses Isserles acknowledged the partnership which existed between the rabbis and Catholic printers and how it benefited Talmudic Judaism:

"Isserles well understood that, ever since Daniel Bomberg had received his monopoly...to print Hebrew Hebrew books, Jews depended heavily on Venetian Christian printers for print editions of foundational rabbinic texts. Indeed, Giustiniani's edition of the Talmud, which the Venetian patrician had begun to print, tractate by tractate in 1546, was designed to meet the needs of Polish *yeshiviot* (rabbinic schools)—and became the standard for all subsequent editions. Isserles recognizes in his ruling that one might claim that 'these (Christian) printers have taught Torah and without them, Heaven forbid, the Torah would have already forgotten Israel, and thus it is appropriate to assist this mission so that there will be no ruin." [57]

From time to time Rome believed it necessary to placate outraged conservative Catholic opinion by mounting a farcical assault on the modernizing innovation of Catholic sponsorship of antichrist rabbinic books. Hence, in 1548, the Church of Rome instituted a new measure, through the Senate of Venice, forbidding Judaic persons from employment at Catholic publishing houses in any capacity, whether as printers,

---

[56] After Bomberg's death, Rabbi Meir Katzenellenbogen commissioned the reprinting in 1550 of Bomberg's edition of the *Mishneh Torah*, by the Venetian Catholic printer Alvise Bragadini, under a printing license granted to Bragadini at the request of Katzenellenbogen, by Katzenellenbogen's cousin, Rabbi Moses Isserles ("the Rema"), one of Ashkenazi Judaism's supreme legal authorities at the time, and the author of the authoritative body of rabbinic law, *HaMapah*. The authority of Isserles' *responsum* (rabbinic decree) extended throughout Europe, in this case from Krakow to Venice. Cf. Neil Weinstock Netanel, *From Maimonides to Microsoft: The Jewish Law of Copyright* (2016), pp. 69-106.

[57] Ibid, pp. 107-108.

typesetters or editors. The next year, in 1549, legislation governing the Venetian Printer's Guild declared that no one could work as a printer unless they were members of the Catholics-only guild. This was red meat to Conservatives, and then as now, they were gulled by what was efectively a hoax: "The prohibition against Jews working in presses...was not rigorously enforced. Witness Katzenellenbogen's collaboration with Bragadini to print the *Mishneh Torah*. For that matter the Venetian printer's guild was not actually established until 1567." [58]

For those who can penetrate the vast apparatus of "The Inquisition"—the intellectual construct that brooks no dissent from the florid image of wretched Italian Judaics besieged by a veritable holocaust of repression and book burnings—the delight of encountering a concealed truth awaits them. The rabbis experienced a Renaissance of their own under the sixteenth century Neoplatonic-Hermetic-Kabbalistic popes of Rome. Beneath the reverberating anathemas and denunciations issued by the Counter-Reformation, it was principally the thunderbolts hurled at Protestants that were backed with consistent, violent repression across decades, unrelieved by any interregnum or respite. *Many rabbis thrived in papal Italy during the Renaissance*. Two momentous achievements by the papists: the execution of Girolamo Savonarola toward the end of the fifteenth century, and the neutralization of the campaign of Johann Pfefferkorn early in the next one, ended, for all intents and purposes, the possibility of any grassroots holy war on the occult popes and their enormous networks of banking, nepotism and patronage.

The life of Rabbi Judah ben Joseph Moscato (ca. 1533-1590) in Catholic Italy (he was a native of Osimo in the papal states), is the epitome of this closeted reality. He was a prominent representative of what has come to be known as "the Italian-Jewish Renaissance." The Mantua-based rabbi was the author of an erudite commentary on Judah Halevy's anti-Christian polemic, *Kuzari*, which was published by the Catholic printing house of Giovanni di Gara in Venice in 1594. Moscato's scholarship reflected "deep engagement with Renaissance culture, both in its humanist and its Platonic/Hermetic

---

[58] Ibid., p. 110.

manifestations...Moscato was a Jewish chauvinist, but his version of chauvinism allowed him to engage with secular culture, since he strongly believed that all that was worthwhile in secular culture ultimately derived from Jewish culture...He...cites a number of Jewish authorities on the theft of philosophy and sciences from the Jews, reaffirming a Jewish version of the *prisca sapientia*." [59]

The Renaissance popes made certain to protect their Kabbalistic allies. If Rabbi Moscato's name had been Luther or Calvin he would have been burned in short order. Instead, he flourished in the homeland of the popes. Despite the diversionary palaver about a "witch hunt against Jews" by Renaissance pontiffs, "Northern Italy was the center of Hebrew printing from the late fifteenth through the early seventeenth centuries, and by the middle of the sixteenth century, print was the preferred, indeed even assumed, medium of publication for Italian Jews, and numerous editions of medieval and classical Hebrew texts had been issued." [60]

During the Renaissance, the Church of Rome was responsible for the diffusion and popularization of the Talmud and Kabbalah throughout Europe and the Middle East: "Italy's importance was magnified by its geographic centrality in the Jewish world. The Jews of northern Italy traded with Jews throughout the early modern Jewish world, from Germany and Poland-Lithuania to the Ottoman Empire and North Africa, by way of ports in Venice and other cities and overland routes across the Alps. Books printed in Italy circulated to all these areas, and books printed in the farther reaches of Jewish settlement made their way to Italy. Moreover, northern Italy drew in Jews from a wide variety of Jewish communities—from Iberia, southern France, southern Italy, former Byzantine lands, Germany, and the Middle East—who brought with them their medieval traditions and manuscripts, leading to rich possibilities for textual production and publication. Italy continued to be an important print center into the late

---

[59] Adam Shear, "Judah Moscato's Scholarly Self Image and the Question of Jewish Humanism," in *Cultural Intermediaries: Jewish Intellectuals in Early Modern Italy* (2004) pp. 165-166.

[60] Adam Shear, "Judah Moscato's Sources and Hebrew Printing in the Sixteenth Century," in *Rabbi Judah Moscato and the Jewish Intellectual World of Mantua* (2012), p. 123.

seventeenth and eighteenth centuries..." [61] This distribution network included Britain and the Protestant nations of Europe, and having erased the network's existence from their comical histories, Catholic apologists of the nineteenth and twentieth centuries proceeded to excoriate Protestants for "initiating the Judaizing of the West from their publishing base in Amsterdam."

According to William Popper, rabbinic books were unmolested from the pontificate of Leo X until 1550 and the election of Pope Julius III. "...at the beginning of the pontificate of Julius III the Golden Era of Jewish literature continued as a reflection of the sunshine of papal favor...(Even) after the pope had issued a bull on April 29, 1550, repealing all previous permission which might have been given to possess or read forbidden books, as far as the Jews were concerned he still acted generously, instructing cardinals and papal delegates to respect Jewish religious observances, and not to annoy them in any way." [62]

Even under pressure from conservative Catholic cardinals, as late as December 5, 1553 Julius III renewed papal privileges for the rabbis of Ancona. "The Pope had shown himself especially friendly to the Jews of that city." Carafa's plan for a "general destruction of Hebrew works...was clearly more than the Papal court at Rome had originally planned." [63]

Half a rabbinic loaf being better than none, Pope Julius III conspired to preserve one part of the Talmud from interdiction: "...in the catalogue of prohibited books which the Inquisition published in Milan and Venice in this year (1554), while the 'Talmuth' is mentioned as one of the works forbidden to the faithful, nothing is said of other Hebrew books...Julius III issued a bull on May 29, 1554 which cited the edict of the Inquisition directed against the *'ghemarat Talmud'* and which ordered its surrender, under penalty of death. But by emphasizing the term *'gemarah,'* (Gemara) the inference was

---

[61] Joseph R. Hacker and Adam Shear, *The Hebrew Book in Early Modern Italy* (2011), p. 10.

[62] Popper, op. cit., pp. 29-30.

[63] Ibid., pp. 36-37.

allowed that other works, and even the *mishnayoth* (Mishnah) as such, were not subject to destruction..." [64]

In other words, the first part of the Babylonian Talmud containing the Mishnah, the foundational core of the Oral Law traditions of the Pharisees contemporary with Jesus, was permitted publication even in 1554.

"But the Church burned the Talmud!" the traditionalist papists will say in defense of their idolatrous destroyers of Catholicism. Right. It was burned. But that came after Leo X, and even then the destruction was fraught with compromise, trade-offs and skullduggery. *After* the Talmudic horse had decisively departed the Augean stables of the Vatican, *only then* was there a public show of hostility toward the Talmud. We call it a show because much, though not all, of the "destruction" was a sop to orthodox Catholics and the masses, to maintain their belief in the myth of an anti-Talmudic, anti-Kabbalistic papacy. The limited incidents of destruction, deliberately magnified by the Cryptocracy into an image seared into our minds of a vast bonfire of Judaic books over centuries, was an operation that was never intended to return the Talmud and Kabbalah to the place they had occupied in the Catholic Middle Ages, when they existed only as hard-written copies of what amounted to rabbinic hate speech, studied and analyzed by Catholic scholars for purposes of refutation and apologia.

A few examples: Pope "Saint" Pius V is an unassailable icon in the eyes of "conservative" and "traditional" Catholics, in part because he assisted in organizing and inspiring the defeat at the naval battle of Lepanto of a formidable Turkish invasion fleet. Decades before this, the Kabbalist conspirator Giles of Viterbo had opened the Fifth Lateran Council with a call for a crusade against the Muslims. These facts of themselves exonerate no one of the crime of betrayal of Jesus Christ. They act as a signature image; a general branding which is supposed to represent the sum of the churchman under study. Need we know nothing else about Giles other than the fact that he was an anti-Muslim orator? Is Lepanto the sole alpha and omega of the papacy of Pius V? The dark forces intend for us to neglect the details of the lives and acts of these churchmen based on

---

[64] Ibid., p. 38.

generalized, supposedly signature events which have the effect of being investigation-stoppers. Yet if we look deeper we discover Cardinal Giles Viterbo was at the heart of the conspiracy to silence Pfefferkorn and exonerate Reuchlin, and at the center of the revolutionary papal publishing enterprise that saw the unprecedented dissemination, in handsome heirloom editions, of the Talmud and Kabbalah.

Looking deeper into the pontificate of Pius V we see him acting as the patron and protector of an important occult infiltrator, Sixtus of Siena (1520-1569), a Judaic pseudo-convert to Catholicism. Sixtus' Kabbalistic recidivism was detected by true Catholics and he was imprisoned, and then released from prison by order of Pope Pius and given safe haven within the Dominican Order, again at the request of the pope. In 1559, "the pope dispatched Sixtus to burn the Talmud in Cremona, Italy," which he did. We could end our narrative there, as do the majority of historians, and another gem would be added to the spiritual tiara of Pius V.

The Cremona Conspiracy: The truth is very different from the appearance, however. Like many Renaissance pontiffs, Pope "Saint" Pius V seems to have been inordinately fond of the Kabbalah and the necessity of its dissemination. When he was Cardinal Michele Ghisleri, seven years before he would be elected pope, he was *sacro totius Christrianae Inquisitionis Senatui praeesset* (head of the Christian Inquisition). He learned that a treasure trove of two thousand copies of the Kabbalah were sitting in Cremona vulnerable to being burned. How might the future Pius V rescue that precious horde without causing a scandal among Conservatives and possibly blowing the cover of the Hermetic-Kabbalistic conspiracy of the Renaissance prelates and pontiffs?

The provenance of those Kabbalistic books, specifically hundreds of copies of the *Zohar*, is itself deserving of mention. They were published in 1559 by the Catholic printer Vincenzo Conti in association with Vittorio Eliano, the grandson of Elias

Levita, whose patron and protector had been Cardinal Giles of Viterbo. [65]

Conti served as the publisher for the textbooks used in Rabbi Yosef Ottolenghi's *yeshiva* (rabbinic school). Ottolenghi was also "editor in chief" at Conti's Catholic printing house! [66] Catholics in Cremona campaigned against this obscenity and petitioned the Inquisition for the destruction of Conti's entire print run of the *Zohar*. But Conti operated with the knowledge and permission of the future Pope "Saint" Pius V. A clever ruse was then devised to protect the beloved copies of Satan's *Zohar*. Sixtus of Siena was dispatched to Cremona on a devious mission: find and burn to great fanfare any copies of the Talmud. *The official account stops there.*

Hence, the myth has it that the future pope ordered the burning of the Talmud and his sincere Judiac convert protégé faithfully performed his duty on behalf of the Inquisition. The Talmud was burned in Cremona; end of story.

Here, as Paul Harvey would say, is *the rest of the story*: the Talmud-burning was a diversion. In the midst of the spectacular bonfire, Sixtus requisitioned the two thousand copies of the *Zohar* and placed them in safety. "Sixtus came to destroy, and he did destroy, but he returned from his journey to Cremona with...the satisfaction of having saved the edition of the *Zohar* that had just been produced by Vincenzo Conti." [67]

The Cremona Conspiracy: *Two steps forward, one step backward.*

For the Renaissance papacy and its top theologians and intellectuals—such as Francesco Giorgio, Paul Ricci, Ludovico Lazzarelli, Petrus Galatinus, Cardinal Giles of Viterbo,

[65] "From 1515 Egidio (Giles of Viterbo) had in his household at Rome the German-born Jewish scholar and grammarian Elias (also spelled Elijah) Levita (1468-1549). Their partnership was of enormous significance..." Robert J. Wilkinson, op. cit., p. 48. "For years, Giles supported Elijah Levita...Levita and his family lived for thirteen years as devout Jews in the Roman palace of Cardinal Giles of Viterbo." Levita's "*Sefer ha-Bahur* (1518) was not only dedicated to Giles but also printed in Rome with the official approbation of Leo X." David H. Price, *Johannes Reuchlin* (2011), pp. 183-184.

[66] Cf. Shlomo Simonsohn, "A Contract for Publishing Hebrew Books in Cremona," in *Shlomo Umberto Nachon* (Shlomo Meir Institute [Jerusalem], 1978), pp. 143-150.

[67] Saverio Campanini, "The Editio Princeps of the Sefer Yesirah," in *Rabbi Judah Moscato and the Jewish Intellectual World of Mantua* (2012), p. 254.

Agostino Steuco, Antonius Hieronymus Lunarius de Recaneto, and Johannes Reuchlin—the Kabbalah, and in particular the Kabbalistic book of the *Zohar* and the *Sefer Yetzirah* ("Yesirah") had canonical status. As the Counter-Reformation came into its own in the sixteenth century, and began to more vociferously and publicly lay claim to the medieval Catholic mantle of anti-Judaism, the Talmud was increasingly the subject of both real and theatrical, criticism and suppression.

According to plan, the many thousands of magnificent copies of the Talmud already published by Italian Catholic printers with the permission of popes from Leo X forward, and distributed and secreted throughout Europe by rabbis and gentiles alike for decades, made the prospect of the Talmud's extirpation only a few decades later, during the Council of Trent, exceedingly difficult and improbable. But as theatre, and for rhetorical purposes, the declamations contra the Talmud made for an effective buttress for the propaganda that the Church of Rome was the relentless foe of the Talmud.

While punitive attention in this time period was focused on the Talmud, simultaneously in Catholic Europe: "there was an explosion of Kabbalistic publications in the years immediately following the burning of the Talmud (1553 in the papal states; 1559 in Cremona, as we have seen)..." [68]

Heinrich Graetz (1817-1891), a German-Judaic historian, believed that he detected the Hermetic-Kabbalistic hand of the papacy in this stratagem. He argued that the *Zohar* volume of the Kabbalah was: "*Schoßkind des Papstums*" ("the favorite child of the papacy"). His thesis was that the early modern popes believed, in keeping with their covert Hermetic theology, that the mysticism of the *Zohar*, and the books of the Kabbalah in general, were more compatible with the Renaissance-Catholic religion than the Talmud. [69]

From the mid-fifteenth century onward, Kabbalistic popes were a dime a dozen. Paul III (Alessandro Farnese, pontiff from 1534 to 1549), was the acclaimed "Counter-Reformation pope," convener of the Council of Trent, bane of adulterous English King Henry VIII, patron of the founding of the Jesuit Order,

---

[68] Campanini, op. cit., p. 255.

[69] Heinrich Graetz, *Geschichte der Juden* (Leipzig: Oskar Leiner, 1877), p. 369.

and of Michelangelo's *Last Judgment* in the Sistine chapel. Paul III's curriculum vitae is sure to warm the heart of the "traditional" and "conservative" Catholic. A closer examination of Paul's papacy vis a vis the occult conspiracy is in order, however. Pope Paul III put the fox in charge of the hen house when, in 1538, he appointed as Director of the Vatican Library, the Neoplatonic-Hermetic Kabbalist Agostino Steuco.

"Still more favored were the Jews by Paul III. (1534-50)...Paul permitted all the Jews who had been banished from Naples, as well as those coming from Palestine and Africa, to settle in Rome. He abolished the passion-plays in the Colosseum, at which Jews had often been murdered, and he granted permission (1545) to Antonio Bladao, Isaac ben Immanuel de Lattes, and Benjamin ben Joseph Arignano to establish a Hebrew printing-press in Rome." [70]

Furthermore, Paul III was the patron of Michelangelo and Loyola in public, but in private he was an equally momentous patron of the Catholic-Kabbalist who published under the unwieldy moniker, "Antonius Hieronymus Lunarius de Recaneto."

Like Giles of Viterbo before him, Recaneto envisioned the papacy as the chosen vehicle for ushering in the Kabbalistic age. Where Cardinal Giles hallowed Leo X as the holy enabler of that magical epoch, Recaneto assigned the role to Pope Paul III and dedicated his book of Kabbalah advocacy (*Discursus de Reformatione Ecclesiae*) to the pontiff.

In neither case did either man suffer any punishment of any kind from the popes to whom they dedicated their occult blasphemies. On the contrary, Kabbalistic papalolaters like Recaneto and Giles of Viterbo were protected and elevated. Cardinal Viterbo was nearly elected pope in 1522.

As we have noted, legend has it that Leo X did get around to issuing a censure of Reuchlin in June, 1520, years after Reuchlin's case had been made, his career and reputation secured and his book rendered a *cause célébre*.

In 1511, Reuchlin had published his *Augenspiegel* in time for the Frankfurt Autumn Fair, where it attracted attention and sympathy. Reuchlin challenged not only the ban on rabbinic literature, but Pfefferkorn's theological patron, the highly

---

[70] Joseph Jacobs and Schulim Ochser, op. cit.

regarded conservative Dominican theologian Fr. Jacob von Hoogstraeten (1460-1527), prior of the Dominican monastery in Cologne, who judged the *Augenspiegel* a subversive defense of the Talmud. The local Dominican Order in Cologne insisted on a trial and Reuchlin was prosecuted in a church court in 1513. Pope Leo X manipulated the outcome to obtain the exoneration of Reuchlin. Just as a guilty verdict was about to be read on October 12, the local ordinary, Uriel, the Archbishop of Mainz, ordered the court shut down, the lengthy written verdict suppressed and the four conservative theologians trying the case, dismissed.

Reuchlin's colleague, Bishop Georg of Speyer, was appointed by the Vatican to hear Hoogstraeten's appeal in the German church's appellate court. Speyer in turn stacked the kangaroo court by naming two lead justices and three co-judges. They were all humanists and opposed to Hoogstraeten. Of the five, four were personal pals of Reuchlin. The case dragged into 1514. During one hearing, Johann Pfefferkorn courageously appeared at the door of Speyer's court and nailed an announcement declaring that the ecclesiastical court in Cologne had already condemned *Augenspiegel*.

Only an intervention from Pope Leo X could rescue Reuchlin. Leo delivered. The pontiff ruled that no other court had jurisdiction over Reuchlin and his book than Speyer's tribunal, which had sole papal authorization. Pfefferkorn was rebuked and nearly excommunicated. The Cologne theological court's verdict was nullified and on April 24, 1514, Bishop Georg and his trial judges completely exonerated Reuchlin's writings about Jews and Judaism. The humiliated Hoogstraeten was ordered to pay all court costs, as well as damages to Reuchlin personally in the amount of 111 gulden. If Hoogstraeten failed to do so, then he who was one of the leading Catholic theologians in Germany at the time, would be excommunicated. The Catholic world was being sent a message: Johannes Reuchlin must be given a free hand with which to operate his Neoplatonic-Hermetic mission on behalf of the Talmud and Kabbalah. *Any* churchman of whatever distinction who obstructed him would be fined and degraded, or even excommunicated. Truth was no defense.

Truth may have been no defense, but Hoogstraeten and Pfefferkorn believed it would prove sufficient in the eyes of God. The Prior of the German Dominicans proceeded with another appeal and here we take note of the extensive judicial process which was in place and which represented the legacy of medieval Catholic justice, though now it was tragically sullied at the hands of a Medici pope. In the late summer of 1514, Hoogstraeten was buoyed by news of a condemnation of Reuchlin's Judaic apologia issued by the most prestigious of all theology faculties, the University of Paris. Their assessment was subsequently published as *The Acts of the Parisian Doctors Against the Augenspiegel*.

The appeal hearing in Rome in January 1515, featured two appointed judges, Domenico Grimani and Pietro Accolti, who were well-disposed toward Reuchlin. Grimani rebuked Hoogstraeten for seeking the judgment from the University of Paris theology faculty. The court's rebuke served to neutralize the Paris judgment in terms of its impact on the legal case. By the summer of 1516, Leo X's cousin, Cardinal Guilio de' Medici (the future Pope Clement VII) was added to a "commission" of assessors who would assist in hearing the appeal.

Among the judicial commission members was the Superior General of the Franciscans (Bernardo Prati), and of the Dominicans (Thomas Cajetan). Also serving on the commission was the Superior General of the Augustinians, Giles of Viterbo. The appeal was heard partly (two of four sessions) in the Sistine Chapel, where Cardinal Giles spoke on the value to Christianity of the teachings of the Talmud and Kabbalah. The final session on July 2, 1516, of what turned into yet another kangaroo legal spectacle, produced a nearly unanimous decision to sustain Bishop Speyer's exoneration of Reuchlin on all the charges brought against him by the Dominican theologian Hoogstraeten. The acquittal of the certainly guilty Reuchlin caused outrage among true Catholic theologians. A scandal simmered for years, with conservatives appealing to Leo X to reverse the rigged verdict, unaware that the pontiff to whom they were appealing was responsible for Reuchlin's exoneration. Great pressure from on high had been bought to bear on behalf of the guilty Talmudic apologist and popularizer.

So commanding was Reuchlin's influence with the pontiff, curia and among the *haute monde* of Renaissance humanists led by Erasmus, that for *three years* Pope Leo resisted all calls for a reversal of the verdict. The Dominican theologian Hoogstraeten meanwhile, was left to twist in the wind. The fledgling Protestant movement was emboldened by the sight of the vulnerable Hoogstraeten, a leading member of the Inquisition in Germany, left hanging in an anxiety-ridden limbo. One consequence of the Renaissance papacy's Hermetic Neoplatonism was the strengthening of the Lutheran revolution, which was quick to detect a paradigm shift in the bowels of the Roman Church with regard to Reuchlin and the growing circle of Neoplatonist-Hermeticists high in the Vatican and operating under the title of "humanist." As a result, the hierarchy of the Church of Rome was giving a morale boost to the early Protestant movement. As a measure of the symbiosis at work, both among the inner circle of the Church of Rome and among Lutherans, Reuchlin was a sympathetic and favored figure.

Out of anxiety in the face of the growing Lutheran satisfaction over the Vatican's special immunities for Reuchlin, which appeared to pit a Neoplatonic humanist papacy against the Catholic Inquisition in Germany, it was impressed upon Leo X that Reuchlin could be supported and rewarded in private, but that in public, the continuing immunity for the Talmudic-Kabbalist Reuchlin would make it all too glaringly plain where the papacy's sympathies had lain; some facade of inquisitorial anti-Judaism had to be reinstated.

In the aforementioned *Epistolae obscurorum vivorum* written by Reuchlin's secret allies, we find this statement: "Reuchlin hath more friends here (in Rome) than in Germany, and many more cardinals and bishops and prelates and curialists love him." In 1520 Pope Leo revoked the acquittal and condemned the *Augenspiegel*. By this Vatican stratagem, to those without knowledge of the details of the years of papal machinations and delaying tactics in favor of Reuchlin, it can be baldly stated to a clueless posterity, "The record shows Reuchlin was censured by Leo X." Yet this was effectuated long after the censure no longer substantively mattered, on the eve of the publication of the Talmud in Italy: "...the Papal decision came too late...The Reuchlin dispute, thus decided all too late by Rome, was the forerunner of a far more important contest...[71]

---

[71] Ludwig Pastor, *The History of the Popes from the Close of the Middle Ages: Drawn from the Secret Archives of the Vatican and Other Original Sources* (1908), vol. vii, pp. 323-324. Pastor was a Catholic and Professor of History at the Austrian University of Innsbrück.

Luther was not the only irritant. Having rejected the Vulgate, Erasmus was having success with his 1516 Greek New Testament. He was, in his private correspondence, an ally of Reuchlin—but not so private that elite opinion in parts of Europe were unaware of it. In one letter to Albrecht of Brandenburg, in October 1519, which was subsequently leaked beyond Albrecht's immediate circle, Erasmus criticized theologians who resisted Reuchlin and the "blossoming of the humanities." In a reference to Neoplatonism and Hermeticism, Erasmus mocked those who also resented "the revival of the authors of antiquity."

Reuchlin had the support of the rabbinic religious network in central Europe through his ally, Rabbi Josel of Rosheim, who Selma Stern, in her eponymous book, rightly termed the "Commander of Jewry in the Holy Roman Empire." For Rabbi Joel, Reuchlin was a hero, and his work "a miracle within a miracle." Meanwhile, a libel apparatus was set into motion against Pfefferkorn. The leader of this organized false witness in defense of the "upright" Reuchlin, a man of "proven virtue and learning," was Erasmus of Rotterdam who, like Renaissance popes, mounted a traditional smokescreen from time to time by offering stern words of disapprobation for the Talmud and other rabbinic texts. All the while he did the dirty work of the Neoplatonic-Hermetic conspiracy by dragging the name and reputation of the noble Judaic convert Pfefferkorn through the dirt, in a vitriolic tirade:

"Pfefferkorn's writings, and particularly his activist campaign, attracted much attention during the ongoing Reuchlin affair, but his reputation was lastingly damaged by this event. The strong Humanist defense of Reuchlin...and the smears on his (Pfefferkorn's) and his wife's integrity, meant that Pfefferkorn and his writings were literally ignored by later polemicists and scholars.

"Erasmus of Rotterdam's condemning characterization of Pfefferkorn may be representative for other voices. He stated that Pfefferkorn, that 'half-Jew Christian by himself has done more harm to Christendom than the whole cesspool of Jewry' and claimed, 'that fellow chose to be baptized for no other reason than to be in a better position to destroy Christianity, and by mixing with us, infect the whole people with his Jewish poison. Now that he has put on the mask of the Christian, he truly plays the Jew. Now at last he is true to his race. They have slandered Christ, but Christ only. He raves against many upright men of proven virtue and learning. He could not have done a more welcome favor to his fellow Jews than pretending to be an apostate and betraying the Christian cause to the enemy.'

"Erasmus blamed Pfefferkorn for having destroyed the harmony of the scholarly world, and asserted, in another clear reminder of the convert's origins, that it would have been better if 'he were a Jew all over, and that his circumcision extended to his tongue and hands.'

"...Reuchlin was indeed not forgotten...Offered a chair in Greek and Hebrew at (the Catholic universities of) Ingolstadt and then Tübingen, which he held until his death in 1522, he remained highly respected...as a defender of Judaism. Pfefferkorn, however, was forgotten." [72]

The circumstances of Pfefferkorn's death aren't certain. He passed away in obscurity, with no known support from any quarter. Reuchlin, on the other hand, died an honored Catholic professor at prestigious German-Catholic universities. Pfefferkorn was above all the victim of a campaign of lying. The lies of Erasmus in this regard are typical of the tidal waves of libel aimed at Pfefferkorn by the now exceedingly powerful conspiracy inside the Church.

Leo X's legate, Gian Pietro Carafa, who had conferred with Erasmus in England (where Erasmus had arrived in 1511 under the sponsorship of St. John Fisher), forbade the Dominican faculty at Cologne from examining the works of Erasmus for heresy.[73] Fisher himself is an intriguing study. He prized his copy of Reuchlin's *De arte cabalistica* and was highly sympathetic to Reuchlin and the Kabbalah. (Fisher's correspondence with Reuchlin is said to be "lost").

"In June 1516 Fisher praised Reuchlin to Erasmus: 'He seems to me, in comparison with everyone else whose works I have read so far, to be the best man alive today, especially in knowledge of the recondite field that lies between theology and philosophy and touches on both. In a long letter to Reuchlin of that same month Erasmus wrote in detail of Fisher's

---

[72] Diemling, op. cit, pp. 30-31.

[73] Cf. Staehelin, *Gedenkschrift*, pp. 166-169. Carafa was the future Paul IV.

admiration for him: 'No words of mine can possibly express the enthusiasm and deep respect felt for you by the bishop of Rochester." [74]

"It is known from other sources that Fisher read and admired Pico" (i.e. Giovanni Pico della Mirandola)...Pico had rediscovered the cabala, the ancient Hebrew oral tradition of divine wisdom. Christian cabbalism aimed to harmonize all knowledge, and thus effect the conversion of the Jews. Fisher came to see the cabala as analogous to the apostolic tradition, those 'unwritten verities' which supplemented and explained the scriptures." [75]

For years Erasmus acted as a liaison between Reuchlin and Fisher, avidly encouraging their correspondence and Fisher's enthusiasm for Reuchlin, while advising Reuchlin on how he could kindle it; then when questioned about Reuchlin by English Cardinal Thomas Wolsey, Erasmus denied it all. He told Wolsey that he and Reuchlin "were not close," and that he "derived little from the Talmud and Cabala."

The tactics of Erasmus and the authors of the *Epistolae obscurorum vivorum* were predicated on suppression and censorship—the confident expectation that Pfefferkorn's pamphlets could be rendered difficult to find and, what is more, by the time the conspirators were through traducing him, that his reputation would be so trashed that few would trouble to read him even if they could obtain his publications.

There is another dimension to the anti-Pfefferkorn propaganda: the bizarre phenomenon of Jew hate employed to advance Judaism. In the third printing of *Epistolae obscurorum vivorum* it was said that Pfefferkorn "still stank like any other Jew." To the charge that Reuchlin was favorable to rabbis and anti-Christian Judaics, both Reuchlin and the authors of the *Epistolae,* maintained a leitmotif of personal revulsion toward individual Judaic persons. This was a masquerade but it reveals a striking fact: the Church of Rome from the Renaissance to the late nineteenth century maintained a two-pronged strategy of ethnic snobbery and hostility toward individual "Jews" on the part of the lower orders of Catholics,

---

[74] Maria Dowling, *Fisher of Men: A Life of John Fisher* (1999), p. 36. Also cf. James K. McConica, "John Fisher," in *Contemporaries of Erasmus* (1985) vol. 2, p. 37.

[75] Dowling, ibid., pp. 35 and 121.

while the papacy and curia were in thrall to the gnosis of Hermetic-Kabbalism and Platonism. Among parish priests and literate layman, books and pamphlets contrary to Judaic persons were allowed to circulate at the parish-level and in these same circles memories of the inquisitorial, token Talmud burnings were kindled. This was a sophisticated and successful ploy. Judging by the level of anti-Judaic suspicion and wariness among the Catholics in the pews up until the eve of Vatican Council II, a casual observer would conclude that the popes had managed to remain loyal to the Gospel after all.

Yet in fact, throughout the entire post-Renaissance era, Neoplatonic-Hermetic-Kabbalism obtained an ever greater hegemony over the Vatican. Whenever it was a choice between a proven leader of a Catholic-populist movement seeking freedom from rabbinic control and influence, whether led by Fr. Charles Coughlin, or Pfefferkorn, or Savonarola, occult elements at the top of the Church of Rome saw to it that these servants of God were silenced and suppressed. The image, maintained by media and academia, of a relentlessly "anti-Jewish" Church of Rome existing from the Middle Ages through the pontificate of Pope Pius XII, has proved to be a remarkably successful imposture.

In addition to allowing for a measure of populist anti-Judaic action and polemic in the parishes, in elite Renaissance Catholic circles, the all-important rescue of the Talmud and Kabbalah from incineration was based partly upon a premise most of us would find laughable today: the use of the Talmud and Kabbalah as fertile textual sources "for the proselytization of the Jews." From Giovanni Pico onward, a lie of epic proportions was sown among bishops, abbotts, cardinals and popes. It was declared with a straight face that the Kabbalah and the Talmud offered proof that Jesus was the Messiah. Therefore it was proposed that these venerable rabbinic books should be preserved from destruction and distributed. From the hands of Pico, this outrageous falsehood was transmitted by Reuchlin to the numerous eminent churchmen increasingly tainted by the tenets of the Neoplatonists and Hermeticists. One of these was Pietro Galatino, prior of the Franciscans of Bari and Apostolic Penitentiary under Pope Leo X, in his folio-sized volume of 425 pages, *De arcanis catholicae veritatis* ("On the Hidden Catholic Truth," 1518; reprinted in Paris in 1603).

Galatino's work was written for Leo X and includes a servile glorification of the Medici dynasty and a defense of that imperial lawyer ("counselor") of the Holy Roman Empire, Johannes Reuchlin. *De arcanis catholicae veritatis* was self-advertised as a debating manual for use against the "perfidious Jews" by way of quoting from the *Christ-affirming Talmud* (!). The fallacies and non-sequiturs in that premise indicate the extent to which even the educated classes of Europe and Britain largely had no working knowledge of the authentic contents of the Babylonian Talmud, and were prone to believe whatever they were told by "papal theology experts." Sowing deliberate misdirection and misunderstanding, Galatino incorporated broad swathes of material from the massive, medieval *Pugio Fidei,* by the Dominican linguist Raymond Martin ("Raymundus Martini"), [76] regarded by most of our contemporary professorcracy as a massive refutation of the Talmud religion and its rabbis. A cursory reading will confirm that faulty impression. It is a poisoned chalice, however: in many respects a learned work containing many valid criticisms of the Talmud — and one fatal poison that corrupts the whole with deadly efficiency: Martini upholds the ludicrous proposition upon which the Neoplatonic-Heremtic-Kabbalistic conspiracy is founded, that the rabbinic Oral Law of which the Talmud is the most prominent part, "proves Christ is the Messiah." To sustain this claim Martini was impelled to state, "Yet of some such (rabbinic) traditions we can believe..." [77] More than two centuries later, Galatino expanded this hoax exponentially.

In addition to encomiums for Reuchlin, Galatino disparaged Johann Pfefferkorn by degrading Pfefferkorn's patron and advocate, Rev. Fr. Jacob von Hoogstraeten. What was being promoted as an age of Renaissance enlightenment was actually a new dark age of occultism where Catholic intellectuals plunged into delusion.

---

[76] Martin was a Spanish monk, expert in Hebrew and Aramaic (the Talmud was written mainly in Aramaic, not Hebrew). His *Pugio Fidei adversus Mauros et Judaeos* (1800 pages circulated in manuscript in 1278), is a formidable work that includes lengthy quotes from the Babylonian Talmud, the Mishhah, and famed rabbis such as Nachmanides, Abraham ibn Ezra and Maimomides.

[77] Cf. T. and J. Carreras y Artau, *Historia de la filosofi espanola*, v. 1 (Madrid, 1939), ch. 4.

A Pfefferkorn Catechism

Reading the reviled Judaic convert Pfefferkorn is like reading the *Catechism of the Council of Trent*. His texts are a blessed relief from the trending occult deceptions and a model of true Catholic catechesis. Here is an extract from Pfefferkorn's *Der Juden Spiegel*:

"...there are some Jews who would agree that Christ was God and man, but by no means do they want to believe in Mary's virginity or even hear anything about it. Moreover, they assert that it is not natural to give birth to a child as a virgin. And secretly they say among themselves that Mary was outlawed. With such and other abominable words they revile the noble and blessed Mother and Queen of Heaven, Mary, from whom arises all our blessedness. To these blind and stubborn blasphemers of Mary, I answer that I am quite disconcerted by their evil defamations, for they still agree that Christ was God. And in order that they might notice their own ignorance all the better, I want to demonstrate more clearly to them how Adam and Eve were created by God pure and free of any sins. Since God Almighty brought Adam and Eve into this world free of the devil and of any sin, it also suited Him to free Himself and be granted pure birth. For Mary conceived Jesus supernaturally by divine providence without losing her virginity and without having been impregnated. In such a supernatural way and by divine providence, she gave birth, for God has power over all things. And if the Jews came to think about it honestly, they could derive from my words the virginity and purity of noble Mary. In better witness, however, I will put before them and before all of you Jews, your Scripture and ask you to read what is written in the third chapter of Genesis (3:15): "A woman will strike at the serpent's head." Oh, blessed Mary has struck the serpent's head, i.e. his power, and has crushed it completely by her pure, virgin birth, Mother Mary who deserves to be honored.

"...Likewise, the Jews who have been led by the false Talmud to a wrong path, continue to walk on it in good spirits. If, however, learned people were to come to them to make them knowledgeable about the Holy Scripture and were to take the false Talmud away from them, they would learn of the right way and would indeed have to follow it. Therefore, confiscate their books and burn them. Then you will steer them onto the path of truth all the easier.

"One could object to my arguments by saying that it is not right to deprive someone of his possessions by force. Answer: Where you do not do it they will be wronged and oppressed much worse by taxes, customs' fees, interest, and fees for protection, than if one seizes their books. Their salvation must be sought more by this than by money. Moreover, I believe that God, Mary, and the whole heavenly host would be greatly displeased by the books; and because one tolerates such bad books and all kinds of blasphemies in Christianity, although one could get rid of them, I am surprised that God has not punished us yet as he punished Sodom and Gomorrah, etc. So, you rulers, who hold power over people, have heard the...reasons why the Jews remain so obstinate. You could indeed confront them and help them find the way to eternal salvation..." [78]

In concluding his section on Judaism, Pfefferkorn solicits the ruling powers of Christendom to receive Judaic converts to Catholicism with kindness:

"Therefore, you are invited and asked to welcome the Jews kindly and to instruct them graciously when they come to you and want to convert to Christianity. Look with mercy upon these people of God who have miserably left everything they possessed in this world and put all their trust in you and have no other comfort than the pious Christians. Support them, so you will build the path Christ has taught. That way a flock of sheep can develop (cf. John 10:16), and this will undoubtedly happen." [79]

Reuchlin was called upon by civil and church authorities to give testimony on the subject of the confiscation of non-Biblical rabbinic books. In his published *Recommendation* against confiscation, he stated that the Talmud was free of all blasphemy and that the statement by Jesus in John 5:39, "Search the scriptures; for in them ye think ye have eternal life: and they are they which testify of me," was a reference to the Talmud. He plied Giovanni Pico's line that the Talmud and Kabbalah buttressed Christian truth. He denigrated the Good

---

[78] Cape (translator), *The Jews' Mirror*, op.cit., pp. 49-51; 91.

[79] Ibid., p. 97.

Friday liturgy which had the temerity to castigate "perfidious Jews."

When it was published there was a great deal of "noise" inside the Church raised against Reuchlin's *Recommendation*, some of it sincere and some of it doubletalk employed to prop up a facade of orthodoxy among the hierarchy who were conspiring with Reuchlin.

Sincerity poured forth from the theology faculty at the University of Cologne. They issued a thorough examination of Reuchlin's texts in favor of Judaism and called on him to recant his heresy. One can obtain a sense of how well-protected Reuchlin was by higher powers inside the Church from the content and tenor of his rejoinder to Cologne's Catholic theologians, among them the esteemed Arnold van Tongern. With no fear of reprisal, Reuchlin termed them "vile scoundrels, lowlife slanderers" and "wicked dabblers."

"Giorgio Benigno Salviati, titular archbishop of Nazareth at Rome ('*Romae iepiscopus Nazarenus*') and formerly a well-respected humanist professor and a protege of both the Medicis and Cardinal Carvajal, composed *Whether Jewish Books, Which They Call the Talmud, Should he Suppressed or Kept and Preserved*, which Neuenahr published in Cologne in 1517 as the centerpiece of a pamphlet titled the *Defense of the Most Distinguished Man Johannes Reuchlin*. The very title page of this work proclaims that Benigno had been the first member of the Roman commission to cast his vote in favor of Reuchlin. Benigno paints Reuchlin, from Rome's perspective, as the premier humanist of the north...

"In 1519, Reuchlin published a new collection of letters: the *Letters of Illustrious Men*. An important feature of this book is the goal of projecting an image of unity between Reuchlin and the Roman curia. The second volume of this book (the first volume is a reprint of the letters Reuchlin published in 1514), begins with a reprint of Reuchlin's 1498 speech in the Sistine Chapel before Alexander VI and, otherwise includes many letters to and from the most distinguished churchmen of Rome. For example, one 1517 letter from Rome recounts a conversation between Francesco Poggio and Leo X: 'Francesco Poggio of Florence recently beseeched the pope: 'Holy Father, I will take the side of Reuchlin, and I wish to stand in his place. I read all of his research, all that I was able to get. An injustice is happening to that man.' After a while, the pope responded to him: 'Poggio, don't worry. I will not allow that man to suffer any harm." [80]

In 1519 Reuchlin's *Illustrium vivorum epistolae* ("Letters of Illustrious Men"), a summation of support for him from members of the Church hierarchy, was published by Thomas Anshelm and circulated throughout Italy, much of the rest of Europe and Britain. The authenticity of these letters was not challenged. They were documentary evidence of the support for Reuchlin at the highest levels of the Church. They were his allies in spreading the Talmud and Kabbalah. The Kabbalist Cardinal Giles of Viterbo had four of his letters published in *Illustrium vivorum epistolae*. In one of those letters Giles wrote to thank Reuchlin for having "saved the Talmud from the fires." With regard to Reuchlin's trial, in which members of the hierarchy rescued Reuchlin from a guilty verdict, Giles wrote on October 25, 1516, "...in your trial...we understand that we have defended and preserved not you but the law, and not the Talmud, but the Church. It is not that Reuchlin has been saved by us but that we have been saved by Reuchlin." [81]

These words by the Superior General of Luther's own Augustinian order were not by accident. A heresy conviction for Reuchlin due to the efforts of Hoogstraeten and Pfefferkorn would have led to a larger investigation of members of the hierarchy of the Church of Rome and exposed the extent to which the Neoplatonic-Hermetic-Kabbalistic theology had infected the Pope, the Curia and the hierarchy. By saving their co-conspirator Reuchlin, the conspirators were themselves saved from being swept out of the Church with an iron broom. The trial of Reuchlin would be the last time a direct frontal assault was launched on the occult infiltration of Rome. Henceforth, minor occult adepts, scapegoats, rivals and challengers to papal authority would be executed or imprisoned, but never a *deep cover* member of the conspiracy (Giordano Bruno was not deep cover).

---

[80] Price, op. cit., pp. 181 and 183.

[81] *"Denique in hoc iudicio tuo, ubi hac aestate pericoloso aestu laboravimus, non te, sed legem, non Thalmud, sed ecclesiam, non Reuchlin per nos, sed nos Reuchlin servatos et defensos intelligimus."*

Many other members of the hierarchy were on board with Reuchlin, from Jacob Questenberg, the papal proto-notary, to Cardinal Adriano Castellesi, a member of the papal commission that had vindicated Reuchlin. The highest member of the hierarchy to conspire on behalf of the occult conspiracy was Pope Leo X. It was the revolutionary Leo who, in 1520, took the shattering and unprecedented step of explicitly licensing Daniel Bomberg to publish the Babylonian Talmud with overt papal permission.

It was Leo who, in 1517, privately paid homage to the publication of Reuchlin's book of black magic, *De arte cabalistica,* which had been dedicated to him. But so bold was this pope in his diabolism that he permitted a public witness to his private endorsement. On May 25, 1517, he authorized the head of the Vatican library, Philipp Beroaldus the Younger, to write to Reuchlin as follows: "The pope read your book on the cabala avidly, as is his wont when reading good things." These words were published in 1519 in *Illustrium vivorum epistolae* without papal objection.

We scratch our heads today in wonder at how the Pope and his hierarchy could get away with supporting the Neoplatonic-Hermetic-Kabbalistic conspiracy with such brazen *chutzpah.* The impunity was achieved in part by depicting the advancement of the Talmud and Kabbalah in terms of the humanist advancement of knowledge in the field of the language arts, and specifically Hebrew philology. All who obstructed this glorious learning were repellant ignoramuses, as Erasmus stated in a letter to Hoogstraeten on August 1, 1519:

"You will find you have done much, not only for the Dominican Order but also for the whole order of theologians, if you use your authority to suppress the brainless calumnies of some people who pour out their poisonous attacks on knowledge of the ancient languages and humanities, the fair name of which they blacken by prating of Antichrist and heresy and other histrionic stuff..."

Several weeks later, in an October 19 letter to Albrecht of Brandenburg, Erasmus would deny any sympathy for Reuchlin, "For what do I have in common with Reuchlin or Luther?" A little more than a year later, on November 8, 1520, the chameleon Erasmus wrote to Reuchlin, "It has always been my aim to separate your cause from the issue of Luther..."

When papalolaters have endeavored to explain away Reuchlin's diabolism they have stooped to paint him in Lutheran hues, as a crypto-Protestant, when in truth *Reuchlin was an always-faithful papist*. It was popery above almost all other objections, which the Protestant movement protested. Hence, on that single point alone the Reuchlin-was-a-Protestant-sympathizer canard is demolished. *The absolute authority of the papacy was absolutely required for the forward movement of the conspiracy*, from Ficino and Giovanni Pico through Reuchlin and onward. The progression was seamless. That the occult Catholic conspiracy would eventually contaminate certain leaders and movements within Protestantism cannot be gainsaid. To claim that it was Protestants who originated the occult infiltration of Christendom when it was the Church of Rome which had pioneered it, is a shameless act of misdirection and scapegoating that compounds the trail of deceit.

The Fifth Lateran Council's final session (March, 1517) took place during the Reuchlin controversy. The supposed assassination attempt on Leo X in April of that year, was alleged to be a poisoning plot supposedly hatched by the young Cardinal Alfonso Petrucci. The pope ordered the torture of Petrucci's *consigliere*, Marcantonio Nini, who is reputed to have implicated Cardinals Adriano Castellesi, Francesco Soderini, Bandinello Sauli as well as the pope's chamberlain, Cardinal Raffaele Riario. Petrucci was likely guilty of a plot, and he was executed. Riario, a power-broker in the Roman curia was ruined by a huge fine of 150,000 ducats. He died four years later, a broken man.

"G.B. Picotti [82] has reviewed the known facts and documents and...believes that Leo X seized upon Petrucci's indiscretions and intrigues to create a 'plot' against his own life as a means of destroying his opponents, extorting huge sums of money from them (especially from Riario), and preparing the way for the drastic enlargement of the Sacred College (of cardinals) by the appointment of neutral and pro-Mediciean cardinals...Almost as remarkable as the supposed conspiracy by five cardinals to kill the pope was the astonishing

---

[82] Picotti, "La Congiura dei cardinali," in *Rivista storica italiana*, I (1923), pp. 249-267.

nomination of thirty-one cardinals in the great creation of 1 July 1517, after which Leo had a firm hold on the College and the Curia." [83]

The main records of the trial of the putative conspirators is missing. It appears that Leo's friend and ally, Cardinal Pucci of Florence, was the presiding judge. The accused cardinals (other than Petrucci) escaped execution only by confessing guilt and agreeing not to question or appeal the outcome of the "trial."

The thirty-one new cardinals created by Pope Leo on July 1 paid him for the privilege of their office. This simoniacal money-glutton also profited handsomely from the immense fines he exacted from the "guilty cardinals." [84]

Nothing is static in history or inside the Vatican and the endless wheeling and dealing in Rome regularly caused alliances to shift. One of the thirty-one cardinals newly named was Tomasso de Vio ("Cajetan"), a formidable theologian and Superior General of the Dominican Order. He and Erasmus had been bitter rivals since the early sessions of the Fifth Lateran Council when Erasmus attacked Cajetan for writing in favor of the acts of Pope Julius II, who Erasmus vilified in his *Dialogus Julius Exclusus e coelis* (1513), which he published anonymously (his authorship has since been established). In *Julius Exclusus,* Erasmus verbally pummeled Pope Julius for disparaging the French King Louis XII's Council of Pisa. Certain that his cloak of anonymity in *Julius Exclusus* was secure, in correspondence with Leo X and also with Cardinal Campeggio, Erasmus felt confident to denounce the French monarch's 1511 Council of Pisa as "schismatic." To say that Erasmus was two-faced is an error in arithmetic by a factor of five.

While Rome was firmly in the camp of the conspiracy there were two opinions about how the occult should advance inside the Church — slowly and quietly, or rapidly and publicly. Leo X had favored the latter policy, which appeared to be a judicious exploitation of the Renaissance *zeitgeist*. It had infuriated conservatives like Hoogstraeten and the test for the

---

[83] Kenneth M. Setton, *The Papacy and the Levant* (1204-1571), vol. 3, pp. 168-169.

[84] The best investigation extant of this fake conspiracy is found in chapter five ("The 'Conspiracy of 1517") of Kate Lowe's *Church and Politics in Renaissance Italy* (Cambridge University, 2002), pp. 104-113).

psychological warriors in the hierarchy was: how much change can the conservatives bear before they reach the breaking point and revolt, thereby threatening all of the progress made for the past seventy-five years? Reuchlin and his "Cabala" had nearly been canonized. Pfefferkorn's campaign against the Talmud of Babylon had been obliterated when Leo X granted Bomberg permission to print and distribute it.

For the time being fortune favored the bold: in 1519, Reuchlin's second edition of his *Letters of Illustrious Men* (*"Illustrium vivorum epistolae"*) [85] boasted of the support he had received from across the spectrum, from humanist to Lutheran to papal, in the form of endorsements from Erasmus, Martin Luther *and* Pope Leo X!

Furthermore, Count Hermann von Neuenahr published, under the nose of the Dominicans in Cologne, Bishop Giorgio Benigno's *Defense of Reuchlin*. Benigno was Bishop of Cagli in Umbria and a member of the Medici inner circle, from the time of Lorenzo onward. With the fall of the Medici in Florence and the rise of Savonarola, Benigno had been charged with infiltrating Savonarola's followers.

Neuenahr launched an assault on Pfefferkorn's principal ally inside the Church, Jacob Hoogstraeten, the theology professor and Dominican priest who was Inquisitor of the German archdioceses of Trier, Mainz and Cologne. The German people in those archdioceses watched as Hoogstraeten was dragged through the mud in print, along with his Dominican Order in Germany. This was perpetrated by the papal agents Neuenahr and Benigno.

In 1519 the German Catholic warlord Franz von Sickingen was recruited by allies of Reuchlin inside the Church, to harass the German Dominicans in general and Hoogstraeten in particular. Sickingen was the author of a pamphlet, *Demand and Announcement to and against the Provincials, Priors and Convents of the Order of Preachers (Dominicans) in Germany, and Especially Friar Jacob von Hoogstraeten on Account of and in the Name of the Highly Learned and Famous Johannes Reuchlin*. Sickingen ordered the Dominicans to halt the publication of any books harmful to Reuchlin and pay monetary compensation to him.

---

[85] Not to be confused with the *Letters of Obscure Men* (*"Epistolae obscurorum vivorum"*).

Sickingen was a war criminal. This butcher had been turned on the German Dominicans by elements within the Church of Rome. As a result, the German-Dominican Prior General, Eberhard of Cleves, arranged a deal with Sickingen wherein Hoogstraeten would be silenced and further negotiations with Sickingen to arrange for Reuchlin to receive compensation, would be opened. This took place in Frankfurt in May, 1520, before a commission of Catholic judges well-disposed toward Reuchlin. Among the judges were Sickingen's brother-in-law, Philipp von Flersheim, Joanes Vigilius and Simon Ribysen, personal friends of Reuchlin. They stripped Hoogstraeten of all of his offices and forbade him to write against Reuchlin. The Dominican Order in Germany, under duress, had abjectly surrendered to the Neoplatonic-Hermetic-Kabbalistic conspiracy.

Observing this tawdry spectacle of dishonor and disgrace were the German people. They reasoned that if a commission of the Catholic Church in Germany had ruled that the Dominicans were men of low character and deficient in morals and that their leader, Rev. Dr. Hoogstraeten, was a wicked and foul cleric, then it must be true, and Martin Luther had been correct all along. The shabby treatment of Hoogstraeten and the German Dominicans contributed to the growth of the Lutheran movement. Here is an enigma: can it truly be said that this was not foreseen by Rome?

Here is another: with one hand Pope Leo had permitted the situation in Germany and the degradation of the Dominicans and Hoogstraeten. With the other he allegedly acted against Reuchlin, in 1520. But if that is the case, how is it that *no record exists of any direct papal order contra Reuchlin? The existence of the order has the status of hearsay*. The Dominican faculty in Cologne claimed to have seen a copy of the papal order and they claimed that the Pope's order permanently silenced Reuchlin. This we know to be a falsehood. Reuchlin remained a full professor in good standing at a Catholic university. Moreover, even though the rumored papal judgment against Reuchlin was supposed to contain a lifting of the ban on Hoogstraeten and his complete freedom, the record shows that from 1521 onward to the day he died, Hoogstraeten never again spoke against Reuchlin or the Talmud and Kabbalah.

Ingolstadt University Prof. Johannes Eck, Luther's nemesis and the Fugger banking dynasty's Catholic usury advocate, played a cruel game with Hoogstraten, feigning friendship toward the Dominican theologian and enmity for Reuchlin. In a letter to Hoogstraeten of July 24, 1519, Eck sought "to encourage Hochstraten (Hoogstraeten) to use his influence to expedite a decision" by the theology faculty of the University of the Sorbonne in favor of Eck. To gain Hoogstraeten's friendship, Eck posed as Reuchlin's enemy, telling him that Reuchlin and Luther were two *grammatici* (grammarians) from the same noxious root. [86] In the same year that he was peddling this malarkey to Hoogstraeten, Eck was entertaining "Johannes Reuchlin as an honored guest in Ingolstadt." [87] Hoogstraeten, the loyal papist and author of *Destructio cabale seu cabalisticae perdiae,* was surrounded by treachery, most of it emanating from his fellow papists.

When he died on June 30, 1522, in Stuttgart, Reuchlin was a member of the faculty of the Catholic University of Tübingen where he was a professor teaching classes until he became too ill to do so. Daniel Bomberg continued to dedicate books to him. Bomberg reminded the world that Pope Leo X had commissioned the printing of the Talmud, "a work of great labor and expense that the Supreme Pontiff entrusted to me," Bomberg wrote.

The misinformed among Catholics and Protestants imagine that Reuchlin became a Protestant with the rise of Luther. The Luther Monument in Worms, Germany, erected in 1868, perpetuates this hoax. It features life-size sculptures of the "Four Patrons of the Reformation"—Philipp Melanchthon, Philipp of Hesse, Friedrich of Saxony and Johannes Reuchlin. This myth helps assuage illusions on both sides. In truth, Reuchlin was always faithful to the papacy and the Renaissance Church of Rome. The public spectacle of the degradation inflicted on Reuchlin's enemies by papal agents, certainly did give impetus to the Lutheran movement.

---

[86] Much of the agitation in favor of the Kabbalah and Talmud was put forth predicated on new textual discoveries reputedly made by humanists fluent in ancient Hebrew, Greek and Aramaic. Consequently, according to this scam, to oppose the mass publication of the Kabbalah and Talmud was to be an "obscurantist," mindlessly impeding advances in philology and linguistics.

[87] David V.N. Bagchi, *Luther's Earliest Opponents* (1991), pp. 75 and 77. Also cf. Erwin Iserloh, *Die Eucharistie in der Darstellung des Johannes Eck* (1950), p. 19.

In sum, "As he achieved the ability to form independent judgments on Jewish writings, Reuchlin began to question the substance of anti-Jewish innuendos and, through his readings, ultimately came to the conclusion that specific Christian allegations of blasphemy and heresy within the Jewish tradition were either baseless or trivial. He also took the further important step of repudiating the portrayal of post-biblical Judaism as the enemy of Christianity. That Jews and Judaism were not anti-Christian (and not antagonistic forces in a Christian society) was a foundational principle of his *Recommendation*...His historical interest in ancient religions and philosophies and his assumption that elements of an original, true theology (*prisca theologia*) could be discovered in ancient, especially Jewish, texts predisposed him to a favorable reception of historical Judaism..." [88]

Reuchlin faithfully transmitted from Giovanni Pico della Mirandola that which he had received, the "*true theology*," and then extended it in his 1517 book, *De arte cabalistica*. [89] He pimped for the Babylonian Talmud, Judaism's book of hatred, sexual perversion, and bureaucratic micromanagement of Judaic lives, as well as the Kabbalah, Judaism's book of black magic. His prestige was such that those two tomes would serve as the clandestine guiding light of the papacy until emerging in public in the twentieth century through Henri de Lubac, the *eminence grisé* of the Second Vatican Council, and in the post-conciliar pontificate of John Paul II and his successors, Benedict and Francis.

Reuchlin reached the height of his influence under Pope Leo X, who licensed the publication of the Talmud and endorsed Reuchlin's *Art of the Kabbalah*. These facts represent foundational mandates for the development of a secret society inside the Vatican which has never been eradicated.

To what art was Reuchlin referring when he wrote *The Art of the Kabbalah*? It is the "art" of falsifying the Word of God with *gematria* and *temurah*, rabbinic exegetical glosses on Scripture as developed in Kabbalistic works like the *Zohar*.

---

[88] Price, op. cit., pp. 226-227.

[89] Johannes Reuchlin, *On the Art of the Kabbalah,* transl. Martin and Sarah Goodman (1983).

In *gematria* the "mystical secrets" are revealed through the numerology assigned to Hebrew letters in the belief that every Hebrew letter has a numerical equivalent. For example, it is said that 231 is the number of all the possible pairs of letters in the 22-letter Hebrew Alef-Beth ("alphabet"). Hence, number 231 is believed by the Judaic Kabbalists to contain the "mystery of creation," and it is through these letter combinations that Kabbalistic tradition holds that in Prague in the sixteenth century the god-like Rabbi Judah Loew brought a Golem (artificial man) to life. This is of Christ?

The word for an evil individual in Hebrew is *Rasha*. The word for a holy individual is *Tzaddik*. According to Kabbalistic *gematria*, the numerical value of *Rasha* is 570 and the numerical value of *Tzaddik* is 204. The difference between them is 366. The Kabbalist searches for words in Scripture that taken together add up to the number 366. This is supposed to reveal something. What it reveals is that the Kabbalistic soothsayer can manipulate the meaning of the Word of God by choosing whatever letters supposedly are derived from words which, when added together, equal 366. He can then declare that he has solved the "mystery of the creative fire that unites the polarities."

This is the occult "art" derived from Pharaonic Egypt and pagan Babylon. It has no connection to the God of Israel or His Word. A spurious "connection" was forged by deceivers whose spiritual patrimony is the Father of Lies. The *gematria* of which Reuchlin was so inordinately besotted and which infatuated Catholics from St. John Fisher to Pope Leo X, and which only "reactionary-inquisitors" and "Jew-hating calumniators" would oppose, represents an ominous counterfeiting of God's Word. Because it has an avant-garde intellectual patina and is described as "sacred mystical Jewish insight" into the Scriptures such as only God's People could discover, it becomes a matter of "anti-semitism" to declare it for what it really is.

Temurah is a configuration method of magical exegesis that entails replacing letters in Old Testament words by the letter that either precedes or follows it. The absurdly subjective and contrived nature of this substitution is obvious to any reasonably literate person not ensnared in Kabbalistic delusion. It was by means of *Temurah* that Reuchlin "confirmed" Giovanni Pico's declaration that the Kabbalah testifies to the truth of the Holy Catholic Trinity, and serves to prove the identity of Jesus as the Messiah of Israel.

It is painfully obvious that the Talmud and Kabbalah needed good p.r. in the overwhelmingly Christian fifteenth and sixteenth centuries, in order to authenticate the validity of the religion of rabbinic Judaism as the planet's foremost repository of primordial truth, wisdom, kindness and benevolence toward all. The lie required to achieve that objective, that "the Kabbalah confirms the truth of Christianity," is no longer needed in our time, when the Kabbalah's prestige is not dependent on confirming the Catholic dogma of the Trinity, or the messianic identity of Jesus. In the post-modernist era, very few, if any, Judaizing Catholic or Protestant theologians employ this lie which was crucial in ensuring the success of the Neoplatonic-Hermetic conspirators in bringing the Trojan Horse of Talmudic and Kabbalistic Judaism into Catholicism, and later, into *some* centers of Protestantism. [90]

Above all, Johannes Reuchlin was a loyal agent of religious syncretism—the synthesis of Catholicism, Neoplatonic-Hermetic paganism and Judaism into a universal, one world Faith, representative of the "Perennial Tradition," which Plethon, Ficino, Giovanni Pico and their followers believed had always existed on earth. This hybrid Church is an assimilative weapon which has marched relentlessly forward through Catholicism, though on occasion, so as to mislead and placate conservatives and camouflage its true nature, popery has, when necessary, taken one conservative step backward, after having proceeded two or more revolutionary steps forward, in what history teaches has been a remarkably successful and seemingly almost invincible alchemical progression.

We qualify this as "almost" because God is in charge and woe to those who have deceived the world. They shall reap what they have sown.

Jesus Christ promised He would never abandon us, and hell would not prevail against His Church; that His Church exists on earth we do not doubt.

---

[90] We specify only "some" centers because, not being subject to a sovereign occult pontiff, early Protestants could not be so throughly infected by the occult. In certain churches and time periods they had the freedom to defy their religious authorities.

Hermes Trismegistus, guardian deity of the Siena Cathedral.
[Giovanni di Stefano, 1488].

Hermes Trismegistus, (at center under the star), guardian deity of the
papal apartment of Pope Alexander VI.
[Bernardino Pintoricchio, circa 1494].

DIVINI

PLATONIS

OPERA OMNIA

MARSILIO FICINO

INTERPRETE.

Recens editio, summo studio, & diligentia à vitiis ema-
culata, & ad exemplar Græcum fideliter collata.

His accesserunt sex Platonis dialogi, nuper à Sebastiano
Conrado tralati, neque unquam adhuc
in hoc volumen recepti.

LVGDVNI,
APVD ANTONIVM VINCENTIVM.
M. D. LXVII.

Cum priuilegio.

Title page from the *Divini Platonis Opera Omnia* (Lyons, 1567). The text is in Latin. Translated from the original Greek and "interpreted" by Rev. Fr. Marsilio Ficino. 712 pages printed in the 'royal folio' format and illustrated with geometric and cosmological schematic woodcuts. Plato's dialogues are preceded by Ficino's extensive commentaries, which are significant philosophical works in their own right. Plato's text is printed in Roman type; Ficino's commentaries are printed in italic.

Giovanni Pico della Mirandola, 1463-1494.
[Cristofano dell'Altissimo].

℃Q ui ſciuerit quid ſit denarius in Arithmetica formabili:& co
gnouerit natura primi numeri ſpherici:ſciet illud quod ego adhuc apud aliquem Cabaliſtam non legi:& eſt quod ſit fundame
tum ſecreti magni Iobelei in Cabala.

℃Ex fundamento præcedentis concluſionis ſciri pariter poteſt
ſecretum quinquaginta portaru3 intelligentiæ:& milleſimæ ge
nerationis & regni omnium ſæculorum.

℃Per modum legendi ſine punctis in lege : & modus ſcribendi
res diuinas & unialis continentia per indeterminatum ambitum
rerum diuinarum nobis oſtenditur.

℃Per id quod dicunt Cabaliſtæ de ægypto & atteſtata eſt expe
rientia habemus credere ꝙ terra ægypti ſit in analogia : & ſub
ordinatione proprietatis potentiæ.

℃Sicut uera aſtrologia docet nos legere in libro dei:ita Cabala
docet nos nos legere In libro legis.

℃Finis.

℃Impreſſum Romæ opera Venerabilis uiri Eucharii Silber ali-
as Franck.   Anno ab incarnatione Domini.Mcccc.lxxxvi. die
Septima Decembris.   Sedente Innocentio.viii. Pont.Max.
Anno Pontificatus eiuſdem Tertio.

Penultimate page of the first edition of Giovanni Pico della Mirandola's
Nine Hundred Theses. The note at the bottom states that it was printed in
Rome by Eucharius Silber, December 7th, 1486, in the third year of the
pontificate of Innocent VIII.

The Life of John Picus.   25

I. P. MIRANDVLA
The Life of John Picus *Earl of* Mirandula,
who dyed, Anno Chriſti, 1494.

John Picus was born *Anno Chriſti,* 1463. of an ancient and Honorable Family in *Italy,* that derived their pedigree from *Conſtantine* the Great :
a little before his Mother was delivered of him,
there appeared in her Bed-chamber a round flame
of fire hanging (as it were) on the wall for a little
while, and then vaniſhing away, concerning which
                              D d d   there

Sir Thomas More's translation of the biography of Giovanni Pico della
Mirandola, written by Pico's nephew.
The Life of of John Picus of Mirandula was published in England with
excisions and emendations by More.

Statue in Germany of the faithful papist Johannes Reuchlin (1455-1522),
the Church of Rome's defender and promoter of the Kabbalah and
Babylonian Talmud.

[Adolf von Donndorf, circa 1868]

SANCTISSIMO LEONI DECIMO PÓN
TIFICI MAXIMO IOHANNES
Reuchlin ſe ſupplex commendat.

TALICA PHILOSOPHIA BEATISSIMĒ
LEO DECIME religionis chriſtianę Pontifex Maxime
à Pythagora eius nominis parente primo, ad ſummos hoies
excellentibus ingeniis præditos olim delata, perǫ́plurimis
annıs ingenti latratu ſophiſtarum occiderat, tam diu tenebris & denſa no
cte ſepulta, ǫuſcǫ deū fauore Sol ois generis optimorū ſtudiorum clariſſi
mus Laurentius Medices pater tuus, Magni Coſmi propago Florentinæ
ciuitatis princeps exoriret.Quē &ſi nouimus animo & ſcientia gubernādi
Rempub. & domi bellicǫ oīa conſilio ac prudentia gerendi, tam fuiſſe cō
potem ut nemo ætate ſua in ciuili exercitatione uideret magis laudādus, tū
ad hoc nobis eū fateri oportet commodius natū eſſe pinde atcǫ cœlitus de
miſſum, ut poſt eloquentię diſciplinas & bñdicendi artes a Petrarchis, Phi
lelphis, Aretiniſcǫ rhetoribus ante iuuētuti Florētinǫ traditas ǫ̃ eſſe abſcǫ
cōtrouerſia poſſent ciues cunctis nationibus exteris nitidiore ſcribendi cā
lamo & puritate linguę ornatiores, ipſe tandē patrię inferret ǫ̃cǫ illā expul
trice uitiorū ſapientiā & arcanorū inueſtigandi ratione ǫ̃ in libris & monu
mentis priſcorū ad ſua uſcǫ tempora latuiſſent. Ad id prouinciæ diligēter
acciuit undequacǫ doctiſſimos & ueterū autorū peritiſſimos uiros ǫbus
cū rerū ſciētia etiā ſatis eſſet eloquētiæ, Demetriū Chalcondylen, Marſiliū
Ficinū, Georgiū Veſpuciū, Chriſtophorū Landinū, Valorē, Angelū Po
litianum, Ioannē Picum Mirandulę comite, cæteroſcǫ orbis eruditiſſimos
ǫbus antiǫrum ſolertia & arcana uetuſtas malignitate caſuū obliterata in
lucē rediret.Hoc egere ſummi uiri certatim.Nā docuit hic, cōmentabat al
ter, legerat iſte, interpretatus eſt ille, ac linguas uertit in linguas. Marſilius
Græciā duxit in Latium, Romanos in Græciā Politianus reduxit. Inſtabant
omnes operi, nemo non ſummas Medicibus laudes afferens. Hos in he
roas Beatiſs. LEO tuus natalis uirgula, ut aiunt, diuina fœliciter cecidit,
Dıís gratia, certe ut non reſtaret ullum elegantioris doctrinæ genus in ǫ̃
tu non euaſeris peritior, adeo quidem puer amplexus politiſſimi ſuauitatē
Politiani.Quid multis? Florentia illo æuo nihil erat floridius.In qua rena
ſcerentur optimarum artium quæ ante cecidere omnia, nihil remanſit inta
ctum de linguis & literis quo non exercerentur nobiliſſimi Florentini.
Ea fama ego tum quidem uehementer mouebar tactus eius loci cupidi
tate, ac non ſolum magnificentiſſimi & nitieti nobis Hieronymis ædiſici
auitæ domus tuæ, quam Magni Coſmi nominarunt, uerum etiam paren
tis tui deſyderio uiſendi, unde noſtro ſeculo tanta commoda prodiiſſent.

Dedication page from Johannes Reuchlin's
De Arte Cabalistica (1517).
"Dedicated to His Holiness Pope Leo X."

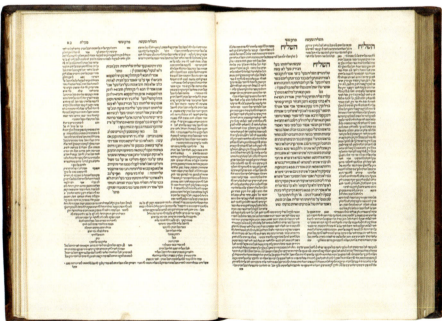

The Papal Edition of the Talmud

At the time of its publication this was the finest edition of the Babylonian Talmud in world history. This printing, under the auspices of the pope, established the text within the canon of rabbinic Judaism for generations to come. [Daniel Bomberg, Venice, 1519-1523].

The serpent with the penis of Biagio da Cesena in its mouth.
Michelangelo, *The Last Judgment*, Sistine Chapel, 1541.

Michelangelo, *The Risen Christ* (1519-1521).
Rome: Church of Santa Maria sopra Minerva.

Partially nude erotica of Our Lord.
[Pietro Perugino, the *Baptism of Christ*, circa 1500].

This painting begs the question, what was Michelangelo's Eve doing before she turned her head? [Sistine Chapel, 1508-1512].

Saint Peter's Basilica, Rome (interior).

Partially nude erotica of Our Lord.

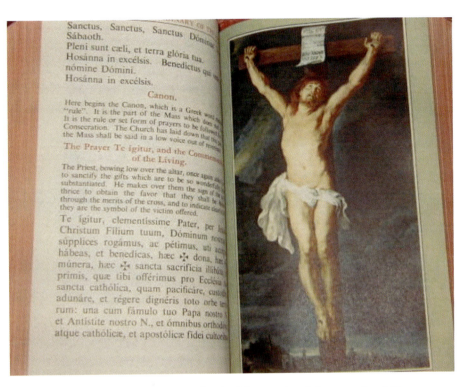

[1950s-era Tridentine Latin Mass missal (prayer book)]

A stone carving of a reclining young man (at left) with a priapic obelisk emerging from his genital region. The carving is at the base of the Monte Citorio obelisk in Rome's Campo Marzio. The obelisk had been toppled by the devout Catholic Duke Robert Guiscard in 1084. It was re-erected with considerable difficulty and expense by Pope Pius VI, in 1792.

Domenico Fontana, the brilliant engineer to whom Sixtus V entrusted the mission of moving an obelisk to St. Peter's Square. He is pictured holding a replica.

[*Della trasportatione dell'obelisco vaticano et delle fabriche di Nostro Signore papa Sisto V*, Rome, 1590].

The obelisk, which is known by different names and under various forms, is a universal signifier of the erect male organ. In the illustration at left, a carved image of the god Shiva stands on the shoulders of a demon in front of an obelisk-shaped *linga*, sacred to the Hindu religion (the same shape is exhibited at right).

[Gudimallam Linga, India, circa 100 B.C.]

Pharaoh's obelisk erected by Freemasons in New York City,
January 22, 1881.

The obelisk presiding over St. Peter's Square, Rome.

The obelisk presiding over the U.S. capitol, Washington, D.C.

The Egyptian obelisk erected by Freemasons in London, England,
September 13, 1880.

The Egyptian obelisk prior to its erection by order of Pope Sixtus V.
St. Peter's Square, Rome, 1586.

[*Della trasportatione dell'obelisco vaticano et delle fabriche di Nostro
Signore papa Sisto V*, Rome, 1590].

A Hermetic Deity

A statue of the Egyptian jackal-headed god Anubis cradling the "Herald's Wand of Hermes" in his left arm, and casting a spell with his right. The statue is sometimes referred to as "Hermanubis." According to Albert Pike in *Morals and Dogma*, the star of the Freemasons is Sirius, the "dog-star." [Circa second century A.D. Egypt (relocated to Rome)].

In 1590 a bronze medal was issued (the rear and obverse of which are pictured above), honoring Pope Sixtus V (Felice Peretti de Montalto), for having ordered the excavation, transport and permanent erection in Rome, of four Egyptian obelisks that had been pulled down by the early Christians.

Ten-euro coin bearing the image of Niccolo Machiavelli, the Renaissance advocate of deceit and treachery. The coin was issued in 2013 by the Republic of San Marino (an independent state within Italy), to commemorate the 500th anniversary of the publication of Machiavelli's best known work, *Il Principe* ("The Prince").

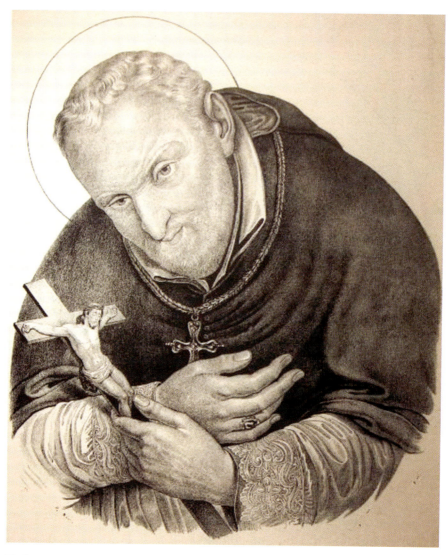

Alphonsus Liguori (1696-1787), a post-Renaissance saint of the Church of Rome whose *Moral Theology* sparked a prolonged controversy in Victorian Britain.

Usury Pope Pius VIII (1761-1830) carried
on the *sedia gestatoria*, a ceremonial Roman throne.

Four Occult Popes of the Renaissance

Top: Alexander VI (Roderic Borgia), 1431-1503. Leo X (Giovanni di Lorenzo de' Medici),
1475-1521. Bottom: Clement VII (Giulio di Giuliano de' Medici), 1478 –1534.
Paul III (Alessandro Farnese), 1468-1549.

The insignia of the Medici usury bank.

Filippo Strozzi the Younger (1489-1538), one of many usury bankers who bought and sold appointments to the Sacred College and other high offices in the Church of Rome.

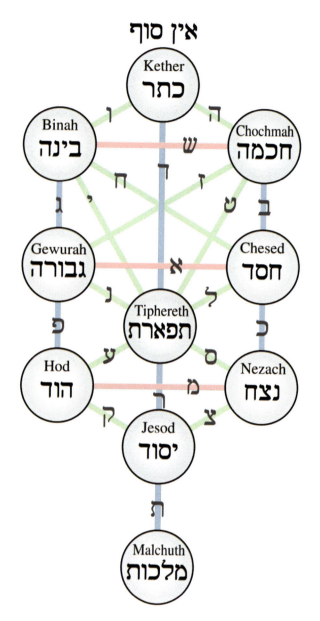

The Sefirotic סְפִירוֹת Tree of the Kabbalistic Ten Emanations.

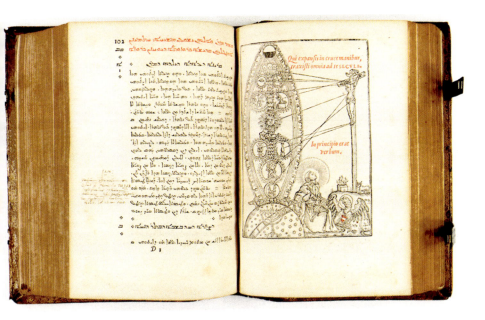

The Holy Roman Emperor's Kabbalah

An illustration of Jesus Christ on the Cross corresponding to the Sefirotic סְפִירוֹת Tree of the Kabbalistic Ten Emanations.

From the Syriac New Testament, published by Ferdinand I (1503-1564), future Holy Roman Emperor, while he was the Catholic King of Hungary and Bohemia, and Archduke of Austria.

[*Liber sacrosancti evangelii de Iesu Christo Domino*, 1555].

Antonin Scalia, Associate Chief Justice of the United States Supreme
Court, in conversation with attorney Nathan Lewin concerning how to
apply Talmudic *halacha* to the American court system.

"Synagogue and State in America," November 6, 2013.
Zahava and Moshel Straus Center for Torah [1]
Yeshiva University, New York.

---

[1] By "Torah" is meant Judaism's supreme law derived from the oral tradition, the
Torah she'Beal peh תורה שבעל פה, i.e. the Talmud Bavli.

2   CAPERTON *v.* A.T. MASSEY COAL CO.

SCALIA, J., dissenting

A Talmudic maxim instructs with respect to the Scripture: "Turn it over, and turn it over, for all is therein." The Babylonian Talmud, Tractate Aboth, Ch. V, Mishnah 22 (I. Epstein ed. 1935). Divinely inspired text may contain the answers to all earthly questions, but the Due Process Clause most assuredly does not. The Court today continues its quixotic quest to right all wrongs and repair all imperfections through the Constitution. Alas, the quest cannot succeed—which is why some wrongs and imperfections have been called nonjusticiable. In the best of all possible worlds, should judges sometimes recuse even where the clear commands of our prior due process law do not require it? Undoubtedly. The relevant question, however, is whether we do more good than harm by seeking to correct this imperfection through expansion of our constitutional mandate in a manner ungoverned by any discernible rule. The answer is obvious.

An excerpt from Associate Supreme Court Justice Scalia's dissent in Caperton v. A. T. Massey Coal Co., 556 U.S. 868 (June 8, 2009).

" Utraque sententia est probabilis, sed prima est probabilior : nam ratio hujus secundæ sententiæ supponit ut certum, tale juramentum sine animo se obligandi emissum, esse verum juramentum. Attamen probabilius est, et commune, ut asserunt *Salm. c.* 1. *n.*] 9. *cum aliis ut supra, et etiam Viva in proposit. 25. Innocent XI. num.* 13. (*contra Less. dict. num.* 37.) quod hujusmodi juramentum non sit verum juramentum : tum, quia caret conditione necessaria ad naturam juramenti promissorii, qualis est animus se obligandi ; tum, quia juramentum sequitur naturam promissionis quam confirmat, ut certum est *ap. Bus. n.* 280. *cum Less. Bon. etc.* At promissio, sine tali animo facta, non est quidem promissio, sed simplex propositum ; ergo, evanescente promissione, evanescit etiam juramentum, et habetur ut factum sine animo jurandi ; quod certe, ut vidimus, nullum est. Si autem nullum existit juramentum, nulla existit obligatio illud implendi.''

At left is an excerpt from the *Moral Theology* of Alphonsus Liguori, [2] in which, concerning oaths sworn by Catholics, this 'Doctor of the Church,' establishes escape clauses, whereby the obligation of Catholics to fulfill what they have sworn to do or uphold, need not be fulfilled:

"Either of the opinions is probable, but the first is more probable: for the reason of the second opinion supposes it as certain that such an oath, made without the mind of binding one's self, is a true oath. But it is a more probable, and common opinion, as *Salm. c. 1 n. 19. with others as above, and even Viva on proposition 25. of Innocent XI. num. 13. (against Lessius in the mentioned num. 37.)* assert that such an oath is not a true oath: both because it wants the necessary conditions to the nature of a promissory oath, such as is the intention of binding one's self; and because an oath follows the nature of the promise which it confirms, as is certain *ap Bus. n. 280. cum Less. Bon. etc.* But a promise made without such a mind is not, indeed, a promise but simply proposed; therefore, the promises being evanescent, the oath is also such, and is considered as made without the mind of swearing, which certainly, as we have seen, is null and void. But if no oath exists, there is no obligation of fulfilling that oath."

---

[2] R.P. Blakeney, *Extracts Translated from the Moral Theology* (1852), p. 130.

The Catholic lay preacher, Brandano da Petroio (1486-1554), scourge of
the occult Church of Rome.

Chapter IX

Renaissance High Art: An Initiation

Some aesthetes believe that the theological abominations of the Renaissance era are vitiated by the fact that it nurtured and played host to the temple of art that is its most renowned achievement. In the introduction to his 1964 translation of Charles Baudelaire's *Flowers of Evil and Other Works*, Wallace Fowlie wrote of Plato's doctrine in *Phaedrus* according to which "beauty is a mark left on the soul which the soul never loses no matter how low it may sink." This is a doctrine of the Kabbalah as it was visually imparted to the masses for the first time in Christendom through Renaissance High Art. Here we have Plato vs. Jesus, who taught no such abomination. If the spirit of a man sinks into depravity, it is not redeemed by possessing "beauty." Transgression of the laws of God removes true beauty from within ourselves. To say that beauty is impervious to the effects of depravity is itself depraved.

What passes for "Catholic art" in the Renaissance by Michelangelo, Botticelli, Pintoricchio and others, is part of a disguise at the heart of the Neoplatonic attitude of contempt for the common man, in line with the words of Horace, "*Odi profanum vulgus et arceo*" ("I hate and avoid the profane crowd"). The common people have no right to the truth, which is reserved for the elite alone, as Giovanni Pico della Mirandola stated, "*Sicut secretam Magiam a nobis primum ex Orphei hymnis elicitam, fas non et in publicum explicare*" ("Just as the secret magic that we first described from Orpheus' hymns is not to be explained in public").

"Michelangelo's works were indeed of pagan inspiration and like other masterpieces of the Renaissance were designed specially for initiates into pagan theology and Neoplatonic thought." [1]

Michelangelo was a creature of the Medici. He lived for two years (1490-1491) in the palace of Lorenzo de' Medici where the frequent visitors and sometime guests were Father Marsilio

---

[1] Edith Balas, *Michelangelo's Medici Chapel* (1995), p. 33.

Ficino and Giovanni Pico. "...in the years after Michelangelo's return to Florence in 1516 he was closely involved in the Neoplatonic circle of Ficino's pupil and philosophical heir, Francesco da Diacetto." [2]

Giovanni Pico della Mirandola is synonymous with religious syncretism, Kabbalah and the occult secrecy and duplicity that inspired Sebastino del Piombo in his letter to Michelangelo of July 17, 1533. In that missive, he urged Michelangelo to disguise Ganymede [3] in his fresco for the Medici chapel, as St. John the Revelator, by giving Ganymede a halo.

Analyzing this epoch's art, Edgar Wind writes that, "...in the study of the Renaissance mysteries...it may help to remove the veil of obscurity which not only distance in time...but a deliberate obliqueness in the use of metaphor, has spread over some of the greatest Renaissance paintings. *They were designed for initiates; hence they require an initiation.*" [4]

When we consider that Michelangelo's Sistine Chapel [5] is regarded as one of the holiest sanctuaries in Christendom, we begin to grasp the depth of human credulity. The Sistine Chapel is the realm of Plato; not Jesus Christ. Our Lord was not a nude, despite the lustful allure of the several revolting depictions of Him hanging virtually nude on the Cross, which we encounter in "Catholic" art after the Middle Ages and which is by no means limited to the Renaissance.

Neither were the apostles, disciples or the holy women who followed Him naked, yet the Church of Rome's Sistine Chapel consists of a riot of nudity which marks one of the most startling departures from the true Church of the previous millennium.

In the western occult imperium there are two phases of time: the time of keeping secrets and the time of revealing

---

[2] Ibid., p. 28.

[3] In mythology, Ganymede is the object of the unrequited homosexual desire of the god Zeus. Ganymede is depicted in Attic vase painting and Hellenistic and ancient Roman art as naked and comely.

[4] Edgar Wind, *Pagan Mysteries in the Renaissance* (Norton, 1968), p. 15; emphasis supplied.

[5] The vault of the Sistine Chapel was commissioned by Pope Julius II. Michelangelo crafted the work from 1508-1512. "The Last Judgment" was commissioned by Medici Pope Clement VII in 1534 and supported by Pope Paul III after Clement's death. Michelangelo completed it in 1541.

them. The former is father to the latter. The Neoplatonist Denys, or Pseudo-Dionysius, (mistaken, as we have noted, for Dionysius the Aeropagite, who was the contemporary of St. Paul), described the stages to be followed in the crucible of change: "...the theological tradition is double, being on the one hand a tradition which is not expressed in words and which is mystical, and on the other hand, a tradition which makes manifest and is better known." [6]

First, the secret gnosis takes deep root, grows and flourishes and hence, must not be made known to the masses of the people of God. Giovanni Pico was adamant about the requirement for absolute secrecy for the ideology, designs and activities of his own work and that of his co-conspirators, lest the still-orthodox Catholic people discover it and demand its extirpation, or effect that extirpation themselves through an uprising. This secrecy was not intended to be perpetual, however. The Renaissance art under consideration, like Renaissance pagan syncretism itself, appears to function as a time capsule consisting of a once-and-future revelation: once for the insiders at the top of the pyramid of gnosis, and then in the future, when the *vulgus* have been so thoroughly processed that the truth "which makes manifest" can be revealed to them without risk of revolt. It seems that this is the stage in which we find ourselves in the twenty-first century, when what would have shocked and enraged our ancestors elicits barely a shrug now.

There were intermediate Thermidorian stages as well. Michelangelo's festival of pagan nudity in the Sistine Chapel was unalloyed for as long as was necessary to firmly initiate the Catholic hierarchy in the pagan ethos. When the arcane ideology had taken complete root and before the Catholic masses could be stirred to wrath by the buck-naked blasphemy, a staged reaction was brought into play by the Vatican masters of psychological warfare. They costumed their "conservative reaction" in inquisitorial habiliments, for the benefit of the uninitiated. Under Paul IV the Roman Inquisition proceeded to denounce nudity in sacred art. Soon after Michelangelo's death in 1564, the genitals of the figures in his "Last Judgment" were

---

[6]   Pauline Moffit Watts, "Pseudo-Dionysius the Areopagite and Three Renaissance Neoplatonists: Cusanus, Ficino and Pico," in *Supplementum Festivum*, p. 28.

daubed over by *braghettoni* (breeches-painters). Later, nudity in sacred places would reappear by papal permission. Situation ethics harnessed to the opportunistic requirements of the Church of Rome as it processed the captive minds of "the Faithful," waxed and waned between stringency and laxity, on the model of the *zugot* pairs in Phariseeism, as personified by Shammai, the strict Pharisee, and Hillel, the lenient one. At any given time after the fourteenth century, within Renaissance parameters and without, one would encounter a Pope Shammai or a Pope Hillel, according to the requirements of their *zeitgeist* god.

Though there were foreshadowings in other pontificates, in the modern era John Paul II was the first openly Neoplatonic-Hermetic pontiff, as his embrace of Talmudic-Judaism in the synagogue in Rome, voodoo in Benin, Islam's Koran, the congress of world religions at Assisi and the Aztec rites during his pilgrimage to Mexico, testify. He instituted the *open fulfillment* of the mandate of Pope Alexander VI and Giovanni Pico della Mirandola. There was little that was disguised or ambiguous about this alleged saint's transgressions against the First Commandment.

What had been performed under the sign of the witch-goddess Isis by the popes in secret, in the six ritual rooms known as the "Borgia Apartment" of the Vatican Palace—as executed by Bernardino di Betto ("Benedetto"), who signed his works "Pintoricchio" (or "Pinturicchio, i.e "little painter"), and designed by Alexander VI, together with Annio da Viterbo, Paolo Cortesi and the Protonotary Apostolic, Francesco Colonna —was performed in the open air as televised in Mexico City in the second year of the second millennium:

"To this day, I recall being in Mexico City with John Paul II in 2002 for the canonization Mass of Juan Diego, and watching a female Mexican shaman perform a dancing purification ritual on the pontiff with a bit of shrubbery during the Mass—in effect, the witch doctor exorcised John Paul." [7]

The pope's Master of Liturgical Ceremonies from 1987 to 2007 was Italian Archbishop Piero Marini who spoke to the press about this pontifical Aztec witch doctor ceremony: "Marini later explained that the ritual is part of traditional

---

[7] John J. Allen Jr., "New Parlor Game," Oct. 28, 2016, cruxnow.com

Mexican religiosity, arguing there's a time-honored thrust in Christianity to 'baptize' such expressions of popular faith." [8]

This is the *prisca theologia* in the raw, without embellishment, or even the familiar duplicitous rhetoric. The pope's Master of Liturgical Ceremonies terms witchcraft, "traditional Mexican religiosity" and "popular faith," and he calls the praxis of Neoplatonic-Hermeticism, "a time-honored thrust in Christianity." The pontiff who publicly took part in this traffic with demons was not excommunicated or otherwise deposed. He was canonized a saint of the Catholic Church. "Conservative" Catholics who look to his pontificate with profound nostalgia refer to him as "John Paul the Great."

These kinds of rites are for initiates, but the fact that they were performed before the eyes of the entire Catholic world in the twenty-first century demonstrates the success of the occult transmutation process in that *we are all initiates now.* How was this virtuoso psychological and spiritual coup set into motion? Through the cultivation, more than five hundred years earlier, of absolute secrecy and plausible denial in service to the alchemical transformation of the traditional theology of Catholicism into the futuristic Church of Rome's modernist pagan syncretism, propelled by the exegetical principles of rabbinic Oral Law dogma. For direction we turn to the youthful Michelangelo's Medici-supported mentor:

"Pico della Mirandola planned to write a book on the secret nature of pagan myths which was to bear the title *Poetica theologia.* 'It was the opinion of the ancient theologians,' he said in his Commentary on Benivieni's *Canzona d'amore,* 'that divine subjects and the secret Mysteries must not be rashly divulged....if committed to writing at all, must be covered with enigmatic veils and poetic dissimulation.... How that was done... by Latin and Greek poets we shall explain in the book of our Poetic Theology.'

"Although the book has not survived (assuming that it was written), the method employed by Pico, as well as some of his conclusions, can be inferred from his other works. He held that pagan religions, without exception, had used a 'hieroglyphic'

---

[8] Ibid. In October, 2016, Pope Francis called Archbishop Marini out of semi-retirement and appointed him to Rome's Congregation for Divine Worship (CDW).

imagery; that they had concealed their revelations in myths and fables which were designed to distract the attention of the multitude, and so protect the divine secrets from profanation: 'showing only the crust of the mysteries to the vulgar, while reserving the marrow of the true sense for higher and more perfect spirits.'

"As an example Pico quoted the Orphic Hymns; for he supposed that Orpheus had concealed in them a religious revelation which he wished to be understood only by a small sect of initiates: 'In the manner of the ancient theologians, Orpheus interwove the mysteries of his doctrines with the texture of fables and covered them with a poetic veil, in order that anyone reading his hymns would think them to contain nothing but the sheerest tales and trifles.' But having studied Plato, Plotinus, and Proclus with care, Pico felt certain that these philosophers had been initiated into the mysteries of Orpheus, and he proposed with their help to penetrate the arcana of the Orphic Hymns.

"*In praising the wisdom of such religious disguises*, Pico claimed that the pagan tradition had a virtue in common with the Bible: there were Hebrew mysteries as well as pagan. The book of Exodus, for example, recorded that on two occasions Moses had spent forty days on Mount Sinai for the purpose of receiving the tablets of the Law. Since it would be absurd to suppose that in each of these instances God needed forty days to hand Moses two tablets inscribed with ten commandments and accompanied by a series of liturgical rules, it was evident that God had conversed with Moses on further matters, and had told him innumerable divine secrets that were not to be written down. These were transmitted among the rabbis by an oral tradition known as Cabala (in which the theory of the *sefiroth* and the absconded God resembled the Neoplatonic emanations and the 'One beyond Being'). In relation to the written law of the Old Testament, the Cabala was thought by Pico to hold the same position as Orphic secrets held in relation to pagan myths. The biblical text was the crust, the Cabala the marrow.

"The law was given to the many, but its spiritual understanding to only a few. With an unanswerable oratorical gesture Pico pointed to 'the tailors, cooks, butchers, shepherds, servants, maids, to all of whom the written law was given. Would these have been able to carry the burden of the entire

Mosaic or divine understanding? [9]

"Moses, however, on the height of the mountain, comparable to that mountain on which the Lord often spoke to his Disciples, was so illumined by the rays of the divine sun that his whole face shone in a miraculous manner; but because the people with their dim and owlish eyes could not bear the light, he addressed them with his face veiled.

"And the same device, Pico observed, was also used by Christ. 'Jesus Christ, *imago substantiae Dei*, did not write the gospel but preached it.' To the common people he spoke in parables, but to a few disciples he explained more directly the mysteries of the kingdom of heaven. 'Origen wrote that Jesus Christ revealed many mysteries to his disciples which they did not wish to put down in writing, but communicated only by word of mouth to those whom they regarded as worthy. And Pico added that this was 'confirmed by Dionysius the Areopagite', that is by the Athenian disciple of St. Paul (Acts xvii, 34), to whom a series of mystical Neoplatonic writings, apparently composed in the fifth century A.D. were piously ascribed by their anonymous author. Dionysius was assumed to have received his mystical initiation directly from St. Paul, again in a secret and purely oral manner; but like the late Cabalists and the Platonic heirs of Orpheus, he—or the late scribe whom he inspired—committed the laudable indiscretion of entrusting the revelation to paper. Without so remarkably universal a breach of etiquette, it might have been difficult for the Renaissance to revive the Orphic, Mosaic, and Pauline secrets.

"In comparing the mysteries to each other, Pico discovered between them an unsuspected affinity. In outward dogma, reconciliation would not seem possible between the pagan, Hebrew, and Christian theologies, each committed to a

---

[9] This is the dichotomy which the Pharisees delineated in their criticism of Jesus: that He was putting the ignorant Jewish masses, the bumpkin *am ha'aretz*, on the same level as the elite Jews (John 7:48-49). All that's missing from Pico's list of dim-witted "tailors, cooks, butchers, shepherds, servants, maids" are *carpenters*. Compare Pico's words with those of the English Protestant reformer William Tyndale, who, while at Little Sodbury Manor, stated to a fellow priest, that he would "make a boy who drives the plough know more of Scripture than the priest himself." Quite the opposite of their publicly stated intentions of higher liberation for all humanity, Rome's occult workers of iniquity establish a duality of "higher and more perfect spirits," contrasted with those who supposedly have lesser ones.

different revelation; but if the nature of the pagan gods were understood in the mystical sense of the Orphic Platonists, and the nature of the Mosaic Law in the hidden sense of the Cabala, and if the nature of Christian Grace were unfolded in the fullness of the secrets which St Paul had revealed to Dionysius the Areopagite, it would be found that these theologies differed not at all in substance but only in name. A philosophy of tolerance was accordingly worked out in the form of a hidden concordance..." [10]

Four hundred years after Giovanni Pico della Mirandola's modernizing theology was in the process of successfully infiltrating and subverting the hierarchy of the Catholic Church, Pope Pius X declared, "Here it is well to note at once that, given this doctrine of experience united with that of symbolism, every religion, even that of paganism, must be held to be true. What is to prevent such experiences from being found in any religion? In fact, that they are so is maintained by not a few...Modernists do not deny, but actually maintain, some confusedly, others frankly, that all religions are true. That they cannot feel otherwise is obvious. For on what ground, according to their theories, could falsity be predicated of any religion whatsoever?" [11]

Why did Pius X fail in his stated goal of defeating the modernist infiltration of the Church? First, because he was himself a modernist, perpetuating the permission for profit on loans and doing absolutely nothing to restore the immemorial dogma forbidding usury. ("Not to oppose erroneous doctrine is to approve of it." Pope Innocent III). Second, because the "holy popes" of the supposed "reaction" (Leo XIII, Pius IX and Pius X), left untouched and intact the Neoplatonic-Hermetic-Kabbalist conspiracy inside the Church.

Clark Trinkaus: "...the underlying vision of reality in the modern age...originates with Renaissance Hermetism, that is the insights based on the Ancient Philosophy (*Prisca theologia*) introduced into European philosophy and theology by Marsilio Ficino in his *Heavenly Gathered Life* (*De vita coelestus*

---

[10] Wind, op. cit., pp. 17-21.

[11] *Pascendi Dominici Gregis: On The Doctrine Of The Modernists*, Encyclical of Pope Pius X, September 8, 1907.

comparata) and by Giovanni Pico della Mirandola in his *Oration on Human Dignity (Oratio de dignitate hominis)...*"

Tutoring Giovanni Pico in Medici Florence was his preceptor, Rev. Fr. Ficino: "Though Pico used the method of mystical reduction for a more radical purpose than Ficino, there can be little doubt that he had it from his teacher. To understand a classical author 'deeply,' Ficino would always turn to a Hellenistic commentary. Even Plato, to whose translation and exposition the major part of his life was devoted, he read with the eyes of Plotinus, in whom he discovered 'an inspiration no less noble but occasionally more profound...His commentary on Plato's *Symposium* was largely derived, as he himself admitted, from the sixth book of the first *Ennead*; and in preparing his readers for the study of Plotinus he paraphrased the relation of this profounder Platonist to Plato by alluding to the descent of the Holy Ghost during the baptism of Christ (Luke 3:22): 'And you may think that Plato himself spoke thus to Plotinus: 'Thou art my beloved son; in thee I am well pleased.' To make Plato appear as God the Father giving his blessing to Plotinus as God the Son is to remove Plato to the inhuman heights of the Almighty, from which Plotinus descends as a philosophical redeemer, a Christ of the Platonic mysteries. That Ficino sensed no blasphemy in the metaphor shows to what extent Christian and Platonic sources of revelation were regarded as concordant and interchangeable." [12]

Pope Paul III "appointed Michelangelo chief architect, sculptor and painter at the Vatican. The instrument is dated September 1, 1535, and the terms with which it describes the master's eminence in the three arts are highly flattering. Allusion is directly made to the fresco of the Last Judgment, which may therefore have begun about this date. Michelangelo was enrolled as a member of the Pontifical household with a permanent pension of 1200 golden crowns..." [13]

After the three hundred ninety figures of "The Last

---

[12] Ibid., pp. 23-24.

[13] John Addington Symonds, *The Life of Michelangelo Buonarroti* (1899), vol. 2, pp. 40-41.

Judgment" were painted, Biagio da Cesena recoiled from it in horror, denouncing it as "disgraceful that in so sacred a place there should have been depicted all those nude figures, exposing themselves so shamefully." Cesena added that the fresco was more appropriate "for the public baths and taverns," than the pope's chapel. Upon learning of Cesena remarks, the vengeful Michelangelo altered the "The Last Judgment" to add figure 391: Cesena himself. Michelangelo placed him in hell and painted him pornographically: with the ears of a donkey and with a snake holding the tip of Cesena's penis in its mouth. According to a contemporary, Ludovico Domenichi, when Cesna protested this pornographic slander to the Pope, Paul III lamely replied that his "jurisdiction does not extend to hell," and that the portrait would remain on the wall of the Sistine Chapel before which the Mass was offered.

The other notable contemporary jeremiad raised in protest of Michelangelo's nude "Christianity" in the Sistine Chapel, was put forth by the Venetian poet Pietro Aretino (1492-1557), whose character has been impugned by Michelangelo's defenders. [14]

Whatever the serious flaws in his own poetic expression however (and there were many), Aretino's observations in his letter to Michelangelo [15] were in fidelity with a thousand years of pre-Renaissance, Bible-centered Catholicism:

"To the Great Michelangelo Buonarroti in Rome

"Sir, When I inspected the complete sketch of the whole of your *Last Judgment,* I arrived at recognizing the eminent

---

[14]   Aretino was certainly an outrageous figure whose command of the language sometimes entailed lubricious verse-satire at the expense of Leo X and Neoplatonic-Hermeticism's grandiose conceits. His reputation has been so thoroughly blackened by the malignant babble of his enemies however, that one should approach their accounts of him with caution. Some of his writings were undoubtedly obscene, but Aretino penned them for the secular world, never for inclusion in a church setting. He excused the nudity of Michelangelo's statue *David,* because it was exhibited in a public square, and not in the sacred sanctuary of a Catholic Church. His objection was to extravagant nudity *in holy places,* and despite his own numerous personal sins and failings, his critique in this regard was valid.

[15]   Cf. Erica Tietze-Conrat, "Neglected Contemporary Sources Related to Michelangelo," in *Art Bulletin,* June 1943. The text of Aretino's letter was translated and published by John Addington Symonds, op. cit., pp. 51-55.

graciousness of Raffaello [16] in its agreeable beauty of invention. Meanwhile, as a baptized Christian, I blush before the license, so forbidden to man's intellect, which you have used in expressing ideas connected with the highest aims and final ends to which our faith aspires. So, then, that Michelangelo stupendous in his fame, that Michelangelo renowned for prudence, that Michelangelo whom all admire, has chosen to display to the whole world an impiety of irreligion only equalled by the perfection of his painting!

"Is it possible that you, who, since you are divine, do not condescend to consort with human beings, have done this in the greatest temple built to God, upon the highest altar raised to Christ, in the most sacred chapel upon the earth, where the mighty hinges of the Church, the venerable priests of our religion, the Vicar of Christ, with solemn ceremonies and holy prayers, confess, contemplate and adore his body, his blood, and his flesh?

"If it were not infamous to introduce the comparison, I would plume myself upon my discretion when I wrote *La Nanna*. I would demonstrate the superiority of my prudent reserve to your immodesty, seeing that I, while handling themes lascivious and immodest, use language comely and decorous, speak in terms beyond reproach and inoffensive to chaste ears. You, on the contrary, presenting so awful a subject, exhibit saints and angels, these without earthly decency, and those without celestial honors.

"The pagans when they made statues I not say of Diana who is clothed, but of naked Venus, made them cover with their hand the parts which should not be seen. And here there comes a Christian who, because he rates art higher than faith, deems a royal spectacle martyrs and virgins in improper attitudes, men dragged down by their genitals, things in front of which brothels would shut their eyes in order not to see them. Your art would be at home in some voluptuous bathhouse, certainly not in the highest chapel of the world.

"Less criminal were it if you were an infidel, than, being a believer, thus to sap the faith of others. Up to the present time the splendor of such audacious marvels has not gone unpunished; for their very excellence is the death of your good

---

[16] Raffaello Sanzio (1483-1520), known to posterity as the painter, "Raphael."

name. Restore it to good repute by turning the indecent parts of the damned to flames, and those of the blessed to sunbeams; or imitate the modesty of Florence, who hides your David's shame beneath some gilded leaves. And yet that statue is exposed upon a public square, not in a consecrated chapel.

"As I wish that God may pardon you, I do not write this out of any resentment." [17]

"Your art would be at home in some voluptuous bathhouse, certainly not in the highest chapel of the world." Pietro Aretino's righteous indignation would be quite out of place among "conservative" and "traditional" Catholics, who esteem Michelangelo's Sistine Chapel as one of the most piety-inducing sacred spaces in Western civilization. People are so far gone into the diabolic that they have lost their ability to delineate right from wrong.

It becomes even more demented for Michelangelo's defenders to attempt to credibly uphold his supposed "Catholic faith," when we examine his disgusting statue of a nude Jesus Christ, sculpted with enlarged testicles, which was successfully hidden from sight from the *post*-Renaissance era until recently. One glance at this supposedly reverent sacred art object crafted by Michelangelo, and the true Christian perceives that it is a Talmudic travesty of the image of the Son of God, and stands as evidence of the identity of the occult Catholic-impersonators who usurped the Petrine Office and patronized Michelangelo, instead of banishing him to the Arctic wastelands after sledgehammering his porn-Christ. Like the Isis worship in the six rooms of the papal palace, the candle-lit obscenities conducted by the hierarchy of the Church of Rome before this striptease Jesus, are from hell.

Rome's eventual reaction against Michelangelo and the Renaissance nudes was, as we have said, liminal and staged, for pragmatic reasons. The ascendance of the Neoplatonic-Hermetic conspiracy required the fixing of its pagan canon in the Sistine Chapel above all other sacred spaces. Once elite Catholic percipients had been conditioned and processed in its presence, and *after* their initiation was successfully concluded,

---

17 The generally accepted date for the letter is November, 1545.

then a reaction was allowed to exert itself, until what was a time capsule containing the Neoplatonic-Hermetic spiritual virus, was reopened on cue. That point was reached in a post-Vatican II pontificate, as confessed in 2014, by Antonio Paolucci, Director of the Vatican Museums, when he conceded that, "the process of obscuring the 'Theology of the Body,'" came to end with the pontificate of Pope St. John Paul II, and his successors. Director Paolucci freely and openly articulates the Renaissance gnosis of the Church of Rome's pagan theology of sacred nudity:

"And there is Michelangelo in the Sistine Chapel...There are the *Ignudi*—the twenty male nudes of the ceiling, 'the most beautiful positions which they variously take on, seated and torisoned in their movements,' as (Giorgio) Vasari wrote and who in the physical magnificence of the male bodies, called upon to glorify the papal oak, saw a sort of homage to the golden age of Pope Julius II. Those young bodies that attempt to take on the most diverse postures...in the anatomies that light and shade modulate from the milky lightness to the lit toes of bronze, there is all of Michelanglo's passionate love for the supreme beauty of the naked male body...

"As regards the 'Last Judgment,' this immense gathering of nudes, a true 'theology of the body'...above all the nudes...all of those breasts, buttocks and sexual organs exhibited in the Chapel of the pope...the Catholic Church...has allowed its artists to narrate the Beauty which is the shadow of God on earth, also by way of the representation of the naked human body." [18]

Would it be far-fetched to note the homoerotic dimension to the preceding male nude celebration?

Would it be irreverent to ask what makes human nudity in the streets outside the Sistine Chapel morally wrong, while representations of that nudity inside the holy precinct where the Sacrifice of Jesus on Calvary is said to be re-enacted in the Mass, is considered a theological virtue?

In the publication of the Pontifical Institute of John Paul II, *A Body for Glory: Theology of the Body in the Papal Collections,*

---

[18] Antonio Paolucci, *A Body for Glory: Theology of the Body in the Papal Collections* (Rome: Pontifico Istituto Giovanni Paolo II, 2014), pp. 7-9.

it is stated on p. 13, "It was Pope John Paul II who described the Sistine Chapel as the sanctuary of the Theology of the Body." This "theology" was reaffirmed by Pope Benedict XVI in his address in the Sistine Chapel, "Meeting with Artists," November 21, 2009.

"...the significance of Hermes for the Renaissance Christian could not have been announced more triumphantly than by his depiction in marble at the very threshold of the great cathedral in Siena, in 1482."[19]

In the order of egregious, pagan Church of Rome Renaissance art, after the Sistine Chapel and Alexander VI's papal apartment, comes the Siena Cathedral, dating from the thirteenth century. The focus of our study is not the medieval part of the cathedral, but the *Renaissance-era* marble pavement which was installed mostly in the fifteenth century. Knowing that St. Augustine had denounced him as an idolater and with no possible excuse of ignorance, the Catholic hierarchy nevertheless proceeded to commission in 1488 in the Siena Cathedral, before the arches of the nave, an exquisitely beautiful, multi-colored marble glorification of "Hermes Trismegistus," by Giovanni di Stefano. This magnificent image of the magician Hermes presides over the entrance to the Cathedral of Siena, an edifice which is supposed to be a temple of the God of Israel.

In a visual age where texts did not appeal to the people as effectively as images, it was this mosaic which had the distinction of manifesting and spreading the cult of Hermes to the laity not in a public square, but in the holy precinct of yet another sacred space where the Mass was offered.

"...in front of the central doorway, where a panel invites the visitor to enter 'chastely into this temple of chastity, dedicated to the Virgin,' *Hermes Trismegistus* is portrayed. As the scroll beneath the imposing figure explains, he was traditionally considered to be a contemporary of Moses. The learned Egyptian, whose doctrine the Humanists preached and studied, rests his hand upon a tablet supported by two sphynxes and offers a book to two figures on his right. They accept it,

---

[19] Angela Voss, ed., *Marsilio Ficino* (2006), p. 16.

respectfully. Inscribed on the tablet is a sentence attributed to *Poimandres* (The Shepherds of Men), a text supposedly authored by Trismegistus:

"Deus omnium creator secum Deumfecit visibilem et hunc fecit primum et solum quo oblectatus est et valde amavit proprium Filium qui appellatur Sanctum Verbum,' [20] while the pages of the open book read: " *Suscipio licteras et leges Egiptiu."* [21] The reference to Egypt, the ancient seat of wisdom, which the two sphynxes also seem to symbolize, is clear. But Egyptian wisdom, entrusted to the peoples of the East and the West, is inseparable from its divine origin (*'Sanctum Verbum'*). The inscription on the right refers to the Creation..." [22]

"As we enter the church and approach the ancient god, a plaque warns us to 'enter with pure heart this purest temple of the Virgin.' Why did the Virgin open her chaste temple to a pagan deity? Can a Christian heart remain pure in the presence of a god whose temple houses demon-souled statues that lived and spoke and worked wonders?" [23]

We find the answer by recourse to our time machine: it is what is known colloquially in the twenty-first century as the "politically correct" response, yet it was the response in 1488 as well: the image of Hermes is appropriate for the cathedral because he is a heathen prophet of Christianity and consequently in the category of pious theology, not diabolic sorcery; that was the insinuation more than five hundred years ago and today it is the openly syncretic explanation. It is a theology alright, but not that of the Church of Christ or of St. Augustine. The defiance is unmistakable.

Augustine "condemned Hermes for being 'friendly to the tricks of demons' even while predicting the fall of Egyptian demonolatry before the irresistible rise of the new faith. He

---

[20] "God, the creator of all, made a visible God to be with Him, and He made Him first and only; He took delight in Him and loved Him greatly as His own Son, who is called the Holy Word."

[21] "Receive Egyptians the laws and letters" (intended as an invocation).

[22] Bruno Santi, *The Marble Pavement of the Cathedral of Siena* (1993), p. 13.

[23] Brian P. Copenhaver, "Hermes Theologus: The Sienese Mercury and Ficino's Hermetic Demons," in *Humanity and Divinity in Renaissance and Reformation* (1993), p. 152.

found Hermes especially perverse for having mourned the collapse of the old religion founded on fraud." [24]

"Hermes...dominates the physical and ideal space of the floor mosaic in the cathedral of Siena, where the sibyls and Hermes himself, as their scrolls show, are clearly connected to the Florentine rebirth of ancient magic and pious theology." [25]

Fraud was the order of the day in Renaissance ecclesiastical art: magnificent beauty married to the infernal.

---

[24] Ibid., p. 159.

[25] Paola Zambelli, *White Magic, Black Magic*, op. cit., p. 72.

Chapter X

The Grand Egyptian Lodge of Vatican City

"Our records inform us that the usages and customs of (Free)masons have ever corresponded with those of the Egyptian philosophers, to which they bear a near affinity. " [1]

Thomas Smith Webb, *The Freemason's Monitor* (1818)

"To come again on Rome...(t)he narrow streets, devoid of footways, and choked, in every obscure corner, by heaps of dunghill-rubbish, contrast so strongly, in their cramped dimensions, and their filth and darkness, with the broad square before some haughty church: in the center of which, a hieroglyphic-covered obelisk, brought from Egypt in the days of the Emperors, looks strangely on the foreign scene about it...It is stranger still, to see how many ruins of the old mythology: how many fragments of obsolete legend and observance, have been incorporated into the worship of Christian altars here; and how, in numberless respects, the false faith and the true are fused into a monstrous union."

Charles Dickens, *Pictures from Italy* (1846)

"I saw the horror and unwholesome antiquity of Egypt, and the grisly alliance it has always had with the tombs and temples of the dead...offering unnameable sacrifices to indescribable gods...And behind it all I saw the ineffable malignity of primordial necromancy..."

H.P. Lovecraft, *Under the Pyramids* (1924)

"...they are your people and your heritage whom you brought out of Egypt, that iron furnace."   I Kings 8:51

When the Fifth Dynasty obelisk which Caligula erected in Rome, circa 40 A.D., was installed in St. Peter's Square in 1586 by Pope Sixtus V, it marked the transformation of the Vicar of Christ into the Pharaoh of the world. The obelisk is symbolic of the reigning occult power as that power is conveyed in the

---

[1] Webb was Grand Master of the Masonic Grand Lodge of Rhode Island.

phallic cult-image. "In Middle Egyptian, obelisks are *thn*; the pyramidion is *bnbn*. Both may be taken to describe the shape of the monument, but they also imply regeneration through sexual action, alluding to the act of 'rising' or 'becoming erect'...The Egyptian monuments employed this common form in part because it was efficacious, suitable to their roles as cult objects." [2]

Representations of the male genital organ in erection are common to pagan religions from Sumer and Egypt onward. "Numerous Sanskrit texts and ancient sculptures such as the Gudimallam lingam from the third century B.C. define this image unequivocally as an iconic representation of the male sexual organ in erection, in particular as the erect phallus of the god Shiva." [3]

A Renaissance illustration depicts Domenico Fontana from *Della transportatione dell'obelisco vaticano et delle fabriche di Nostro Signore papa Sisto V.* [4] Published in 1590, this book describes one of the most impressive engineering feats of the early modern world, Fontana's most famous undertaking, the removal of the Egyptian obelisk (brought to Rome in the first century A.D.), weighing 327 tons, from its place in the circus of the Vatican, and its subsequent erection 275 yards from its old position, at the new one in front of the basilica in the Square of St. Peter's. This engineering achievement took the concerted effort of 900 men, 75 horses and countless pulleys and yards of rope. Fontana gives a detailed account in *Della transportatione dell'obelisco Vaticano e delle fabriche di Sisto V*. A large-format folio, the book contains dozens of full-page plates depicting the engineering processes involved in moving the obelisk. The stunning detail of these drawings invite careful perusal. Many of the images combine detailed architectural depictions with pagan allegorical and mythical figures such as *"Concordia"* and *"Firmitas" who preside over the engineers' labor.*

---

[2] Molly Swetnam-Burland, *Egypt in Italy: Visions of Egypt in Roman Imperial Culture* (2015), p. 69. One of the most ominous depictions of an obelisk in cinema is in the 1981 film, "Clash of the Titans," where an obelisk is shown standing sentry at the entrance to the abode of the Stygian witches.

[3] Wendy Doninger, *The Hindus* (2009), p. 22.

[4] Though the book is designated as "volume one," it was the only volume printed.

It is the gravitational pull of consensus reality which has impaired the vision of the "Faithful" and kept them from a shock of recognition at the sight of the dull totem of pagan Egypt that dominates the square named for Jesus Christ's chief apostle. As part of the majestically clever disinformation saga of the occult Church, its mentally trapped disciples have been led to believe that because the giant obelisk has a tiny cross at the top, that the thing is "a glorious symbol of the defeat of the pagan world by the Cross."

If a giant swastika, 88 feet tall, were placed in St. Peter's Square, with a tiny cross atop it, would people accept the cover story that it was the symbol of Catholicism's supremacy over Nazism? One can hardly glimpse the cross on the top of the obelisk. The overwhelming symbolic reality of the obelisk is the power of the massive iconic imagery of Pharaonic Egypt which dominates St. Peter's Square, where one would expect to find a huge Catholic crucifix, or statuary depicting with the resplendence typical of the astonishing craftsmanship of the sculptors of the Italian Renaissance, the signal event of the cosmos, Jesus Christ's Resurrection, and His victory over the power of death itself.

But those Christian images are not at all dominant amid Gian Lorenzo Bernini's ellipsoid piazza, which has come to be known as "Bernini's Colonnade," and where towers at the center of it the phallic emblem of pharaonic power, as an obelisk also dominates Washington D.C,. and stands as well in the financial capitals of New York and London: all of these centers of power are symbolically connected through the obelisks.

Occult ceremonies have been enacted by Catholics (or rather pseudo-Catholics), in the misnamed "St. Peter's Square." Among the strangest is the mysterious ritual homosexual rape of an unnamed *un puto* (boy), who was the godson of Cardinal Francesco Albizzi. This was a violent rape. It occurred in December, 1670, and it left the sodomized child with several fractured bones. It seems that it was intended that he should have died, but he survived his injuries and identified his attacker as Bernini's own brother, Luigi.

Was it the case that Cardinal Albizzi's nephew was selected as a *giovane agnello di Dio* (little lamb of God), intended as a sacrifice to Satan through an ignominious and torturous death? What we know for certain is that Luigi Bernini sodomized the boy beneath the famed statue of Constantine which had been sculpted by his brother, within his brother's "Colonnade," and in the shadow of the obelisk. We also know that Luigi Bernini was found, but never brought to trial. This rapist, who had nearly killed the boy, suffered no punishment other than a token "fine."

The *Statuta almae urbis Romae* (vol. ii, section 49) prescribed death by fire *in all cases* where "the unspeakable crime of sodomy" had been committed. But the law did not apply to Bernini. Why? By way of a motive, a twenty-first century academic explains that "Luigi must have simply been crazed by sexual frenzy." Perhaps, but that begs the question of how his savage, open-air crime within the sacred precinct of the Vatican, happened to be excused by Pope Clement X, Cardinal Albizzi and the victim's family and extended clan.

Returning to the obelisk itself, the feat of moving it from its old Roman location since the days of the Caesars, to its new location at the heart of St. Peter's Square, was of one enormous expense and effort. Many contemporary engineers doubted that it could be achieved without death and injury to the regiment of workers that would be required, and destruction to the obelisk, yet the monumental task was obsessively pursued on a tight schedule, as if it were a matter of life and death.

Bern Dibner, the eminent historian of science and technology, has written the most comprehensive study in English of how the thing was done and at what expense in treasure and effort. In his paper, *Moving the Obelisks*[5] we read, "Many of these ancient monoliths, taken from Egypt as trophies of conquest and symbols of power through the efforts of extraordinary human labor and engineering ingenuity, were *re-established in the capitals and seats of empire that also inherited Egypt's burden of civilization.*"

Is this what Christ's Church represents, ancient Egypt's "burden of civilization"? What was Pharaonic Egypt's *civilization*, if not the Satanism of Set/Shaitan (Satan)? [6]

---

[5] Bern Dibner, *Moving the Obelisks: A Chapter in Engineering in which the Vatican Obelisk in Rome in 1586 was Moved* (1952).

[6] "Shaitan...derives from the ancient Egyptian god Set...which blackens everything...Modern etymology regards *Sheitan*, or *Shaitan*, as an Arab word, possibly based on the Hebrew Satan..." (Bogdan and Starr, *Aleister Crowley and Western Esotericism* [2012], p. 194).

Inheriting "Egypt's burden of civilization"

Among the very first, prominent agents of the sexual revolution in the United States was Fahreda Mahzar, who, under the stage name "Little Egypt," belly-danced at the Chicago World's Fair ("World Columbian Exhibition") in 1893, violating obscenity laws and becoming a *cause celebré* for early sex activists such as Ida Craddock. "Little Egypt" is a slang term for the geographic region in the American Midwest containing many sites named after those in Pharaonic Egypt, such as Memphis in Tennessee, where the 'King of Rock and Roll' died and the 'Black King' (Rev. Martin Luther King Jr.) was murdered; and Cairo, Illinois where Abraham Lincoln confronted Stephen A. Douglas in fateful debates.

In America's Little Egypt region, the Mississippi River was equated in the minds of Freemasons with the Nile River, and it was in Little Egypt that these and other masons constructed obelisks and conducted processions, pilgrimages and rituals on the geomantic roads and waterways of an *America mystica* about which most Establishment historians are oblivious. With regard to the phenomenon of rock-and-roll (which was originally slang for the sex act), after the assassination of President John F. Kennedy, the binding of the nation's psychic wounds did not begin in earnest until a "rock and roll" band from England named the "Beatles" debuted on the nationally broadcast Ed Sullivan television program in February of 1964, telling America, "I want to hold your hand." The response from the nation was a level of popular hysteria so unprecedented it eventually led the band's leader, John Lennon to opine, "We're more popular than Jesus Christ." Those who believe that "rock music" is both an *excremental* as well as an elemental reversion to the primitive tom-tom rhythm of sub-Saharan Africa, may be interested to know that the "roll" portion of the Beatles "rock" refers to a *dung-roller*.

The Beatles rock band maintained that their name was coined in reference to the "beat" of their sound. It is worth noting however, that according to E.A. Wallis Budge, Keeper of Egyptian Antiquities at the British Museum from 1894 to 1924, "Scarab, or Scarabaeus, is the name given by Egyptologists to the myriads of models of a certain beetle, which are found in mummies and tombs, and in the ruins of temples and other buildings in Egypt...The beetle which was copied by the Egyptians in this manner...compose a very numerous group of dung-feeding Lamellicorns...A remarkable peculiarity exists in the structure and situation of the hind legs, which are placed so near the extremity of the body, and so far from each other, as to give the insect a most extraordinary appearance when walking. This peculiar formation is, nevertheless, particularly serviceable to its possessors in rolling balls of excrementitious matter in which they enclose their eggs...These balls are at first irregular and soft, but by degrees, and during the process of rolling along, become rounded and harder...

These maneuvers have for their object the burying of the balls in holes...and it is upon the dung thus deposited that the larvae, when hatched, feed." [7]

For those who have eyes to see, the obelisk in St. Peter's Square is a symbolic, masonic-type of communication conveying the revelation that the theology of the Church of Rome is dominated by Pharaonic Egypt. The obelisk represents acceptance of the supreme value to the Church of the esoteric Egyptian philosophy (Hermeticism as it came to be known), as channeled by Marsilio Ficino and Pico, who were the ambassadors of Hermes Trismegistus to the Church. The supreme value of Hermetic Egypt above Jesus is conveyed by the scale of Christological images in St. Peter's compared with the Egyptian obelisk that dwarfs them.

"The Masons had always believed their origins went all the way back to ancient Egypt. This was a holdover from the Renaissance when it was widely believed that Egypt was a repository of all lost or mystical knowledge...Obelisks, Freemasonry and Egyptomania had always been closely related...On July 4, 1848, when the cornerstone of the Washington Monument was laid, Washington's brother Freemasons conducted the ceremony." [8]

In addition to Washington D.C., New York City sought its own obelisk—directly from Egypt. The task fell to Freemason Henry Honeychurch Gorringe, a lieutenant commander in the U.S. Navy who succeeded in transporting an obelisk to New York, where Freemasons presided over the civic ceremony of laying the obelisk's foundation. In October 1880, five hundred commanders of masonic lodges converged on the city, where

---

[7] Sir E.A. Wallis Budge, *The Mummy: A History of the Extraordinary Practices of Ancient Egypt* (1989) pp. 231-232.

[8] Bob Brier, *Egyptomania* (2013), pp. 115 and 125.

they led nearly nine thousand of their lodge brothers in a march past the Grand Masonic Temple on 23rd St. and 9th Avenue to Central Park, to lay the cornerstone for the obelisk which had the common name (actually a misnomer) of "Cleopatra's Needle." [9] "In the name of the Grand Lodge of the State of New York I now proclaim the cornerstone of this obelisk, known as Cleopatra's Needle, duly laid in ample form." (The obelisk was not actually erected until January 22, 1881).

The installation of an Egyptian obelisk in a place of honor in the city of London, England was also under the supervision of Freemasons: the engineer John Dixon and Sir Erasmus Wilson. The question of siting the obelisk was of masonic significance. Would it be in a public square like St. Peter's, or imitative of the French masonic-siting of their obelisk at the Place de la Concorde? The masonic duo proposed that London's obelisk, or "Cleopatra's Needle" as it was melodramatically and erroneously called, be erected in front of Parliament. A precise replica made of wood was erected there to win public approval, but Protestant evangelical Bible-believers objected that a symbol of pagan empire had no business in front of the houses of a Christian legislature. The Freemasons relented and decided upon a site at the Adelphi Steps at the Thames Embankment, with the approval of the Grand Lodge of England.

Like the "Grand Lodge of Vatican City," in the modern era sorcerers initiated the process of erecting what is, after the Mummy, the most elemental and recognizable symbol of

---

[9] "Though the (New York) obelisk is often called 'Cleopatra's Needle,' Cleopatra...had nothing to do with its creation....the Obelisk predates her by more than a millennium. Approximately 3,500 years ago in the ancient Egyptian city of Heliopolis, stonecutters carved two obelisks out of granite. Each one was formed from a single piece of quarried stone, and the enormous feat of extracting and erecting the monolith was symbolic of the reigning pharaoh's power. Both obelisks were inscribed with hieroglyphs praising Pharaoh Thutmose III, who reigned from 1479 to 1425 BCE, and were erected outside of a temple. The obelisks were toppled...during an invasion by Persians in 525 BCE; for more than 500 years, they remained buried in sand until Roman Emperor Caesar Augustus discovered and transported them to Alexandria. They were erected in a temple built by Cleopatra to honor Julius Caesar, which may explain how they individually came to be known as Cleopatra's Needle." — http://www.centralparknyc.org/things-to-see-and-do/ attractions/obelisk.html The "needle" moniker derives from the Muslim conquest, when obelisks came to be known in Arabic as "mislah," a sewing needle, and messalat far'un, "pharaoh's needles."

Pharaonic Egypt. The Catholic Church of the early centuries A.D. had no interest in Egypt except as a lesson in what befalls those who become victims of enslaving pagan dictatorships. By around 1150 A.D. of the medieval period, there was only one obelisk still on display in Rome, the one standing next to old St. Peter's, in what had been the "Circus." The others had all been toppled. "Sixtus the V's obelisk specialist, Michele Mercati, reported that the Circus Maximus obelisk showed traces of fire damage and holes drilled for the insertion of toppling levers." [10]

In Italy the obelisk "needle" was known as a *guglia*. The Catholic poet Pietro Aretino, who we met in the previous chapter, used this as a simile in his identification of the obelisk with *magica sexualis*: "In 1524, during a period when Renaissance popes had begun to display a renewed enthusiasm for the excavation and re-erection of obelisks...Pietro Aretino used the term *guglia* to describe the priapic member of his protagonist in...*I modi*." [11]

Priapic symbolism is on view in Rome's Campo Marzio, at the base of the Monte Citorio obelisk, which had been pulled down by the devout Catholic Duke Robert Guiscard in 1084. It was re-erected with considerable difficulty and expense by Pope Pius VI in 1792. [12] The base features a stone carving of a reclining young man with a large, phallic-like obelisk emerging from his genital region.

The early Christians in Rome intended to remove all symbols connected with pagan Egypt as befits a capital city of Christendom. They were dissuaded from dismantling the obelisk in Nero's Circus Maximus however, by a legend that St. Peter had been tortured and murdered in its shadow, which if true, would seem to be more of a reason to take it down than to

---

[10] Brian A. Curran et al., *Obelisk: A History* (2009), p. 308, quoting Mercati, *Obelischi* (Rome, 1589).

[11] Curran, p. 67.

[12] An obelisk that had been erected in A.D. 14 and torn down by the early Christians, was the subject of an attempted erection by Pope Leo X in 1519. In 1587, Pope Sixtus V, who sought a pagan obelisk "in front of every church," succeeded in raising the obelisk in the precinct of Santa Maria Maggiore Basilica, in Esquiline Square. In the 18th century, Pius VI was responsible for the erection of ancient Egyptian obelisks in the Piazza del Quirinale in 1786, and in 1789 (the year of the French Revolution), at the top of the Spanish Steps, in front of the Trinitá dei Monti church.

preserve it. Nevertheless, rescued by the folk tale, the seemingly charmed obelisk remained upright.

An excerpt from Mr. Dibner's distinguished monograph, *Moving the Obelisks* here follows, by which we hope to convey a sense of the immense effort expended, including conferring upon the engineer Fontana draconian conscription, confiscation and police powers, all for the purpose of making an emblem of Pharaonic Egypt the most monumental visual motif at the heart of what was supposed to be Jesus Christ's principal church.

"...With only the main arches and walls of St. Peter's completed and the dome still unbuilt, the College of Cardinals met in 1585 to elect one from among them to become the new pontiff to succeed the deceased Gregorius XIII. The choice was Cardinal Montalto and he ascended the pontifical throne as Sixtus V at the age of 64. He, like Julius II, was destined to imprint his vigorous personality upon the face of Rome. It was his determination to...include the majestic old obelisk that had been standing since Caesar's day on its pedestal behind the sacristy of the new St. Peter's. Alone among the obelisks of Rome, it had stood erect...Not one other of the many obelisks...had remained upright or unbroken...It had no inscriptions on its faces prior to being brought to Rome, so that its more ancient history could not be determined as accurately as those obelisks having hieroglyphic inscriptions....

"It required moving this enormous stone 275 yards from its old position to the new one in front of the cathedral, and it therefore became a topic of major interest among engineers as well as among prelates.... The...ingredient in this formula of success was the engineer and architect, Domenico Fontana (1543-1607). He was born in Mili (now Melide) on Lake Lugano in the Ticino canton of Switzerland. He thus springs from a nation famous for its engineers and also from a family that had given many sons to the constructive profession. He was the son of the architect Matteo Fontana who had been active in Venice in the 1400s. In the 1500s three Fontana brothers, Giovanni, Domenico and Marsiglio, worked in Rome, often together as engineers and architects. The oldest of these, Giovanni (1540-1614), was retained as hydraulic and military engineer by four popes and by the King of Spain....For Cardinal Felice Peretti de Montalto (future Pope Sixtus V), Fontana had worked as the designer and constructor of the mausoleum of Pope Nicholas IV in 1574, and of several palace buildings. He was then building a small chapel of the Sacrament erected in the Santa Maria Maggiore, one of the four prime churches in Rome. This show of magnificence on the part of Cardinal Montalto seems to have displeased Pope Gregorius XIII, who thereupon suspended the Cardinal's income.

"...on April 24, 1585, Montalto became pope. Fontana was immediately repaid out of the papal treasury and was made papal architect. An immediate task assigned to him was to continue the work of Giacomo della Porta (1529-1604) in completing the construction of the dome of St. Peter's, which Michelangelo had left unfinished upon his death.

"It is related that once while Cardinal Montalto and Fontana were crossing the Vatican area, the cardinal remarked that if he ever became pope the obelisk would not long remain in that place...It is therefore not surprising that one of the first official acts of Sixtus V on assuming the papal throne was the appointment, on August 24, 1585, of a special commission to study the problem and to make a recommendation for the transportation of the obelisk...The commission met in the palace of its head, Pier Donato (Cardinal Cesis) and was composed of prominent men of Rome representing both the ecclesiastic and state functions of the papacy. In addition, there was representation from the administrative and legislative bodies as well as the departments of finance and public works. On this commission were such dignitaries as Cardinal Guastavillano, the papal chamberlain; Francesco, Cardinal Sforza; Ferdinando Cardinal de Medici (later Grand Duke of Tuscany), and such functionaries as the Treasurer-General, Commissary-General and Commissioner of Roads. Secular Rome was represented by several Senators and Deputies—in all a commission endowed with a sufficiency of funds and authority and one committed to act. The dream of many popes was now to be realized.

"The commission met immediately after its appointment...The commission...was most impressed by the plan, model and presentation of the engineer Domenico Fontana. He presented his plan and demonstrated how the monolith could be lowered, moved and lifted by a combination of a wooden tower and ropes and pulleys, using as a model a lead obelisk about two feet tall, and a wooden tower with ropes and tackle made to scale. The commission thereupon appointed Fontana engineer-in-chief in charge of the project.

"We are thankful to him not only for performing a most workmanlike job in planning and executing a difficult physical and political task, but like the complete artisan he was, by leaving for posterity a record that, in format, type and engravings, makes one of the handsomest and most complete records of any engineering problem, a prize in the field of bibliography and engraving. His book *Della trasportatione dell'obelisco vaticano et delle fabriche di Nostro Signore papa Sisto V*, was printed in Rome in 1590. It is very rare and has become a classic in engineering literature.

"...The difficulties that Fontana faced were the great weight, the great bulk and the fear of breaking this fragile stone in moving it. It weighed half again more than the obelisk now in New York...First, the edict of authority was issued so that Fontana could obtain the required men, draft-animals, timber, equipment, subsistence and rights-of-way, and at the same time be free from litigation due to possible damage incurred in the operation. The following is the document as issued by the pope and as based on his sovereign right of eminent domain.

"We, Sixtus V, grant power and full authority to Domenico Fontana, architect of the Holy Apostolic Palace, in order that he may more easily and more quickly transport the Vatican obelisk to the Piazza of St. Peter, to make use, as long as this removal lasts, of whatever workmen and laborers, with the apparatus that may be necessary, of whatever kind it may be, and when in need *to compel anyone to lend material to him*, or sell it, he, however, satisfying them with due compensation.

"*That he can make use of all the boards, timbers, and wood of any size, which are in places convenient for his needs, regardless of to whom they belong,* paying, however, the due price to the owner of this lumber, in accordance with the decision of two arbitrators chosen by the parties; and *that he can cut, or have cut, all the wood which may in any way belong to the church of St. Peter, its chapels and canons, particularly in the ground of the Campo Morto, or of the Hospital of San Spirito in Sassia, or of the Apostolic Chamber, without making any payment,* and he can carry this wood to whatever place he desires; and let out to pasture the animals used in this work without incurring any punishment, making up, however, for damage done, according to the decision of experts chosen for this purpose.

"That he can buy and carry away the above-mentioned articles and anything else necessary from any person whatever, without paying excise tax or customs duty of any kind. That he can, without a license, or permit, get together in Rome or in other cities and neighboring places any amount of victuals for his own use and that of his workers and animals.

"That he can requisition and carry away from wherever he finds them, capstans, ropes and cords, whether loose or fixed, undertaking, however, to repair them and make them whole, paying a due recompense; and that in the same way he can make use of all the instruments and apparatus belonging to the edifice of St. Peter, and can order the agents, representatives and officials of the said building in a due space of time to make free and clear the Piazza around the obelisk so that it can be removed and to accommodate him in whatever way necessary in this undertaking.

"That he can (if it be necessary) tear down, or have torn down, the houses near the said obelisk, deciding first on the way in which to compensate the owners for the damage. Finally, authority is given to the said Domenico Fontana to do, command, execute and carry out any other thing necessary to this task, and, moreover, that he, together with his agents, workers and domestic servants in any place and at any time may carry any force of arms necessary, except those prohibited; all the magistrates and officials of the entire estate of the church are commanded to aid and help the said Domenico Fontana in the above-mentioned things, as are all others subject in any way at all to the authority of the Holy See, of whatever rank and condition, under pain of Our displeasure, and a fine of 500 ducats to the Treasury, and other punishments at Our discretion. No one shall dare impede, nor in any way molest the carrying out of this work of the said Domenico, his agents, or workers, but on the contrary without delay or any pretext, everyone shall help, obey and support him; anything to the contrary notwithstanding. Given at Rome in St. Mark's this 5th day of October, 1585.'

"...Fontana was...particularly careful in anticipating the development of cracks in his obelisk by avoiding the strains that would have expanded such cracks into breaks....The combined weight of the protective planking, the blocks, the ropes and bars rose to 56,459 pounds, which were added to the weight of the obelisk, making the total 737,690 pounds which had to be lifted by the ropes and levers. On opposite sides of the tower the main timbers had scantlings attached to them forming ladders that reached up to the top.

"...When the time came for inclining the obelisk after raising it above its base, it was planned to draw the shaft at its foot towards the west into the opening pierced through the sacristy wall. The obelisk foot was to be rested on a timber carriage laid on rollers. Fifty-three men were assigned to the levers in the raising process, 35 to the westerly levers and 18 to the two levers pointing east. Some were to pull directly on the ropes attached to the levers, others to bear on the capstans attached by rope to the levers. Additional men with sledges and mauls clambered through the tower and obelisk, driving wedges to tighten the binding members and stiffen the system. As in any similar modern job, these men wore metal helmets to protect them from objects falling from above.

"...In addition to the tall barricade enclosing the working area, stringent orders were published that prohibited anyone beyond the barricade from passing the barriers or hindering the workmen in any way, nor might they speak, spit or make any loud noise, under penalty of severe punishment, *"including death."* This was intended to make it easier for orders to be heard over the noise of 900 moving men and 74 horses and over the scrape and rumble of ropes, blocks, capstans and timber. Police were assigned to carry out this strict order and the resulting silence gave rise to one of the prettiest legends in engineering history. This story has, through the last two centuries, become so much a part of the general story of the erection of the Vatican obelisk that, in permitting its refutation, one owes to tradition, at least, the kindness of its repetition.

"It seems (so the legend goes) that at one point of the operations the silenced multitude (who were threatened with death if they uttered a word) noted that all was not going well with the strained ropes. One version has it that the speed and strain of winding caused the ropes and blocks to get dangerously hot, another version has it that they stretched so much that they piled up on the capstan drums, the leverage ratio dropping so low that the horses and men could no longer continue to pull.

"At this critical moment, a lusty voice rang out from

someone in the silent crowd—it was the voice of an old Genoese sailor named Bresca di Bordighera, and it called out *'Aqua alle funi!'* ('Water on the ropes!') Thereupon water was poured on the failing ropes, they grew taut they held, and the obelisk was saved! Instead of condemning the spirited and brave sailor to death the legend has it that honors were bestowed on him and his family, and that to this day his descendants have the exclusive privilege of selling palms used in the procession on Palm Sunday in St. Peter's.

"The date for the lowering operations of the obelisk was set by Fontana as April 30, 1586. A last preparatory task was the removal of the ancient metal ball still at the obelisk top, placed there by the old Romans and believed to contain the ashes of Julius Caesar. The ball was removed but no ashes were found there. The tower was complete, blocks were in position, capstans and ground tackle fixed in their places. The men were divided into their respective crews, assigned to their posts and again drilled each in his special task. Their equipment and supplies were distributed and last minute checks were made. An air of expectancy fell upon the metropolis.

"...by sunrise (of the 30th) every man and horse was at his post ready to proceed. The morning was a typically clear and serene Roman spring day and all Rome moved towards the Piazza to witness the event that had held their interest so deeply and for so long a time. The great personages of Rome and the nobility of all Italy were present. The majority of the College of Cardinals and the city officials were there. Upon roofs and windows facing the square and upon the walls and scaffolding of the incomplete St. Peter's there were crowds of onlookers. The city police was reinforced by the Swiss Guards and a detachment of cavalry kept the swarming populace in order.

"...upon his (Fontana's) signal the trumpet sounded and over 900 men and 74 horses bore on their lever-arms. The gear groaned, ropes tightened and the great stone budged with a rumble that Fontana describes as like an earthquake. The bell was then rung and positions were held as the foremen inspected the equipment. It was found that the top one of the horizontal bands had burst. Evidently the radial component of tension on this band had been underestimated in arrangement of the blocks. Repairs were made and in twelve additional moves the shaft was raised more than two feet above its pedestal. This permitted the timber carriage, moving over rollers, to be slipped into the gap, completing the first phase of the operation. By 10 o'clock that evening the quitting-signal was sounded. The success of this first step was celebrated by the firing of a signal gun which was answered by a burst of artillery from the city's batteries and great joy was shown by the multitude.

"Upon re-examination of the results of the first move in the operation it was found that not only the top band had broken, but that all nine bands had suffered somewhat—some had slid from their positions, others had twisted or had developed breaks in their sections. To prevent further slippage, rope slings were passed under the obelisk foot, for it was found that none of the rope lashings had suffered as had the iron ones, and this added precaution had saved the old stone. It was also found that some of the vertical bars had also been broken at their eyes. Evidently the bars had not been adjusted to share the load equally as no adjustment mechanism (turnbuckles or wedges) had been provided and the "cascading" of such breaks had not yet been a province of study. The result was the shearing of pins and jaw-members in the hand-forged, and therefore ill-fitting, elements. Fontana did not understand 'shear' and was mystified by the clean break that looked 'as if cut by a knife...'

"For the lowering operation three new steps were taken. The first of these was to shift the system of pulleys from the east face of the obelisk to the other three faces so that this face, being the bottom one when resting on the carriage, would have no encumbrances in the descent. The second step was to introduce a sliding brace, having its top bear upon the underside of the lowering obelisk and having its foot slide outward as the stone came slowly down....The third innovation was a group of four blocks that were attached to the foot of the obelisk and the ropes from these were passed through a corresponding set of blocks positioned on the west face of the sacristy. The purpose of this was to be sure that the base of the obelisk would be properly drawn through the opening made in the eastern sacristy wall as the obelisk moved away from its vertical into its horizontal position. This would also help keep the main ropes in a vertical position, thereby avoiding lateral strain. However, these elaborate precautions seemed quite unnecessary because when the shaft was half-way down, there was shown a tendency for the carriage on its rollers to slide westward without any aid; in fact, the slide had to be controlled by rigging up ropes in the opposite direction from that originally intended. To avoid the danger of impact developing from a jerky or too rapid motion of such a great and fragile weight, it was deemed necessary to add a bridle by attaching five additional blocks to the top of the obelisk and to connect these by rope to five equivalent pulleys suspended from the top of the sacristy. It had required eight days to make these preparations for lowering the shaft, the date of lowering up to May 7. In this, the initial raising of the shaft, the same signals were used, but in reverse order. At the trumpet blast, the main capstans paid out rope while the capstans connected at the base wound theirs up, thereby pulling the base westward. As the bell sounded work stopped, the gear was examined, and the ropes were tightened equally.

"The operation ran smoothly with no unexpected occurrences. By 10 o'clock that night the obelisk had been completely lowered and rested properly blocked up on its carriage. The master engineer of this operation then received his due reward by being accompanied to his home by an honor guard of drums and trumpets. The next four days were required to prepare for the next phase of the operation, transporting the obelisk. The capstans, rigging and tower had first to be dismantled and this required rolling the sleeping monument out of range of possibly falling iron or timber. With bolts loosened, the tower members and rigging were then removed to the new site and work was begun clearing the obelisk pedestal of its 1500 years of accumulated earth and debris which had buried it almost up to the base of the shaft. The solidly-packed earth about the stone pedestal made it possible for Fontana to lay the planks for the rollers and carriage right under the obelisk itself. Fontana planned to replace the obelisk pedestal in its new position in a condition as much like the original as he could. He therefore moved the metal corner astragals and then the pedestal stone, which stood eight feet six inches high and was nine feet six inches square and weighed 55 and1/2 tons.

"Beneath it and occupying a narrower space was a rougher stone weighing 63 tons. The next courses were of white marble connected by iron clamps encased in lead. Fontana was surprised to find the iron of the clamps in a perfect state of preservation. The lowest courses were of travertine forming three steps that rested on decomposed concrete. Because the top stone was damaged in removing the astragals, two inches of the pedestal had to be cut away. In the new pedestal, between the two lower strata of marble, was placed a new stone bearing the names of Sixtus V and Fontana and giving an account of the transportation...

"The distance from the old position (of the obelisk) to its new in the center of the recreated Piazza is only about 275 yards and covers an elevational drop of nearly thirty feet. This was of great advantage to Fontana for it enabled him to bridge the distance by a causeway of increasing height so that the obelisk could be swung right over its newly reconstructed pedestal without having to be raised the corresponding height.

"...The preparations for resetting the obelisk over its new base consisted of reversing the procedure in having it lowered. The tower timbers were dragged to the new site and re-erected on the broadened section of the causeway. On the tower were hung pulleys and riggings for the raising operation and the rope and pulleys were attached to the bands of the three free faces of the obelisk after it had been moved on its carriage to its position over the pedestal. Because of the spread length of the obelisk in its prone position and the increased stresses in the raising (as against the lowering) process, the number of horses was increased from 74 to 140. Of the 48 capstans set out for the raising process, 40 were assigned to the lifting tackle, and in the east end four were intended to drag the obelisk base forward to the central position.

"On September 10, 1586 dawn found every detail ready...At the east end of the ramp a command tower was built for Fontana and his deputies. With the experience gained in the lowering phase the raising moved much more quickly and smoothly. When the obelisk was at about 45° angle, it was buttressed by timbers and the tackle was made fast. The crew (of eight hundred men) were then permitted to eat and rest. At sundown that day the shaft was hanging vertically over its pedestal after 57 pulls and pauses. The joy of the great crowd and the holiday atmosphere of the occasion gave rise to spontaneous jubilation.

"The next day, again as in the lowering stage, levers were in use to raise the shaft over the pedestal. There were clear vertical spaces under the north and south faces. With the obelisk raised, blocks and wedges were driven between its base and pedestal and the carriage was thus free to be rolled out of the way. The capstans were then tightened and the bronze astragals, now in the form of gilded bronze lions (the work of the sculptor Prospero Bresciano), were set in stress-equalizing lead at the four corners. These astragals were not level, thereby requiring metal shims to be inserted until the shaft stood perfectly vertical.

"In eighteen days the tower, cribs and scaffolding had been cleared and on September 18, 1586 the obelisk appeared in full view and was duly consecrated. It had taken Fontana just one year from the time of winning his commission to complete his task and to leave the obelisk standing practically as we see it today. Only the bronze eagles at its base and a more elaborate balustrade were later added...

"Rewards and honors were then showered upon Fontana. He was made a Palatine Count and a Knight of the Golden Spur and he was also granted a pension of 2000 gold scudi as well as the recipient of an immediate gift of 5000 more. He received, gratis, all the wood and equipment left over from the operation.

"Architectural commissions also were thrust upon him. He was required to supervise the restoration and erection of three additional obelisks in Rome. One, a few feet shorter than the Vatican obelisk, was re-erected by him in the Piazza del Popolo, the second he placed in the Piazza di San Giovanni Laterano. This is the tallest obelisk known, even though we think that part of the base of the shaft had, at some time, already been cut away. The third is behind the church of Santa Maria Maggiore and stands 48 and 1/2 feet tall. However, the pedestal upon which it stands is 17 feet high, thereby giving it the appearance of good overall height. Two of the above, those at San Giovanni and Santa Maria, had been buried and lost, but once in a conversation between Sixtus, Fontana and Mercati it was urged that more obelisks be hunted. Fontana, using an iron bar, probed the fill in the Circus Maximus and came upon two obelisks, both fallen and both broken into three parts. Fontana joined the broken sections with the use of stone dove-tail mortises.

"...At the time of Fontana's obelisk operations the facade facing the Piazza consisted of an assembly of five old buildings. These were torn down and the grand facade of St. Peter's, as we know it today, along with the additional portico, were built by Fontana's nephew, Carlo Maderno, but this was not completed and consecrated until 1626, nineteen years after the death of Domenico Fontana. The old facade was demolished in 1605 and the nave was lengthened in the direction of the obelisk. The familiar encircling colonnade moving out in a converging line and then embracing the piazza with the obelisk as its center was not built for another 71 years (1656-1657): it consists of four rows of 284 Doric columns and 88 pillars, surmounted by some 300 statues and was the masterpiece of Giovanni Bernini (1598-1680).

"Of the two fountains flanking the obelisk, one was set there by Sixtus V, and the other by Clement IX (1700-21). In 1723 a rose-of-the-winds was placed around the foot of the obelisk, and in 1817 the astronomer Gilii traced a meridian curve around it. To the balustrade and four small posts that Fontana added to protect the odd base of the obelisk pedestal against vehicles, eight more posts were added by Urban VIII (1623-1644). Under Clement IX (1700-1721) the original four columns were replaced by a larger ornamental marble balustrade and a quadrature of sixteen heavy granite circular columns surrounded by a circular travertine walk. To cover the unsightly holes that remained when the old Roman ornaments were removed, the architect Lodovico Sergardi added a gilt bronze garland of oak leaves surmounted by an eagle, on each of the four faces of the obelisk." (End quote from Bern Dibner).

Honor is due to Fontana and his crew for their genius and daring. If this had been an installation at a secular museum of Egyptian antiquities, completely separate from the Church and its environs, we could also congratulate the Bishop of Rome on saving a historical artifact for study by future generations. Most people will feel that we have placed an over-emphasis on what is essentially a relatively benign restoration of a monumental art work. This is the liberal-humanist view and in our post-modernist world it will appear eminently reasonable and compelling. For Christians it is another matter entirely, however: *the claims of Jesus Christ are total and exclusive.* For believers, who are obviously in the minority (Matthew 7:14), and who are faithful to those claims, the erection of Pharaoh's obelisk at what is supposed to be the heart of the Christian Church, will be seen for the occult pagan exaltation which in fact, it is.

It is advantageous for the Cryptocracy that the civic bonds of the Rome-London-NY-Washington nexus should be strengthened through the placement of obelisks, and that the public should espy in both masonic capital cities and the capital of the Church of Rome, a towering obelisk, conveying to percipients an unmistakable and ultimately demoralizing message of a control system of lithic continuity.

The main motor of Freemasonry was papally-enabled Hermetic Neoplatonism, which had translated ancient Egypt into a living mythos in the Renaissance Church of Rome. The erection of the obelisk in St. Peter's is the culmination of a process which began to reach its summit with the idolization of the legendary figure of Hermes Trismegistus and the secret knowledge his cult personified. The erection of the obelisk of the Pharaohs in the sacred precinct of St. Peter's basilica had been prepared ritually and visually in stages prior to that—in the pope's apartment, and in the Cathedral of Siena, where unambiguous veneration had been paid to Hermes, and in the former case, to an elaborate allegory centered on the Egyptian goddess Isis, who in mythology is "equated with Sothis (Sirius)" and "the snake goddess."[13] Occult images were enshrined in the apartment of the "Vicar of Christ on earth," and a cathedral church, and no pretext of having altered the nature of these icons of demonic deities through the sprinkling of holy water, or papal circumambulations, or other forms of putative exorcism or baptism, cancels the blasphemy of their installation in the name of Jesus Christ. Centuries later these fetishistic monstrosities remain in place in the "Eternal City," no less hallowed than before.

---

[13] Hornblower, op. cit., *The Oxford Classical Dictionary Third Edition*, p. 768.

Chapter XI

The Cabal's Co-conspirators

Ludovico Lazzarelli (1447-1500; also spelled "Lodovico"), referred to his birth on February 4 as inauspicious, in keeping with traditions of the ancient Roman calendar: "A troublesome day for Egypt, and no less for me" (*De Gentilium Decorum Imaginibus*). "Throughout the Middle Ages the belief was also widespread that certain days were inherently ill-omened, especially the so-called Egyptian Days, which derived from the ancient Roman belief that Egyptian magicians had determined certain days to be unlucky...[1]

The most likely candidate as Ludovico Lazzarelli's Judaic handler in his youth is Leone Ebreo, a physician and alchemist in Lazzarelli's home town of San Severino, where Alessandro Lazzarelli, Lodovico's father, was physician to the Christians.

In his most famous work, *Crater Hermetis,* Lodovico Lazzarelli casts Ferdinand I, King of Naples and Sicily and nicknamed "Ferrante," as his pupil. Ferrante was the ally of Pope Pius II in the war with Duke Jean II d'Anjou. From 1462-1464 Lazzarelli lived in the household of, and was tutor to, the son of Duke Matteo di Capua, who at the time was the governor of Atri under Ferrante. Beginning in 1464 and for the next two years, he obtained a position with Bishop Giovanni Antonio Campano. Bishop Campano was a patron of Rev. Fr. Marsilio Ficino. In 1466 Lazzarelli relocated to Venice for reasons that remain unclear. What we know is that while still a youth he had been marked for promotion and prestige. At age twenty-one his high level contacts with Pope Pius II took him to meet the Emperor Frederick III, who crowned Lazzarelli with laurels in San Marco church in Pordenone, Italy on November 30, 1468. By 1473 he was in the company of the astrology-obsessed Lorenzo Zane of Venice, the future Catholic Patriarch of Antioch, with whom he entered Rome. Here Lazzarelli joined the Roman Academy, ostensibly dedicated to keeping alive the classical heritage of the Rome of the Caesars, but in fact a secret society comprised of the lay elite of the

---

[1] Michael David Bailey, *Magic and Superstition in Europe* (2007), p. 88

Church of Rome (Paolo Marsi, Aurelio Brandolini, Publio Astreo, Bartolomeo Platina and Sulpizio da Veroli), engrossed with reenacting pagan rituals in the ruins of the city and accused of ceremonial sodomy. With the death of Paul II and the election of Sixtus IV, the Academy reinvented itself as the "pious" Catholic *Societas Literatorum S. Victoris in Esquilis*.

In 1480 Lazzarelli dedicated his long Hermetic poem *Fasti* to Pope Sixtus IV, the Ferrantes and King Charles VIII of France. In it Lazzarelli positioned the usual markers of the syncretic religion which was enveloping Rome and the papacy: "Jesus is the Logos and the Word, the Mind and Wisdom, who first was Pimander [2] in the mind of Hermes...called Thrice Greatest." [3]

Giovanni Mercurio da Correggio. Some time around November 12, 1481, Lazzarelli fell under the influence of a mysterious, peripatetic false-messiah figure, Giovanni Mercurio da Correggio, who had addressed the College of Cardinals in Rome. As Correggio's disciple, Lazzarelli subsequently became ever more immersed in "alchemy, magic and astrology." [4] Correggio "came from a well-known, old and powerful family belonging to the higher nobility..." [5] Correggio mixed traditional medieval eschatological preoccupations with the doctrines of Hermes Trismegistus. Lazzarelli called his spiritual master Correggio, by Hermes' alternate name, Mercury/Mercurio, and addressed Correggio in writing as follows, "You alone have gone through the secret caves of father Hermes, by roads unknown to all, and have returned from there."

Correggio suffered various arrests and brief imprisonments, episodically in the 1480s. The year 1497 found a costumed Correggio free and out and about in Venice, preaching Hermetic occultism from street corners and calling himself

---

[2] Pimander is another name for the *Corpus Hermeticum* translated by Father Ficino.

[3] Cf. Marco Bertolini, ed., *Lodovico Lazzarelli: Fasti Christianae Religionis* (1991).

[4] Eugene F. Rice, *The Prefatory Epistles of Jacques Lefévre D'Estaples*, n. 3, p. 136.

[5] Wouter Hanegraaff, *Lodovico Lazzarelli: The Hermetic Writings*, p. 23

"Mercurio." Now he worked completely untouched by the Catholic authorities. His exhortations were published in Rome in 1499. Lazzarelli excerpted parts of Correggio's writing in his books, the *Fasti* and the *Crater Hermetis*. Though he posed as a mendicant, Correggio had sufficient funds from mysterious sources. These in turn supported his large family and funded their trips around Italy and France. In the latter nation, upon meeting King Louis II, he gave the king a costly sword as well as magical books (including the *Corpus Hermeticum*), and delivered occult speeches to the French court, proclaiming himself Hermes/Mercurio, master-magician of all knowledge. He arrived at the court of the French king in ritual attire, riding on an ass, holding a scimitar and a mirror-like shield, "shining like the sun." Correggio received gold from King Louis, who sought his counsel, as did the king's physician, Symphorien Champier, who, in 1507 would publish Lazzarelli's occult book, *Diffinitiones Asclepii*. [6]

Correggio subsequently roamed freely across Catholic Europe proclaiming himself the Hermetic Christ, a reader of minds, teller of fortunes, and herald of the coming syncretic religion that bears remarkable resemblance to what emerged in the Church of Rome in the pontificate of Pope "Saint" John Paul II. Correggio, it seems, was protected by forces inside the Church. In 1506 he published a foul work of alchemy and magic dedicated to Pope Julius II (Giuliano della Rovere): *De Quercu Julii Pontificis sive de lapide* ("The Oak of Pope Julius," [7] or the Philosopher's Stone"). No inquisition laid a hand on him. He suffered no fate in anyway similar to that of Savonarola. His doctrine subsequently spread into the bowels of the Church, as it was intended to do.

Correggio was Lazzarelli's occult master and in turn Lazzarelli's pupil, Angelo Colocci, who he initiated into the mysteries of occult regeneration, became a member of the papal court of Julius II and eventually personal secretary to Popes Leo X and Clement VII. Colocci was later named Bishop of Iesi. Throughout his long ecclesiastical career he proved himself another immune and untouchable 'Catholic' Neoplatonic-

---

[6] Hanegraaff, *Lodovico Lazzarelli,* op.cit., pp. 40-41.

[7] The "Oak of Pope Julius"—the Rovere family's coat of arms included an oak tree.

Hermetic syncretist. Correggio is the man of whom Lazzarelli wrote, "Dear teacher, dearly beloved father Giovanni Mercurio —I have become so absorbed in the study of the divine books of Hermes Trismegistus and also in the most holy words of Moses and the prophets, and most of all in those of Jesus Christ our savior, that all other writings, whether of ancients or moderns, have completely lost their appeal to me...Father Mercurius, teacher by fatherly love, hail to you who are like a god to me."

Circa 1494 Lazzarelli finished his magnum opus, the *Crater Hermetis*, also known as *A Dialogue on the Supreme Dignity of Man: The Way of Christ and the Mixing Bowl of Hermes*.[8] This is a typical Renaissance work of syncretic Hermetic-Catholicism. It concludes by offering a path to becoming a god.

To Pontano ("Pontanus"), a scholar who was a member of the court of Ferrante of the King of Aragon and Naples, Lazzarelli wrote, "I am a Catholic, Pontanus, but I am not ashamed to be a Hermetist as well. If you would study his (Hermes) teachings you would find they do not clash with Christian doctrines." Other founts of wisdom for Lazzarelli were the writings of Maimonides and "Denys" or "Pseudo-Dionysius." These texts, with emphasis on Platonic-based "divinization" of humans, have considerable influence in twenty-first century "conservative" and "traditional" Catholic circles, being published by the conservative Jesuit Ignatius Press, and sold in "traditional" Catholic bookstores, as we have noted previously, William Riordan's Neoplatonist *Divine Light: The Theology of Denys the Areopagite*.

Perish the thought that this god-making would evoke associations with magic. The deniers say that this is not magic, but "the mystery of Christian regeneration." But is it really? It seems it has more in common with the serpent in the Garden of Eden and the rabbinic Judaism which kept that gnosis alive, emerging in the 13th century writing of Eleazar of Worms, who gave explicit instructions for making an artificial man in his *Pe'ullath Ha-Yetzirah*—arcana that was conveyed to Giovanni Pico della Mirandola as well as Lodovico Lazzarelli.

This Frankenstein thaumaturgy, the apologists tell us, cannot have an evil origin, because unlike the black magic of witches, this is the pure gnosis of the benevolent Judaism

---

[8] The reference is to part 4 of the *Corpus Hermeticum* titled, "A Discourse of Hermes...Mixing Bowl or the Monad."

espoused by our elder brothers in the faith, who do not practice magic, but rather, "divine secrets." As Lazzarelli writes in *Crater Hermetis*: "For about the word in Genesis: 'And Abraham gave all that he had to Isaac, but to the sons of the concubines he gave gifts,' the Kabbalists say that what was given to the sons of the concubines were the *Scemoth Sceltoma*, that is to say, the names of impurity, namely the magical arts. But the things that were given to Isaac were certain divine secrets, which they call *Kabbalah*[9] (because they are passed down from mouth to mouth). And that name is beginning to be known to some people in our days."

The Catholic occult magus is the divinely perfect man, by definition; and also by definition, this god-man has the ability to create life. From this Catholic template, arose Protestant variants, most notably in the work of Dr. John Dee, who was inspired by the Catholic Abbot Trithemius and his disciple Henry Cornelius Agrippa. Dr. Dee prophesied with hopeful anticipation, a future occult imperium led by England, in which the animation of dead matter (as in *The Asclepius*), would arise and reign over humanity. In our time this hope is centered on autonomous machine super-intelligences. The point at which these stand-alone artificial intelligences (AI) surpass their creators' intelligence is termed *Singularity*. We have a generation among us so disconnected from Biblical wisdom that they ardently long for this event. "...non-evil people might find it in their self-interest to risk propelling humanity into a Singularity even if they know that it has a high chance of annihilating mankind." [10]

Lazzarelli's *Crater Hermetis* was deeply influenced by the *Zohar* and *Sefer Yetzirah* books of the Kabbalah; in particular the passage in the *Sefer Yetzirah* dealing with instructions for the creation of life. [11]

Ludovico Lazzarelli died in his hometown peacefully at age 53 from some type of pulmonary complaint. He is entombed at

---

[9] Specifically, the Kabbalistic text, *Sefer Yetzirah*; of this genre is the aforementioned text by Eleazar of Worms.

[10] James D. Miller, *Singularity Rising,* p. xviii. For a study of the probable dire consequences of Singularity, cf. James Barrat, *Our Final Invention: Artificial Intelligence* (2015).

[11] Claudio Moreschini, *Hermes Christianus: The Intermingling of Hermetic Piety and Christian Thought,* transl. Patrick Baker (2011).

the Church of San Lorenzo in San Severino. No inquisition touched him. From the time of his death his influence inside the Church and among Catholic intelligentsia and royalty grew exponentially.

Superficial profiles of Franciscan Fr. **Pietro Galatino** (1460-1540), who was one of Medici Pope Leo X's most heavily favored Vatican scholars and who also enjoyed the protection and favor of Pope Paul III, present him as an "anti-Semitic Catholic friar" who wrote "against the Jews." Score one for the orthodoxy of Leo X and the Renaissance Church, yes? If image prevails over reality, then yes. If truth matters, Galatino emerges as a very different creature altogether, in keeping with the chameleon character of the operatives under examination. Galatino was commissioned to mount a defense of the Kabbalist Johannes Reuchlin by Pope Leo X.[12]

As Italian scholar Caesare Vasoli has demonstrated, the deceitful pope executed this sleight of hand commissioning Galatino to come to Reuchlin's rescue in 1518, with the publication of his treatise *De arcanis Catholicae veritatis*. We are dealing with both a two-faced pope and a covert support network inside papal Rome. In the papally-authorized *De arcanis*, Galatino praised the ancient rabbis who compiled the Kabbalah. Reprinted in 1550, 1561, 1603 and 1672, Galatino's *De arcanis* "was one of the most widely dispersed books of the Renaissance." Though modernist Catholics and academics describe it as representing the "familiar medieval anti-Jewish polemic," this is a superficial reading. *De arcanis* mixes cosmetic denunciations of contemporary Judaism while putting forth a sympathetic "change in attitude toward the Talmud," while offering a "real appreciation of the substantive and independent value of Kabbalah for Christians." [13] In order to perpetrate this hoodwink, Rev. Fr. Galatino:

"...included both material from the long-standing tradition of Christian controversial writing against the Jews, and alluring scraps of Christian Kabbalah. He praised the ancient

---

12 Caesare Vasoli, "Giorgio B. Salvati, Pietro Galatino e la edizione di Ortona -1518- del De Arcanis Catholicae Fidei," in *Cultura Humanistica* (L'Aquila, 1984), pp. 183-210.

13 Robert Wilkinson, *Orientalism, Aramaic and Kabbalah in the Catholic Reformation*, p. 59; and Wilkinson, *Tetragrammaton*, p. 329.

rabbis who, he claimed, had forseen the coming of Jesus and proclaimed, long in advance, the truths of Christianity. But he damned their more recent successors, who had corrupted the true doctrines of Judaism in order to support their own stiff-necked refusal to convert." [14]

This split-personality type of doctrine is a template of the *modus operandi* of the Church of Rome.

In a burst of claims predicated on a Judaizing delirium, about which Isaac Casaubon was dubious, occult priest Galatino alleged that the rabbis he quoted in *De arcanis* had made accurate prophecies concerning the Virgin Mary, the Messiah and the Catholic doctrine of the Eucharist. Galatino stated, "He (Rabbenu Haccados; i.e. the "Holy Sage," "Holy Rabbi"), was rightly called the holy teacher, since with the inspiration of the Holy Spirit he opened up all the mysteries of Our Lord Jesus Christ so clearly...Casaubon simply could not accept the idea that an otherwise unknown sage had spoken 'a good bit more clearly about the mysteries of our faith than the prophets...but also more openly in many cases than the Evangelists or the Apostles." [15]

In Galatino's defense of Reuchlin and the Kabbalah in *De arcanis Catholicae veritatis,* written under the patronage of Pope Leo X, he avers that the Pharisee Rabbi Simeon the Just ("Shimon Ha Tzaddik") blessed the baby Jesus in the Temple. Here we encounter the profession of one of the oldest of the legends of the Cryptocracy, that the Simeon mentioned by St. Luke in Luke 2:25-35, is actually Rabbi Simeon the Just. This tangled papist legend is part of the larger object of the rehabilitation of the Pharisees in general and Hillel and Gamaliel specifically, by means of the repetition of the myth of Simeon the Pharisee blessing Our Lord.

"Simeon the Just" was a Pharisee who was the son of Hillel, and the father of Gamaliel. The documentary record provides no knowledge of the identity of the Simeon that St. Luke mentions. His identity is unknown to history, but amply illustrated in the rabbinic fantasy concerning him, which was dutifully imported into the disinformation of the Church of

---

[14] Grafton and Weinberg, *I Have Always Loved the Holy Tongue,* (op. cit., 2011), p. 37.

[15] Ibid., pp. 39-40.

Rome, which advanced it. The Pharisee Simeon the Just is reputed to have led the Sanhedrin. He was a hero in the annals of the Talmud:

"As *Kohen Gadol* and head of the *Sanhedrin,* he embodied both religious and political power...The Talmud relates that five miracles occurred in the *Bais Hamikdash* during his tenure. First, the red string that was hung in the *Bais Hamikdash* during the Yom Kippur services turned white, symbolizing Israel's purity. Second, on Yom Kippur two sacrificial goats were designated—one to be offered in the *Kodesh HaKodoshim,* one to be cast off a cliff. The *Kohen Gadol* drew lots in each hand to determine which goat should be used for which purpose. During Shimon *HaTzadik's* 40 year-tenure, the lot indicating the goat to be offered in the *Kodesh HaKodoshim,* always turned up in his right hand, a sign of Divine favor. Third, every evening a full night's supply of oil was put into each lamp of the *Menorah.* Miraculously, the oil put into the western lamp burned for twenty-four hours, demonstrating the constant presence of G-d in the *Bais Hamikdash.* Fourth, although each *Kohen* received only a small portion of the *Lechem Hapanim* (the showbread), he felt satiated as if he had eaten a full meal. Fifth, the fire on the Altar burned steadily without constant addition of wood. Sadly, after Shimon *HaTzadik's* death miracles of such magnitude were no longer manifest in the *Bais Hamikdash.*" [16]

Simeon the Just is consequential to Catholic occultists both as a channel for synthesizing rabbinic Judaism with Catholicism, and in terms of the occult use of the name of God, the Tetragrammaton YHVH (Yahweh), in pagan magical rituals. Yahweh's Divine Name was forbidden to Catholics and Protestants in worship and verbal prayer by Scripture translators from St. Jerome onward to the King James scribes. They placed the commands of the rabbinic Mishnah in this regard above the Word of God—which states that His people shall be known by His name. Instead, His Name was suppressed and clandestinely reserved for use in occult rituals of crucial significance to the Cryptocracy. A good deal of the prolix texts of the Neoplatonic-Hermetic theology are derived

---

[16] Yosef Eisen, *Shimon Ha Tzaddik (Simeon the Just),* http://www.chabad.org/library/article_cdo/aid/2833935/jewish/Shimon-Hatzadik-Simeon-the-Just.htm

from, or concerned in some way with, the correct employment of the wonder-working power of the Hebrew name of God—reserved for the occult-Catholic elite and denied to what we can term the latter-day Catholic *am ha'aretz*. To ensure the efficacy of Yahweh's name in their magical ceremonies, papal Rome in the Renaissance continued its suppression in the liturgy and verbal prayer life of the Church. As recently as the pontificate of Pope Benedict XVI this prohibition against the use of the name of Yahweh was reinstated. In Judaic lore and the Neoplatonic-Hermetic-Catholicism that is guided by it, Simeon the Just is considered to be the last Jewish High Priest to employ the Tetragrammaton in the Temple rite.

The enthusiasm for the murderous Sanhedrin-Pharisees among "traditional" Catholics is a perverse residue of the superstitions and rabbinic folklore emanating from deep within the Church of Rome's Neoplatonic-Hermetic Cryptocracy. The conspirators inside the Renaissance Church were the forefathers of our contemporary "traditional" Catholics, who fantasize that the good Simeon of St. Luke was the son of Hillel, i.e. "Simeon the Just," the leader of the Jewish Sanhedrin. [17] Subversive operatives and useful idiots [18] inside "traditional" Catholicism today have made a saint out of the evil Hillel, just like the modern secular world, which lauds him as the "good Pharisee" whose "benevolence" is equivalent to that of Jesus. For evidence of the quasi-canonization of this archetypal Pharisee by "traditional" Catholics, consult the article, "Saint of the Sanhedrin" which was published in the December 2009 issue of *The Angelus* magazine, an official periodical of the SSPX "traditional" Catholic priests' fraternity in the U.S. (the "saint" in the headline is a reference to Hillel).

Jean Thenaud (1480-1542) was a Frenchman "born near Poitiers into the household of Louise of Savoy, the mother of King Francois I. Thenaud was instrumental in enticing the

---

[17] Upon Hillel's death the mantle of the School of Hillel was passed to his son Simeon. Upon Simon's death the mantle of the school of Hillel passed to Gamaliel. This Gamaliel is mentioned in Acts 5:34-39. He was the teacher of Saul the Pharisee (Acts 22:3), the future St. Paul.

[18] "Useful idiot": for an account of how revolutionary change agents exploit gullible persons who are not in themselves conspirators, cf. chapter 3, p. 17 of usurer Ludwig von Mises' treatise, "Planned Chaos," reprinted in *Socialism: An Economic & Sociological Analysis* (1951).

King into a fascination with the "Catholic" Kabbalah. In response to the King's requests, he produced a manuscript, *Le saincte et trés chrétienne cabale* (circa 1519).[19] Thenaud draws heavily on Pico's *Heptaplus,* Ficino's *Platonic Theolgia* and Reuchlin's *De arte cabalistic.* In Thenaud's own 1521 volume, *Traicté de la cabale*, he makes a show of attacking the Kabbalah's superstitions and deceptions and were we to quote solely from those passages, an impression of stalwart Catholic orthodoxy would be conveyed. Thenaud's attacks however, were merely frosting intended to sweeten his advocacy of Kabbalah and his many "positive assessments of the many layers of meaning in Hebrew letters" and "Thenaud's interest in Kabbalah is apparent in his fascinating diagrams and also in his angelic cosmology, much indebted to Pythagoreanism, Neoplatonism and pseudo-Dionysius...based upon Reuchlin's *De Arte Cabbalistica.*" [20]

"A reading of the *De perenni philosophia libri decem*, a long work by **Agostino Steuco** (1497-1549), Bishop of Gubbio and a learned fixture of the Vatican Library...The author's basic position consists in maintaining that the similarities, even the superficial ones, between Christianity and ancient philosophies (from those of Hermes, the Chaldaeans, and Orpheus, down to Plato) derive from a common point of inspiration; thus he ignores the fundamental differences between Christian dogma and pagan thought. Like Lazzarelli, Steuco takes up Ficino's concept of *pia philosophia*...Steuco's demonstration of a continuity between Christian revelation, on the one hand, which occurred in a specific time and place with the coming of Christ, and the theosophies that preceded it, on the other, is based on continuous scholarly research....Steuco's work adheres to a fundamental concept, that of *philosophia perennis*, which he adopts as a kind of motto of his thought.

"In his *De perenni philosophia libri decem* Bishop Steuco writes: 'In order to realize that all ages, all places, all peoples concur in preaching the truth, you must read what Mercury Trisemegistus has to say about this Mind...' Steuco is "seeking

---

[19] Robert Wilkinson, *Tetragrammaton: Western Christians and the Hebrew Name of God*, p. 337.

[20] Robert Wilkinson, op. cit., p. 338.

the harmony among Greeks, barbarians and Christian theologians in their teaching of a single 'pious theology.'...For Steuco...this search is constituted by the simple juxtaposition of ancient theological writings (Chaldaean, Hermetic, Orphic) for the purpose of drawing from them the essential conclusion."

Bishop Steuco taught that "Mercury, a most ancient theologian, who lived around the time of Moses, knew the Holy Spirit, since he called it 'fine intelligent spirit.'...In the (rabbinic) book *Beresit Rabba*, that is, *maximus genesis*, this spirit is said to be the spirit of the Messiah..." [21]

Prof. **Francesco Patrizi** of Cherso (1529-1597), of the papal university, was born "to an Italianized noble Croatian family in Cherso (Cres) Dalmatia, a city that is now part of the republic of Croatia but which in Patrizi's day was ruled by the Venetian Republic." [22]

"Not to be confused with the earlier humanist and political theoretician, Francesco Patrizi of Siena (1413-1494)...Patrizi began his initial scholarly training in his home city, followed by studies in Venice and Ingolstadt, before enrolling at the University of Padua in 1547." [23] "There, Patrizi moved in important circles, being associated with men like Niccolo Sfondrati, later Gregory XIV; Ippolito Aldobrandini, later Clement VIII; and Gerolamo della Rovere (nephew of Sixtus IV), Scipione Valiero and Agostino Valiero, who would all end as cardinals."[24]

With reference to his future impact, we read, "That Hermeticism is still so deeply engrained in the mind of a pious Jesuit as late as the seventeenth century, may suggest that (Francesco) *Patrizi*'s advice to the Jesuits to take up Hermeticism was not out of place....in this survival in seventeenth-century Jesuitism of the most enthusiastic type of Renaissance religious Hermeticism we have something like

---

[21] Moreschini, op. cit., pp. 245-247; 250.

[22] Leijenhorst, "Francesco Patrizi's Hermetic Philosophy," in Van den Broek and Hanegraaff eds., *Gnosticism and Hermeticism* (1998), p. 125.

[23] Moreschini, op.cit. and http://plato.stanford.edu/entries/patrizi/

[24] Leijenhorst, op.cit., p. 125.

another of those esoteric channels through which the Hermetic tradition is carried on..." [25]

After Patrizi published his heretical occult treatise, *Nova de universis philosophia* [26] Pope Clement VIII promoted Patrizi to Professor of Philosophy at the papal university of Rome, the Sapienza. Patrizi was thereby directing the channel of Hermetic diabolism into the youthful elite of the Church.

In his *New Philosophy of Everything,* the Renaissance papacy's Professor of Platonism celebrated the replacement of fixed dogma, as represented by Thomistic scholasticism, with the situation ethics of Neoplatonism. Patrizi taught that "On the basis of what the most illustrious and ancient wise men said (i.e. Zoroaster, Hermes...Orpheus, Pythagorus)...it can then be deduced that a most ancient doctrine was passed down according to which the world has a soul." [27]

In his appendix to the *Nova,* Patrizi celebrates the *Oracula Chaldaica,* a compendium of Platonic, neo-Pythagorean, Gnostic and Persian doctrines. In his introduction to the *Oracula,* "Patrizi affirms that it contains 'such admirable, such divine laws concerning the Trinity, the divine orders (celestial hierarchies), and the excellency of the soul...Zoroaster can be seen, not without justification, as the one who before all others as it were, laid the foundations of Catholic faith, however unpolished they may be...Plato...transmitted the Hermetic-Zoroastrian 'secret doctrine' of the Chaldeans and Egyptians orally to his pupils." [28]

Patrizi was professor at the Sapienza, imparting the occult stew of Neoplatonic Hermeticism to a new generation and enjoying the protection of Cardinal Ippolito Aldobrandini (the future pope). By 1594 his book had been in print for nearly three years. During those years Vatican Prof. Patrizi was invulnerable from repression under the supposedly harshly anti-occult Pope Clement VIII. This protection continued until significant unrest arose among orthodox Catholic churchmen, which in turn led to the *Nova de universis philosophia* being placed on the Index of Prohibited Books. It is at this point in

---

[25] Yates, *Giordano Bruno and the Hermetic Tradition*, pp. 421-423.

[26] "New Philosophy of Everything" (Ferrara, 1591).

[27] Moreschini, op. cit., p. 263.

[28] Leijenhorst, op.cit., pp. 133-134.

Patrizi's biography where, typically, New Age writers as well as Church of Rome apologists, halt their accounts. They surmise that Patrizi's career was "destroyed" by "bigoted prelates" (the New Age tale), or "vigilant conservative prelates" (the papist's story). Despite this disinformation from two symbiotic wings of consensus history, in reality, *Patrizi's occult paganism inhered in the Renaissance Church and was never extirpated.*

The case of Patrizi is instructive for the purposes of our study. His career illustrates the Machiavellian tactics whereby the papacy would promote radical occult syncretists. Then, when there was a sustained outcry from true Catholics, a token gesture of disciplining or punishing the occultist was performed in public. Patrizi was one such occultist. Catholics point to the Index's theatrical ban on his book *Nova de universis philosophia*. They don't see (or refuse to see) what came before the discipline, and more importantly what came afterward, in terms of how Patrizi fared in his future life and prospects:

"Patrizi developed a thorough and vehement critique of the then still-dominant Aristotelian-Scholastic philosophy and his own alternative Hermetic-Platonist system, *which was to replace the former at the curricula of the universities of all Christendom.* Patrizi's plea for a new Hermetic-Platonist philosophy fully in accord with Catholic faith at first seemed to find considerable resonance. None other than the pope himself (Clement VIII, as indicated, a former fellow student at Padua), called Patrizi to the newly created chair of Platonist philosophy at the Sapienza, the papal university in Rome." [29]

---

[29] Ibid., p. 127 (emphasis supplied). The preceding six occult agents who were adherents of popery, Lazzarelli, Correggio, Galatino, Thenaud, Steuco and Patrizi, are but the tip of the proverbial iceberg in terms of the personnel who played a significant part in transforming the Catholic Church into the occult Church of Rome. There are of course many more listed in these pages (chapter VIII alone yields a harvest of Judases).

Chapter XII

The Moral Theology of Mental Reservation and Equivocation in the Church of Rome

With Special Reference to Alphonsus Liguori

"With St. Augustine...strong convictions were established on the subject of veracity. During the Middle Ages scholastic theologians accepted and expanded upon, but never deviated from Augustine's definition of a lie and his teaching that to utter the opposite of what one holds to be true is intrinsically evil. In the 16th century this tradition began to weaken..." [1]

There cannot be a Church that is eager to have the Neoplatonic-Hermetic doctrines, the Babylonian Talmud, and later the Kabbalah, published and distributed far and wide throughout its intellectual circles, without paying a severe and tragic price for this treachery. The measure that was meted out[2] after the spread of the Neoplatonic-Hermetic, Talmudic and Kabbalistic theology, occurred within the hierarchy, and later, through the Confessional, it was transmitted to the Catholic people in general.

It is true that casuistry had been a "religious science" as far back as the Catholic Middle Ages. Yet, it had remained, in that age, largely anchored to the requirements and verities of Scripture, and the sound traditions derived from the lives of the orthodox Fathers and other holy persons. After the genie of Neoplatonic-Hermeticism and the Talmud and Kabbalah had been released from the lamp where they had been confined by the Church for centuries, casuistry became another name for a highly evolved sophistry, which concealed a method of justification for sin, by means of shrewd alibis and elaborate rationales by which the law of God could be circumvented under the direction of charlatans posing as His priests and theologians.

---

[1] *New Catholic Encyclopedia* (1967), vol. 9, p. 662.

[2] "...with what measure ye mete, it shall be measured to you again." Matthew 7:2.

The reanimation of pagan Greek thought in the Renaissance brought with it a renewed appreciation for a school of sophistry centered on Protagoras (490-420 B.C.). Sophistry seems to have begun with the study of techniques of argument and persuasion, thereby constituting a branch of the classical and legitimate art of rhetoric. Under Protagoras however, the sophists became associated with techniques for making lies appear true, and crimes, virtues. Protagoras himself is reputed to have alluded to these reversals of fact with his claim to "make the weaker argument the stronger."

Plato was far too serious a dissembler to seriously commit in public to the principles of sophistry, which he denounced. A true master of sophistry would be the last to admit it. In one illustrative case, Plato's stirring accusation of mendacity against poets, "proves on closer analysis to be a condemnation of their failure to use their lies on behalf of the state, rather than a condemnation of lies as such." [3]

Talmudic Oath-Breaking
A Pattern for the Church of Rome

The Renaissance witnessed the rise of a theology which legitimated deception, lying and oath-breaking startlingly similar to Judaism's notorious *Kol Nidrei* rite of nullification of promises, vows and oaths. Before we proceed into the Church of Rome's theology of oath-breaking and sundry forms of deception, the reader should be acquainted with the Talmudic *Kol Nidrei*. On Yom Kippur Eve the promise-breaking *Kol Nidrei* ritual is conducted in the synagogue.

The Babylonian Talmud in Mishnah Hagigah 1:8 (a) admits that there is no Biblical basis for the *Kol Nidrei* rite. Rabbi Moses Maimonides confirms that the *Kol Nidrei* ceremony is not in any way Biblical: "The absolution from oaths has no basis whatever in the Written Torah." [4]

The Talmudic law concerning the *Kol Nidrei* rite is as follows: "And he who desires that none of his vows made during the year shall be valid, let him stand at the beginning of the

---

[3] Ann Jefferson, *Times Literary Supplement*, June 3, 2016, p. 5.

[4] *Mishneh Torah*, Sefer Haflaah, Hilkhot Shevuot 6:2.

year and declare, 'Every vow which I make in the future shall be null." [5]

Note that the Talmud declares that the action nullifying vows is to be taken at the beginning of the year and with regard to *promises made in the future*. This distinction is critical. It contradicts what the deceivers tell the public: that *Kol Nidrei* is a penitential service for begging forgiveness for promises broken in the past, rather than what it is: a nullification made in advance for vows and oaths yet to be made (and deliberately broken with impunity).

This "advance stipulation" is called *bitul tenai* and it is the basis for a Judaic person being absolved ahead of time for violating future oaths and promises, or to use the rabbinic lawyer's jargon: "declaration of intent for the anticipatory invalidation of future vows."

This corresponds to the Talmudic lesson that God rewards clever liars (Kallah 51a). One pities the poor people ensnared in this sordid charade of cajoling God into helping them cheat; and more so for those supposed conservative and traditional Catholics who imagine they can follow the clever liars among the Church of Rome's popes, prelates and theologians into "Catholic" forms of oath-breaking, while priding themselves on being part of a "Catholic Faith" that is anti-Talmudic. Satan is a mocker and here is his mockery, helped along by those who have curtailed their divinely-bestowed powers of discernment in subservience to their *religiose* beliefs.

While officially condemned in 1679, the sanction for lying and deceit continues to form a powerful underground current among the personnel of the Church of Rome. The ascendance of the Money Power, Judaism and the occult, the Second Vatican Council, the post-conciliar Judaism adopted by the popes, and the relentless deception mounted to defend serial child molesters and their enablers among the bishops, cardinals and pontiffs, stem from the moral disease that arose during the Renaissance.

From the days of the Gospel to that of St. Augustine in the fourth century, mendacity and dissimulation were condemned as attributes of the devil. Eight hundred years later St. Thomas

---

5 BT Nedarim 23a and 23b.

Aquinas and his cohort, using the analytical tools of scholasticism, affirmed the condemnation. Then, beginning with the Renaissance, a theology of lying derived from casuistry, gained purchase within the Church.

There are two types of casuistry. The first, *classical casuistry*, pre-dates the Renaissance. It concerns "the art or science of bringing general moral principles to bear upon particular cases." Deception and prevarication are not intrinsic to *classical casuistry*, though it can become subject to hair-splitting and the lawyer's tendency to exculpate based on procedural minutiae and special pleading. *Renaissance casuistry* however, is another matter altogether—the degenerate stepchild of classical casuistry, representing a brazen phenomenon centered on the question of *how to avoid telling the truth without appearing to be lying.*

This conundrum was solved by the employment of two Talmudic tactics: *equivocation* and *mental reservation* (also known as mental restriction). Both of these techniques exist in rabbinic texts under other names.[6] Prior to the Renaissance, these were generally despised and opposed in Christendom. Commensurate with the abandonment of God's immutable laws against usury,[7] and the support for the Kabbalah and Talmud from the late 1400s onward, the Church proceeded to harbor in its inner councils and missionary precincts, equivocation and mental reservation.

Equivocation

With verbal equivocation it is not a lie to make a statement which possesses both true and false meanings, provided that it is true according to one's own sense and intention. In its

---

[6]   Cf. Hoffman, *Judaism Discovered*, pp. 593-612; also cf. 149-152, and 169-174.

[7] "In this modern period of moral theology the sufficiency of attrition without any strictly so-called initial charity on the part of the penitent as a proximate disposition for the remission of sin in the sacrament of Penance may be considered as established. The changed conditions in our modern capitalist society have had their effect on moral questions, for morality must always take account of altered circumstances. Perhaps the chief result in this direction is that a practical solution has been attained of the long controversy about the lawfulness of taking interest for a loan of money. The lawfulness of the practice is now admitted; the only moral question is concerning the amount which may be exacted." Rev. Thomas Slater, S.J., *A Short History Of Moral Theology,* (1909), sec. III: The Modern Period.

mildest form, equivocation is little more than a lawyer's trick, a "little white lie" as they say, centered on the principle that the equivocator does not deceive, but rather he allows his interlocutor to deceive himself. According to Jesuit seminary rector Fr. Robert Persons (1544-1610, also called "Parsons"), where a man is "unjustly questioned"...and where "the first and principal intention of the answerer is not to hurt or impugn others, but to defend and cover himself...it followeth evidently, that it can be no lie, nor deception on his part, though by his manner of answering they deceive themselves, which is not to be imputed to any fault of his." [8]   As late as 1595 among shocked Catholic lay people in England, equivocation by priests "caused general disquiet...and was much wondered at." [9]

The concept of a questioner being allowed to "deceive themselves" is a loophole that *permits the deceiver to proceed with his deception by assigning responsibility for it to the victim of the ruse*, predicated on the concept that the other person has no legitimate right to be told the truth. This is dangerously close to the rabbinic deprecation of the rights of the gentile, consonant with equivocation: that the gentile is not owed a candid answer.

By now readers might be nodding their heads in recognition at what they regard as a proprietary Jesuit technique. Yet certain distinguished non-Jesuit Catholic theologians were no less smitten with this stratagem, which gained acceptance from the concept that certain persons do not have a right to the truth. In the *Summa de casibus conscientiae*, published in 1488, the Franciscan theologian Angelus de Clavasio (1411-1495) asserted that an "unjustly questioned" man could reply by saying "what is true according to his own meaning, even if it is false according to the understanding of the hearer." This is harmless and patently ethical when an eight-year-old child asks his parents who have just emerged from their bedroom what they have been doing inside of it. It is another matter entirely when applied to an adult, particularly one in authority. Imagine a man who was speeding in his automobile justifying telling a policeman that he had not been speeding, after the officer asked him about it, because the speeder

---

[8] *A Treatise tending to Mitigation towardes Catholicke-Subjectes in England* (1607).

[9] Antonia Fraser, *Faith and Treason* (Doubleday, 1996), p. 241.

decides that the policeman is "unjustly interrogating me" or is "someone who does not have a right to the truth."

When Church of Rome Bishop William Skylstad of Spokane, Washington, was repeatedly questioned by lawyers concerning a child-molesting priest who flagrantly raped boys in a rectory which the priest shared for years with Skylstad, when the latter was pastor, Bishop Skylstad would not give a straight answer. The repeated failure on the part of clerics and prelates around the world to straightforwardly answer questions about molester priests who they shielded and enabled, demonstrates that the legacy of equivocation and *mental reservation* (a false statement contradicted silently and internally in the mind of the liar, or by an inaudible whisper made by the liar), remains intact.

As someone who is not himself a cardinal or bishop, the interrogator therefore is, according to the doctrine of equivocation, not entitled to a candid answer. This type of thinking emanates from a superiority complex and is not confined to the Catholic hierarchy. The English Puritan theologian Richard Baxter wrote, "If I am unjustly interrogated by someone who has no authority to question me, I may lawfully answer him in such doubtful words as purposely are intended to deceive him, or leave him ignorant of my sense, so be it they be not lies or false in the ordinary usage of those words." [10]

First among Catholics, and later Protestants, a rabbinic type of escape clause was created during the Renaissance to justify deceptive speech. Whereas the rabbis justified deception against the *goyim*, the Christian cleric rationalized deception with regard to someone who, it was decided, did not have the "right" or "authority" to question them. This was a revolutionary break with Christ's command — "Let your yes be

---

[10] *A Christian Directory: or a sum of practical theologie and cases of conscience* (London, 1673), p. 430. Baxter was one of the earliest Puritan advocates of redefining what constitutes usury (cf. *Usury in Christendom*, p. 49). The legacy of this Renaissance sophistry continues: Ted R. Weiland is a contemporary Protestant exegete in Nebraska. He writes: "No one who is seeking to do us evil...is entitled to the truth. More than that, it can with scriptural grounds be called an evil to tell the truth to evil men...people who do not distinguish between righteous and unrighteous lying fall under the Apostle Paul's description of people who use Yahweh's laws unlawfully..." ("Righteous Lying," in *The 9th Commandment: Thou Shalt Not Bear False Witness*).

yes, and your no be no, anything else is of the devil" (Matthew 5:37). The devil was shockingly proximate in the Renaissance, and his cunning human agents processed the clergy by first offering cases of supposedly "harmless" dissimulation that only a fanatic would denounce. One of the most famous examples circulated throughout the Church, was put forth by the Dominican theologian Dominico Soto (1494-1560) in his *De Justitia et Jure libri decem*. It concerns a priest-confessor who is asked a question which he can only answer from knowledge he gained in secret in the confessional, from a penitent. The priest therefore replies to the questioner, "No, I don't know" and then, using the other deception technique, mental reservation, says mentally to himself inwardly, "not in such a way that I can reveal it."

Notice the clever example: deception is perpetrated for the good cause of protecting both the confidence of a penitent and the integrity of the process whereby sinners reveal their transgressions to the priest. Without being fearfully cognizant of the Biblical injunctions and the church law and practice institutionalized for centuries, it is difficult to argue against the example given.

We do have from the life of Jesus Christ a warrant for the right to remain *silent*, as Our Lord was silent before the Jewish court, and later before Pontius Pilate, in certain parts of their exchange. As St. Augustine writes, "Although every one who tells a lie may wish to conceal what is true, yet not every one who wishes to conceal what is true tells a lie."

These are the only options available to the Christian who does not want to hate his master who said, "If you love me, keep my commandments" (John 14:15). Against the truth of God is arrayed the worldly-wise Talmudic-Renaissance lawyer's stratagems. The priest who knows the secret sins of the penitent can remain silent in the face of a question about those sins, but he cannot answer falsely, if he loves his Savior.

In an old story, another widely disseminated sucker-bait offered to persuade Christian religious personnel of the morality of equivocation (deceptive speech), involves self-protection. It seems that a certain Christian traveler, upon arriving at the gates of a foreign city, is interrogated by the guards concerning whether he is coming from a town believed to have the plague. Here the tale varies somewhat: in one version the traveler knows for a fact that his town does not have the plague; in another version the plague is raging in his town but he knows he has not been infected by it. If he tells the truth about coming from the town, then the sentries will bar him from their city. He has nowhere else to seek shelter, and there are wild beasts and brigands outside the gates of the city. According to the Dominican theologian Silvestro ("Sylvester") Mazzolini da Prierio (1460-1523), who was the protégé of Pope Leo X and a director of the Inquisition in Rome, [11] the traveler in the story has no obligation to answer the question correctly, but he does have an obligation to assure them that his entry will not endanger the welfare of the city. Consequently, 1. the traveler decides that the real question is not about what town he comes from, but rather, whether or not he is a carrier of contagion. 2. The traveler also decides that the guards have the right to know whether or not he is infected. Since he believes he is not carrying the plague, he is allegedly morally in the right when he states to the guards that he is not from the town in question. Rather than a lie, the theologian Prierio adduces the traveler's answer to be an "ambiguous reply" and therefore, "truthful under the circumstances."

The tactics on display in the preceding tangled web of deceit are inculcated into clients a hundred times a day in law offices throughout America. They are "clever" and "sophisticated" devices, yet they possess none of the vulnerability of Christ: "...power resides in a complete abandonment and surrender to the will of God and His laws, a faithful reliance that says, 'If God is truth, he will be found only within truth, and not in a lie.' This is the sort of heart-over-head theology that invites mockery, even as it zeroes in on Christ's urging toward 'childlike faith.'" [12]

Instilled in the practitioners of the vice of equivocation is a situation ethic whereby cheating under certain circumstances is permissible, and it is the cheater who decides when the circumstances arise. A Christian society cannot function as God intended with this type of rationalization, which reflects the morals of the Babylonian Talmud (Yoma 83b; Yevamot 65b and 106a; Nedarim 62b). Jesus prayed that His Father's Will be done on earth as it is in heaven (Matt. 6:10). Is there deception

---

[11] http://www.ccel.org/s/schaff/encyc/encyc09/htm/iv.iv.liv.htm

[12] Elizabeth Scalia, "Defending Christine O'Donnell," *First Things*, September 21, 2010.

in heaven? Will the Gospel gain adherents—will we convert the teeming masses of China and India—by Christians being known as sly operators who speak with a forked tongue "under the circumstances"?

Another rationale for deceptive speech and expression is a resort to those cases in the Old Testament where deceit occurred, as for example Abraham counseling Sarah to tell the Pharaoh that she was his sister and not his wife (Genesis 12: 11-20). This is classic equivocation on the rationale that Sarah was (in fact) Abraham's half-sister. There are other Old Testament examples. First, we observe that there is nothing of deceit, equivocation or mental reservation in Jesus Christ or His Gospel. Neither are there injunctions incumbent upon the Christian, as there were in the Old Testament which were incumbent in certain circumstances upon the Israelites, to extirpate pagan peoples who, by means of *magica sexualis,* propitiated false gods. The Old Testament is the chronicle of fallen man in exile from Eden on the pilgrim road to the coming of the Messiah, the new Adam who regenerates man's relationship with God. In the Christian believer's living covenant, our regenerated relationship with the Son of God, the vengeance of old (Deuteronomy 32:35), *continues* to be visited upon hard-hearted wrong-doers, but that vengeance is now visited *soley* by Our Lord and Savior Jesus Christ (Hebrews 10:30). [13]

---

[13] Some people use as their alibi for rejecting Scripture, the claim that God's war in the Old Testament on hostile aliens (*nokri*) who employed sex magic in the course of their idolization of demon gods, was barbaric in its violence, and consequently, the God of the Bible cannot be the true God. Douglas Wilson, writing in the wake of the Jan. 21, 2017 "women's marches" protesting against the newly-inaugurated President Donald Trump, which had as their principal theme, "reproductive rights" (i.e. abortion on demand), addressed the issue as follows: "These are the people who, if you were talking to them about the authority of the Scriptures, would protest that the Bible cannot be taken as the Word of God because it required the extermination of Canaanite men, women and children. These are the same people who, just two days ago, were out there marching in the defense of their own right to slaughter their own children. In short, they do not object to taking of human life, but rather they object to the taking of Canaanite life by the God of Scripture. They object to this because they are obviously Canaanites, and so the whole set up makes them nervous. They do agree that the deity has the right to take life as the deity wills it—they just insist on the right to be the deity." ("Nasty Canaanite Women," Blog and Mablog, January 23, 2017, https://dougwils.com/s7-engaging-the-culture/nasty-canaanite-women.html).

With this in mind, let us take the New Testament view of an Old Testament figure often cited as a righteous liar. Rahab was a harlot in Jericho who hid Joshua's two spies. She hid them under drying stalks of flax on her roof. Rahab deceived the pursuers of the pair by sending them off on a false trail, thereby saving the lives of Joshua's men. Rahab is referred to in the New Testament in Hebrews 11:31 and James 2:25. "Significantly, the passages cited do not single out her deception as a praiseworthy act. Heb. 11:31, emphasizing the faith of each cited individual, refers simply to Rahab's having 'received the spies with peace'—no mention of the deception. Similarly, James 2:25, emphasizing the life of action which follows from regeneration, only mentions that 'she had received the messengers, and had sent them out another way.' Rahab, at great personal risk, sent them out by lowering them from the back window on the city wall (Joshua 2:18). For this risky act of rescue she is commended in the New Testament." [14] There is no hint of commendation of her for any other reason. How could there be, in view of the life of Jesus which was without spot or blemish? Our Redeemer taught us to be on the watch for two characteristics of the devil: 1. He is "a *murderer* from the beginning, who *abode not in the truth*, because *there is no truth in him*." 2. "When he speaketh a lie, he speaketh of his own: for *he is a liar, and the father of it*."

Anyone who can glean from the preceding words a warrant for equivocation or mental reservation is intellectually this writer's superior, since we can see nothing of the kind. Do Christians abide in the truth when they equivocate, or allow other persons with whom they are conversing to "deceive themselves"? Are the survival tactics of clever lawyers the Way of Christ? Was it as lawyers that the early Christians went forth to the lions? Did they conquer pagan Rome by cunning speech, or was it their complete innocence and vulnerability that disarmed their enemies?

"It is evident from all this that by the end of the sixteenth century there was impending *a total change in the doctrines and practice of the Church* with regard to sin and the means of its avoidance and cure." [15]

---

[14] "Deception is Impermissible," in *Antithesis*, vol. I, no. 3; May/June 1990.

[15] Henry Charles Lea, *History of Auricular Confession* (1968), vol. 2, p. 301 (emphasis supplied).

Studying the layers of bureaucracy that began to erupt from casuistry during the Renaissance, we encounter a hair-splitting lawyer's maze of subtle craft that came to be known as "probabilism," which took the morally depraved and indeed diabolic position that where two conflicting theological views were advanced, the perspective that had *the least amount of support in the Bible, and was thus the least "probable," could be accepted as grounds for Catholic judgment, direction, and action.* The theological impetus for probabilism seems to have originated with Spanish Jesuit priests, among them Tomás Sanchez (1550-1610, cf. his *Opus Morale),* and Gabriel Vazquez (1551-1604), as outlined in the latter's 1597 treatise on St. Thomas Aquinas, *Prima Secundae.*

The renowned Francisco Suarez (1548-1617) was professor at the Jesuit College in Rome and then at Coimbra. In his *Tractatus Quintus de Juramento et Adjuratione* [16] he offered various rationales for employing "ambiguous language" to swear an oath without committing perjury. He explained that a lie is that which is contrary to one's own mind, rather than contrary to the minds of one's interlocutors. He has a reputation for being conservative in the application of mental reservation, however on closer examination it appears that he mainly hedged the practice with lofty rhetoric, calling it allowable only when someone was unjustly compelled to swear an oath or divulge a fact. When it was not used for just cause he warned that it constituted a grave sin. The expansive hole in that statement is the license that mental reservation extended to the potential perjurer who was the ultimate decider of whether his judges and interrogators were deserving of a correct answer from him, or were even in a position to judge him. Human nature being what it is, an accused person will be prone to a subjective view of his accusers and judges. One of the methods of restriction which Suarez recommended to those believed they were being unfairly oppressed by police and judges, was to answer out loud the question of whether one did or did not commit a crime as follows: "I did not do it." This was to be followed by the whispered word "today."

Lest we imagine that this despicable trickery could some how be confined to a legal setting, young Catholic men who

---

[16] Book 3, chapters 9-11 in *Opera Omnia*, 24 vols. (Paris, 1859), vol. 14.

wanted to gain sexual favor from a young women would tell her audibly, "I love you," and then inaudibly mumble, "for tonight." Suarez would have denounced the practice, but how is the barn door of mental reservation closed in one instance when it has been opened in another? A culture of deceit inevitably spreads its contagion when immoral acts are condoned by religious authorities. In a society ensnared thus, the lie told in court before an "unjust judge" may be seen to justify, in the eyes of a young man, a lie told to an "impure" woman.

The mental reservation allowed by certain of Rome's early modern theologians is an end-justifies-the-means practice which is unscriptural and ungodly. A lie does not stop being a lie because of a just end. To surmount this objection, Suarez, like many of his brother Renaissance-era theologians, implicated Jesus in the justification of lying. Suarez wrote that when Jesus stated concerning Judgment Day, "But of that day and that hour no man knows, not the angels which are in heaven, neither the Son, but the Father only" (Mark 13:32)— He was using mental reservation. Suarez proposes that Our Lord actually knew the day and the hour but the disciples did not deserve to know that, so he lied to them— or rather He "mentally restricted" His statement.

The defenders of Suarez will reply that he wrote many hundreds of pages of very edifying teachings. This is true. But ten thousand such tomes cannot cancel the disastrous consequences of teaching that the Son of God was a deceiver.

Another key figure was a member of the Augustinian Order, Martin de Azpilcueta, the Renaissance Catholic canon lawyer (1493-1586, nicknamed "the *Navarrus*" after his native land, Navarre), who was the author, in 1553, of the wildly popular *Enchiridion sive Manuale Confessariorum et Paenitentium* ("Handbook for Confessors and Penitents"), eighty-one editions of which were published in less than seventy-five years. Azpilcueta had powerful allies in Rome, among them Pope St. Pius V and Charles Borromeo, the Counter-Reformation dynamo who would be canonized a saint. Borromeo gave Azpilcueta a pivotal appointment as lead canonist in the Apostolic Penitentiary, charged with oversight of the theology of the Confessional and the Sacrament of Penance. Like Liguori's impact in the eighteenth century, this signified that Azpilcueta's probabilism would be directed toward the theology of the Confessional, and through that sacrament to the masses of the Catholic world.

Borromeo may have been the patron saint of the Counter-Reformation, but Azpilcueta was the patron saint of perjury. In the *Enchiridion* he ruled that a Catholic witness who is being questioned by a judge who the witness regards as having "exceeded his competence," or "proceeded unlawfully," in that case is fully warranted in swearing an oath that is not true. The self-serving nature of permitting a Catholic witness or defendant to personally determine to his own decidedly partisan satisfaction, that his judge is incompetent or unlawful, and therefore undeserving of the truth, renders the courtroom a theatre of falsehood and destroys the basis of jurisprudence. These are the tactics of the synagogue and the masonic lodge. They have no place in any theology bearing the name of Jesus Christ, although Our Lord is dragged into these sordid deceptions through refinement of Azpilcueta's recommended courtroom tactics. He suggests that one way to lie under oath to a judge and not commit perjury is to respond with "mixed speech" that is part verbal and part mental. It's true overall even though the verbal part is a lie, but since Jesus can hear the mental part, the Catholic is therefore speaking the truth before God.

The Jesuit casuists of the sixteenth and seventeenth centuries were coining a Newspeak lexicon in which black was white; in which lies were not-lies—they were legitimate means of withholding truth. The degradation of the language through redefinition would become one of the principal engines for the legalization of usury: it was redefined as not-usury, a legitimate means of earning a living.

Due to their prestige, Suarez and Azpilcueta's doctrines achieved an unparalleled renown in the Catholic world and inspired Jesuits such as English Father Robert Persons/Parsons (*A Treatise tending to Mitigation towardes Catholicke-Subjectes in England,* 1607); Louvain Prof. Leonard Lessius (*De Justitia et Jure,* 1605); Ingolstadt Prof. Gregory de Valencia (*Commentariorum Theologicarum,* 1619); Théophile Raynaud's *Disputatio de Veritate Morali cum Mendacio & Locutionibus Aequivocis ac Mente Restrictis Comparata,* 1665; and the moral theology of the Redemptorist "Saint" Alphonsus Liguori in Italy.

While dozens of tomes have been written to explain it and justify it, probabilism is just a fancy word for relieving the Catholic's obligation to obey the law of God. According to probabilism, a single "Catholic authority" (such as Alphonsus Liguori), is adequate for rendering a theological opinion "probable," and therefore worthy of being taught in seminaries and imparted to penitents in the confessional. Here is the lawlessness which Martin Luther with his "Sin boldly" comment on God's mercy, has been branded. If a Catholic wants to commit a sin of lust, of lying, thievery, etc., and he can locate a recognized theological authority who will furnish him with ingenious grounds for indulging in that sin, then he has the liberty to proceed. This is probabilism. Predicated on a probable opinion, the Catholic taking the lenient view on the sin he wishes to commit, cannot be condemned. After all, his moral agency is not part of the equation. He is acting not by the light of Scripture, or even his own conscience, but through obedience to the guidance of a Catholic authority. This distinction is termed in Rome's theology, *probabilitas extrinseca*.

While it would be wrong to describe as the "new art of lying," the sewer stream from hell which erupted on earth from Rome's casuistic probabilism—since Satan has been the Father of Lies from Genesis 3 onward— it was most certainly a recrudescence of perjury and false witness which was now rendered the integral core of the West's most dominant institution.

In light of the extent of lying in our 21st century world, where one is considered a fool not to pad one's resumé, exactly how does deceptive speech harm the well-being of our culture and commonweal? Does it not compound the evil of our times? St. Augustine raised the spectre of the double heart, "When regard for truth has been broken down or slightly weakened, all things will remain doubtful." What happens to us as a people when we catch the virus of deviousness and think, "everyone else deceives when the circumstances call for it, why shouldn't I?"

Within the Church a hue and cry was raised against the moral theology of the Jesuits, in particular their probabilism, mental reservation (also called "mental restriction"), and equivocation. Among the leaders of this protest was the French theologian Rev. Fr. Antoine Arnauld (1612-1694). His argument was made in his study, *Théologie morale des Jesuites*. The Catholic mathematician Blaise Pascal (1623-1662) preceded Arnauld's attack, with his *Provincial Letters*, which took the Jesuits to task for the same reasons. Pascal's book was translated into English by Henry Hammond. It corroborated the suspicion among the English that the Church of Rome was synonymous with underhanded tactics of deceit. Despite the "Jansenist" cloud that hung over the reputations of both individuals, Pascal and Arnauld were Catholics of rectitude.

The Oxford Professor, Anglican priest, and commissioner of education for England,[17] Rev. Frederick Meyrick (1827-1906), wrote:

"In his books *De Mendacio* and *Contra Mendacium*, St. Augustine enumerates eight sorts of lying. Every one of these he rejects uncompromisingly. He denies that we may at any time be guilty of moral falsehood under whatever temptation we may be. The sin of the tongue in violating veracity is as great, he says, as the sin of the hand in theft or in murder, or, at least, we are no more justified in committing the former than the latter. He discusses all the examples of apparent falsehood in the Old and New Testaments, to which those who had a theory of lying appealed in his days as they do now, and concludes that 'for the examples which are brought forward out of the Holy Scriptures, either they are not falsehoods or, if they are falsehoods they are not proposed as objects of imitation...

"Now we can conceive the possibility of a case arising in which the two virtues of veracity and charity might so clash as to make it at least pardonable to deflect somewhat from the rigid observance of the former. St. Augustine does not admit of such a possibility. 'You must not destroy your own soul,' he replies, 'for any supposed good of your neighbor, spiritual or temporal."

Augustine "nowhere makes a distinction between lying and equivocating. Equivocating is in his estimation lying...The 'double heart' is, according to his teaching, the source of the

---

[17] His official title was, "Her Majesty's Inspector of Schools." Meyrick served in that capacity from 1859-1869.

accursed thing and any man 'who has one thing in his mind, and enunciates another by words or any sort of signs,' is guilty of sin. Word-jugglery is a thing unknown to him, for the sage of Hippo was...too honest to deceive others by such a transparent fallacy as that which lies at the bottom of the justification of equivocation....And yet it is to St. Augustine that (Catholic "Saint" Alphonsus) Liguori refers in justification of his Equivocation and non-pure Mental Reservation, which, according to St. Augustine's definition, are merely forms of expressing a lie." [18]

What happened to our moral fibre as a nation after it was revealed that we went to war in Iraq in 2003 with assurances from our highest leaders that the Iraqis threatened the world with weapons of mass destruction? Since then it has been insinuated that we shouldn't anguish over the consequences of this serious breach of the nation's trust, since we were deceived for a good cause, the liberation of Iraq from the tyrant, Saddam Hussein. This type of thinking breeds a corrosive cynicism, the effects of which are difficult to gauge but are most certainly destructive of the virtue of integrity as a non-negotiable standard.

What is your opinion of the man or woman in your neighborhood who has a sterling reputation for strict adherence to the truth? Can you do otherwise than to admire and have faith in such a person? The erosion of mutual trust— the old-fashioned business deal that is closed with a handshake —is a barometer of our nation's decline. St. Augustine put his finger on it sixteen hundred years ago when he wrote: "Every liar breaks his faith by lying, since he wishes the person to whom he lies to have faith in him, and yet he does not keep faith with that person when he lies to him. Whoever breaks faith in this manner is guilty of iniquity."

The sly equivocator will here attempt to inject a loophole by alleging that Augustine was referring to boldface lying, not to "mild" types of deception such as equivocation. *Wrong.* Augustine *did* include the tactic of intending to deceive in his definition of lying. One of his definitions of what constitutes lying is "a false signification told with a desire to deceive." He

---

[18] Frederick Meyrick, *Moral and Devotional Theology of the Church of Rome* (London, 1857), pp. 39-41.

forbids any equivocation and quashes any rationale for such tactics: "He who says that there are some just lies must be regarded as saying nothing else than that there are some just sins."

The Priscillianists were a heretical sect which justified lying as a form of concealment and self-protection. An orthodox Christian heresy-hunter, Consentius, advocated lying to these liars — in order to identify them and snare them in their heresy. Augustine addresses himself to Consentius concerning the consequences of becoming a knave to catch a knave — "Do you not see how your argument in favor of lying to the Priscillianists supports their views concerning the permissibility of lying?...They must be refuted, not imitated."

Augustine's main teachings concerning lying are: Lying is sinful; it brings death to the soul and must not be indulged in for the temporal safety of anyone. One must not lie for the sake of preserving bodily chastity. It is not permissible to lie even to secure eternal salvation for others. The emphasis is on the Scripture: "The son that keeps the word shall be free from destruction." [19] The corollary to strictly truthful speech in a Christian society is respect for the right to silence. For truth to prevail in our hearts and on our lips, we should respect the right to be silent in the face of questions that invade privacy and answers that are not owed to gossips—or an intrusive and oppressive government, for that matter: "And the high priest stood up in the midst and asked Jesus, 'Have you no answer to make? What is it that these men testify against you?' But He remained silent and made no answer." (Mark 14: 60-61; for the silence of Jesus before Herod, cf. Luke 23: 8-9).

From the founding of the Church to the time of the Renaissance, *nothing more was permitted to Christians who did not wish to answer other than silence.* We can find no Christian justification for any other response; neither could the Church, until the coming of the Renaissance. [20]

---

[19] For St. Augustine's writings on this subject, *De mendacio* and *Contra mendacium,* cf. "Lying" and "Against Lying" in *The Fathers of the Church: Saint Augustine: Treatises on Various Subjects* (1952), especially pp. 51-107.

[20] On the American guarantee of the right to remain silent, cf. Leonard W. Levy, *Origins of the Fifth Amendment: The Right Against Self-Incrimination* (1986). For a survey of the permission to lie as specified in the sacred books of Judaism, cf. this writer's *Judaism's Strange Gods* (2011), pp. 146-163, 256, 300-302, 335-343.

Mental Reservation

Mental reservation proceeds from equivocation and represents a more grievous transgression of the obligation to be truthful. On the positive side, it is not so well camouflaged in its moral failing as is equivocation, and can be better seen for what it is, and therefore, it is a somewhat more easily discerned indictment of those who advocate it.

There are two types of mental reservation advocated by two different schools of theologians. "Pure" mental reservationist-casuists placed few strictures on the practice. On the other hand, "conservative" or "broad" exponents of mental reservation hedged it with qualifications they believed rendered it morally permissible. The latter appears more hypocritical than the former. [21]

Mental reservation is such an odious example of lying that it is problematic to distinguish any significant difference between these two schools of thought. In mental reservation a false statement is supposedly made true by the addition of words that are "reserved" within one's own mind and which thereby serve to cancel the spoken or written lie. Once again, as a kind of marketing strategy, seemingly benign case histories of self-protection were put forth to show that lying verbally and then adding an escape clause mentally, was morally permissible, at least in certain circumstances. A "benign" example was given of a man who had been waylaid by robbers. They take all the possessions he has on his person and then make him promise that he will open his storehouse that evening if they release him immediately. The victim agrees to meet the robbers and promises to give them his remaining possessions later that night. He then mentally adds the reserved clause, "If I lawfully owe it to you." Most people, when faced with this man's predicament, would agree that his mental reservation was appropriate and sensible. *Once the principle of mental reservation was established in this extreme case, however, it was then extrapolated to many others.*

According to the Spanish Jesuit Gregorius de Valentia (1549-1603), in his *Commentarium Theologicorum Tomus Tertius* (Venice, 1598), there was a "general precept obliging men to tell the truth, combined with a precept in which certain

---

[21] One of the most eloquent jeremiads against mental reservation was issued by the Catholic mathematician Pascal in his *Pensées*.

circumstances permitted or even obliged men to say what they believed to be deceptive falsehoods." We are here approaching an approximation of the rabbinic theology behind the *Kol Nidrei* nullification of vows:

"Mental reservation undermined traditional ideas not only on intentionally deceptive statements, but also on promises and oaths. By including a mental reservation in a promise, a man could evade the obligation to perform that which in spoken words he undertook to perform....Of course, if we follow Valentia in holding that there is a positive precept of truthfulness, we will regard a man who unjustifiably uses mental reservation in a promise, as guilty of infringing the precept. But it looks as though such a man would still evade the obligation to perform in spoken words what he said he would perform. Suppose that I borrow $1,000...promising to repay it on the first day of next month....In making my promise I mentally reserve some such clause as 'provided that I choose to repay the money.' I ought not to make this reservation, but having done so I am under no obligation to return the money unless I choose to....The point about promises was well-made by Henry Mason in *The New Art of Lying, covered by the Jesuits under the Vaile of Equivocation* (London, 1624), pp. 105-106: 'And if he promises to me a sum of money, how can I tell that he keepeth not a reservation behind, that may disannull his promises aforehand...?" [22]

The Benedictine monk John Barnes, in his *Dissertatio contra Aequivocationes* (Paris, 1625), wrote, "You should not lie, even to save your life." A direct command from God would be the sole exception. Biblical liars had either obeyed a divine compulsion or had acted wrongly. Prior to the judicial murder of Jesuit priests in England during the reign of Elizabeth I, equivocation and mental reservation were largely unknown to lay people. Knowledge of the practice had been maintained as something of a clerical secret, though it was present in various arcane volumes of Latin theology, yet these would have been indigestible to all but the most enterprising laymen. Elizabeth's regime refined torture to an art form and in order

---

[22] Johann P. Sommerville, *Conscience and Casuistry* (Cambridge University Press, 2002), p. 176.

not to divulge the identity of fugitive priests or those who harbored them, the hunted Jesuits resorted to equivocation and mental reservation when under interrogation. Since show trials of these persecuted priests were another feature of Elizabethan policy, equivocation and mental reservation on the priests' part were exposed and came into public view. Inspired by Martin Azpilcueta (recall that he termed his volume on permissible dissimulation, "*novus modus*" [new measure]), Father Robert Southwell "...used this practice (and ingenious theory) of equivocation, though unsuccessfully, when he was tried for treason in London in 1595....Henry Garnet, superior of the English Jesuits from 1586 until his arrest in 1605, sought to explain Southwell's use of equivocation in the large treatise on the topic that he probably wrote in the late 1590s. Writing to his fellow Jesuit Robert Persons, Garnet explains that he 'wrote a treatise of equivocation to defend Father Southwell's assertion, which was much wondered at by Catholics and heretics....

"For Azpilcueta, Garnet and Robert Persons, who also wrote (the aforementioned) treatise on equivocation (*A Treatise tending to Mitigation towardes Catholicke-Subjectes in England*), first published in 1602 and reissued in 1607, an equivocal statement can be distinguished from a lie because in the former type of discourse, the whole truth is present in the discourser's mind and is indeed communicated to the primary audience of all discourse, God." [23]

This is similar to the rabbinic rationale for mental reservation used by a "revered sage" in the Babylonian Talmud, in its account of how Rabbi Eliezer supposedly tricked Blessed Mary into admitting that she conceived Jesus while she was menstruating. Eliezer uses mental reservation to falsely promise Mary that he will guarantee her a future life in heaven if she will tell him the truth about the circumstances of Christ's conception. Concerning his offer of a guarantee, Mary in the Talmud allegedly tells him, "Swear it to me." The

---

[23] Margaret W. Ferguson, *Dido's Daughters* (University of Chicago, 2003) p. 277. "Persons cleverly insists that it is not the producer of the utterance but rather the recipient, whether reader or auditor, who is ultimately responsible for making it conform to a 'truth'..." (Ferguson, p. 281). This is the attitude of the Talmudic rabbi toward the *goy*.

Talmud states that Rabbi Akiba, *"took the oath (to her) with his lips but annulled it in his heart."* [24]

In accord with Renaissance Church of Rome theology, the oath is a lie only if taken in isolation. The rabbi's equivocation is not a deception if viewed within the entire context of the expression: the whole that was heard and supposedly approved by God, but not by Mary. It is no coincidence that Renaissance Christians were weaving a corresponding web of Talmudic deceit commensurate with the unprecedented rise of the prestige of the Talmud and the Kabbalah within Catholic intelligentsia of that time.

"As a central figure in the English Catholic community and a proponent of equivocation, Garnet was one of the Crown's most important prisoners, even though he played a minor role in the Gunpowder Plot itself...Scholars cite the equivocation jokes within the Porter scene (of Shakespeare's Macbeth) as topical references to Father Garnet's infamous equivocation when questioned about his role in the Gunpowder Plot." [25]

Fr. Garnet's *A Treatise of Equivocation*, which was circulated secretly in manuscript but not published until 1851 (under the editorship of David Jardine), was political dynamite. Until recently, authorities in the Church of Rome issued what appeared to be plausible denials of Fr. Garnet's authorship. As much as we wish to show respect to martyred priests who were victims of cruel, hypocritical Protestants, we are duty-bound to mention the sad fact that *A Treatise of Equivocation* bears Talmudic-like aspersions on the character of Jesus Christ. Fr. Garnet's situation was so desperate in terms of the intensity of the hunt for him, and Judaism's arcane teachings having circulated and radiated from Renaissance Italy as never before, it appears that the combination of the two led him to pen a how-to manual of deceit that also manages to libel Our Lord, as related by Margaret W. Ferguson:

"Garnet, himself executed for treason after his (ambiguous) role in the Gunpowder Plot was discovered, made an important contribution to the evolving arena of contest around

---

[24]Babylonian Talmud, Kallah 51a. Also cf. *Judaism Discovered* (2008), p. 383.

[25] Rebecca Lemon, *Treason By Words: Literature, Law and Rebellion in Shakespeare's England* (2006), p. 186. Readers are also referred to the oath of office administered by the U.S. government which specifically names and forbids "mental reservation."

equivocation. This area dealt with the philosophy and politics of language as much as with issues of religious doctrine. Garnet adapts Azpilcueta's formulations about equivocation in ways particularly suited to the situation of Catholics in England. Garnet defends equivocation as a verbal practice of legitimately 'hiding' the (whole) truth, and insists that this practice was authorized and illustrated by Christ himself in various New Testament passages of great hermeneutic difficulty. Such passages come to be the model for what counts as a 'literary' language of irony, indirection and 'dark conceit.'"[26]

Here the plot thickens for, as was previously noted, Garnet's first motive in writing *A Treatise of Equivocation* was to "defend Father Southwell's assertion." According to a theory advanced by historians Clare Asquith and Peter Milward, William Shakespeare was Robert Southwell's clandestine Catholic disciple. [27] Milward writes:

"We may do well to remember that Shakespeare was no innocent bystander in all the events leading from the Essex Rebellion to the Gunpowder Plot, nor was he likely to have been deceived by the elaborate working of the government propaganda machine to cast discredit on the English Catholics. 'Not only was Robert Catesby (accused Gunpowder plotter) his (Shakespeare's) cousin on his mother's side, but it is also surprising to see how many of Essex's supporters as of the gunpowder plotters came from the same part of the English Midlands and met not infrequently at the same Mermaid Tavern in London....when it came to the Jesuit theory and practice of equivocation, we may safely say that not only did the dramatist feel no horror at it, but he even commended its use, even in terms beyond what the Jesuits themselves would

---

[26] Ferguson, op.cit., p. 227.

[27] Cf. Asquith, *Shadow Play: The Hidden Beliefs and Coded Politics of William Shakespeare* (New York, 2005), pp. 65, 72, 114-115, 291, 294; Peter Milward, S.J., *Shakespeare the Papist* (Sapientia Press, 2005), pp. 101-102, 106, 110, 186-187, 204-205, 210, 233. Milward writes: "...the theme of equivocation is taken up not only by the Porter but by Macbeth himself, as when he later complains of 'the equivocation of the fiend that lies like truth' (act 5),' his use of the word was no chance phenomenon...it may have found its way into the mouth of Hamlet, speaking of the cosmic gravedigger...It even looks...as if the Jesuits were responsible...for the vein of indignation that seems to enter deeply into the composition of *Macbeth*" (p. 204).

have acknowledged...when he professes horror, with Macbeth, at 'the equivocation of the fiend' he can hardly be thinking of the Jesuits, whom he would have known as innocent victims, but of their persecutors in those 'cunning times'..." [28]

Religiously authorized deception came as a shock to the Christian yeomanry in England, Protestant and Catholic alike:

"Hitherto most laymen, Catholic as well as Protestant, had been ignorant of mental reservation. Now they reacted to it with horror. Catholic vernacular writings, aimed at a lay audience, had inculcated virtues of honesty and truthfulness, claiming that it was heretics who lied. To unsophisticated laymen, however, mental reservation itself seemed no more than downright lying or, worse still, lying of a new and devious variety...

"As early as the 1590s, a manual of casuistry written for the use of Catholic priests on the mission to Protestant England warned that deceptive statements should not be made to Protestant interrogators in the presence of 'rude and simple' Catholic laymen who, 'being ignorant of the difference between pretense and lying...will immediately think that the priest is denying the faith if he uses pretense and...will be confused and inwardly despair if they see a priest do such a thing.' Mental reservation might be justifiable, but it should not be used if it led to bad publicity for the church and its priests. When priests responded to Protestant criticisms of the doctrine, their posture was defensive...The Jesuit Parsons...claim(ed) that Catholic thinkers *permitted* but did not *recommend* the use of mental reservation: they 'do allow and like far better of simple, plain and resolute speech in all Catholics,' but tolerated mental reservation in a few cases since 'perfection is one thing, and obligation another." [29]

Parsing "the difference between pretense and lying," and "perfection and obligation," is a Talmudic enterprise which brought disrepute upon the Church that bore the name Catholic, even as Protestant equivocators such as Richard Baxter and William Perkins, who developed the concept of

---

[28] Ibid., Milward, p. 205.

[29] Sommerville, op. cit., p. 177.

dolus bonus ("good deceit"), and mental reservationists like Elizabeth I and her chief co-adjutant, William Cecil, who engaged in that very practice when they were at the mercy of Queen Mary, escaped the opprobrium associated with it and bear no stigma even unto our own time, while Jesuits and Catholics generally bear the brunt of it. Public relations, it seems, is everything. Or as Ronald Reagan told the Governor of New Hampshire, "Image prevails over reality."

We would like to be able to say that since the hunted Catholic priests labored daily under the threat of capture and death by torture, that some amount of equivocating word play, while a moral failure, would be understandable, though not condoned. This may have been true of rank-and-file priests. It does not deserve to be offered in defense of their leaders, Garnet and Persons/Parsons, both of whom wrote manuals of equivocation which dared to implicate Jesus Christ as the father of equivocation, which is an inexcusable act of character assassination.

Having said that, the feigned horror of the Elizabethan regime and the indignation of their Anglican clergymen and Puritan supporters over the means by which some fugitive Catholics fleeing execution may have shaded the truth, is the height of *chutzpah*. At the time the pirate queen's crew were railing in high dudgeon against "Jesuit deceit and mendacity," Sir Francis Walsingham's English Secret Service had carved a niche for itself as the supreme masters of disinformation, covert operations, treachery and deviousness; a reputation well-deserved three hundred fifty years later when the British Secret Intelligence Service tricked America into entering the fratricidal First World War on behalf of "the Crown." While the Jesuits became a byword for dishonesty in the Protestant world, that same world came to adulate Elizabeth and her coruscanting cronies of corruption, as a fine new paradigm of Christian rule and rectitude. Eventually, the vertiginous interpretations and equivocating strategies of the casuists, which were strikingly similar to the convoluted hermeneutic gymnastics of the Talmud, entered Protestantism itself: "In a fine irony of history, a 'science' developed by the Roman Catholic Church to resolve problems of moral choice 'that arose from the 'equal poise' of conflicting laws, obligations and loyalties' was appropriated by both the government and the church of Tudor England, and hence assumed a central place in the legal, political and theological documents of a Protestant realm." [30]

Mental reservation, in the form of the propositions of Rome's Renaissance theologian Tomás Sanchez, were finally and formally condemned in 1679, by Pope Innocent XI (Benedict Odeschalchi, 1611-1689; pontiff from 1676-1689). [31] Innocent was flawed, and compromised by having done, like his Renaissance predecessors and his post-Renaissance successors, nothing to restore the *de fide* laws against profit on loans, a root of all evil. We cannot, therefore, say, 'this was a great pope,' or even 'this was a good pope.' Taking the New Testament at its word forbids us from granting our Catholic readers respite from our relentless exposé of the popes. It would be a relief to grant it, if only to relieve the monotony. Yet we would be guilty of overturning the truthful thesis of this book if we were to opine that 'with the exception of his tolerance for usury, Innocent XI was in many respects a pontiff worthy of admiration.' We wish we could say so, if it were not an offense against truth.

Would it be better to draw a phrase from nineteenth century literature and refer to Innocent XI as a prostitute with a heart of gold? The appellation would probably satisfy very few, and needlessly antagonize very many, so we will refrain from it and state instead: this was a bad pontiff who did good things on many occasions. His life is a complexity and mystery and we leave the unraveling of it to the Almighty.

Among the good that Pope Innocent XI accomplished was his courageous defiance of an entire entrenched school of powerful ecclesiastics with the explicit anti-mental reservation stance which his papacy had taken. "Out of the sixty-five laxist propositions condemned by Innocent XI and the Holy Office in

---

[30] Ferguson, op. cit., p. 282.

[31] Innocent XI was strenuously opposed by the French monarchy in its Gallican period. For an informative analysis of Gallicanism, cf. Joseph Bergin, "Introduction," in *The Politics of Religion in Early Modern France*, (Yale University, 2014). Pope Innocent "worked tirelessly to unite Christian princes both Catholic and Protestant" against the growing threat of the Muslim-Turk invasion of Europe. The crushing victory of Christian forces over the Turks at the Gates of Vienna, Austria on Sept. 11, 1683, was attributed to the leadership and financial support of this pope. After Vienna, Muslim conquerors would not imperil Europe again until the immigration invasion which began in the late 20th century.

1679, two concerned the doctrine of equivocation. The twenty-sixth concerned the right to use mental reservation under oath, and the twenty-seventh concerned the justification of such use because of a just cause..." [32]

Johann Lorenz von Mosheim, the Protestant Chancellor of the University of Göttingen, had qualified praise for Popes Innocent XI and XII:

"This respectable pontiff acquired a very high and permanent reputation by the austerity of his morals, his uncommon courage and resolution, his dislike of the much grosser superstitions that reigned in the Romish church, his attempts to reform the Romish clergy, and to abolish a considerable number of those fictions and frauds that dishonor their ministry...But it appeared manifestly by his example, that those pontiffs who respect truth and act from virtuous and Christian principles, may indeed form noble plans, but will never be able to bring them into execution, or at least to give them that measure of stability...which is the object of their wishes. By his example and administration it appeared that the wisest institutions and the most judicious establishments will be unable to stand firm for any considerable time, against the insidious stratagems or declared opposition of a deluded multitude, who are corrupted by the prevalence of licentious morals, whose imaginations are impregnated with superstitious fictions...whose credulity is abused by pious frauds...

"Be that as it may, all the wise and salutary regulations of Innocent XI were suffered almost to ruin by the criminal indolence of Peter Ottoboni, who was raised to the head of the Romish church in the year 1689, and assumed the name of Alexander VIII. A laudable attempt was made to revive them by Innocent XII, a man of uncommon merit and eminent talents whose name was Pignatelli, and who in the year 1691 succeeded Alexander in the papal chair; nor were his zealous efforts absolutely destitute of success. But it was also his fate to learn by experience that the most prudent and resolute pontiffs are unequal to such an arduous task, such a Herculean labor, as the reformation of the church and court of Rome; nor

---

[32]   Stefania Tutino, *Shadows of Doubt: Language and Truth in Post-Reformation Catholic Culture* (2014) p. 35.

were the fruits of this good pope's wide administration enjoyed long after his decease." [33]

Prior to Innocent XI, mental reservation's soul-rot had progressed so far that the proposition that calumniators, witnesses and unjust judges may be murdered if there is no other way of avoiding their attacks, was accepted in some quarters. [34]

Despite Pope Innocent XI's ban however, the Renaissance scourge of mental reservation and equivocation were not eradicated from the Church, much less from its very dogma as pronounced by a "saint" declared to be a "Doctor of the Church" (i.e. a theologian of unimpeachable integrity and authority).

Alphonsus Liguori, "Doctor of the Church" Patron Saint of Liars and Thieves

The preceding headline is probably sufficient to ensure this writer's lynching, if not literally, at least rhetorically, at the hands of the devotees of "Saint" Alphonsus Liguori (1696-1787), who is one of the most revered of all post-Renaissance Catholic thinkers; a canonized saint and "Doctor of the Church" esteemed as an incomparable pillar of conservative morality, and what is for many Catholics at least as important, an advocate of the Blessed Virgin Mary. To rectify the perception of this scoundrel among Catholics is a tall order.

Liguori nullified the decree of Pope Innocent XI against pure mental reservation ("restriction") by making a distinction, by clever word jugglery, between "pure" and "non-pure" mental reservation; yet it was a distinction without a difference. He redefines pure mental reservation as non-pure mental reservation ("restriction") and recruiting Jesus to the deceiver's side:

"On the contrary, it is allowable to use non-pure mental restriction, even with an oath, if it can be discovered by

---

[33] *Ecclesiastic History Ancient and Modern*, transl. Archibald MacLaine (London, 1782), vol. 5, pp. 101-103.

[34] Cf. Meg Lota Brown, *Donne and the Politics of Conscience in Early Modern England*, (1995) p. 42. n. 22; quoting Kenneth E. Kirk, *Conscience and Its Problems* (1927), p. 118.

circumstances. This is proved by John 7:8, where Christ said, 'I go up not to this feast,' and yet Scripture says that He afterwards went up." [35]

In cases where the person under interrogation decides that the individuals asking questions are "unjust questioners," the respondent could answer *audibly* one way, and then inaudibly, with an unspoken thought that contradicted his verbal statement. By this and numerous other subterfuges and loopholes of escape, Pope Innocent XI's condemnation was evaded and effectively rendered meaningless by the "saint" whose *Moral Theology* for confessors was accepted as the leading authority, and occupied an authoritative position in the curriculum of the seminaries of Latin Christendom.

The Cryptocracy often makes certain that Church of Rome modernizers and change agents become renowned as the Blessed Virgin Mary's champion on earth. When Pope John Paul II's liberal innovations emerged early in his papacy, it was floated by the Vatican and their assets in the Establishment media that the pope was Mary's special defender, "the Blessed Virgin's own pontiff," whose personal motto with regard to her was, *"Totus tuus"* ("totally yours"). Liguori's dreadful doctrines are rendered nearly invulnerable among the pious by the same ruse. He wrote the book *The Glories of Mary,* therefore he is untouchable in the eyes of those Catholics for whom conformity to the truth of Jesus Christ is second to the exaltation of Mary. In stating this unvarnished fact about mariolatry in the ranks of the papists, we do not intend by any means to diminish, as very many Protestants do, *the proper honor* paid her by the true Catholic Church as ever-virgin, and the most noble human in the history of the human race, whose faith, obedience to the will of God, and long suffering, are worthy of emulation and the highest commemoration, thanks and praise. She was the new Eve, God's best and most faithful servant on earth.

Some Protestants suffer from an emotionally constrained aridity because they have no significant mother figure in their theology. Here we do not speak of anything approaching a goddess, or "co-redemptrix." The Russian and Greek Eastern Orthodox Church guards against any such error by most often

---

[35] *The Christian Remembrancer*, January, 1854, pp. 41-42.

only depicting a *Hodegetria* image of Mary, i.e. a portrait of her embracing—or accompanied—by Jesus, thereby symbolically demonstrating that *He is the source* of her redemption and ours; her importance being subsidiary, and dependent on her relationship with Her Divine Son.[36]

It is not our purpose to enter the lists of the controversy which has raged among learned theologians Catholic and Protestant, concerning the subject of proper reverence for Blessed Mary, as opposed to mariolatry. The heat of that debate has disquieted the Church and the lack of moderation on both sides begets ill blood in the body of Christ. Let us recall and heed Jesus' explicit instruction, that *any Christian may be said to be the most blessed of all, by becoming one of those "who hear the word of God and observe it"* (Luke 11: 27-28). Before the Renaissance, few Catholic theologians sought to make of the humble Israelite Mary a goddess or "co-redeemer"; nor did they seek to level her down to a vague personage whose life and example is less often invoked by Christians than that of Protestant heroines such as Susanna Wesley or England's "New Isis," Elizabeth I.

Blessed Mary has also been distorted into an Isis figure by New Age initiates. We have seen American converts to Buddhism pray the rosary and maintain images of both the Dalai Lama and "Mother Mary" together on an altar or mantlepiece, as a veiled propitiation of the mother goddess in one of her thousand forms. This pagan perversion of the holy image of the Blessed Virgin Mary is also found in Voodoo and Santeria. These perversions, whether Buddhist/New Age or the Voodoo manifestions, subvert the First Commandment, and the Scriptural principle of Patriarchy. The *perversion* of her image however, in no way obviates its *legitimate* display, or justifies the iconoclastic vandalism which accompanied the Protestant Reformation in places such as Scotland, England and the Huguenot regions of France. A Christian is not required to possess depictions of Mary, or even of Jesus for that matter; though clearly the authentic Catholic Church taught that in their proper place, reverent artistic depictions can be an aid to contemplation and sanctification. On the other hand, neither is it *required* that true worship be conducted in a church that

---

36 This type of image is not unknown in the Western Church, under the title *Madonna Della Strada* ("Our Lady of the Way").

resembles a warehouse, stripped of all reverent artist depictions of the sacred. It is most unfortunate that man-made "requirements" issued from both extremes have resulted in discord, hatred and bloodshed, causing the Gospel to be held in disrepute, as all violence between Christians tends to do.

Alphonsus Liguori was beatified in 1816 by Pope Pius VII. On July 5, 1831, the Sacred Penitentiary of the Apostolic See reaffirmed complete approval for Liguori's moral theology around the same time that this body, by direction of the pope, issued the revolutionary directive that no Catholic usurer was obliged to confess or seek absolution for his usury. "The followers of St. Alphonsus may point to the official declaration of the Church that...his teaching has never been censured. To these advantages must be added the great personal authority of the...founder of the Redemptorist Order." [37]

Liguori was canonized a saint in 1839 by Pope Gregory XVI, and declared a Doctor of the Church in 1871 by Pope Pius IX. After this "Doctor" status had been conferred on Liguori, English Cardinal Henry Edward Manning described in 1887 his impact on the Church: "Doctor of the just mean, his influence on hearts has ever increased...This influence has passed from one nation to another, from one church to another, from one diocese to another, from one confessional to another. The spirit of Alphonsus...(has) penetrated everywhere and...triumphed in all Catholic countries...hold(ing) sway over the entire Church of God." [38]As recently as 1950, Pope Pius XII named Liguori "Heavenly Patron of Confessors and Teachers of Moral Theology." Pius XII explained his declaration as follows: "He (St. Alphonsus Liguori) left, both in speech and in writing, for the education and direction of confessors, a remarkable moral and pastoral teaching which has been the most highly esteemed in the whole world up to our present age..." In 1967, *New Catholic Encyclopedia,* published by the Catholic University of America, stated: "The influence of St. Alphonsus on moral theology has proved durable, and the practical direction traced by him has been substantially adopted by the Church."

---

[37] Anton Koch, *A Handbook of Moral Theology* (1918),vol. 1, pp. 232-233).

[38] Théodule Ray-Mermet, *Moral Choices: The Moral Theology of Saint Alphonsus Liguori* (Liguori Publications, 1998), pp. 142-143.

The papal-ecclesiastical approbation for Liguori was a notorious and scandalous fact among evangelical Protestants. Rev. A.C. Coxe, writing in his *The Novelty and Nullity of the Papal Dogma* (1855): The Church of Rome "openly authorizes the morals of Alphonsus Liguori, and has actually made a saint of the man who teaches that there are no less than thirty different methods of swearing falsely without guilt; and that, for what one deems good cause, it is lawful to use equivocation, and to confirm it with an oath..." [39]

The papalolaters two main defense strategies are, on one hand, to say that Liguori is thoroughly orthodox, and on the other to equivocate, as Cardinal John Henry Newman did, and state that though Liguori was a great and wonderful saint, Catholics are not obliged to follow him. Notice the dissembling spirit of the double mind in this line of defense. Liguori is a saint, a Doctor of the Church and Heavenly Patron of Confessors and Teachers of Moral Theology, but "no Catholic is bound to follow him throughout." Yet Cardinal Newman understood very well indeed that it was not up to the laymen in the pews, the pray-pay-and-obey parishioners, to reject or embrace Liguori. As the Pope declared in 1950, and the *New Catholic Encyclopedia* stated as recently as 1967, his moral theology "has been substantially adopted by the Church"—in other words, at the top of the hierarchy—among the teachers of moral theology and the confessors who advise, admonish and absolve penitents.

Liguori's theology, disguised as mercy for sinners, against the Jansenist error of the time, of letter-of-the-law severity, propelled Machiavellian, post-Renaissance situation ethics to new heights undreamed of by "conservative" and "traditional" Catholics, who generally don't have a clue as to what Liguori actually taught, since his *major* works have never been translated from ecclesiastic Latin.

For instance, consider the situation after Vatican Council II, in the "post-Conciliar" years, when, in spite of Paul VI's thoroughly orthodox encyclical *Humane Vitae*, thousands of confessors were advising troubled husbands and wives that birth control was permissible. This betrayal of Catholic dogma on the part of lax confessors has been attributed to the bad

---

[39] Cf. St. Alphonsus Liguori, *De juramento*, Lib. iv., cap. 2.

fruits of the 1960s-era Council. In actuality however, what had occurred was that Liguori's diabolic laxity concerning birth control for Catholic married couples, which had been part of his recommended confessional praxis for two centuries after he wrote his Church-approved *Moral Theology*, had finally lost its shame and brazenly emerged from the shadows and into the glare of the garish light of the late 1960s.

In terms of that endorsement, let the record show that in teaching the lawfulness of Liguori's demonic dementia, the Church of Rome approved it *totally*. He died in 1787. In May, 1803, the Sacred Congregation of Rites decreed "that *in all the writings of Alphonsus Liguori, edited and unedited, there is not a word that could be justly found fault with.*" Pope Pius VIII approved the decree. Rome proclaimed that in Liguori there is nothing to be censured:

"...that his whole teaching is altogether free from all error. That in the whole of his moral theology not one principle is disapproved of; that there is not in it any opinion contrary to faith or good morals, new, opposed to the sense of the Church, heretical erroneous, approaching to error, savoring of heresy or error, suspected of error, rash, scandalous, offensive to pious ears, ill-sounding, such as to lead the simple astray, schismatical, harmful, impious, blasphemous."

Bishop Asti, Prince Prelate of the Papal Household, published the decree "that the examination of Liguori's work had been conducted with particular severity, that his System of Morality had been more than twenty times discussed by the Sacred Congregation, and that all had agreed *voce concordi, unanimi consensu, uno voce, una mente.* On July 5, 1831 the Sacred Penitentiary (charged with imparting the laws of God and the Church to priest-Confessors in their directions to penitents in the Sacrament of Penance), formally stated that Liguori's ruling can be followed without moral qualms of any kind. No Confessor need be disturbed by anything he has written." The Cardinal-Archbishop Rohan-Chabot soon afterward directed all of his clergy commanding that "the judgment of Rome should be fully adhered to, and that the opinions of Blessed Alphonsus de' Liguori should be followed and reduced to practice, all doubt whatever being cast aside."

"In the words of the Preface to his Life, edited by the Fathers of the Oratory, and approved and recommended by Cardinal Wiseman, 'the morals of this saintly Bishop cannot be censured, without setting up as a censor authority itself; without, in fine, censoring the decision of the Holy See." [40] It cannot be denied that Liguori is the authoritative exponent of Rome's moral teaching.

Equivocation and mental reservation are not just sins in themselves in terms of the individual situation in which they gull and deceive the individuals to whom they are specifically addressed. Rather, they infect the hierarchy and the intellectuals of the Church. What one scholar described as the effect on Judaic persons of the *Kol Nidrei* rite's sanction for cheating, applies to the use of equivocation and mental reservation among Christians, *"the inevitable moral abasement that this sort of treachery fosters in its practitioners."* [41]

This inevitable abasement manifests in the occlusion of the good sense and judgment of the followers of the Church of Rome, whose powers of reason have become so atrophied they are nearly incapable of seeing how *the "infallible" papacy has become, since the Renaissance, the engine of the transformation of the ecclesia from the Catholic Bride of Christ to the papal Judas of Christ.*

What is "traditional" about those who sacrifice the Catholic Church to the god they have made out of the Bishop of Rome? They are modernists, not traditionalists. In Catholicism's first millennium, propitiation of this pope-idol would have looked as though it had come straight out of Antichrist's rules for radicals (as so often it has).

The apologists for the usury permitted by the Church of Rome in our time play Talmudic games with the definition of usury. They deny that the accurate definition of usury consists in the statement that *any gain by the lender that exceeds the amount of the loan to the debtor is usury.* That this is the correct definition of usury from the beginning of the Christian Church to the dawn of the Renaissance is as plain as the sun at noonday, but equivocation of the papist theological species will have it otherwise. The Renaissance papists claim other escape clauses founded in part in the concept of *lucrum cessans* (the

---

[40] Meyrick, *Moral Theology of the Church of Rome: No. II Certain Points in S. Alfonso de' Liguori's Moral Theology Considered in Nineteen Letters* (London, 1855), p. 61.

[41] William N. Grimstad, *Talk About Hate* (1999); emphasis supplied.

loss of a profit which a lender might otherwise have gained from his money if he had not loaned it to a debtor), which testifies to the spirit of mental confusion and deceit applied to the history and theology of usury. [42]

So much of this justification of the nullification of what was the *sensus fidei,* that which had been taught always and everywhere (*quod ubique, quod semper, quodo ab omnibus creditum est*),[43] camouflages the sophistry that is at its center. What is being obscured is the power of the "Sovereign Pontiff" to do whatever he likes with Jesus Christ's Church, such as canceling the ban on profits on loans by calling those profits by another name, when it is expedient to do so according to the so-called economic "realities" of the situation. Christ's Church thereby becomes subject to the whims of the Bishop of Rome. The dogma of His Church can be reworked, reformulated and remade, along with the Word of God itself, by an exalted man on a throne in Rome. For instance, according to the teaching of Benedict XIV in his encyclical *Ex Quo Singulari,* the question of whether the continued observance of the *ceremonial* precepts of the Old Law is permitted, depends, according to the pontiff, on the character and motivation of the observances in question:

"Although the ceremonial precepts of the old Law have come to an end with the promulgation of the Gospel, and the new Law does not contain any precept which distinguishes between clean and unclean foods, nevertheless the Church of Christ has the power of renewing the obligation to observe some of the old precepts for just and serious reasons, despite their abrogation by the new Law."

Here is the overthrow of the Bible by the whim of Benedict XIV, who dares to accord to himself the title, "the Church of Christ." In the New Testament however, he and all other usurping human authorities, are unmasked: "Therefore *let no one pass judgment on you in questions of food and drink...*These are a shadow of the things to come, but the substance belongs to Christ. Let no one disqualify you...If with Christ you died to the elemental spirits of the world, why, as if you were still alive in the world, do you submit to regulations— 'Do not handle, Do not taste, Do not touch' (referring to things that all perish as

---

[42] Cf. *Usury in Christendom,* pp. 392-393.

[43] St. Vincent of Lerins, *Commonitorium,* (II, 5, PL 64, 149).

they are used)—*according to human precepts and teachings? These have indeed an appearance of wisdom in promoting self-made religion* and asceticism and severity to the body, but they are of no value..."(Colossians 2:16-18; 20-23; emphasis supplied).

The Word of God states that no human being can pass judgment on our choices of food and drink, and that any such judgments are human precepts and teachings of a religion that is not of God—it is a self-made religion. Only people sunk in a mentality of bipolar falsehoods can call themselves Bible believers while adhering to the "sovereign" spiritual supremacy which Pope Benedict XIV, and dozens of pontiffs like him, reserved for themselves alone.

This spirit is visible in the case of another celebrated, virtually canonized Church of Rome intellectual, Hilaire Belloc, whose prowess as a wordsmith cannot be denied and is rightly acknowledged, *caeteris paribus.* In the matter of his books of history [44] and his writing on usury however, he is a true son of Liguori. For example, concerning usury he is an innovator and no enemy of the Money Power (unless it is a Money Power that he denominates as "Calvinist" or "Bank of Amsterdam"). Belloc was a change agent in the same vein as bankers such as Fugger. The spirit of the lawyer and the equivocator has penetrated the marrow of the latter day Church of Rome to such an extent that the former scions of Thomistic reason have degenerated into the children of sophistry. Hilaire Belloc, in line with the modernist trend of his times, redefined usury so as to qualify it as not-usury: "Usury, then, is a claiming of interest on an unproductive loan, or of interest greater than the real increment produced by a productive loan." [45]

With this statement Belloc issued a *prozbul* worthy of Rabbi Hillel. He is saying that usury is permitted when a loan is "productive" (when the lender loans to a business). This is the

---

[44] Belloc's "histories" of the anti-Puritan Stuart monarchs are a palimpsest of fraud amounting to little more than pedestrian propaganda indifferent to facts. Belloc traffics in cliches and is ignorant of the authentic diplomatic history and legislation of the era. His "histories" are avidly published and parroted by contemporary "conservative and traditional Catholics." Cf. Hoffman, "Right Wing Myths with an Endless Shelf Life," in *Revisionist History*, no. 74.

[45] Hilaire Belloc, "On Usury" in *Essays of a Catholic Layman in England* (1931).

Machiavelli/Renaissance/Liguori/post-Renaissance doctrine. "Liguori's system...neutralizes God's law by sophistical distinctions..." [46]

Because he did not go all the way into libertarian extremism concerning usury, he is mistaken, by economic reformers and "Distributists" affiliated with the Church of Rome, for an archetypal enemy of usury. Good luck trying to wield facts of the documentary record to convince these individuals concerning the truth about Belloc. The same of fog of casuistry used to enshrine his legend is employed to deny the existence of papally-condoned Renaissance-Catholic usury. Equivocation and mental reservation have bred a rabbinic type of dialectic among some "Catholic" intellectuals which is largely impervious to truth.

One rather large problem for the post-Renaissance papist deceivers, at least in Britain anyway, was the publication of accurate English translations by two scrupulous Anglican scholars, Frederick Meyrick and R.P. Blakeney, of Liguori's magnum opus: *Moral and Devotional Theology of the Church of Rome According to the Authoritative Teaching of S. Alfonso De' Liguori*. These translations were called into action against the Anglican Church's most troubling "apostate."

The Cardinal Newman Controversy

"St. Alfonso certainly says that a play upon words is allowable; and, speaking under correction, I should say that he does so on the ground that lying is not a sin against justice, that is, against our neighbor, but a sin against God. God has made words the signs of ideas, and therefore if a word denotes two ideas, we are at liberty to use it in either of its senses..." John Henry Newman, *Apologia pro Vita Sua*.

Catholic Cardinal John Henry Newman (1801-1890), celebrated scholar and author, had been the ornament of High Church Anglicanism before becoming the most eminent English convert to Romanism in England in centuries, even though in the early years of his career as a convert in the Church of Rome he was barely visible. He made up for that initially marginal existence with an eventual celebrity that was remarkable.

---

[46] Frederick Meyrick, op.cit., p. xiii.

In the words of David Newsome in his book *The Parting of Friends*, many Anglicans were keen to "mend the breaches made by the secession of Newman to the Roman Church." In the act of that attempted "mending," Newman was confronted by Anglicans who forbore to analyze Alphonsus Liguori's recondite doctrine on mental reservation and equivocation and confront Newman with it. Among them was the Rev. Charles Kingsley, author of the classic books *Westward Ho!*, *Hypatia* and his juvenilia, *The Water Babies*. Kingsley sparked a literary conflagration when he wrote in the January, 1864 issue of the widely read, *Macmillan's Magazine*, "Truth for its own sake had never been a virtue with the Roman clergy." Kingsley questioned Newman's credibility: "How can I tell I shall not be the dupe of some cunning equivocation, of one of the three kinds laid down as permissible by the blessed St. Alfonso Liguori and his pupils even when confirmed by an oath, because: 'Then we do not deceive our neighbor, but allow him to deceive himself?'"

Newman had enemies inside the Roman Church as well. An influential group of ultramontane Romanists had accused the convert of Protestant tendencies. Two of his early projects, the Irish university and his editorship of *The Rambler*, had flopped. Since 1845 his existence as a Catholic had been largely an obscure one. The Anglican challenger, Kingsley, was what would be called nowadays a "best-selling author," and the fact that he picked a fight with the besieged Newman gave the latter a golden opportunity of putting his impressive command of the English language to use in ably defending many authentic, traditionally Catholic doctrines which Kingsley had disparaged, and which pre-dated the Renaissance.

Our concern however, is with Newman's qualified defense of Liguorianism, which was the paramount and indeed most explosive aspect of Kingsley's criticism, in branding all Catholic priests as equivocators (which is, of course, an unfair generalization). The debate played out in an exchange of pamphlets subsequently published in Newman's *Apologia*. The original edition of his *Apologia* differs from editions made popular later in the twentieth century. In its first edition, the *Apologia* began with the debate, "Mr. Kingsley and Dr. Newman: A Correspondence on the Question Whether Dr. Newman teaches that Truth is No Virtue" (London, 1864), after which followed the cardinal's autobiography, and then an appendix which replied to Kingsley and the "39 blots" (a satire on the Anglican Church's *39 Articles*).

Wilfrid Ward, [47] the editor of the authoritative 1913 Oxford edition of the *Apologia,* pronounced Newman the winner over Kingsley by a mile: "Newman...emerged triumphant. The *Apologia* carried the country by storm..." This sunny view of Newman's "triumph" is the general verdict of the papists and the intellectual elite of the English-speaking world generally. It is true that Newman convinced the Tories and upper classes of Britain that his defense of equivocation was correct. But what was the *locus* of those classes in terms of their ethics? At this stage in the Victorian era, the British upper and middle classes, in what was termed the Establishment Tory wing of the Church of England [48] (e.g. "the Liberalism which today inundates the English intelligent classes," to use Newman's own description), were desirous of moral support for their own acts of equivocation. Hence, some significant portions of the Protestant Overlord class in Britain welcomed Newman when he provided that support. Those Anglicans who were not seduced by modernist trends and not convinced by Newman's qualified defense of Liguori, tended to be "Evangelicals," who at the time numbered in the millions.

Newman proposed through the medium of the elegance of his much admired prose, what would come to be applauded as a nuanced understanding of equivocation, along with a subtle dig at the Italian character, which had only just been held up to national contempt in Britain by Wilkie Collins in his popular, 1859 mystery novel, *The Woman in White,* in which the figure of the loathsome "Count Fosco" is rendered as the epitome of menace and treachery.

Newman presented to the liberal Protestant lords and ladies of Britain the ethical cover they were seeking for their own considerable violations of the requirement for absolute fidelity to truthful speech, and they accepted his thinking with the *frisson* of having obtained it from a romantic rebel who had turned the tables on what was perceived as the holier-than-

---

[47] Wilfrid Ward's daughter Maisie founded, with her husband Frank Sheed, the distinguished publishing house of Sheed and Ward.

[48] As demarcated in Newman's instructive survey of the competing Anglican factions, in the appendix to the 1866 French language edition of the *Apologia,* which was reprinted in the 1913 Oxford edition, pp. xxii-xxx.

thou faction of the Church of England. From then until now, Newman's *Apologia* has been celebrated as the triumphal refutation of an ugly strain of pig-headed evangelical Protestantism on the part of a more reasonable and humane Catholicism. This myth is sustained by internal and external omissions: a failure to closely examine Newman's text in terms of the ramifications of his qualified support for Liguori, and beyond the text of the *Apologia* itself, the fact that Newman ran away from his most formidable opponent, Prof. Frederick Meyrick of Oxford, who he did not scruple to endeavor to answer in public, or even to name, as he had done with the less theologically talented Mr. Kingsley.

The version of the *Apologia Pro Vita Sua* which is now the standard text in schools and Roman Church circles after it was re-edited by its author, is a redacted version which takes the focus off of Kingsley and Liguori, on the queer pretext, as articulated by Wilfrid Ward, that the censorship was necessary so that the volume might metamorphose into "permanent literature." [49] Ward wrote:

"It became a classic of the language, and it had to be re-edited that its form, as well as its substance, might befit its permanent character. Its form had to be no longer that appropriate to a *controversy of the hour* which rapier thrusts and colloquialisms were suitable weapons, but that of an earnest autobiography which could stand side by side with those of St. Augustine and Rousseau...What was justified only as a retort made in heat and on the spur of the moment, to words blurted out by Kingsley himself in a moment of anger, was withdrawn. The last chapter was no longer called, 'General Answer to Mr. Kingsley;' it became, 'The position of my mind since 1845.' Such omissions and alterations indicate the general principle on which the book was re-edited." [50]

Was the contest with Newman concerning Church-sanctioned verbal and literary deceit really just a "controversy of the hour," or was it one for the ages? Is "a classic of the language" created by confecting a cosmetic edition of a text which has been drained of its most dangerous polemics? Or are

---

[49] The Liguori controversy remains present in the 1913 edition of *Apologia Pro Vita Sua,* but it has been toned down and signal particulars omitted.

[50] Wilfrid Ward, "Introduction," in *Newman's Apologia Pro Vita Sua* (1913), pp. vii and viii; emphasis supplied.

Ward and the Newman faction he represented, guilty of censoring a narrative which is potentially damaging to the reputation of the Church of Rome and Cardinal Newman? Is the falsification any less morally troubling because it was admitted publicly by Wilfrid Ward?

Kingsley had raised a number of points. The issue of Liguorianism was only one of them, though it proved the most contentious. Cardinal Newman did not entirely endorse Alphonsus Liguori's teaching on deceiving others, though one could say that Newman himself nearly equivocated concerning it when he wrote:

"I cannot think what it can be, in a day like this, which keeps up the prejudice of this Protestant country against us (Catholics), unless it be the vague charges which are drawn from our books of moral theology; and with a short notice of the work in particular which my accuser (Kingsley) especially throws into our teeth, I shall in a very few words bring these observations to a close.

"St. Alfonso Liguori, then, it cannot be denied, lays down that an equivocation, that is, a play upon words, in which one sense is taken by the speaker, and another sense intended by him for the hearer, is allowable, if there is a just cause, that is, in an extraordinary case, and may even be confirmed by an oath. I shall give my opinion on this point as plainly as any Protestant can wish; and therefore I avow at once that in this department of morality, much as I admire the high points of the Italian character, I like the English character better; but in saying so, I am not, as will shortly be seen, saying anything disrespectful to St. Alfonso, who was a lover of truth, and whose intercession I trust I shall not lose, though, on the matter under consideration, I follow other guidance in preference to his. [51]

Newman goes on to list four distinguished Protestants (Anglican Bishop Jeremy Taylor, Anglican Archdeacon William Paley, and from the world of letters, Puritan John Milton and Anglican Samuel Johnson). He examines the views of these four luminaries over the course of six pages, adducing evidence

[51] *Apologia Pro Vita Sua: Being a History of His Religious Opinions* (Longmans, 1904), pp. 169-170.

for his assertion that they supported either equivocation or mental reservation, or both. For example, he cites Johnson thus: 'The general rule is, that truth should never be violated; there must, however, be some exceptions. If, for instance, a murderer should ask you which way a man is gone."

Furthermore, Cardinal Newman states as his own preference that the "Italian character" is liked less than the English character. Is this not a gentleman's way of framing racial defamation of Italians? How is it that Liguori has come to be identified with the Italian character as a whole? What a tragedy for Italians that by the Victorian Age they were no longer the people of Saints Anthony of Padua and Francis of Assisi, and of the poet Dante Aligheri, but of Liguori, so that even the Church of Rome's own John Henry Newman had to parse the assessment of the national character of Italy based on the impact of Liguori, whose influence even he admitted, by a circuitous route, had rendered the Italian character second to the English.

Note too that concerning Liguori, Newman describes him as a "lover of truth." If that false statement is not a case of mental reservation, what is? How can Newman's *Apologia* be celebrated as a triumph over Kingsley when Newman resorted to such demonstrably false statements? If Liguori is such a "lover of truth" why does Newman confess that "in the matter under consideration, I follow other guidance in preference to his"? This is classic equivocation—whereby Newman permits us to deceive ourselves. Equivocation and mental reservation in just one paragraph. How then did Newman supposedly win the debate with Kingsley?

The consensus in Britain was that Newman had exonerated himself of Kingsley's accusation that Newman had been infected with Liguori's morality; though it was less clear as to whether he had managed to rescue the reputation of Liguori and the Church of Rome from the charge of institutionalizing lying and deception. Among those who were not persuaded was Newman's renowned Catholic friend and correspondent, Lord Acton (John Emerich Edward Dalberg Acton, 1834-1902), who stated, "Newman wrote a book to deny Liguori, but ended by invoking his intercession. Therefore I differ from N. (Newman) exactly as I do from Lig. (Liguori). Clearly he does not think it sinful to lie. It is not enough to disapprove lies if we say they are not sins."

As noted, Newman lists several of England's most distinguished Protestant literary figures who he says were in favor of untruthful speech in certain circumstances: "...great English authors, Jeremy Taylor, Milton, Paley, Johnson, men of very distinct schools of thought, distinctly say, that under certain special circumstances it is allowable to tell a lie. Taylor says: 'To tell a lie for charity, to save a man's life, the life of a friend, of a husband, of a prince, of a useful and a public person, hath not only been done at all times, but commended by great and wise and good men. Who would not save his father's life, at the charge of a harmless lie, from persecutors or tyrants?' Again, Milton says: 'What man in his senses would deny, that there are those whom we have the best grounds for considering that we ought to deceive—as boys, madmen, the sick, the intoxicated, enemies, men in error, thieves? I would ask, by which of the commandments is a lie forbidden? You will say, by the ninth. If then my lie does not injure my neighbor, certainly it is not forbidden by this commandment.' Paley says: 'There are falsehoods, which are not lies, that is, which are not criminal."

Newman added, "...in truth, a Catholic theologian has objects in view which men in general little compass; he is not thinking of himself, but of a multitude of souls, sick souls, sinful souls, carried away by sin, full of evil, and he is trying with all his might to rescue them from their miserable state; and in order to save them from more heinous sins, he tries, to the full extent that his conscience will allow him to go, to shut his eyes to such sins, as are, though sins, yet lighter in character or degree. He knows perfectly well that, if he is as strict as he would wish to be, he shall be able to do nothing at all with the run of men; so he is as indulgent with them as ever he can be. Let it not be for an instant supposed, that I allow of the maxim of doing evil that good may come; but, keeping clear of this, there is a way of winning men from greater sins by winking for the time at the less, or at mere improprieties or faults; and this is the key to the difficulty which Catholic books of moral theology so often cause to the Protestant. They are intended for the Confessor and Protestants view them as intended for the Preacher...

"This is pretty much the answer I make, when I am considered in this matter a disciple of St. Alfonso. I plainly and positively state, and without any reserve, that I do not at all follow this holy and charitable man in this portion of his teaching. There are various schools of opinion allowed in the Church; and on this point I follow others. I follow Cardinal Gerdil, and Natalis Alexander, and St. Augustine....Augustine is the doctor of the great and common view that all untruths are lies, and that there can be no just cause of untruth.

"I will quote one passage from Natalis Alexander:—'They certainly lie, who utter the words of an oath, without the will to swear or bind themselves: or who make use of mental reservations and equivocations in swearing, since they signify by words what they have not in mind, contrary to the end for which language was instituted, viz. as signs of ideas. Or they mean something else than the words signify in themselves and the common custom of speech.'

"And, to take an instance: I do not believe any priest in England would dream of saying, 'My friend is not here;' meaning, 'He is not in my pocket or under my shoe. Nor should any consideration make me say so myself. I do not think St. Alfonso would in his own case have said so...

"And now, if Protestants wish to know what our real teaching is, as on other subjects, so on that of lying, let them look, not at our books of casuistry, but at our catechisms. Works on pathology do not give the best insight into the form and the harmony of the human frame; and, as it is with the body, so it is with the mind. The *Catechism of the Council of Trent* was drawn up for the express purpose of providing preachers with subjects for their sermons; and as my whole work has been a defense of myself, I may say here that I rarely preach a Sermon, but I go to this beautiful and complete catechism to get both matter and doctrine. There we find..notices about the duty of veracity..." [52]

And there too we find notices about the duty of not charging interest on loans which is just as studiously ignored as "the duty of veracity." Newman's postulation of two sets of books is as bankrupt in religion as it is in accounting. The books of casuistry direct the conscience of the papist. What is performed in the Sacrament of Confession is supposed to enforce the laws

---

[52] John Henry Newman, "Answer to Mr. Kingsley," in *Newman's Apologia Pro Vita Sua* (1913), pp. 367-369.

of God. Newman would have us look to the declarations of Trent as indicative of the faith of the Church of Rome. The trumpeting of the mere fact of the *existence* of Trent's decrees has been misleading generations of Catholics, many of whom remain convinced that the Church of Rome continues to ban profit on loans and strictly forbids lying, deceit and theft. The situation ethics of the Liguorian and other papist systems demonstrates that the reverse is true, and now that we have some inkling of the extent of the plague of child molestation inside the Church, we can better understand how the Liguorian and other casuist systems have served as a bulwark against the exposure and prosecution of child-molesting priests.

In light of the fact that in print Newman debated Rev. Kingsley, who was not a theologian, while evading Meyrick, who was a formidable Protestant theologian, and whose documentation and arguments it may be that Newman could not answer, the histrionic assessment of Newman's alleged complete victory over his lesser opponent Kingsley is wearying in its bombast:

"The rough handling of Kingsley by his opponent was a marked feature in the original *Apologia*...It succeeded so completely and issued in such an acknowledged and crushing defeat for Kingsley that Newman's warmest friends found themselves feeling sorry for the man...A fine literary critic among Newman's Oratorian entourage—Father Ignatius Dudley Ryder—wrote at the time...the following note of his own impressions on reading Newman's scathing denunciation of his assailant...this polemical annihilation...In reading the tremendous handling of his opponent in the introduction and conclusion of the *Apologia*, it is impossible, I think, whatever may be one's sympathies, to avoid a sense of honest pity for the victim as for one condemned though by his own rashness to fight with gods or with the elements." [53]

Mr. Ward's belief that Newman was nearly universally recognized as the victor in the exchange with Kingsley does not bear up under scrutiny. Church of England Bishop Samuel Wilberforce viewed Newman's response to Kingsley as "special pleading" of a type which had not succeeded in freeing the Church of Rome from complicity in the errors of Liguori: "In

---

[53] Ward, "Introduction," in *Newman's Apologia Pro Vita Sua*, op. cit., p. x.

truth there is against him here that consensus of living authority to which in matters ecclesiastical Dr. Newman attributes so indisputable a power." [54] *The Spectator* was not persuded that Newman had carried the day, writing that Kingsley had not been proved wrong in his main point, that "truth for its own sake" was not a high point in the Roman priesthood.

The bragging of the Newmanites repels the revisionist reader who has witnessed similar boasts and congratulatory back-slapping predicated on a hoax that maintains credibility from the fact that the favored party commands the attention of the press and the masses, while opponents languish in obscurity. The advantage is solely in terms of public relations, not the truthfulness of the "winning" side. Because Newman refused to face Frederick Meyrick, a first class opponent, his followers were able to crown him with the laurel wreath of unconditional victory over a second rate, "annihilated" opponent, and this has become the judgment of consensus history.

Here we glimpse more of the deceit of which the august Cardinal Newman may be guilty. In the face of his glorification, a scrupulous Newman would have interrupted to say, Gentleman, you do overpraise me, for if I have triumphed it is because I have been too exhausted and perhaps too timid to deign to answer the charges made by the Oxford theologian Rev. Meyrick, whose special knowledge of these matters is far above that of the children's book author, Mr. Kingsley.

No statement of that tenor came from Cardinal Newman. With the hindsight of nearly one hundred fifty years, no similar statement has emanated from Newman's prominent supporters and enthusiasts who have erected and maintained the Newmanite legend. Prof. Meyrick was the author of some seventy books and pamphlets on theology and history. He was a specialist on the moral theology of Alphonsus Liguori and no bigot, being an admirer of Innocent XI. In a pamphlet dated March 18, 1864 entitled, "But Isn't Kingsley Right After All?" Meyrick, who had met Newman years before, took the battle to him:

---

[54] Samuel Wilberforce, "Dr. Newman's Apologia," *Quarterly Review*, October 1864, pp. 680-681.

"...is not Mr. Kingsley substantially right?...is he wrong in stating that you—Dr. Newman the individual man, and Dr. Newman the representative of a school—are unable to declare what we in England mean by untruthfulness to be immoral?"

Meyrick then quoted profusely from Liguori on equivocation. As previously observed, Newman would not reply in public to Meyrick. Prof. Meyrick and his challenge to Newman constitute a virtual cipher in mainstream biographies of Cardinal Newman and accounts of his defense of Liguori. It is the memory hole all the way for Meyrick. Newman's reputation is sustained only when Meyrick is made to disappear. How dishonest is that? Late in 1864, Meyrick again challenged Newman with his study, *On Dr. Newman's Rejection of Liguori's Doctrine of Equivocation* (an intentionally ironic title), which Wilberforce, the Anglican Bishop of Oxford, considered "unanswerable." Meyrick put forth an analogy which deflates Newman's own equivocation: "Dr. Newman holds very much the same relation towards S. Alfonso and Equivocation as a monogamist Mormon would hold towards Polygamy...He has amply vindicated for himself the character of an honest and truthful Englishman...but by that vindication he has the more deeply (in)criminated his Church, which sanctions what he rejects, and which will not allow him to condemn as a Roman Catholic what he scornfully refuses to practice as a man."

The only Catholic scholar writing in English (of whom we are aware), who has taken any significant notice of Meyrick's challenge to Newman, is Joseph L. Altholz, who wrote, "Meyrick was a controversialist of greater substance than Kingsley; but his pamphlet went virtually unnoticed in the glow of Newman's triumph with the *Apologia*. Newman does not appear to have taken any cognizance of him, and his unanswered pamphlet was the last blow of the controversy." [55]

And so it goes—the familiar furrow is plowed and the seeds by which posterity judges a controversy are planted; one undeserving celebrity is crowned king, while the man with truth slowly sinks into the shadows like a sputtering twenty

---

[55] Altholz, "Truth and Equivocation," in *Church History*, March 1975, pp. 82-83. Newman did privately correspond with Meyrick, but in public he would not respond to his challenge.

watt bulb, leaving the celebrity's partisans to crow, "Twas a famous victory." [56]

Newman has been accused by his Right-wing Romanist critics of not being sufficiently Catholic, i.e. in not supporting the Ultramontane party; as well as in some instances (and here we think his Roman critics were on firmer ground)—for his unfortunate theory of the *development of doctrine*. [57] One thing he was not, was an ecumenist; that is, assuming that he was not equivocating when, in 1862, he called Protestantism "the dreariest of possible religions...the city of confusion and the house of bondage." Newman's understanding of papal infallibility was of interest for its marketing brilliance, contrasted with the inept marketing by the adherents of Ultramontanism. Newman wrote attractively that, "the Holy See has no magical power of teaching new truth infallibly, but represents the conservative element which preserves the original deposit of faith." (It was by the advancement of this claim that the First Vatican Council's doctrine was sold to the sheeple). But whether the pope's power is magical or not, it is power nonetheless; the power of an absolute monarch. It was that power which was used from the Renaissance forward in a mission to derogate or nullify ancient truths from the Deposit of Faith, while elevating heresies. This is a diabolic process, which, believe it or not, was *praised by Newman* in later editions of the *Apologia,* in this manner: "Heretical questionings have been transmuted by the living power of the Church into salutary truths."

This is a statement of an extraordinary candor concerning the effect of the power of the "sovereign pontiff" to transmute,

---

[56] This is a reference to Robert Southey's ironic and scathing use of the term in his poem, "The Battle of Blenheim."

[57] For example, in the course of elucidating his theology on the development of doctrine (which is actually a type of situation ethics), Newman admits that the belief in the pope's universal jurisdiction was largely unknown in the early Church, viz. that it was "...only partially apprehended in the early age of the Church. It required time for Christians to enter into the full truth...I believe (in) whatever has been and shall be defined as revelation by the Church." Cf. Mark D. Chapman, *The Fantasy of Reunion: Anglicans, Catholics, and Ecumenism* (2014), pp. 144-145.

for example, usury, from a mortal to sin to something that need not even be confessed for reception of the Eucharist.[58]

(To his credit, and though in our opinion he was resoundingly confuted, English Cardinal Henry Manning, Rome's "Lord Archbishop of Westminster," did not evade a debate with Meyrick over Liguori. It took the form of a public exchange of nineteen letters, which Meyrick subsequently published in *Moral and Devotional Theology of the Church of Rome).*

In the midst of the muck and mire of equivocation and mental reservation, let us restate the doctrine of the ancient, True Catholic Church. Scott M. Sullivan, of the University of St. Thomas: "But let your speech be yea, yea: no, no: and that which is over and above these, is of evil. (Matthew 5:37) (St.) Augustine's position on this matter is well known and needs little elaboration. Lying is always a sin. Purity of soul is preferable to bodily purity and this holds without exception....Augustine does not change his mind in the *Contra Mendacium,* written decades later. A lie is still not allowable even if to save one from injury. *Biblical examples to the contrary, like that of Jacob, Augustine maintains are not lies, but mysteries.* Augustine remains constant in this position through the *Enchiridion.* There are no lies that are not sins...every lie must be called a sin...

"Aquinas prohibits truthful speech spoken with intent to deceive. A good thing can be done for the wrong intention, and just like one who goes to Church in order to steal, likewise, speaking truthfully with the intention to deceive is a form of lying. Even though the speech is true, the intent to deceive renders it as a species of lying."[59]

There are surely numerous truthful adherents of the Church of Rome. The catastrophe is this: as long "Saint" Liguori's revival of the Renaissance doctrine of permissible deceit and

---

[58]   Cardinal Newman substituted the word Church for pontiff. The indefectible Catholic Church of Jesus Christ is not responsible for transmuting heresy into truth, however.

[59]   Scott M. Sullivan, "In Defense Of The Falsiloquium," University of St. Thomas (http://scottmsullivan.com/articles/Falsiloquium.pdf)

falsehood is a theological legacy for leaders of the hierarchy of the Church of Rome, who put it into practice in their own criminal careers, while transmitting it to penitents in the confessional, and to criminal clergy involved in facilitating or actually perpetrating child molestation—this circumstance goes a long way toward explaining the stubborn survival of the epidemic molestation of children which has been shrouded in the deepest institutional secrecy, protected by equivocation and mental reservation.

Some will say it is an anti-Catholic act to call so eminent a "saint" as Alphonsus Liguori to task for his counsels on this head. On the contrary, let it be said that *it is a profoundly anti-Catholic act to do as the equivocators and mental reservationists do and proceed to approve of deception and double-dealing in the name of the Church*, thus defaming her and giving powerful ammunition to Talmudists, those Protestants who are bigots, and other enemies of the authentic Catholicism that existed for fourteen hundred years.

The system of moral theology which would later become Liguori's specialty first gained prominence during the Renaissance, almost two centuries before his birth. According to Redemptorist theologian Rev. Théodule Ray-Mermet, CSsR., "The phenomena of moral systems appeared during the sixteenth century to face the complexity of a new world whose problems agonized consciences and divided scholars."[60] Fr. Ray-Mermet's preceding words constitute a modernist statement. He implies that times change in "the complexity of a new world." What actually happened was that the *zeitgeist* embraced the sophistry of lawyers with strong similarities to the Talmudic and Kabbalistic system. In the Talmudic system, stringent and less stringent are represented by the *zugot* pairs, one of the earliest of which was represented by the "schools of Shammai and Hillel" (supposedly contemporary with Christ), which in turn personified a rabbinic dialectic, represented symbolically by the two "pillars of the Temple," *gevurah* (severity) and *chesed* (mercy). In the predominant moral theology of the post-Renaissance Church of Rome these antipodes are designated as *rigorist* and *laxist*. They were definitively demarcated and explicated in a dense work that has the heft and prolixity of the Talmud—the *Theologia*

---

60 Théodule Ray-Mermet, op. cit., p. 66.

Moralis of Alphonsus Liguori, the sixth edition of which was completed in 1767 when he was seventy-years of-age. Between 1791 and 1905 sixty complete editions were published.

Liguori, who had been a lawyer before he became a priest, created a theological system that approximated the Jesuit-dominated theology of probabilism,[61] but which, for purposes of camouflage, he named "Equiprobabilism." [62] The *Catholic Encyclopedia* states, "Equiprobabilism opposed to either a lax or rigorous moral position, was not a compromise between the two, but a *higher equilibrium*." [63] In Kabbalistic Judaism the mean between the two pillars of *gevurah* and *chesed* is known as "the knowledge of the *higher equilibrium*."

In Orthodox Judaism, among the Ten Commandmants, the command, "Thou shalt not steal," is not applied mechanically, that is to say, in every case equally. In certain instances, Judaic persons may steal from gentiles without incurring sin.[64] The *New Catholic Encyclopedia* writes, "In Alphonsian moral theory the study of the concrete circumstances of action rules out the mechanical application of a system, however sound it

---

[61] Probablism is a moral theology "according to which in a doubt of conscience about the morality of a particular course of conduct, a person may lawfully follow the opinion of liberty, provided it is truly probable, even though the opinion for law is definitely more probable." *New Catholic Encyclopedia* (Catholic University of America, 1967), v. 11, p. 814. This is the convoluted thinking of lawyers and rabbis furnishing escape clauses from God's law. This aspect was astutely detected by the Dominican theologian Servais Pinckaers in *Ce qu' on ne peut jamais faire* (Fribourg, 1986): "In casuistry everything occurs as though the subject, impelled by freedom, was always seeking to escape universal laws by means of particular circumstances, or at least to loosen the hold of such laws...Within this context...it is difficult to uphold the universality of the laws in the face of a freedom that employs all its ingenuity in finding exceptions through the use of extreme cases and that is constantly tempted to appeal to them to break through the law itself. In the view of Saint Thomas, by contrast...dealing with difficult and unusual cases is an exercise in judiciously applying laws according to their spirit, rather than seeking a loophole to escape from them" (pp. 128-129).

[62] *New Catholic Encyclopedia* v. 1, p. 340: states, "...he was constrained to veil his thought somewhat because of anti-Jesuit persecutions."

[63] Ibid. Emphasis supplied.

[64] Cf. BT Sanhedrin 57a; BT Sanhedrin 76a; Baba Mezia 24a; Baba Kamma 37b; Baba Kamma 113b. Also: Rabbi Ezra Basri, *Ethics of Business Finance & Charity* (Jerusalem: Haktav Press, 1988), vol. two, chapter 13 ("No obligation to be fair to gentiles"). Basri was chief justice of the Jerusalem district court). Also cf. *Judaism Discovered*, pp. 357-361.

may be." Liguori was "(a)lways disposed to prefer reason to the authority of moralists."[65] Here is a succinct summation of the modernist mentality of Liguori which nullifies the Ten Commandments ("mechanical application of a system") and prefers "reason" to the authority of "moralists." Who are these denigrated "moralists"? Are they not Jesus, St. Paul, St. Peter, et. al? Alphonsian moral theory is the theology of Renaissance, post-Renaissance and modern popes from John XXIII onward. Hence, when "traditional" Catholics approach the Vatican and demand the restoration of the faith "in line with the teachings of St. Alphonsus Liguori" they perform a ceremony of ignorant self-mockery which identifies them to the hierarchy of the Church of Rome as infants babbling about matters of which they know nothing. "Traditional Catholics" defend a pre-1960s Catholicism which, being "Renaissance-Catholicism" is the essence of the forked tongue and the double cross, and they wonder why they can't win their battles and must resort to apocalyptic prophecies from obscure nuns and hoaxed papal chronologies about the "Glory of the Olive" (Benedict XVI) and "Peter Romanus" (Pope Francis). The Overlords in Rome are more than happy to watch them retreat to this ghettoized playpen for, after all, according to the equivocator's motto, "they have deceived themselves."

As previously noted, Liguori perpetrated his swindle on the Catholic world by making himself known as a supreme champion of Mary. His book The *Glories of Mary* is far better known among the common people than his *Moral Theology* (*Glories of Mary* "has been translated into over eighty different languages and 800 known editions"). [66] As we pointed out earlier with regard to the pious Marian front mounted by John Paul II, some Catholics are convinced that any reputedly dedicated advocate of Mary must be theologically sound.

Liguori's extensively argued theology of equivocation and mental reservation will be found only in the *uncensored, complete* edition of his *Moral Theology*. Excerpts in English appear in the Blakeney and Meyrick translations. We believe that these two individuals accurately and scrupulously translated the portions of *Moral Theology* containing the

---

[65] *New Catholic Encyclopedia*, op. cit. pp. 340-341.

[66] Frederick M. Jones, C.S.s.R., *Alphonsus De Liguori: Saint of Bourbon Naples* (1999), p. 274.

approval by Liguori, "under certain circumstances," of trickery, dissimulation, mendacity, misdirection and almost every species of duplicity. In Meyrick's case he was not a bigot. He seems to have been a seeker after Christ's truth wherever it might be found. If it could be found in a pope of Rome, so much the better. He esteemed Pope Innocent XI as an enemy of equivocation and mental reservation. Meyrick wrote concerning him:

"Innocent XI of the house of Odescalchi, was a pope meek and mild in manner, but firm and high in purpose...A man of uncompromising and inflexible integrity, he naturally leaned toward the Jansenist codes of morality and had little sympathy for the system...However...Jansenism has always been worsted in its conflicts with Jesuitism. The Moral Theologians set to work...(g)iven the problem how to retain a certain practice, and at the same time pay an outward respect to a papal decree forbidding it, the method to be adopted is the following—Take the thing condemned and divide it into two species, distinguished from each other by a distinction without a difference. Assume that the papal condemnation applies to either one of these species, but not to the other. Range everything which you wish to do under the uncondemned head; whatever you have no temptation towards under the other. The result will be the conclusion desired. Thus, the Pope (Innocent XI) condemned mental restriction (and) immediately afterward mental restriction is divided into two kinds (by theologians like Liguori), pure mental restriction and non-pure mental restriction. There is no moral difference between them, but the papal condemnation is declared to be confined to the former and so the old practice goes on as securely and merrily as ever."[67]

"Thou shalt not steal." — God, Exodus 20:15.

"What is theft? It is the secret and unjust taking-away of a thing belonging to another, when the owner is reasonably unwilling."
— "Saint" Alphonsus Liguori, *Theologia Moralis*, iv, 518.

---

[67] Meyrick, op. cit., pp. 37-38.

Notice the chasm-like loophole provided for a thief by Liguori. If the thief can convince himself that the rightful owner is *reasonably willing* to having his property stolen, then the Catholic thief is free to take it.

Liguori characterized his opponents as "overstrict" and "extremely rigid" theologians, but he is sly enough to make it appear as though he favors the teaching of Augustine and Innocent XI on the need for absolute truthfulness, after which he cynically proceeds to subvert them both by boring several large loopholes in their doctrine. Where, for instance, Pope Innocent XI condemned the proposition that domestic servants may, from their masters *"possunt occulte heris suis surripere ad compensandam operam suam, qua majorem judicant salario quod recipiunt"* ("steal secretly for the purpose of compensating themselves for their own labor which they judge to be greater than the salary they receive"),[68] Liguori wrote, "the pontifical decrees are not designed to lay servants under an unjust obligation." [69]

How much does Liguori allow the servant to steal? The "saint" states that the amount is to be determined by the thieving servant himself, "according to his own judgment...if the servant, or any other hired person, be prudent, and capable of forming a correct judgment, and be certain concerning the justice of the compensation, all danger of mistake being removed." [70]

Some of Liguori's *Moral Theology* descends into the realm of the ridiculous, such as when he rules that while it is a mortal sin to steal a small relic "in the district of Rome," outside of Rome it would be only a venial sin to steal a small relic, provided that the thief does not deform or diminish it (*"ipsam reliquiam non deformans, neque minuens illius*

---

[68] *Salm.* de 4. praec. n. 130.

[69] R.P. Blakeney, *Saint Alphonsus Liguori: Extracts Translated from the Moral Theology*, (1852), p. 183. The Latin language being more familiar to the intelligentsia of the nineteenth century than in our time, Rev. Blakeney proceeded to publish on each page, Liguori's original Latin text next to Blakeney's English translation. Had Blakeney tampered with Liguori's words it would have been apparent to scholarly readers, and the Church of Rome would have had grounds to cry foul. No objection from any quarter was raised regarding the veracity of his translation.

[70] Blakeney, ibid. pp. 184-185.

aestimationem"). An exception is to be made if the relic is very rare, as for example a piece of the true cross or a hair from the head of the Blessed Virgin Mary. In both cases the theft of those relics would be considered mortally sinful no matter where they occurred.

Liguori had no scruple against blasphemy since he accused Jesus Christ of lying. Referring to mental reservation as "mental restriction," he wrote: "...it is allowable to use non-pure mental restriction, even with an oath, if it can be discovered by circumstances. This is proved from John vii: 8, where Christ said, 'I go not up to this feast,' and yet Scripture says that He afterward went up." (p. 5). [71]

Here is the passage in the Gospel to which Liguori alludes, implicating Jesus in Liguori's immoral theology: John 7: 8-10: "Go ye up unto this feast: I will not go up yet unto this feast: for my time is not yet come. These things he said unto them, and abode still in Galilee. But as soon as his brethren were gone up, then went he also up unto the feast, not openly, but as it were in private."

Was Jesus a deceiver, as the leaders of the Jews and the Gnostics declare, and Liguori insinuates, when "Saint" Alphonsus claims Our Lord used "non-pure" mental reservation?

When Jesus' time had come, he went up to the Feast (of Booths). He did so secretly because He and His followers were under threat (John 7:13). Liguori claims to be a follower of St. Augustine. Can he be ignorant of St. Augustine's own commentary on John 7: 8-10? Augustine, in a homily on this passage, rejects with indignation and horror the Liguorian-type of twisting of the words of Jesus. Augustine, with no axe to grind in favor of justifying deceit, in godly and reverent terms, would rather give Our Savior the benefit of the doubt, and believe that Our Lord was deceived by others, rather than, as Liguori blasphemously implies, that He Himself had deceived

---

[71]Liguori distinguishes between "pure" and "non-pure" mental reservation ("restriction"), as follows: "The condemnation passed by the pontiff (Innocent XI) on mental restriction is rightly to be understood of restriction purely and strictly taken, for that alone ought to be called true mental restriction which takes place solely in the mind, and there remains concealed and can by no means be discovered from outward circumstances." (Blakeney, op. cit., pp. 5 and 6).

others (*"falli enim pertinet ad infirmitatem, mentiri ad iniquitatem"*).

When lying to a questioner about whether someone is present in a building or not, Liguori prefers the phrase "He is not here," to "He is not at home." Alphonsus states that the latter is a material falsehood, whereas to tell a questioner that someone "is not here" meaning not at the door, or not at the window, or not in sight, involves no deceit. [72]

Under certain circumstances, when a wife who is being questioned about having broken her marriage vows and being guilty of adultery seeks to lie to her husband about the extra-marital tryst which she has committed, she may do so, according to Liguori, the canonized Doctor of the Church and founder of the Redemptorist Order, under the following stipulation: "She may equivocally assert that she has not broken the marriage, for it still exists.

"If she has sacramentally confessed her adultery, she may answer, 'I am innocent of this crime,' because it has already been taken away by confession." [73]

How many thousands, or tens of thousands of times, were these hellish alibis which are evocative of the seediest shyster, whispered into the ears of female adulterers in the confessional, based on the *Moral Theology* of Liguori? How can this be of Christ, or of His Church? Is it not of Satan? And is it not put forth by an enemy of the True Catholic Church, desirous of wrecking the reputation of Christ's Church, to say nothing of the purity, integrity and honor of its wives and mothers?

When it comes to making a promise, Liguori furnishes a *Kol Nidrei*-type of exit strategy: "We must mark here as certain that no promise binds although it has been accepted by the other party, if afterwards it becomes impossible, or very harmful, or unlawful, or inexpedient, and, generally speaking, whenever any notable change of circumstance takes place, so that if it had been foreseen, the promise would not have been made; because a promise is always supposed to be made under such a tacit condition."

---

[72] Blakeney, p. 13.

[73] Blakeney, p. 15.

If a promise can be broken because it is "inexpedient" or "whenever any notable change of circumstance takes place," what good is it? How can it be called a promise?

"Saint" Alphonsus has theologized an evil and iniquitous teaching for the direction of priests and prelates in the Confessional, revealing of the perverted nature of his disordered mind and soul: whereby, promises of marriage by Catholic noblemen to women who are commoners may be freely broken, if it is to the advantage of the aristocrat to do so. It was Protestant scholars who discovered and published this authenticated teaching after intensive investigation of Liguori's writings. No official of the Church of Rome had been forthcoming in this regard. The popes after the eighteenth century were content to keep Liguori's reprehensible teaching in the Latin language and made known only inside the Church to tens of thousands of Catholic priest-Confessors who resorted to Liguori in these matters, or who were instructed second hand, by seminary professors and the theology faculty of Catholic universities. This morally diseased doctrine about women, reflecting the double standard of a pagan potentate in ancient Babylon, was defended in pages of convoluted lawyer's casuistry in the leading Catholic publication in Britain at the time, Cardinal Nicholas Wiseman's *Dublin Review* (published in London, Edinburgh, Paris and New York,) after it had been exposed in the Protestant journal, *The Christian Remembrancer,* to nation-wide revulsion and disgust in Britain. [74] It is not a simple matter to ascertain which is more perverse, Liguori's warrant for seduction and abandonment of women who are not aristocrats, by Catholic men who are, or the *Dublin Review's* attempt at defending it, as follows:

"But suppose the man is very far superior to the woman in rank and condition, is he still bound to marriage? The question must be considered under the further supposition of whether the promise was real or feigned...what shall be said if the marriage must almost necessarily be crowned with social and moral disorders of the gravest character?...the whole character of a nation (is) dependent upon the due observance of grade in

---

[74] Nicholas Cardinal Wiseman (1802-1865), founded *The Dublin Review* in 1836. Cf. Dom Paschal Scotti, "English Catholicism and the Dublin Review," in *Out of Due Time: Wilfrid Ward and the Dublin Review* (2006). Ward was Wiseman's biographer (*The Life and Times of Cardinal Wiseman* [1897]).

the structure of society, and regard(s) the interchange of marriage between high and low as the very source of corruption of a whole people. Rightly then, as it seems to us, do theologians make exceptions to the general rule in favor of cases where nothing but the worst results, *'pessimus exitus,'* could be expected from the marriage." [75]

Liguori's depraved theology is reflected in this defense, published more than six decades after his death. The defense, such as it is, adds qualifications which Liguori never made; that is its first fallacy. *Liguori stated baldly that aristocrats need not keep promises of marriage to women of a lower social class.* His apologist in *The Dublin Review* insinuates that Catholic men of the upper class are usually morally superior to women of the lower class, whether Catholic or not. On no grounds whatever, she is assumed to be the potential "source of corruption." Cardinal Wiseman's theological journal then proceeds to traduce these girls even further, placing the onus of blame for a broken promise of marriage on them, because "the woman could easily have detected the fraud, either from the man's words, or other circumstances, or according to some theologians, from the fact of very great disparity in rank...." [76]

In other words, a beautiful young Catholic girl, when courted by a Catholic aristocrat, must possess the self-realization that she is very inferior compared to him, and on that basis should rebuff his attempts at courtship almost immediately in order to free herself from the likelihood that he will callously break his promise to her — in which case it will be her fault that he does so! Is it any wonder that hundreds of thousands of the peasants of nineteenth century Italy fled the country of their birth for Protestant America, where the Church of Rome dared not exact so heavy a toll of injustice upon the daughters of the poor and middle classes?

We regret to say that there is more of this disgusting theology: "Some theologians also say that she cannot, by the strict letter of the law, claim any compensation because, says St. Liguori, she ought to look upon the injury she has received

---

[75] "St. Alphonsus and the Christian Remembrancer" in *The Dublin Review*, December, 1854, collected in *The Dublin Review Volume 37* (London: Thomas Richardson, 1854), pp. 391-392.

[76] Ibid., p. 393.

as a just punishment for her own carelessness and levity of conduct." [77]

Protestant theologian Frederick Meyrick observed with indignation, "We hope that the aristocratic parents will, for their sons' sake, duly appreciate these novel privileges of the nobility. For ourselves we are well content that the right of seducing maidens on promise of marriage, and then refusing to keep the promise, should remain a privilege of the nobles of those countries alone where Rome's religion is professed and Rome's teachers have sway."

"Saint" Liguori also furnishes the moral theology of perjury —how Catholics can be justified in committing it in a court of law: "A witness or defendant when not legitimately questioned by the judge, may swear he does not know a crime that he really does know, understanding to himself that he does not know a crime about which he can be legitimately questioned, or that he does not know it so as to give evidence about it...

"When, however, the witness or defendant is legitimately questioned by the judge, he must not use any equivocation, because he is bound to obey the rightful precept of his superior.

"...Even when legitimately and juridically interrogated you are not bound to give evidence in the following cases...If notable harm will result to yourself or any belonging to you from your testimony...

"If the man (the defendant) probably did not commit sin in what he did, owing to ignorance, or because he took something by way of compensation for a debt, and for doing so was charged with theft.

Liguori on bribery: "...Does a man commit sin who offers a bribe to a judge or to his ministers?...If he gives without good reason, he commits sin by cooperating in an unlawful receiving, but not if he gives with a reason, namely, to free himself from annoyance which he does not deserve...what the laws intend is to provide against men giving money, and so corrupting the judges by bribes, not to prevent them from getting a just sentence." [78]

---

[77] Ibid., p. 394.

[78] Blakeney, pp. 22-24.

The Pope of Rome made Alphonsus Liguori a canonized saint, and one of only thirty-three formally declared "Doctors of the Church," an exalted theological rank which Liguori shares with Saints Ambrose, Augustine, Basil, Jerome, Cyril of Alexandria, Gregory of Nazianzus, John Chrysostom and Thomas Aquinas.[79] Liguori's sainthood and "Doctor of the Church" status are a pathological joke worthy of the "Franciscans of Medmenham" (i.e. the Hell-Fire Club). [80]

Liguori's *Moral Theology* is so crammed with nostrums for lying and dissembling in the guise of equivocations, mental restrictions and a multitude of distinctions and qualifying factors, as well as ecclesiastical permission to lie classed under the headings of dispensations, commutations and remissions, that one does not know where to begin or end in quoting, in context, this despicable liar's "theology." When studying "Saint Alphonsus Liguori, Doctor of the Church," one feels as though one has been studying the Talmud.

---

[79] During the time of the faithful Catholic Church, Aquinas ruled that papal infallibility is not a doctrine that can command the dogmatic assent of Catholics. It has only the standing of a pious belief: "Since, as Thomas (Aquinas) says, no damnable error can exist in the Church and since it would be a damnable error for the faithful to honor a saint in hell, therefore no canonized saint can be in hell...Thomas articulated, for the first time, the infallibility of the papacy in the glorification of the saints. For him, though, the definition of dogma is a very strict business. Since nothing without at least its seed in the scriptures can be an article of faith, Thomas would not call infallibility in canonization in itself a dogma. He makes a rather fine distinction...since it cannot be absolutely derived from the scriptures, the doctrine of the infallibility of the pope in canonization is a matter of pious belief only." Donald S. Prudlo, *Certain Sainthood: Canonization and the Origins of Papal Infallibility* (2015), pp. 128-129.

[80] At a meeting of the Hell-Fire Club, Robert Vansittart (1728-1789), Regius Professor of Law at Oxford University, presented with great pomp, a baboon, "to which Sir Francis Dashwood was accustomed to administer the eucharist at their meetings." (Sidney Lee, *Dictionary of National Biography* [1909], vol. xx, p. 145). The Hell-Fire club enshrined mockery of God as among the most potent of Satanic acts. This cabal was heir to the conspirators who had installed pornographic "art" in the Sistine Chapel where the Mass was offered; and to the legacy of the Franciscan priest Francois Rabelais's books, *Gargantua* (1535) and *Pantagruel* (1532). Rabelais mocked Christ on the Cross when Jesus called out, "I thirst," by depicting a drunk in *Gargantua* saying the same thing. ("Thelema," the utopian "abbey" in Rabelais's *Gargantua*, [cf. ch. 55], which allegedly has only one rule, "Do what thou wilt," is a signature ideological meme of the post-Renaissance western secret societies). In our Revelation of the Method era, ridicule of Jesus is freely performed in public: in movies, television, theater and "art" exhibitions.

Recall that Newman, in distancing himself from Liguori, made reference to preferring English over Italian ways. Between Machiavelli and Liguori, Italy in general and Rome in particular became synonymous in the English-speaking world with "*Arte*," in the sense of the intrigue of the diabolist. The early English essayist William Harrison protested that in Italy a man is "accounted most wise and politic that can most of all dissemble."

"Insofar as Catholics were said to lie for Rome, it might be concluded that their integrity and freedom of action were compromised...a number of ethical tracts...vigorously criticized...the effect of Italian manners and mores. Italian culture and society were said to be debased by papism and court intrigue...Italian influence was seen as corrupting honest English manners, including plainness, sincerity, directness, simplicity and openness. An 'English man Italianated' was putting at risk the authentic moral basis of his gentility....The earl of Cork sent his sons on the standard Continental grand tour in the 1630 and 1640s, while expressing an increasing Protestant wariness about the possibility of infection by the 'Roman disease' (lying)...In much English commentary Italian and French deceitfulness was associated with the Roman Catholic Church..." [81]

Concerning the *Moral Theology* of Liguori, Prof. Meyrick wrote, "It is strange that the courts of justice are what they are in Spain, in Rome, in Naples? Look at the case of witnesses. The distinction between legitimate and non-legitimate interrogation is enough to destroy all hopes of arriving at the truth. If a man is anxious to conceal the truth, he has only to say to himself that the judge is questioning illegitimately, and then he has no obligation to speak the truth."

Since we have conceded that there are Protestant theories countenancing equivocation and mendacity, what is there to distinguish between the two, that of the Romanists and that of the "Reformers"? First, in that there is no Protestant theologian so hallowed and authorized as Liguori, among the pro-equivocation and mental reservation Protestant advocates. Second, while Anglicans invested their monarchs with divine right and absolute or near absolute authority, they were not

---

[81] Steven Shapin, *A Social History of Truth* (1995), pp. 96-98.

viewed in a dogmatic ecclesiastical sense either as "the Vicar of Christ on earth," or infallible interpreters of the Word of God, as is the Pope of Rome. Here is where Protestants differed with Catholics: "...it was very widely understood in sixteenth and seventeenth-century English society that the possession of great power and responsibility might compromise integrity and that places of power were places where truth could thrive only with greatest difficulty. The (English) court was, therefore, the major target of claims that the early modern period was an 'age of dissimulation." [82]

From the Renaissance onward, the Church of Rome promoted a hierarchical reversal of this wisdom which amounted to its overthrow, reverting to the ancient Pharaonic leadership pyramid, where error is believed to be more likely found among the people at the bottom, and truth and rectitude among those at the top. The elite Pharisees of Jerusalem mirrored this Egyptian dichotomy with their disparagement of the lowly Israelite *am ha'aretz* who valued the words of Jesus.

It was Newman's erstwhile friend Lord Acton who famously said, in the wake of the First Vatican Council decree on papal infallibility that "Power corrupts and absolute power corrupts absolutely." Catholics responded that the pope has resorted to "infallible" declarations only sparingly. This may itself be an argument from equivocation since it so blatantly ignores the corollary to papal infallibility—that the Bishop of Rome invested with it is assumed to have a much greater likelihood of inspiration from the Holy Spirit.

It is only very recently, prior to the ascent of Pope Francis, after some of the most appalling outrages committed by Popes Paul VI and "Saint" John Paul II, that one heard Catholics begin to question the pope in any serious manner, and these few were quickly taken to task by the majority. Moreover, it is taught that the Pope is the earthly representative of God Himself, "the Vicar of Christ on earth." From the Renaissance through to the 1960s, the popes of Rome exerted a cult-like hold over Catholics who stood in awe of them as personifications of the teaching authority of God Almighty. To be highly suspicious and wary of the seductive danger posed by the pontiffs' monarchial power in the realm of the spiritual was

---

[82] Shapin, op. cit., p. 100.

regarded as little more than a Protestant heresy. As a result, usury crept up on Catholics unawares. Had not the popes always condemned it? Sodomy in rectories, monasteries and chanceries flourished undetected and unguessed at. Today Catholics attempt to put a start date for the wave of predation against children, claiming that it was a product of the hippie Sixties, or the Second Vatican Council or modernism. Where is there any evidentiary grounds for limiting the child predation epidemic to modern times, or the time during and after Vatican II? In western Montana, in the Diocese of Helena, priests as well as the Ursuline Sisters of the Western Province have been implicated in the molestation of dozens or perhaps even *hundreds* of American Indian children and other youngsters in their care at the Ursuline Academy in St. Ignatius, *dating from the 1940s and the pontificate of Pope Pius XII*. Between 1950 and 2010, almost half—more than forty percent—of all the religious who were members Australia's St. John of God Brothers' Order, were child molesters.

In Catholic Ireland, widespread clerical pederasty and sadism has been found to have occurred *as early as the 1920s*.[83] Why is it difficult to believe that these crimes occurred in "traditional times" when the thought of daring to question the integrity or morality of a "Prince of the Church" was nearly unthinkable? The degree to which Catholics, like Mormons under Joseph Smith, Chinese under Mao Tse Tung or Germans under Adolf Hitler, failed to dispute, question, investigate, overrule and prosecute the criminals among their leaders and rulers, they are complicit in the destruction of the souls of the defenseless molested children of many generations and centuries. The ineluctable product of Alphonsus Liguori's *Moral Theology* of cozening, dissembling and flat-out lying, was the shield it fashioned for guilty perpetrators of molestation and sodomy to outwit both secular authorities and credulous Catholics, so as to remain immune from detection, apprehension and prosecution.

"Traditional" Catholics seek no reform of the Pharaonic model of papal and prelatical power. Rather, they pray for a Right-wing pope after their own liking who would once again

---

[83] Cf. ch. 13 herein, as well as Peter Tyrrell, *Founded on Fear: The Hidden History of a Childhood with the Christian Brothers*, Diarmuid Whelan, ed. (Irish Academic Press, 2006).

wield the absolute dictatorial power of the papacy concentrated in one man, and launch a new inquisition against modernizers and liberals. The terrible potential of frail and fallen human nature—from the occupant of the papal throne on downward, as elucidated in Lord Acton's maxim—to abuse power, would once again be ignored.

These supposed conservatives and traditionalists do not see that *it was papal power that cast aside God's law against the love of money as practiced in the charging of interest on loans*; that *it was papal power that cast aside their beloved Tridentine Mass and sent its worshippers into a liturgical desert.* They do not see that it was *the sovereignty of the pope and the total secrecy by which he and his minions operated, that robbed hundreds of thousands of innocent and largely helpless Catholic souls of their childhoods.*

The continuation of absolute monarchial power in the Bishop of Rome ensures more of the same. The notion that only *after* the Second Vatican Council did the popes work to nullify the Word of God and install the situation ethics that extruded Biblical and Patristic doctrine, ensures more of the same crimes crying unto heaven for vengeance. The continuation of belief in the myth that the Renaissance Church of Rome was the faithful and orthodox representative of the Gospel of Christ until subverted in the eighteenth century by the forces of the Enlightenment and the French Revolution, also guarantees more of the same.

Superiority and inferiority of position, deference and condescension, mastery and subjection, are constituent factors in the system that nurtures the crimes of the papalolaters. Inferiors are not entitled to know the minds of their superiors or the acts of their superiors, much less that of the mind or the hidden deeds of "The Vicar of Christ on earth." This attitude is appropriate to the Egyptians under the Pharaohs, not the followers of Christ who, ultimately, are to be under no one but God, as represented by those men who acknowledge their fallibility and submit to examination and correction by their fellow Christians, and whose rights are seen to be no more nor less than that of any other believer.

The post-Renaissance Catholic Church enshrined as its doctor of moral theology a so-called "saint" who gave permission for theft, under particular conditions. This should not surprise us in the least since the Renaissance and later popes had given permission for interest on loans of money, which was always defined as theft by the true Catholic Church.

Much of the Liguorian *Moral Theology* has striking similarities and parallels with the Babylonian Talmud. For instance, Liguori taught that a servant may steal from his master under the following circumstances: "A servant can, according to his own judgment, compensate himself for his labor if he without doubt judges that he was deserving of a larger stipend. Which indeed appears sufficiently probable to me and to other more modern learned men, if the servant or any other hired person be prudent and capable of forming a correct judgment and be certain concerning the justice of the compensation." [84]

Liguori gives moral consent to aristocrats who steal: "What if a nobleman is very much ashamed to beg or to work, can he provide for himself out of other people's goods?...Viva says yes, and Roncaglia and Mazzotta, as well as Lessius, Palao and Diocastillo in Croix; so do Bannez and Serra. This seems to me to be the 'more probable,' if he is so ashamed of begging he would rather die." (*Theologia Moralis* iv. 520). [85]

"Six times in the course of three pages in his *Homo Apostolicus*, sixteen times in the course of his *Theologia Moralis*, Liguori lays down the principle that, as soon as a man is reduced to extreme necessity, all goods become common and, more than this, that the thief has a right to what belongs to others...The ingenuity which he has contrived to bring the distressed nobleman into the category of those laboring under extreme necessity, is as commendable as the Unjust Steward's own cleverness." [86]

Liguori states, "If a man, on an occasion arising, only steals a little, whether from one or from more, not intending to acquire much himself, nor to do great harm to his neighbor by his several thefts, he does not sin gravely, nor do all these

---

[84] Blakeney, op. cit., pp. 184-186.

[85] Frederick Meyrick, *Moral Theology of the Church of Rome No. III: S. Alfonso de' Liguori's Theory of Theft* (London, 1855), p. 11.

[86] Ibid. For a discussion of the correct understanding of Christ's meaning in the "Parable of the Unjust Steward," and His teaching concerning the "Mammon of Unrighteousness," cf. this writer's *Usury in Christendom*, pp. 53-58.

taken together constitute one mortal sin..." (*Theologia Moralis,* iv. 533).

Liguori decrees that a wife may steal from her husband in matters where "husbands often don't understand and it would be of no use to ask them." According to the "saint," a wife commits no sin in secretly "subtracting" (*subducendo*) from his wealth (*Theologia Moralis,* iv. 541). A son under certain circumstances may steal from his own father (*Theologia Moralis,* iv. 543, and iv. 488.3).

Liguori writes on the subject of a wife who does not pay her dowry to her husband and therefore is rightly reduced by her lawfully wedded husband to the degraded status of a mere servant and nothing more:

"Is the husband bound to keep or support his wife if her dowry has not been paid? The Doctors in common say no, if it is the fault of the promiser that it has not been paid. So Sanchez, Bonacina, Bossius, the Salamanca Doctors, Fagundez, Trulenchius and others, saying that the object of the dowry is that the husband may keep his wife with it. Except, however, 1., if the husband married without a dowry being promised, and, 2., if the wife pays obedience to her husband, for then he is at least bound to keep her as a servant. So say the Salamanca Doctors, with Abbas, Lupo etc. quoted by Sanchez. Sanchez however, with Surdus and others, does not allow the second exception because (as he says) the wife is bound to pay her husband both a dowry and obedience, and therefore it is not necessary for him to maintain her if she only pays obedience. But I rather adhere to the opposite opinion, because the law of nature itself teaches you to keep one who occupies himself in being your servant." (vi. 939).

According to Liguori, a son who curses his father commits only a venial sin. The curse does not become a grave sin unless he actually means the curse to take effect, otherwise, *si oretenus tantum maledixerit,* it is venial (iv. 334). Liguori does not stipulate at how young an age children may curse their parents and still only incur a venial sin.

Another Talmudic example (one may rightly term it demonic), concerns Liguori's aforementioned permission for servants to steal from their masters. As we noted earlier, Innocent XI condemned similar permissions like this. Liguori eats the heart out of the pope's condemnation in a masterful exhibition of exceedingly cunning exceptions which had the effect of nullifying the decree of the Pope. Alphonsus Liguori:

"The Salamanca Doctors and others, speaking of this condemned proposition say, 1. That a servant can *not* afterwards make himself compensation if he makes his bargain freely with his master for a lower sum, without necessity; *but* that he is not forbidden to do so, if he agrees on wages considerably less than are just, from necessity; namely to lighten his own distress. The reason is that Pontifical decrees do not mean to bind a servant contrary to justice." (iv. 522). Neither, it seems, do the decrees of the Ten Commandments, Jesus Christ and the New Testament bind contrary to Liguori's casuistry.

When Frederick Meyrick and his party of English travelers were in Italy seeking lodging, they found a house for rent which suited them well and was priced lower than the other houses that were for let in that particular Italian vicinity. Ignorant of Liguori's compensation principle as elucidated above, they rented the lower-priced accommodation and took up residence. They soon discovered that their personal articles, including clothing, had gone missing. A careful search of the house revealed that their property was hidden in out-of-the-way places throughout the house. Confronting the dishonest landlords, they denied the theft. Meyrick writes, "They knew, from their attendance at the confessional, that household servants might 'compensate' themselves...if they had wages lower than their services deserved, and they knew that tailors, tradesmen etc. were justified in purloining little pieces of cloth, using short measures, etc. 'if they would otherwise make no profits, or if they ought to raise their price and then would find no customers' (Liguori, iv. 533).

"Being gifted with reasoning powers, they inferred that as they had let their apartments at a lower rate than their neighbors, and as they 'ought' to have raised their price, but very likely would not, they thought, having then found lodgers, they were fairly entitled to make up their profits by secret compensation. This they accordingly did..." [87]

Liguori states that "The servant may steal small amounts of food and drink from his master without troubling himself over

---

[87] Meyrick, *Liguori's Theory of Theft,* pp. 38-40.

much on account of it, if the items are not locked up and are not stolen for purposes of re-sale." (iv. 545). Prof. Meyrick: So much for the guileless uprightness and security of any home where reside servants who make confession to confessors who adhere to the theology of Rome's 'Patron Saint of Confessors.' Under Liguori's system and that of his fellow casuists, the wife pilfers from her husband and taking care that he not know of it; servants pilfer to recompense themselves for wages they regard as too low. The name of *home* cannot be applied to places where these dishonest practices are but trifling affairs, except in mockery."

Liguori on restitution: "If the theft is uncertain — i.e. if it is not known who the person is to whom the damage is done — the penitent is to be bound to make restitution for the purpose of having Masses celebrated, or giving alms to the poor, or making gifts to holy places, and, if he is poor himself, *he may apply it to himself, or to his family.* [88]

The Roman Cicero famously expressed his fierce indignation at a brazen swindle that the politically-connected Governor of Sicily, Gaius Verres, arranged through his partner Lucius Rabonius, in order to give *himself* a security deposit that was intended as compensation for damage he caused others: *"Deridet quum sibi ipsum jubet satisdare Rabonium."* [89] Cicero called Gaius Verres the "king of hell." What would Cicero have called a Liguorian Catholic who stole and then made *"restitution"* to himself with his ill-gotten gains, with the approval of one of the highest moral authorities of the Church that bears the name of Rome? [90]

Here we witness the power of criminal politics. Exposure of the criminal ideology of Alphonsus Liguori which brings the Catholic Church into grave disrepute and instructs the

---

[88] *Praxis Confessarii,* Cap. ii. 44, emphasis supplied.

[89] Cicero's Orations Against Gaius Verres, *Actionis Secundae: De Praetura Urbana.*

[90] In his *Oration,* Cicero's case against Verres for extortion, embezzlement, violation of human rights and impiety, represents an intrepid prosecution of a powerful politician who possessed a network of dangerously influential cronies in the judiciary and senate. As the charge of impiety shows, Cicero was a follower of the traditional religion, yet he was also an enemy of criminal politics. On the strength of the truth of Cicero's oratory alone, Verres fled Rome in disgrace.

followers of the Church of Rome on the best methods of lying and thieving within Talmudic-like perimeters, will bring down upon the head, name and reputation of the person exposing Liguori, the most fearsome calumny. This occurred when we published just a few facts about the Italian saint in our *Revisionist History* newsletter. Like Judaics defending a criminal rabbi, we were showered with cries of rage, such as "How dare you besmirch the author of *The Glories of Mary!*" (or with reference to one of the other titles of mystical devotion that the "saint" penned).

"...in *The Glories of Mary* Ligurori peppered the text with spurious quotes and citations, and a heretical theology which teaches that hardened sinners who mumble Hail Marys while half asleep, or wear her scapular while committing crimes of blasphemy and Satan worship, will be preserved from damnation by being given the grace of final repentance. [91] In the first instance, Rev. Meyrick is referring to the following passage from *The Glories of Mary*:

"It is the opinion of many theologians and of S. Thomas in particular, that for many who have died in mortal sin the Divine Mother has obtained from God a suspension of their sentence...Trustworthy authors give us many instances in which this has occurred...the Divine Mother has been able to deliver from hell even some who have died in sin...

"In the year 1604, in a city in Flanders, there were two young men, students who, instead of attending to their studies, gave themselves up to a life of debauchery. One night they were both in a house with an evil companion, when one of them, named Richard returned home, leaving his companion there. After he got home, and had begun to undress, he remembered that he had not that day said some 'Hail Marys' that he was in the habit of reciting. Feeling very sleepy he was loath to say them; he did himself violence and repeated them, though without devotion, and half asleep.

"He then laid down, and had fallen into a sound slumber, when he was suddenly roused by a violent knocking at the

---

[91]Meyrick, "St. Alphonsus de' Liguori's 'Glories of Mary," *Christian Remembrancer,* October, 1855, in *The Christian Remembrancer*, Vol. 30 (London, 1855), pp. 417-467.

door, and without its opening he saw his companion deformed and hideous standing before him. 'Who art thou?' he cried out. 'What! Dost thou not know me?' 'Ah! yes, but how thou art changed; thou seemest to me a devil.' 'Truly,' he exclaimed, 'poor creature that I am, I am damned, and how? When I was leaving that wicked house a devil came and strangled me: my body is in the street, and my soul is in hell; and thou must know,' added he, 'that the same fate awaited thee had not the Blessed Virgin preserved thee in consideration of that little act of homage of the 'Hail Mary.'...With these words he opened his mantle, and showing the flames and serpents by which he was tormented, he disappeared." [92]

Liguori's iniquitous theology does not register with his followers. We observed a similar phenomenon in the matter of the child molestation facilitator Cardinal Castrillon Hoyos, a strong proponent of the Tridentine Mass, who wrote a letter to Bishop Pierre Pican, bishop of Bayeux-Lisieux in France, congratulating him on shielding a molester-priest, Father René Bissey, from the police. Father René Bissey was guilty of raping minors. According to Vatican analyst Jean-Marie Guenois, the Congregation for the Clergy, under Cardinal Hoyos, argued for protective treatment of accused molesters.[93] After his criminal cheerleading for Bishop Pican was published and made known to the world, as far as we could detect it detracted not one iota from the illustrious standing of Cardinal Hoyos among "traditional Catholics." We have preserved the record of the numerous "traditional Catholic" media outlets, some internationally renowned, which had nothing meaningful to say concerning Hoyos' letter to the bishop, while continuing to celebrate him as a bastion of fidelity to "traditional Catholicism," which can only signify that one of the "traditions"

---

[92] *The Glories of Mary Translated from the Italian of St. Alphonsus de' Liguori by A Father of the Same Congregation* (Redemptorist Fathers, 1852), pp. 188-189; 190-191.

[93] Jean-Marie Guenois: http://blog.lefigaro.fr/religioblog/2010/04/le-poids-dune-larme.html?xtor=RSS-59 (April 22, 2010). "Castrillon pressured Bishop Manuel Moreno, who was bishop of Tucson, Arizona from 1982-2003, to allow a priest sex abuser to take a pension and work outside the diocese. Fr Robert Trupia 'sexually abused dozens of minor boys' before he was defrocked in 2004, according to documents in a civil case." Jason Berry, *National Catholic Reporter*, April 22, 2010.

of "Catholicism" is the facilitation of child molestation. What counted in the eyes of those many persons who dare to self-describe themselves as "traditional Catholics" was Hoyos' devotion to an ancient rite of worship; clouds of incense serving to obscure (or minimize) the molestation of children.

A similar absolution for the prelate who grants freedom to ceremony while committing heresy is the "traditional" Catholic nostalgia for Pope Benedict XVI after he abdicated. We are here tracking criminal politics. With the Word of God as our guide, we mark the love of money as manifested in rule by the Money Power as the root of all other crime, after which we acknowledge Jesus Christ's cosmic battle with the God-defying, Scripture nullifying "Scribes and Pharisees" as having established the nature and identity of His principal enemies. In the matter of Benedict XVI, he is culpable for supporting rule by the Money Power through the permission for usury and "Catholic" usurers, which he continued as part of the dreadful legacy of his predecessors. On the second count he continued the abominable practice of Pope "Saint" John Paul II of entering synagogues in order to win the favor of the Christ-deniers within its walls, and failing to contend with them for the faith. Let us compare the behavior of Pope Benedict XVI with St. Paul:

"Every sabbath he held a disputation in the synagogue, trying to convince both Jews and Greeks by confronting them with the name of the Lord Jesus. Just at the time when Silas and Timothy arrived from Macedonia, Paul was much occupied with preaching, while he bore witness to the Jews that Jesus was the Christ. But they set their faces against it and talked blasphemy, until he shook the dust out of his garments, and said to them, Your blood be upon your own heads; I am clear of it....he spared no pains to refute the Jews publicly, proving from the scriptures that Jesus was the Christ." [94]

When did Pope Benedict have a *disputation* in the synagogue(s) he entered and prayed within? When did Pope Benedict in the synagogue "bear witness to the Jews that Jesus was the Christ" and without Him they were lost? When did Pope Benedict "spare no pains to refute the Jews publicly"?

He did nothing of the kind. Quite the contrary, he betrayed our Lord Jesus Christ by confirming the unbelieving people in

---

[94] Acts 18: 4-6; 28. Ronald Knox translation.

the synagogue, in their sins and blasphemy by upholding, through his presence and his weasel words, Pope "Saint" John Paul II's disastrous "elder brothers in the Faith" theology. What is the "traditional" Catholic response to Pope Benedict XVI, whose burlesque of the Christian witness and mission of Jesus Himself classes him as a turncoat? From a leading "traditional" Catholic pundit on the "Benedictine Respite":

"During the seven-year Benedictine Respite, the post-conciliar revolution in the Church seemed to have lost its momentum, even if it was far from being in retreat. Traditional Catholics rejoiced to see a series of papal acts favorable to Tradition: the promulgation of *Summorum Pontificum* (2007), bringing an end at last to the insane suppression of the traditional Roman Rite...and the long-overdue correction of the errant, doctrinally defective translations of the Latin typical edition of the Novus Ordo Missal...Also cause for rejoicing was Benedict's return to dignity and decorum in the papacy as befits the august Vicar of Christ...Pope Benedict returned to the line of his preconciliar predecessors, issuing prophetic warnings...In his Address to the Parish Priests and Clergy of Rome on February 14, 2013, given on the heels of his staggering announcement that he was abdicating the papacy, Benedict...conceded what traditionalists have been contending since the post-conciliar crisis began: that the entire program of 'updating' the Church in the name of the Council had been a disaster...during the Benedictine Respite the revolution did seem to lose momentum, while a Latin Mass revival was gaining momentum all over the world...With Pope Benedict's abdication, however, the promising signs of renewal during the Respite were soon overshadowed..." [95]

Too often — *far too often* — the devil uses the human fascination with pietism, ceremonies, long robes (*"cappa magna"*), bells, chants, incense, candles and all the outward signs of antiquarian devotion, as a substitute of that for which there is no substitute, *obedience to the law of God.* When an agent of the devil advocates for pious customs and venerable, Latin-rite traditions and is then seen to defend them, that is all

---

95   *The Remnant* ("A National Catholic Bi-Weekly based in St. Paul, Minnesota"), May 20, 2014, pp. 1 and 8.

that most "conservatives" and "traditionalists" need to know. It is the ceremony, the outward show, the deceptive theatricals, that register as sure signs of Christian faith in the eyes of these deluded persons. The Cryptocracy has used "traditional" Catholicism with as much effectiveness and potency as it has exploited Liberalism, to obstruct God's will being done on earth. In fact, one might go so far as to venture to say that it has wrought more damage through "traditional" Catholics, because of the pharisaical pride of many within this movement, who regard themselves as infinitely morally superior to a Liberal; and, due to the stealth by which the beautiful, outward trappings of "traditional" Catholicism have served to conceal the horribly disfigured and deceitful theology which "Popes and Saints" of the ilk of John Paul II, Benedict XVI and Alphonsus Liguori have injected into the bowels of the Church of Rome.

In Benedict XVI's case we see that one can be both a Judaizer and "the august Vicar of Christ," he who personifies "dignity and decorum in the papacy" (inside a synagogue); a pontiff "opposed to the updating of the Church," who caused "the revolution to lose momentum," yet who also de facto canonized Judaism's post-modernist "Shoah" theology of Holocaustianity, suspended the evangelization of the Jews and buttressed the synagogue system of the rabbis as a legitimate forum for the worship of God without Christ. Ah, but he advanced the Latin language, the Latin Mass, the smells, the bells and "the decorum." Obviously the aesthetic's the thing. Here we have the "theology" of the interior designer and the hairdresser.

The legacy of Romanist equivocation, and of Liguorianism, is a mental fog that seeps into the mind like gas under a door, emitted by an ecclesiastical milieu that is permeated with it from the Confessional to the court— the *il fumo di Satana* revealed by Pope Paul VI; the reason why so many Catholics cannot think straight concerning these issues; why they prefer image to reality, and "rejoice" over a Judas pope who they consider "favorable to *Tradition*." When one sees this reference to a "Tradition" one is reminded of that *"Faith"* in which John Paul II situated the "Jews" as our "elder brothers." The question arises, whose Tradition is being referred to here, and *which Faith is it in which the "Jews" are our elders?* Collaborating with the deniers of Christ is not a tradition of the ancient Catholic Church. *The Faith wherein faithless Jews are the elders cannot be the Christian Faith* (1 John 2: 22-23). The Faith of Antichrist cannot be "our" Faith.

The "Tradition" of placing denial of Auschwitz gassings on a vastly higher plane of cosmic transgression than denial of the Resurrection of the Son of God, as Pope Benedict's Vatican Secretariat of State did when it suspended the episcopal functions of Bishop Richard Williamson for questioning the existence of homicidal gas chambers in Auschwitz-Birkenau, had no precedent beyond the papacy of John Paul II; if it is a "Tradition" it has been observed heretofore only in hell.

"Saint" Alphonsus Liguori on Contraception

Two thousand years ago the attitude of servile obedience represented by clericalism and immersion in priestcraft was the mental attitude that kept the Jewish people away from Jesus Christ, who had been branded an *apikoros* (wicked rebel against the *Torah SheBeal Peh* oral law). Whoever followed Christ when He walked on earth had to be an independent thinker free of the religious authority that controlled the Temple and had condemned Him. But "traditional" Catholics" don't question the pieties, legends and lies that came before Vatican Council II on the part of saints and popes labeled conservative. Liguori is part of that pantheon.

Right to life activists in the Church of Rome have campaigned since the 1960s against the relaxed attitude in the Confessional toward husbands and wives who practice artificial contraception. To be fair it must be admitted that Pope Paul VI promulgated a traditional Catholic teaching on this subject, *Humane Vitae*. His teaching was firmly supported by the hierarchy of American bishops, [96] *but it was defeated in the Confessional.* Newman and other apologists for Liguori's Machiavellianism allege that we should look to the Council of Trent for Catholic theology and not in Liguori's *Moral Theology* which, they say, was intended as a guide for confessors and pastors. Even if this assertion were true, it is a patently foolish one. Theology is an academic exercise if it does not serve as a rule of life for the Catholic. The Church's teaching on contraception was undermined and then subverted not by some abstract theological treatise issued by an ivory tower dissident.

---

[96] *Human Life in Our Day: A Collective Pastoral Letter of the American Hierarchy* (Washington D.C: United States Catholic Conference, 1968).

It was overthrown in the Confessional. Many Catholics will be appalled to learn that in the 1700s, *long before Vatican Council II or the modernism condemned by Pope St. Pius X, subtle moral vagaries amounting to tacit permission for birth control were put forth by "Saint" Alphonsus.* This fact is known to the Charles Currans of the Church of Rome but not to the lay people in the pews. Who has conspired to keep the laity in the dark?

Liguori is the ultimate author of the nullification of the laws against contraception. Why wouldn't modernists follow his lead when he was cited by Pope Pius XII a few years before the onset of the Second Vatican Council as the supreme clerical authority on the shepherding of the conscience of penitents? Imagine the smirks of the modernist theologians when "traditional" Catholics charge them with heresy for permitting artificial birth control. Gales of clandestine laughter must surely be the response in the chanceries of the dioceses. "Your own patron Saint Liguori is the author of our innovations!" is very likely the private thought of the liberal prelatical insiders and theologians that causes them so much mirth in the face of the pitifully gullible "traditionalists" who imagine they fight for Christ while following Liguori. Once again we observe that "traditional" Catholics, burdened with ignorance and a terminal case of the double mind, are hopelessly outclassed by their enemies.

"In Liguori the decline of the old Augustinian position on non-procreative intercourse is evident. As he customarily did in his *Moral Theology*, he used as his text the seventeenth-century German Jesuit, Herman Busenbaum (1600-1668), and he quoted Busenbaum's opinion that there is no sin in intercourse 'to avoid danger of incontinence in oneself or one's partner." [97]

"In the Augustinian tradition the norm of the actual openness of sexual intercourse to creation was an absolute norm...St. Alphonsus Liguori taught that even in questions of the natural law there is room for *epikeia*[98]...he applies the

---

[97]   John T. Noonan Jr., *Contraception: A History of its Treatment by the Catholic Theologians and Canonists*, p. 320.

[98]   *Theologia moralis* 1: I: tr. II,c. IV, n. 201.

possibility of *epikeia* explicitly to *coitus interruptus,* [99] which at that time was the only...method of birth control, and the cooperation of the wife who knows her husband is going to use this method...he explicitly mentions cases in which couples have good reason to want the marriage act not to lead to conception...such refinements of moral theology...justify the refusal of the faithful in their perceived circumstances to follow *Humanae Vitae...*" [100]

Liguori advised confessors to permit birth control for some married couples in certain cases: "Ligouri proposed this course of action. If a priest thought that the penitent, *after* being informed of the sinfulness of coitus interruptus, *still might not cease* performing that act, then the priest was not to disturb the conscience of the penitent. The confessor should not put his penitent 'in bad faith." [101]

There will be diehards who, even after acknowledging the probable veracity of our documentation concerning Liguori, will nevertheless insist that by disclosing his teaching we have irreparably harmed the reputation of a saint of the Catholic Church, and therefore of the Church itself.

We reply that it was not the Catholic Church that canonized this scoundrel in 1839. It was the post-Renaissance, Neoplatonic-Hermetic-Kabbalistic Church of Rome that did so, led by the thieves who stole the holy name of Catholic and appended it, *mala fide*, to their robber Church.

We further reply that the name and reputation of the Catholic Church is degraded and soiled not by truth-divulgers, but by those "Holy Fathers," and prelatical "Eminences" and "Excellencies" who maintain that Alphonsus Liguori is an authentic saint of the One, Holy, Catholic and Apostolic Church, and that his doctrines are free of error.

---

[99] *Coitus Interruptus* = the sin of Onan (onanism); always proscribed by the Catholic Church prior to theologians such as Liguori.

[100] Mark MacGuigan, *Abortion, Conscience and Democracy* (1994), p. 30.

[101] Liguori, "Opera Moralia" IV, Book 1, numbers 4 and 5 in *Theologia Moralis* (Graz, 1954); and Robert Obach, *The Catholic Church on Marital Intercourse*, (2009), p. 115.

The Irrational Principle in Orthodox Judaic
Hermeneutics and the Church of Rome's Probabilism

Though it would require an additional volume to document all of the correspondences between rabbinic-Talmudic-Zoharic theology and the theology of the Church of Rome, at least one of these parallels is worth noting here.

A hermeneutic principle of Orthodox Judaism employed for allegedly divining the authentic meaning of the Old Testament, is termed *Gezara shava*, by which two Scripture passages often having nothing more in common than a single, inconsequential word, are said to be inter-dependent and linked by a common significance. [102] So that, for example, the word "guilty" in Deuteronomy 25:2 is linked by the rabbis to the same word occurring in Numbers 35:31, in support of expanding the passage in Deuteronomy concerning corporal punishment, to include capital punishment, which is, quite frankly, incoherent and demented, since there is no connection between the two citations, except that both are the word of God.

In the Church of Rome's Probabilism, as we have seen it employed, where two conflicting theological views are advanced, the perspective that has the least amount of support in the Bible, and was thus the least "probable," could indeed be accepted as grounds for Catholic judgment, direction, and action.

Each of these methodologies is clearly irrational, yet each enjoys acceptance from among some of the most esteemed and authoritative theologians in both religious traditions. Some will say that this is a coincidence. In fact, it is one among many instances in which the Satanically deranged Talmudic and Kabbalistic mentality is mirrored in Rome's own Renaissance and post-Renaissance theology.

---

[102] For more on *Gezara shava*, cf. *Judaism Discovered*, pp. 170-171.

Chapter XIII

Ecclesiastical Sodomy and its Root

"...the history of the church has shown this vice to be a
peculiarly clerical 'contagion...'" [1]

Rome's reliance on secrecy has been nearly total. Together
with clericalism it is the engine of its pandemic plague of child
molestation. Secrecy confers on clerics—who are revered as
persons possessed of sacred faculties (priesthood) and
miraculous powers (transubstantiation)—power over laymen
and their children. As Richard Seymour has written, "I don't
accept the explanations of child rape within the Catholic
church which attribute it to Catholic practices producing
sexual repression—as if were priests allowed to marry, they
would not be tempted to abuse boys from the laity...I doubt that
it (celibacy) produces predatory child rapists. *The rape of
children typically takes place in institutions and situations
where adults have too much unaccountable power over
children.*"

From whence does this immunity, this freedom from
accountability arise? The founder of the Jesuits, Ignatius of
Loyola, wrote, "Rules for Thinking with the Church." These
appear in his *Spiritual Exercises* of 1548, which remain in use
around the world. Loyola's "Rule 10" counsels secrecy with
regard to sins and crimes perpetrated by clerics:

"To be eager to commend the decrees, mandates, traditions,
rites and customs of the Fathers in the Faith or our superiors.
As to their conduct; although there may not always be the
uprightness of conduct that there ought to be, yet to attack or
revile them in private or in public tends to scandal and
disorder. Such attacks set the people against their princes and
pastors; we must avoid such reproaches and never attack
superiors before inferiors."

"*Never attack superiors before inferiors.*" There has seldom
been a more pithy summation of the occult command system.

---

[1] Mark D. Jordan, *The Invention of Sodomy in Christian Theology*, p. 154.

This Jesuit clericalism permitted molesters of children who were priests, bishops or cardinals to be protected from exposure in front of "inferiors" (the laity). The prime mandate is to protect *"princes and pastors"* from being *"attacked."* Their victims are not even mentioned. This was *taught in "the good old traditional Church" in 1548, not 1968.*

Beginning in the 1990s we learned of widespread molestations of children by priests and monks of the Church of Rome, facilitated by bishops, cardinals and popes such as "Saint" John-Paul II, for the main purpose of protecting Rome's institutional reputation and global financial operations, as well as the "sacred person" of individual priests who are taught in traditional seminaries the Kabbalistic heresy that the souls of priests are of a higher order than that of the laity, contravening the anti-Kabbalist teaching of Jesus Christ (Matthew 20:24-26).

The laity who believe that they are of a lower order of humanity compared with the ordained priest, embrace clericalism, deferring to priests in the craven manner observed in many Latino and Oriental nations, as well as among the post-modernist churchlings termed (ironically and falsely) "traditional Catholics." *This deference has been a contributing factor in the virulence of criminal child molestation*: as "Saint" Ignatius of Loyola stipulated, "Father" must be protected at all costs, including suppression of police and media investigations. Here we observe parallels with rabbinic doctrine concerning informants. In Orthodox Judaism, those who turn a molester-rabbi over to the police are *"mosers"* (an informer, denunciator; synonyms are *"masor, mesirah"*). According to the *Jewish Encyclopedia* (1906), "Nothing was more severely punished by the Jews...the sages of the Talmud compared the '*moser*' to a serpent."

The *systematic molestation of children by priests* occurred at least *nine hundred years before the Second Vatican Council*. The most stirring protest and exposé of homosexual predators in clerical ranks was registered by a medieval Benedictine monk and saint, Peter Damian (1007-1072), in his Letter XXXI, *Liber Gomorrhianus* ("Book of Gomorrah"), addressed to Pope

Leo IX in 1049,[2] wherein he refers to "improper leniency on the part of prelates" toward sodomite Catholic priests. Later it was suppressed: "He wrote a scathing tract against homosexual practices that Pope Alexander II (1061-1073) discretely locked up."[3]

St. Peter Damian had long served as prior of the hermitage of Fonte Avellana near Gubbio, while Leo had been bishop of Toul for about two decades before his election to the papacy early in 1049. This pope was a sleuth in matters of clerical sexual corruption, outlining in his biography of St. Romuald of Revenna written circa 1042, how homosexual priests and monks intimidated other clerics from exposing them by claiming the accusers were also guilty of the sin, and bringing trumped up charges against them.

According to St. Peter Damian, St. Romuald "himself used to say that he knew that this kind of thing went on in the hermitage he had just left..."[4] The uncensored edition of St. Peter's singular Latin text is in print in an accurate English

---

[2] St Peter Damian, "The Letters of Peter Damian," (Letter 31), in *The Fathers of the Church: Medieval Continuation*, transl. Owen J. Blum, O.F.M.(1990). Leo IX responded to Damian's *Liber Gomorrhianus* with his own *Ad splendidum nitentis*, excommunicating priests and prelates who engaged in sodomy in the form of anal sex: "...there may be no hope of recovering their rank for those who are tainted with...what is horrible to mention as well as to hear—who have fallen into anal relations." Leo's excommunication of anal sodomite priests and prelates is cited in Catholic University of America Professor Uta-Renate Blumenthal's work, *Papal Reform and Canon Law in the 11th and 12th Centuries* (1998). The excommunication was presumably issued at the 1049 Council of Reims.

[3] Robert Hale, "St. Peter Damian" in *Encyclopedia of Monasticism* (2000), p. 357.

[4] *American Historical Review*, February, 2013, p. 234. Leo IX seems to have been a sincere campaigner against simony (the sale of ecclesiastic offices). It was on his watch that the Eastern Church at Constantinople was lost to Rome. For an account of the bungling in this regard cf. John Julius Norwich, *Absolute Monarchs* (2011), 97-99.

translation by Owen Blum. [5] Pierre S. Payer assesses its rarity as "an indispensable work...the only extended, serious treatment of the subject in the formative period of the Christian West." [6]

St. Peter Damian did not address this sin against nature as a theoretical exercise. He well understood that celibate males living in close proximity and isolated must be vigilant. It would be wrong to say that by their living circumstances alone they are "prone" to sodomy, as some Protestants assert in intemperate agitation against "monkery" (monastic life), which are in fact indirect aspersions on Christ and the Apostle Paul and other holy persons who took upon themselves the honorable vocation of a single, unmarried life. It cannot be said that the condition among Christian brethren of celibate group life is *ipso facto* homo-erotic or homosexual. However, complacency is the other extreme failing in assessing this state in life, and where a "Yes, Your Lordship!" hierarchy of inferiors/superiors is in place, together with clerical secrecy, there are always grounds for concern and watchfulness without which, "the wantonness of the foul impurity" will "spread unpunished" unless "repelled by proper repressive action of apostolic severity..." [7]

Writing in the eleventh century, St. Peter Damian, in line with Biblical, Apostolic and Patristic doctrine stated: 1. Definition: Clerical sodomites are members of a "Satanic tyranny."

2. Prevalence: "the cancer of sodomy is, in fact, spreading through the clergy like a savage beast...raging with shameless abandon through the flock of Christ." St. Peter understood that it was so virulent in the eleventh century that:

---

[5] An earlier translation is by P.S. Payer, *Peter Damian: Book of Gomorrah, An Eleventh-Century Treatise Against Clerical Homosexuality* (1982). The Payer volume is a censored edition and is not recommended, except, as it so happens, for Payer's invaluable introduction (also cf. Payer's 1985 study, *Sex and the Penitentials: Formation of a Sexual Code 550-1150*). Two pro-"gay" treatises nevertheless offer a wealth of documentation, despite the extent to which their interpretations elide traditional morality: Derrick Sherwin Bailey's *Homosexuality and the Western Christian Tradition* (1975), and Louis Crompton's *Homosexuality and Civilization* (2006).

[6] *Peter Damian: Book of Gomorrah*, p. 5.

[7] St. Peter Damian, *The Fathers of the Church*, op. cit., p. 4.

"Unless immediate effort be exerted by the Apostolic See, there is little doubt that, even if one wished to curb this unbridled evil, he could not check the momentum of its progress." [8]

St. Peter was writing in a conservative age when there was no "gay" rights movement, no pornography industry and no doctrinal dilution of the ancient Biblical law concerning the sin of Sodom, and yet sodomy among the clergy was "raging with shameless abandon through the flock." Since this was an epidemic in the Middle Ages, an age that was exponentially light years ahead of our time in terms of recognizing and enforcing right-and-wrong, it is not far off the mark to perceive that where special powers and immunities are granted to clerics within a milieu of secrecy, sodomy among single, unmarried men living in close quarters is a constant threat. St. Peter writes of a priest who "known to have committed this sin with eight or ten equally foul companions is still permitted to continue in his rank." [9]

One section of St. Peter Damian's Letter 31 is devoted to "Bishops who practice impure acts with their spiritual sons." He writes, "Who can expect the flock to prosper when its shepherd has sunk so deep into the bowels of the devil? What man will continue to be under his authority...?"

In the 21st century we have many such bishops in the Church of Rome. Because of clerical secrecy we do not know who among them are active practitioners of sodomy, but we know who among the hierarchy are recruiters for the seducers. A few examples:

•Chicago Archbishop Blase Cupich who, when Bishop of Spokane, Washington permitted homosexual dances held by the "gay" students' club in Cataldo Hall on the campus of Jesuit Gonzaga University. (Cupich was elevated to the rank of cardinal by Pope Francis in November, 2016).

•Cardinal Godfried Danneels who, in 2013 referred to the "marriage" of sodomites as a "positive development." Cardinal Danneels was recorded urging a 13-year-old male victim of

---

[8] Damian, ibid., p. 6.

[9] Ibid., pp. 7-8.

sexual abuse at the hands of his friend and colleague Bishop Roger Vangheluwe, not to go to the police.

•Cardinal Timothy Michael Dolan, the archbishop of New York, who led the 2015 St. Patrick's Day parade as grand marshal after praising as a "wise one" the parade organizers' decision to allow right-to-sodomy groups to march in the event.

•Archbishop Bruno Forte, of the diocese of Chieti-Vasto, Italy, who drafted the homosexuality section of the midterm report of the 2014 Synod on the Family that spoke of "accepting and valuing ['gay'] sexual orientation." When questioned about his declaration, Archbishop Forte stated that sexually active homosexuals have "rights that should be protected," calling unions of sodomites an "issue of respect," and stating: "...connected to homosexual unions it has to be noted that there are cases in which mutual aid to the point of sacrifice constitutes a precious support in the life of the partners." (*Relatio post disceptationem*, Oct. 13, 2014).

•Cardinal Angelo Sodano, the dean of the Vatican's College of Cardinals, attempted to halt investigations into sex crimes committed by Fr. Marcial Maciel Degollado, the wealthy founder of the Legionaries of Christ.

•Cardinal Raymundo Damasceno Assis, the archbishop of Aparecida, Brazil, and president of Brazil's National Conference of Bishops, who praised the "softer and tolerant rhetoric of Francis, especially regarding homosexuality."

•Pope Francis, the "Vicar of Christ," on earth stated, concerning homosexuality, "Who am I to judge?" ("Pope Says He Will Not Judge Gay Priests," *NY Times* [online], July 29, 2013). Yet, on January 20, 2017 in an interview with the Spanish newspaper *El Pais*, he was asked, "Trump is just now being sworn in as president of the United States...What do you make of it?" Francis answered, "We will see what he does and will *judge accordingly.*" [10]

• Cardinal Desmond Connell (1926-2017) was educated by the Jesuits at Belvedere College in Dublin and attended Clonliffe College, Dublin's diocesan seminary. He was ordained in 1951 and earned a doctorate in philosophy at University College, Dublin.

---

[10] Cf. http://elpais.com/elpais/2017/01/21/inenglish/1485026427_223988.html (emphasis supplied).

Connell became a professor of general metaphysics and dean of the philosophy faculty there. Pope "Saint" John-Paul II appointed the "conservative Catholic scholar" Archbishop of Dublin in 1988.

Connell was a facilitator of child molestation in his archdiocese. The crimes first began to emerge after the Rev. Brendan Smyth, a Northern Irish priest, was convicted of child sex abuse in 1994. The next year Archbishop Connell denied that the archdiocese had paid compensation to victims of abuse by its priests. But in 1998, it emerged that he had quietly lent archdiocesan money to an abusive priest, the Rev. Ivan Payne, who then paid an abuse survivor, Andrew Madden. Three years later Pope "Saint" John Paul II elevated Connell to the rank of Cardinal.

In 2002, the Irish national television network RTE broadcast "Cardinal Secrets," a report by the investigative journalist Mary Raftery exposing the archdiocese's protection of eight priests who had sexually abused children. An independent commission was established to investigate the archdiocese's handling of 325 claims of child molestation.

Cardinal Connell mounted a High Court challenge to block the inquiry from gaining access to 5,500 files on priests and molestation allegations. He secured a temporary injunction, before withdrawing his action later amid public outrage.

After retiring in 2004, Connell lived in comfort, provided by the Church. He was never prosecuted.

In 2009 the government of Ireland mounted a commission of inquiry led by Judge Yvonne Murphy, which resulted in the 2009 Murphy Report. "The Dublin Archdiocese's preoccupations in dealing with cases of child sexual abuse, at least until the mid-1990s, were the maintenance of secrecy, the avoidance of scandal, the protection of the reputation of the church and the preservation of its assets," the commission found. "All other considerations, including the welfare of children and justice for victims, were subordinated to these priorities."

Cardinal Connell's remains were on display in state at St Mary's Pro-Cathedral, Dublin February 23rd-Feb. 24, 2017. Accompanying two archbishops in receiving the remains at the pro-cathedral were Bishop Walsh, and fellow Auxiliary Bishop of Dublin Ray Field, Bishop of Clonfert John Kirby, Vicar General in Dublin Msgr Paul Callan, Fr Damian McNeice who worked as spokesman for Cardinal Connell, and Canon Damian O'Reilly, administrator at the pro-cathedral. In the eulogy, Bishop of Dublin Eamonn Walsh spoke of the late cardinal's "deep, deep faith" his gifts "as a philosopher, historian and lover of classical music." Internment was in the crypt of the cathedral.

The Murphy Report revealed that four archbishops in Dublin – John Charles McQuaid, who died in 1973, Dermot Ryan, who died in 1984, Kevin McNamara, who died in 1987, and retired Cardinal Connell – failed to report their knowledge of child sexual abuse to the Garda (Irish Police), from the 1960s to the 1980s. The report, launched by the Irish Attorney General Dermot Ahern, also concluded that the vast majority of priests and bishops turned a "blind eye" to abuse. One priest was found to have abused more than one hundred children. Another confessed under questioning that he had committed abuse every two weeks for more than 25 years.

The Commission's investigation disclosed that senior members of the Irish police regarded priests as being outside their investigative jurisdiction. The relationship between some senior police officers and priests and bishops was labeled a criminal coverup of "dreadful crimes." The Murphy Report stated that rather than investigate complaints from children, the police simply reported the matter to the Dublin Catholic diocese, and that the structures and rules of the Church facilitated the conspiracy. It found that government officials participated in the cover-up by allowing the Church to exist beyond the reach of the law.

His critics believed that Cardinal Connell had a talent for equivocation. For example, he initially denied using diocesan funds to compensate victims—but later said he had used the present tense to say that payments were not being made at that moment. He had not said that payments had not been made in the past.

Some contemporary Catholics imagine that these facilitators, apologists and recruiters for homosexuality are mostly a product of the 1960s. Actually, the contemporary "gay" rights sympathizers are emboldened by the knowledge of the clandestine chronicle of homosexual practices and predation in the Catholic Church *extending back more than a thousand years* to those supposed halcyon "traditional Catholic" times, when bishops, cardinals and popes were costumed in elaborate lace, gowns and similar effeminate attire and paraphernalia resembling the outfit of a female impersonator.

Who was there to protest when one or more of these "princes of the church" quietly selected a young Catholic male for a night of sodomy from among the ranks of those boys who had been accepted at puberty to enter pre-seminary facilities, and who grew up to be monks, friars and priests without any experience of women, or of any world other than the all-male clerical preserve? How would these activities leak out when the reputation of the prelate was held to be of greater importance than God's justice and divine law?

Child Oblation

"In the early Middle Ages, the practice known as child oblation had been common in Benedictine monasteries in western Europe for six hundred years. Oblation, which properly means the giving of a child in permanent (irrevocable) gift to a monastic community, could provide vicariously for the donors' own spiritual welfare...by the beginning of the seventh century both ecclesiastical and secular law in Europe stipulated that children given in infancy were not to leave the cloister in maturity." [11]

According to historian Sarah Foot, the scripture text quoted to justify the practice of a child's involuntary lifetime obligation to a monastery was I Samuel: the dedication in the Temple "of the infant Samuel to the priesthood soon after his birth." Of course, the ancient temple of Israel was not a cloistered monastery. In 726 Pope Gregory II ruled that a child-oblate was effectively a slave, bound for life. Neither departure nor marriage was permitted to the oblate, even after reaching adulthood: "This we absolutely forbid, since it is an impious

---

[11] Cf. Sarah Foot, *Monastic Life in Anglo-Saxon England*, c. 600-900, p. 141. On the practice of child oblation cf. Patricia A. Quinn, *Better Than the Sons of Kings: Boys and Monks in the Early Middle Ages* (1989), and Mayke De Jong, *In Samuel's Image: Child Oblation in the Early Medieval West* (1996). De Jong argues that parents viewed their oblate children as a *holocaustum,* a sacrifice wholly consumed by fire, i.e. completely given to God. De Jong argues against John Boswell's abandonment thesis in his book, *The Kindness of Strangers* (1989), as well as the common idea that oblates were a family's supernumerary offspring. The most famous bound-for-life English oblate was Venerable Bede.

thing that the restraints of desire should be relaxed for children given to God." [12]

"Children as young as five would be placed in cloistered communities...But by the twelfth century...the tide was turning and the practice of oblation became much less common. Part of the problem may have been that sexual relations were taking place between boys and monks...In England, the *Regularis concordia*, a code of monastic observance approved by the Synod of Winchester ca. 970-973, had ruled against physical contact between older and younger monks..." [13]

"In the monastery moreover let neither monks nor abbott embrace or kiss, as it were, youths or boys (*adolescents uel puerulos*); let their affection for them be spiritual, let them keep from words of flattery, and let them love the children reverently and with the greatest circumspection. Not even on the excuse of some spiritual matter shall any monk presume to take with him a young boy alone for any private purpose but, as the Rule commands, let the boys always remain under the care of their master." [14] This was "a statement echoing earlier warnings against the temptations offered by the residence of young males in monastic environments: *De renuntiatione saeculi* attributed to Basil the Great (ca. 330-79) and remarks by Pope Gregory III (690-731) on sodomitic practices among the ordained..." [15]

Another grave threat to the modesty of boys in the care of clergy or prelates: an offending pontiff, cardinal, bishop or abbott had the power to absolve the one he seduced (or raped) of the sin of passive cooperation with sodomy, just as a co-conspirator among the hierarchy could immunize the man who was the active sodomite: the prelate himself. This was a common tactic in 1049, as St. Peter Damian testified:

---

[12] Sarah Foot, ibid., p. 142. Gregory II was in this respect abrogating the Rule of St. Benedict as well as St. Basil's teaching. Benedict required consent from a self-determining adolescent. Basil specified the age of consent at 16 or 17 years.

[13] *Regularis concordia Anglicae nationis monachorum sanctimonialiumque*, 7-8.

[14] Robert Mills, *Seeing Sodomy in the Middle Ages* (2015), pp. 215-216 and 339. Mills cites Payer's bowdlerized text of Damian's letter 31.

[15] Mills, ibid.

"...some of those who were shot through with the poison of this crime, when their conscience began to trouble them, confess to one another...they themselves become judges and each happily grants to the other blanket forgiveness that he aspires to acquire for himself." [16]

In this explication of sodomite priests confessing to other sodomite priests there is an intimation of a network of sodomites. This network would seem to extend beyond circles of individual priests to the principal authors of ecclesiastical laws. Some canon laws at the time of Damian were written and published for the purpose of enacting leniency for clerics engaged in sodomy. The saint exposes these: he cites canon laws that permit priests to be punished lightly and laymen to be punished more stringently for the same sodomite crimes. [17]Here again we encounter the clandestine Church of Rome doctrine of two types of souls, that of the higher dimension-soul of the priest (in Judaism: *"ruchniyus"*); and that of the layman, which is the equivalent to the Pharisaic doctrine of *shnei minim nifradim,* regarding the superiority of Judaic souls compared with the souls of the *goyim.* Countless souls have been sent to ruin in this life and perdition in the next so as to protect the clergy from exposure.

There is evidence that in medieval society sodomy was viewed as a mortal sin *prevalent* among priests and monks. This extends as far back as 969 A.D. and the suspicion by Rather of Verona of institutionalized sodomy among clerics. [18] This was a view also expounded by William the Conquerer's chaplain, Serlo of Bayeux (ca. 1036-1104) and other medieval advocates of an option for married clergy.

Remedies according to St. Peter Damian: priests who engage in anal intercourse "for even a short period " have lost "all hope of recovering their priesthood" and are to be defrocked. It is "utterly preposterous for those who are habituated to the filth of this festering disease to present themselves for (holy) orders or to remain in them if they are already ordained." Damian

---

[16] Damian, op. cit., pp. 16-17.

[17] Ibid., pp. 26-27.

[18] Peter L.D. Reid, *The Complete Works of Rather of Verona* (1991).

stipulated a remedy for priests who stop short of anal intercourse in sexual dalliance with men or boys:

"Of Clerics or Monks Who Are Seducers of Men: any cleric or monk who seduces young men or boys, or who is apprehended in kissing or in any shameful situation, shall be publicly flogged and shall lose his clerical tonsure...bound in iron chains...(for) six months of close confinement...Following this period, he shall spend a further six months living in a small segregated courtyard in the custody of a spiritual elder, kept busy with manual labor and prayer, subjected to vigils and prayers, forced to walk at all times in the company of two spiritual brothers, and never again allowed to associate with young men for purposes of improper conversation or advice."

Sodomy, Contraception and the Natural Law

St. Peter Damian's definition of sodomy was derived from the consensus of the early medieval Church, which was reflected even in the theology of Luther and Calvin, both of whom declared contraception to be a type of sodomy. [19] For Peter Damian, sodomy consisted of both anal intercourse and any act, including masturbation, which resulted in the squandering of semen.

Rather than being some far-out stipulation from the moral manual of a Catholic fanatic, this doctrine was common to the *natural law* (not Neoplatonic creeds) [20] taught by certain Greeks who prized fertility (as did even pagan societies in antiquity).

---

[19] Cf. Charles D. Provan, *The Bible and Birth Control* (1989).

[20] For instance, usury was generally viewed as a foul deed by ancient Roman statesmen and poets, who were in turn admired in the Christian West for the stance they took, consonant with their alignment with the Natural Law, *which is not derived from pagan religion.* What distinguishes acknowledgement of the flicker of Natural Law in some pre-Christian people from the heresy of the *prisca theologia* of the syncretists, is this: a person in antiquity living before knowledge of Christ and the gospel, is certain to have a distorted vision, even of the Natural Law, because "the stance and vision of the unregenerate" is a fault related to their existing in Original Sin, which "distorts whatever reality they apprehend." God dispenses "common grace," of which an inclination to adhere to the Natural Law is a part, in conjunction with "God's work of preserving order and limiting the damage that accrues from the worst consequences of human folly." (Cf. Stephen J. Grabill's discussion of Henry Stob's theology in *Rediscovering the Natural Law in Reformed Theological Ethics* [2006]).

"The *Preambles to the Laws*, a Hellenistic treatise penned under the pseudonym 'Charondas' advocates procreationism in an unambiguously strict sense. This work was in circulation prior to the mid-first century B.C...Cicero (106-43 B.C.) mentions it....Charondas assumes that each man has or should have a wife and that the married couple should reproduce...He stipulates in no uncertain terms that the man must climax with his penis located nowhere else besides in his wife's vagina and for the purpose of reproduction alone...'Each man must love his legitimate wife and procreate with her. Into nothing else should he ejaculate...Nature made seed for the sake of producing children, not licentiousness...Only deliberately procreative sex acts in marriage remain permissible....Semen is the 'seed of a man's children' and as such must be used strictly to reproduce them.

"...This solemnity about semen comes to the fore particularly...(when) Charondas deplores its misdirected use. A man who misdirects his semen 'kills' and 'wastes' both 'his children' and even the entire 'human race." [21]

Scripture-Twisting

One of the oft-quoted leaders in the sodomite denial movement is Prof. Michael Carden of the University of Queensland. In his influential book, *Sodomy: A History of a Christian Myth,* he twists the Genesis 19 account of the city of Sodom in a manner pleasing to those who wish to engage in anal intercourse without the burden of Biblical transgression being attached to it.

We can find no other motive for his writing, which makes no sense as an interpretation of the text, but a great deal of sense from the vantage of an apologia for buggery.

---

[21] Kathy L. Gaca, *The Making of Fornication: Eros, Ethics and Political Reform in Greek Philosophy and Early Christianity* (2003), pp. 108-109. Typical of the situation ethics of the pre-Christians, Plato lent only qualified support to this view: his support was *contingent* on the period of time it takes a couple to conceive the required number of children, *after which Plato wrote that they were free to do as they pleased* (in other words, to *waste semen as they pleased*, which reduces the argument against contraception to situation ethics.)

The traditional orthodox Catholic understanding of the Biblical account of Sodom in Genesis is as follows: 19:1-3: "Two of the 'men' who visited Abraham are now called *angels.*

19:5: *Know them.* Have sex with them. Sodom was guilty of unnatural sexual lust, highlighted here in its homosexual violence.

19:9 *Pressed sore.* Pressed hard. The wicked Sodomites responded to Lot's rebuke by accusing him of presuming to be their judge. Nothing but men would satisfy their lusts.

19:29: *God remembered Abraham.* The Lord answered Abraham's prayer not by saving the city of Sodom, which did not have ten righteous people within it (Genesis 18:32), but by having mercy on its only righteous man." [22]

The modernist falsification of Genesis 19 has many sources. We will begin with the Rev. Dr. Derrick Sherwin Bailey's 1955 spin on Sodom in Genesis, in his book *Homosexuality and the Western Christian Tradition.* Here one will find one of the most enduring of all the sodomite-exculpatory shibboleths which liberal church-goers continue to parrot: that what was punished by God in Sodom was a breach of etiquette, a refusal of hospitality to strangers, absent a sexual dimension.

To accept this notion one must ignore the sexually charged statement in Genesis 19:5, "And they called unto Lot, and said unto him, Where are the men which came in to thee this night? Bring them out unto us, that we may *know them.*" The Hebrew denotation of the English rendering of the words *"know them"* is a direct reference to having sex with them, as a comparison of the use of the term in Genesis 4:1 ("And Adam *knew* Eve his wife and she conceived"), 24:16 ("And the damsel was very fair to look upon, a virgin, neither had any man *known* her"), and 38:26, will readily demonstrate.

A more sophisticated falsification is offered by the *New Bible Dictionary Third Edition* (Inter-Varsity Press, 1996), which states, "...the sin condemned was attempted homosexual rape, not a caring homosexual relationship between two consenting partners" (p. 479).

---

[22] *Reformation Heritage KJV Study Bible* (2014), pp. 36-37.

Prof. Carden offers a similar alibi in his *Sodomy: A History of a Christian Myth:* "Pack rape at the hands of a mob would be a particularly brutal death. Pack rape of a defenseless stranger is a particularly apt symbol of injustice and abuse of the helpless, which I would argue are the real sins of Sodom...and not same-sex desire and its mutually consenting expression...the very name of Sodom and its inhabitants can be used figuratively to signify the ungodly life, resulting in sodomy's first rehearsal—to denote not homoeroticism, but arrogant self-indulgence and luxurious living...." [23]

If the Bible intended to offer support for this conclusion that anal or oral sex ("homosexual relationship") was condoned by God if both men consented to the act, it would have so stated. But there is no such condonation of sodomy by consent, anywhere in Scripture. The consent or lack thereof of men who play the part of a woman, serving as passive receptacles for the sex action of a man, is irrelevant in Leviticus 20:13. There is no other possible context in keeping with the spirit and intent of the text than the fact that for a man to act the part of a woman in having sex with another man is a capital offense: "If a man also lie with mankind, as he lieth with a woman, both of them have committed an abomination: they shall surely be put to death; their blood shall be upon them."

Moreover, *male homosexual acts were intrinsically violent*, whether or not the two transgressors willingly consent to being overtaken by their lust for each other. *This violence is intrinsic to the waste of the male seed.* This waste is not modified in the severity of its transgression by the fact of consent, because no one can give consent to a lawless act.

The authors of the *New Bible Dictionary Third Edition,* and *Sodomy: A History of a Christian Myth,* have declared, based on their personal beliefs, that the waste of the male seed is no transgression in the eyes of God.

This is a conclusion that requires the falsification of Leviticus 20:13; the falsification of the account of Onan's capital crime in Genesis 38; as well as the overthrow of the Apostle Paul's dogmatic condemnations in Romans 1:23-27, I Corinthians 6:9 and I Tim. 1:9. Prof. Carden furnishes a disquisition on rape which he terms a "queering approach," transforming rape by homosexuals in Sodom into:

---

[23] Carden, pp. 27 and 117.

"an act of homophobic...violence." Consequently, if his "queering approach" is accepted, then the males in the city of Sodom in Genesis 19 who desired to sodomize the other men who were not homosexuals, are perpetrating this sexual violence from a fear of homosexuals! Carden's fantasy on Genesis is queer indeed. On the basis of imaginings like these, the "gay" lobby raises pseudo-intellectual objections to the application of the words sodomy and sodomite in Christendom, asserting that the use of these terms is little more than a *late medieval* prejudice. [24]

In Bishop Hincmar of Reims's ninth century treatise on divorce, relating to the attempt of Lothair II to divorce his wife Theutberga— *De divortio Lotharii regis et Theutbergae reginae,* —(not to be confused with his nephew of the same name)—he employs the term *scelus sodomiae* for all those sexual acts ruled to be "against nature." Hincmar's application of the term was derived from an earlier usage by Pope Gregory the Great, in the pontiff's letter in the sixth century containing the statement, "*Sodomitae illum sceleremaculatum.*" [25] The sixth century is not "the late medieval" period. [26]

---

[24] A similar tactic has been used with regard to Purgatory, to suggest it too was an invention of "late medieval popery." Isabel Moreira observes to the contrary: "It was Bede (writing in the early 700s) who first provides purgatory with an orthodox, theological justification...In Bede's work we encounter the culmination of centuries of purgatorial thinking." Cf. *Heaven's Purge: Purgatory in Late Antiquity* (2010), p. 16. On p. 40 of her study, Moreira traces articulation of Purgatory as far back as Clement of Alexandria (200 A.D.). Before Protestants dismiss this out of hand due to the indulgence-money racket that grew up around it hundreds of years later, consider the *sheol* (not "hell"), into which Jesus descended after His resurrection. It was neither heaven nor *gehenna* (hell), but an intermediate stage. This interim state was referred to in the Early Church as *refrigerium*, a term that appears on "numerous Christian grave inscriptions in the Roman empire." (Eliezer Gonzalez, *The Fate of the Dead in Early Third Century North African Christianity* [2014], p. 139).

[25] "Stained with the sin of the sodomite." Gregory the Great, *Registrum Epistularum*, 10.2, (Norberg). This was the pope's allusion to a sex crime that had been perpetrated by a sub-deacon.

[26] For a refutation of Prof. Mark Jordan's thesis in this regard in his book *The Invention of Sodomy in Christian Theology, cf.* Glenn W. Olsen, *Of Sodomites, Effeminates, Hermaphrodites and Androgynes: Sodomy in the Age of Peter Damian*, pp. 33-36. "...there was from the beginning a rhetorical excess in Jordan's claim that sodomy was invented in the mid-eleventh century..." (Olsen, p. 36).

The two male forms of ecclesiastic celibacy, priesthood and monasticism, faced the constant threat of auto-eroticism. Masturbation and its more extreme manifestation (auto-fellatio) were a problem for the Church from the beginning of the monastic orders; to what extent is debatable, though we note that pornographic images of these and other homosexual acts appear in sacred Catholic Church sculpture, on the facades of churches such as the Collegiate Church of St. Peter of Cervatos in Cantabria, Spain; the Church of Saint Pierre, Passirac, France; the Church of Semur-en-Brionnais, Saône-et-Loire, also in France, and others in Europe, Britain and Ireland. [27]

"The 'world without women' of the high and late medieval religious community, school, friary or university continued a homosocial ethos favorable to homoeroticism." [28] There is some validity to this thesis, but it risks succumbing to a Freudian distortion of the state of celibate men in community, about which there is nothing necessarily pathological or sinful, assuming that rigorous safeguards are in place.

The larger question of homoeroticism with regard to liturgical vestments has not been addressed inside the Church, as well as other possible ecclesiastical trappings of the homoerotic aesthetic.

One is struck by the fact that Pope Francis visited the U.S. for several days in September of 2015, and gave a huge gift to the American homosexual culture (it is no longer a "subculture"), by refusing to say a word about the recent legalization of sodomite marriage in the U.S.

Yet at the same time much was made of his finger-wagging platitudes against the molestation of Catholic boys by priests. Can his gestures be serious when the pontiff, by his silence, uttered absolutely nothing concerning the newly legitimate marital arrangement, whereby men may "marry" other men? Is the pope's double-mind a product of modern post-Vatican II perversion alone, or an outward sign of an underground clerical current with a pedigree of many centuries?

---

[27] Cf. Anthony Weir and James Jerman, *Images of Lust: Sexual Carvings on Medieval Churches* (1999).

[28] Cf. Glenn W. Olsen, ibid., p. 165. Also cf. David F. Noble, *A World Without Women: The Christian Clerical Culture*, pp. 57 and 154-155.

The homosexual orientation of the Church of Rome since the Renaissance is no longer the deep secret that it once was.

A hoax has been put forth in the name of Christ's True Catholic Church; that hoax emanates from the top-down. It is long overdue for it to receive its comeuppance, particularly so in light of the canonization on April 27, 2014, of Pope John-Paul II on whose watch the *epidemic* of molestations of defenseless children occurred. Pope John-Paul II granted to Cardinal Bernard Law, a notorious facilitator of child-molesting priests in Massachusetts, safe haven in Vatican City from criminal prosecution. Cardinal Law was honored by the "saint" with the administration of a basilica in Rome. He officiated at the public funeral of John-Paul II. Any church that would raise to sainthood a pope like this individual whose criminal indifference toward molestation, and outright collusion with child-molestation facilitators such as Father Marcial Maciel, of the Legionaries of Christ, Cardinal Roger Mahony, Bishop William Skylstad (named during John Paul's pontificate as head of the National Conference of Catholic Bishops *after* his facilitation of child-molester priests came to the attention of the courts and the media), the aforementioned Bernard Law, and dozens of other bishops and some cardinals, who constitute the corrupt of the earth, is a *Judas church* that will increasingly incur the wrath of God.

The child molestations perpetrated by "Money bags Maciel" were repeatedly reported to Pope "Saint" John Paul II, yet the pontiff "led massive celebrations to mark both the fiftieth and sixtieth anniversaries of Father Maciel's priestly ordination."

In light of the canonization of the patron saint of molesters, Pope John Paul II, the thought of Catholics praying to this criminal in front of a statue of him, evokes the starkest Protestant portrayals of Catholics sunk in a swamp of credulity and idolatry. [29]

---

[29] For documentation of these charges, cf. Jason Berry and Gerald Renner, *Vows of Silence: The Abuse of Power in the Papacy of John Paul II* (2004). On the horrors inflicted on Irish children during the "traditional Catholic" years, cf. Mary Raftery, *Suffer the Little Children* (2002); and Peter Tyrrell, *Founded on Fear* (2006).

Chapter XIV

The Hermetic Prince
of the Second Vatican Council

"The theological *eminence-grisé* of Vatican II was Jesuit Fr. Henri de Lubac (1896-1991). Under theological interdict for many years, "The reversal of his ten years of ostracism resolved slowly and gradually, culminating in the invitation from Pope John XXIII to be a consultant for the preparatory Theological Commission of the Second Vatican Council...At the Council itself he was a *peritus* (theological expert) and was associated with the work on the documents *Dei Verbum, Lumen Gentium,* and *Guadium et Spes.*" [1]

The "ostracism" and "theological interdict" were strange in that De Lubac was not formally questioned by either his Jesuit superiors or any member of the curia or Holy Office. He was not asked to recant, or provide a retraction. Was the whole episode a charade calculated to burnish his reputation and create a high profile aura for him as a dissident and make a *cause célebré* of him and writings? Certainly he came to prominence during the time of his "ostracism."

Prof. Jacques Prévotat of the University of Lille-III writes:

"From the time of his nomination as a consultor to the Preparatory Theological Commission in July, 1960, then as an expert on the Doctrinal Commission, Father de Lubac was an active participant in or witness to all the diverse aspects of the council: the general congregations, the Doctrinal Commission...meetings of the French and foreign bishops on fundamental questions, various conversations, preparation and clarification of interventions at the council at the request of numerous bishops, lectures in front of audiences of bishops...Father de Lubac was always present." [2]

---

[1] Susan K. Wood, *Spiritual Exegesis and the Church in the Theology of Henri de Lubac* (1997), p. 5.

[2] Introduction to the *Vatican Council Notebooks I of Henri de Lubac* (Ignatius Press, 2007), pp. 10-11.

Both of these appraisals are modest ones. In truth, *Henri de Lubac was the guiding theological light of the Second Vatican Council*. "After the Council, Paul VI appointed him one of the original members of the International Theological Commission, where he worked with Hans Urs von Balthasar and Joseph Ratzinger, the future Benedict XVI." [3] On February 2, 1983, Pope St. John-Paul II elevated Father De Lubac to Cardinal without his having first been consecrated a bishop.

The Jesuit theologian who began his career as a Liberal ended it with the reputation of a Conservative, which is an abuse of the term when we consider that Lubac wrote books in defense of the Piltdown Man hoaxer and New Age evolutionist Pierre Teilhard de Chardin, S.J., and one other *miscreant* who should by now be familiar to the reader: "Toward the end of his career he wrote a very favorable monograph on the Renaissance Platonist Giovanni Pico della Mirandola...His assessment of the work of the Renaissance philosopher Pico della Mirandola could fairly be applied to his own: 'A stand for intellectual pluralism against the narrowness of the school." [4]

Balthasar, upon whom John Paul II conferred the Paul VI Prize, was also under the influence of Giovanni Pico della Mirandola:

"Balthasar ends his study, somewhat abruptly, with some remarks on de Lubac's study of the Renaissance Christian-Platonist and lay Dominican Pico della Mirandola. Leaving aside the banal consideration that *Pic de la Mirandole* was the last of de Lubac's books to reach Balthasar, the reason for choosing this finale was probably the—altogether admirable— way Pico combined spiritual independence with catholicity of attitude. His anthropology begins from human freedom, but this is no closed humanism: the goal of that freedom is the supreme peace of all things in union with God...Pico treats man as an essentially ecstatic being who must model himself on Thrones and Seraphim...His gleaning husks of pagan wisdom (the *prisca theologia* he sought among the ancients, classical and otherwise), puts one in mind of de Lubac's raids on Asiatic wisdom as well...

---

[3] David Grumett, *De Lubac: A Guide for the Perplexed*, p. ix.

[4] Ibid., pp. ix and 8.

"A Renaissance man can form the climax of a study of—and by—a modern priest-student of the Catholic tradition in all its length and breadth, height and depth, precisely because Balthasar shared the view that the Renaissance was not anti-Catholic...but simply 'a period in which men were trying to find a new, more personal piety, and personal expressions of religious thought.' So why *not* end with Pico as, like de Lubac, a wonderful *homo ecclesiasticus*?" [5]

Analyzing Lubac's book-length salute to the Neoplatonic-Hermetic Kabbalist Pico, Hans Urs von Balthasar writes: "...more than four hundred pages are dedicated to Pico della Mirandola. Why Pico? Certainly not only because he needed to be vindicated of a thousand misrepresentations, restored from layer upon layer of paint, and given back to the great Christian tradition. Pico...presents a rounded image of what de Lubac stands for...he so much points the way to greater openness of spirit and indeed with the same spiritual 'independence,' the same instinct for the right direction that strives toward the universal, the catholic, as de Lubac himself. When Pico focuses on freedom as man's innermost essence, he stands in the great tradition of Christian humanism...yet he keeps an accent as personal as, for example, Tielhard had, when he spoke of the creature's elan toward God. Imperceptibly, but unerringly, Pico goes his way, which leads him out of the closed sphere of the humanism of his time. He no longer understands the *'desiderium naturale'* [6] naturalistically, as Ficino did, and man is more for him than a mere microcosm. He gathers up all of tradition—the four senses of Scripture—elevating it in a *'Concordia,'* a synthesis, a universal *'Pax'* that hovers before

---

[5] Aidan Nichols, O.P., *Divine Fruitfulness: A Guide through Balthasar's Theology* (Catholic University of America), pp. 72-73.

[6] In the theory of the *desiderium naturale*, "At issue is whether a natural desire to see the divine essence can be reconciled with the necessarily supernatural and gratuitous manner of this desire's fulfillment. The 16th century Dominican, Cardinal Cajetan strove to mollify the problem by proposing a duplex *ordo* in which the hypothetical state of pure nature would have its own natural end distinct from man's supernatural end. This ostensible solution to the issue was regnant until the broad-ranging criticisms of the *Nouvelle Theologie* in the 20th century (represented especially by Henri de Lubac). The theologies of grace, which emerged after this critique— most notably that of Karl Rahner—sought to remedy the Neoscholastic separation of nature and grace..." Alexander S. Rosenthal, "The Problem of the Desiderium Naturale," *Verbum*, vol. 6, no. 2.

him...Pico knows, as does de Lubac, that all concepts and systems are indeed indispensable but limited; that their construction is due to a deeper force that also strives farther and beyond them." [7]

Let us turn now to the words of Cardinal de Lubac himself concerning the Renaissance Pico:

"A closer examination of the texts, of the dates and facts has shown that there never was, on Pico's part, any intention or gesture of revolt or disloyalty; and on the part of the Holy See (and of Garcia himself), [8] no mark of any lack of esteem toward his person, quite the contrary. The inquisitorial tribunal that was for a moment constituted seems never to have really functioned at all. The *Apologia* [9] that Pico presented of his theses prior to any sentence from the pope did not give rise to an examination followed by judgment...From the time the fugitive returned to Paris, a more or less tacit compromise was established, and...all was soon smoothed out by the Brief of Alexander VI." [10]

All of the preceding is correct. Pico della Mirandola enjoyed a high-level immunity after a pro forma theatre of critical examination involving his "persecution" and dramatic "flight." (The parallels with de Lubac are intriguing). Some otherwise ferocious inquisitors became strangely meek in the presence of the case of Giovanni Pico, for example Marco Maroldi and Gioacchino da Vinci. Pope Alexander convened a commission of investigation in 1493, staffed by three cardinal-inquisitors: Giambattista Orsini, Francesco Todeschini-Piccolomini and Giorgio Costa. Acting as *peritus* for the

---

[7] Hans Urs von Balthasar, *The Theology of Henri de Lubac* (1991).

[8] Pedro Garcia (also: "Garsias"), Master of the Papal Chapel, Bishop of Ales (Uselli) Italy, and later of Barcelona, Spain. He was Giovanni Pico's occasional antagonist. He died in 1505.

[9] Pico's *Apologia* was a bold justification, and in no way a recantation, of his theology.

[10] Cardinal Henri de Lubac, S.J., *Theology in History* (1996), p. 42.

commission was the illustrious Paolo Moneglia [11] The commission concluded that Pico should be fully rehabilitated and the pope concurred, issuing the "Brief" to which de Lubac referred, *Ominum Catholicorum*, on June 18, 1493. [12]

De Lubac:

"...all had admired his (Pico's) 'Discourse on the Dignity of Man,' as it was called, in which they thought to see a 'manifesto,' the 'manifesto of the Renaissance'...This celebrated discourse...was received very favorably in religious circles. Going through the libraries and archives of Rome, Father John W. O'Malley has found a whole series of sermons dating from the last years of the fifteenth century and from the first third of the sixteenth, in which several use—let us even say plagiarize —Pico's discourse. Some of them come from preachers at the Roman court and are not in any way worldly sermons. This discovery will contribute to restoring, for a wider circle, the true face of Pico della Mirandola." [13]

It is somewhat remarkable that with the palaver about the theological origins of the Second Vatican Council mainly focused on 1. the late nineteenth and early twentieth century modernism denounced by Pope St. Pius X; and 2. the masonic ideas of the secularist French Enlightenment; that in spite of De Lubac and Balthasar being cited as the intellectual lodestars of the Council, almost no prominently published and heralded work has been undertaken the study of the momentous implications of the devotion of De Lubac and Balthasar to Giovanni Pico della Mirandola, who is among the foremost papist exponents in history of the books of the Kabbalah.

---

[11] Paolo Moneglia, Doctor of Theology at the University of Pavia and Chair of Thomistic Theology (*ad lecturam operum beati Thomae*). On June 6, 1490 he was elevated to the curia by Pope Innocent VIII. He was Dominican inquisitor in Genoa from April, 1494 to February, 1497. In 1498, the pope named him Inquisitor of Rome.

[12] Cf. Giovanni Di Napoli, *Giovanni Pico della Mirandola e la problematica dottrinale del suo tempo* (Rome, 1965), for an account of the commission's investigation (pp. 81-137), and the text of Pope Alexander's *Ominum Catholicorum* (pp. 116-118).

[13] De Lubac, *Theology in History*, op.cit., p. 43.

The silence is deafening. Is the silence accidental? Opening the door to Giovanni Pico's diabolism inevitably leads to Johannes Reuchlin and his enabler, Pope Leo X. From there, the investigator encounters the network of occultists occupying the Church of Rome at all levels, from 1525 to 1965, and into the present era. Yet this has been "missed." How does one miss the elephant in the room? The two leading Catholic theologians of the twentieth century, who were disciples of the most admired Catholic, Neoplatonic-Hermetic Kabbalist of the fifteenth century, exercised a decisive influence on Vatican II, perhaps more than any other Catholic other than Pope Paul VI.

Yet "traditional and conservative Catholics" are united in almost always listing as the *principal* ideological godfathers of modernism and Vatican II, the *philosophes* of the eighteenth century Enlightenment: Jean-Jacques Rousseau, Immanuel Kant, Denis Diderot, David Hume, "Voltaire" (François-Marie Arouet)—seemingly everyone *except* the Church of Rome's most guilty spiritual and theological progenitors of the Second Vatican Council: Nicholas of Cusa, Ficino, Pico, Reuchlin, Alexander VI, Leo X, Clement VII, Paul III, Giles of Viterbo, Ludovico Lazzarelli, Francesco Giorgio, Sixtus of Siena, Johannes Trithemius, Francesco Patrizi, Agostino Steuco, Giovanni Nesi, Foix de Candale, Lefevre d'Etaples and hundreds more.

One gasps at the extent to which the guilty parties of an entire epoch in the history of the occult Church have vanished, and are missing from virtually every page of the voluminous output of the "conservative" and "traditional" Catholic *oeuvre* (innumerable newsletters, pamphlets, journals, bulletins, magazines, books, blogs and websites).

The neglect is appalling, and the question arises, as it always does when there is a gaping memory hole in a highly controversial historical subject: is this erasure the result of rank ineptitude and willful blindness, or a deliberate conspiracy?

De Lubac's fascinating, book-length encomium for Pico, *Pic de la Mirandole: études et discussions* (Paris, 1974) is a major statement, yet it has not been translated into English. William G. Craven writes concerning *Pic de la Mirandole*: "It is a series of essays by the French Jesuit Henri de Lubac...A prefatory note refers to a personal interest in Pico extending over half a century. The great merit of the book is that it makes the point, with a wealth of learning, that Pico's language, figures of speech and ideas were thoroughly traditional..." [14]

Giovanni Pico della Mirandola: *traditional Catholic*. This is the bad joke that "Saint" John-Paul's august Cardinal de Lubac peddled to the theological overlords of the Church of Rome. It was indeed Pico's "tradition" that informed the theology of Vatican II. In a sense, it is in fact a theology with a tradition, having a patrimony in the Church of Rome of more than five centuries, which is one reason why the adjective "traditional Catholic" is such a source of confusion and misdirection useful to the Cryptocracy.

From Jesuit theologian Henri de Lubac's *Pic de la Mirandole* (Part I, "Liberty" Ch. 3, "Limits of the Thesis," p. 77-78): [15]

"There is no denying that the serious warning of the year before and the situation that resulted from it helped the young intellectual to become more mature and wiser. But from granting this to presenting the *Heptaplus* [16] as a minor work, lacking originality, marred by the intention that gave rise to it and not representing the real Pico, would be going too far. The new work is, on the contrary, the fruit of an intense, personal labor in the highest degree. [17]

"...In 1488, at Florence, Pico made the acquaintance of another learned Jew, Jochanan Alemanno, as intelligent as he was erudite, as much poet as philosopher, of a great elevation of soul, and soon the two men became quite intimate. Jochanan

---

[14]*Giovanni Pico della Mirandola: Symbol of his Age. Modern Interpretations of a Renaissance philosopher* (Librairie Droz, 1981), p. 18.

[15] The English translation of Henri de Lubac's *Pic de la Mirandole* in these pages is by our translator, A.M. Stinnett. Except for the note below, all of the other footnotes linked to this English translation are *original to De Lubac's French text.* In this section, they are his footnotes; not ours.

[16] Pico's *Heptaplus* interprets the Book of Genesis through the prism of the Kabbalah.

[17] Here begin's de Lubac's own notes: Giuseppe Barone justly ranks it, as do the older publishers, among the three *Opere maggiori*, with the *De onte et uno* and the *Disputationes adversus astrologos: Giovanni Pico della Mirandola*, (Milan-Rome, 1948) ch. 2.

completed Pico's Hebraic culture; he guided him in the knowledge of the Talmud and of the Kabbalah. If he moderated certain aspects of his youthful ardor, he confirmed several of his first intuitions.

When he was writing the *Conclusiones* and the *Oratio*, Pico had waxed too enthusiastic over what he believed was the prophetic content of the books of the Kabbalah; Jochanan made him better understand its method, with its possible applications in the philosophico-religious domain. [18] But his Kabbalistic fever did not abate (it never completely left).[19]

In the *Heptaplus* he makes no effort to dissimulate it. On the contrary, in it he proclaims that his method of interpreting the Book of Genesis, based on Kabbalah, is something quite new: "*hoc novum illud et intactum adhuc quod nos afferre temptavimus.*" He provides as an appendix to the work (as a crown, Sixtus of Siena will say[20]), the most cabalistic page, one could almost say the only one, of his entire work: it is an explication of the first word of the Bible, 'In principio' (*beresit*), based on the divers combinations possible of the Hebraic letters that compose it.

He declares himself amazed by all the discoveries he made, far beyond his expectation and his hope. [21]

We can see from the preceding passage by Cardinal De Lubac how normative is the Catholic application of Kabbalah for comprehending the Scriptures. He continues:

"Indeed, as M. Eugenio Garin correctly writes, if the *Heptaplus* testifies to Pico's greater maturity, it certainly does not represent a sort of humiliated retreat in comparison to his earlier positions; it is, on the contrary, 'the work which best

---

[18] Dell'Acqua, 162166. On the friendship of Pico and Jochanan, see *infra*, III, 7.

[19] N. 4: "There is evidence that he continued to study the Kabbalah long after his so-called conversion." Dulles, 23.

[20] *Biblioteca sancta*, 1, 4; t. 1, Lyons, 1575, 292: "...*Additur veluti pro coronide specimen quoddam octavae explanationis Kabalisticae... quae non solum ex singulis sententiis ac dictionibus multos sensus elicit, sed ex singulis Hebraicis literis uniuscujusque syllabae mysteria pene infinita deducit.*"

[21] "*Praeter spem meam, praeter opinionem, inveni quod neque inveniens ipse credebam, neque credere alii facile potuerunt, universam de mundi rerumque omnium creatione rationem in una ea dictione apertam et explicatam...*" 376.

expresses his Kabbalistic phase, and the one in which his vision of reality is the most organically composed, in its order, in the correspondence of its various planes, in its link with man, the ideal center of creation." [22]

In the preceding, De Lubac notes that Giovanni Pico was not intimidated by the displeasure of Pope Innocent VIII in reaction to his thesis. Pico knew he had "protection" and there would be no need for any "humiliated retreat." De Lubac esteems Pico's Kabbalistic peregrination (this is from de Lubac's chapter five, "Pagan Prophecy"):

"As all had for centuries, [Pico] believes in the high antiquity of 'Mercury' (Hermes Trismegistus) and his writings, the Greek text of which had been recently brought to Florence and which Marsilius Ficinus had translated into Latin under the title of *Pimander* (1471) at the behest of Cosmo de Medici. Tommaso Benci had just procured a Tuscan version of it (which would not be published until later); Lorenzo de Medici sang its praises in verse, which Gelli set out in dialogues. [23] This Mercury, he thinks, was both 'a very great philosopher, a very great priest, and a very great king; it is thus (M. Ficinus just explained in his preface) that one commented on his last name of Trismegistus, the thrice great.' [24] He wonders at seeing him 'in accord with Moses,' and 'approaching his thought.'[25] Concerning the faith of Christian antiquity, [26] Pico equally upholds the authenticity of the 'Chaldean Oracles,' of which he will not delay in discovering a much more recent origin; but for

---

[22] 1937, 39: "*...non rappresentava certo una dimessa palinodia rispetto al precedente atteggiamento... Quanto l'opera piacque ai dotti, altrettanto dispiacque alla Chiesa che vi trovo piuttosto della pertinacia che della sottomissione....*" 1963, 50.

[23] Cf. Kristeller, *Studies*, 221-247.

[24] P. 94, n. 5. "*Ter maximus*": Bucer will apply this epithet ironically to Erasmus. Cf. Nicole Peremans, *Erasme et Bucer* (Liege, 1970), p. 98.

[25] P. 95, n. 1: Conversation with Savonarola and Lawrence, reported by Crinito, Bk. 3, Ch. 2, 104-5.

[26] Cf. Edouard des Places, "*Les Oracles chaldaiques dans la patristique africaine,*" in *Studia patristica*, 11 (Berlin, 1972), 27-41; and "*Histoire et survie des Oracles...*" in introduction to the Chaldean Oracles, *Belles Lettres* (1971), 8-52.

the moment, their discovery enthused him so much that he set himself immediately the task of mastering their language. [27]

By a more consequential allusion, in the fervor of his initiation, he believes that he has found 'the golden thread'[28] that will enable him to unify everything: it is the question of the Kabbalah, this 'divine science,' already mentioned, defined, and praised in the *Commento*.[29] Does it not come from Moses by way of the men he had chosen at the Lord's behest and who used it to hold in Israel the place that the cardinals hold today in our Church? [30]

"(Pico) persuades himself that he can justify thinking so because of a recent, august example: Had not Sixtus IV, the immediate predecessor of the reigning pontiff, 'personally seen to it with enthusiasm that these books (of the Kabbalah) were translated into Latin for the use of our faith?' Already, 'at the time of his death, three of them had been translated.' [31] It has been supposed that the story was wholly fabricated by (Flavius) Mithridates, who boasted of having preached a set speech on the Passion mingled with Arabic and Hebrew names before the pontiff for two hours straight with great success.[32] Perhaps the story has a foundation in the fact that several Roman theologians, encouraged by Sixtus IV, had interested themselves in the Kabbalah with an apologetic intention that preceded that of Pico." [33]

---

[27] Cf. his two letters to Ficinus and to an unknown friend, Nov. 1486; *Opera*, 367-368 and 384-386.

[28] Expression of [author] Eugenio Garin.

[29] *Commento particolare*, v. *finem: "Cabala si chiama, che significa recezione, perchè non per scritti ma per successione a bocca l'uno dall' altro la ricevono. Scienzia per certo divina e degna di non participare se non con pochi, grandissimo fundamento della fede nostra* etc." 580-581. And the *Oratio*, 156-158.

[30] *Apologia: "...quorum locum mihi videntur tenere Cardinales in nostra Ecclesia." Opera*, 177.

[31] *Oratio*, 158-160. The thing is not impossible.

[32] Secret, 24-26. *Sermo de passione Domini*, ed. C. Wirszubski (Jerusalem, 1963).

[33] Raffaello Morghen, *Medioevo cristiano* (Bari, 1962), 146: "...Perfino dei teologi della corte del papa Sisto IV, come ha provato in un acuto studio il Moore, 'credevano che la *Kabbala* contenesse dimostrazioni accettabili della dottrina cristiana e la fecero oggetto di attento studio e di meditazione'."

In his *Oration on the Dignity of Man*, Pico published the fact that Pope Sixtus IV had, "for the common good of those of our faith," the rabbinic books of the Kabbalah published in Latin. De Lubac refers to the controversy that arose when Sixtus IV's enthusiasm for the Kabbalah began to become known to Catholic Conservatives in the hierarchy. To answer the pope's orthodox critics, the Vatican floated the rumor that the Judeo-Catholic Kabbalist Flavius Mithridates, preacher to the pope's own household, concocted the story about the pontiff issuing the Kabbalah in Latin. De Lubac writes that it was "supposed that the story was wholly fabricated by Mithridates."

Supposed by whom? Few historians of the era believe the rumor to be credible. De Lubac then covers all the bases when he writes, "Perhaps the story has a foundation in the fact that several Roman theologians, encouraged by Sixtus IV, had interested themselves in the Kabbalah"—for "apologetic intentions."

Here is that slippery indeterminancy which is the very marrow of the arcane command ideology of the Church of Rome. We encounter it consistently throughout the history of the Renaissance and post-Renaissance papacy. These weasel methods permitted the popes to evade the consequences of their revolutionary actions. Leo X's Bull, *Inter multiplices* of May 4, 1515, appears as though it is rebuking usury when in fact it is extending, with qualifications, feints, sideshows and distraction, an escape clause for usury in the form of the good cause of helping the poor. "Sin for a good cause" the pope's argument could be called, if indeed it could be nailed down. A similar pattern of plausible denial and permissible dissimulation occurred in Pope Benedict XIV's *Vix Pervenit* of November 1, 1745, which has been often quoted to us as the definitive rebuff to all who dare to assert that the Church gradually made the mortal sin of taking a profit on loans into no sin at all. In fact, after reams of impressive-sounding anti-usury blabber, Benedict provided a loophole for usury. [34]

The hot button question during the 2014 and 2015 synods that led to the Apostolic Exhortation *Amoris Laetitia* (March 19, 2016), was whether divorced and remarried Catholics could receive Communion. Pope Francis addressed the point only in a

---

34 Hoffman, *Usury in Christendom* (2013), pp. 380-382.

footnote (no. 351) in the document. The footnote seemed to perhaps constitute a "yes" answer to the question, but not in a way that *explicitly* altered Church law or teaching. This ambiguity allowed local bishops to interpret the signals from the pope's *Amoris Laetitia* differently, with some promulgating a stringent interpretation and others a more lenient one, yielding the historical indeterminancy and potential for plausible denial which we observe in papal documents from the Renaissance onward.

Almost all of the Babylonian Talmud at one time or another can be valid and authoritative in Judaism, depending on the circumstances of the time. In Erubin 13b, we observe that the school of Hillel and the school of Shammai differed. These schools are depicted as disputing for three years over whose ruling constituted the *halacha*. In this case, even though it was subsequently determined that the *halacha* was according to Hillel, it is written that both Shammai and Hillel represent the words of God. [35]

Since both schools of rabbinic thought represent the word of God according to the belief of Orthodox Judaism, both represent the *Torah sheBeal peh*, (the Oral "Torah" which rabbinic Judaism claims Moses gave to the ancient Pharisees embodied by *Chazal,* the collective Pharisaic and Talmudic "sages" who concocted the *halacha).* Viewed within the perspective of the rabbinic hermeneutic—which is so often denied in public—the exchanges between competing rabbinic views within the Talmud are 1. the basis of rabbinic law (*halacha*); and 2. have authority and validity even when in certain historical periods another view predominates.

This too is the method and outlook employed by the papal Cryptocracy. Their "god" is the *zeitgeist*. The Renaissance "happened" partly because the timing was right. There is an argument that can be made that it could not have happened in the Middle Ages. How that timing is determined and why it is a ruling principle, is difficult to explain without entering into a disquisition on one of the more recondite secrets of the occult: *the confirmation by what could be described as the "god of*

---

[35] Cf. Bar-Ilan University Prof. Avi Sagi, "Both are the Words of the Living God: A Typological Analysis of Halakhic Pluralism," in *Hebrew Union College Annual* no. 65 (1995). Also cf. Prof. William "Zev" Kolbrenner, "Chiseled from All Sides: Hermeneutics and Dispute in Rabbinic Judaism," in *Association for Jewish Studies Review*, no. 28 (2004).

*power," of any behavior that is successfully conducted — on the
basis that it was successful.* While the expression, "might is
right" does not alone account for what is also at work here
(ritual manipulation in time and place to achieve success), the
epigram "nothing succeeds like success" gives a hint of the
wind that powers these sails. There is no morality or ethics to
the process. Yet it has been the engine of the Church of Rome's
dominion for many centuries.

Another arcane doctrine of the Church of Rome is situation
ethics, the long history of which is seldom detected in all
respects or analyzed comprehensively by Rome's true believers.
A true believer will sometimes detect one significant instance
of situation ethics, as for example, the situation ethics entailed
by the syncretist Assisi prayer meetings of Pope St. John Paul
II and his successors, or in the marriage controversy of *Amoris
Laetitia.*

But Conservatives who detect some modern instances
almost always frame the situation ethic they are denouncing as
a radical "aberration" and "departure" from what has otherwise
been ("prior to Pope Francis," or "antecedent to John Paul II,"
or "before to Vatican II"), the supposedly unchangeable Roman
Catholic Church.

This is a lamentable spectacle to witness in folks who are
otherwise often people of integrity, possessed of a selfless
dedication to the Faith. But in consideration of the actual
documentary record, which has seen the Church of Rome
discard immemorial Scriptural dogma on Jews and Judaism,
and profit on loans of money, for centuries, their ignorance (or
willful blindness) ensures the defeat of their Cause. As we have
noted in another chapter, the prelates who are the heirs of the
Neoplatonic-Hermetic Renaissance command ideology,
privately laugh in contempt at the *schmucks* who appeal to
them for "faithful adherence to the unchanging Church," based
on a naive and cockamamie misapprehension of the history of
the Church of Rome.

We left De Lubac at the point in which he cited the
apologetic uses of the Kabbalah. This too was Pico's line, as De
Lubac quotes him:

"I find in these books,' the latter said, 'God is my witness,
the religion, not so much of Moses but of Christ. I see in it the
mystery of the Trinity, the Incarnation of the Word, the

divinity of the Messiah; original sin, its expiation by Christ, the fall of the bad angels, the angelic choirs, purgatory, the pains of hell, I read there the same things that we read every day in Paul and Denys, in Jerome and Augustine." [36]

Pico the acclaimed scholarly prodigy, by the waving of the wand of spiritual transposition, sees Christ in the Kabbalah. What exotic substance was he smoking when he saw this hallucination? De Lubac would not agree with our irreverent dismissal of Pico's papist Kabbalism, however. For him, Pico is the paradigm of a truly pious, Roman Catholic intellectual:

"It is thus to a vast enterprise of spiritual transposition or, as Salutati said, to a 'pious interpretation' that Pico intends to devote himself. And if he proceeds in the company of so many strangers summoned from everywhere, it is always in order to come (back), as Manetti had already done, to 'our Fathers,' to those whom Manetti called 'our Catholic doctors,' as to 'the only port of salvation.' [37] In the works of both writers, these expressions above all designate, not those whom we call today the Fathers of the Church, but their Fathers as well as ours, the sacred authors of both Testaments: 'the patriarch Jacob'; Moses; the Apostle Paul, and his interpreter Denys." [38]

De Lubac hopes that we will believe that Giovanni Pico della Mirandola's theology is thoroughly Biblical and orthodox. It seems that the litany of our Fathers in Faith consists of Moses, Jacob, St. Paul and—"Denys"?

As we have noted previously, the strange texts of the hoaxer known by nearly a half-dozen names (Pseudo-Dionysius, Dionysius the Pseudo-Areopagite, Denis, Denys and Dionigi), are falsely attributed to Dionysius the Areopagite, the Christian who is mentioned in the Book of Acts (17:34), as

---

[36] (P. 96, n. 1:) *Oratio*, 160. *Ibid.* "In plenum nulla est ferme de se nobis cum Hebraeis controversia, de qua ex libris Cabalistarum ita redargui convincique non possint, ut ne angulus quidem reliquus sit in quem se condant..." The inexact interpretation of Jean Delumeau, *Naissance et affirmation de la Réforme* (PUF, 1965), 70: Pico would have thought "that the Bible offered to the Christians of his time was incomplete and that a part of Divine Revelation had thus far escaped the Church." See below, III, 6.

[37] [p. 97, n. 6]

[38] [p. 98, n. 2]

having been converted by St. Paul. Denys lived some five hundred years after Paul. As recently as the nineteenth century, scholars such as John Parker continued to believe in the first century provenance of the Denys writings. We do not know the identity of "Denys." The actual author was a hoaxer: he did his best to make his 525 A.D. writing appear to be authentic apostolic documents from the first century A.D. (through manipulation of manuscript titles and headings, such as the address of a "letter" supposedly intended for "the monk Gaius;" and another addressed to John, the inspired author of the Book of Revelation "on the isle of Patmos" (*Letter 10*).

De Lubac regurgitates Pico's detritus about Kabbalah being a support for Catholic truth:

"Finally, if our exegete (Pico) consults the secret books of Judaism, it is not at all in order to 'reinterpret Christianity thanks to the Cabala.' [39] It is to wrest from the Synagogue, as from the Egyptians, the Greeks, or the Chaldeans, the part of the truths that they unjustly hold, and to give it to the Christians, the only 'legitimate Israelites.' [40] It is to force it despite itself to bear witness to the mysteries of Christ and his Church.[41] In short, it is always, following in the footsteps of an Origen and a Hilary, 'with a view to confirm the sacrosanct Catholic faith." [42]

In the preceding statement we see De Lubac adopt the tough-sounding rhetoric against the Jews that the endlessly duplicitous occult Renaissance Judaizers would employ whenever it was absolutely necessary to do so for the sake of the rescue of their campaign of rehabilitation of the Talmud or Kabbalah.

There is nothing that these conspirators would not say or do to advance their objective, including taking *one step backward*

---

[39] Helen Védrine, *Les philosophies de la Renaissance* (PUF, 1971), 38.

[40] [p. 98, n. 7].

[41] P. 98, n. 8: (Latin extract). The famous convert Drach, in the 19th century, will not speak otherwise.

[42] P. 98, n. 9: Citation. Or, as (his nephew) John-Francis said, he wants to show how the poetic theology of the ancient sages can be placed at the service 'of the mysteries of our theology.'

—it is "the Synagogue" that "unjustly holds" the parts of the truth that the Kabbalah contains. It is the Christians who are "the only legitimate Israelites"— in order to *advance two steps forward*: "...despite itself" the Kabbalah "bear(s) witness to the mysteries of Christ and his Church'... 'with a view to confirm the sacrosanct Catholic faith."

In apprehending De Lubac's doubletalk we are afforded a front row seat at the spectacle of Vatican public relations methodology. It arose in the Renaissance and hundreds of years later in the mind and spirit of De Lubac.

He wishes us to accept that Satan's book of black magic "confirms the Catholic faith" and bears witness to the mysteries of Christ.

This contemptible folderol is presented by the learned Jesuit Cardinal with a reputation as a towering intellectual figure in modern Catholic theology. It is repeated later in his book (p. 295):

"If he (Pico) is so greatly interested in the books of Kabbalah, it was on the contrary because he believes he finds there the announcement under a form more or less veiled, of precise dogmas 'of the Catholic faith of Christians,' above all, those of the Trinity,[43] and of the divinity of Christ."

In the very name of Jesus, interpreted according to the method and principles of the Kabbalah, he sees these two fundamental dogmas revealed with precision. He likes to discover divers symbols of the Trinity in the 'Orphic Theology.' At least that was his conviction at the time of the *Conclusiones*, of the *Apologia,* and still of the *Heptaplus*." [44]

---

[43] *Conclusiones cabalisticae*, 5 and 33... We do not see on what M. J. Delumeau is basing himself when he says "the count of Mirandula seems to prefer Judaic monotheism to the Christian Trinity."

[44] P. 289, n. 7: Exp. 6, proem. 308-319: "Est Trinitatis divinae in creatura multiplex vestigium, etc."; cf. 228. He takes up the old doctrine according to which "in animo Trinitatis imago repraesentatur": Exp. 5, c. 6; 302. Dulles, 56, observes that he thinks, contrary to Scotus, with Henry of Gand, that the three Persons participate in the creative act, not indistinctly, but each according to His own function.

Another reconciler of Christianity and paganism in Cardinal De Lubac's syncretic pantheon is Rev. Fr. Marsilio Ficino:

"At Florence, one knows how (John) Argyropoulos (Neoplatonic teacher and philosopher funded by Cosimo de Medici; member of the papal court of Sixtus IV from 1471 onward), attempted to unite Aristotle, Plato, Plotinus, and Proclus. The synthesis sought by Marsilio Ficino was different. He received impetus from Plethon, but he does not set out in the same direction. He does not neglect the text of Aristotle; he meditates on the works of Plato (then Plotinus), those of St. Augustine and St. Thomas, especially the *Summa contra Gentiles*; he adds to them all he can find of the 'ancient theologians.' In conformity with a tradition one of whose most eminent representatives was Olivi,[45] he wants to liberate philosophy, this sacred gift of God, from 'impiety,' and at the same time liberate religion from an 'execrable ignorance.' [46]

"That's why, in this Neoplatonic atmosphere, he undertakes to construct a 'pious philosophy,' which he also calls a 'philosophical religion'...in order to oppose the incredulity of 'the majority of peripatetics' (followers of Aristotle) who see, he says, 'in the common religion old wives' tales' [n. 2]. His *Platonic Theology* is a propaedeutic [introductory study], with no ambition to be more. Far from having for himself to 'try to reconcile Christianity and Platonism' [n. 3], he thinks he finds in the latter the better introduction to the former and its best defender: *ad Christum per Platonem*, as in our own century Simone Weil (1909-1943) will say. His influence was to be extensive and long-lasting.

"It has been remarked that the term *'philosophia perennis,'* which will later on experience a renewed fortune by changing meaning, was coined by one of his disciples 'to denote the Christian tradition and the Platonic tradition studied in its

---

[45] *Lectura super Apocalypsim:* By following Averroes, the disciples of the Antichrist have meditated 'profunda et voraginosa dogmata obscurantia solem christianae sapientiae et evangelicae vitae et purum aerem religiosi status ipsius.' Text published by Gregory in *L'Attesa*, 277.

[46] P. 250, n. 1: *De christiana religione*, 1 and 2. There was a bit of over-reacting in the warning addressed to him by the Hungarian John Pannonius: "*Caveas ne forte curiositas quaedam isthaec renovatio antiquorum (sit?) potius quam religio.*"

wake.' [47] Agostino Steuco (1497-1548), who was bishop and prefect of the Vatican, was to dedicate to Paul III in 1540 the ten books of his treatise *De Perenni Philosophia*, which would be republished more than once; there he constantly refers, not only to Plato and his disciples, but to Pythagoras, to Trismegistus, to the Chaldean Oracles, to Sibyls, etc., with an intention that could be called 'ecumenical.' [48]

"A few months after the death of his young friend (Pico), whom he doubly mourned, Marsilio Ficino knew how to show that he bore him no ill will. In the letter he addressed on 23 March 1495 to Germain of Ganay, he made a generous and tender elegy...'He is the chief of Concord since he reconciled the Jews with the Christians, the Peripatetics with the Platonists, the Greeks with the Latins.'

"Without being complete, the enumeration at least implies that in the grand design of Pico, philosophical reconciliation was not all. It was only to be a basis, a point of departure. A real peace had to be established among men, and this could only be solidly established by religious unity."

Notice that De Lubac momentously states, though *en passant*, that "the term *'philosophia perennis'*...will later on experience a renewed fortune by changing meaning..." Is not this *'philosophia perennis,'* under a different coloring, the *genius locus* of Vatican II, Pope Paul VI and his successors?

De Lubac's previously nuanced approach to Pico, accompanying his Kabbalism and pagan syncretism with qualifying statements and modifiers, and assertions of strict orthodoxy and sublime Catholic piety, is undercut when Cardinal de Lubac puts forth "the cosmic Christ," the specialized term of the Hermetic Theosophists, together with his litany of syncretist eminences of the Church of Rome (p. 339):

---

[47] Page 250, n. 4: Kristeller, *Thomisme*, 103-104.

[48] Page 250, n. 5: Lyons, 1540. In the *Opera*, Vol. 3 (Paris, 1578), fol. 1-245. The "ecumenical philosophy" dreamt of by Gratry (*Logique*, Vol. 2, 249) corresponds rather well to this first concept of a "perennial philosophy."

"Apropos the doctrine of Nicholas of Cusa, it has been asked: 'In so far as he is the *Jesus semper benedictus*, an historical person, can (the Christ) become the *fundamentum inconcussum* of an ontology? The problem is grave.[49] It is grave, but it greatly exceeds their two cases. Is not what it expresses the central paradox of the Christian faith, the very paradox of the Incarnation? It does not only appear in subsequent theologies, but already in the texts of St. Paul and St. John.

"The Jesus of history and the 'cosmic Christ' are but one. It is the same paradox that is affirmed in our century in the doctrines of the concrete personal-universal such as they are propounded by a Maurice Blondel, a Pierre Teilhard de Chardin, an Urs von Balthasar; and one must always keep oneself from confounding it with a gnosis, precisely because they always involve *Jesus semper benedictus*.[50]

This is not to be construed as any part of the occult gnosis, De Lubac assures us, because the blessed name of Jesus is always invoked by the ecumenical syncretists. Hence, all is well.

De Lubac takes up the definitive defense of Pico by Pope Alexander VI, after the bull *Et si injuncto nobis* of Pope Innocent VIII, dated August 4, 1487 (but not publicly issued until December 15), condemning seven of the conclusions in Pico's *Nine Hundred Theses*, and censoring six more, which is a measure of tolerance worthy of note in that many hundreds of Pico's other heretical conclusions in the *Nine Hundred Theses* were passed over without censure of any kind by Innocent VIII. His other Kabbalistic magical treatises in his other books were "overlooked" by the reputedly "stern and vigilant" pontiff. As De Lubac also points out:

"Not for an instant does Pico endeavor to justify or to explain his exaltation of human freedom. It needed no defense

---

[49] P. 339, n. 2: L.-J. Bataillon and C. von Schonborn, giving an account of the work of K. Jacobi, *Die Methode des cusanischen Philosophie* (Fribourg-Munich, 1969), in the *Rev. des sc. philos. et theologiques*, 1972.

[50] P. 339, n. 4: Cf. Henri de Lubac, *The Eternal Feminine* [French] (1968) 193-202 and 279-294. As much will be said for the generation that followed Pico, that of a Lefevre d'Etaples, then a Luis de Leon.

because it had never been contested (by Innocent VIII). The reason is simple: the *Oratio* (*Oration on the Dignity of Man*), in which this 'celebration' is found, had not been examined. It was, let us repeat, totally outside the debate. Whatever one may think of the doctrine contained in this work, it must not be forgotten that it was never pronounced upon, nor subject to an examination by any censor" (p. 401). "None of the writings of Pico della Mirandola was ever listed in any catalogue of the *Index of Prohibited Books*" (p. 412).

At this juncture we note that Lorenzo de Medici and Pope Innocent VIII were political allies. Lorenzo's daughter married Innocent's natural son. Lorenzo and the pontiff shared a grandson, the future cardinal, Innocenzo Cibo. [51]

As previously stated, Pico fled to France the next year where he was briefly imprisoned by order of the Duke of Savoy. He was soon after released by French King Charles VIII and returned to Florence and the lap of Medici luxury, a "heretic" who now lived exempt from any further interdiction by the pontiff.

Conservative Catholics were placated by the ostentatious "dramatic moves against Pico" and hoped there would be more to come. There was a theatrical aspect to the papal intervention, the "flight into France" and the subsequent return to the comfort and safety of Lorenzo the Magnificent's city of Florence, where Giovanni Pico settled in a palatial villa and continued his heretical writing as before. In the summer of 1489 he published *Heptaplus,* his Kabbalistic falsification of the book of Genesis. De Lubac, in asserting Pico's alleged orthodoxy, writes (pp. 401; 410 and 411):

"...one will object, what about the Bull of Innocent VIII?... [Upon the accession of Rodrigues Borgia to the pontificate under the name of Alexander VI, Pico had delivered to him a model letter insinuating his request to be rehabilitated...] [p. 409]. During the first year of his pontificate, Alexander VI, ratifying the conclusions proposed by three cardinals and the

---

[51] Pope Innocent VIII (Giovanni Battista Cibo) publicly acknowledged as his natural son, the scoundrel Franceschetto Cibo, who was married to Maddalena de' Medici, Lorenzo's daughter. The eldest of their six children was Innocenzo Cibo (1491-1550), who, in 1513, would be made a cardinal by his uncle, Pope Leo X (Giovanni de' Medici).

master of the Sacred Palace, wrapped up the whole affair by a letter addressed 'to our dear son, the noble Giovanni Pico, Earl of Mirandola.' Of course, it was a political gesture, 'a homage rendered to Peter de Medici given the current political situation in Italy'; but the gesture nonetheless came at the conclusion of a seriously conducted investigation...

"Was Alexander VI's *Brief* a simple absolution granted to Pico or a rehabilitation pure and simple, which could be viewed as a retraction on the part of the Holy See? In our opinion, the truth seems to lie between the two, closer, however, to the second hypothesis. A close reading of the document is the best way to ascertain this. It is composed of two parts: an exposition of the facts that occurred under Innocent VIII, then, by reason of the new inquiry, the decision of Alexander. The exposition of the facts attenuates the rigor of the measures taken previously; it was merely a matter of protecting the faith of believers and especially of the simple, because the wording of some of the propositions could have led them into error.

"Pico is always shown in a good light: the fact that the *Nine Hundred Conclusions (Theses)* had been proposed for the discussion of the learned under the pope's control is advanced in his favor, and that their author always showed himself to be disposed toward an entire submission. The *Apologia* is presented entirely to Pico's credit: with a sincere faith he interprets the contested propositions in a Catholic way. [52] Then the pope pronounced his judgment. He begins by conditionally absolving Pico from every censure he may have incurred by reason of perjury, in order to bring to his soul perfect tranquility. Then he declares 'extinct *(motu proprio et ex certa scientia)*, all the grounds for complaint [grievances] raised against him by the previous commission. He assures him that he committed no fault, has incurred no penalty, has not fallen under suspicion of heresy *'propter editionem Declarationum et*

---

[52] P. 410, n. 3: "*...te quemdam alium librum Apologeticum edidisse, in qo easdem conclusiones in meliorem et catholicum sensum declarans interpretabaris, et circa eas intellectum sincerae fidei explicabas...*" The word "*meliorem*" allows the inference that Pico, in explaining himself, was able on one point or other to rectify his doctrine. Thus the self-esteem of the censors is saved.

Apologetici.'[53] Finally, he forbids anyone from picking a quarrel with him over any of these past events. The *Brief* was skillfully drafted. Without contradicting Innocent, Alexander did more than absolve Pico.[54] He praised him, and basing himself on his *Apologia*, he approved his doctrine. That is why John-Francis (his nephew, Gianfrancesco) was able to have a new edition of his uncle's *Apologia* published in 1495..."

De Lubac herewith follows the trail of Pico's influence in the Church of Rome in the centuries that followed his death, including with Reuchlin (notice his dig at Hoogstraeten [below] as guilty of "petty...provincialism" like Pico's alleged adversary Pedro Garsias), though he omits Francesco Giorgi and Agrippa. Nonetheless, De Lubac adds to our knowledge of the Neoplatonic-Hermetic-Kabbalistic Catholic personnel, and the "clean slate" that constituted Pico's Catholic status:

"Thus it is in complete security that the hot-headed defender of Pico's Christian Kabbalism, Archangelus de Borgo Novo (Angiolo Pozzi, author of *Interpretationes in Cabalistarum selectiora dogmata* of 1569), will in 1564, in the preface of a book directed against Pedro Garsias,[55] contrast the grandeur of his hero with the petty, pretentious provincialism of those who had wanted to stifle his voice. 'Fallen,' he wrote, 'into the nets set out for him by the clever folly of his judges, Pico, the noblest of the learned and the most learned of the nobles, more eloquent than the ancient wise men, more illustrious, holy, and of a purer taste in every genre of life and of doctrine, poured

---

[53] This is indeed how the document is cited in the edition of the *Opera* and in Napoli, 117. The *Civilta Cattolica*, cited elsewhere, deemed that it should have read: "propter editionem et declarationem Apologetici," because the "Conclusiones" were not "Declarationes." For the general meaning of the Brief, this discrepancy seems to us to be unimportant.

[54] When Alexander says *"Pro potiori cautela tua, ab omni reatu perjurii si quem etim forsan indirecte, dicto juramento tuo... aliquo modo contraveniendo incurrisses, absolventes,"* he relieves (*absolvit*) Pico of an hypothetical censure; he does not absolve him from any fault of heresy or of bad doctrine, of which he declares him, on the contrary, exempt, given the explications of the *Apology*: he *nullifi (extinguimus)* the cause inaugurated by the theologians of Innocent VIII.

[55] Published at Bologna, the book, several times reprinted, was never censured. Secret, 256, 268, 343. Garsias has been justly compared to the Cologne Dominican Hoogstraeten, the implacable adversary of Reuchlin.

into his *Apology*, a small book of immense erudition, gems more precious than gold.'

"Such will be, in the following century, the opinion of the renowned Jesuit Kabbalist Athanasius Kircher, who will include Pico della Mirandola among the sources of his monumental *Oedipus Aegyptiacus.*[56] He will adopt his interpretations of Orpheus and will cite them in commenting 'according to their legitimate sense' in order to give an '*anakephalaiosis*' of his own thought, seven of the *effata mystica*, chosen among the *conclusiones secundum Proclum* (Nos. 2, 8, 11, 15, 49), *secundum propriam opinionem de modo intelligendi hymnos Orphei* (No. 28) and *cabalisticae* (No. 13).[57]

"There is no mention of him in the fourteen books *Adversus omnes haereses* published under Paul III at Venice in 1546 by Alphonsus de Castro Zamorensis, O.M.

"The *Treatise of Heresies* published in 1661 by Louis Abelly, which aims at a complete inventory century by century and which does not spare Raymond Lully, breathes not a word about the (*Nine Hundred*) *Conclusions* or the *Apologia*. One would also seek in vain the name of Pico in the *Istoria di tutte l'eresie* of Domenico Bernino in the chapter that relates the errors condemned under the pontificate of Innocent VIII."

As Cardinal De Lubac attests through his sources, *Pico's rehabilitation by the papacy was complete*. His diabolic slate had been wiped clean, even by the "Counter-Reformation Pontiff" Paul III. It has remained so over the centuries, up to the present. Alleged "counter-occult" popes of the post-Renaissance Church of Rome, such as Leo X and Pius X, had not a word of disapprobation for this preeminent worker of iniquity. "Conservatives" and "traditionalists" likewise view him as benign. His syncretic occult religion has been a smashing success. His dream of a public fusion between Catholicism, Hermeticism and Judaism has come to fruition. Giovanni Pico della Mirandola is the true father of the Second Vatican Council and the "post-Conciliar Church."

---

[56] P. 413, n. 1: Vol. 2, Part I (Rome, 1653), 151, 186-189.

[57] P. 413, n. 2: Pico, *Opera*, 75, 76, 78, 107, 109. This is last of de Lubac's notes reprinted in these pages.

Chapter XV

Neoplatonic-Hermetic Kabbalism in the Modern Era

I

Eliphas Lévi: Patriarch of the incognito Hermetic "Traditional Catholic" movement

It was the ultra-montane Catholic layman Joseph de Maistre (1753-1821), "a proponent of traditionalism," Minister to Russia under King Victor Emmanuel I, and Minister of State in Sardinia, who worked on behalf of an Illuminati "tradition" in league with the Church of Rome and consonant with the absolute obedience owed to the pontiff. A monarchist and one of the founders of the ultramontanist movement, De Maistre was from 1774 to 1790 at the same time a Freemason of the various masonic orders, among them the powerful Illuminist Scottish Rite (the Chambéry lodge "La Sincérité," led by Jean-Baptiste Willermoz), as well as simultaneously a member in good standing of the Jesuit penitential order, Grande Congrégation Notre Dame de l'Assomption.

Maistre's occult master, Willermoz, was part of the Catholic-Kabbalist movement under the papist occultist Martines de Pasqually (d. 1774), [1] who required that members of his inner Order of Elect Coens (*Ordre des Elus Coëns*), join the Catholic Church, devoutly and faithfully attend the Catholic Tridentine Mass and receive the sacraments from bona fide Catholic priests. Here was another transmission of the Neoplatonic-Hermetic "Perennial Philosophy," i.e. the Renaissance Catholic "Marsilio Ficino's original Perennialism," together with Pico and Recuhlin's Kabbalism, manifested within Martinism in the eighteenth century, and through it, the Church of Rome's

---

[1] Gérard van Rjinberk gives the year of Pasqually's birth as circa 1709. Other documents indicate circa 1726.

doctrine of papal infallibility, as well as the "staunchly Catholic" Right-wing ultramontane movement. [2]

In his unfinished *Les Soirées de Saint-Petersbourg*, which is a defense of the Kabbalist-papist Martinist movement, Maistre wrote that certain forms of Illuminism, such as that of Louis-Claude de Saint-Martin (1743-1803), help to erase the disunity caused by Protestantism, through the maintenance of a secret tradition across confessional boundaries. His book *Du Pape* (1820) served as a groundwork for the papal infallibility movement that culminated in Vatican Council I, decades later. In it he stated, "no sovereign pontiff has ever made a mistake in speaking on matters of faith."

The heir to this occult pottage was the "always faithful Catholic" Alphonse Louis Constant, known by his *non de plume*, Éliphas Lévi (1810-1875). He is the spiritual patriarch of the mostly incognito Hermeticists who have infiltrated the contemporary "traditional Catholic" Latin Mass movement of our time. Ordained a deacon at the Catholic seminary of Saint-Sulpice under the papist-occultist Abbé Frére-Colonna, with the patronage of the Archbishop of Paris, he obtained a supervisory post at the Catholic Collége de Juilly and preached in churches in the vicinity of Solesmes. Devoted to mariolatry (Jesus' mother as a kind of goddess), in his *Le rosier de mai ou la guirlande de Marie* ("The Rosebush of Mary's Garland"), he indulges in erotic vignettes of Mary's dolorous plight, and in *La Mére de Dieu*, Mary is the Co-Redemptrix of the Universe. Constant/Lévi was all over the occult map of France, presenting the Kabbalah to French masonic initiates and among the circle of Edward Bulwer-Lytton in England, as well as in his books, among them his manual of Kabbalistic magic and gematria, *La clef des grands mystéres* (1861). Constant/Levi, despite his Satanic rites and writings (cf. his *Dogme et rituel* chapter on Necromancy), and rumored summoning of demons (according to his housekeeper and nurse, Madame Gebhardt), and as reported by associates of Bulwer-Lytton (for

---

2 Cf. Mark Sedgwick, *Against the Modern World: Traditionalism and the Secret Intellectual History of the Twentieth Century* (Oxford University, 2004) pp. 40-41.

instance in London, in July, 1854), *was never disciplined by the Catholic hierarchy and freely spread his occult contagion.* [3]

The appearance of "bleeding hosts" (a "host" is a name for the Catholic communion wafer) is often taken as proof of Transubstantiation, the belief that when a validly ordained Catholic priest who has the proper intention, consecrates a host during the Mass, it literally becomes the flesh of Jesus Christ. For the occult circle of Constant-Levi, these "bleeding hosts" were manifestations of transcendental magic—and masonic and Hermetic symbolism: "Eliphas Lévi combined his occultism with a strong adherence to Catholicism...Lévi was...shocked when the Abbé showed him an album containing pictures of miraculous hosts, three of which particularly caught his attention because of the signs that they bore. The first was stamped with the star of the microcosm, or the magic pentagram...It is the five-pointed star of occult masonry, the star with which Agrippa drew the human figure...The second host bore the signs of two intertwined hermetic serpents." [4]

Inspired by the Kabbalistic popery of Constant/Lévi, an Anglican priest, the Right Rev. C.W. Leadbeater (1854-1934) became a leader in the "Theosophical" movement. [5] Some theosophists combined devotion to the Tridentine Latin Mass with a movement to bring the Antichrist to earth. One hesitates to state a fact so lurid, yet there it is. Beginning in 1909, Leadbeater proposed a Hindu youth in India, Jiddu Krishnamurti, as the "World-Teacher." (This writer was first

---

[3] One of Constant/Lévi's followers lectured at the seminary of the "traditional Catholic" Society of St. Pius X (SSPX) in Winona, Minnesota in the 1990s. As of this writing, he continues to give interviews on "Catholic radio," and to lecture and write on behalf of ultramontane "traditional Catholicism," monarchy, and the Anglo-Catholic-masonic Stuart dynasty.

[4] Christopher McIntosh, *Eliphas Lévi and the French Occult Revival* (State University of New York, 2011), pp. 109 and 171.

[5] "The occultist group that (Rene) Guenon joined in 1906, and from which he developed his 'Vedanta-Perennialism,' was the Martinist Order. It had been established in about 1890 by Gérard Encausse (famous as 'Papus')...The Theosophical Society was established in New York in 1875...by...Colonel Henry Olcott. Olcott wanted the Theosophical Society to...find 'ancient wisdom,' especially in the 'primeval source of all religions, the books of Hermes and the Vedas'—in other words, the Perennial Philosophy." (Mark Sedgwick, *Against the Modern World* [2004], p. 40). For the role of Papus in helping to erode the institution of the Tsar in Russia, cf. Sergei O. Prokofieff, *The Spiritual Origins of Eastern Europe* (2016), pp. 208-211.

confronted with the alleged perspicacity of this Krishnamurti individual, by an affluent "traditional Catholic." Our failure to agree that this Krishnamurti Antichrist was an astute truth-teller, put an end to our acquaintance).

Leadbeater is claimed as an inspiration by many wings of the occult. He is of interest in our study for his advocacy of the Tridentine Latin Mass. In his book *The Science of the Sacraments*, Leadbeater unveils what he alleges are the occult secrets of the Mass. Leadbeater was part of the occult gnosis which saw in the old Catholic Mass the fulfillment of magical doctrines. Catholics should be aware that when the Tridentine Mass is made an idol in itself, it can become the object of a cult subject to mystification, private revelation and magical thinking that is indifferent to the primacy of Biblical standards. Antiquarians who imagine that the revival of the old Mass is the primary means of sanctification, no matter which pederastic priest or bishop celebrates it, or how sleepy, apathetic or superstitious is the congregation, are in line with Leadbeater's occult thinking.

On the other hand, Protestants who seek to abolish the liturgy of the Eucharist, which was clearly a part of the first century worship of the Early Church, are as much in error as those Catholics who imagine that Jesus preached a religion of magic. *What Jesus did at the Last Supper was not magic*, and Catholics who treat the Eucharist as if it were, build the empire of the occult, not the Kingdom of God.

II

Tridentine Judaism

Ever since the pontificate of John-Paul II, we have witnessed the rise of the religion of Holocaustianity, formerly known in theology as *YomHaShoah* (or *Shoah*, for short), the doctrine of the Israeli state inside the Church of Rome. Some "traditional Catholic" leaders, both clerical and lay, have declared that the infiltration of the *Shoah* theology into the Church of Rome has "no bearing on faith and morals."

The old Catholic Mass rite alone, when separated from ancient Christian truth (which is now outlawed by means of the "antisemitism" canard), becomes merely a type of High Church Anglicanism, in which one emasculated wing of the Hegelian synthesis is allowed to participate in the dialectic for considerations of aesthetics and enhancing organizational discipline. This is not Scriptural. The prayer of the Church is a mere totem if it is immersed in a milieu which overthrows the doctrine of the Gospel.

Under High Church Anglicanism, the Elizabethan Isis-gnosis was not challenged, but rather, was accommodated as a *quid pro quo* for the High Church faction being permitted the liturgy of Edward VI.

Under Pope Benedict XVI, the masonic, post-conciliar, Hermetic-Talmudic-rabbinic gnosis was not challenged, but rather is accommodated as a *quid pro quo* for the traditionalist faction being permitted the liturgy of Pius V.

The medieval prayer of the Church without the medieval belief of the Church is not a remedy, it is an abomination and an alchemical mockery. Many on the Right said in his defense that Pope Benedict was execrated and opposed by the Left, as if this hatred on the part of some Leftists is the universal solvent that reconciles all contradictions. Few seem to be cognizant of elementary principles of human alchemy and mind control as practiced by the Cryptocracy by means of the Hegelian dialectic. The thesis is always played against the antithesis, i.e. the Right is always a stage prop against the Left. The opposition of zealous Leftists to the pontificate of Benedict XVI did not render Benedict a true Catholic. Leftists are enraged that Benedict did not modify church edicts against contraception and women priests. But of what genuine significance is this particular "conservatism," when a Neoplatonic-Hermetic revolution against the Gospel itself—the radical overthrow of nearly 1500 years of Christian teaching on Judaism—is implemented by Pope Benedict?

The Left-wing oppositional *thesis* does not absolve Benedict XVI of his complicity in Paul VI's 1965 *Nostra Aetate,* or John-Paul II's *Shoah* business. Benedict's *synthesis* of the Leftist *thesis* and the Rightist *antithesis* culminated in his continuing perpetuation of the calamitous "Elder brothers in the faith" fraud, and "Holocaust" mania. Both of these modernist innovations were as strong as ever under Benedict's pontificate and thanks to his astute maneuvering, were repeated by "Roman Catholic conservatives and traditionalists."

The mixing of irreconcilable opposites is a hallmark of the human alchemy of the Cryptocracy. This virtuoso amalgamation is what we have in the infernal marriage of the Old Catholic Mass with the new Catholic belief in Holocaustianity, and the notion that Orthodox Judaism does not seriously threaten Catholicism, and is at least somewhat benign, at least in comparison with Islam.

Benedict XVI cloaked his modernism in the venerable attire of the Latin liturgy of the high civilization of the European past. He revived the old ceremonies because he and his Vatican understood that it is increasingly difficult to successfully maintain organizational discipline and the loyalty of an increasingly wayward laity under the exclusive auspices of the mediocre reductionism which often attends Pope Paul VI's "Novus Ordo" Mass.

Benedict's cloak fell at least somewhat when he issued the following document, "Letter of his Holiness Benedict XVI to the Bishops of the Catholic Church Concerning the Remission of the Excommunication of the Four Bishops Consecrated by Archbishop Lefebvre." Note the dialectical jargon in the pope's first paragraph:

"...A gesture of reconciliation with an ecclesial group (the SSPX) engaged in a process of separation...*turned into its very antithesis: an apparent step backwards with regard to all the steps of reconciliation between Christians and Jews taken since the Council – steps which my own work as a theologian had sought from the beginning to take part in and support.* That this overlapping of two opposed processes took place and *momentarily upset peace between Christians and Jews,* as well as peace within the Church, is something which I can only deeply deplore....

"Certainly, for some time now, and once again on this specific occasion, we have heard from some representatives of that community many unpleasant things – *arrogance and presumptuousness, an obsession with one-sided positions* etc.

"...Dear Brothers, during the days when I first had the idea of writing this letter, by chance, during a visit to the Roman Seminary, I had to interpret and comment on Galatians 5:13-15. I was surprised at the directness with which that passage speaks to us about the present moment: 'Do not use your freedom as an opportunity for the flesh, but through love be servants of one another. For the whole law is fulfilled in one word: 'You shall love your neighbor as yourself.' But if you bite and devour one another, take heed that you are not consumed by one another.' *I am always tempted to see these words as another of the rhetorical excesses which we occasionally find in Saint Paul. To some extent that may also be the case...*" [6]

Pope Benedict accuses the Apostle Paul of exaggeration ("rhetorical excesses") and admits that "reconciliation between Christians and Jews" has been his goal as a theologian from the beginning of his career —not the *conversion* of Judaics, but "reconciliation." How can two opposites reconcile? Where in scripture is the mandate for a "reconciliation between Christians and Judaics" warranted? The Vatican worships the god of the United Nations, the mainstream media and the spirit of the world (1 Cor. 2:12). In our media age the concept of reconciliation with evil (except the unpardonable supposed "evil" of obstructing Talmudism and Kabbalism), is a politically correct idol to which the Vatican has submitted.

Pope Benedict exhorted Catholics to work for "peace between Christians and Jews." What sort of "peace" was there between Jesus and the Pharisees? How can there be peace with the successors of the Pharisees, except by diluting the Catholic

---

[6] March 10, 2009; published on March 12; excerpts with emphasis supplied.

Faith with the leaven of the Pharisees? With reference to supporters of Bishop Williamson, Pope Benedict wrote of their: "...arrogance and presumptuousness, an obsession with one-sided positions..."

Holocaustianity

In the Neoplatonic-Hermetic theology of the Church of Rome, the "Holocaust" or *Shoah*, represents the sublimation of our Lord Jesus Christ. His subsidiary status is a type of blasphemy since it is brought about by the idolatry inherent in *Shoah* theology, viz. Holocaustolatry. Consider the fact that Cardinal Sean O'Malley of Boston made the astonishing declaration on February 23, 2009, that the "Holocaust" was the "worst crime" in history. Calvary? What's that? A footnote, at best.

We also observe the effects of Holocaustolatry in the increasingly bold and public Talmudic mockery and denigration of Jesus by Hollywood (as for example by repeatedly taking His name in vain; Exodus 20:7; Philippians 2:10), and in the deadly anti-Christian libel that constitutes denial of His Resurrection, as personified by the "Discovery" cable television channel with its worldwide broadcast of "Titanic" movie director James Cameron's documentary claiming to have found the burial tomb of the "dead" Jesus Christ. Needless to say, Hollywood moguls are not jailed for blaspheming Jesus or denying His Resurrection. Furthermore, all the hot air blown by the Right-wing over Obama, abortion, Islam etc. is nowhere to be found assailing the *Talmudic source* of the media's blasphemies, which strike at the heart of the Christian Faith (1 Corinthians 15: 14-15).

Meanwhile, revisionist historians serve prison sentences in Germany for blaspheming Judaism's sacred Auschwitz, which is far more sacred in our modern world than the immolation of the Son of God on Calvary. In Europe, faith in the alleged homicidal gas chambers is state-mandated and papally promulgated. Their status as a sacred relic is vastly superior to the Crucifixion of the Son of God. There is no civic protection for Jesus Christ and no Vatican promotion of His Gospel as salvation to the Jews. Rather, the Neoplatonic-Hermetic popes of the modern era, in *Nostra Aetate* ("In Our Time") and subsequent post-conciliar and papal decrees, have twisted scripture to rehabilitate Christ's assassins, the Pharisees.

The roots of Holocaustianity's Catholic-S*hoah* cult pre-date 1965 and the Second Vatican Council. Talmudism and neo-Platonic Kabbalism were, as has been demonstrated in these pages, powerful currents in the Renaissance and that era's popes succumbed to the allure. The protagonists behind *Nostra Aetate* were Popes John XXIII and Paul VI, and the "Secretariat for Promoting Christian Unity" led by Jesuit Cardinal Augustin Bea and Bishop Johannes Willebrands, with assistance from Bea's *peritus* ("theology expert"), Jesuit Father Malachi Martin (who intermittently wrote for Zionist publications under a pseudonym). Josef Ratzinger (the future "Benedict XVI") was also a player.

In June, 1960, Pope John had a fateful meeting with Jules Isaac, an 81-year-old French Zionist who founded the *Amitié Judeo-Chrétienne*, a Paris-based study group of approximately sixty Judaics and "Christians." As far back as 1947, *Amitié* had proposed "correcting" what it described as "theologically inexact concepts and presentations of the Gospel of Love" that place Judaics in spiritual and physical ghettos. Mr. Jules Isaac had prepared for the Roman Church a study that sketched the history of its teachings, legislation and actions toward Judaics. Isaac's unedited memoirs record his conversation with John XXIII. He noted that "the teaching of contempt for the Jews, in essence anti-Christian, should be purified..." Could not the pope, "a voice from the summit, show the true path?" Pope John XXIII asked Isaac to meet with Cardinal Bea. On September 18, the pope and Bea weighed Isaac's positions and proposals. Upon Bea's recommendation, John XXIII mandated that the Secretariat for Promoting Christian Unity should facilitate "reflection" on "the Jewish question" during its preparation for the Second Vatican Council. The fostering of a spiritual, theological and catechetical revolution became the objective. Nathum Goldmann, president of the World Jewish Congress and co-chairman of the World Conference of Jewish Organizations was advising the Vatican at this time. Goldmann and Cardinal Bea met in the latter's private quarters three weeks before the Secretariat's first plenary session. [7]

The Vatican II Kabbalist-sage Rabbi Abraham Heschel candidly admitted that his dialogue with Catholicism was really about attacking Christians' souls with 'Holocaust' guilt. Heschel actually said, *"I want to attack their souls."*

"In *Spiritual Radical*, the biography of the Hasidic change agent, Rabbi Abraham Heschel (by Edward K. Kaplan, Yale University Press), is an account of an interview Rabbi Heschel gave during the time the Vatican II document *Nostra Aetate*, which Heschel collaborated on, was being deliberated.

The interview reveals an attitude of remarkable hostility to Christians, which should come as no surprise to those knowledgeable of the rabbinic tradition. What may surprise some (but shouldn't at this point) is that such a hostile character would be invited by Vatican officials to participate in the writing of a Church council document.

"First some background: in Heschel's many meetings with Vatican officials (as a representative of the American Jewish Committee) regarding *Nostra Aetate*, mostly with Augustin Bea, but including a secretive meeting with Paul VI, Heschel was most adamant that the document should clearly proclaim his belief that it is unacceptable for Christians to seek the conversion of 'Jews.'

Heschel's *chutzpah* in peddling this absurd idea (which consequently would undercut Christ's incarnation, evangelical mission and sacrifice), went to the extreme of appealing to the non-Biblical, relativistic, Talmudic anti-principle, *mipnei darchai shalom* [8] during his meeting with Paul VI.

---

[7] http://www.americamagazine.org/content/article.cfm?article_id=4431

[8] This is a legal category derived from Mishnah Gittin 5:8, which lists various laws centered upon the custom, under certain circumstances, of *mipnei darchei shalom* (giving the appearance of benevolent acts toward gentiles). Behind this camouflage is the actual *halachot* (law)—the *mishum aivah*, denoting actions performed "because of animosity." The teaching is that where Judaism encounters powerful opposition it is best to wear a mask of benevolence until such time as Israel is supreme; at which time the pretense is no longer necessary and can be dropped.

"During the deliberations, a draft of the *Nostra Aetate* document was leaked to the press which did not include the prohibition against converting 'Jews' which Heschel desired. This infuriated Heschel, and in response he wrote an editorial published both by the *New York Times* and *Time* magazine in which he proclaimed, 'As I have repeatedly stated to leading personalities of the Vatican, I am ready to go to Auschwitz any time, if faced with the alternative of conversion or death.'

"Heschel's biographer Kaplan (citing Schuster's notes on record at AJC/Paris), writes that the American Jewish Congress's European director, Zachariah Schuster, warned Heschel that this outburst had been embarrassing to their Vatican collaborators, but that Heschel replied undauntedly, 'I had my own private reasons for making this remark.'

"Heschel later revealed to a female Stern Gang terrorist, Geula Cohen, what those private reasons were, in an interview for the Israeli newspaper, *Ma'ariv*. In interviewing Rabbi Abraham Heschel, Cohen made reference to his hysterical 'ready to go to Auschwitz' statement, saying she was proud of it, but that she would have handled it differently. She wrote:

"This statement of yours made me proud. Yet, I would have written it differently, saying: 'if this were the only way in which I would be permitted to live, I would have endeavored to send them (Christians) to Auschwitz.'

"Cohen relayed that Heschel was not shocked by her words, but explained that his statement was stronger than hers...Heschel further clarified, explaining the private reasons he earlier said he had for making the 'Auschwitz' statement: "(Christians) correctly understood that I was comparing them to the Nazis. If I had made the statement in a straightforward fashion saying 'you are Nazis,' it would have sounded ridiculous. My style of writing is by hinting, because truth is in the depths. There are those who would like to attack their bodies. *I want to attack their souls*. Today, there is no longer any place for religious wars as such. Today there is occasion for conversation and discussion. Do you consider the desire to discuss a sign of weakness?" [9]

---

[9] Rabbi Abraham Heschel, interviewed by Geula Cohen for *Ma'ariv*, January 4, 1965, as translated by AJC/Paris; emphasis supplied.

There we have the motivation behind "dialogue" with "elder brothers" succinctly summarized by one of the esteemed pioneers of interfaith "dialogue," who participated in the writing of a Church Council's document, *Nostra Aetate*. Rabbinic warfare against Christian souls is not fought with guns and bombs as often as with "conversation" and "discussion." Here we see the subtlety of rabbinic warfare..." [10]

Nostra Aetate ("In Our Time")

Declaration on the Relationship of the Church to Non-Christian Religions
Second Vatican Council, October 28, 1965.
Passed by a vote of 2,312 bishops pro, and 88 con.

"Sounding the depths of the mystery which is the Church, *this sacred council remembers the spiritual ties which link the people of the new covenant to the stock of Abraham.* The Church of Christ acknowledges that in God's plan of salvation the beginnings of its faith and election are to be found in the patriarchs, Moses and the prophets.

"It professes that all Christ's faithful, who as people of faith are daughters and sons of Abraham (see Gal 3:7), are included in the same patriarch's call and that the salvation of the Church is mystically prefigured in the exodus of God's chosen people from the land of bondage. On this account *the Church cannot forget that it received the revelation of the Old Testament by way of that people with whom God in his inexpressible mercy established the ancient covenant.* Nor can it forget that it draws nourishment from that good olive tree onto which the wild olive branches of the Gentiles have been grafted (see Rom 11:17-24).

"The Church believes that Christ who is our peace has through his cross reconciled Jews and Gentiles and made them one in himself (see Eph 2:14-16). Likewise, the Church keeps ever before its mind the words of the apostle Paul about his kin: 'they are Israelites and it is for them to be sons and daughters, to them belong the glory, the covenants, the giving of the law, the worship, and the promises; to them belong the patriarchs, and of their race according to the flesh, is the

---

10   http://mauricepinay.blogspot.com/2007/12/vatican-ii-kabbalist-sage-rabbi-abraham.html

Christ' (Rom 9:4-5). It is mindful, moreover, that the apostles, the pillars on which the Church stands, are of Jewish descent, as are many of those early disciples who proclaimed the Gospel of Christ to the world." (End quote; emphasis supplied).

Nostra Aetate is sometimes defended in the following terms: "It lifts collective guilt for deicide off the shoulders of the Jewish people." This fact is supposed to be a conversation-stopper which 1. proves *Nostra Aetate* is consonant with scripture and tradition, and 2. acts as a rebuke to "anti-Semites."

The problem is that *Nostra Aetate* is a great deal more than just a single declaration. Its defects are to be found in its other, mostly unexamined declarations. There is nothing particularly sinister in the portion of *Nostra Aetate* which we have quoted, except for the ominous racial emphasis on the "stock of Abraham." From here onward in modern Catholic theological pronouncements, we encounter the lineaments of what this writer terms *Ku Klux Judaism*.

The Neoplatonic-Hermetic papacy proclaims to the world that "the Jews" among us are still the Holy Race. This is occult Jew-hate, not love. Observe the demonic insinuation (for it is never stated openly), that contemporary Judics are saved—or at the very least—rendered sacred in God's eyes, by their alleged descent from Abraham.

Catholic liberals *and* conservatives imagine that this proposition is some sort of lofty and radical challenge to craven "anti-Semitism" and a "prophetic call" to humility on the part of Christians.

In truth, this proposition is Jew-hate par excellence, for *it encourages the deadly race pride that has blinded Judaics to Jesus Christ across the centuries, and thereby consigns them to eternal perdition.* But to speak this paradoxical truth is forbidden (I Thess. 2:16).

In a few respects *Nostra Aetate* makes valid points. For example it says to the proponents of the Wagnerian/neo-Nazi theory of a non-Judean "Aryan Christ," and to the Manichaean and Mariconian haters of the Old Testament, that Jews and the Old Testament are integral to the Church and form its root. This is true.

Nostra Aetate: "As holy scripture testifies, Jerusalem did not recognize God's moment when it came (see Lk 19:42). Jews for the most part did not accept the Gospel; on the contrary, many opposed its spread (see Rom 11:28). Even so, the apostle Paul maintains that the Jews remain very dear to God, for the sake of the patriarchs, since God does not take back the gifts he bestowed or the choice he made. Together with the prophets and that same apostle, the Church awaits the day, known to God alone, when all peoples will call on God with one voice and serve him shoulder to shoulder (Soph 3:9; see Is 66:23; Ps 65:4; Rom 11:11-32)."

The misuse and distortion of St. Paul is a keystone of Holocaustianity. We have here the emphasis on *the implication that the Apostle is sanctioning a saved-by-race happy ending to the Judaic drama of rejection of their Messiah*. All that Paul has ever said on this subject amounts to Jews being saved at the end of time *because they will be numbered among the Christians*.

This is the meaning of the authentic reconciliation referred to in Ephesians 2:14-16: Jews are reconciled with gentiles *through the Cross*. Jews who are not saved by faith in Christ are, according to St. Paul, "under wrath...contrary to all men." (1 Thess. 2:14-16). *Nostra Aetate* omits this harsh truth. In the lexicon of the Neoplatonic-Hermetic papal subversives, "reconciliation" between Christians and Jews connotes the appeasement of rabbinic Judaism and its unscriptural[11] claim to having a divine relationship with God the Father while rejecting his Divine Son.

Nostra Aetate: "Even though the Jewish authorities and those who followed their lead pressed for the death of Christ (see John 19:6), neither all Jews indiscriminately at that time, nor Jews today, can be charged with the crimes committed during his passion."

The first statement is true, the second is conditional. Anyone, be they "Jew" or gentile can be charged with crimes "committed during his passion" if they share in the spiritual ideology of the Pharisees who railroaded Him to His death. This includes blond British Freemasons and dusky, curly-

---

[11] John 14:6; I John 2:23.

haired Hasidim. No one is guilty solely by virtue of being of a particular ethnicity. But there can be no immunity for Antichrist Judaics (or gentile sinners, which includes us all— Romans 3:10), from bearing *spiritual guilt for the Crucifixion*, even in the present age.

Nostra Aetate: "It is true that the Church is the new people of God, yet the Jews should not be spoken of as rejected or accursed as if this followed from holy scripture. Consequently, all must take care, lest in catechizing or in preaching the word of God, they teach anything which is not in accord with the truth of the Gospel message or the spirit of Christ."

An ambiguity is being manipulated and exploited in this paragraph. How is the Vatican Council defining "Jews" — by race, or by religious ideology? It is entirely Biblical to regard the adherents of contemporary Orthodox Judaism who perpetuate the beliefs of the Pharisees, as exactly what Jesus said they were (and are), "accursed." (Matthew 21:19).

The accursed fig tree was carnal Israel, which gave the appearance of fertility but was actually barren (Hosea 9:10). Galatians 1:8 states that those who come preaching a false, modern gospel are "accursed." It is entirely within the right of the Catholic to employ this term *accursed* as Jesus and Paul applied it.

Nostra Aetate has no power to cancel a Scriptural warrant, except by the same power that the Talmud uses to cancel the Old Testament. Furthermore, it is politically correct modernism *in extremis* to suggest that "preaching or catechizing" Judaics must be limited or modified.

Nostra Aetate: "Indeed, the Church reproves every form of persecution against whomsoever it may be directed. Remembering, then, its common heritage with the Jews and moved not by any political consideration, but solely by the religious motivation of Christian charity, it deplores all hatreds, persecutions, displays of antisemitism directed against the Jews at any time or from any source."

From correct denunciation of racial animus, *Nostra Aetate* branches out to extrapolate a Neoplatonic-Hermetic conclusion for which, once again, there is no basis in the Scriptures:

"...deplores all...persecutions...directed against the Jews at any time or from any source." Here is the great departure from historic Christian teaching, and a repudiation of all Christian saints throughout history who exposed rabbinic Talmudic-Phariseeism, from Vincent Ferrer to Queen Isabella of Spain.

And what of those *Christians who were persecuted by Judaics?* Do their persecutors come in for the Council's sweeping condemnation "for all time" and from "any source?" In the face of the Judeo-masonic holocaust of Catholics in the Vendee region of France and of the Cristeros in Mexico; and of the Judeo-Bolshevik holocaust of Orthodox Christians in Russia, the pontificating moral conscience of *Nostra Aetate* is silent. The post-Renaissance Vatican's memory of those other holocausts is blank. This too is a fruit of the religion of Holocaustianity: *amnesia concerning the history of the persecution of Christians by Judaics.* The smoke of Talmudic immunity and entitlement has entered the Church.

Taking *Nostra Aetate* to its logical conclusion, the enemies of Christ, call them Freemasons, rabbis, Communists or neocons —if they happen to be of Judaic descent—cannot be exposed. Saints who did so in the past were mistaken and are now rebuked and repudiated. "The Church...reproves, as foreign to the mind of Christ, any discrimination against people...on the basis of their...religion." How is this foreign to the thinking of Jesus when He called the followers of the religion of the Pharisees the "children of hell"? (Matthew 23:15).

Do the authors of *Nostra Aetate* expect us to believe that Christians are not to "discriminate" against the modern followers of the old Talmudic creed of the Pharisees who break the commands of God for the sake of their rabbinic traditions? Truly, *Nostra Aetate* is another gospel, and a descendant of the Neoplatonic-Hermetic theology.

Pope Paul VI built upon *Nostra Aetate* and prepared the ground for the acceptance of the Israeli-*Shoah* theology of Pope John-Paul II. In Paul VI's *Guidelines and Suggestions for Implementing the Conciliar Declaration Nostra Aetate,* published under the signature of Cardinal Willebrands in his capacity as President of the "Commission for the Catholic

Church's religious relations with the Jews," [12] there are two instructive declarations. 1. "The history of Judaism did not end with the destruction of Jerusalem, but rather went on to develop a religious tradition. And, although we believe that the importance and meaning of that tradition was deeply affected by the coming of Christ, it is still nonetheless rich in religious values." 2. Paul VI's document also objects to the fact that the words 'Pharisee' and "Pharisasim' have taken on a largely pejorative meaning."

On January 10, 1975, Paul VI gave an address to the liaison committee between the Catholic Church and world Judaism: "...as we look at history as a whole, we cannot fail to note the connections, often too little remarked upon, between Jewish thought and Christian thought. We may here merely recall the influence...of the philosopher and theologian Thomas Aquinas, who died...in the year 1274, there very naturally come to our mind the numerous references of our Angelic Doctor to the work of the rabbinic scholar from Cordoba, who died in Egypt at the dawn of the thirteenth century, Moshe ben Maimon, in particular his explanations of the Mosaic Law and the precepts of Judaism."

Pope VI played quite a joke on the Catholic world with his pretense that Aquinas was a disciple of the Maimonides who taught that Jesus got exactly what He deserved when He was executed. Maimonides also advocated the murder of Christians by stealth. *Aquinas was aware of none of this.* Paul VI is either ignorant or lying when he claims that Aquinas admired Maimonides for his "explanations of the...precepts of Judaism." Aquinas knew next to nothing about Maimonides and referred to him mainly due to what he had seen of the rabbi's arguments against atheism. There is nothing in the voluminous writings of St. Thomas revealing any sympathy whatsoever with rabbinic Judaism or any of its "precepts." Aquinas challenged Judaism at its radix, he did not accommodate it. [13]

---

[12] Instituted by Pope Paul VI on October 22, 1974, for the ninth anniversary of the promulgation of *Nostra Aetate*.

[13] Cf. *Judaism Discovered*, [2008], p. 421.

John-Paul II, was a subversive revolutionary change agent, like his Renaissance predecessors. Cardinal Karol Wojtyla, Archbishop of Krakow in Poland, was elected pope in 1978. His teachings are diametrically opposed to the truth as declared by the Word of God. Hence, we have a choice concerning Judaism: we can believe the Bible or we can believe the Pope-Saint. We observe Wojtyla's Hermetic theology as early as 1980: "The Holy Father has stated th(e) permanent reality of the Jewish people in a remarkable theological formula, in his allocution to the Jewish community of West Germany at Mainz, on November 17th, 1980: 'The people of God of the Old Covenant, which has never been revoked." John-Paul's pontificate also produced *Notes on the Correct Way to Present the Jews* (June 24, 1985). The pope's document propounds the big lie put forth by Pico della Mirandola, Johannes Reuchlin and Neoplatonic-Hermetic 'Catholicism,' stated as follows: *"An exclusively negative picture of the Pharisees is likely to be inaccurate and unjust."*

The Polish Pope has done to the New Testament what the rabbis of Orthodox Judaism have done to the Old Testament. The New Testament was reversed and overthrown by John-Paul II, the pope of Holocaustianity, which is the religion of Judaism for gentiles, e.g. for those who do not formally convert to Judaism. Open conversion from Christianity to Judaism has a strong connotation of betrayal of Jesus Christ, to whom many people are attached by nostalgia, social status and custom. Consequently, the discreet way such people can adopt Judaism is through a Christian front, which Holocaustianity's *Shoah*-Catholicism affords. A principle of this new theology is the rehabilitation of the Pharisees. If the Pharisees can be rehabilitated, then the rabbis of Orthodox Judaism regain their teaching role, and certain Talmudic and Kabbalistic dogmas gain entrance to the Church and become obligatory for Catholics. Since the Renaissance this has the objective of the Neoplatonic-Hermetic conspiracy.

Modern Orthodox Judaism is the continuation of the ideology of the Pharisees whom Jesus encountered. Writing in his book *Rabbinic Judaism* (1995), Rabbi Jacob Neusner, a colleague of Pope Benedict XVI, stated:

"This book introduces the structure and the functioning system of Rabbinic Judaism...the particular religious system set forth by sages, or 'rabbis' who flourished in the first six centuries C.E."

During the pontificate of John-Paul II, Cardinal Joseph Bernardin of Chicago, in a speech to Israelis, moved to suppress "anti-Semitic" portions of the Gospel of John. [14]

Bernardin was a favorite of the papal-"saint."

On June 24, 1985, in the pontificate of John-Paul II, Rome issued its teaching document, the *Vatican Commission for Religious Relations With The Jews: "Notes on the correct way to present the Jews and Judaism in Preaching and Catechesis in the Roman Catholic Church."* The rehabilitation of the Pharisees was the central teaching of this Commission, which declared, "His (Jesus) relations with the Pharisees were not always or wholly polemical. Of this there are many proofs: it is Pharisees who warn Jesus of the risks he is running (Lk 13:31); some Pharisees are praised e.g., 'the scribe' of Mk 12:34; Jesus eats with Pharisees (Lk 7:36; 14:1)."

Let us evaluate each of these "proofs" provided by Pope "Saint" John-Paul's theologians.

1. "Pharisees who warn Jesus of the risks he is running." This is a reference to Luke 13:31: "At that very hour some Pharisees came and said to him, 'Get away from here, for Herod wants to kill you.'"

John-Paul II's theologians want us to believe that these were friendly Pharisees who were trying to save Jesus' life. Where is the evidence for this spin? All of the evidence is to the contrary. Christ's true *ecclesia* always faithfully taught the following regarding this passage: "...our Savior was at this time in Galilee, for that was the tetrarchy or province of Herod Antipas, who is the Herod here mentioned. Whether these Pharisees came of their own heads, or as sent by Herod is not so plain...If they came of their own heads, it is certain they came not out of kindness, for the whole history of the gospel lets us know, that the Pharisees had no kindness for Christ, but were his most implacable enemies, and continually consulting on how to destroy him...they either came to scare him out of Galilee...or to drive him into the trap which they had

---

[14] "Address to the Hebrew University of Jerusalem," March 23, 1995, in *Selected Works of Cardinal Joseph Bernardin: Homilies and Teaching Documents* (2000), pp. 285-299; with a forward by child-molestation facilitator Cardinal Roger Mahony.

laid for him in Judea...it is most probable that they came as secretly sent by Herod...This opinion looks more probable because in verse 32 our Savior sends them back with a message to Herod ("Go and tell that fox, 'Behold, I cast out demons and perform cures today and tomorrow, and the third day I finish my course").[15]

2. "...some Pharisees are praised e.g., 'the scribe' of Mk 12:34." This passage in Mark reads: "And when Jesus saw that he answered wisely, said to him, 'You are not far from the kingdom of God." There is no proof that this scribe was a Pharisee. For the Pope-Saint's Vatican to assert definitively that the scribe was a Pharisee is a falsehood. Moreover, this passage is not an indication of benevolence toward Jesus on the part of a supposed Pharisee, but rather of a loosening of the hold of the scribal mentality over this man, and his willingness to begin to move toward embracing the doctrine of Jesus Christ, as did the Apostle Paul. As such, this scribe foreshadows the convert Paul, rather than serving as an indication that a committed Pharisee exhibited some kindness to Christ and was praised for it.

3. This is the most familiar—and threadbare—of all the apologies for the Pharisees: "Jesus eats with Pharisees (Lk 7:36; 14:1)." Yes, indeed our Lord did so because He came for sinners and as He said, sinners need a physician. Jesus sought to convert them by dining with them. The need for conversion is the underlying motive for sharing the meal. Luke demonstrates what John-Paul II's Vatican denies, *that Pharisees (and their modern rabbinic heirs) are in need of conversion.* Let us see what actually came of one of these supposedly "non-polemical" dinner engagements:

"While Jesus was speaking, a Pharisee asked him to dine with him, so he went in and reclined at table. The Pharisee was astonished to see that he did not first (ritually) wash before dinner. And the Lord said to him, 'Now you Pharisees cleanse the outside of the cup and of the dish, but inside you are full of greed and wickedness. You fools! Did not he who made the outside make the inside also? But give as alms those things

---

15 Matthew Poole, *A Commentary on the Holy Bible*, v. 3, p. 241.

that are within, and behold, everything is clean for you. But woe to you Pharisees! For you tithe mint and rue and every herb, and neglect justice and the love of God. These you ought to have done, without neglecting the others. Woe to you Pharisees! For you love the best seat in the synagogues and greetings in the marketplaces. Woe to you! For you are like unmarked graves, and people walk over them without knowing it." (Luke 11:37-44).

These are the words spoken by Christ at the meal which was, according to the pope-saint's devious theologians, not "wholly polemical."

Next, the canonized pontiff's theologians teach: "Jesus shares, with the majority of Palestinian Jews of that time, some pharisaic doctrines: the resurrection of the body; forms of piety, like alms-giving, prayer, fasting (cf. Mt 6:1-18) and the liturgical practice of addressing God as Father; the priority of the commandment to love God and our neighbor (cf. Mk 12:28-34)."

What a clever ruse—to attribute to the Old Testament-nullifying Pharisees what are in fact *Old Testament doctrines*. If the Pharisees cling to a few vestiges of the Old Testament, these did not exonerate their own man-made traditions from being wholly evil. How dare the Vatican under the papal "Saint" claim that Jesus believed in some doctrines of the Pharisees! *They are disseminating a blasphemous fable which makes a liar out of Jesus Christ.*

In Luke 12:1 our Lord speaks of their doctrines as the "leaven of the Pharisees." What did Jesus mean by this? How does leaven work? Silently, and the smallest particle of it, when spread to other dough, will ferment the whole of it.

What then, is Jesus warning of? He was exhorting us to beware of t*he smallest particle of the doctrine of the Pharisees*, lest it infect the whole of the community of believers. Yet under John-Paul's pontificate we were taught to believe that Jesus did indeed "share...some pharisaic doctrines."

The pope's theologians also cite Acts 23:8: "For the Sadducees say that there is no resurrection, nor angel, nor spirit, but the Pharisees acknowledge them all." *True*. But the Pharisees denied the Resurrection of Jesus Christ, so what is the benefit of holding to a Biblical concept theoretically, and rejecting the most obvious, and compelling example of resurrection—by the Son of God?

This denial makes them more guilty than the Sadducees, since the latter could not even entertain the idea of resurrection, whereas the Pharisees professed belief in it and then obstinately denied it with regard to Jesus. What is there to praise in this?

The 1985 "Saint" John-Paul Commission document continues: "Paul (cf. Acts 23:8)...always considered his membership of the Pharisees as a title of honor (cf. ibid. 23:6; 26:6; Phil 3:5)."

In Acts 21-23 Paul is facing a violent Jewish mob and a Sanhedrin that seeks to kill him. As a divide-and-conquer tactic he identifies himself as a Pharisee in order to sow discord between the Sadducees and the Pharisees. The passage, when taken in context (Acts 23:6-7) reveals this: "Now when Paul perceived that one part were Sadducees and the other Pharisees, he cried out in the council, "Brothers, I am a Pharisee, a son of Pharisees. It is with respect to the hope and the resurrection of the dead that I am on trial." And when he had said this, a dissension arose between the Pharisees and the Sadducees, and the assembly was divided."

Nowhere does Scripture denote, suggest or imply that Paul considers the title of Pharisee to be "honorable." Reading from Acts 21-17 to Acts 23:35 we see that St. Paul is not relaxing on a seaside veranda teaching disciples while at his ease. He is in peril of his life. Nonetheless, no matter what duress he is under, Paul's intention is not to deceive anyone by his statement. Instead, he is humbly informing the sinful Pharisees that, as you are now, I once was. In his public confession in Acts 22:3-5, he convicts himself of Pharisaic sins: "I am a Jew, born in Tarsus in Cilicia, but brought up in this city, educated at the feet of Gamaliel according to the strict manner of the law of our fathers, being zealous for God as all of you are this day. I persecuted this Way to the death, binding and delivering to prison both men and women, as the high priest and the whole council of elders can bear me witness."

Does the Vatican expect us to believe that the Apostle Paul regards it an "honor" that he "persecuted to death" those of the "Way" (of Christ)? Paul's statement in Acts 23:6 that, "I am a Pharisee" must be read in the context of his statement that precedes it in Acts 22:20: "And when the blood of Stephen your witness was being shed, I myself was standing by and approving and watching over the garments of those who killed him." Where is Paul saying there is honor in being a Pharisee?

In support of their claim, John-Paul II's theologians also cite Acts 26:6, which is irrelevant and contains no reference to the Pharisees. They also cite for support Philippians 3:5. An analysis of this passage reveals the extent of the rabbinic-like deceit by which the Pope's Vatican falsifies the Bible. Let us take the passage in context (Philippians 3:4-6): "If anyone else thinks he has reason for confidence in the flesh, I have more: circumcised on the eighth day, of the people of Israel, of the tribe of Benjamin, a Hebrew of Hebrews; as to the law, a Pharisee; as to zeal, a persecutor of the Church; as to righteousness under the law, blameless."

Would even a school child adduce the preceding passage as support for the claim that for Paul "membership in the Pharisees" was "a title of honor"? Paul in this section is addressing the Judaizers in the Church, attempting to persuade them of the errors of their ways. He is making his statement not on the basis of the disingenuous Vatican proposition that he was showing forth the honor of being a Pharisee, but to demonstrate that in opposing the Judaizing of the *ecclesia* of Christ, he himself did not lack a Jewish pedigree.

Pope "Saint" John-Paul and his magisterium were applying midrashic and Talmudic exegesis to the New Testament. Yet this tendentious hair-splitting and outright falsification will not avail the post-Renaissance, Neoplatonic-Hermetic Church in its objective of reducing and softening the opprobrium with which the New Testament brands the Pharisees and their oral traditions.

Since 1965, when it comes to the Pharisees, the papacy won't stand for any strictly good-versus-evil dichotomy. Toward the Pharisees the Vatican under "the saintly pontiff" harbored a morally ambiguous, shades-of-gray attitude: "If in the Gospels and elsewhere in the New Testament there are all sort of unfavorable references to the Pharisees, they should be seen against the background of a complex and diversified movement... An exclusively negative picture of the Pharisees is likely to be inaccurate and unjust..."

Who is the Vatican accusing of being unjust and "inaccurate"? Is this not *a covert dig at Jesus Himself*?

Christ must be the one who is "unjust" and "inaccurate" since His *unrelievedly negative characterization* of the Pharisees as *the children of hell* (Matthew 23:15) who are *doomed to eternal damnation* (Matthew 5:20) demolishes Neoplatonic-Hermetic theology. The two cannot coexist. The teaching issued in "Saint" John-Paul II's pontificate is covert Talmudic denigration of Jesus.

From 1965 onward the Catholic Church succumbed to the post-modernist notion that after the Nazi massacre of Judaics it is incumbent on the Church to modify the politically incorrect truths of the New Testament and through distortion and misrepresentation, make them appear to blend with the dogma of Holocaustianity. For the World War II theology to supplant the New Testament theology, it was necessary to invoke "*The* Holocaust" as inaugurating an era in which many Biblically-derived Christian verities are suspended, or indicted as having been accessories to the supposed cosmic crime of the "*Shoah.*" All of history and all of humanity must henceforth make every other martyrdom and victimization secondary, including Christ's sacrifice on Calvary, while submitting to the universally enforced dogma that declares that protecting Judaics from being victimized by yet "another Holocaust" is the highest duty of the Church of Rome.

To promulgate this revolutionary alteration of the mission of the New Testament, extreme Leftist hermeneutics common to the modern humanist theology of mainline Protestant churches have been adopted by the Church of Rome. The Talmud decrees that the Old Testament does not mean what it says. The Catholic *Shoah* theology of John-Paul and his successors suggested rather than declared (through omission and distortion), that the New Testament does not mean what it says.

This error is much more dangerous when it manifests in the Church of Rome than in Protestant congregations which are free to reject it, since among Catholics it is advanced within a structure of authoritarian obedience demanded of the faithful, who are subject to the pope and the authority of the "magisterium."

The unstated axiom of the Church of Rome's dogma of Holocaustianity is fundamentally Talmudic: a higher value is placed on Judaic life compared with the lives of non-Judaics. The advancement, edification and protection of Christians and

Christianity is made subsidiary to the advancement, edification and protection of Judaics who reject Jesus Christ. This is Renaissance humanism married to Talmudic particularism. Scripture-quoting is the mask by which the intellectually dishonest infiltrators cloak their Talmudic theology in order to give it a Christian facade.

The theology of Holocaustianity denies the Biblical doctrine that there are severe repercussions and punishments for the crime of unrepentant rejection of Jesus. While Christians may not engage in vengeance or violence, when God allows or initiates these things against evil-doers would it be proper for the Christian Church to adjust its doctrine out of sympathy and solidarity with the evil-doers? The truth is that all those who reject Christ and are spiritual (*not* necessarily racial) heirs of those who crucified Him, are under wrath. This has been the teaching of the Catholic Church from the first century A.D. until the Renaissance. In Matthew 10:14-15, Jesus declares, "And if anyone will not receive you or listen to your words, shake off the dust from your feet when you leave that house or town. Truly, I say to you, it will be more bearable on the day of judgment for the land of Sodom and Gomorrah than for that town." Jesus is uttering this prophecy of doom upon those who reject the words of true Christians. These opposers, according to Jesus, are worse than the residents of Sodom and therefore, *worse than sodomites*.

Many of the Judaics who were killed by the Nazis rejected the words of Christian evangelists. St. Paul described unbelieving Jews as those "Who both killed the Lord Jesus, and their own prophets, and have persecuted us; and they please not God, and are contrary to all men: Forbidding us to speak to the Gentiles that they might be saved, to fill up their sins always: f*or the wrath is come upon them to the uttermost*." (1 Thessalonians 2:15-16; emphasis supplied).

"Wrath has come upon them to the uttermost." By what right do popes and cardinals overthrow Biblical theology out of remorse for the fulfillment of Biblical prophecy? The true Church's way of protecting the Jews is for Jews—like all other people who desire God's blessing and favor—to bear good fruit, cease persecuting Christians, express remorse for the murder of Jesus by the founders of Orthodox Judaism, and have faith that He is the Son of God who died on the Cross for their sake.

If they do not, then Christ Himself, in His parable of the vinedressers, has prophesied a miserable destiny for them.

There is a wretched end predicted for those who killed the Son of God, both for those who had a literal, physical hand in it, as well as all of those who share in and continue the spiritual ideology that is based on the ideology of the killers. God sent to the 'vinedressers' prophets, and they killed the prophets. He sent them His Son and they even killed Him (Matthew 21:33-39). In our modern age, the spiritual and ideological heirs of the 'vinedressers' continue to teach and uphold that their murder of the prophets of God was legitimate (Babylonian Talmud: Yebamoth 49b). The vinedressers continue to teach and uphold that their murder of God's Son was legitimate (Babylonian Talmud: Sanhedrin 43a). These are the teachings of the religion of the Pharisees as it exists in our world today, in the form of Orthodox Judaism.

"Therefore, when the owner of the vineyard comes, what will he do to those vinedressers?" God said in Matthew 21 that He would destroy these wretched vinedressers *miserably*. Therefore, when calamity befalls the rabbis of Judaism and their adherents in one 'holocaust' or another, why do supposed Christians regard it as shocking, or an injustice?

Vile Nazis killed many innocent people, including countless Christians, and many others of ethnic Judaic descent who rejected, or at the very least were indifferent, to the Talmud and Judaism, and we sincerely mourn those deaths and condemn the murderers responsible. But facts are facts. Those who fit Christ's description of evil "vinedressers" and who died miserably under the Third Reich, were suffering the curse of God, as foretold in Matthew 21. Many times in the Old Testament history of Israel, God sent wicked armies to chastise the equally or still more wicked Israelites. The post-Renaissance Church of Rome, when it overthrows Biblical theology in order to make amends for the Nazis having been the instruments of God's curse on the "vinedressers," are perpetrating a liberal humanist reversal of God's Will.

Due to camouflage afforded by their conservative position on abortion and contraception, the papist Church is believed by many persons to be loyal to the ancient verities. In fact, Rome is smitten with a Talmud-centric hermeneutic advanced by scriptural exegetes such as Amy-Jill Levine and Bart D. Ehrman.

The latter, in his book *Jesus Interrupted,* judges the Church mainly by the degree to which it is either pro or anti-Judaic. This is Ehrman's chief criterion for assessing the good or evil of the historic Christian ecclesia. Following the rabbinic party line, Ehrman claims, along with Prof. Levine and other falsifiers, that Jesus did not come to found a religion substantially different from "Judaism." Mr. Ehrman goes so far as to claim that, "The charge of deicide first occurs in the writings of a late-second-century writer..." Apparently Ehrman has not read the gospel of Matthew and John, or the letters of Paul the Apostle.

The following could have been written by Ehrman, Amy-Jill Levine, or dozens of other Bible-falsifying liberal scripture "scholars." But these were the words of "Saint John-Paul the Great": "We must remember how much the balance of relations between Jews and Christians over two thousand years has been negative. We must remind ourselves how *the permanence of Israel is accompanied by a continuous spiritual fecundity, in the rabbinical period*, in the Middle Ages and in modern times, taking its start from a patrimony which we long shared, so much so that 'the faith and religious life of the Jewish people as they are professed and practiced still today, can greatly help us to understand better certain aspects of the life of the Church...The permanence of Israel (while so many ancient peoples have disappeared without trace) is a historic fact and a sign to be interpreted within God's design. *We must in any case rid ourselves of the traditional idea of a people punished, preserved as a living argument for Christian apologetic. It remains a chosen people*, 'the pure olive on which were grafted the branches of the wild olive which are the gentiles." [16]

These are the words of Antichrist. We will not modify this judgment with weasel words "out of respect for the Holy Father." The idea that an evil-doer cannot be exposed, or his soul-destroying poison curbed because he is an exalted personage ("pope"), is unscriptural.

God is no respecter of persons (Acts 10:34) and neither is any Christian. The notion of immunity for the lies and deceit of a supreme religious leader is priestcraft. This "John-Paul II" Judas wants us to "rid ourselves of the traditional" Catholic-

---

[16]   John-Paul II, March 6, 1982, alluding to Romans 11:17-24; emphasis supplied).

patristic doctrine concerning the unbelieving Jews, who have been preserved throughout history to be punished as a "living argument for the Catholic apologetic." We are to eradicate the wisdom of the Catholic saints and patriarchs who, before the Renaissance, always taught and always believed these truths. John-Paul II's revolutionary teaching that rabbinic Judaism has a continuous "spiritual fecundity" is of a piece with the cries of the Renaissance heresiarchs on behalf of the fecundity of the Talmud and Kabbalah. But never was the cry so effective in alchemically processing humanity as when it was uttered by the "pro-life, conservative" Papal Saint.

On March 12, 1998 the Vatican issued the pontiff's declaration, *The Tragedy of the Shoah and the Duty of Remembrance* concerning the cosmic suffering of the "Jews" under the Nazis. Nothing approaching this document has ever been issued by Rome concerning the Communist holocaust against millions of Christians. Conforming to the Talmudic belief that only Jews are fully and completely human, the Church of Rome elevates the sufferings of the World War II-era Judaics far above that of Christian mass murder victims. In his epochal adoption of the innovative creed of Holocaustianity, The Polish Pontiff declared:

"The 20th century...has witnessed an unspeakable tragedy which can never be forgotten: the attempt by the Nazi regime to exterminate the Jewish people, with the consequent killing of millions of Jews....Before this terrible genocide... no one can remain indifferent, least of all the Church, by reason of her very close bonds of spiritual kinship with the Jewish people and her remembrance of the injustices of the past. The Church's relationship with the Jewish people is unlike the one she shares with any other religion. However, it is not only a question of recalling the past...we ask all Christians to join us in meditating on the catastrophe which befell the Jewish people and on the moral imperative to ensure that never again will selfishness and hatred grow to the point of sowing such suffering and death...

"While *bearing their unique witness to the Holy One of Israel and to the Torah*, the Jewish people have suffered much at different times and in many places. But *the Shoah was certainly the worst suffering of all*...such an event cannot be fully measured by the ordinary criteria of historical research alone. It calls for a 'moral and religious memory...

"The fact that the *Shoah* took place in Europe, that is, in countries of long-standing Christian civilization, raises the question of the relation between the Nazi persecution and the attitudes down the centuries of Christians towards the Jews...

"In the Christian world—I do not say on the part of the Church as such—*erroneous and unjust interpretations of the New Testament regarding the Jewish people and their alleged culpability have circulated for too long,* engendering feelings of hostility towards this people...

"Such interpretations of the New Testament have been totally and definitively rejected by the Second Vatican Council Despite the Christian preaching of love for all, even for one's enemies, the prevailing mentality down the centuries penalized minorities and those who were in any way 'different.' Sentiments of anti-Judaism in some Christian quarters and the gap which existed between the Church and the Jewish people led to a generalized discrimination, which ended at times in expulsions..."

The pontiff's 1998 declaration is a regurgitation of the cliches of rabbinic nullifiers of the New Testament. He declares the Judaic people to be what they see themselves to be, through the warped lens of their own egotistical narrative: the "unique witness to the Holy One of Israel and to the Torah." But Talmudic Judaism is nothing of the kind. How can those who falsify the Word of God with their Mishnah, Gemara and Zohar, and deny that Jesus is the Son of God, "bear witness to the Torah"? Pope John-Paul II preached the doctrine of the Talmud, in line with Pope Leo X, the Talmud rescuer and publisher.

Observe John-Paul's mystification of history: "the *Shoah*...cannot be fully measured...by...historical research alone...It calls for a...religious memory." In other words, where research conflicts with a "religious memory" of World War II, research is discarded. This is why scientific research cited by revisionist historians will not be countenanced. In fact, it is a sin to do so. This sort of procustean superstition is a step backward to the worst excesses of the Inquisition. As for loving one's enemies, where does that interfere with guarding against their sins? John-Paul's crack about "expulsions" is a dig at

Queen Isabella, who ruled Spain, and whose canonization has been obstructed, perhaps permanently, in deference to the protests of the rabbis, while the Polish pontiff who fulfilled the dreams of the Neoplatonic-Hermetic Kabbalists, has been canonized.

John-Paul II's lead theologian and the "prefect" of his Congregation for the Doctrine of the Faith was Joseph Ratzinger, who succeeded him as Pope Benedict XVI, before resigning. Benedict confirmed the Holocaustolatry of his predecessor and expanded upon it, rendering it more oppressively rabbinic than it was under John-Paul. As Cardinal Ratzinger he had a formative hand in its infiltration of the Church and its development therein. Ratzinger was a theological prodigy who blasted a beachhead for Holocaustianity inside Catholicism, based on his gravely distorted interpretation of the Bible.

Cardinal Ratzinger's landmark, 200-page theological statement, *The Jewish People and their Sacred Scriptures in the Christian Bible,* was published in 2001 by the Pontifical Biblical Commission.

This official document, composed by the cardinal and twenty-three Vatican scholars under his direction, in addition to being rife with apostasy, demonstrates the future Pope Benedict XVI's thorough knowledge of the basics of the Talmud, so that it cannot be said that he promulgates errors about Orthodox Judaism from ignorance. He had a good grasp of the Mishnah and the "seven *middoth*" that form the rabbinic exegesis of scripture.

Cardinal Ratzinger mirrors with considerable fidelity the influential modern fulfillment of the occult Renaissance contention that Jesus was under the influence of the Pharisees. To sow this confusion is essential because it is an effective way of shaking the believer's confidence in the existence of an *unambiguous condemnation* in the New Testament of a rabbinic gnosis which, beginning in the late fifteenth century, covertly steered the *sotto governo* of Catholic Italy.

To achieve this end, mitigating factors must be marshaled which present Jesus as thinking like a Pharisee. Hence, Cardinal Ratzinger stated that the use by Jesus of "analogy" and "*a fortiori* argument" (a corollary implied by a stronger claim), demonstrates the influence on Jesus' thinking of the "first two middoth (rules) of Hillel the Pharisee, '*qal wa-homer* and *gezerah shawah*."

The assignment of the latter *gezerah shawah* (more commonly spelled *gezera shavah*) sophistry to Jesus Christ, is a blasphemy against Him, since the rabbinic *gezera shavah* entails the attribution of a grotesquely *falsified meaning to scripture*; a transgression of which Jesus is obviously innocent. As for analogy and *a fortiori* argument, these are found in the pure Word of God in the Old Testament, uncontaminated by the human imaginings of the traditions of the Pharisees.

To establish a proprietary relationship between these methods and the proto-Talmudic *middoth* of the Pharisee Hillel, is a fallacy intended to dilute the Truth of Jesus by watering it with the imputation of a Pharisaic influence. Cardinal Ratzinger dared to say that in Jesus' words can also be discerned the influence of "rabbinic midrash." The Midrash is accurately described as a book of old wives' (*bubbe-meises*) tales, as well as outlandish fables such as claiming that Noah was sodomized on board Noah's Ark, and other equally pornographic fables. This is what influenced Jesus Christ?

Ratzinger sought to associate the words of Jesus with this mad heritage. The claim that Jesus used the reasoning methods of the Pharisees is a degenerate libel. The truth is that Jesus' used the reasoning methods *imparted to Him by His Father in Heaven*, and not the depraved lawyer's entrapments and salacious fables that were the specialty of the successors of the Pharisees.

It gets worse: Cardinal Ratzinger argued in *The Jewish People and their Sacred Scriptures in the Christian Bible,* that in the wake of the "Holocaust," Christians can learn much from the Talmud. In conjunction with the positing of this doctrine of Giovanni Pico della Mirandola and Johannes Reuchlin, Cardinal Ratzinger contradicted it in passing, and by so doing, provided himself with a loophole:

"Should not Christians henceforth read the Bible as Jews do, in order to show proper respect for its Jewish origins? In answer to the last question, a negative response must be given for hermeneutical reasons. For to read the Bible as Judaism does, necessarily involves an implicit acceptance of all its presuppositions, that is, the full acceptance of what Judaism is, in particular, the authority of its writings and rabbinic traditions, which exclude faith in Jesus as Messiah and Son of God."

Ratzinger's loophole serves as an escape clause that offers an alibi to double-minded papalolaters who argue that the pope is not a Hermetic agent and that we are misquoting the "Holy Father." Many people want to be deceived (2 Thess. 2:9-12). They seize on one half of modern papal double-talk, the orthodox half, *and ignore the Kabbalistic half.* Cardinal Ratzinger's Pontifical Bible Commission document reflects the confusion of the insane. After saying we shouldn't read the Bible as Judaism does, the Commission document states: "Christians can and ought to admit that the Jewish reading of the Bible is a possible one, in continuity with the Jewish Sacred Scriptures from the Second Temple period."

The Vatican is sunk so far down in the thick mud of the Hegelian dialectic that they don't know which end is up. Straight talk is foreign to them. They can't set pen to paper without lying. They tell us we shouldn't read the Bible as Judaism does, but the Jewish reading of the Bible is a "possible one."

Here is a bipolar mind for all who have a sufficient love of the truth to readily perceive. The future Pope Benedict, in his text, *The Jewish People and their Sacred Scriptures in the Christian Bible,* then proceeds to make the following astonishing statement: "Christians can, nonetheless, learn much from Jewish exegesis practiced for more than two thousand years."

Jewish exegesis of two thousand years: the Talmud, Midrash, Kabbalah, Mishneh Torah, Shulchan Aruch, Mishnah Berurah, etc. From 2,000 years of an enormous heap of delusions, lies and blasphemy against Jesus and Mary, Christians can "learn much."

Wrapped in the mantle of the "struggle against Holocaust denial and antisemitism," Holocaustianity becomes the alibi for the completion of that which was launched in the Renaissance, the revolutionary overthrow of the authentic Catholic teaching on rabbinic Judaism and the Talmud. At the same time, it nearly completely smothers the gospel call to unconverted Judaics to obtain freedom from the bondage that oppresses them.

Cardinal Ratzinger's document, *The Jewish People and their Sacred Scriptures in the Christian Bible,* presented a long and convoluted analysis of the St. Paul's statements on the Jewish people, twisting his words to make it appear as though the Talmudic doctrine of the racial prestige of the Jews is valid. The future pope ignored the Biblical warning in Rev. 2:9 and 3:9 about counterfeit Israel, and the critically important fact that Jesus did not believe that the Jews who confronted Him qualified as authentic descendants of Abraham: "They answered him, "Abraham is our father.' Jesus said to them, 'If you were Abraham's children, you would be doing the works Abraham did, but now you seek to kill me, a man who has told you the truth" (John 8:39-40).

Ratzinger's theology culminates in his confirmation of post-Renaissance Catholicism's proclamation of a new "elder brother" status for the unbelieving Judaics who reject and oppose Christ: "It is because of our common roots and from this eschatological perspective that the Church acknowledges a special status of 'elder brother' for the Jewish people, thereby giving them a unique place among all other religions."

John-Paul's "elder brothers" declaration, confirmed by the future Pope Benedict, is predicated upon the overthrow of the Biblical teaching on the Christian's *exclusive covenantal relationship with God.* Once again we see a regurgitation of the Judaizing that began in earnest in Medici Florence five hundred fifty years ago. Instead of correcting these errors, Cardinal Ratzinger incorporated them into the official teaching of the Church of Rome. The myths he perpetuated are not difficult to refute, but their virulence emanates from the ecclesiastical authority by which they are propounded. Witness the mendacity of the future Pope Benedict XVI: "For Paul, Jesus' establishment of 'the new covenant in (his) blood' (1 Cor. 11:25), does not imply any rupture of God's covenant with his people, but constitutes its fulfillment. He includes 'the covenants' among the privileges enjoyed by Israel, *even if they do not believe in Christ* (Romans 9:4). Israel continues to be in a covenant relationship and remains the people to whom the fulfillment of the covenant was promised, because *their lack of faith cannot annul God's fidelity* (Romans 11:29). Even if some Israelites have observed the Law as a means of establishing their own justice, the covenant-promise of God, who is rich in mercy (Romans 11:26-27), cannot be abrogated.

"Continuity is underlined by affirming that Christ is the end and the fulfillment to which the Law was leading the people of God (Gal. 3:24). For many Jews, the veil with which Moses covered his face remains over the Old Testament (2 Cor. 3:13-15), thus preventing them from recognizing Christ's revelation there. This becomes part of the mysterious plan of God's salvation, the final outcome of which is the salvation of 'all Israel' (Romans 11:26)."

Could Ratzinger have forgotten that Israel's sin abrogated the Mosaic covenant, the only one of the covenants that is not eternal? God replaced it with a new covenant and a new Israel. Except among those Judeans ("Jews") and other Israelites who *through Faith* believe that Jesus is the Messiah of Israel who died on the cross for the sins of mankind, *racial Israel is no longer part of God's covenant* (Hebrews 8:7-13 and Jeremiah 31:31-34).

Employing Romans 11:29, Cardinal Ratzinger stated: "Israel continues to be in a covenant relationship and remains the people to whom the fulfillment of the covenant was promised, because their lack of faith cannot annul God's fidelity (Romans 11:29)."

Here the future pope accuses God of being unfaithful were His covenant with racial Israel to be annulled. This level of presumption is rabbinic in its brazen accusation against God. The Holy Bible says of God, "In speaking of a new covenant, He makes the first one obsolete. And what is becoming obsolete and growing old is ready to vanish away." (Hebrews 8:13).

If we accept the future Pope Benedict's interpretation of Romans 11:29, we have to discard the gospels of Matthew and John; as well as 1 John; the Book of Hebrews; Jeremiah 31 and the teaching of the whole of the Book of Romans itself, when taken in context.

Let us read Romans 11 from verse 26: "And in this way all Israel will be saved...as regards election, they are beloved for the sake of their forefathers." Verse 29: "For the gifts and the calling of God are irrevocable."

Liberal and neocon papists and Protestant dispensationalists alike interpret this passage to mean that the election of carnal Israel is irrevocable because of God's love for the patriarchs of Israel. Cardinal Ratzinger and the Zionists of Churchianity propose with their theory of salvation by race, two different paths to salvation, one for the Jews without Christ, and one by Christ for gentiles. This is an abomination.

Can it be regarded as prudent or edifying to take a few lines from the Book of Romans in order to contradict the entire doctrine of Jesus Christ?

This is not only a case of twisting Romans 11—*in the sense it is explained by Cardinal Ratzinger*—vs. the doctrine of Jesus— it is also a case of Romans 11 vs. the doctrine strongly emphasized in Paul's other writings. For example, in Galatians 3:7 and 28-29, Paul teaches that *the Church is the true Israel of God*.

How can racial Israel be irrevocably saved by virtue of God's love for the patriarchs of Israel when, according to Jesus, and Paul himself in 1 Thessalonians 2:15-16, *it was racial Israel that killed and opposed the prophets*? Jesus said to the leaders of Israel, "Thus you witness against yourselves that you are sons of those who murdered the prophets" (Matthew 23:31). God is going to save Antichrist-racial Israel *for the sake of the prophets they killed?* This is a gospel of occult popery, not the true Catholic Church.

If the future Pope Benedict's's Hermetic exegesis was correct, and God's covenant with carnal Israel has never been revoked and can never be revoked, then we must ask, why did Israel need restoration in the first place? Why did the lost sheep of the House of Israel need Jesus Christ (Matthew 15:24), if those sheep are saved by their ethnic connection to God's beloved Biblical patriarchs of old?

We can't find any saved-by-racial-heritage doctrine in Romans 2:6-8: "He will render to each one according to his works: to those who by patience in well-doing seek for glory and honor and immortality, he will give eternal life; but for those who are self-seeking and do not obey the truth, but obey unrighteousness, there will be wrath and fury."

We can't find any saved-by-racial-heritage doctrine in 2 Corinthians 3:10-11: "...what once had glory has come to have no glory at all, because of the glory that surpasses it. For if what was being brought to an end came with glory, much more will what is permanent have glory." With the arrival of the new covenant, the old covenant has no glory whatsoever. Consequently, God has *brought to an end* (Greek: *katargeo*) the glory of the old covenant.

There is another serious problem with supporting the claim that "Jews" can be saved apart from faith in Christ: what if many of these self-proclaimed "Jews" are not in fact Jews at all and are not descended from Abraham? This writer has long asked a simple question of those who accept that Judaics who say they are "Jews" should be automatically taken at their word: where is the *evidence* and where are the *records* that prove their Jewish genealogy? No one today can furnish such documentation (Titus 3:9). Yet, with hypnotic verisimilitude it is universally accepted that those followers of Judaism who self-advertise as the "Jews" of the Old Testament are to be regarded as credible.

Moreover, we discern here the clandestine operation of an anti-Judaic, diabolical trap: many Judaics who imagine that they are "Jews" destined to be saved by their alleged ethnic descent from the patriarchs will have no such salvation, since in fact they are not racial "Jews" at all. The seeding of this *false racial hope* is almost never factored into the struggle over the misuse of Romans 11:26-29. Who has planted this futile expectation, which leads to the eternal damnation of Judaic people? Is it not the Judaic-hating devil himself, operating through Protestant fundamentalism, post-Renaissance Catholicism and Judaism?

Scripture exegete Bob Burridge writes, "During the first century, the Jews were the greatest antagonists to the gospel. It was the apostates among the Jews who stirred up the Romans to hate the Christians by slandering them. As more of the Gentiles came into the Church, the olive tree became less 'Jewish.' This fulness of the Gentiles marked the end of physical Israel as God's people. God even used pagan Rome in 70 AD to crush Jerusalem, to destroy the temple the Priests had defiled, and to mark the final end to the special privilege of the physical seed of Abraham. It is by this process that all Israel will be saved. The words describe the process by which God's true Israel will be saved. It is not a prediction of some yet future event.

"Those who see here a future promise for the abandoned and apostate nation of Abraham, are missing Paul's point about what constitutes the truly good olive tree. It is not just Physical Israel. It is the outward Covenant Family of God. In the time between Abraham and Jesus, the tree was the nation of the Jews. In the time after Jesus, the tree is the Apostolic church,

God's Spiritual Israel (see Romans 9:6). *As the elect from all nations are evangelized and brought in*, the tree grows toward fulness. As the apostate and unbelieving are removed, the tree improves in purity. *It is in this way that all of God's true Israel will be saved. The New Testament Church does not replace Israel. The Church is Israel in her completed form*...the apostate children of Israel were never more than outwardly consecrated to God. At the time Paul wrote this letter to the Romans, God was using his grace toward the Gentiles to provoke the elect among the Jews to believe." [17]

What a blessed relief is Mr. Burridge's affirmation of Christian Truth, contrasted with the twisted perversion of it promulgated by the infallibly canonized Pope John-Paul II, and that palladin of the "conservatives," Pope Benedict XVI.

In studying Ratzinger's document we discover an assertion that is startling. In addition to claiming that St. Paul taught the doctrine of salvation by Israelite ethnicity, we come across the future Pope Benedict's identification of Paul as someone not fully converted to Christianity from rabbinic Judaism: "In his writings, as was mentioned above, we find not only continual references to the Old Testament, but many traces of Jewish traditions as well."

Notice the distinction made between the Old Testament and Jewish tradition. Is this accusation against Paul—of being under the influence of non-Biblical traditions—based on arcana from the Vatican archives? The "many traces" of "Jewish traditions" alleged to be present in the writings of Paul would be the "traditions of men" which Jesus condemned in Mark 7 and Matthew 15, because they nullify the Word of God. Cardinal Ratzinger's assertion that Paul's writings reflect "Jewish traditions" is a reference to doctrines not found in the Old Testament.

In other words, the future pope is indicating that Paul's teachings reflect the doctrines of the Oral Law of the Pharisees. This atrocious attack on the Apostle Paul, as being not fully converted to Christ, and still clinging to proto-Talmudic beliefs, accounts for the Church of Rome's emphasis on him as a

---

[17] Bob Burridge "God's Olive Tree," http://www.genevaninstitute.org/2012/02/gods-olive-tree/ Emphasis supplied.

teacher of race-based salvation, since racism is a fixture of Pharisaic Judaism. Cardinal Ratzinger's theology in *The Jewish People and their Sacred Scriptures in the Christian Bible* would seem to lend new support to the old accusation that Paul founded a new religion contrary to the teachings of Jesus.

If St. Paul is indeed guilty of teaching salvation for ethnic Jews independent of Jesus Christ, "for the sake of God's love for the Old Testament patriarchs," then he was not teaching the gospel of Jesus Christ, but rather the race pride traditions of the Pharisees. In Matthew 3: 9-10, John the Baptist, in line with Jesus, teaches that in order to inherit the promise of God it is not enough to be a descendant of Abraham. One must also bear good fruit or be cut down and thrown into the fire. No misinterpretation of the words of the Apostle Paul can possibly nullify this truth.

From the annals of the Fathers of the early Church we learn that, "Before Clement of Alexandria (150-215 A.D.), no patristic writer apparently commented on (Romans) 11:26. Those of the first three centuries who know of Paul's teaching fail to mention a coming salvation of the Jews." [18]

Let us recall St. Peter's warning, which we would do well to apply to the distortion of Romans 11:26-29 by lawless, post-Renaissance popes and cardinals: "Our beloved brother Paul also wrote to you according to the wisdom given him, as he does in all his letters...There are some things in them that are hard to understand, *which the ignorant and unstable twist to their own destruction*, as they do the other Scriptures. You therefore, beloved, knowing this beforehand, take care that you are not carried away with the error of lawless people and lose your own stability." (2 Peter 3:15-17).

"Our Elder Brothers in the Faith"

"Our Elder Brothers in the Faith." This slogan would appear to be an occult mockery. By classifying as our "elder brothers" those who cling to the religion and heritage that rejected Jesus, Popes John-Paul II and Benedict XVI were nullifying the Bible and appealing to fallen natural man's family and clan structure. Whereas the Mafia and the pagan order teach,

---

18 Joseph A. Fitzmyer, *Romans: A New Translation with Introduction and Commentary* (2008), p. 620.

"Don't ever go against the family," throughout the Bible, God demonstrates that He represents a radically different order, in which truth often predominates over family ties and hierarchical succession. This truth is so important that *God gives us a reminder of an evil elder brother immediately at the start of the New Testament*, in the geneology of Christ Himself, in the gospel of Matthew, where four women appear in the list of the ancestors of Jesus: Tamar, Rahab, Ruth and Bathsheba. It is Tamar with whom we are concerned.

As we have already observed, Tamar was the widow of Judah's *evil firstborn son, who God had killed* (Genesis 38:7). After that son's death, Tamar was married to Judah's next eldest son, Onan, who practiced contraception in his marital relations with Tamar and who God did therefore also kill. Another son, Shelah, was promised to be Tamar's husband by Judah her father-in-law, but Judah broke his promise. Tamar then disguised herself as a roadside prostitute and Judah, not recognizing her, asked to pay her for sex. She complied, after which Judah left her, not knowing she was Tamar. Then Tamar put away the disguise of a harlot and resumed her life as a widow. Three months later, when Tamar's pregnancy from her union with Judah became obvious, she was accused of harlotry, and Judah ordered her to be burned. But she kept documentation of his coupling with her (his signet, cord and staff), and when confronted with these, Judah admitted what he had done with her, thinking her to be a prostitute. Judah confessed, "She has been more righteous than I" (cf. Genesis 38: 13-26).

Here we encounter an example of evil elder brothers creating the conditions that led to Tamar's sordid predicament.

There is more: Tamar becomes pregnant with Judah's twin sons. At birth, the elder brother, Zerah, is passed over in favor of the younger brother, Perez (Genesis 38: 27-30), a switch of momentous consequence, for God chooses the younger brother Perez, to be the ancestor of the royal house of David, the root of Jesse, the line of descent of Our Lord Jesus Christ (Ruth 4:18-22). *Thus does God overthrow elder brother customs for the sake of His Divine Will.* Why then do the recent pontiffs render the "Elder Brother" a special theological category of divine endearment, and spread this misbegotten concept throughout the Church?

The figure of the evil elder brother is not an isolated case. Abel is preferred to his elder brother Cain who persecuted him, Jacob is preferred to his elder brother Esau, who persecuted him. In Galatians 4:28-30, St. Paul identifies Christians and freedom with the younger brother, Isaac. He identifies enslavement and persecution of Christians with the elder brother, Ishmael: When Hagar conceived Ishmael, "she looked with contempt on her mistress" (Genesis 16:4).

Regarding Talmudists and Zionists, the papal coining of the phrase "Elder Brothers in the Faith" is most ominous in light of what we have demonstrated from the Bible about certain elder brothers. Rabbinic texts are full of commands to yield to the elder brother. Hilchot Mamrim (6:15): "It is *mid'Rabanan* that one must honor his older brother just as he honors his father."

Bishop Bernard Fellay, the Superior-General of the Society of St. Pius X, the "traditional Catholic" fraternity of priests, adopted the papal *mantra* in a January 31, 2009 statement to the French Catholic weekly *Famille Chrétienne*: "The Jews are 'our elder brothers' in the sense that we have something in common, that is, the old Covenant." Bishop Fellay then added an escape clause: "It is true that the acknowledgment of the coming of the Messiah separates us."

This compels us to query Bishop Fellay as follows: is the arrival of the Messiah a mere detail, and hence the "separation" a minor one, or is it a definitive break in our alleged relationship with these "elder brothers"? If it is the latter, why bother to use this post-Conciliar Newspeak at all, except as an equivocation intended to curry favor with the papacy by being seen to parrot its post-Renaissance Judaizing?

The subterranean processing of humanity is worked partly by means of the Hermetic-Kabbalistic/alchemical distillation of the *conjunctio oppositorum* ("conjunction of opposites"), which was weaponized in the dialectical epistemology of G.W. Hegel in the early 19th century.

In Hegel's dialectic, allegiance to eternal truth is considered an anachronism, a species of naiveté. The rabbinic theology of the "Holocaust" and its *Shoah* Newspeak were incorporated into the post-Renaissance Church of Rome to appease rabbinic and Zionist power and complete the magical mandate of Hermetic-Kabbalism, in conformity with the dialectical model which mandates the institutional accommodation of change for the sake of changing times.

This change is almost always accompanied by the imposition of mystifying language ("Holocaust" and "*Shoah*") that seriously undermines the clarity that comes from literal language which denotes or represents something precisely. "Holocaust" and "*Shoah*" constitute the Hegelian jargon of mystification—they are deliberately vague and emotion-laden; they connote many different things to different people. In the dialectic, language becomes "speculative," the embodiment of the "dynamic process" of "double usage."

John Rees, a leading Hegelian, states in *The Algebra of Revolution*, "Ordinary language assumes that things and ideas are stable, that they are either 'this' or 'that'...the fundamental discovery of Hegel's dialectic was that things and ideas do change —empires rise and fall, likewise religions and schools of philosophy....of ideas and concepts which we tend to regard as 'absolutely firm and fast,' Hegel said, 'We look on them as separated from each other by an infinite chasm, so that opposite categories can never get at each other. The battle of reason is the struggle to break up the rigidity to which the understanding has reduced everything.' It is to this end that Hegel deliberately chooses words that can embody dynamic processes: 'The double usage of language, which gives to the same word a positive and negative meaning, is not an accident...We should...recognize in it the speculative spirit of our language rising above the mere Either-or of understanding." [19]

While it is true that Christianity is resisted by formidable intellects and sophisticated systems of deception, in the end, guilt for the subverted condition of Christ's *ecclesia* must first be apportioned not so much according to the conspiratorial plots of the few, as by the hypnotic sleep of the many. While the New Testament teaches that unbelieving Jews are under wrath, an even more damning sentence falls upon the *baptized*, who, under the spell of a paralyzing lassitude, quietly trade their obligation to bear witness to the truth, for the pottage of human respect and the promise of material security in a conforming world.

---

[19] Rees (1998), p. 41.

Under Pope Francis the Pontifical Commission for Religious Relations with the Jews, on December 10, 2015, issued *The Gifts and Calling of God are Irrevocable*:
"The Catholic Church neither conducts nor supports any specific institutional mission work directed towards Jews...it does not in any way follow that the Jews are excluded from God's salvation because they do not believe in Jesus Christ as the Messiah of Israel and the Son of God."

In light of what this Pontifical Commission teaches, it would appear that the New Testament is a fraud, at least as it applies to Jews. All of the preachings and disputation to the Jews in the New Testament were for no purpose if we accept the "reasoning" of the Pontifical Commission for Religious Relations with the Jews and the papally-endorsed document, *The Gifts and Calling of God are Irrevocable*. Why did Jesus persist in causing a great deal of difficulty for the Jews by insisting they had to be born again, they had to believe He was their Messiah, they had to stop following their Oral Law traditions of men, and that they couldn't have eternal salvation unless they believed that He was the Son of God?

The Francis Papal Commission instructs so-called Jews in the true path to their salvation: their race. It is all they need and all they have ever needed according to the popes. God has a covenant with their genes and it is their covenanted genes that save them. The Church of Rome is tolerated by the rabbis because it is no longer the Catholic Church. No Church of Jesus Christ could teach that it has no "mission work directed towards Jews."

This statement is so preposterous it almost does not merit a response, other than derisive horse laughter at the *chutzpah* that so bald a betrayal manifests. It ignores Revelation 2:9 and 3:9 which prophesies the existence of false Jews. If the majority of disbelieving Israelis are not descended from the patriarchs, but are in fact Khazars, by what means other than faith in Jesus Christ, can they be saved? The answer is, *none. They are damned*. They can thank Popes John-Paul II, Benedict XVI and Francis for formulating the theology of their perdition, based on the arcane theology of the Renaissance.

Despite the public relations folderol, nothing about the religion of the Pharisees—Orthodox Judaism—has changed, except that it is increasing in depravity and political and religious power. Students of Judaism know what this increase signifies because we have read the texts of Rabbi Moses Maimonides, the leading religious authority for Israelis of European and American background. Maimonides ruled that when Judaic persons are weak they should feign friendship for Christians as a way of gaining power over the Christians. But when Judaics are dominant, Maimonides ruled, they may kill or oppress anyone who obstructs their supremacy. The outcome of the papal and Protestant Fundamentalist surrender to the Sanhedrin will be the extirpation of Christians, as the world witnessed when Soviet Russia was ruled by the children of the rabbis. [20]

The Church of Rome for centuries has certainly had some things in common with Judaism. It must relish the fact that Orthodox Judaism permits the molestation of boys under age nine by the Pharisee Hillel's permission. Molester priests and the bishops and popes who facilitate their molestation can go wild under Talmudic law. The rabbis made their religion desirable for sex perverts. Children may be molested at a young age with no penalty for the adult Judaic molester. Rabbis may have sex with boys under nine [21] and with girls under age three. [22] Mothers may engage in sexual activity with their male sons under the age of nine. [23]

---

[20]   Cf. "When Israel is Mighty," a video interview with Israeli Yossi Gurvitz ,http://bit.ly/1LtBWLk (in Israeli-Hebrew with English subtitles).

[21]   "This Baraita supports Rav, for it teaches that if a man engaged in homosexual intercourse with a child under nine, he is exempt from liability... "Since a child less than nine years old cannot commit sodomy, he can also not be the object of sodomy." Cf. *The Talmud: The Steinsaltz Edition* (1991), vol. XVIII, p. 77; Sanhedrin 54b). Rabbi Moses Maimonides confirmed the ruling. Cf. *Issurei Biah* 1:14.

[22] *The Talmud: The Steinsaltz Edition* (Random House, 1991), volume VII, p. 145; Ketubot 11b.

[23] In the Babylonian Talmud, Sanhedrin 69b, a woman having sex with a boy less than nine-years-of-age is an act that is exempt from punishment (and therefore permissible), and does not render her a *zonah* (trollop), or disqualify her from marrying a *kohen* (priest), because sex with male children less than age nine is not a regarded as a sex act. The reference in Sanhedrin 69b is to incest between a mother and her son. If the woman's son is less than nine years-of-age, then it is rabbinically permissible for her to have sexual intercourse with him, according to the *halacha* of the Talmud Bavli.

III

Tridentine Judaism according to the "Traditional Catholics"

Since the mainstream of "traditional Catholic" theology in our time preaches servile submission to almost all the popes prior to Paul VI (or prior to John XXIII), and because the priority is personal piety and the recitation of x number of rosaries and novenas, attendance at "First Fridays" and "First Saturdays," and scapular-wearing, they are highly susceptible to the allurement of Neoplatonism and Hermeticism, enveloped as it is in the clouds of incense and Latin ceremony in which the Renaissance conspirators shrouded themselves and which "traditional Catholicism" is committed to reviving, without sufficient regard to, or vigilance over, who is stage-managing the revival. Powerful occult forces are operating inside contemporary "traditional Catholicism," whose clerical leaders are not routinely answerable to the laity except in emergency terms of threats of lawsuits or withholding donations.

How do occult forces manifest inside "traditional Catholicism"? Primarily in the same manner they chiefly (though not exclusively) manifest inside the post-Renaissance Church of Rome: as an adjunct of Neoplatonic-Hermetic-Kabbalistic advancement of gnosis, through commission or omission. The hybrid abomination we style *Tridentine Judaism* can be seen controlling the "traditional Catholic" movement. This union of irreconcilable opposites is known in alchemy as *individuation*. In Freemasonry it is symbolized by *tessellation*.

Their movement is open to this exploitation because "traditional Catholics" are far more devoted to the incense, bells, sacred music and ceremonies of the Tridentine Latin Mass of old, than they are to *the substance of the true Church's dogma of rabbinic Judaism's perfidy*. The exterior of the Mass has been retained but the interior of its Biblical, Patristic and medieval theology has been hollowed out and replaced by apathy toward accommodations with Talmudic Judaism and the betrayal of Jesus that they symbolize.

Most laity as well as even priests and bishops have little accurate knowledge of the legal basis of Ashkenazic Orthodox Judaism: the Talmud Bavli, Maimonides' *Mishneh Torah*, Joseph Karo's *Shulchan Aruch*, Shlomo Ganzfried's *Kitzur Shulchan Aruch*, or the *Mishna Berurah*. As a result of this ignorance, in February 2016, two "prestigious traditional Catholic" organizations, the "International Federation Una Voce" and the "Latin Mass Society of England and Wales" issued a position paper defending the Talmud, fulfilling the mandate of Mirandola and Reuchlin and the other Renaissance subversives. *Plus ça change, plus c'est la même chose.*

Their position paper is titled *The Good Friday Prayer for the Jews in the Extraordinary Form* (an allusion to the Tridentine Latin Rite "form" as it is now called in the Vatican). This text from Una Voce and the Latin Mass Society is a farrago of illiteracy with regard to the Talmud and its opponents. The paper dares to traduce the medieval Franciscan Nicholas Donin, a saintly Judaic convert to Catholicism, for having allegedly sparked "a tragic phase in the Church's history." Here is an excerpt from the text issued by Una Voice International and Britain's Latin Mass Society. It is, not surprisingly, perfectly consonant with Renaissance occult theology:

"...official theological resistance to anti-Semitic violence was itself challenged, however, in the 13th century. Notably, in 1238 Nicholas Donin attacked the Talmud as leading the Jews into error and blasphemy, undermining the notion of the Jews as bearing witness to the truth. In the following centuries Jewish religious writings were seized for examination or destruction, sometimes by Papal mandate; synagogue services were disrupted and aggressive proselytization attempted by members of religious orders; mass expulsions were carried out from many European countries...It must be underlined that this tragic phase in the Church's history cannot be blamed on the theology of the Fathers...Throughout the period attempts were made to defend the Patristic view, notably by St Thomas Aquinas, and to refute Donin's claims about the Talmud, a refutation definitively accepted following the Council of Trent."[24]

This text is a nearly verbatim repetition of the rabbinic propaganda about the despised convert Nicholas Donin. He is execrated by the rabbis because this Catholic friar had inside knowledge of the Talmud and used it to damaging effect against rabbinic Judaism. This servant of God has the distinction of being the first Catholic in the history of Christendom to cause the Talmud to be formally put on trial. This occurred in Paris in 1240, before a papally commissioned jury of university scholars, with Donin valiantly acting alone as prosecutor. It required an entire team of rabbis from northern France to endeavor to refute him. The rabbis were under no coercion and they safely returned to their homes after the trial, which convicted the Talmud of being a heinously evil, anti-Christian text constituting blasphemy against the holy name of Jesus.

For this tremendous feat his reputation is sullied by "traditional Catholics," on the preposterous grounds that Donin's anti-Talmudic theology runs counter to the Fathers of the Church.

From the earliest history of the Catholic Church, Judaism and Judaizers inside the Church ("*nostri Judaizantes*") were condemned in no uncertain terms by the *Fathers of the Church*. In the first century St. Ignatius of Antioch declared that nothing unconverted Jews could teach Christians was of any use, and that all such teachers were to be shunned. (*Letter to the Philadelphians* [1]). St. Ignatius stated that to profess Jesus Christ while Judaizing was a monstrosity, and that there is no salvation for those who follow Judaism. (*Letter to the Magnesians*). In St. Justin Martyr's second century *Dialogue with Trypho,* and in the fourth century St. John Chrysostom's *Adversos Judaeos* and his *Discourses Against Judaizing Christians* (in particular the first, second and fourth discourses), Chrysostom declares that both Jewish synagogues and Jewish souls are dwellings of demons. These Patristic

---

24 Cf. The Foederatio Internationalis Una Voce (FIUV) and the Latin Mass Society of England and Wales (LMS) Position Paper 28: The Good Friday Prayer for the Jews in the Extraordinary Form. The whole text with footnotes is online here: http://rorate-caeli.blogspot.com/2016/03/good-friday-prayer-for-jews-new.html#more

dogmas derived from the Bible were upheld by the Council of Antioch (341 A.D.) and the Council of Laodicea (circa 363 A.D).

It is even alleged by "traditional Catholics" that attempts were made by St. Thomas Aquinas to combat the anti-Talmudic "tragic phase in Church history" by upholding the Fathers of the Church, who, it is insinuated, would have also opposed the "tragic phase." Where does Aquinas have one good word to say about the Talmud, or one bad one for Nicholas of Donin? How can it be said that the Fathers of the Early Church would have opposed militant challenges to rabbinic Judaism when those challenges were founded in part on their theology?

We can laugh at these assertions in the hope that derision will put paid to the falsehoods. It would be comforting to be able to say that anything so utterly ludicrous should be ignored. Why bother to challenge this tissue of absurdities? For one thing, these "traditional Catholics" confirm a portion of our thesis regarding the Renaissance Church. Una Voce and the Latin Mass Society *openly acknowledge that the Renaissance Church compromised with Talmudic Judaism*! They allege that a refutation of Donin was accepted "definitively" by the Renaissance Catholic Church at the Council of Trent.

The authors of *The Good Friday Prayer for the Jews in the Extraordinary Form* make this claim by extrapolating from the datum which they themselves correctly put forth: that during the Renaissance the Vatican permitted the publication of the Talmud. As we have seen, this publishing enterprise was made possible under the influence of the occult Neoplatonic-Hermeticism-Kabbalism which had infiltrated the papacy and the curia.

One of the representatives of the Latin Mass Society in Britain promoting and defending the position paper, *The Good Friday Prayer for the Jews in the Extraordinary Form*, is a "traditional Catholic" and an academic. He corresponded with us with regard to our concerns. What he wrote on March 15, 2016 contains a noteworthy admission:

"The paper, as you quote it, does not say that St Thomas Aquinas defended the Talmud. That distinction goes to

Raymond Martin. [25] His judgement, that only a few verses of the Talmud needed to be censored, was confirmed by the Congregation of the Index, which was asked to look into the matter again by the Council of Trent. That decision was never overturned, and in that sense proved definitive."

In 2016 the "Latin Mass Society" leader conceded that the Renaissance Church of Rome had no major objection to the contents of the Babylonian Talmud, with the exception of "a few verses" out of its thousands of pages.

Moreover, the "distinction" of "Raymond Martin" in his *Pugio Fidei*, one of the formative philo-rabbinic texts which predates the Renaissance, which yet remained influential in the Neoplatonic and Hermetic papal networks, is his defense of the Talmud. As we stated previously, Martin was a clever operator. His book was officially anti-rabbinic, as its full title attests (*"adversus Mauros et Iudaeos"*). It formed the literature of Rome's Machiavellian, one-step-backward-two-steps-forward deceit mechanism. The *Pugio Fidei's* key thesis was that which Giovanni Pico della Mirandola put forth two centuries later: that rabbinic books such as the Talmud contain proof of Jesus being the Messiah. Martin wrote:

"As often as the Talmud offers us some prophetic proof text, interpreting it concerning the messiah or concerning those things known to relate to the messiah, if it has expounded the text well, it should be admitted in argument. For honey, as the wise man knows, is consumed eagerly, even though, if it is examined carefully, it proves to be the spittle of bees...I found in the Talmud and *midrashim*—that is, glosses—and traditions of the ancient Jews which I gladly raised up like pearls out of an enormous dung heap...Certain (traditions) which know the truth and in every way reveal the doctrine of the prophets and holy fathers, wondrously and incredibly bespeak the Christian faith too, as will become obvious in this book. They destroy and confound the perfidy of modern Jews..."

---

25 Ramon Marti, a.k.a. Raymond Martin, *Pugio Fidei adversus Mauros et Iudaeos* ("Dagger of Faith Against Muslims and Jews," circa 1278).

The "Talmud and midrashim...destroy and confound the perfidy of modern Jews." This is an unintentionally hilarious statement, but there is nothing humorous about it since this notion gained increasing traction over the centuries, and was one constituent part of the successful occult movement to rehabilitate rabbinic Judaism and its Babylonian Talmud.

In our exchange of correspondence, the individual representing the Latin Mass Society added: "The reference to Aquinas is connected with his more general defense of the Patristic view of the role of the Jews in the economy of salvation, by contrast with the views of Scotus and others. Also of note is his refutation of the charge of decide, made against the Jews...On the Talmud, the (position) paper refers to an article by John Lamont which is available online, in the *Homiletic and Pastoral Review*, which goes into more detail."

Our point of contention is not "the role of the Jews in the economy of salvation." The reference to it would seem to be a diversionary tactic. We are not contending against the Old Testament, or the Book of Romans, chapter eleven. *The point at issue is Talmudic Judaism.* The Latin Mass Society wants us to believe that the Roman Catholic Church was always, even prior to the Renaissance, a politically-correct ally of Pharisaic Judaism's diabolism, and that Aquinas is noteworthy for "his refutation of the charge of decide, made against the Jews."

As for deicide, concerning culpability for the hatred that motivated His crucifixion, Jesus said: "If I had not come and spoken to them, they would not have been guilty of sin, but now they have no excuse for their sin. Whoever hates me hates my Father also. If I had not done among them the works that no one else did, they would not be guilty of sin, but now they have seen and hated both me and my Father. But the word that is written in their Law must be fulfilled: They hated me without a cause." (John 15: 22-25).

St. Thomas Aquinas on deicide stated, "...their ignorance did not excuse them from crime, because it was, as it were, affected ignorance. For they saw manifest signs of His Godhood. Hence, He Himself says of them in John 15:22: 'If I had not come, and spoken to them they would not have sin; but now they have no excuse for their sin.' And John 15:24 'If I had not done among them the works that no other man had done, they would not have sin....

"Bede likewise says, 'It is to be observed that he does not pray for those who, understanding Him to be the Son of God, preferred to crucify Him rather than acknowledge Him.'...

"All this shows that while they beheld Christ's marvelous works, it was owing to their hatred that they did not allow him to be the Son of God...The rulers of the Jews knew that he was Christ: and if there was any ignorance in them, then it was affected ignorance, which could not excuse them...Among the Jews, some were elders, and others of lesser degree...those of lesser degree—namely the common folk...The Jews of the common order sinned most grievously as to the kind of their sin: yet in one respect their crime was lessened by their ignorance...they were deceived ...by their rulers so that they did not believe Him to be the Son of God or the Christ." [26]

St. Thomas Aquinas has succinctly summarized a thousand years of Catholic teaching regarding the words of Jesus Christ in this regard, and no amount of spin from agents of the post-Renaissance Church of Rome, whether Latinists or not, can alter that fact.

The leader of the "Latin Mass Society of England and Wales" with whom we corresponded, made a further revelation of a once suppressed secret: "The Congregation for the Index asked only that a very small number of verses referring to Our Lord be removed. Their ruling meant that the Talmud could be freely printed and distributed, as far as the Church was concerned."

Yes indeed, the papists, more than any other power on earth, and certainly more so than Protestants of that era, were the principal enablers of the Babylonian Talmud.

The person in the Latin Mass Society with whom we corresponded stated further, "On the Talmud the paper refers to an article by John Lamont which is available online, in the *Homiletic and Pastoral Review*, which goes into more detail."

---

26 *The Summa Theologica of St. Thomas Aquinas*, part III, question 47, articles 5-6. Aquinas here distinguishes between the less culpable *am ha'aretz* and their more guilty leaders.

The Una Voce/Latin Mass Society publication, *Good Friday Prayer for the Jews in the Extraordinary Form*, is sourced as follows in its own footnote no. 17: "Professor John Lamont in the *Homiletic and Pastoral Review*."

According to another of Lamont's publishers, the "traditional Catholic" website OnePeterFive.com: "Dr. John R. T. Lamont is a Canadian Catholic philosopher and theologian. He studied philosophy and theology at the Dominican College in Ottawa and at Oxford University, and has taught philosophy and theology in Catholic universities and seminaries."

The *Homiletic and Pastoral Review* is a publication of "Conservative Catholics" who are not necessarily dedicated to restoration of the Tridentine Latin Mass. The article by Prof. Lamont published online by *Homiletic and Pastoral Review*, "Why the Jews Are Not the Enemies of the Church," is, we regret to say, an embarrassment. One wonders how a "Catholic philosopher and theologian" could make so many erroneous statements, and how leaders of national "Latin Mass societies," and priestly "Pastoral reviews" could be so maladroit as to imagine Prof. Lamont has expertise in the field of Talmudic Judaism. Yet, his farrago is endorsed by *Homiletic and Pastoral Review* and Tridentine Latin Mass groups. Perhaps the folly of Lamont's article is not the point. Perhaps the point is to put forth anything with an appearance of scholarship that is sufficient to recruit large segments of what is known as "traditional Catholicism" into the ranks of the movement to appease the Talmudic spirit of the age, and fulfill the Renaissance-papal occult mission.

The devolution of "traditional Catholicism" from offering resistance to Talmudic Judaism, into a Trojan Horse which embraces it (with the requisite qualifications and cautions, i.e. the two-steps-forward-one-step backward tactic), is not entirely unexpected. "Traditional Catholicism" with its servile allegiance to the Renaissance and post-Renaissance pontiffs, has always contained within it seeds of contradiction which doomed it from the outset, and those seeds have come to fruition.

The following is an excerpt from Dr. Lamont's article, "Why the Jews Are Not the Enemies of the Church": [27]

"The reason why Rabbinic Jews are not enemies of the Church can be put briefly. Such Jews do not seek to convert Christians to Judaism, or to prevent non-Jewish Christians from exercising their faith. They only refuse to become Christians themselves, which does not suffice to make them 'enemies' of the Church...Rabbinic Jews make no effort to prevent the preaching of the Gospel to Gentiles..."

One doesn't know whether to laugh or cry in confronting the preceding statement from a professor of theology at a Catholic university. "...Jews do not seek to...prevent non-Jewish Christians from exercising their faith. They only refuse to become Christians themselves..."

In truth, the rabbinic legal authorities of Orthodox Judaism decree that the worship of Jesus Christ as the Second Person of the Blessed Trinity constitutes nothing less than idol worship ("avodah zarah"). [28] Idol worshippers are liable to the death penalty under the Talmudic "Noahide Laws." [29]

All of the inhabitants of the world are compelled to accept the Noahide Laws. If any non-Jew does not accept those laws he should be killed.

---

[27] Readers are encouraged to study Dr. Lamont's text in its entirety online, at: http://www.hprweb.com/2014/03/why-the-jews-are-not-the-enemies-of-the-church/

[28] Cf. *Mishneh Torah*, Hilchot Avodat Kochavim 9:4; *Teshuvos Pri ha-Sadeh* 2:4 and *Igros Moshe*, Y.D. 3:129-6.

[29] Babylonian Talmud, Sanhedrin 57a.

The preceding is the doctrine of Rabbi Moses Maimonides. [30]

Rabbinic authorities decree that a building (i.e. a church) set aside for actual (rather than feigned) worship of Jesus Christ is a house of *avodah zarah*. [31]

In traditional Orthodox Judaism, Western civilization is both *malkhut zadon* ("the empire of insolence") [32] and *"kochi ve'otzem yadi of Edom,"* ("the wicked progeny of Esau"). The Talmudists have sacred festivals and curses that are aimed at precipitating the ritual downfall of the gentile nations. One such festival is the rabbinic holy day known as the Ninth of Av (*Tisha B'Av*). [33]

According to a textbook authored by Rabbi Saadya Grama, "Jewish success in the world is completely contingent upon the failure of other peoples. Jews experience good fortune only when gentiles experience catastrophe...The difference between Jews and gentiles is not historical or cultural, but rather genetic and unalterable." [34] Rabbi Grama is a distinguished alumnus of the prestigious Beth Medrash Govoha "Lakewood Yeshiva." Grama's book *Romemut Yisrael Ufarashat Hagalut* carries the endorsements of the most revered religious leaders

---

[30] Cf. *Mishneh Torah*: Hilchot Melachim U'Milchamoteihem ("Laws of Kings and Wars"), Section 8, Halacha 10. This passage from "Hilchot Melachim" deals with battle captives, but in the course of elucidating those laws pertaining to captives, Maimonides is drawing on the larger corpus of laws having to do with non-Jews; i.e. the Seven Laws (of the Noahide). (Maimonides is specifically cited in this regard in Tosefot Yom Tov, Avot 3:14]. The call to execute all those "among the nations" (*goyim*) who do not accept the Noahide laws (not just those who are prisoners of war), is indubitably present in Hilchot Melachim 8:10. In the early 21st century, this killing may occur in Palestine, where the Israelis are supreme. In Europe and America Judaic executions of those who worship Jesus Christ as God, or refuse to submit to the Noahide laws, cannot take place at this time. This is due to the fact that Maimonides decreed that killings of obstreperous non-Jews can only occur in those places where "the hand of Israel is powerful over them." In other words, where Judaic supremacy is complete. Cf. Hilchot Melachim 8:9.

[31] Cf. Yayin Malchus, 234-237. Minchas Elazar 1:53-3. Yechaveh Da'as 4:45. Darchei Teshuvah 150:2. Tzitz Eliezer 14:91.

[32] The Judaic who undertakes the virtue of harming western civilization earns the honorific, *makhnia' zedim* ("he who degrades the insolent").

[33] Cf. *Judaism Discovered*, pp. 653-656.

[34] *Romemut Yisrael Ufarashat Hagalut* ("Israel's Supremacy and the Question of Exile"; Lakewood, New Jersey, 2003).

of the yeshiva, including the *rosh yeshiva* (head of the school), Rabbi Aryeh Malkiel Kotler.

The rabbinic gentile-murder-manual *Torat Ha'Melech* ("The King's Torah"), is a guidebook of 230 pages on the religious laws concerning the killing of non-Jews. According to the book's co-author, Rabbi Yitzhak Shapira, "Non-Jews are uncompassionate by nature," and should be killed in order to "curb their evil inclinations...If we kill a gentile who has violated one of the seven commandments there is nothing wrong with the murder," Shapira declared.

"Citing rabbinic law as his source he stated: "There is justification for killing the babies of the *goyim* if it is clear that they will grow up to harm us, and in such a situation they may be harmed deliberately, and not only during combat with adults."

Shapira is the head of the Israeli Od Yosef Chai *yeshiva* (rabbinic school). According to journalist Max Blumenthal: "Od Yosef Chai has raked in nearly fifty thousand dollars from the Israeli Ministry of Social Affairs since 2007, while the Ministry of Education has pumped over $250,000 dollars into the yeshiva's coffers between 2006 and 2007. The yeshiva has also benefited handsomely from donations from a tax-exempt American non-profit called the Central Fund of Israel. Located inside the Marcus Brothers Textiles store in midtown Manhattan...

"...Shapira counts Israel's leading fundamentalist rabbis among his supporters. His most well-known backer is Dov Lior, the leader of the Shavei-Hevron yeshiva at Kiryat Arba, a radical Jewish settlement near the occupied Palestinian city of Hebron and a hotbed of Jewish terrorism.

"Lior has vigorously endorsed *Torat Ha'Melech*, calling it 'very relevant, especially in this time.' Lior's enthusiasm for Shapira's tract stems from his own eliminationist attitude toward non-Jews. For example, while Lior served as the Israeli military's top rabbi, he instructed soldiers:

'There is no such thing as civilians in wartime...A thousand non-Jewish lives are not worth a Jew's fingernail!'

"...Besides Lior, *Torat Ha'Melech* has earned support from another nationally prominent fundamentalist rabbi: Yaakov Yosef. Yosef is the leader of the Hazon Yaakov Yeshiva in Jerusalem and a former member of Knesset (the Israeli parliament). Perhaps more significantly, he is the son of

Ovadiah Yosef, the former chief rabbi of Israel and spiritual leader of the Shas Party that forms a key segment of Netanyahu's governing coalition. Yaakov Yosef has brought his influence to bear in defense of *Torat Ha'Melech*, insisting at the August 18 (2010) convention in Jerusalem that the book was no different than the *Hagadah* that all Jews read from on the holiday of Passover." [35]

Until the Renaissance, rabbinic Judaism was considered the enemy of Western Christian Civilization for the most fundamental reason of all, it was guilty of implacable hatred toward Jesus Christ, the founder of that civilization. This hatred manifests as lies about Him, His mother and His followers. These lies were considered so malignant that our civilization deemed them blasphemy.

At the dogmatic Fourth Lateran Council of 1215, Pope Innocent III issued the following binding decrees upon Catholics:

Canon 68: "[Jews] are not afraid to mock the Christians who maintain the memory of the most holy Passion (of Jesus Christ). This, however, we forbid most severely, that any one should presume at all to break forth in insult to the Redeemer. And since we ought not to ignore any insult to Him who blotted out our disgraceful deeds, we command that such impudent fellows be checked by the secular princes by imposing on them proper punishment so that they shall not at all presume to blaspheme Him who was crucified for us."

Canon 69: "Since it is absurd that a blasphemer of Christ exercise authority over Christians, we, due to the boldness of these transgressors, renew in this general council what the Synod of Toledo wisely enacted in this matter: we prohibit Jews from occupying positions of public office."

The Talmudists will be enemies of the West, and the canons of Innocent III will be valid and in force, for as long as the adherents of rabbinic Judaism ceremonially curse Jesus Christ, His Blessed Mother and the "*min*." How could it be otherwise? How could it be said they don't wish us, or Christianity harm?

---

[35] Blumenthal, "How To Kill Goyim And Influence People: Leading Israeli Rabbis Defend Manual for For Killing Non-Jews" (Aug. 31, 2010). http://maxblumenthal.com/2010/08/how-to-kill-goyim-and-influence-people-leading-israeli-rabbis-defend-manual-for-for-killing-non-jews/

This is not a complex issue. Yet the willful blindness concerning this uncomfortable truth is often overwhelming.

Babylonian Talmud tractate Shabbat 116a orders that the New Testament be burned. The rabbinic rite of cursing Christians is now well-documented. Judaism from its Pharisaic beginnings is replete with hate speech, superstitiously charged curses, gematria [36] and evil eye looks. Nonconformists in Orthodox Judaism are subject to the *cherem* curse of excommunication, wherein a rabbi holds a Torah scroll illuminated by candles that are then blown out, accompanied by blasts from a shofar and the pronouncement of a lengthy list of curses targeted at the nonconformist.

Certain Israeli rabbis such as Rabbi Yosef Dayan from the West Bank settlement of Psagot take credit for placing the *pulsa d'nura* ("whip of fire") death curse on Israeli Prime Ministers Yitzhak Rabin in 1995 (because he sought peace with the Palestinians), and on Ariel Sharon in 2005 (for expelling "settlers" from the Gaza Strip).

The curse against Sharon was carried out at the grave of the Zionist terrorist Shlomo Ben Yosef, who was executed in the 1930s during the British Mandate, for atrocities that included shooting at a bus carrying Arab civilians. Rabin died from a bullet fired by a Talmud student. Sharon fell into a coma from which he never awakened.

In 1988, in the course of laying the cornerstone of the state-sponsored synagogue disguised as the "US Holocaust Memorial Museum," President Ronald Reagan, acting as the dummy of his ventriloquist "speech writer" John Mordechai Podhoretz, gave the keynote address in which he predicted that long after our western civilization had fallen, the "Jewish people would survive to "cast their blessings." [37]

Mr. Podhoretz must have had a hearty laugh at the words his presidential mannequin mouthed and the *goyim* in

---

36 Rabbinic Judaism teaches that the meaning of the Bible is to be found in the interpretation of letters, words and combinations of words having a numerical value that conveys secret meanings. This *gematria* is a superstition worthy of the soothsayers of Babylon, not the Israel of God.

37 Reagan's spiel constitutes an over-the-top muttering of *meshugganah* megalomania on behalf of the Zionists. It was spoken by a man who has been enshrined by the Right-wing as one of our most celebrated Conservative exemplars. As of this writing his 12 minute oration can be viewed online: www.youtube.com/watch?v=CoA83ZREL_U

attendance applauded, because in the heads-is-tails world of the Talmudic religion, one of the most prominent of these "blessings" is in fact a curse, as we demonstrated in chapter eight. The *halachic* authority "Rambam," (Maimonides) wrote: "In the days of Rabban Gamaliel, the *minim* became numerous in Israel and they caused trouble for the Jews, seducing them to turn away from God. When they saw that this was more significant than any other human need, Rabban Gamaliel and his court acted and established an additional blessing that would include a petition before God to make the *minim* perish. He established it in the *amidah* so that it would be set in everyone's mouths. Consequently, the number of blessings in the *amidah* is nineteen." [38]

This is a reference to the *Amidah* "prayers of benediction," the *birkat haminim*, which, as we have seen, contains the murderous, ritual curse on the Christians (i.e. the "*minim*"), a curse which has echoed perpetually down the corridors of time since at least the days of Rabbi Gamaliel, when it was enacted at the rabbinic academy of Yavneh (known in Greek as the academy of "Jamnia"), in the late first century A.D.[39]

Dr. Lamont of the Catholic *Homiletic and Pastoral Review* seems to be unaware that Orthodox, Talmud-faithful (*frum*) Judaic persons have had a large role in harassing and extruding Arab-Christians in Palestine; or that Bolsheviks raised in Talmudic homes in Russia were in the forefront of the leadership of Lenin and Stalin's holocaust against Orthodox Christianity in the U.S.S.R. Sever Plocker, writing for the Israeli "Ynetnews" agency in 2006 states:

"Almost 90 years ago, between the 19th and 20th of December 1917, in the midst of the Bolshevik revolution and civil war, Lenin signed a decree calling for the establishment of The All-Russian Extraordinary Commission for Combating Counter-Revolution and Sabotage, also known as Cheka. Within a short period of time, Cheka became the largest and cruelest state security organization. Its organizational structure was changed every few years, as were its names:

---

[38] *Mishneh Torah,* Hilkhot Tefillah Unesi'at Kapayyim 2:1.

[39] This is a reference to Rabban Gamliel II, who is reputed to have survived the destruction of the Temple in 70 A.D.

From Cheka to GPU, later to NKVD, and later to KGB. We cannot know with certainty the number of deaths Cheka was responsible for in its various manifestations, but the number is surely at least 20 million, including victims of the forced collectivization, the hunger, large purges, expulsions, banishments, executions, and mass death at Gulags. Whole population strata were eliminated: independent farmers, ethnic minorities, members of the bourgeoisie, senior officers, intellectuals, artists...Lenin, Stalin, and their successors could not have carried out their deeds without wide-scale cooperation of disciplined 'terror officials,' cruel interrogators, snitches, executioners, guards, judges, perverts, and many bleeding hearts who were members of the progressive Western Left and were deceived by the Soviet regime of horror and even provided it with a kosher certificate....And us, the Jews? An Israeli student finishes high school without ever hearing the name Genrikh Yagoda,' the greatest Jewish murderer of the 20th Century, the GPU's deputy commander and the founder and commander of the NKVD. Yagoda diligently implemented Stalin's collectivization orders and is responsible for the deaths of at least ten million people. His Jewish deputies established and managed the Gulag system. After Stalin no longer viewed him favorably, Yagoda was demoted and executed, and was replaced as chief hangman in 1936 by Yezhov, the 'bloodthirsty dwarf.' Yezhov was not Jewish but was blessed with an active Jewish wife.

"In his Book *Stalin: Court of the Red Star,* Jewish historian Sebag Montefiore writes that during the darkest period of terror, when the Communist killing machine worked in full force, Stalin was surrounded by beautiful, young Jewish women. Stalin's close associates and loyalists included members of the Central Committee, and Politburo (member) Lazar Kaganovich...Many Jews sold their soul to the devil of the Communist revolution and have blood on their hands for eternity....Leonid Reichman, head of the NKVD's special department and the organization's chief interrogator... was a particularly cruel sadist. In 1934, according to published statistics, 38.5 percent of those holding the most senior posts in the Soviet security apparatuses were of Jewish origin...Turns out that Jews too, when they become captivated by messianic ideology, can become great murderers, among the greatest known by modern history. The Jews active in official communist terror apparatuses (in the Soviet Union and abroad) and who at times led them, did not do this, obviously, as Jews, but rather, as Stalinists, communists, and 'Soviet people.' Therefore, we find it easy to ignore their origin and 'play dumb.' What do we have to do with them? But let's not forget them.

"My own view is different. I find it unacceptable that a person will be considered a member of the Jewish people when he does great things, but not considered part of our people when he does amazingly despicable things. Even if we deny it, we cannot escape the Jewishness of 'our hangmen,' who served the Red Terror with loyalty and dedication from its establishment." [40]

Can Prof. Lamont actually expect us to believe that very few of these Judaic-Communist killers of Christians developed their detestation for Christians from having been raised, as was often the case, in a Talmudic religious environment seething with hostility toward the followers of Jesus in Russia?

Talmudic Judaism is implacably opposed to Christianity. Where is there any proof or evidence that anything has changed since the time of St. Paul? By the example of Jesus Christ and Paul, every Christian has the right *and the warrant* to speak to the leaders of Judaism as they did. Situation ethicists pretend that time has changed the truth, or that those who follow the Talmud-religion are not currently the heirs of the religion of Pharisaic Judaism that gave birth to the Talmud.

Rabbinic Judaism poses as "the religion of the prophets." This is the motto of the "liberal progressive 'peace' rabbis" such as Michael Lerner of *Tikkun* magazine. This is a lie. Judaism is not the religion of the prophets. According to Jesus, *Judaism is the killer of the prophets.* Yahweh (YHVH), the God of the Prophets, is not the deity of Judaism. Judaism's god is in the lower case, a devil-idol, the spirit that entered Judas (John 13:27).

If one were to ask this writer to distill all that we know about Judaism's object of worship to one sentence, we would

---

[40] Sever Plocker, "Stalin's Jews: We mustn't forget that some of the greatest murderers of modern times were Jewish." www.ynetnews.com, December 21, 2006.

reply as follows: the god of Judaism is their own self-pride. This self-pride is the idol at the core of rabbinic propitiation. "For the true Deity of the Jews is not Yahweh, but the Jewish people itself." (Miguel de Unamuno). Everything in Judaism exists for the Judaic ego and for it alone. God has nothing to do with it.

According to Maimonides, any gentile religion is illicit; the only alternatives for gentiles are conversion to Judaism or observance of the rabbinic "Noahide Laws," which by definition exclude any gentile religion. [41]

The fifteenth century Spanish-Judaic Talmudist, Rabbi Isaac Abravenel asserted that God will wipe out the Christians for their "transgression" of attributing corporeality to God. Abarbanel further decreed that Christianity was more wicked than the paganism of savages. [42]

In the *Avodat Kochavim,* Rabbi Maimonides declares a divine mandate to kill the "wicked" Jesus Christ, all Jews who follow Jesus and all those who do not follow the Talmud: "It is a *mitzvah* (religious duty highly pleasing to God), to destroy Jewish traitors, *minim,* and *apikorsim,* and to cause them to descend to the pit of destruction, since they cause difficulty to the Jews and sway the people away from God, as did Jesus of Nazareth and his students, and Tzadok, Baithos, and their students. May the name of the wicked rot."

Catholic Professor Lamont:

"...the *Talmud* is an attempt to preserve the beliefs and practices of the scribes and Pharisees of the latter part of the Second Temple era (the era from 530 B.C. to 70 A.D., when the second Jewish Temple was in existence). It contains some inaccuracies and expansions of these beliefs and practices, but not enough to constitute Rabbinic Judaism as a new religion, or even as a substantially new form of an older religion."

---

[41] Cf. *Hilkhot Melakhim* 10: 9; R. Zvi Hirsch Chajes, *Kol Sifrei Maharatz Chajes* (Jerusalem, 1958), vol. 2 p. 1036; Moshe Feinstein, *Iggerot Moshe* (New York, 1973), Yoreh Deah II, p. 9.

[42] David Berger, "Al Tadmitam shel ha-Goyim ba-Sifrut ha-Pulmusit ha-Ashkenazit," in *Yehudim mul ha-Tselav,* p. 90.

In other words, according to this Catholic professor, the religion of the Pharisees was the religion of the Old Testament, and Jesus' statements concerning their teachings being not of God, but of man, and nullifying the Word of God, are wrong. Judaism's Babylonian Mishnah and Gemara contradict the Old Testament many thousands of times. Those seminal rabbinic texts even nullify God's sabbatical year with *prozbul* contracts still being issued in the twenty-first century. Rabbi Jacob Neusner: "We have already seen substantial evidence that any notion of Pharisaism (or later rabbinic Judaism) as the true and direct descendants of the Old Testament is contradicted by one Mishnah-tractate after another. These stand wholly separate from the Priestly Code...and generally contradict it!"[43]

Prof. Lamont: "The Talmud permits Jews to behave immorally towards Gentiles.' This claim is supported by quoting a number of Talmudic texts as, for example, a text that says that even the best of the Gentiles should be killed. These texts are, however, taken out of context, and their use reflects a misunderstanding of the way that the Talmud works...The nature of Talmudic discussions means that, in practice, rabbis are not trained simply by study of the *Talmud*, because such study on its own is too difficult. Instead, they study the standard legal codes and commentaries on the *Talmud* (principally those of Maimonides, Rashi, and Joseph Karo), which give an organized presentation of the conclusions of Talmudic discussions. None of these codes and commentaries make the immoral assertions that are ascribed to the *Talmud*, and no Rabbinic Jew is free to disagree with their consensus."

Lamont alleges that in the texts of Maimonides, Rashi and Joseph Karo there are none of the immoral assertions found in the Talmud! Either Lamont has read all of the thousands of pages written by these three and *doesn't know what he's read*, or he is relying on someone else he does not name for his *demonstrably false statement*. The texts of Maimonides and Karo are replete with numerous "immoral assertions." Has Lamont read the uncensored *Mishneh Torah* of Moses Maimonides where Maimonides states that Jesus and His

---

[43] Neusner, *A History of the Mishnaic Law of Purities* (1974), p. 7.

followers should be destroyed? Has he read the uncensored, Shlomo Pines translation of Maimonides' volumes, *Guide of the Perplexed,* in which the rabbi states that Black people are sub-human?

Lamont's thesis is that if you're a gentile or a Christian, Judaism is not interested in harming or dominating you. Yet, as we have already noted, Maimonides decreed, "All of the inhabitants of the world are compelled to accept the Noahide laws. If any non-Jew does not accept these laws he should be killed."[44] As for Karo, he upheld one of the most notorious *halakhot* in all of the Talmud Bavli: the permission for a woman to have sex with a boy under the age of nine (Sanhedrin 69b), even if she is the boy's mother. In the *Shulchan Aruch,* Karo decrees that the original ruling by the ancient Pharisee Hillel, that the incestuous molesting mother was nonetheless still eligible to marry a Jewish priest, was valid.

Catholic Prof. Lamont: "...The accusation that the *Talmud* was immoral and anti-Christian, through and through, originated largely with Jewish converts to Christianity of this period, such as Nicholas Donin. One may guess that these converts were influenced in these accusations by a reaction against their former religious position, and by feeling a need to prove their loyalty to Christianity."

Prof. Lamont assumes the best about obstinate Judaics who reject Jesus, but is willing to "guess" that the motives and truthfulness of heroic Judaic converts to Catholicism were motivated by other than honorable motives.

How dare he calumniate Donin on no evidence, and speculate, Freudian-like, on his supposed ulterior motives? The converts who testified that the Talmud was thoroughly immoral and anti-Christian were not doing so truthfully, Lamont asserts, but, "one may guess" they prevaricated "to prove their loyalty to Christianity."

It should not surprise us that these aspersions on Donin, the Catholic convert from Judaism, originate with the rabbis who he defeated in debate. Is it necessary to say anything more

---

44 Maimonides, *Mishneh Torah: Hilchot Melachim U'Milchamoteihem* ("Laws of Kings and Wars"), Section 8, Halacha 10.

about the historical perspicacity of this accredited authority of the Latin Mass Society?

Catholic Prof. Lamont: "The inaccuracy of these accusations made them ineffective for missionary purposes, which, in turn, led to Catholic theologians making a thorough study of the *Talmud*."

The only ones who charged Donin with "inaccuracy" were his rabbinic adversaries. Medieval Catholic authorities did not. Lamont takes the word of the rabbis over the medieval Catholic authorities.

Catholic Prof. Lamont: "A commission of Jews approached the Council (of Trent) to request that it rule that the *Talmud* could be printed. The Council passed their request on to the Congregation for the Index, which again ruled that it could be printed if any anti-Christian statements were removed. This evaluation of the *Talmud* was more positive than that given to the works of Luther, Calvin, Peter Abelard's *Introduction to Theology*, and Samuel Richardson's *Pamela*–all of which were banned in their entirety by the Church..."

We have no argument with the preceding correct observation by Prof. Lamont, which points out that the Renaissance Church of Rome censored Luther and Calvin completely ("were banned in their entirety"), while leaving the Talmud of Babylon nearly intact. This approach is mirrored in "traditional Catholic" chapels as of this writing, where priests routinely sermonize on the pitfalls of Protestantism, while hardly daring to utter a word of disapprobation for the Talmud or the religion established upon it.

Catholic Prof. Lamont: "Rabbinic Judaism preserved much of the atmosphere and beliefs of the world of religious thought in which Christ and the apostles lived. These beliefs were often accepted as divinely revealed by Christ, and the authors of the New Testament books and, hence, it is true that Rabbinic Judaism contains elements that are of divine origin. A study of Rabbinic Judaism can, thus, illuminate, although not add to, the revealed deposit of faith that originates in Christ; this has been shown in detail through scholarly studies of the New Testament." (End quote from Dr. John Lamont).

These giddy assertions are all too similar to Amy-Jill Levine's dreary opus, *The Misunderstood Jew: The Church and the Scandal of the Jewish Jesus*, an exegesis predicated on liberal rabbinic fantasies regarding the New Testament. It seems to this writer that Dr. Lamont, traditional Catholicism's Talmud-explainer, may have proceeded *a priori* to absolve Talmudic Judaism of its Satanic malevolence toward Christ's true Catholic Church, and then cherry-picked a few supposed "facts" to suit his purpose, for which he has gained plaudits from many corners of the "Conservative" and "traditional Catholic" world. [45]

Amid the hand-clapping, we hope we won't be faulted for hearing, if ever so faintly, the screams of the Christian children ritually murdered by members of the religion of Judaism, as documented by Israeli Prof. Ariel Toaff, son of the late chief rabbi of Rome, in the uncensored first edition of his 2007 masterpiece, *Pasque di Sangue* ("Blood Passover"), [46] wherein he fully upholds the testimony of Catholic witnesses concerning the torture-execution of two-year old St. Simon of Trent, and other Catholic children killed by Ashkenazic persons.

We can rest assured that all is well, however. The principal from the Latin Mass Society of England and Wales with whom we corresponded in March, 2016, stated that the "position paper" his group was advancing concerning the non-malevolence of rabbinic Judaism toward Christianity, cannot be rejected by any reasonable person:

"The paper relies on the scholarship referred to in the footnotes. This is current and respectable; we don't expect everyone to agree, but we do expect reasonable people to accept that the position the paper takes is itself reasonable."

George Bernard Shaw observed that "all progress depends upon the unreasonable man." In the context of the low quality of the material being presented as unassailably "reasonable" scholarship, we will take Bernard Shaw's position.

On July 29, 2016 Dr. Lamont published another troubling essay, "The Catholic Church and the Conversion of the Jews,"

---

[45] No accusation of wrong-doing is here leveled at Professor John Lamont. His blunders, though most regrettable, are surely not deliberate; nor are they malicious.

[46] http://bloodpassover.com/xbp.pdf

which appeared on a "traditional Catholic" website, OnePeterFive.com.[47] In this study, Lamont proposes the theory that the expulsion of Talmud-believers from Christian lands was mainly the result of the ascent of the theology of the antinomian Duns Scotus and the Nominalist school. Lamont asserts that Aquinas was hostile to the expulsions in all cases. Yet, the theological basis for expulsion, in some grave cases of national crisis, of unconverted Judaics, does not derive its justification from Duns Scotus. It is Biblical and truly Catholic: separation, by extrusion, of a racist, Antichrist group of people who might otherwise gain malevolent ascendance over Christians and *goyim*. This separation was *prescribed* in Canons 68 and 69 of the Fourth Lateran Council.

Moreover, in "The Catholic Church and the Conversion of the Jews," Prof. Lamont equates the masonic-secular Enlightenment with Jew-hate, rather than with the enormous advancement of the power and influence of anti-Christian Judaics. His most egregious oversight is found in the course of his argument decrying (quite rightly) racial animus against Judaics even when they converted to Christ. A key datum that he overlooks however, is that Catholic conspirators who advanced the prestige of the Babylonian Talmud inside the Church launched savage, racist attacks on Judaic converts to Catholicism who dared to reveal the evil of the Talmud. We saw this with Nicholas Donin, and even more so in the vile, racist campaign against the Judaic convert Johann Pfefferkorn by "progressive" Catholic forces heavily invested in the rehabilitation of the Talmud. Dr. Lamont is oblivious.[48]

Tridentine Judaism is not confined to the Una Voce and the Latin Mass Society of England and Wales. Other groups, such as the Society of St. Pius X (SSPX) publish Judaizing absurdities consonant with the Neoplatonic-Hermetic gnosis and John-Paul II/Benedict XVI theology. In the SSPX article

---

[47]   OnePeterFive.com describes itself as "Rebuilding Catholic Culture. Restoring Catholic Tradition."

[48]   In December, 2016, Dr. Lamont lent his pen in support of the "Conservative Catholic" campaign of the four cardinals (Brandmüller, Burke, Caffarra and Meiser) who questioned the Apostolic Exhortation, *Amoris laetitia,* of Pope Francis: cf. http://rorate-caeli.blogspot.com/2016/12/article-considerations-on-dubia-of-four.html#more

"Saint of the Sanhedrin," [49] Hillel, who concocted methods for nullifying the Old Testament, including the *prozbul* to nullify the aforementioned sabbatical law on cancellation of debt, and who condoned sexual molestation of boys under the age of nine, is lauded as "an instrument of heaven."

To this heavenly accolade is added highly speculative conjecture which the SSPX published in *The Angelus* asserting the fundamental benevolence of Phariseeism concerning the patrimony of Simeon as conveyed by Gamaliel to Saul of Tarsus. This leaves the SSPX in the awkward predicament of having to explain how it was that Saul mercilessly persecuted Christians and may have had a hand in the murder of St. Stephen, when he had been taught such exemplary Pharisee ethics as a youth. The origin of the legend about Simeon being the son of Hillel, though ascribed to various Church Fathers, is actually derived from a rabbinic source, the *Pirke Avoth*. The SSPX essay in their *Angelus* magazine imagines that St. Paul was taught the Gemara (the second section of the Talmud) when he was fifteen years of age. The Gemara, however, would not be written for at least another two centuries after Paul.

In "Saint of the Sanhedrin," the "traditional Catholic" *Angelus* presents rabbinic delusions as fact and promotes the Pharisee Hillel as a virtual holy man of God. The great confusion among "traditional" Catholics concerning Judaism is only exacerbated by this type of Judaizing coming from an official organ of the leading "traditional Catholic priestly fraternity."

The objective of the major "traditional Catholic" organizations is to secure the growth of the Tridentine Latin Mass and all other pre-Vatican Council II rites and rituals, bells, incense, lace, processions and the whole panoply of old ceremonies. They imagine that an ingenious strategy for ensuring the success of this objective, which has Christ's gospel hollowed out of it in true Renaissance fashion, is to offer one or more compromises on the "small matter" of Judaism; the gospel truth on that subject being considered a distant second to having the Latin ceremonies permanently reinstated.

---

[49] *The Angelus,* December, 2009, pp. 29-34.

A Supremely Talmudic Supreme Court Justice

Antonin Scalia, was a much-admired and extolled "traditional Catholic" as well as Associate Justice of the United States Supreme Court. If it appears that we take joy in the sad task of debunking his record, we do not; neither do we shrink from it, however, in deference to anyone's illusions. The process of deprogramming, i.e. *disenchanting* the previously enchanted is almost always painful. [50]

"Traditional Catholics" and alleged "Conservative" Protestants offered up extravagant accolades for the late Supreme Court Justice Antonin Scalia, who passed away at age 79 on February 13, 2016. Justice Scalia, an adherent of the old Latin Tridentine Mass, was the son of Sicilian immigrants. Through hard work and a high IQ, he rose to the top of the judiciary in America. He and his wife had nine children. He was said to be an opponent of abortion, illegal immigration and some aspects of gun control. Legend has it that he was a proponent of a strict construction (interpretation) of the Constitution as it was originally written.

The preceding curriculum vitae is attractive indeed, and if we were fixated on symptoms, surface appearances and situation ethics we too would join the fanfare for the judge. Alas, we cannot. Perhaps Mr. Scalia's enthusiasts don't discern as we do the power of an evil in this world that emanates directly from the Crucifixion of Jesus Christ on Calvary. Perhaps they do not suffer as we do from that power. The *ideology* that wrought that evil is alive and more virulent than ever.

It is an ideology, *not a race*. The racial heirs to the evil have long since been dispersed to the four corners of the earth and throughout mankind. We can no more genetically determine who is a descendant of the Pharisees of A.D. 33 than we can identify a descendant of the Caesars. The infamous statement, "Let his blood be on us and our children" refers to a few generations of Jews in the first century, not to the Khazars and mixed multitude who masquerade as Jews today. Yes, of

---

[50] "Enchantment" is a word is derived from late Middle English, denoting "under a spell" and "deluded." To term something "enchanting" or as offering "enchantment" is considered a high accolade in our world. The vocation of the disenchanter is a lonely one. Yet, to attempt to behold things as they are one must dispel enchantment.

course, there are still authentic racial Judeans ("Jews") on earth, but in general we know them not.

The virus of the mind that killed Jesus Christ can, however, be readily identified. It is a spiritual force that radiates from within Orthodox Judaism and its Kabbalistic offshoots. Among Republicans, conservative Protestants and "traditional Catholics" there is alarm over the supposed "imminent threat of the imposition of Islamic Sharia law on America" Meanwhile, there is little evidence of awareness that Talmudic *halacha* (rabbinic law) has already been imposed on the United States; *a grievous transgression against the Gospel of Christ which the late Justice Scalia aided and abetted,* as his numerous activities on behalf of Talmudic training for American lawyers and his own statements testify, such as his March 9, 2001 letter written on Supreme Court stationery, to Rabbi Noson Gurary of the Chabad Lubavitch sect of Christ-haters.

It was perhaps not a coincidence that Scalia wrote his letter to Gurary on Purim, the rabbinic festival of revenge against gentiles, which was marked in 2001 on March 9 (14th of Adar 5761). In his letter he recommends Marshal Breger, vice-chairman of the extremist Neocon, war-Zionist Jewish Policy Center, and a teacher of Talmudic *halacha* at the Catholic University of America, in helping Rabbi Gurary discover "what works" in disseminating "Jewish law" at the University of Buffalo.

These facts are public knowledge, as an informed reading of Scalia's dissent in the Supreme Court's Caperton v. A.T. Massey Coal ruling, will show. There he refers to the "Babylonian Talmud" as a "divinely inspired text." The Talmud-ignorant will argue that Scalia is referring not to the Talmud but to "Scripture" as divinely-inspired. We are however, in the precarious realm of rabbinic word play here and scholars would do well to carefully scrutinize their terms.

The Talmud tractate cited by Justice Scalia, Aboth, is referring to *rabbinic* scripture, which is the Mishnah, chapter V, *not* the Bible. When we examine Mishnah Aboth 5:21, the verse that precedes Mishnah Aboth 5:22, we see that it contains a reference to the *primacy of the Mishnah as scripture.* Hence, the text that advises one to "turn over and over" is not in fact "with respect" to Old Testament "Scripture."

The context of the rabbinic quotation which Justice Scalia employs is a reference to "turning over and over" the Mishnah, a sacred *rabbinic* scripture of supreme authority in Judaism.

Scalia's claim to fame among Conservatives is that he was a "strict constructionist." Yet Scalia championed the bane of our American court system—*the making of law not by the legislature, but by judicial decision—which is the fundamental principle of the law-making ideology of rabbinic halacha*. This is Judaism 101, and it is almost impossible that a lawyer of Scalia's erudition and intellectual gifts would be unaware of it. How was the abominable crime of conferring "marriage" upon sexually active homosexuals made the law of the land?

It was accomplished by a Supreme Court engaged in *legislating through judicial decision*—which happens to be *the foundation of the Talmudic method of law-making*. Justice Scalia consistently failed in his duty to alert the American people to the rotten rabbinic root of a judicial process that rendered "gay" marriage the law of the land. He did not support the "gay" rights law itself, only the rabbinic legal philosophy that made it possible, which is a distinction without a difference.

Justice Scalia approved and participated in the training of a generation of American lawyers in the *halacha* of legislating through judicial decision. No aspect of Sharia law has had any impact on America anywhere near comparable to the impact of *halachic* law on our nation. Mr. Scalia's vast fan club howl their outrage at "gay" marriage, to zero effect. They battle the dragon's fire but leave the dragon intact, as did their darling, when he voted against legalizing the marriage of sodomites *while refusing to reveal the* halachic *modus operandi that effected it*.

He was not only guilty of cooperating with rabbinic *halacha* and the Babylonian Talmud, Justice Scalia, like many of Rome's intellectuals who are concerned with this issue, was an active participant in burnishing the reputation of those dark doctrines and spreading their diabolical influence. He openly worked for what his handlers termed the rise of "Synagogue and State."

This "traditional Catholic" Latin Mass worshipper and supposed "great friend of the Republic" *directly assisted with the Talmudic training program for future lawyers* at numerous Talmudic institutes, such as the Benjamin N. Cardozo School of

Law, which is part of the Talmudic Yeshiva University in New York. On November 6, 2013, at the "Synagogue and State" conference at Yeshiva University's Zahava and Moshael Straus Center, Rabbi Dr. Meir Soloveichik, director of the Straus Center, introduced Justice Scalia, along with Yeshiva alumnus Nathan Lewin, "whose extraordinary legal career is a source of great pride to our University." *Scalia and Lewin then proceeded to laud Talmudic* halacha *as a system of justice for America.*

Scalia's close friend and Talmudic crony, Nathan Lewin, served as the attorney for AgriProcessors, allegedly one of the worst and most inhumane kosher slaughterhouses in the nation. Lewin is on record advocating that the *families* of Palestinian suicide bombers should be executed. In 1994, in the case of Board of Education of Kiryas Joel Village School District v. Grumet, Lewin argued before the high court for the creation of a school district based on the boundaries of the Satmar (Hasidic) synagogue-community. Justice Scalia also believed that Talmudic synagogue-schools should have taxpayer support. He wrote a passionate defense of his vote in favor of the taxpayer subsidy advocated by his pal, Lewin.

In 2009, Judge Scalia took an active part in advancing the Institute of American and Talmudic Law, chaired by Rabbi Shlomo Yaffe and Rabbi Noach Heber. The Institute operates under the auspices of the Chabad Lubavitch Hasidim, who place a heavy emphasis on the inculcation of the doctrines of the Kabbalah. Chabad-Lubavitch was founded by Rabbi Shneur Zalman. Its most revered text, after the Talmud and the *Zohar,* is Zalman's *Tanya,* which decrees that gentiles are "supernal refuse" and that Jesus Christ was a diabolic imposter.

At the Institute of American and Talmudic Law, Justice Scalia, the alleged "traditional Catholic" paladin of the movement to restore America and the Constitution, apologized to the three hundred assembled rabbis and other "dignitaries," over the fact that he had not managed to study a page (*Daf Yomi*) of the Talmud every day (which is strongly advised for Orthodox Judaic males). Scalia said, "I assume I'm here to talk about federal law because I must confess that my *Daf Yomi* attendance has been lackluster." His defenders say that he was only joking. Imagine the reaction if Scalia had participated in a daylong conference of German nationalists and "jokingly" apologized for not reading *Mein Kampf* daily.

The outcry would have been explosive and nearly ceaseless. But a "traditional Catholic" Supreme Court judge who fronts for the Talmudic infiltration of America's legal system, and grovels before hundreds of rabbis about his neglect of a demonic book, is no less a "great American" and a "devout traditional Catholic" for having done so? Here we glimpse the farce that is so-called Conservative and Traditional Catholicism. "Pragmatists" will say that we are setting too severe a standard; that Justice Scalia was loathed by the Left and many secular Zionists, and that, while not perfect, he did his best to slow the decay process sweeping the land. In return, they suggest that we should overlook the fact that he made common cause with the heart of evil. This argument reflects the moral pathology of the Right-wing: compromise with evil for the sake of some imaginary greater good.

Under color of his Catholicism and defiance of various *symptoms* of evil, Judge Scalia advanced the powerful Talmudic institutions which enlarge the stature and authority of *halachic* law over our nation and help to ensure its infiltration of our institutions. He also helped to burnish the reputation of Talmudic rabbis and their unholy Talmud in Catholic circles. No liberal could have accomplished this betrayal of our once Christian country so well as "Conservative" Antonin Scalia. If we are labeled "extremists" because we won't partake of these Faustian bargains, and wink at the profound confusion and misdirection sown by Justice Scalia, then we accept the designation.

Jesus would have us be either hot or cold. After a time the "pragmatism" which confers hero status upon Scalia begins to look a lot like a chain of retreat and compromise that spells defeat for Our Lord's commission to us that His Father's will "be done on earth as it is in heaven." A Right-wing that imagines that the Talmudic rabbis are our allies in the struggle for family values, or at most a subsidiary adversary far down the list of threats, has lost the battle before the first shot is fired. The more we mistake symptoms for causes, while shying away from the root of the iniquity that is tearing at the foundations of our civilization, the more we dig the graves of our children. A movement that has for its paradigm Justice Scalia's simulacrum of Christian Conservatism, will be lethally compromised by the self-sabotaging contradictions of a double-mind.

My Memories of Nino Scalia
The Most Jewish Gentile on the Supreme Court

By Nathan Lewin

When there was no Jewish justice on the Supreme Court, Antonin "Nino" Scalia told me, "I considered myself the Jewish justice." After Abe Fortas resigned in May 1969, there would be no Jewish justice on the court for nearly a quarter of a century, until President Bill Clinton named Ruth Bader Ginsburg to the court in 1993. Scalia had been on the Supreme Court since Ronald Reagan appointed him in 1986, so there were seven years during which Scalia saw himself as the court's guardian of Jewish heritage.

Scalia's admiration for Jews and Jewish learning explains the frequent references in his opinions to the Talmud and other Jewish sources, and the significant number of Orthodox Jewish law clerks he hired.

We were both in the Harvard Law School class that began in 1957 and graduated in 1960. Scalia and his wife were guests in our *sukkah*. He accepted my recommendations to attend and address Orthodox Jewish gatherings such as colloquia run by Chabad-Lubavitch, sessions and dinners with Agudath Israel of America, and a mass meeting at Yeshiva University where he and I discussed current issues of constitutional law and public policy.

There is universal agreement that Nino Scalia was brilliant, amazingly articulate and a real *mensch*...all must concur that he was a great man, that the United States he loved is greatly diminished by his loss, and that he greatly revered Jews and Jewish tradition. [51]

---

[51] Jewish Telegraph Agency, February 15, 2016.

Chapter XVI

The Breeders of Money
Gain Dominion over the Church of Rome

Our book, *Usury in Christendom: The Mortal Sin that Was and Now is Not* [1] is a history of the rise of the Money Power inside the Church and readers may wish to access it for the depth at which it attempts to explore the subject matter. It would be redundant to reprint substantial portions of it in this volume. [2]

In these pages we will summarize our thesis and present additional research that has come to light since our book was published. Let us commence our pursuit of that goal by surveying the actual teaching of St. Thomas Aquinas, who is often misrepresented by papist usury apologists and others, as having tolerated escape clauses in the Church's immemorial proscription against profit on loans.

Aquinas confronted the loophole which the money-lenders and their agents sought to implement to their advantage: theological relativism that renders usury evil only because it is prohibited (thus leaving the door open to a future time when it will not be forbidden by the Church and therefore not evil). Aquinas replied, in *De malo*, that usury is not sinful because it is forbidden, rather, it is forbidden because it is a grave sin, *secundum se*. Historian Christopher A. Franks elaborates on the Christian economics of Aquinas:

"(St.) Thomas's position on usury depends, not on a particular way of configuring money, but on the very notion of abstractable exchange value that any understanding of money presupposes. Thomas argues that abstracted exchange value as

---

[1] Independent History and Research, 2013; paperback, 416 pages. The book's index is online at http://bit.ly/2fIfk0q

[2] We believe that any comprehensive analysis of Christ's teaching on money must include a commentary on His "Parable of the Talents," and "Parable of the Unjust Steward" and the "Mammon of Unrighteousness." The misunderstanding of these discourses has been used to portray Our Redeemer as a usury advocate, or at the least an apologist; cf. *Usury in Christendom*, pp. 50-58.

such cannot have a vendible use value in addition to the exchange value it abstracts. To believe that it does indicates that a spurious 'usefulness' humans can attribute to something has been mistaken for true use value. Further, Thomas goes on to consider other possible justifications for interest on a loan, and he faults them not for misconstruing the nature of money, but for presumptively seeking a security against the future that denies the deferent receptivity necessary to humans as members of an antecedent natural order that sustains us. Thus, we can see Thomas's adherence to the usury prohibition not as evidence of his obscurantism in the face of 'economic realities,' but as his resistance to the presumption inherent in emerging economic practices...

"Thomas's economic teachings reflect an assumption that justice in exchange depends on commensurating the terms of exchange with the shape of the provision God unfolds for human beings.

"When Thomas says, 'one man cannot overbound in external riches without another man lacking them,' we are tempted to read it as a mere pious assertion to shame the rich. But it is firmly rooted in Thomas's assumptions about how God provides for human beings through fruitfulness of nature...To make a claim to wealth that outstrips that provision, as usury does, is to produce injustice.

"...Thomas's centerpiece argument attacks the very notion of usury, but he supports it with other arguments about a variety of possible titles to interest. In both cases his arguments are meant to preserve justice by rejecting inordinate claims to wealth...

"Thomas's centerpiece argument does not hinge on an antiquated understanding of money. Thomas sees in the very notion of an abstracted exchange value the possibility of economic activity that obscures the primacy of use values....

"What all of Thomas's positions on titles to income from money show is an insistence that profit can only come from nature's goods, which always requires the patience and vulnerability that waits to see what nature offers. Thomas refuses the presumption against God's providence that would seek to secure a claim to wealth that outpaces that provision.

"...to contract a price for the use of money in addition to the principal is to sell a use that does not and cannot exist...Thomas's arguments, by uncovering the most basic reason against usury (that it sells a metaphysical impossibility), confirm the rationale of the usury prohibition even in productive loans where the borrower is not needy. Thomas is concerned not only for charity, but for keeping all exchanges answerable to the contours of real wealth...

"The consumptibility argument is not meant to destroy all possible arguments for a return on one's money...The *lender at interest* presumes by staking a claim to wealth — possible future wealth — that is not disciplined by any receptivity to what God's providence may actually end up providing.

"The *investor* does not presume, but takes the risk of waiting to see what comes of it. He does not hold the title to the return of all his money, but rather makes himself vulnerable to the contingencies of how God's provision may or may not smile on the efforts of the merchant or craftsman to whom the money is entrusted...

"What if the borrower is an incompetent businessman, while the lender could quite reliably have turned a profit with his money somewhere else? This argument Thomas rejects, again because of its presumption. This is the notion of *lucrum cessans*, the notion that a lender has a title to compensation beyond the principal for forgoing the gain he might have otherwise made with his money...The reason Thomas finds it presumptive is that, unlike a risky investment, a loan involves a contract obliging the borrower in advance to compensate the lender for a potential gain the actual realization of which could only be determined by waiting to see...However reliable the alternative investment, it would involve vulnerability to the contingencies of the unfolding of God's provision, a vulnerability that *lucrum cessans* circumvents. To establish a title to such wealth irrespective of the actual possibilities and provisions the future may turn out to hold, is to set up an artificial invulnerability...One contemporary manifestation of this drive toward invulnerability is the imperative 'to convert wealth into debt in order to derive a permanent future income from it — to convert wealth that perishes, into debt that endures, debt that does not rot, costs nothing to maintain, and brings in perennial interest." [3]

Because of the penchant of the Church of Rome for word games, subterfuge and doubletalk, the strictest, clearest and best definition of the sin of usury as originally understood by the Biblically-based Early Church (not the Romans, Greeks or other pagan nations), is any loan in which more than the principal is returned to the lender. An elementary expression of this process is "money breeding money."

There is nothing inherently inaccurate with calling money gained by a lender from a borrower which exceeds the principal, *interest.* The *Oxford English Dictionary* defines interest as: "Money paid for the use of money lent (the principal)." *Webster's Third International Dictionary* (1971), denotes it as: "the price paid for borrowing money."

But to make black into white and papal usury not usury, games with words must be played, otherwise the stage magic cannot operate, and the situation ethic that made the mortal sin of usury not mortally sinful, cannot be made to vanish, and the papacy of the sixteenth and following centuries cannot be exonerated of the charge of incrementally rendering profit on loans not sinful.

The first two steps in this legerdemain entail exploiting confusion over the old Roman word *interesse,* and to impose the mantle of St. Thomas Aquinas on the scam. Before we furnish a textbook example, let us define the Roman empire's *interesse*: "that which is between." Specifically "damages arising from a borrower's default on the loan."

When papist apologists conflate *interesse* with usury (interest), the Renaissance and post-Renaissance popes can be indemnified against the consequences of their gradual alteration of unalterable dogma. To work this deception, all of the usury-profit on loans which the papacy incrementally permitted, must be grouped under the category of "damage or loss caused by the lending of money."

As a student of the Babylonian Talmud, this writer is reasonably familiar with the duplicitous lawyer's mentality

---

[3] *He Became Poor: The Poverty of Christ and Aquinas's Economic Teachings,* pp. 71-83 (emphasis supplied.) In *He Became Poor* Prof. Franks refutes charges by John T. Noonan (*The Scholastic Analysis of Usury*), of discrepancies in the teachings of St. Thomas Aquinas on this subject.

that pervades it, and which can be summarized as self-deception coupled with the attempt to overcome God Himself, a feat which the Talmud proclaims the rabbis managed to achieve, when, in tractate Bava Metzia 59b it is reported that God gladly admitted to them, "My sons have defeated me! My sons have defeated me!" [4]

This is the rabbinic egotism and insane pride that informed the mentality of the original Sanhedrin, and the latter day Sanhedrin in the Vatican. [5]

In studying the deceptions of the apologists for papal usury permissions, we are in the realm of lawyers who call themselves Catholic historians, economists, theologians, and so forth. Observe this sleight of hand: "...passages from the writings of St. Thomas Aquinas can serve as representative of the development of the definition of, and rationale for usury...St. Thomas explains: 'A lender may without sin enter an agreement with the borrower for compensation for the loss he incurs of something he ought to have, for this is not to sell the money but to avoid a loss." [6]

Aquinas is being smeared as "representative of the development of the definition of, and rationale for usury," because he allowed for a charge to the borrower for a loan that was not repaid in the time specified. A borrower paying a reasonable fine of some type for refusing to repay a loan according to the time-frame mutually agreed upon when the

---

[4] This brag about defeating God is not something Judaism is ashamed of, or even one that Talmudists always deny. England's "Lord Rabbi Jonathan Sacks," who is celebrated in the corporate media as a "liberal, humane, progressive of the highest moral rectitude," announced that he positively loves this announcement that the rabbis have defeated God. In his review of Jonathan Rosen's book *The Talmud and the Internet,* "Lord Sacks," who was the Chief Rabbi of the United Hebrew Congregations of the Commonwealth of Britain, wrote: "Rosen loves, as do I, that extraordinary moment in the Talmud in which God is outvoted on a point of Jewish law and celebrates the fact that His children have defeated him. In the world of the rabbis, not only do men study the word of God; God studies the words of men." (*The Guardian,* December 21, 2001). "The Oral Law is determined by majority rule; hence, the Sages can overrule not only Rabbi Eliezer but even God Himself." —Rabbi Shlomo Riskin, "Halacha is not Decided in Heaven," *The Jewish Week,* May 23, 2011. "God must submit to the decisions of a majority vote of the rabbis."—BT Bava Metzia 59b.

[5] This is an example in the Talmud of Kabbalistic man-as-god mentality.

[6] Brian M. McCall, *The Church and the Usurers: Unprofitable Lending for the Modern Economy* (Ave Maria University, 2013), pp. 66 and 69.

loan commenced, is not the same as the mortal sin of renting money. It is a penalty for the sin of avarice on the part of the borrower, who can be as guilty of such a transgression as a lender. A good-hearted Catholic lender may wish to privilege Bob with a loan for a certain amount of time, and when the money loaned is returned on the schedule agreed upon, he may then wish to privilege Bill with the same, or a similar loan. If Bob withholds repayment then Bill does not have access to the loaned money in the time he needs it. It does not make St. Thomas Aquinas any kind of "developer" or "rationalizer" of usury because he clarified the point that a lender, like a borrower, has rights within the laws of Christian charity. It is outrageous that for the sake of rescuing the credibility of the Church of Rome's usury, the reputation of Aquinas is sullied.

The next step in the prestidigitation is to enlarge the categories of losses incurred by the lender for which he should be "compensated" under the category of interest. But perish the thought that this interest is profit for renting money. Certainly not. George Orwell would have loved it: don't call interest "profit"; call it "avoidance of loss":

"St. Raymond of Penafort's explanation of interest and why it is permitted to be collected notwithstanding the prohibition of usury: 'Interest is never thought of as payment on a loan; it is the 'difference' to be made up to a party injured by the failure of another to execute his obligations. The common distinction is between *usura* and *interesse, id est non lucrum sed vitatio damni'* (which means 'it is not profit but avoidance of loss'). Interest is purely compensatory. It is accidentally and extrinsically associated with a loan...'

"Two expressions of this right to damages (or interest) were *damnum emergens* [7] (damage emerging) and *lucrum cessans*. [8] These titles arose not as a right of payment on account of making a loan from the outset, but represented compensatory expectation damages due to the actual fault of the debtor." [9]

Woe unto the lawyers who gathered and asked among themselves, how can we gain for the lender interest on a loan that will not appear to be usury? We will term it, "compensatory expectation damages due to the actual fault of the debtor," and we will expand the definition to include loss of the use of the money loaned during the time the borrower possessed it, when it could have been invested in something more beneficial to the lender.

In addition to the aforementioned escape clauses, the Church of Rome in its "development of doctrine" (*dissolution of dogma* is the more candid term), hit on another loophole in charging for loans: the excuse that the loans were to the poor, from banks named Mountain of Compassion (*Monte di Pieta*), and the charges were not profits accruing from the loans themselves, but the costs that came from *administering the loans*.

Originally the true Catholic Church, with the compassion typical of an ecclesia that was as old as the idea of Europe and had founded great charitable institutions such as the earliest

---

[7] A financial loss incurred by the creditor during the time his money was loaned out, rather than being put into some other investment. As a result of *damnum emergens* it was theorized that the lender was "entitled" to be paid interest. This could be legitimate, viz. when a simple loan without usury went unpaid and the debtor owed the creditor the amount loaned; or it could become a loophole-exception to the moral law against usury from which permission for charging interest on money was derived. Thomas Aquinas opposed *damnum emergens* exceptions, ruling that the lender should have foreseen the consequences of making the loan.

[8] *Lucrum cessans*: (Lost potential); the loss of a profit which a lender might otherwise have gained from his money if he had not loaned it to a debtor. Under *lucrum cessans* a charge for a loan of money was justified as "damages," on the basis that the creditor had reserved his money for the debtor instead of putting it into some other investment. St. Thomas Aquinas "denied the lender's right to demand compensation for *possible* lost profit, since doing so involved selling what had only been *probable*, rather than real existence. He wrote, 'one should not sell something which one has not yet got and which one may be prevented in many ways from getting.'"

[9] Ibid., McCall, p. 70.

hospitals and schools, encouraged, in accordance with the spirit of the gospel, societies of *mons pietatis,* wherein Catholic volunteers and philanthropists offered loans to borrowers which, when repaid on time, *were free of charges of any kind.* The borrower repaid the principal and not a penny more, as God ordained. These arrangements operated for centuries under other names and in one form or another, to the glory of God and the testimony of His Church. With the passage of time however, situation ethicists who were at work in the bowels of the Church more than four hundred fifty years before the Second Vatican Council, "discovered" that usury had to be paid on the "charitable" loans — under the euphemism "administrative costs." According to this line of thought, Jesus Christ's command to lend expecting nothing in return was unworkable and required modification. What was actually afoot? The creation of the first, papally-approved Catholic usury banks. The alibi for this swindle, as issued to the gullible, is here outlined:

"As the *montes* began operating it soon became apparent that they would eventually exhaust their ability to serve the poor; if they merely received back the amount loaned, their donated capital would be depleted in paying their costs of operation, including salaries to employees. It was thus proposed that those benefiting from their operation share the costs of the operation in proportion to the benefit received, that is, the amount of the loan borrowed and repaid. Said another way, those who actually benefited were bound in justice to contribute back to the *mons* to compensate for the loss occasioned by the benefit...In practice these charges amounted to 5% per annum, on average. The *montes* represent an *excellent example of the application of the collection of interest merely as the right to charge the reimbursement of the cost of making the loan...*" [10]

It was Medici Pope Leo X who formalized this hoodwink with a bull in May 1515, after which, entirely by coincidence no doubt, the Medici-operated *mons pietatis* grew into full-blown international usury banks—templates for the seventeenth

---

[10] Ibid., p. 77, emphasis supplied.

century Protestant Bank of England and the Calvinist Dutch usurers who serve as stock villains in the pages of Right-wing tracts, where the names Leo X, Medici and *monte* are conveniently absent.

Pope Leo X initiated a process of gradualism, whereby the Church's immemorial dogmatic law against the charging of interest on loans of money was incrementally relaxed and diluted, leading to a papal revolution, culminating in the complete abolition of all ecclesiastical penalties for usury by Pope Pius VIII in his bull of Aug. 18, 1830, *Datum in audientia*, as well as the absence of all such penalties in the 1917 and 1983 Codes of Canon Law. No Renaissance or post-Renaissance pontiff from the sixteenth century to our time, restored the divine law proscribing profit from loans. All the popes from that time period either cooperated with the revolution or did nothing to halt it and left it in place. Some, like Pope Leo XIII, waxed eloquent in his encyclical *Rerum Novarum,* contra greed and the oppression of workers, but left untouched the root of those mortal sins — profit on loans; *usury.*

We begin, as often seems inevitable in a survey of the early Renaissance, with the Medici. But first let us take note of two pernicious historical myths in this field of study. The first is the rumor, disseminated by the major usurious banking houses and later perpetually recycled by the Right-wing, that the so-called "Jews" were the major financial force implicated in this usury.

There is not one Judaic banking house that is of over-arching significance in this early period; not one. Every bank we will implicate *in this epoch* is primarily of the Church of Rome. Yet who gets the blame for usury in this epoch? "The Jews." What's behind this? It is deliberate misdirection concealing the fact that the conspiracy operates just as smoothly in the gentile Right-wing as it does from within Judaism itself.

Notice that we state, "in this epoch." Later, Judaic banking houses such as the Rothschild bank, will become dominant, but the initial massive profits from the Renaissance papacy's gradual relaxation of the laws against usury were gained first by the gentile banks. The company of Vieri di Cambio de' Medici was the original foundation of the great Medici bank of the 15th century, and papal Rome was at the center of this banking dynasty's business empire. The papacy obtained usury loans from the Medici bank in the late 15th century by borrowing directly at stated rates of interest.

Giovanni di Lorenzo de' Medici, Pope Leo X, initiated a revolution that would only completely come to power some three centuries later, in 1830, under Pope Pius VIII, and confirmed in the Canon Law codes of 1917 (by omission) and in 1983 (by slightly less devious means).

Pope Leo X's new teaching consisted of an incremental step on the road to the permission for usury. In his Bull of 1515, *Inter multiplices,* Leo wrote that, "provided no profit be made," a "moderate fee" could be charged to borrowers to cover "administrative costs" of the operation of the bank known as the *Monte di Pietà.*

Medici Pope Leo, whose extended clan was deeply entrenched in Florentine banking and upon whom the pontiff had already bestowed many favors, was empowering the usury networks in Italy with his Bull. Apologists for the pope have asserted that the *montes* that developed in the wake of Leo X's bull were mostly pawnshops operating on the repossession of items pawned, not in making loans. They forget, however, that under *Inter multiplices,* the pawnbrokers could sell unredeemed pawns at a profit. They seem to think that Leo X was so obtuse that he did not foresee the loophole in his "provided no profit be made" provision. *Au contraire,* such profits were inevitable and the pontiff was no ingénue when it came to worldly affairs or financial transactions.

In practice, the pope's bull helped to establish usurious entities operating in the name of charity but functioning as for-profit businesses. Prior to the pope's revolutionary encyclical, truly Christ-like *montes* had donated their administrative costs. As a charity fund, the *montes* should not have been allowed to charge a middleman's 5% for "administrative fees," due to the obvious potential for abuse which such a "fee" represented. With the pontificate of Leo X the five percent so-called "administrative costs" were permitted. The five percent figure was ominous in that this was the rate which the Renaissance-Catholic nominalists and the usurious Catholic Fugger banking dynasty had set, through its theological mouthpiece Johann Eck, as a "moderate" rate of return on a loan.

In submission to a Scriptural standard, no Christian lender may gain a profit from a loan by charging fees that substitute for an interest rate. In all cases where a borrower repays a loan on time and in full, any charge of any kind beyond the return of the principal represents a profit to the lender and a loss to the borrower and constitutes usury. The rabbinic-style loopholes are the "extrinsic" titles which, under this and other deceptive euphemisms, in most cases lead to profit on a loan at the expense of the borrower. No previous pope in the course of fifteen hundred years had ever *formally* permitted such "fees" (though there had been some disgraceful accommodations made informally, such as by the Apostolic Chamber in 1486).

"Pope Leo X's *monte di pieta* was a bank to be plundered by his Florentine-merchant relatives and cronies. Charity for the poor was the necessary front used to vindicate the once forbidden usury. It didn't take long for the mask to fall, however: 'Never did the *monte's* officials recognize any irony in the fact that the *monte*, like the Jewish pawnbrokers it sought to replace...could sell unredeemed pawns at a profit...in the fall of 1529 the regime (in Florence) commanded the officials of the *monte di pieta* to assign it credits from the resources...this money amounted to an interest-free loan to the regime. There is no record that collateral was offered...By 1533 the city of Florence itself was guaranteeing the solvency of the *monte di pieta* and offering to pay interest of five percent on its deposits. All this in the name of poor relief (profit was guaranteed to any depositor willing to subsidize the *monte's* 'charitable activities').

"In 1486 the Apostolic Chamber took the first step toward regularizing the debt through an agreement with a consortium of bankers according to which they would advance loans over a number of years in return for their control over consolidated revenues...the number rose to forty-six (bankers), most of them Genoese and Florentines. A full funding of some of the debt occurred with the establishment of the Monte della Fede in 1526, and over the course of the century forty other *monti* were set up. These were funds raised through sales of shares that paid interest guaranteed by assignment of specific revenues for this purpose...These shares...paid interest in perpetuity and were therefore inheritable...Through the *monti* the papacy institutionalized its borrowing, creating a permanent funded debt..." [11]

Where were the poor, on behalf of whom this particular *monti* racket was instituted by the Bull of Leo X?

The Renaissance Church of Rome incrementally extended ever greater latitude to usurers, knowing that once the Money Power was unleashed it would eventually gain dominion (*omnia per pecuniam facta sunt*), by choosing the personnel of what was supposed to be Christ's Church, because the papacy would sometimes pay back what it owed to the banks by selling ecclesiastical offices to the highest bidder:

"The fact that the titles of more than 258 offices passed through the hands of Filippo Strozzi during his service as banker to the Medici popes in the early sixteenth century indicates something of the traffic in this kind of investment." [12]

"...the bankers organized themselves to handle their enormous collective business with the papacy...this can be illustrated by the career of Benvenuto di Paolo Olivieri... Olivieri held the post of depositary of the Apostolic Chamber from 1540 to 1543 and from 1545-1546. During these years his company was advancing loans to the papacy in about every possible way, usually jointly with other bankers...all the while he was buying and selling credits in several *monti*...This complex and variable web of Olivieri's credit ties to the papal government also extended underground, so to speak...

"By Olivieri's time the enormous increase in the number of fiscal offices in the Papal states, of *monti,* and of other investment opportunities attracted bankers from many places."[13]

The American Right's go-to villains, "greedy Calvinist bankers of Holland" and "Protestant predators behind the Bank of England" were not yet born when the maze-like labyrinth of usury operations were being established and enlarged among Renaissance popes and "Catholic banking houses" and dynasties. As we noted earlier, the House of Fugger, the fabulously wealthy German-Catholic usury

---

[11] Richard A. Goldwaithe, *The Economy of Renaissance Florence* (2011), pp. 251.

[12] Ibid., Goldwaithe, pp. 250-251.

[13] Ibid., pp. 252-254.

dynasty who were the bankers behind one of religious history's most notorious shakedowns—the sale of indulgences which sparked the Protestant Reformation—have formed barely a blip on the radar screen of economic reformers who have had the meme of "Calvinist usury" seared into their minds. Backed by the Hapsburg rulers of Catholic Spain and Austria, the Fuggers supervised the financial transfers from the German church to the papacy. Their loans to the pope gained for them the portfolio of revenue-collecting privileges.

"With his (Jacob Fugger's) support, Augsburg schoolmaster Sebastian Illsung wrote a defense of lending by focusing on the narrow subject of the Augsburg Contract—the legal agreement Fugger signed with depositors that promised them 5 percent. Illsung argued the contract was valid if the lender, like the borrower, risked bankruptcy.

"Then a young theologian named Johannes Eck caught Fugger's eye by echoing Illsung's arguments in a university lecture. Fugger asked Eck to write a dissertation on the Augsburg Contract and enter a debate—a public showdown with scholars as judges—to validate it.

"Fugger was taking a risk...If Eck lost the debate and the judges declared the contract usurious, Fugger's depositors would refuse to give him money. This would be lethal. It was one thing to operate in a gray area. It was another to engage in a practice specifically ruled heretical. Fugger must have felt extremely confident because he sought nothing short of a Scopes trial, a winner-take-all smackdown pitting dogma against modernity...He had at least one precedent on his side. After theologians squared off over the subject of annuities—the interest-earning pension schemes that cities sold to raise money—the pope had sanctioned them.

"Maybe Pope Leo, who had replaced the 'Warrior Pope' Julius II earlier that year, would do the same with the Augsburg Contract. There was also the fact that Leo was a member of the Medici banking family. Legalization would serve his personal interests. Even better was that Leo himself was a borrower of Fugger's. It goes without saying that Leo would be favorably inclined towards someone who gave him money.

"...Fugger and Eck turned to Italy where, thanks to Venice and Florence, the universities were open-minded about lending. They found a willing (debate) participant in the

University of Bologna, Europe's oldest university and among its most prestigious. Thomas Becket, Erasmus, Copernicus and (Pico) Mirandola had studied there. On his way to Bologna, Eck passed through Augsburg. Fugger assigned him a translator and other assistants....(In the debate) Eck avoided scriptural references and focused on intent. Only evil intentions could make a transaction usurious, he declared. A lender committed usury if he aimed to harm the borrower. But he acted legally if he had a legitimate business interest...

"The judges...refused to call the Augsburg Contract heretical. Eck...had presented a cut-and-dried case of charging interest on loaned money, and had given the judges a perfect chance to confirm Luke 6:35. But the judges refused to make a call, a call that could have put Fugger out of business. That was tacit approval. What's more, Fugger's letter to Pope Leo had gotten through and made an impact.

"Leo ignored the question about debate venues but, in a decree issued that same year, Leo went to the heart of the matter and signed a papal bull that...acknowledged the legitimacy of charging interest...

"According to the new doctrine of the church, usury was no longer strictly about what Jesus said about charging interest. It was about charging interest without labor, cost or risk. And what loan didn't involve one of the three? As long as a loan passed that easy test, the lender was off the hook.

"Fugger's lobbying had paid off in spectacular fashion. He and others were now free to charge borrowers and pay depositors interest with the full blessing of the church. Leo's decree, issued in conjunction with the Fifth Lateran Council, was a breakthrough for capitalism. Debt financing accelerated. The modern economy was under way...Eck earned a spot in history by going to Rome and successfully persuading the pope to excommunicate Luther..." [14]

In 1514 Eck would have another debate concerning his advocacy of a five percent rate of interest. His opponent was Martin Luther.

"The Fugger Company, one of the biggest financial corporations of the age, headed by Jakob Fugger, and after his

---

[14] Greg Steinmetz, *The Richest Man Who Ever Lived: The Life and Times of Jacob Fugger* (2015), pp. 107-11.

death in 1525, Anton Fugger (his nephew), acted as bankers for the Curia in the same way they did for the (Holy Roman) emperor. They were the main agents remitting indulgence money collected in the German lands to Rome. Such payments came to the tune of several hundreds of thousands of florin or gulden per year—at conservative estimates. The general indulgence collector for the German lands, Cardinal Albrecht of Brandenburg (1490-1545) allegedly used half of the sums collected in Germany to repay his debts to the Fuggers, because in a not unusual manner he had accumulated a number of high-ranking church positions as Archbishop of Magdeburg, Halberstadt and Mainz, which made him elector and a powerful ruler in sixteenth century Germany. For this he had to pay dearly, in cash. Thus the circle closed. Only half of the indulgence money collected under Albrecht actually made it to Rome.

"The other half went into the coffers of some of the richest and biggest private business corporations of the age...Jakob and Anton Fugger shuffled millions of florins across Europe within weeks...the indulgence campaign headed by Albrecht would have represented a minor branch of their financial business in the early 1500s and 1510s.

"...Indulgences, as practiced around 1500, represented the perversion of an originally much more innocent idea, which had put the task of repentance at the center of the exercise, and the monetary donation accompanying the indulgence only as a secondary...requirement, underlining—but never replacing it for—one's good intentions to repent." [15]

Until circa 1550, the Catholic Fugger bank was wealthier than any Italian financial institution. They were eventually eclipsed by Catholic usury establishments in Genoa, such as the House of Cattaneo, and the usury firm of Alessandro Strozzi and Zanobi Carnesecchi. Toward the end of the century (circa 1589), Florentine-Catholic usurers such as Luigi Capponi were back in the papal saddle, helping to form the large Catholic banking consortium of Doria-Velluti-Amatto.

Martin Luther's opposition to profit on loans was fierce and sincere. Nonetheless, as an innovator who had launched into

---

[15] Philipp Robinson Rössner, introduction to *On Commerce and Usury* (Anthem Press, 2015), pp. 20-21.

Christendom the concept of "justification by faith alone," he did not uphold the early and medieval Church dogma against usury seamlessly, or with the same absolutism as Catholics had done from Apostolic times to the eve of the Renaissance.

The distinction here is between the kind of Renaissance Catholic casuistry and equivocation that Pascal excoriated in *The Provincial Letters,* and Luther's attempt to destroy usury banking with a new approach. The defense of the Renaissance and post-Renaissance Church's morally reprehensible novelties rests chiefly in Talmudic-type quibbles and dissimulation which negate Christ's test of the nature of a thing: by its fruits we will know it. Renaissance Church apologists assert the contrary: they say that modernist Catholic canonists, theologians and popes only made way for a new type of contract, while preserving the basic law and theology of the anti-usury dogma. They assert this in nearly every case where it can be shown that the highway to total usury legalization was paved with furtive innovations imposed incrementally in the name of necessity, or lofty motives, such as relieving the plight of the impoverished. Post-Renaissance Catholic casuists have a psychological disposition to deny what the revolution has wrought. They see its ravages, but can't account for its roots, except as a mist-enshrouded act of the devil; a ghostly ectoplasm that arose spontaneously out of erewhon. The fact is, the devil leaves hoof prints and these can be detected, beginning with the concealment of interest devices by means of evasive glosses.

Blaise Pascal wrote concerning the mentality which empowers this process: "Accordingly...our casuist has suggested a general method for all sorts of persons...and a very simple process it is...consisting only in the use of certain words to be pronounced by the person in the act of lending his money; after which he may take his interest for it without fear of being a usurer..." [16]

For the words, "fear of being a usurer" substitute "fear of being a Judaizer" and one can spot the same process in the casuist reinterpretation of Judaism, or any other deceptive revolution that has infiltrated the Church on the heels of clever wordplay and the infinite human capacity for self-deception.

---

[16] *The Provincial Letters* (1997), p. 71

Luther breathed fire on usurers in sermons of power and conviction, such as his *Long Sermon on Usury* (1520), *Preface to an Ordinance of the Common Chest* (1523), and *Trade and Usury,* which was published in 1524. In these writings he pits the German nation against the Money Power of the Renaissance Church, as it was promoting profit on loans both covert and overt, in Church and State. Luther's argument was consonant with classic medieval Catholicism:

"...the greatest misfortune of the German nation is certainly the traffic in annuities. If that did not exist, many a man would have to leave unbought his silk, velvet, golden ornaments, spices, and luxuries of every sort. The system has not existed much over a hundred years, and has already brought almost all the princes, foundations, cities, nobles, and heirs to poverty, misery, and destruction. If it shall continue for another hundred years, Germany cannot possibly have a *pfennig* left and we shall certainly have to devour one another. The devil invented this system, and the pope by confirming it has injured the whole world. Therefore, I ask and pray that everyone open his eyes to see the ruin of himself, his children, and his heirs, which not only stands before the door but already haunts the house; and that emperor, princes, lords, and cities arrange that this trade be condemned as speedily as possible and henceforth prevented, without considering the opposition of the pope and all his justice and injustice, nor whether benefices or endowments depend upon it. Better a single benefice in a city based on an honest freehold revenue, than a hundred based on an annuity; yea, a single endowment based on an annuity is worse and more grievous than twenty based on freeholds."

Addressing himself in 1523 to a "community chest" project which had been expropriated from Roman ecclesiastical foundations that had been the beneficiaries of usury, Luther declaimed, "Part of the possessions of monasteries and foundations, and a great part of the prebends are based upon usury, which now calls itself everywhere 'interest' (*widderkauf*), and which has in but a few years swallowed up the whole world. Such possessions would have to be separated first of all, like leprosy from those possessions which consist of simple bequests...

"Interest bearing foundations...may rightly be regarded as usury; for I have never yet seen or heard of an ethical annuity that bears interest. It would be necessary, therefore, in such a case, to make restitution of the usury, by returning to each one his interest payments, before allowing such a possession to go into a common chest; for God says, 'I hate robbery for burnt offering' (Isaiah 61:8). If it prove impossible to find the persons who sustained loss by paying interest, the common chest might then receive the possession...This matter is altogether one of the most urgent to which emperors and kings, princes and lords, and everyone else should give attention..."

In Luther's time the German concept of *zinskauf* ("interest purchase") represented *both* scripturally-permissible income on rents and redeemable security in lands, as well as usurious financial instruments. "*Rente*" was a specified annual return (in the form of produce, livestock etc.) from a tenant for the use of land. A landlord could sell to a third party the contract with his tenant. The contract, which did not entail usury, was called "*rentenkauf*," and was later grouped under the general heading of *zinskauf*, even though other contracts under the heading of *zinskauf* were usurious. Luther denounced the usurious variety of *zinskauf* (wuchrische *zinskauf*), which was permitted by the Renaissance papacy.

Luther channeled the classic Catholic teaching in his commentary on Luke 6:34-35: "If we look the word of Christ squarely in the eye, it does not teach that we are to lend without charge, for there is no need for such teaching, since *there is no lending except lending without charge*, and if a charge is made, it is not a loan. He wills that we lend not only to friends, the rich, and those to whom we are well disposed, who can repay us again, by returning this loan, or with another loan, or by some other benefit; but also that we lend to those who cannot or will not repay us, such as the needy and our enemies..."

Inspired by Luther, Jakob Strauss, a native of Basel and a preacher at Berchtesgaden, and later pastor of Eisenach, advocated the implementation of Mosaic Law according to the light of Christ, in the struggle to abolish interest on debt in the name of Christian love. Strauss's *Fifty-One Theses Against*

Usury banned the taking of even a penny of interest. [17] He believed that the Protestant faith made a mockery of Christ's injunction to love one another if it permitted the charging of interest on a debt. [18]

Eventually, Luther would soften — though not do away with — his anti-usury campaign. He did so for the same reason that he would eventually make slavish obedience to the ruler of a Lutheran state a pre-requisite of his church — his trepidation at the prospect that the peasant revolutionaries in Germany would cite him as the inspiration for their violence and uproar. He was horrified by the demands of the armed anti-usury insurgents in Erfurt in 1525, who sought to pay their creditors only the principal and not the interest on their loans, and enforce their will at the point of a lance.

Concerning Pastor Strauss, Luther appreciated his efforts in honoring the Biblical "Sabbatical Year of Release from Debt" (Deut. 15:1-5), which Luther termed a "most beautiful and equitable law...Were it to be adopted today, the governors of the world would be saved endless legal business and disturbance...debts...would all be terminated at one time and not be allowed to plague people forever. Moreover, men would be careful not to lend a greater sum of money than they could hope to have restored before the seventh year."

Luther's sentimental regard for the Sabbatical Year was derogated however, by his famous "Law and Gospel" dichotomy. If he were emperor he said he would choose to reenact the Sabbatical Year, but he also stated that heads of state were under no obligation to do so. This law-as-option element he imparted to the portions of the Old Testament that are not ceremonial, and which are in fact, eternal divine law (Matthew 5:17), thereby undercutting the ability of German Christians to fulfill God's will on earth.

Luther parted ways with Strauss in the matter of the latter's declaration that the debtor was guilty for having paid interest to a creditor, which set up a revolutionary situation in which German peasants felt justified in violently revolting against lenders; a revolt Luther feared as part of his general revulsion against social disorder in Protestant lands. Luther

---

[17]   Strauss, *Hauptstücke und Artikel christlicher Lehre wider den unchristlichen Wucher.*

[18] Strauss, *Das Wucher zu nehmen* (1524).

informed Strauss that the Bible did not teach that debtors were complicit in usury by paying interest. Christ had said that His followers were to surrender even their cloaks and tunics to oppressors.

The German reformer detested usury but he did not maintain the medieval standard of complete abolition. In his conceptualization of divine grace and Christian liberty, he made the individual conscience the supreme guide to economic relations and affairs, until such time as the state, in the form of an emperor or prince, would abolish usury by edict.

In *Trade and Usury,* he set the bar at the very top of New Testament ethics, allowing oneself to be robbed of one's material possessions and goods by unregenerate men (Matthew 5:40), if necessary.

According to Luther, the Christian was to give money freely to whoever was in need of such a gift (Matthew 5:42 and Luke 6:30),[19] or at the very least to lend money rather than to give it away, while expecting no return on what had been loaned.

His private opinion, in his last days, was that Protestant ministers should urge their people not to engage in usury. He sincerely believed that the best way to overcome the curse of profit on loans was to teach the Gospel in such a way that the German nation would voluntarily resist profit on loans, until such time as a Lutheran ruler would ban it outright. Lutheran ministers were to proclaim the Gospel prohibition on interest on money in no uncertain terms, leaving legislation and enforcement to the princes.

Luther was never an agent of the banks or the Money Power. It should be conceded that Luther did not traffic in papal and Vatican doubletalk and duplicity on the subject of usury. There is no clever wordplay in his writing and sermons on the subject. He spoke his mind plainly and boldly.

---

19   According to University of Regensburg Prof. Hans Schwarz, Luther qualified this as follows: "...this does not include those...who do not want to work...It also does not mean giving if you do not have what you yourself need, nor does it mean to give away everything, because then you could not give anything tomorrow if need arises. Freely giving should not imply that one becomes a beggar. It is also not so that one reaps benefits from it, or is celebrated for this deed." Cf. Schwarz, *True Faith in the True God* (Augsburg Fortress Press, 2015), p. 260.

"Luther...was led by his keen sense of justice to a vigorous assertion of the (medieval) canonical determinations on usury in opposition to the casuists' hair-splitting attempts to circumvent the very laws they were pledged to uphold." [20]

Catholics on the Right tend to overlook the papal accommodation of usurers which eventually led to the Church of Rome's overthrow of the divine, true Catholic Church proscription on profit on loans.

Calvin and Luther are branded the originators of miserly shylock banking in Christendom. It's ludicrous, but the Big Lie has stuck. The degree of denial and myopia is a wonder to behold. In the summer of 2016 a group of prominent "traditional Catholics" issued their "Lake Garda Statement Regarding the 'Catholic' Apotheosis of Luther":

"...a massive attempt to masquerade the truth regarding their real character and practical alliance is being mounted in conjunction with the five hundredth anniversary of Martin Luther's devastating appearance on the public scene in 1517...to masquerade what Luther and his 'freedom' wrought. For what they *truly* wrought was ultimately nothing other than what Richard Gawthrop identifies as that 'Promethean lust for material power that serves as the deepest common drive behind all modern Western culture'...it did not take long for the freedom of depraved man in depraved nature *from* the restraints of a supposedly impossible Law—in the name of an openness to unmerited grace—to be seen as the providential tool for molding unbridled human thoughts and actions into the building blocks of a new Age of Gold." [21]

Luther is scapegoated for the acts of the Catholic usury bankers, the Catholic Augsburg Diet of 1500 and the popes of usury, all of whom in their betrayal of the true Catholic Church, pioneered in Christendom the "new Age of Gold."

Many "Conservative" and "traditional" Catholics of the twentieth-first century are nothing of the kind. They ally with renegade, Renaissance proto-modernist bishops of Rome who were popes not of Catholicism but of the cash nexus. The Right-

---

[20] Walter I. Brandt, *Luther's Works,* v. 45 (Muhlenberg Press, 1962), p. 305.

[21] The Lake Garda Statement, July 7, 2016; signed by Dr. John C. Rao, President of the Roman Forum; Christopher A. Ferrara, President of the American Catholic Lawyers Association; Rev. Richard A. Munkelt, Ph.D; Prof. Dr. Thomas Heinrich Stark; and Michael J. Matt.

wing "Catholic" idolatry of these men has supplanted *the loyalty due to the Catholic Church of the previous fourteen hundred fifty years.* Luther suffered a spiritual crisis when he finally became cognizant (and it took him some time to do so; his evaluation was not rash), that the papacy in the Renaissance was no longer the guarantor of Catholic orthodoxy, but its gravedigger. This shock of recognition led to a psychological crisis which produced in Luther a disfigurement that led him into excesses and distortions, and an abiding pride. It is distressing however, that in reflecting upon Lutheranism, the history of the Neoplatonic-Hermetic-Kabbalistic takeover of Rome is whisked away and it is Luther who is stigmatized as money's prophet.

If there actually were traditional Catholics on earth today (and surely there is a remnant), they would believe as the Roman Catholic Church had always believed until the Renaissance usurpation:

"Lord, who shall abide in thy tabernacle? Who shall dwell in thy holy hill?...He that does not ask interest on loans, and cannot be bribed to victimize the innocent." [22]

St. Clement of Alexandria (second century A.D.): "taking profit from loans to fellow Christians partaking of the Logos, is a transgression against the law of God."

The Council of Elvira, circa 300 A.D., decreed that lay and clerical usurers are to be excommunicated.

St. Jerome (fourth century) quotes Ezekiel 18:13, "Hath given forth upon usury, and hath taken increase: shall he then live? He shall not live: he hath done all these abominations; he shall surely die; his blood shall be upon him."

St. Basil (fourth century): "Whenever you have the intention of providing for a poor man for the Lord's sake, the same thing is both a gift and a loan, a gift because of the expectation of no repayment, but a loan because of the great gift of the Master who pays in his place, and who, receiving trifling things through a poor man, will give great things in return for them. 'He that hath mercy on the poor, lendeth to God.' Do you not wish to have the Lord of the universe answerable to you for payment?"

---

[22] Psalm 15: 1 & 5.

St. Ambrose (fourth century): *"Si quis usuram accipit, rapinam facit, vita non vivit."* ("If someone takes usury, he commits robbery, he shall not live").

Other fourth century Fathers: St. Gregory of Nicea, St. Leo the Great, and St. John Chrysostom, all condemned taking profit on loans; that is to say all profit (even a penny) on any kind of loan.

St. Augustine (354-430 A.D.): *"Homo miser, cur foenearis homini? Foenerare Deo et centuplum accipes vitam aeternam possidebis."* (Miserly man, why do you lend compound interest to men? Lend to God a hundred-fold you will have eternal life").

In the eleventh century, St. Edward the Confessor, the Anglo-Saxon Catholic King of England, declared, *"Usura radix omnia malorum."* ("Usury is the root of all evil").

Gratian's *Decretum* (circa 1140), the oldest and most extensive cornerstone of the *Corpus iuris canonici* (body of Canon Law): *"Usurae arte nequissima ex ipso auro aurum nascitur."* ("By the detestable art of usury gold gives birth to gold").

The Fourth Lateran Council of 1179, decreed that those who gain profit from loans are to be excommunicated and denied Christian burial.

Pope Urban III (1185-1187) quotes Luke 6:35: "Lend, expecting nothing in return."

Pope Gregory IX in 1234 commanded all Christian rulers to expel all usurers and to nullify all wills and testaments of unrepentant usurers.

Pope Innocent IV (1200-1254): "Usury is generally prohibited because if it were allowed all manner of evils would ensue...It is clear that practically every evil follows from usury." (*Commentaria super libros quinque Decretalium*).

The Council of Lyons (1274) extended the restrictions on lenders-for-profit based on the Decree on Usury of Pope Gregory X (1210-1272):

"Although manifest usurers may have commanded that satisfaction be made for the usury they received in express quantity or indistinctly in their final will, nonetheless, they are to be denied ecclesiastical burial until full satisfaction has been made for the very usury (as their faculties permit) or to those to whom restitution must be made, if they are on hand, or to others for whom they can acquire it, or in their absence the local ordinary or his vicar, whether the rector of the parish in which the testator lives, in the presence of some trustworthy members of the parish (for whom it is permissible for the ordinary, vicar, and rector in the aforementioned way to accept this warning in their name by the authority of this current constitution in such a way that action is gained for them), or that it be properly entrusted to a public servant at the command of the same ordinary concerning the making of restitution. For the rest, if the quantity of the usury received is clear we want that to be always expressed in the aforesaid warranty, otherwise we want another warranty of the receiver to be controlled according to such a will; the same person, however, knowingly controls not less than is reasonably believed, and should he do otherwise, let him be obliged to make satisfaction for the rest.

"We decree that all the religious and others who have dared to admit manifest usurers to ecclesiastical burial against the form of present sanctions are subject to the punishments of the Lateran Council promulgated against usurers. No one is to take part in the wills of manifest usurers, or admit them to confession or absolve them unless the have made restitution for usury, or afford a fitting warranty about making restitution according to the strength of their faculties."

The Council of Vienne (1311) ordered the excommunication of any ruler who condoned profits on loans or who forced debtors to pay usury. It presciently warned of those who seek to open cracks in the laws against usury by camouflaged contracts that hid usury under "diverse colors."

Contra the Money Power in The Arena Chapel

High Catholic art *before the Renaissance* was often a glory to God, and among the artists who personified the medieval aesthetic at the masterpiece level were the virtuosos Giotto di Bondone, known to history by his first name, and the master stone carvers Arnolfo Pisano, his chief assistant Arnolfo di Cambio, and his son Giovanni Pisano. The Christian who would seek edification, sobering reflection and a sermon in paint will visit and ponder the Arena Chapel in Padua, a city in Italy that had been the base, seventy-two years earlier, of St. Anthony of Padua, the hammer of usury heretics who was one of the most phenomenal preachers of the Gospel of Jesus Christ in the post-apostolic history of Christianity. [23]

The chapel is a sacred edifice founded on a plea for forgiveness as a means of making restitution. The Dominican Pope Benedict XI (Niccolo Boccasino) named it the "Chapel of Santa Maria della Caritá." It was dedicated to the Blessed Virgin Mary on the feast of her Annunciation,[24] March 25, 1303.

It is extraordinary for being the most prominent monument in Christendom to the Catholic belief in the divine dogma that profit on loans is a sin that imperils the soul and requires, after confession, expiation. The chapel was founded, designed and dedicated while Dante Aligheri, the preeminent poet of the Gospel over the Money Power, walked the earth.

In *Usury in Christendom* (pp. 344-350), we give an account of a seldom remarked upon miracle of St. Anthony of Padua and reproduce a photograph of Tullio Lombardo's harrowing sculpture depicting it:

"It is not an easy matter to find a full account of St. Anthony's 'Miracle of the Usurer's Heart,' since it is a huge embarrassment to 'Christian' usurers and a devastating rebuke to the contemporary Church which permits their trade. Consequently, the miracle has been classed as too parochial and dated, and has been renamed. When it is presented to the public it is no longer a parable about a money-lender who grew wealthy from charging interest on debt. It has been rewritten as "The Miracle of the *Miser's* Heart," and the dead man's sin is not specifically usury, but the more generic theme of parsimony. By means of this falsification, the people do not learn of the degree of hostility which medieval Catholic culture—and one of the most esteemed of all saints of the Church—harbored for the sin of charging interest on loans of money.

"...long after the Renaissance, Catholic culture at the folk level persisted in execrating usury. St. Anthony's example of righteous wrath against the den of thieves who sought a place

---

[23] The Arena Chapel is so called because it is situated on land where in ancient times stood a Roman amphitheater, or "arena," located just outside the walls of the "old city" of Padua.

[24] The events described in Luke 1: 26-39 are referred to in Catholicism as the "Annunciation."

in the Church in spite of their intractable addiction to money breeding, resonated among the lay people down through the centuries, commemorated in magnificent art works by Francesco Pesellino, Domenico Campagnola and Tullio Lombardo, and contributing to a living culture of revulsion toward the sin of usury among the Catholic people for hundreds of years, even while their cardinals and popes trafficked in and profited from partnering with capitalism's immensely powerful banking houses.

"What the old Church had believed and taught left deep traces in the cultural memory of the Catholic people for many centuries during the time that usury was being rehabilitated from on high. This holy memory persisted long after the theology itself had decayed. Lowly parish priests and laymen preserved indignation over income derived from interest into the nineteenth and even the twentieth century. Many were outraged to discover, in the 1800s, that when impenitent usurers complained to the Catholic hierarchy about priests who refused to grant them absolution in the confessional, the hierarchy stood with the unrepentant sinners against the confessors. [25]

The miracle God worked through St. Anthony has for its scripture text Matthew 6:2: "It happened that while blessed Anthony was preaching the Word of God, a murmur spread through the assembly that a great moneylender had passed away. Seeing the agitation in the crowd and hearing the murmur, Anthony questioned them. They answered that a rich usurer had just died. All murmured to one another, and he said to them: 'Behold how the word of the Lord is revealed as true; for He said, 'Where your treasure is, there will your heart be also.' Then Anthony said, 'Go to his strongbox and in the largest moneybag his heart will be found.' So it was done. And proving true the prediction of the holy man, they then cut open the corpse and, not finding the heart, they all praised God and His servant, blessed Anthony." [26]

---

[25] *Usury in Christendom: The Mortal Sin that Was and Now is Not*, pp. 345-346.

[26] Cf. Vatican Library, MS lat. 7592; and Vergilio Gamboso, *Testimonianze minori su S. Antonio* (2001).

The Ten Sermons of Saint Anthony of Padua

"...some of the most scathing sermons against usury that survive were authored by Saint Anthony. Unsurprisingly, Saint Anthony defines usury strictly: in a sermon for the first Sunday of Lent, he writes, quoting (the canonist) Gratian: 'To take any return over and above the principal is called usury.' But his sermons are often far more vivid than this statement suggests. In another sermon, he writes: 'Just as birds and beasts will scatter the cadaver, so demons will scatter the heart of the miser and the usurer.' In another, his sermon for Sexagesima Sunday, he fulminates:

"The accursed race of usurers has multiplied upon the earth, with teeth like the teeth of a lion. The lion has two characteristics: a stiff neck containing only one bone, and stinking teeth. The usurer is likewise inflexible, neither fearing God nor regarding man. His teeth stink because the dirt of money and the dung of usury are always in his mouth.'

"We may observe three kinds of usurers: those who lend money privately, who may be described as creeping things without number; those who do so openly, but only in a small way, so as to seem merciful—these are the small beasts—and the faithless, hopeless and open usurers who, as openly as in a marketplace, take interest from all and sundry.

"These are the great beasts, more cruel than all the rest. They will be pursued by the demon huntsmen and slain with an eternal death, unless they restore their ill-gotten gains, and do penance. To give them the opportunity to do so, there go the ships among them, the preachers of the Church who pass among them and sow the seed of God's word. Yet, though our sins need it, the thorns of riches and wild beasts of usury choke the word sown so devotedly, so that it does not produce the fruit of penance." [27]

---

[27] Anne Derbes and Mark Sandona, *The Usurer's Heart* (2008), pp. 39-40 and 174. "Anthony excoriates usurers in a number of other sermons, including those on the Feast of the Nativity (*Sermones*, ed. Costa, 3:5); the first Sunday in Lent (1:69,71); the Second Sunday in Advent (2:482-83); the third Sunday in Advent (2:502); the ninth Sunday after Pentecost (2:25), the tenth Sunday after Pentecost (2:40); the Feast of St. Stephen (3:18-20); the Feast of the Chair of St. Peter (3:123); and the Feast of the Birth of St. John the Baptist (3:267)." Ibid., p. 174.

"Anthony's fiery sermons drew enormous throngs in Padua, but even after his lifetime, as we have seen, his sermons lived on, serving as sourcebooks for friars and cathedral canons alike...Clearly then, anyone earning a livelihood from money-lending (at a profit) ran the risk of enormous penalties in this life and even more horrific punishment in the next. And neither social status nor ecclesiastical connections could ensure the salvation of the usurer. The only hope for such sinners was to renounce the practice, repent, and make full, unambiguous restitution." [28]

In the contemporary Church of Rome, whether styled traditional, conservative or progressive Catholic, St. Anthony is known almost exclusively as the patron saint of the return of lost articles ("Dear St. Anthony please come around, something is lost and must be found"), and as the friar who was granted the miraculous privilege of holding the infant Jesus in his arms. The preeminent object of the saint's preaching ministry —at least ten sermons blasting the diabolic Catholic traffic in profits from loans, and one miracle involving a usurer's heart— are almost completely erased from the record of St. Anthony's hagiography. This relentless campaigner for Biblical economics has been reduced in popular Catholic piety to an innocuous searcher-after lost things, and it is a grotesque irony that knowledge of the hellfire homilies he repeatedly hurled at Catholic bankers and other usurers, are, for all intents and purposes, *lost*.

A testimony to the degeneracy of the churches in the twenty-first century, both papist and otherwise, is that the consciences of Protestants and Catholics are seared by the thought of the wanton woman with whom they committed adultery; the beating they administered while drunk to an innocent passerby, or the bribery they offered to a bureaucrat.

---

[28] Ibid., p. 40. Of course Anthony was not alone in his fury toward lenders who charged interest. In a Lenten sermon, the Dominican Jacobus de Voragine (1230-July, 1298), the eventual Archbishop of Genoa and reputed compiler of the famed collection of the lives of the saints known as *The Golden Legend*, stated that a lender who takes profit from a borrower "is similar to Judas Iscariot in sin and he will be similar to him in punishment...The usurer will not live in heaven, but in hell with the demons, because he ruined mankind." *Sermones quadragesimales: Edizione critica* (2005), pp. 242-243.

But remorse for acquiring money from profits on loans is as distant from their conscience as the GN-Z11 galaxy. A testimony to the presence of the true faith in an authentic follower of Jesus is sorrow for having benefited from the mortal sin of interest on money. Even the thought of such sorrow would be a bizarre anomaly to the hearers if it were preached from almost any pulpit today. The extent to which the ungodly and unnatural predation emanating from profit on loans is mistaken for permissible "free enterprise" is all-encompassing. In our time the Church of St. Anthony of Padua has been almost, though not completely, eclipsed (Luke 18:8).

The Scrovegni Penance

In the Christendom of the Middle Ages, with all its other failings and shortcomings, the fear of God (and hence, "the beginning of wisdom," Proverbs 9:10), was paramount, and the terror at having offended God by breeding money from money, was overwhelming. Reginaldo Scrovegni had been a notorious medieval Italian usurer who Dante, in Canto XVII of *The Inferno,* placed in the seventh circle of hell. [29]

The heir to Reginaldo's fortune (worth an astounding half-million lire), was his son, Enrico, and it was he who spent the equivalent of millions of dollars in today's money to erect a Christian palace of repentance for his father's financial crimes and for his own (he had taken up usury banking in his youth while serving as his father's apprentice). Crooked churchmen had taken loans from the firm of Scrovegni and Son, and Reginaldo Scrovegni's operations were protected by the corrupt bishops of Padua and Vicenza and certain lawyers on the faculty of the University of Padua College of Law, including Giovanni Forzaté, whose son was the beneficiary of a lucrative arranged marriage with a daughter of Reginaldo. With this background in mind, we turn to Ursula Schlegel, the principal and most astute scholar of the Arena Chapel:

---

[29] Scrovegni is identified by Dante having alluded to the sow azure on the Scrovegni coat of arms: "And then I heard (from one whose neat, white sack was marked in azure by a pregnant sow): 'What are you after in this awful hole?" (*The Divine Comedy*, translated by Robin Kirkpatrick [Penguin Books, 2013]), p. 76. The "white sack" is shown by Dorothy L. Sayers to have been a usurer's money purse, and the seventh circle of hell in this scene is inhabited by Florentine usurers. Cf. Sayers, *Dante Hell* (Penguin Books, 2001), p. 111.

"Enrico Scrovegni owed his immense fortune to his father, Reginaldo, who had acquired his riches not through honest work but through base usury, which in medieval times was considered by the Church a mortal sin.

"After the Lateran Council of 1176, whose declaration was reaffirmed in 1274, usurers were not to be permitted to receive Holy Communion or to have Christian burial if they died without atonement...Enrico, received absolution from Benedict XI...

"Enrico's absolution must have taken place shortly before the start of the decoration of the Chapel, because Pope Benedict reigned from October 1303 until July 1304. We do not know the conditions of Enrico's absolution. The erection of the church, however, and its particularly resplendent decoration must have been one of them..." [30]

"He had it built with his own money in compensation for the many usurious deeds of his father, doing so at the command of Pope Benedict XI." [31] It was this pontiff in his commentary on the Gospel of Matthew, who emphasized a particular insight into the nature of the betrayal of Jesus, when he stated that Judas was *"cupiditate pecuniae ductus"* (led by his passion for money). [32]

Concerning the Chapel's art, Schlegel writes, "Judas hangs in Giotto's Hell, and behind him we see three other damned men who must atone for their sins in the same way; their torture, however, seems to be increased, since they have been hanged with the strings of their own money purses. In a particularly prominent place, to the right, below the cross and above the curve of the door arch, a usurious peasant with a fat money bag on his back is led into the abyss of hell by a devil who holds the peasant's promissory notes in his claw. Another of the damned who likewise cannot separate himself from his money bag, despite the fact that a devil pulls on it vigorously, must go the way down to the abyss behind the peasant.

"The depiction of the hanged Judas in the *Last Judgment* is rare...in Padua, Judas is in the middle of Hell in a very

---

[30] Ursula Schlegel, "On the Picture Program of the Arena Chapel'" in *Giotto: The Arena Chapel Frescoes* (1995), p. 185.

[31] Giuseppe Gennari, *Annali della Citta di Padova* (1804), volume III, p. 89.

[32] Pope Benedict XI, *In evangelium D. Matthaei*, 11. col. 1.

conspicuous place: he hangs exactly in the center, between the cross and the jaws of Hell...Horizontally, there is a straight line leading, at the right, from the head of Judas to the jaws of Hell, and at the left, through the cross and the model of the Chapel, to the head of Enrico.

This allows us to place (the figure of) Enrico, even though he kneels with the Blessed, in a very special relationship to Judas, for it is no less obvious that the misers and usurers populating the part of Hell around Judas correspond to the group with Enrico Scrovegni below the Blessed on the other side of the cross, and that the misers and usurers suffer the same punishment as Judas.

"We assume that Enrico wished to atone for his father's sin of usury, the price of which is Hell. For this reason he joined the lay order of the Cavalieri di Santa Maria, whose aspiration it was to lead a model life and whose most significant duty was to combat usury, and for this reason he built the Chapel and gave it to the order as its church.[33]

"The basis for atonement, however, is the confession of the sin, for every sin is a betrayal of Christ. And here the confession is made through the representation of the greatest betrayal of all, the betrayal by Judas. And since it happened that Enrico's father Reginaldo betrayed Christ for money just as Judas did, *The Betrayal of Judas* is located on the triumphal arch wall in the consciousness of guilt and as its confession. We should, therefore, not look at this representation as the criticism of the father by the son, but only as the confession of guilt of his own — rendered in a language equal in its pitiless candor to Dante's in the *Inferno*." [34]

In the *Chronica Patavina* (Vatican library MS5290), circa 1335, we find this description of Enrico: "He built a temple in the Arena to the honor of the Virgin Mary and for the salvation

---

[33] "As can be gathered from the Bulls of Gregory IX and Urban V: 'No one is to be received into the order...who either has gained any other good through usurious wickedness, or through other illicit or unjust means for himself or for others who succeed him by will or intestate, if he does not first make restitution of everything he holds illicitly or unjustly...' Thus the membership of Enrico in his order by itself means such a break with the habits of his father that, according to the customs of the Church, it must have considered it an act of contrition. We may also consider the construction of the church as such an act." Schlegel, op. cit., p. 188, n. 17.

[34] Schlegel, op. cit., pp. 187-189.

of his family and especially for the soul of his father Reginaldo who, since he was of common status occupied himself with infinite usuries..."

In Enrico's Last Will and Testament, written a few months before his death in 1336, we find these words commanding that restitution be made: "I wish, order and command that all of my ill-gotten gains (*male ablata*), if it should be that such be found, and these were not restored, and all the ill-gotten gains of my grandfather Ugolino, my father Reginaldo, by brother Manfredo, and his son Manfredo the Younger, for the one-third part that I am legally held to restore— these ought to be restored and paid with any expenses incurred at that time, to all petitioners without any lawsuit, controversy, trial, condition or pact." [35]

Many other usurers, under severe pressure from their confessors or from their own consciences (often as they neared death), made restitution for their thieving, including as in some cases, as Enrico had, by constructing and donating a church, school, hospital or monastery. Among Enrico's penitent contemporaries and countrymen who constructed religious edifices we find former captains of banking such as Pietro da Marano, Guglielmo Castelbarco and Marsilio da Carrara. Among lesser fry, the whole of their estates were simply divided among those who could be found to have paid them anything above the principal loaned. Penance and restitution by usurers was public. [36]

The medieval Paduan Arena Chapel is a sermon in paint and sculpture, and the explication of its elaborate symbolism would require a book solely dedicated to that end. [37] Suffice it to say for our purposes, that Derbes and Sandona point to a central theme in the iconography of the Chapel, that of Judas contrasted with the Blessed Virgin Mary. Our Lady's exemplification of charity diametrically opposed to the greed of Judas, occupies "extraordinary prominence" in the Arena.

---

[35] Benjamin G. Kohl, "The Scrovegni in Carrara Padua: And Enrico's Will," in *Apollo: The International Magazine of the Arts* (December, 1995).

[36] Cf. for example, Mary C. Mansfield, *The Humiliation of Sinners: Public Penance in Thirteenth Century France* (1995).

[37] Cf. Derbes and Sandona, *The Usurer's Heart*, op. cit.

We took Michelangelo to task for it, so it is incumbent on us to note that Giotto also employed nudity in his work. Like Michelangelo in the Sistine Chapel, in the Arena Chapel Giotto executed a version of *The Last Judgment* in which the damned are nude. The difference between the Michelangelo *Judgment* and that of Giotto however, is the difference (if we may be so bold) between the spirit of the Renaissance and the spirit of the Middle Ages. With Michelangelo, whether damned or not, the naked humans often exude an eroticism. *In Giotto the nudity only heightens the sense of shame and degradation,* such as Adam and Eve experienced in the Garden after the Fall. Public nudity of the type displayed in the Sistine Chapel is utopian. It is a way of expressing the heresy that on earth, in this life, we can return to Eden. For Giotto, as for the Early and Medieval Catholic Church, public nudity, except when portraying pre-pubescent humanity, is mainly a sign of disorder and concupiscence, or damnation.

The medieval pontiff who may have came closest to St. Anthony of Padua in spirit was the ill-fated monk-hermit, Pope Celestine V (1215-1296), who was "elected after more than two years of deadlock in the hope that a saint might transform the Church...the unworldly old man (eighty-five when elected)...was a visionary, the founder of a brotherhood of hermits with strong links to the radical Franciscans. [38] He therefore represented precisely that dimension of the thirteenth-century Church which detested the wealth, worldliness and legal and political entanglements of the papacy. His election fed apocalyptic hopes of a *Papa Angelicus*, a holy and unworldly pope who would cleanse the Church and prepare the world for the advent of Christ. The notion of an unworldly pope, however, was by now almost a contradiction in terms...Celestine's election highlighted just how incompatible these two visions of the Church had become. Faced with political and financial complexities which prayer and fasting seemed powerless to untangle, Celestine resigned after six months." [39]

---

[38] These were the "Spirituals" who were faithful and zealous for the original teaching of St. Francis of Assisi concerning wealth and the scourge of avarice.

[39] Eamon Duffy, *Saints & Sinners: A History of the Popes* (2006), p. 159.

His resignation appears to have been engineered by Benedetto Caetani, his successor, who would become the tyrant Pope Boniface VIII. It was Caetani who produced canon lawyers to justify Celestine's abdication and it was Caetani who wrote Celestine's abdication speech. After Caetani was made pope, Celestine fled. "Determined to avoid any... (resistance) from the outraged 'spiritual' element in the Church who had looked to Celestine to redeem the papacy, Caetani tracked down his predecessor.." [40] Benedict VIII had this holy ex-pontiff kidnapped, tortured, and imprisoned until Celestine's death in 1296.

A "worthy pope," you say? Let him proclaim, *ex cathedra,* a declaration along the lines of the following statement. When he does so, we will know that the war of the Church contra the Money Power, engendered by the root of all evil (I Timothy 6:10), has been revived:

All usury—*any* gain on a loan above the return of the principal—is a grave transgression against the law of God. In order to obtain absolution, reception of the Eucharist and a Catholic burial, all usurers must confess their mortal sin, avoid the near occasion of sin by halting their involvement in banks and businesses lending at interest; and by lenders expiating their sin of usury through restitution of all monies paid by debtors to the lenders above the principal. Impenitent, practicing bankers (usurers) are not to receive the Eucharist and are to be refused a Catholic burial. In Catholic nations, the civil authorities are urged to seize the assets of usurers after death to restore the interest stolen from debtors. Obstinate usurers are excommunicated.

The preceding, if pronounced *ex cathedra,* would be the dogmatic statement of a real *alter Christus,* a true *Papa Angelicus* and Petrine guardian of Biblical and Patristic Tradition, who does not weaken the fabric of truth by subterfuges and tricks with words, but whose yes is yes, and whose no is no. Whether such a bishop of Rome arises or not, the true Christian's war with the Money Power is perpetual.

---

40 Ibid.

The Vatican went into hock to the Rothschild bank in the the nineteenth century, when priests had to admit unrepentant practicing usurers to Communion. The Catholic laity were kept in the dark and pacified by thunderous bulls and encyclicals anathematizing Judaism, Freemasonry and avarice. Machiavelli could have devised an elementary con like this before his first cappuccino of the morning: denounce the Kings of the Deal all you like; if you permit them to control the money supply of the Church, then they are the rulers of the Church, post-Renaissance papal anathemas and the enforced ignorance of the pay-pray-and-obey sheeple, notwithstanding.

With respect to Pope Benedict XIV's 1745 encyclical *Vix Pervenit,* which has the reputation among Catholics of being a lofty and definitive rebuke to usury, we draw the reader's attention to the fact that the pope declined to apply any enforceable prohibition to the specific usury contracts he was addressing in the encyclical. We do not believe this was a mere oversight. Observe the methodology: the vast majority of the text of Pope Benedict XIV's encyclical is devoted to excoriating usury, while a small portion of it, what might be described as the document's "fine print," contains a loophole for profit on loans large enough to accommodate Catholic usury-banking. As far as imposing enforceable penalties and obstructions on Catholic lenders at interest, *Vix Pervenit* was an exercise in toothless semantics. Post-Renaissance predatory capitalism on the part of the followers of the Church of Rome continued to flourish in the wake of *Vix Pervenit.*

Far from being the ballyhooed bulwark against usury, *Vix Pervenit* was so ambiguous it generated tremendous confusion. Observe the testimony of the Bishop of Rheims as recorded in Denzinger 1609: "There is bitter dispute over the meaning of the Encyclical Letter, '*Vix pervenit*'...On both sides arguments are produced to defend the opinion each one has embraced, either favorable to such (usury) profit or against it."

Vix Pervenit is part of the papal lexicon of trickery, employed by Pope Benedict XIV in 1745, and Pope Francis two hundred seventy-one years later. The same stratagem at work in Benedict's *Vix Pervenit* is visible in the *Amoris Laetitia* of Francis:

"*Amoris* does *not*—again, let me repeat, does *not*—declare ministers of holy Communion bound to give the sacrament to divorced-and-remarried Catholics living as if married. Francis' phrasing in several key passages of *Amoris* is, I have argued, malleable enough to allow bishops such as Chaput and Sample to reiterate the traditional Eucharistic discipline or, as the Buenos Aires bishops did, simply to pass ambiguous criteria down to local pastors to sort as best they can. But precisely because key passages of *Amoris* are also flexible enough to allow bishops to do as the Maltese have done and require Church ministers to distribute the Eucharist to Catholics who engage in 'public and permanent adultery" (CCC 2384)—not to mention conferring absolution on penitents who express no purpose of amendment in regard to such conduct—all this, without doing violence to the actual text of *Amoris*." [41]

Neoplatonic-Hermeticism has no fixed abode in the household of dogma. Its god is the *zeitgeist*. When the Church of Rome gradually changed its position on God's immemorial laws against profit on loans in accord with "changing times," this revolution sent an electrifying message to insiders within and without the hierarchy: since Rome changed its prohibition on usury, Rome can change its dogma on contraception, divorce, premarital and extramarital sex, women priests and homosexual behavior.

The bane of Christian society is *situation ethics*, the substitution of human standards relative to the circumstances and context of the times, for immutable divine law. Let us recall that Rome continued to agitate against usury from the pulpit at the parish level, and kept the ignorant laity in the dark concerning the incremental revolution that had been put into motion in elite circles of Catholic banking; that was the genius of their process which would eventually create a legend that usury permission was a Protestant phenomenon.

We are largely defenseless today against the ravages of situation ethics due to the nullification of the mortal sin of interest on money, from which proceeds every other evil (I Tim. 6:10). Apologists argue that the Church of Rome has not nullified this mortal sin because it has "not promulgated any

---

[41] Edward Peters, Jan. 15, 2017, canonlawblog.wordpress.com/.

doctrinal decree on the subject." [42] Surely the papists have heard it said, "By their fruits ye shall know them." This criterion was given by God Himself as the supreme discernment. May we dare to ask, what have been the fruits of the post-Renaissance Church with regard to the ascendance of the Money Power? Millions of Catholic usurers are free to practice their mortally sinful trade and receive the Eucharist, without either confessing or receiving absolution. "Catholic" institutions of usury have been established throughout the world, including in Vatican City. Perhaps we would better discern the degree of transgression at work here if, for usury, we were to substitute prostitution. If prostitutes, pimps and those who frequent them were to receive Holy Communion without having to confess their sin, and were given freedom, under papal auspices, to spread their moral contagion wherever it was allowed by secular law, including by establishing a brothel *coram populo* in Vatican City, could it still be asserted by sane persons that the Church of Rome had not, in practice, changed the dogma against fornication? Or would we salve our consciences by assuring ourselves that since no *ecclesiastical edict* had been pronounced in favor of it, the Church still upheld the mortal sinfulness of prostitution? At what point does a claim that theology has not been formally declared to have been altered, become little more than a double-minded alibi in the face of the *massive practice* of a soul-destroying transgression of God's law?

The allowance for usury and usurers in good standing in the post-Renaisance Church of Rome cannot be merely a sin of omission. This is not a matter of failure to enforce a dogma, it is *the active overthrow of the dogma* as shown by the rulings of the Holy Office and Penitentiary in the nineteenth century, beginning with the Pontificate of Pius VIII and his Bull *Datum in audientia* of Aug. 18, 1830, which granted absolution to usurers *who intended to persist in their usury.*

---

[42] With regard to the 1917 and 1983 Codes of Canon Law, the ambiguity of the 1917 Code permitted usury to flourish as usual. Canon 1294 of the 1983 Code, written when, then as now, usury dominated the world of investment, orders that ecclesiastical monies must be carefully invested—without issuing a word of caution against the ubiquity of usurious investments. Canon lawyers of the Church of Rome have interpreted the 1983 Code as permission for lending money at interest.

The 1917 Code of Canon Law promulgated by Pope Benedict XV, (though composed by churchmen appointed by Pope St. Pius X), which went into effect May 19, 1918, declared, "in the loan of a fungible thing, it is not by itself illicit to reap a legal profit." The 1983 Code of Canon Law promulgated by Pope John Paul II, in canons 1294 and 1305 repeat the permission for usury granted in the 1917 Code, and exceed it by requiring clerics in charge of church funds to invest them "profitably"—in other words by the readiest means available for doing so, whatever that might be according to the law of the land.

The *formal* overthrow of usury dogma in the 19th and 20th centuries by Popes Pius VIII, Benedict XV and John-Paul II, and the founding of the Vatican Bank in the 1940s by Pius XII, did not arise out of thin air. As with the nullification in Judaism of the Old Testament Law of God by gradual Talmudic modification and evasion, the loophole for profiting from loans of money under the name "extrinsic titles" and similar escape clauses, contributed significantly to the erosion and the overthrow of the Church's dogma against usury.

Once the precedent for tampering with the Word of God has been established, our consciences and Christendom itself are henceforth ordered by the situation ethics intended to fit the occasion of our human wants and desires. Beware: our children are watching. Amid a world of exceedingly seductive sins that beckon to them on the basis that *the times they are a changin,'* and that the laws decreed by God "require a new understanding," our accommodation of the Money Power through profiting from loans of money, furnishes our young people the leeway to engage in mortal sins of *their choosing*, as the "situation" and the *zeitgeist* demand. As usual, Jesus is the antidote to this diabolical confusion. He presents us with a blessed alternative, giving direction on how we can become sons of the Most High God and receive a great reward: "Love your enemies...and lend, hoping for nothing in return." (Luke 6:32-36).

Chapter XVII

A Prophecy Fulfilled

"Bartolomeo Brandano da Petroio of Siena (1488-1554) was born to a peasant family in Petroio, in the domain of Siena, presumably in 1488; his father was named Savino, the mother Meia, short for Bartolomea. It is uncertain whether the surname Carosi or Garosi, with which his descendants were known, among them the painter Ansehno...was already in use at this time. (His) nickname (was) Brandano, with which he was known during his preaching. The earliest records date from an autobiography, dictated at the end of his life to a follower, the Augustinian 'John the Baptist,' covering the years 1526 to 1535. It was during Lent of 1526 which established his conversion, occasioned by listening to a sermon of Brother Serafino from Pistoia, after which Brandano was converted from a life of 'great blasphemy, full of every vice,' which he exchanged for a preaching mission to 'take back and call to penance wretched and obstinate sinners.' There followed heavenly visions of Christ, the Virgin Mary, the saints, and some say, even the stigmata. He became an apocalyptic preacher of doom and he was initially greeted by blatant mockery; persecuted and ridiculed though this did not discourage him from his mission. Exhorting prelates, clergy and people with a crucifix in one hand and a skull in the other, pronouncing penance, prophecy and invective in rhyme that made him famous, he attracted crowds willing to heed his drastic exhortations. Throughout the course of his itinerant preaching, which lasted about a decade, he preached in Rome, Narni and Siena in 1527; Orvieto and perhaps in Camerino in the following year; Volterra in 1529; in Tuscany in 1530; in 1531 in Atri; Bologna and Modena in 1532; and in the same years, repeatedly, to Loreto on a pilgrimage to the sanctuary, and in Spain, to Santiago de Compostela in 1530, the year in which it was remembered that he was in Madrid; the following year, he was reported in Zaragoza; in 1532. He apparently preached in Germany, 'where he would also argue with many Lutherans.' He expressed the sufferings of the common people with exhortations to sorrow for sin and penance, dramatic references to the passion of Christ, and announcements of impending disasters." [1]

Brandano had a particular antipathy toward the rise of the usury banks which he blamed on the Medici. Whether because, since the days of Dante's *Inferno*, the sterility of usury was regarded as equivalent to sodomy, or due to having knowledge of actual homosexual acts by Medici Pope Clement VII, during Lent of 1527 he preached against the pontiff in Rome. For his trouble, Clement had him tossed into the Tiber river chained inside a chest. Legend has it that he survived the ordeal and emerged from the water unharmed.

During Holy Week in the same year Rome experienced what were regarded as ominous portents, including lighting strikes on the Vatican. Consequently, it was not a relaxed atmosphere when, as Clement VII was, per the annual papal custom, blessing the crowds on Maundy Thursday, Brandano da Petroio approached him and shouted, *"Bastardo sodomita! Per i tuoi peccati Roma sarà distrutta"* (Sodomite bastard! For your sins Rome will be destroyed").

He was immediately seized by Clement's Swiss Guards and jailed, an arrest which did not sit well with the large crowds of penitents gathered at St. Peter's. For fear of disorder, he was released to fanfare, as "a show of mercy" by the pope. This was a ruse, however. Three days later, on Easter Sunday, the pope had him quietly apprehended and imprisoned. Concerning whether it was intended that this should be a sentence of life imprisonment, the historical record is silent. What we do know is that a few weeks after Brandano had thundered his prophecy in the face of Clement VII, and while he languished in the pope's prison, the armies of the night approached the gates of Rome. Over the next several months the city would experience death and destruction on a scale seldom seen since the fall of the Roman empire and the invasion of the pagan hordes. Brandano da Petroio's prophecy was fulfilled in what has come to be known to posterity as the "Sack of Rome." Roberto de Mattei provides this account:

---

[1] Cf. Gaspare De Caro, "Bartolomeo da Petroio, detto Brandano," in *Il Dizionario Biografico degli Italiani* (1964), vol. 6, pp. 752-755.

"On Sunday May 9, 1527, an army descending from Lombardy reached the Janiculum. The (Catholic Holy Roman) Emperor, Charles V, enraged at Pope Clement VII's political alliance with his adversary, the King of France, Francis I, had moved an army against the capital of Christendom. That evening the sun set for the last time on the dazzling beauties of Renaissance Rome. About 20,000 men, Italians, Spaniards and Germans, among whom were the Landsknecht mercenaries of the Lutheran faith, were preparing to launch an attack on the Eternal City. Their commander had given them license to sack the city.

"The Swiss Guards lined up around the Vatican Obelisk, resolute in their vow to remain faithful unto death. The last of them sacrificed their lives at the high altar in St. Peter's Basilica. Their resistance allowed the Pope along with some cardinals, the chance of escape. Across the Passetto di Borgo, the connecting road between the Vatican and Castel Sant'Angelo, Clement VII reached the fortress, the only bastion left against the enemy. From the height of the terraces, the Pope witnessed the terrible slaughter which initiated with the massacre of those who were crowding around the gates of the Castle looking for refuge, while the sick of Santo Spirito Hospital in Sassia were massacred, pierced by spears and swords.

"This unlimited license to steal and kill lasted eight days and the occupation of the city nine months. We read in a Veneto account of May 10, 1527, reported by Ludwig von Pastor, [2] "Hell is nothing in comparison with the appearance Rome currently presents" The religious were the main victims of the Landsknechts' fury. Cardinals' palaces were plundered, churches profaned, priests and monks killed or made slaves, nuns raped and sold at markets. Obscene parodies of religious ceremonies were seen, chalices for Mass were used to get drunk amidst blasphemies. Sacred Hosts were roasted in a pan and fed to animals, the tombs of saints were violated, heads of the Apostles, such as St. Andrew, were used for playing football on the streets. A donkey was dressed up in ecclesiastical robes and led to the altar of a church. The priest who refused to give it

---

[2] *The History of Popes*, (Desclée, Rome 1942), vol. IV, 2, p. 261.

Communion was hacked to pieces. The City was outraged in its religious symbols and in its most sacred memories.' [3]

"...On October 17 the imperial troops abandoned a city in ruins. A Spanish eyewitness gives us a terrifying picture of the City a month after the Sack: 'In Rome, the capital of Christendom, not one bell is ringing, the churches are not open, Mass is not being said and there are no Sundays nor feast days. The rich merchant shops are used as horse stables, the most splendid palaces are devastated, many houses burnt, in others the doors and windows broken up and taken away, the streets transformed into dung-heaps. The stench of cadavers is horrible: men and beasts have the same burials; in churches I saw bodies gnawed at by dogs. I don't know how else to compare this, other than to the destruction of Jerusalem. Now I recognize the justice of God, who does not forget, even if He arrives late. In Rome all sins were committed quite openly: sodomy, simony, idolatry, hypocrisy and deceit; thus we cannot believe that this all happened by chance; but for Divine justice". [4]

"...Everyone understood that it was a chastisement from Heaven. There were no lack of premonitory warnings: lightening striking the Vatican and the appearance of a hermit, Brandano da Petroio, venerated by the crowds as 'Christ's Madman,' who, on Holy Thursday 1527, while Clement VII was blessing the crowds in St. Peter's shouted: "Sodomite bastard, for your sins Rome will be destroyed. Confess and convert, for in fourteen days the wrath of God will fall upon you and the City." [5]

Brandano had been freed. He was released "during the sack by the mercenaries who seemed to have an extraordinary respect..."

After the rampaging troops of the Holy Roman Emperor departed, calm was restored and the destruction in Rome was surveyed. In the following March (1528), Brandano followed

---

[3] Cf. André Chastel, *The Sack of Rome*, (Einaudi, Turin, 1983); and Umberto Roberto, *The Sack of the City from the Gauls to the Landsknechts*, (Laterza, Bari, 2012).

[4] L. von Pastor, *History of Popes*, op. cit., p. 278.

[5] Roberto de Mattei, (transl. Francesca Romana), *Corrispondenza Romana*, December 3, 2015, http://rorate-caeli.blogspot.com

Pope Clement to Orvieto, where the remains of the papal court had been temporarily established, and haunted him there with more public preaching against his pontificate; only now the pope did not hazard to harm him.

Brandano's polemic against the rich and the corrupt continued to take the form of dramatic gestures of revolt and menace: as in Zaragoza, in 1531, when he called on the surrender of the usurious 'loot of all the religious and the rich.' So too in Bologna, the following year, when he preached against the clergy collections for the establishment of the *monte' di pietá* bank, an institution which he detested. He transformed it into a collection for the poor of Bologna, distributing the monies directly to them. [6]

In 1539 the tatterdemalion ceased his peripateticism and settled in Siena, his birthplace, where he enjoyed the protection of the people, and of the local nobility. He is reputed late in life to have joined the Congregation of the Augustinians of Lecceto. He worked in Siena's hospital of Santa Maria della Scala until he became too weak to do so. He died of natural causes on May 24, 1554, aged sixty-eight.

His body lay in state for three days in the Church of St. Martin before his burial, and here we encounter something of a minor mystery. Brandano asked that the location of his grave be left unknown, though whether from reasons of humility, or apprehension over the likelihood of the desecration of his remains by his enemies, has not been determined.

In 1612 local church authorities in Siena issued an edict proclaiming him "Blessed Brandano." This recognition of his sanctity was never confirmed by any pontiff however, and therefore he remains officially, perhaps as he would wish to be known, simply as Brother Brandano.

Historian Judith Hook has penned his most pithy epitaph: "Bartolomeo Carosi da Petroio, known to the Sienese as Brandano (Brendan), whose opposition to urban values was as staunch as any medieval saint. His hatred of the market knew no bounds and he attributed all human misery to banks." [7]

---

[6] Cf. De Caro, op.cit.

[7] Judith Hook, *Siena: A City and Its History* (1979), p. 137.

Chapter XVIII

An Occult Miscellany

I

A Commentary on a Kabbalistic image printed in the Syriac New Testament

The cover of this book reprints an illustration from the *Liber sacrosancti evangelii de Iesu Christo Domino* of 1555, which marked the first time in the West that the *Peshitta* ("simple") edition of the New Testament in Syriac (a variant of Aramaic), was published, and which caused a sensation in Europe and Britain. [1] Our cover reprints the woodcut which precedes the Gospel of John in this Syriac New Testament. This illustration was added to the text by two of the Church of Rome's Kabbalists. It is the most elaborate of the volume's six illustrations. It portrays the evangelist at the foot of a crucifix made to resemble a *Sefiroth*, emanating symbolic Kabbalistic representations of each of Jesus Christ's wounds. It is one of the most unabashed symbols of the Church of Rome's Kabbalistic orientation outside of the secret archives of the Vatican itself.

The volume containing the illustration was funded by the future Holy Roman Emperor, Ferdinand I, as part of what was known at the time as the Catholic school of "Orientalism." The Syriac New Testament was dedicated to "Ferdinand, King of Hungary and Bohemia, Archduke of Austria and Duke of Burgundy." Ostensibly published for Syriac-speaking Christians who had long sought a New Testament in their own language, with the inclusion of the Kabbalistic illustration, the book was an opportunity for visually propagating a Renaissance *revelation*: the identification of Jesus Christ with Kabbalistic arcana.

---

[1] The first edition had a print-run of one thousand copies, of which three hundred were given to Moses of Mardin to take to the Patriarch of Antioch. A second edition was produced by Michael Zimmermann ("Cymbermannus"), in 1562, after obtaining an imperial license to use the prized Syriac type.

This was similar to the propaganda by which Reuchlin's Kabbalism had been puffed in Christendom: as a progressive development in the language arts. With the publication of the Syriac New Testament, the Kabbalah/Christ symbolism printed within it was given wide dissemination by virtue of its inclusion in what became a treasured volume in the library of the leading Orientalists of the age. In both Reuchlin's case and here, with this Syriac text, moral objections by true Catholics to the introduction of Kabbalistic gnosis were characterized as the reactionary ignorance of backward ultraconservatives who were obstructing Renaissance learning and progress.

Teseo Ambrogio (1469-1540), Canon of the Lateran Church, and "Egidio da Viterbo" (Cardinal Giles of Viterbo), "were the main scholars in the construction of Orientalism, within which the first printed Syriac New Testament was produced...This *editio princeps* of the first printed Syriac New Testament was the product of...cooperation between a Syriac scribe sent by the Patriarch of Antioch, Moses of Mardin, and two (Catholic) scholars, (Rev. Fr.) Guillaume Postel (1510-1581), and Johann Albrecht Widmanstetter (1506-1557), working under the patronage of Ferdinand I...The Gospel of John...is illustrated with the Sefirotic tree (a *sefirot* being a divine incarnation of God in the Kabbalah), which is a Tree of Life with ten attributes..." [2]

"...the northern scholars who had been involved in the production in Vienna of the 1555 e*ditio princeps* of the Syriac New Testament...are most helpfully characterized as Christian Kabbalists." [3]

---

[2] Cf. Max Engammare, *Renaissance Quarterly* (Winter, 2008), p. 1315.

[3] Robert J. Wilkinson, *The Kabbalistic Scholars of the Antwerp Polyglot* (2007).

Widmanstetter, with help from Postel,[4] published the superb *editio princeps* of the Syriac New Testament in Vienna in 1555. The edition features a symbolic Kabbalistic illustration, a woodcut of the Apostle John receiving the inspiration for his Gospel, which links both a crucifix and a *sefirotic* tree, "thus neatly symbolizing the confluence of Christian gospel and Jewish mysticism." [5]

"The Kabbalistic symbolism in the illustration, making the Crucifixion and the wounds of Christ analogous to the Ten Sefiroth of the Kabbalah is ascribed to Postel, who claimed it as his own work in *De Magia orientali*: 'Postel writes mentioning the editio princeps and the Sefirotic Tree as his work.'

"The symbolism includes the chalice of the Holy Sacrifice of the Mass, 'marking the point of contact between upper and lower worlds. The world is clearly represented by the orb and the Zodiac band and set in front of it is the Menorah. The Evangelist's symbol, the eagle, is present wearing a Hapsburg shield on its breast." [6]

---

[4] Catholic priest Guillaume Postel contributed to the rise of Rosicrucianism, having exerted a significant influence on several circles linked to the Rosicrucian movement: "The meaning of the mysterious name of the (Rosicrucian) Brotherhood seems to have a relationship to Postel and his self-designated name Rorispergius...both *ros* and *rosa* are significant for Postel. By his name Rorispergius, Postel claimed to be the one chosen to scatter God's dew (*ros*)...Postel constantly uses the word *ros* in the context of resurrection and rebirth, or a general resurrection of mankind into a new spiritual man (which) was the very foundation of the general reformation or rebirth which the Rosicrucian documents proclaim...In 1623 Gabriel Naudé, in his *Instruction a la France sur verité de la Roze-Croix*...devotes ten pages in his rather short book to Postel...indicative that Postel had been associated in the minds of his contemporaries with the strange new movement, the Rosicrucians, and that this association continued into the seventeenth century and later...Variations of Postel's symbol(ism) can be seen in numerous Rosicrucian documents...The documents and drawings associated with Rosicrucianism have their counterparts in texts of Postel..the language which Postel uses to describe...the 'chemical marriage of the sun and the moon....Frances Yates numbers him among the Illuminati in *The Rosicrucian Enlightenment*." Cf. Marion L. Kuntz, *Guillaume Postel: Prophet of the Restitution of All Things* (1981), pp. 106 and 174-177.

[5] Robert J. Wilkinson, *The Kabbalistic Scholars*, pp. 77-78.

[6] Robert J. Wilkinson, *Orientalism, Aramaic and Kabbalah in the Catholic Reformation*, pp. 184-185.

"At the top, the illustration carries the words, *Quis expansis in cruce manibus, traxisti omnia ad te Secula* ('Thou who spreading out thy hands upon the Cross, drew all the ages to thyself'). This expression is Patristic, rather than Biblical. A version of it was used by Irenaeus, Athanasius and Cyril of Jerusalem, emphasizing Christ's arm, hand or extremities in relation to *raising* the Kingdom of God and *delivering* His people." [7]

Postel's colleague, Johann Albrecht Widmanstetter (1506-1557), was a protégé of Johannes Reuchlin. He studied law at Tübingen, Basel and Heidelberg universities. In 1530 he was mentored by "Samuel Abrabanel (or Abarbanel), the head of the Neapolitan Jewish colony, and deepened his knowledge of Talmud..." He was invited to Rome by Cardinal Giles of Viterbo in 1532. In 1533 he became secretary to Pope Clement VII and then in 1534, the Kabbalist Widmanstetter became secretary to Pope Paul III, and from 1535-1537 secretary to Cardinal Nikolaus of Schönberg. Afterward he was "secret counselor of the Germans (*Geheimrat der Deutschen*) in the Holy See, and in 1541 emissary of Duke Ludwig X of Bayern-Landshut to the Reichstag of Regensburg. Under King Ferdinand I, he was appointed Chancellor of lower Austria in 1553, and later Superintendent of the University of Vienna. He was ordained a Catholic priest months before he died on March 28, 1557. His tomb is in Regensburg cathedral." [8]

In the illustration linking Jesus to the Kabbalistic tree, Postel and Widmanstetter, were faithfully executing the Kabbalistic vision of their patron, the late Cardinal Giles of Viterbo who associated the ten sefiroth with the "Tenth Age"— the pontificate of Pope Leo X. Viterbo believed that as a Medici, Pope Leo was of Etruscan origin and thereby destined for a cosmic role by hereditary right. Like Ficino and Pico and the overwhelming majority of the Catholic occult-conspirators we have tracked, Giles of Viterbo dedicated his occultism in total fealty to the popes, as heralds of what the Cardinal termed the Catholic-sefirotic, "Tenth Age" of Kabbalistic glory. In Viterbo's occult schema, Pope Leo X is hailed as the first pope of the

---

[7] Cf. Wilkinson, *Orientalism, op.cit.,* p. 183.

[8] Cf. Ulisse Cecini, "Johann Albrecht Widmanstetter," in *Christian-Muslim Relations: A Bibliographical History,* vol. 7 (2015), pp. 235 and 242.

Tenth Age, when, "All secrets will be revealed: those of the divine world through the Kabbalah, and those of the created world by voyages of discovery. Mankind will be brought into a new intellectual and religious unity under the Papacy." [9]

Widmanstetter stated in the Syriac book's dedication to Ferdinand (who in 1558 would succeed Charles V as Holy Roman Emperor), that more scholars than ever were qualified to read Syriac, Hebrew and Chaldean. Widmanstadt made no direct reference to the illustration itself. Thus by misdirection, a blasphemous image associating Jesus Christ and rabbinic magic, successfully infiltrated a valuable Catholic volume of the New Testament, aimed at a highly literate and elite readership.

---

[9] Wilkinson, *Orientalism*. op. cit., p. 39.

II

Pa-pa Francis and his parrot familiar

News agencies reported in January, 2014: "Among the newest recipients of Pope Francis' good will is the parrot of Francesco Lombardi, a male stripper-turned-pornographic film actor (stage name: 'Ghyblj'). Pope Francis gladly blessed and held a green parrot named *Amore* that was offered to him by his owner, Lombardi. In the pope-mobile during his general audience, Francis initially drove by the parrot, but then doubled back and took the bird on his finger.

The parrot *Amore* ('Love'), was passed to the Pope. The crowd watched as he (Pope Francis) leaned from the pope-mobile in St. Peter's Square to hold the bird on his finger and bless it. Later, Lombardi told the media that *Amore* said 'Pa-pa' during the encounter, mocking the people's chant." [10]

Wolfgang Amadeus Mozart's *Die Zauberflöte (The Magic Flute)*, which premiered in 1791, featured rituals of the Freemasons. "*The Magic Flute*..is a *Singspeil*—a spoken play comprising substantial music scenes set in a vaudeville Egypt, typically outfitted with hieroglyphic stage sets and partly based on pseudo-Egyptian (Rite of Memphis and Mizraim) Masonic rituals. Furthermore, one of its crucial themes is the contrast between discursive language and some more powerful means of communication..."

In *The Magic Flute,* a central character is "Papageno—his name is Italian for parrot...(he) is dressed in a costume of feathers—can't stop talking, boasting, telling lies...a priest threatens him with the direst punishment by thunder and lightning if he says one word— but of course he can't be quiet for even a minute. When at last the merciful theocrats forgive him his blabbering, and even provide a little wife (Papagena) for him, the parrot-pair bursts in full crow: Pa-pa..." [11]

---

[10] Associated Press, January 29, 2014; and *Time magazine,* January 31, 2014.

[11] Daniel Albright, *Untwisting the Serpent: Modernism in Music, Literature and Other Arts* (University of Chicago, 2000), p. 42.

Papageno possesses a set of magic bells. He is half-man, half parrot and works as a bird catcher.

The opera's libretto was written by Emanuel Schikaneder with assistance from Mozart. The two were Masonic lodge brothers. [12]

"Immediately after the solemn gathering of Sarastro and his priests, Papageno and Tamino are visited by two priests, who ask them what has led them to this place. Tamino gives a straight answer: he is in search of teachings of wisdom, *'Weisheislehre.'*
"The priest then asks Papageno: Do you also want to struggle for the love of wisdom?
"Papageno replies: "Struggling is not my thing. Basically, I really do not need any wisdom at all...'
"Papageno is Hermes Mercurius..." [13]

"When he was twelve years of age, Mozart composed *Bastien and Bastienne*, a small work still performed occasionally; its first performance was in the gardens of Dr. Anton Mesmer, a member of the Egyptian Rite of Masonry whose 'animal magnetism' is today known as 'mesmerism." [14]

"The reigning pontiff, Nicholas V...dreamed of rebuilding the whole city (of Rome) on Renaissance principles...part of the dream was partly realized and the *Cortile del Papagallo* (Parrot's Court) became the centerpiece of a new palazzo." [15]

"We can now behold the massive substructure of the Sistine Chapel, which mounts high into the air besides St. Peter's. A plain portal inserted in the buttresses of the building gives access to the *Cortile della Toree Borgia* (Court of the Borgia

---

[12] M. F. M. Van Den Berk, *The Magic Flute: Die Zauberflote. an Alchemical Allegory* (Brill, 2004) cf. chapter one: "On the Trail of Hermes," and pp. 156-167.

[13] Van Den Berk, ibid.

[14] Cf. Jacques Chailley, *The Magic Flute, Masonic Opera: An Interpretation of the Libretto and the Music*.

[15] George L. Hersey, *High Renaissance Art in St. Peter's and the Vatican* (University of Chicago, 1993), p. 98.

Tower). A few steps more and we reach the *Cortile del Papagallo* (Parrot's Court)...Later, all the papal palaces in Italy, and even that in Avignon, possessed a *Sala dei Papagalli* (Parrot's Hall)." [16]

The "Courtyard of the Parrot" is located in the oldest part of the Vatican Palace proper, between the *Sala Ducale* and the apartment of Alexander VI.

The familiar of the pirate is a parrot.

Rather than using a broomstick, Mary Poppins flies through the air by means of a parrot-handled umbrella.

"Black Magic...has always one definite characteristic. It is the tendency to use people for some, even the best of aims, without their knowledge and understanding...by producing in them faith and infatuation...."

P.L. Travers

---

[16] Ernesto Begni, *The Vatican: Its History, Its Treasures* (New York, 1914) pp. 25-26.

Papageno the bird-catcher, in *The Magic Flute*.

CITTÀ DEL VATICANO - PALAZZO PONTIFICIO
CORTILE DEI PAPPAGALLI

Appendix

The Influence of Neoplatonic Thought on Freemasonry: Pico della Mirandola and his *Oratio de Hominis Dignitate*

Fabio Venzi [1]

...we shall attempt to find references, within the thought and work of Pico, through which, to demonstrate, the link with the Masonic project of the "construction of man." Among the numerous definitions of Freemasonry in circulation, I must confess that few seem to me to be comprehensive. In my opinion, Freemasonry is not an "orthodoxy"; instead, it has the characteristics of an "orthopraxy," a code, to personal and social conduct, based on ethical-moral principles, substantially separated by a real theoretical essence.

In the light of such a statement, where can we find the connection with the thought of Pico? The answer is to be found by analyzing Pico's concept of "Dignity." If Freemasonry is a code of conduct, the dignity of man is a journey, a route, which may lead to the transcendent, to God, or rather, to the Great Architect of the Universe. So, Freemasonry is a code of conduct, but has a transcendent aspect to it, due to its desire for identification, to become nearer to an absolute, irrepresentable. This absolute irrepresentable, is the Great Architect of the Universe

In the Neoplatonic thought, the human soul, is directed, both toward God and toward the body, that is, both toward the intelligible, and toward the corporeal world. These ideas are embodied in Ficino's scheme of a universal hierarchy in which the human soul occupies a privileged, central, place: God, the Angelic Mind, the Rational Soul, Quality and Body.

---

[1] Venzi is, as of this writing, Grand Master of the Regular Grand Lodge of Italy. The Regular Grand Lodge of Italy is affiliated with the United Grand Lodge of England and Scotland, and the Grand Orient of Italy.

The same ideas, are taken up, and further developed by Pico, in his famous *Oratio of the Dignity of Man*. Pico stresses, especially, man's freedom to choose his way of life. Consequently, man no longer occupies any fixed place in the universal hierarchy, not even the privileged central place, but he is entirely detached from that hierarchy, and constitutes a world in himself:

"I have given thee, Adam, no fixed seat, no form of thy very own, no gift peculiarly thine...In conformity with thy free judgment in whose hands I have placed thee, thou art confined by no bonds, and thou wilt fix the limits of thy nature for thyself.... Neither heavenly nor earthly, neither mortal nor immortal have We made thee. Thou...art the moulder and maker of thyself... Thou canst grow downward into the lower natures which are brutes. Thou canst again grow upward from the mind's reason into the higher natures which are divine."

Pico's originality of thought stems from his hermeneutic approach, which is not to be found in any other thinker of his time. In fact, his interdisciplinarity is a unique case in the history of Renaissance philosophy, with his attempts to find "agreement" between Platonism and Aristotelianism, and the religious syncretism present in his own Christian Cabalism.

Pico goes even further, and emphasizes that all religious and philosophical traditions have a share in a common, universal truth. Pagan, Jewish and Christian theologians and also all philosophers who supposedly contradict each other, Plato and Aristotle, Avicenna, and Averroes, Thomas and Scotus, and many others, have had a good many insights into truth. When Pico included propositions from all these authors among his *Nine Hundred Theses*, it was his underlying intention to illustrate this universality of truth, which justified his endeavor to incorporate and defend doctrines from so many different sources. This syncretism of Pico provided the foundation for a broad conception of religious and philosophical tolerance.

...(In) *The Oration*...as the great Eugenio Garin recalls: "there are only a few pages, but they mark an era, ancient and still contemporary. They ask for peace between doctrines, a concordance of beliefs; they tell of the continuity and convergence of man's efforts, to pursue the light; they realize the significance of man in the world, and of his vocation. Man's importance is in his responsibility; in his freedom. Man is the only being in reality that chooses his own destiny; only he affects history and frees himself from the conditions of nature; he dominates nature...The conscious image of man typical of the modern world comes from there: man is involved in the act which constitutes him, and has the ability to set himself free. In this concept there is the condemnation of every oppression, slavery and conditioning."

According to Pico, God did not create man in his own image, as the Catholic orthodox theologians stated; rather, he gave man the faculty to create his own image. This extolling of man's creative faculties, of his chosen freedom, has led many scholars to identify within the concept of "free will," which distinguishes man from the rest of humanity, the most important concept in the thought of Pico about man.

But what interests us most of all for the purposes of this essay, is the ethical thought of Pico, and without doubt the *Oration* can be defined as the quintessence of Pico's ethical-moral speculation. The fundamental similarity between the three fundamental stages on man's path of accession to the supreme good, found in the *Oration* and the three degrees on the Masonic path to perfection of the individual (Entered Apprentice, Fellow of the Craft and Master Mason), is one of the key points of our belief in the influence of Pico's ethics, on Masonic philosophy.

If, in fact for Pico, the first of his three stages is the "purification of vices with the help of ethics," for Freemasonry the first of its three degrees is characterized by "principles of morality and virtue," and we can therefore, rightly define it as a degree of ethics. The second stage of Pico's path is the "perfection of reason, by means of dialect, and natural philosophy," which corresponds to the second Masonic degree, that of Fellow of the Craft. In fact we see, in the Ceremony of Passing from the degree of Entered Apprentice, to that of Fellow of the Craft, the Worshipful Master turns to the Brother and says: "as you learned the principles of moral Truth and Virtue in the previous degree, now you may extend your enquiries to the hidden mysteries of Nature and Science."

Therefore in this second degree, the Freemason perfects his consciousness, through "human reason." The third and final stage of Pico's ethical thought, contained in the *Oration*, is the consciousness of the Divine, which corresponds to the third degree of Freemasonry, that of Master Mason, which concludes the esoteric path of Freemasonry. In fact, we read in the ritual, that the Worshipful Master says to the Brother: "Advancing further, still guiding your progress by the principles of moral truth, may you be steered into the second degree, to see the intellectual faculty of it, and track your development in it, through the paths of celestial science, unto the throne of God himself." And he continues, "Allow me now to point out to you, that the light of a Master Mason is darkness visible, which serves only to express that shadow, which shrouds future prospects. That is the mysterious veil, which the eye of human reason cannot penetrate without the help of the Light, which comes from above."

...We can conclude that, just as in Masonic thought, ethics, the philosophy of nature, and the approach to the Divine represent the principal degrees of consciousness in Pico's ethics, through which man must pass. A first preparatory stage of consciousness, represented by Ethics, that is moral science, requires that man be set free by a passion for pleasure. For Pico, it is only through Ethics, that the destruction of men between different states may be ended, and long-lasting peace be established on earth.

In the next stage, the *Philosophia Moralis* gives way to the *Philosophia Naturalis*, which leads man along the road to consciousness of reality. It is through philosophy that the secrets of nature are revealed to man, and this is the principle function of philosophy. The final stage is that in which human reasoning, prepared and educated by philosophy, will reveal a consciousness of the deepest secrets, concerning the system of the universe.

Who, in philosophy, has represented better than Pico, the fundamental Masonic allegory of coarse stone, after hard work, being turned into smooth stone? Throughout the *Oration*, man is portrayed, as moulder of himself, in an absolutely arbitrary way...

For the Mirandolian in fact, man's happiness does not come from the possession of truth, but solely from pursuit of the typical platonic concept of Eros.

For Pico and for the Freemason, it is not possessing the truth that is important, but its pursuit, the enquiry that we undertake, in order to investigate it, and it is in this extreme display of free will, that one's spiritual power is demonstrated. In light of this, any constraint in religion according to Pico, is absolutely reprehensible, and the *Libertas credendi* is essential, because true faith can only be borne out of freedom.

According to Pico, "even man's sin does not constitute, an ineradicable defect in his nature, because in his nature one can only see the correlative and the opposite of something different, and superior. It was necessary that man be capable of sin, so that he may become capable of good." Pico's fundamental concept is that man, in good as in evil, is never concluded; he may never rest secure in good, and is never in the power of evil without hope of redemption.

Lives, which lead to good and evil, are never precluded from one another, and the decision lies in his own hands: thus, according to a follower of Pico, man's sin is not merely a fault, on the contrary it is an expression of that force which makes the same man capable of doing good. And his freedom may demonstrate all its power only when he is capable of moulding his own existence, and to do this, it is necessary to pass through the various stages of existence. [2]

---

[2] www.cornerstonesociety.com (2004).

Bibliography

Abbott, Walter M., ed., *The Documents of Vatican II* (America Press, 1966).

Abraham, Lyndy, *A Dictionary of Alchemical Imagery* (Cambridge University, 1998).

Adkins, Lesley, *The Keys of Egypt* (HarperCollins, 2000).

Adler, Jeremy, "Book of Splendour," *Times Literary Supplement*, November 4, 2016.

Agrippa, Henricus Cornelius, *Declamation on the Nobility and Preeminence of the Female Sex* (University of Chicago, 1996).

Agrippa, Henricus Cornelius, *Three Books of Occult Philosophy*, transl. James Freake (Llewellyn, 2004).

Akerman-Hjern, Susanna, "De Sapientia Salomonis: Emanuel Swedenborg and the Kabbalah," *in Lux in Tenebris: The Visual and the Symbolic in Western Esotericism* (Brill, 2007).

Albertini, Rudolf von, *Firenze dalla Repubblica al Principato Storia e Coscienza Politica* (Einaudi, 1970).

Aligheri, Dante, *The Divine Comedy*, transl. Robin Kirkpatrick (Penguin Books, 2013).

Allen, Michael J.B., *Plato's Third Eye: Studies in Marsilio Ficino's Metaphysics and its Sources* (Ashgate, 1995).

Altholz, Josef L., "Truth and Equivocation," *Church History*, March 1975.

Amram, David, *The Makers of Hebrew Books in Italy* (London: Holland Press, 1963).

Anderson, Charles A., *Philo of Alexandria's Views of the Physical World* (Mohr Siebeck, 2011).

Angus, Samuel, *The Mystery-Religions and Christianity* (University Books, 1966).

Aquinas, Thomas, Saint, *Summa Contra Gentiles*, 4 vols., transl. Vernon J. Bourke (University of Notre Dame, 1975).

Aquinas, Thomas, Saint, The Summa Theologica, 5 vols., (Christian Classics, 1981).

Armogathe, Jean-Robert, "Caramuel: A Cistercian Casuist," in *Juan Caramuel Lobowitz: The Last Scholastic Polymath* (Institute of Philosophy, 2008).

Augustine, Saint, *The City of God Against the Pagans*, transl. R.W. Dyson (Cambridge University, 2011).

Augustine, Saint, "Against the Manicheans" and "Against the Domatists," in *A Select Library of the Nicene and Post-Nicene Fathers of the Christian Church*, vol. 4 (Eerdmans, 1996).

Austin, Eugene, *The Ethics of the Cambridge Platonists* (University of Pennsylvania, 1935).

Austin, Kenneth, *From Judaism to Calvinism: The Life and Writings of Immanuel Tremellius* (Ashgate, 2007).

Backus, Irena, "Jacques Lefévre d'Etaples: A Humanist or a Reformist View of Paul?" in *A Companion to Paul in the Reformation* (Brill, 2009).

Bagchi, David V.N., *Luther's Earliest Opponents: Catholic Controversialists, 1518-1525* (Fortress Press, 1991).

Bailey, Derrick Sherwin, *Homosexuality and the Western Christian Tradition* (Archon Books, 1975).

Bailey, Michael David, *Magic and Superstition in Europe* (Rowman & Littlefield, 2007).

Baker, Nicholas Scott, *The Fruit of Liberty: Political Culture in the Florentine Renaissance, 1480-1550* (Harvard University 2013.)

Bakhtin, Mikhail, *Rabelais and His World* (Indiana University Press, 2009).

Balas, Edith, *Michelangelo's Medici Chapel* (American Philosophical Society, 1995).

Baldassarri, Stefano Ugo (ed.), *Images of Quattrocento Florence: Selected Writings in Literature, History, and Art* (Yale University, 2000).

Balthasar, Hans Urs von, *The Theology of Henri de Lubac* (Ignatius Press, 1991).

Barrat, James, *Our Final Invention: Artificial Intelligence* (St. Martin's Press, 2015).

Basri, Rabbi Ezra, *Ethics of Business Finance & Charity* (Jerusalem: Haktav Press, 1988).

Basser, Herbert W., "Kabbalistic Teaching in the Commentary on Job," in *Biblical Interpretation in Judaism and Christianity* (T&T Clark International, 2006).

Baumann, Priscilla, "The Deadliest Sin: Warnings against Avarice and Usury on Romanesque Capitals in Auvergne," in *Church History*, March 1990.

Baxter, Richard, *A Christian Directory: or a sum of practical theologie and cases of conscience* (London, 1673).

Bedouelle, Guy, *Jacques Lefévre d'Etaples et l'intellegence des Ecritures* (Droz, 1976).

Beitchman, P., *Alchemy of the Word: Cabala of the Renaissance* (State University of New York, 1998).

Bellarmine, Robert, *Doctrina Christiana: The Timeless Catechism of St. Robert Bellarmine,* transl. Ryan Grant (Mediatrix Press, 2016).

Belloc, Hilaire, "On Usury" in *Essays of a Catholic Layman in England* (Sheed and Ward, 1931).

Bertolini, Marco, ed., *Lodovico Lazzarelli: Fasti Christianae Religionis* (Naples, 1991).

Berger, David, *The Jewish-Christian Debate in the High Middle Ages* (1996).

Berry, Jason, *Render unto Rome: The Secret Life of Money in the Catholic Church* (Random House, 2011).

Berry, Jason, and Renner, Gerald, Berry *Vows of Silence: The Abuse of Power in the Papacy of John Paul II* (Free Press, 2004).

Bietenholz, Peter G., and Deutscher, Thomas B., (eds.), *Contemporaries of Erasmus, Volumes 1-3* (University of Toronto, 2003).

Bjornstad, James and Johnson, S., *Stars, Signs and Salvation in the Age of Aquarius* (1971).

Black, Crofton, *Pico's Heptaplus and Biblical Hermeneutics* (Brill, 2006).

Blakeney, R.P., *Saint Alphonsus Liguori: Extracts Translated from the Moral Theology,* (London, 1852).

Blanchett, M.H., *Georgios Gennadios Scholarios* (Paris, 2008).

Blau, J.L., *The Christian Interpretation of the Cabala in the Renaissance* (Kennikat Press, 1965).

Blumenthal, Uta-Renate, *Papal Reform and Canon Law in the 11th and 12th Centuries* (Ashgate, 1998).

Bogdan, Henrik, and Starr, Martin P., *Aleister Crowley and Western Esotericism* (Oxford University Press, 2012).

Bono, James J., *The Word of God and the Languages of Man: Interpreting Nature in Early Modern Science and Medicine—Volume I: From Ficino to Descartes* (University of Wisconsin).

Borchardt, Frank L., "The Magus as Renaissance Man," in *Sixteenth Century Journal* (no. 1, 1990).

Bori, Pier Cesare, "The Historical and Biographical Background of the Oration," in *Pico della Mirandola Oration on the Dignity of Man: A New Translation and Commentary* (Cambridge University, 2012).

Brackett, John K., "The Florentine Onestá and the Control of Prostitution, 1403-1680," in *Sixteenth Century Journal* (no. 2, 1993).

Brann, Noël L., *Trithemius and Magical Demonology* (State University of New York, 1999).

Brier, Bob, *Cleopatra's Needles: The Lost Obelisks of Egypt* (Bloomsbury, 2016).

Brier, Bob, *Egyptomania: Our Three Thousand Year Obsession with the Land of the Pharaohs* (Palgrave Macmillan, 2013).

Brod, Max, *Johannes Reuchlin und sein Kampf: Eine historische Monographie* (1965).

Brown, Driver and Briggs, *A Hebrew and English Lexicon of the Old Testament* (Oxford University, 1972).

Brown, Meg Lota, *Donne and the Politics of Conscience in Early Modern England*, (Brill, 1995).

Bruno, Giordano, *Giordano Bruno: Cause, Principle and Unity* (Cambridge University, 1998).

Bruscoli, Francesco Guidi, *Papal Banking in Renaissance Rome: Benvenuto Olivieri and Paul III, 1534-1549* (Ashgate, 2007).

Budé, Guillaume, *Annotationes in quattuor et viginti Pandectarum libros* (1508).

Budge, E.A. Wallis, *The Mummy: A History of the Extraordinary Practices of Ancient Egypt* (Random House, 1989).

Bull, Malcolm, *The Mirror of the Gods: How Renaissance Artists Rediscovered the Pagan Gods* (Oxford University, 2005).

Bullard, Melissa, *Filippo Strozzi and the Medici: Favor and Finance in Sixteenth Century Florence and Rome* (Cambridge University, 1980).

Burkert, Walter, *Lore and Science in Ancient Pythagoreanism* (Harvard University, 1972).

Burnett, John, *Early Greek Philosophy* (Meridian, 1965).

Burnett, Stephen G., *Christian Hebraism in the Reformation Era* (2012).

Byrne, Susan, *Ficino in Spain* (University of Toronto, 2015).

Cajetan, Cardinal Thomas, *On Exchange and Usury* (CLP Academic, 2014).

Calcidius, *On Plato's Timaeus*, transl. John Magee (Harvard University, 2016).

Caldiero, Frank M. "The Source of Hamlet's 'What a Piece of Work is a Man!'" *Notes and Queries* 196 (1951).

Calvin, John, *Institutes of the Christian Religion: Calvin's Own Essential Edition* (Banner of Truth Trust, 2014).

Campannini, Saverio, "Introduction," in *The Book of Bahir: Flavius Mithridates' Latin Translation, The Hebrew Text, and an English Version.* [The Kabbalistic Library of Giovanni Pico della Mirandola, vol. II], (Torino: Nino Aragno Editore, 2005).

Campannini, Saverio, "On Abraham's Neck: The Editio Princeps of the Sefer Yesirah," in *Rabbi Judah Moscato and the Jewish Intellectual World of Mantua* (Brill, 2012).

Campannini, Saverio, *"Pici Bibliotheca Cabbalistica Latina: Sulle traduzioni latine di opere cabbalistiche eseguite da Flavio Mitridate per Pico della Mirandola,"* in *Materia Giudaica* v. 7, no. 1 (2002).

Campannini, Saverio, "Talmud, Philosophy and Kabbalah" in *The Words of a Wise Man's Mouth are Gracious* (Walter de Gruyter, 2005).

Campbell, Joseph, *Mythic Worlds, Modern Worlds* (2003).

Cape, Ruth I., *The Jews' Mirror* (Center for Medieval and Renaissance Studies, 2011).

Caramuel, Bishop Juan, *Theologia moralis as prima eaque clarissima principia reducta* (Louvain, 1645).

Carrafiello, Michael L., *Robert Parsons and English Catholicism, 1580-1610* (Susquehanna University, 1998).

Cassirer, Ernst, "Giovanni Pico della Mirandola: A Study in the History of Renaissance Ideas." *Journal of the History of Ideas* 3 (1942): 123–144.

Catena, Girolamo, V*ita del gloriosissimo papa Pio Quinto* (Rome, 1586).

Catholic University of America, *New Catholic Encyclopedia*, 15 vols. (Catholic University of America, 1967).

Ceccarelli, Giovanni, "L'usura nella trattatistica teologica sulle restiuzioni dei *male ablata*," in Diego Quaglioni et. al, *Credito e usura fra teologia* (École Francaise de Rome, 2005).

Cecini, Ulisse, "Johann Albrecht Widmanstetter," in *Christian-Muslim Relations: A Bibliographical History,* vol. 7 (Brill, 2015).

Celanese, Christopher S., "Giovanni Nesi and Pythagoras: Between Ficino and Savonarola," in *Piety and Pythagoras in Renaissance Florence: the Symbolum Nesianum* (Brill, 2001).

Celenza, Christopher S., *Machiavelli: A Portrait* (Harvard University, 2015).

Chadwick, Henry, *Priscillian of Avila: The Occult and the Charismatic in the Early Church* (Oxford University, 1976).

Chapman, Mark D., *The Fantasy of Reunion: Anglicans, Catholics, and Ecumenism* (Oxford University Press, 2014).

Chlup, Radek, *Proclus* (Cambridge University, 2012).

Churton, Tobias, *The Invisible History of the Rosicrucians* (Inner Traditions, 2009).

Clarke, Elizabeth, *Politics, Religion, and the Song of Songs in Seventeenth Century England* (Palgrave, 2011).

Clarke, Paula, *The Soderini and the Medici: Power and Patronage in Fifteenth Century Florence* (Oxford University, 1991).

Cochrane, Eric, *Florence in the Forgotten Centuries, 1527-1800: A History of Florence and the Florentines in the Age of the Grand Dukes* (University of Chicago, 1973).

Cohen, Jeremy, *The Friars and the Jews* (Cornell University, 1984).

Cooper, Roslyn, "The Florentine Ruling Group," in *Studies in Medieval and Renaissance History* no. 7 (1985).

Copenhaver, Brian P. "Astrology and Magic," in *The Cambridge History of Renaissance Philosophy*, edited by Charles Schmitt, Quentin Skinner, Eckhard Kessler, and Jill Kraye (Cambridge University, 1988).

Copenhaver, Brian P., "Hermes Theologus: The Sienese Mercury and Ficino's Hermetic Demons," in *Humanity and Divinity in Renaissance and Reformation* (Brill, 1993).

Copenhaver, Brian P., *Magic in Western Culture* (Cambridge University, 2015).

Corkery, James, and Worcester, Thomas (eds.), *The Papacy Since 1500: From Italian Prince to Universal Pastor* (Cambridge University, 2010).

Cotts, John D., *The Clerical Dilemma: Peter of Blois and Literate Culture in the Twelfth Century* (Catholic University of America, 2009).

Coudert, Allison P., and Shoulson, Jeffrey S., eds., *Study of Judaism in Early Modern Europe*, (University of Pennyslvania, 2004).

Coudert, Allison P., *The Impact of the Kabbalah in the Seventeenth Century* (Brill, 1990.

Couliano, Ioan, *Eros and Magic in the Renaissance* (University of Chicago Press, 1987).

Crompton, Louis, *Homosexuality and Civilization* (Harvard University, 2006).

Cumont, Franz, *The Oriental Religions in Roman Paganism* (Chicago, 1911).

Curl, James Stevens, *The Egyptian Revival* (Routledge, 2005).

Curran, Brian A. et al., *Obelisk, A History* (Burndy Library, 2009).

Daileader, Philip, *Saint Vincent Ferrer, His World and Life* (Palgrave-Macmillan, 2016).

Damian, St. Peter, "The Letters of Peter Damian," (Letter 31), in *The Fathers of the Church: Medieval Continuation*, transl. Owen J. Blum, O.F.M.(Catholic University of America, 1990).

D'Amico, John F. "Humanism and Pre-Reformation Theology," in *Roman and German Humanism 1450–1550* (Ashgate/Variorum, 1993).

Dan, Joseph (ed.), *The Christian Kabbalah* (Harvard College Library, 1997).

David, Rosalie, *Religion and Magic in Ancient Egypt* (Penguin Books, 2002).

Davies, Brian, *Thomas Aquinas's Summa Contra Gentiles: A Guide and Commentary* (Oxford University, 2016).

Davies, Jonathan, *Florence & its University during the Early Renaissance* (Brill, 1998).

Davies, Owen, *Gimoires: A History of Magical Books* (Oxford University, 2010).

De Boer, Jan-Hendryk. "Faith and Knowledge in the Religion of the Renaissance: Nicholas of Cusa, Giovanni Pico della Mirandola, and Savonarola," in *American Catholic Philosophical Quarterly* 83 (2009).

De Caro, Gaspare, "Bartolomeo da Petroio, detto Brandano," in *Il Dizionario Biografico degli Italiani* (Rome, 1964), vol. 6.

De Jong, Mayke, *In Samuel's Image: Child Oblation in the Early Medieval West* (Brill, 1996).

De-Léon-Jones, Karen Silvia, *Giordano Bruno & the Kabbalah* (University of Nebraska, 2004).

De Lubac, Henri, *Theology in History* (Ignatius Press, 1996).

De Molina, Luis, *A Treatise on Money* (CLP Academic, 2015).

Dennison, William A., *Paul's Two-Age Construction and Apologetics* (University Press of America, 1985).

Denzinger's Sources of Catholic Dogma, Roy J. Deferrari, transl. (Loretto Publications, 2004).

De Quincey, Thomas, "Historico-Critical Inquiry into the Origins of the Rosicrucians and the Freemasons," in *De Quincey's Collected Writings,* 14 vols. (Adam and Charles Black, 1890), vol. 13.

Derbes, Anne and Sandona, Mark, *The Usurer's Heart: Giotto, Enrico Scrovegni and the Arena Chapel in Padua* (Pennsylvania State University, 2008).

D'Evoli, Cesare, *De divinis attributis quae sephirot ab Hebraeis nuncupata* (Venice, 1573).

Dickens, Charles, *Pictures from Italy* (Penguin Books, 1998).

Dibner, Bern, *Moving the Obelisks: A Chapter in Engineering History* (Burndy Library, 1952).

Diemling, Maria, "Conversion, Anti-Judaism, Controversy: The Rise and Fall of Johannes Pfefferkorn," in *The Jews' Mirror* (Arizona Center for Medieval and Renaissance Studies, 2011).

Dillon, John M., "Dionysius the Aeropagite," in *Interpreting Proclus: From Antiquity to the Renaissance* (Cambridge University, 2014).

Dillon, John M., *The Middle Platonists: 80 B.C. to A.D. 220* (Cornell University, 1996).

Di Napoli, Giovanni, *Giovanni Pico della Mirandola e la problematica dottrinale del suo tempo* (Rome, 1965).

Doninger, Wendy, *The Hindus: An Alternative History* (The Penguin Press, 2009).

Dougherty, M.V. (ed.), *Pico della Mirandola: New Essays* (Cambridge University, 2008).

Dover, K.J., *Greek Homosexuality* (Harvard University, 1978).

Dover, K.J., *Greek Popular Morality in the Time of Plato and Aristotle* (Oxford University, 1974).

Dowling, Maria, *Fisher of Men: A Life of John Fisher* (St. Martin's Press, 1999).

Drelichman, Mauricio and Voth, Hans-Joachim, *Lending to the Borrower from Hell: Debt, Taxes and Default in the Age of Philip II* (Princeton University, 2014).

Duffy, Eamon, *Saints & Sinners: A History of the Popes* (Yale University, 2006).

Duffy, Eamon, *Ten Popes Who Shook the World* (Yale University, 2011).

Dulles, Avery. *Princeps Concordiae: Pico della Mirandola and the Scholastic Tradition* (Harvard University, 1941).

Dunand, Francoise, Zvie-Coche, Christiane, *Gods and Men in Egypt: 3000 BCE to 395 CE* (Cornell University, 2004).

Dunn, Geoffrey D. (ed.), *The Bishop of Rome in Late Antiquity* (Ashgate, 2015).

Dunn, James D.G., *Neither Jew Nor Greek: A Contested Identity* (Eerdmans, 2015).

Ebeling, Florian, *The Secret History of Hermes Trismegistus: Hermeticism from Ancient to Modern Times*, transl. David Lorton (Cornell University, 2007).

Edelheit, Amos, *Ficino, Pico, and Savonarola: The Evolution of Humanist Theology 1461/2-1498* (Brill, 2008).

Edighoffer, Roland, "Rosicrucianism I," in *Dictionary of Gnosis and Western Esotericism*, (Brill, 2006).

Egan, Kathleen Crozier, "On the Indignity of Man: The Quarrel between Boiardo and Pico della Mirandola," in *Fortune and Romance: Boiardo in America* (Medieval and Renaissance Texts and Studies, 1998).

Eisenbichler, Konrad (ed.), *The Cultural Politics of Duke Cosimo I de' Medici* (Ashgate, 2001).

Eisenbichler, Konrad, and Pugliese, Olga Zorzi, *Ficino and Renaissance Neoplatonism* (University of Toronto, 1986).

Elliott, J.K., (ed.), *The Apocryphal New Testament* (Oxford University, 1993).

Encausse, Gérard, ("Papus"), *Catholicisme, satanisme et occultisme* (Paris, 1897).

Eisenmenger, Johann Andreas, *Entdecktes Judenthum*, two vols., (1700).

Evans, R.J.W., *Rudolf II and His World: A Study in Intellectual History, 1576-1612* (Oxford University, 1973).

Everson, Jane and Zancani, Diego, *Italy in Crisis, 1494* (European Humanities Research Center, 2000).

Evola, Julius, *La tradizione ermetica* (1931).

Fages, Pierre-Henri Dominique, *Historie de Saint Vincent Ferrier* (Louvain, 1901).

Faivre, Antoine, *Eternal Hermes: From Greek God to Alchemical Magus* (Phanes Press, 1995).

Farmer, Stephen A., *Syncretism in the West: Pico's 900 Theses (1486): The Evolution of Traditional Religious and Philosophical Systems* (Medieval and Renaissance Texts and Studies, 1998).

Ferguson, Margaret W., *Dido's Daughters* (University of Chicago, 2003).

Ferrer, Vincent, *A Christology: From the Sermons of St. Vincent Ferrer* (London: Blackfriars, 1954).

Ficino, Marsilio, *Platonic Theology*, ed. and transl. Michael J.B. Allen and James Hankins, 6 vols. (Harvard University, 2001-2006).

Ficino, Marsilio, *Commentaries on Plato,* 2 vols., ed. and transl. Maude Vanhaelen (Harvard university, 2012).

Firpo, Luigi, "Il processo di Giordano Bruno," *Rivista storica italiana* (Napoli), LX, 1948, pp. 542-597.

Fishman, Talya, *Shaking the Pillars of Exile: 'Voice of a Fool,' An Early Modern Jewish Critique of Rabbinic Culture* (Stanford University, 1997).

Fitzmyer, Joseph A., *Romans: A New Translation with Introduction and Commentary* (Yale University Press, 2008).

Flatto, Sharon, *The Kabbalistic Culture of Eighteenth-Century Prague* (The Littman Library of Jewish Civilization, 2010).

Fleming, Julia A., *Defending Probabilism: The Moral Theology of Juan Caramuel* (Georgetown University, 2006).

Fletcher, Joseph, *Situation Ethics: The New Morality* (Westminster John Knox Press, 1966).

Fonbaustier, Laurent, *La déposition du pape hérétique Une origine du constitutionnalisme?* (Bibliothèque des thèses, 2016).

Foot, Sarah, *Monastic Life in Anglo-Saxon England, c.600-900* (Cambridge University, 2009).

Fosi, Irene Polverini, "Justice and Its Image: Political Propaganda and Judicial Reality in the Pontificate of Sixtus V," in *Sixteenth Century Journal* (no. 1, 1993).

Foxe, John, *Acts and Monuments of the Latter and Perilous Days* (1563).

Franks, Christopher A., *He Became Poor: The Poverty of Christ and Aquinas's Economic Teachings* (Eerdmans, 2009).

Franz, Raymond, et al., *Aid to Bible Understanding* (1971).

Fraser, Antonia, *Faith and Treason* (Doubleday, 1996).

Freedman, *Harry, The Talmud: A Biography* (Bloomsbury, 2014).

Freidman, Jonathan, et al., *The Trial of the Talmud: Paris, 1240* (Pontifical Institute Mediaeval Studies, 2012).

Fuchs, Joseph, "Epikeia Applied to Natural Law?" in *Personal Responsibility and Christian Morality* (Georgetown University, 1983).

Gabrieli, Vittorio. "Giovanni Pico and Thomas More," *Moreana* 4 (1967).

Gaca, Kathy L., *The Making of Fornication: Eros, Ethics and Political Reform in Greek Philosophy and Early Christianity* (University of California, 2003).

Galatino, Pietro, *De arcanis catholicae veritatis* (Paris, 1603).

Ganzfried, Shlomo, *Kitzur Shulchan Aruch*, transl. Avrohom Davis, 2 vols. (Metsudah, 1996).

Garfagnini, Gian Carlo, *Marsilio Ficino e il ritorno di Platone: studi e documenti*, two vols. (Olschki, 1986).

Garin, Eugenio, *History of Italian Philosophy*, vol. 1, transl. Giorgio Pinton (Rodopi, 2007).

Garrison, Daniel H., *Sexual Culture in Ancient Greece* (University of Oklahoma, 2000).

Gatti, Hilary, *Essays on Giordano Bruno* (Princeton University, 2011).

Geanakoplos, Deno John (ed.), *Constantinople and the West: Essays on the Late Byzantine (Palaeologan) and Italian Renaissances and the Byzantine and Roman Churches* (University of Wisconsin, 1989).

Geisst, Charles R., *Beggar Thy Neighbor: A History of Usury and Debt* (University of Pennsylvania, 2013).

Gennari, Giuseppe, *Annali della Citta di Padova* (1804), volume III.

Gersh, Stephen, *From Iamblichus to Eriugena: An Investigation of the Prehistory and Evolution of the Pseudo-Dionysian Tradition* (Brill, 1978).

Geyraud, Pierre, *Les Réligions nouvelles de Paris* (Paris, 1939).

Geyraud, Pierre, *Les Sociétiés secrétes de Paris* (Paris, 1939).

Gill, Joseph, *The Council of Florence* (Cambridge University, 1959).

Godman, Peter, *From Poliziano to Machiavelli: Florentine Humanism in the High Renaissance* (Princeton University, 1998).

Godwin, Joscelyn, *The Pagan Dream of the Renaissance* (Weiser, 2005).

Goering, Joseph, *William de Montibus (c. 1140-1213): The Schools and the Literature of Pastoral Care* (Pontifical Institute of Mediaeval Studies, 1992).

Goldberg, Edward, *Jews and Magic in Medici Florence* (University of Toronto, 2011).

Goldschmidt, E.P., *The First Cambridge Press in its European Setting* (Cambridge University, 1955).

Goldwaithe, Richard A., *The Economy of Renaissance Florence*, (Johns Hopkins University, 2011).

Gonzalez, Eliezer, *The Fate of the Dead in Early Third Century North African Christianity* (Mohr Siebeck, 2014).

Goodman, Lenn E., *Neoplatonism and Jewish Thought* (State University of New York, 1992).

Goodrick-Clarke, Nicholas, *The Western Esoteric Traditions* (Oxford University, 2008).

Gordon, John Steele, *Washington's Monument and the Fascinating History of the Obelisk* (Bloomsbury, 2016).

Gouwens, Kenneth and Reiss, Sheryl E., *The Pontificate of Clement VII* (Ashgate, 2005).

Grafton, A., "Protestant vs. Prophet: Isaac Casaubon on Hermes Trismegistus in *Journal of the Warburg and Courtauld Institutes*, no. 46 (1983).

Grama, Saadya, *Romemut Yisrael Ufarashat Hagalut* (Lakewood, New Jersey, 2003).

Grice-Hutchinson, Marjorie, *Early Economic Thought in Spain, 1177-1740* (Liberty Fund, 2015).

Grumett, David, *De Lubac: A Guide for the Perplexed* (T&T Clark, 2007).

Guizot, Francois, "Calvin," in *Museé des protestants célébrés* (1822).

Gundersheimer, Werner L. "Erasmus, Humanism and the Christian Cabala," *Journal of the Warburg and Courtauld Institutes,* Vol. 26, No. 1/2 (1963).

Guthrie, William Keith Chambers, *A History of Greek Philosophy: Volume 4, Plato: The Man and his Dialogues: Earlier Period* (Cambridge University, 1986).

Guthrie, William Keith Chambers, *A History of Greek Philosophy: Volume 5, The Later Plato and the Academy* (Cambridge University, 1986.

Guthrie, William Keith Chambers, *A History of Greek Philosophy: Volume 6, Aristotle (Cambridge University, 1990).*

Haas, Guenther H., *The Concept of Equity in Calvin's Ethics* (Paternoster Press, 1997).

Häberlein, Mark, *The Fuggers of Augsburg* (University of Virginia, 2012).

Hacker, Joseph R., and Shear, Adam, *The Hebrew Book in Early Modern Italy* (University of Pennsylvania, 2011).

Hadas, Morton, et al., *Heroes and Gods: Spiritual Biographies in Antiquity* (Routledge and Kegan Paul, 1965).
Hale, Robert, "St. Peter Damian" in *Encyclopedia of Monasticism* (Routledge, 2000).

Hall, Joseph, *The Peace of Rome Proclaimed to All the World by Her Famous Cardinal Bellarmine and the No Less Famous Casuist Navarre* (1609).

Hanegraaff, Wouter J. (ed.), *Dictionary of Gnosis and Western Esotericism* (Brill, 2006).

Hanegraaff, Wouter J., *Esotericism and the Academy* (Cambridge University, 2012).

Hanegraaff, Wouter J., and Bouthoorn, Ruud M., *Ludovico Lazzarelli: The Hermetic Writings and Related Documents* (Arizona Center for Medieval and Renaissance Studies, 2005)

Hankins, James, *Plato in the Italian Renaissance* (Brill, 1990).

Hankins, James and Meroi, Fabrizio, *The Rebirth of Platonic Theology* (2013).

Harrie, Jeanne Helen, "Francois Foix de Candale and the Hermetic Tradition in Sixteenth Century France" (PhD. thesis, University of California, 1975).

Heřůfek, Jan. "Giovanni Pico della Mirandola's Encounter with Jewish Intellectuals," *Acta Comeniana* 25 (2011).

Hertz, Joseph, *The Authorized Daily Prayer Book* (New York, 1948).

Hess, Jonathan M., *Germans, Jews and the Claims of Modernity* (Yale University Press, 2002).

Hoffer, Eric, *The True Believer: Thoughts on the Nature of Mass Movements* (Harper and Row, 1951).

Hoffman, Michael, *Judaism Discovered: A Study of the Anti-Biblical Religion of Racism, Self-Worship, Superstition and Deceit* (Independent History & Research, 2008).

Hoffman, Michael, *Usury in Christendom: The Mortal Sin that Was and Now is Not* (Independent History & Research, 2013).

Holmes, P.J. (ed.), *Elizabethan Casuistry* (Catholic Record Society, 1991).

Hook, Judith, *Siena: A City and Its History*, (Hamish Hamilton, 1979).

Hornblower Simon and Spawforth, Antony (eds.), *The Oxford Classical Dictionary* (2003).

Hornung, Erik, *The Secret Lore of Egypt and its Impact on the West* (Cornell University, 2001).

Horton, Michael, *The Christian Faith: A Systematic Theology* (Zondervan, 2011).

Hotchkiss, Valerie, and Price, David, *Miracle with a Miracle: Johannes Reuchlin and the Jewish Book Controversy* (University of Illinois Urbana-Champaign, 2011).

Howe, John, Before the Gregorian Reform: *The Latin Church at the Turn of the First Millennium* (Cornell University, 2016).

Hubbard, Thomas K. (ed.), *A Companion to Greek and Roman Sexualities* (Blackwell, 2014).

Hughes, Philip Edgcumbe, *Lefévre: Pioneer of Ecclesiastical Renewal in France* (Eersmans, 1984).

Huizinga, Johan, *Erasmus and the Age of Reformation* (Harper and Row, 1957).

Hutten, Ulrich von, and Rubeanus, Crotus, *Letters of Obscure Men* [English translation of *Epistolae obscurorum vivorum*], (University of Pennsylvania, 1964).

Iamblichus, *On the Mysteries,* transl. Clarke, Dillon and Hershbell, (Society of Biblical Literature, 2003).

Ickert, Scott, *Defending and Defining the Ordo Salutis: Jacob von Hoogstraten vs. Martin Luther* (Archiv für Reformationsgeschichte, 1987).

Idel, Moshe,"Hermeticism and Judaism" in *Hermeticism and the Renaissance*, Ingrid Merkel and Allen Debus, eds. (1988).

Idel, Moshe, "Jewish Kabbalah in Christian Garb," in *Kabbalah in Italy: 1280 to 1510* (Yale University, 2011).

Idel, Moshe. "The Magical Interpretation of Kabbalah and Pico's View of 'Books,' in *Absorbing Perfections: Kaballah and Interpretation* (New Haven: Yale University Press, 2002).

Irenaeus of Lyons, Saint, *Against the Heresies,* 3 vols. (The Newman Press, 1992 and 2012).

Iserloh, Erwin, *Die Eucharistie in der Darstellung des Johannes Eck* (Aschendorff, 1950).

Iversen, Erik, *The Myth of Egypt and its Hieroglyphs in European Tradition* (Princeton University, 1993).

Jacobs, Joseph, and Ochser, Schulim, "The Community Organized" in the *Jewish Encyclopedia* (1906), topic: "Rome." http://jewishencyclopedia.com/articles/12816-rome

Jonas, Hans, *The Gnostic Religion* (Beacon, 1963).

Jones, Frederick M., C.S.s.R., *Alphonsus De Ligurori: Saint of Bourbon Naples* (Liguori Publications, 1999).

Jones, G. Lloyd, *The Discovery of Hebrew in Tudor England: A Third Language* (Manchester University, 1983).

Jones, Malcolm, *The Secret Middle Ages: Discovering the Real Medieval World* (Sutton, 2002).

Joost-Gaugier, Christiane L., "Pico's Venerable Pythogoras: Fountainhead of Wisdom," and "Pico's Version of Pythagoreanism," in *Pythagoras and Renaissance Europe: Finding Heaven* (Cambridge University, 2009).

Jungmann, Josef A., S.J., *The Mass: An Historical, Theological and Pastoral Survey*, transl. Julian Fernandes, S.J. (Liturgical Press, 1976).

Kant, Immanuel, "On a Supposed Right to Lie from Benevolent Motives," in *The Critique of Practical Reason and Other Writings in Moral Philosophy* (University of Chicago, 1949).

Katz, Steven T., ed., *The Cambridge History of Judaism: Volume Four, The Late Roman-Rabbinic Period* (Cambridge University, 2006).

Keech, Dominic, *The Anti-Pelagian Christology of Augustine of Hippo, 396-430* (Oxford University, 2012).

Kent, Dale, *Cosimo de' Medici and the Florentine Renaissance* (Yale University, 2000).

Kiesewetter, Carl, *Geschichte des neueren Occultismus*, 2 vols., (Leipzig, 1981-1895).

Kindleberger, Charles L., *A Financial History of Western Europe* (George Allen & Unwin, 1984).

King, Ross, *Michelangelo and the Pope's Ceiling* (Penguin, 2003).

Kirk, Keneth E., *Conscience and Its Problems* (Longmans, 1927).

Kirk, Russell, "Pico della Mirandola and Human Dignity," reprinted as "Introduction" in Giovanni Pico della Mirandola, *Oration on the Dignity of Man*, translated by A. Robert Caponigri (Regnery Publishing, 1956).

Kisch, Guido, T*he Jews in Medieval Germany: A Study of their Legal and Social Status* (New York, 1970).

Knecht, R.J., *Renaissance Warrior and Patron: The Reign of Francis I* (Cambridge University, 1994).

Knight, Gareth, *A Practical Guide to Qabalistic Symbolism*, two volumes (Helios Book Service, 1965).

Koch, Anton, *A Handbook of Moral Theology* (London, 1918).

Kolbrenner, William Zev, "Chiseled from All Sides: Hermeneutics and Dispute in Rabbinic Judaism," in *Association for Jewish Studies Review*, no. 28 (2004).

Krabbenhoft, Kenneth, "Syncretism and Millennium in Herrera's Kabbalah," in *Jewish Messianism in the Early Modern World* (Springer, 2001).

Kraye, Jill (ed.), *The Cambridge Companion to Renaissance Humanism (Cambridge University*, 1998).

Krey, Philip D., and Krey, Peter D.S., *The Catholic Luther: His Early Writings* (Paulist Press, 2016).

Kristeller, Paul Oskar, *Eight Philosophers of the Italian Renaissance* (Stanford University, 1964.)

Kristeller, Paul Oskar, "Jewish Contributions to Italian Renaissance Culture," in *Studies in Renaissance Thought and Letters IV* (Edizioni di Storia e Litteratura, 1996).

Kristeller, Paul Oskar, *Marsilio Ficino and his Work after 500 Years* (Olschki, 1987).

Kuntz, Marion L., *Guillaume Postel: Prophet of the Restitution of All Things* (Springer, 1981).

Laertius, Diogenes, *Lives of Eminent Philosophers*, vol. I and II (Harvard University, 1925).

Lamm, Norman, *The Religious Thought of Hasidism* (Yeshiva University Press, 1999).

Langer, Ruth, *Cursing the Christians?* (Oxford University Press, 2012).

Langholm, Odd, *The Aristotelian Analysis of Usury* (Oxford University Press, 1985).

Lawee, Eric, "The Messianism of Isaac Abarbanel," in *Jewish Messianism in the Early Modern World* (Springer, 2001).

Lea, Henry Charles, 3 vols., *History of Auricular Confession* (1968).

Lee, Alexander, *The Ugly Renaissance* (Random House, 2013).

Leijenhorst, Cees, "Francesaco Patrizi's Hermetic Philosophy," in *Gnosis and Hermeticism from Antiquity to Modern Times* (State University of New York, 1998).

Leinkauf, Thomas, "Reuchlin und der Florentiner Neuplatonismus, in *Reuchlin und Italien* (Stuttgart, 1999).

Lemon, Rebecca, *Treason By Words: Literature, Law and Rebellion in Shakespeare's England* (Cornell University, 2006).

Lev, Elizabeth and Granados, José, *A Body for Glory: Theology of the Body in the Papal Collections* (Rome: Pontifico Istituto Giovanni Paolo II, 2014).

Lévi, Eliphas (Alphonse-Louis Constant), *Dogme et rituel de la haute magie* (Paris, 1856).

Lévi, Eliphas (Alphonse-Louis Constant), *Transcendental Magic: Its Doctrine & Ritual* (Senate, 1995).

Levy, Leonard W., Levy, *Origins of the Fifth Amendment: The Right Against Self-Incrimination* (Macmillan, 1986).

Lewy, Hans, *Chaldean Oracles and Theurgy* (Paris, 1978).

Liguori, Alfonso de, *Moral and Devotional Theology*, Frederick Meyrick transl. (London, 1857).

Livanos, Christopher, "The Conflict Between Scholarios and Plethon," in *Modern Greek Literature: Critical Essays* (Routledge, 2003).

Lohr, Charles H., "Metaphysics," in *The Cambridge History of Renaissance Philosophy* (Cambridge University, 1992).

Long, Pamela O., *Openness, Secrecy, Authorship: Technical Arts and the Culture of Knowledge from Antiquity to the Renaissance* (Johns Hopkins University Press, 2004).

Lord, Evelyn, *The Hell-Fire Clubs* (Yale University, 2008).

Löw, Andreas, *Hermes Trismegistos als Zeuge der Wahrheit* (Berlin, 2002).

Lowe, Kate J.P., *Church and Politics in Renaissance Italy: The Life and Career of Cardinal Francesco Soderini* (Cambridge University, 2002).

Luchinot, Cristina Acidini, *Pintoricchio* (Scala, 1999).

Luther, Martin, "Trade and Usury" (1524), in *Luther's Works* vol. 45 (Muhlenberg Press, 1962).

MacGuigan, Mark, *Abortion, Conscience and Democracy* (Toronto, Canada, 1994.

Machiavelli, Niccolo, *The Prince* (Cambridge University, 2000).

Matt, Daniel, transl. *The Zohar: Pritzker Edition*, 9 vols. (Stanford University, 2003-2016).

Majercik, Ruth, *The Chaldean Oracles: Text, Translation and Commentary* (2013).

Maifreda, Germano, "The Jews: Institutions, Economy and Society," in *A Companion to Late Medieval and Early Modern Milan* (Brill, 2015).

Maimonides, Moses, *Guide of the Perplexed,* transl. Shlomo Pines, 2 vols. (University of Chicago, 1963).

Maimonides, Moses, *Mishneh Torah,* transl. Eliyahu Touger, 25 vols. (Mozaim Publishing, 1989-1999).

Malloch, Archibald, "Father Henry Garnet's Treatise of Equivocation," in *Recusant History*, vol. 15, no. 6 (1981).

Mallerais, Bernard Tissier de, *The Biography of Marcel Lefebvre* (Angelus Press, 2004).

Mansfield, Mary C., *The Humiliation of Sinners: Public Penance in Thirteenth Century France* (Cornell University, 1995).

Manuel, Frank E. "Pico della Mirandola and His Jewish Mentors," in *The Broken Staff: Judaism through Christian Eyes* (Cambridge, MA: Harvard University Press, 1992), 37–44.

Martines, Lauro, *Fire in the City: Savonarola and the Struggle for the Soul of Renaissance Florence* (Oxford University, 2007).

Martini, Annett. *The Kabbalistic Library of Giovanni Pico della Mirandola*, vol. IV (Torino: Nino Aragno Editore, 2010), 163–218.

Martyn, J. Louis, *History and Theology of the Fourth Gospel* (Westminster John Knox Press, 2003).

Masai, Francois, *Plethon et le Platonisme de Mistra* (Paris, 1956).

Mason, Henry, *The New Art of Lying Covered by Jesuits Under the Vale of Equivocation* (London, 1624).

Masters, G. Mallory, "Renaissance Kabbalah," in *Modern Esoteric Spirituality* (Crossroads, 1992).

Maurer, Wilhelm, "Reuchlin und das Judenthum," in *Theologische Literaurzeitung* (1952).

McBrien, Richard P., (ed.), *Encyclopedia of Catholicism* (HarperCollins, 1995).

McCall, Brian, *The Church and the Usurers* (Sapientia Press, 2013).

McClean, *The Art of the Network: Strategic Interaction and Patronage in Renaissance Florence* (Duke University, 2007).

McConica, James K., "John Fisher," in *Contemporaries of Erasmus* (University of Toronto, 1985).

McGinn, Bernard, "Cabalists and Christians" in *Jewish Christians and Christian Jews* (1994),

McKnight, Stephen A. "Ficino, Pico, and the New God: Anthropos," in *Sacralizing the Secular: The Renaissance Origins of Modernity* (Louisiana State University Press, 1989).

McKnight, Stephen A., *The Modern Age and the Recovery of Ancient Wisdom* (University of Missouri, 1991).

McIntosh, Christopher, *Eliphas Lévi and the French Occult Revival* (State University of New York, 2011).

McIntosh, Christopher, *The Rosicrucians: The History, Mythology and Rituals of an Esoteric Order* (Weiser, 1998).

Medvedev, Igor P., *Neue philosophische Ansätze im späten Byanz* (1981).

Menéndez Pelayo, Marcelino, *Historia de los heterodoxos espanoles* (Madrid, 1992).

Menning, Carol Bresnahan, "The Monte's 'Monte': The Early Supporters of Florence's Monte di Pietá," in *Sixteenth Century Journal* (no. 4, 1992).

Meyrick, Frederick, *Moral and Devotional Theology of the Church of Rome* (London, 1857).

Meyrick, Frederick, "St. Alphonusus de' Liguori's 'Glories of Mary," *Christian Remembrancer,* October, 1855, in *The Christian Remembrancer,* Vol. XXX (London, 1855).

Miller, James D., *Singularity Rising* (2012).

Mills, Robert, *Seeing Sodomy in the Middle Ages* (University of Chicago, 2015).

Mirandola, Giovanni Pico, *On the Dignity of Man,* (trans. Charles Glenn Wallace; 1998).

Mirandola, Giovanni Pico, "Proem to the Third Book, Third Exposition: Of the Angelic and Invisible World" in *On the Dignity of Man, On Being and the One, Heptaplus,* transl. by Douglas Carmichael et al. (Bobbs-Merrill, 1965).

Mirandola, Gioovanni Pico, "The Nine Hundred Theses," in *Syncretism in the West: Pico's 900 Theses* (Medieval and Renaissance Texts, 1998).

Mitchell, R.J., The *Laurels and the Tiara: Pope Pius II, 1405-1464* (Doubleday, 1962).

Mithridates, Flavius, *The Book of Bahir* (Institut für Judaistik, 2005).

Molho, Anthony, *Florentine Public Finances in the Early Renaissance* (Harvard University, 1971).

Molnar, Thomas, "The Gnostic Tradition and Renaissance Occultism" in *The Journal of Christian Reconstruction* (Winter, 1974).

Molnar, Thomas, *The Pagan Temptation* (Eerdman's, 1987).

Molnar, Thomas, *Utopia: The Perennial Heresy* (Sheed and Ward, 1967).

Monfasani, J., "A tale of two books: Bessarion's *In Calumniatorem Platonis* and George of Trebizond's *Comparatio Philosophorum Platonis et Aristotelis,*" in *Renaissance Studies 22* (2008).

Montgomery, John Warwick, *Principalities and Powers* (Bethany Fellowship, 1973).

More, Henry, *Conjectura Cabbalistica* (London, 1653).

Moreira, Isabel, *Heaven's Purge: Purgatory in Late Antiquity* (Oxford University, 2010).

Moreschini, Claudio, *Hermes Christianus: The Intermingling of Hermetic Piety and Christian Thought* (Brepols, 2012).

Morrisson, Mark S., *Modern Alchemy: Occultism and the Emergence of Atomic Theory* (Oxford University, 2007).

Morley, Henry, *The Life of Henry Cornelius Agrippa* (Chapman and Hall, 1856).

Mormando, Franco, *Bernini: His Life and His Rome* (University of Chicago, 2001).

Mosheim, Johann Lorenz von, *Ecclesiastic History Ancient and Modern*, transl. Archibald MacLaine (London, 1782), vol. 5.

Muggeridge, Anne Roche, *The Desolate City: Revolution in the Catholic Church* (Harper & Row, 1986).

Myers, Ellen, "Thomas Molnar: A Christian Scholar for our Time," in *Creation Social Science & Humanities Society Quarterly Journal*, (vol. 9, no. 4, 1987).

Najemy, John M., *A History of Florence: 1200-1575* (Wiley-Blackwell, 2008).

Najemy, John M., *Corporatism and Consensus in Florentine Electoral Politics, 1280-1400* (University of North Carolina, 1982).

Netanel, Neil Weinstock, *From Maimonides to Microsoft: The Jewish Law of Copyright* (Oxford University, 2016).

Neusner, Jacob, *A History of the Mishnaic Law of Purities* (Brill Academic, 1974).

Neusner, Jacob, *The Mishnah: A New Translation* (Yale University, 1988).

Newhauser, Richard, *The Early History of Greed: The Sin of Avarice in Early Medieval Thought and Literature* (Cambridge University, 2000).

Niccoli, Ottavia, *Prophecy and People in Renaissance Italy* (Princeton University, 1990).

Nicholson, M.H. and Hutton, S. (eds.), *The Conway Letters: The Correspondence of Anne, Viscountess Conway, Henry More and their Friends* (Oxford University, 1992).

Noblecourt, Christine Desroches, *Gifts from the Pharaohs: How Egyptian Civilization Shaped the Modern World*, transl. Jonathan Sly (Flammarion, 2007).

Noonan, John T. Jr., *Contraception: A History of its Treatment by the Catholic Theologians and Canonists* (Harvard University).

Norena, Carlos G., *Studies in Spanish Renaissance Thought* (Martinus Nijhoff, 1975).

Norwich, John Julius, *Absolute Monarchs* (2011).

Nuovo, Angela, *The Book Trade in the Italian Renaissance* (Brill, 2013).

Obach, Robert, *The Catholic Church on Marital Intercourse*, Lexington Books, 2009).

O'Callaghan, Daniel, *The Preservation of Jewish Religious Books in Sixteenth Century Germany: Johannes Reuchlin's Augenspiegel* (Brill, 2013).

Ocker, Christopher, "German Theologians and the Jews in the Fifteenth Century," in *Jews, Judaism and the Reformation* (Leiden, 2006).

Ogren, Brian, *Renaissance and Rebirth: Reincarnation in Early Modern Italian Kabbalah* (Brill, 2009).

Oleck, Howard L., "Historical Nature of Equity Jurisprudence," in *Fordham Law Review,* vol. 20, no. 1 (1951).

O'Malley, John W., *Giles of Viterbo on Church and Reform: A Study in Renaissance Thought* (Brill, 1968).

O'Meara, Dominic J., *Neoplatonism and Christian Thought* (State University of New York, 1981).

Page, Sophie, *Magic in the Cloister: Pious Motives, Illicit Interests, and Occult Approaches to the Medieval Universe* (Penn State Press, 2013).

Paoletti, John T., et al., *Art in Renaissance Italy* (Laurence King, 2005).

Parks, Tim, *Medici Money: Banking, Metaphysics and Art in Fifteenth Century Florence* (Norton, 2005).

Partner, Peter, "The Papacy and the Papal States," in *The Rise of the Fiscal State in Europe: 1200-1815* (Oxford University, 1999).

Pascal, Blaise, *The Provincial Letters* (Wipf and Stock, 1997).

Pastor, Ludwig, *The History of the Popes from the Close of the Middle Ages: Drawn from the Secret Archives of the Vatican and Other Original Sources* (J. Hodges, 1891-1953), 40 vols.

Patrides, C.A., *The Cambridge Platonists* (Cambridge University, 1969).

Patrizi, Francesco, *Discussiones peripateticae* (1581).

Patrizi, Francesco, *Nova de universis philosophia* (1591).

Payer, P.S., *Peter Damian: Book of Gomorrah, An Eleventh-Century Treatise Against Clerical Homosexuality* (Wilfred Laurier Press, 1982).

Payer, P.S., *Sex and the Penitentials: The Development of a Sexual Code: 550-1150* (University of Toronto, 1985).

Pearson, Birger, *Gnosticism, Judaism and Egyptian Christianity* (Fortress Press, 1990).

Pereira, Michaela, "The Alchemical Corpus Attributed to Lull," in *Warburg Institute Surveys and Texts* (1989).

Persons, Robert S.J., *A Treatise tending to Mitigation towardes Catholicke-Subjectes in England* (London, 1607).

Peters, Edward N., *The 1917 Pio-Benedictine Code of Canon Law* (Ignatius Press, 2001).

Peterse, Hans, *Jacobus Hoogstraeten gegen Johannes Reuchlin* (Philipp von Zabern, 1995).

Petrarch, Francesco, *Letters on Familiar Matters* (Italica Press, 2005), volumes I-III.

Petrarch, Francesco, *My Secret Book,* transl. Nicholas Mann (Harvard University, 2016).

Pfefferkorn, Johannes, *Der Juden Spiegel* (Cologne and Nuremberg, 1507).

Pfefferkorn, Johannes, *Handt-Spiegel wider die Juden, und Jüdischen Thalmudischen Schrifften* [Hand Mirror Against the Jews and the Jewish Talmudic Writings], (Mainz, 1511).

Pfefferkorn, Johannes, *Ich bin ein Buchlein der Judenveindt ist mein namen* (Augsburg, 1509).

Pfefferkorn, Johannes, *Judenbeichte* (Cologne and Nuremberg, 1508).

Pfefferkorn, Johannes, *Speculum adhortationis judaice ad Christum* [Latin translation of *Der Juden Spiegel*], (Cologne, 1507).

Pfefferkorn, Johannes, *The Jews' Mirror,* transl. Ruth I. Cape (Medieval and Renaissance Texts and Studies, 2011).

Picotti, G.B., "La Congiura dei cardinali," in *Rivista storica italiana*, I (1923).

Pincus, Steve, "Gallicanism, Innocent XI and Catholic Opposition," in *Shaping the Stuart World, 1603-1714* (Brill, 2005).

Pinckaers, Servais, *Ce qu' on ne peut jamais faire* (Fribourg, 1986).

Plato, *Plato's Cosmology: The Timaeus of Plato*, transl. Francis Cornford (Hackett, 1997).

Plato, *Timaeus and Critias*, transl. Robin Waterfield (Oxford University, 2009).

Pocock, J.G.A., *The Machiavellian Moment: Florentine Political Thought and the Atlantic Republican Tradition* (Princeton University, 2003).

Pool, Matthew, *Annotation Upon the Holy Bible* (1685).

Popkin, R.H. and Weiner, G.M. (eds.), *Jewish Christians and Christian Jews from the Renaissance to the Enlightenment* (Kluwer, 1994).

Popper, William, *The Censorship of Hebrew Books* (KTAV Publishing, 1969).

Price, David H., *Johannes Reuchlin and the Campaign to Destroy Jewish Books* (Oxford University, 2011).

Proclus' Commentary on Plato's Parmenides, Glenn R. Morrow and John M. Dillon, transl. (Cornell University, 1992).

Provan, Charles D., *The Bible and Birth Control* (Zimmer, 1989).

Prudlo, Donald S., *Certain Sainthood: Canonization and the Origins of Papal Infallibility* (Cornell University, 2015).

Pullan, Brian, "Good Government and Christian Charity in Early Modern Italy," in *With Us Always: A History of Private Charity and Public Welfare* (Rowan & Littlefield, 1998).

Purnell, Fred, "A Contribution to Renaissance Anti-Hermeticism" in *Das Ende des Hermetismus* (Tübingen: Mohnr Siebeck, 2002).

Popper, Karl, "Epistemology and Industrialization" in *The Myth of the Framework: In Defense of Science and Rationality* (1996).

Prokofieff, Sergei O., *The Spiritual Origins of Eastern Europe* (2016).

Quinn, Patricia A., *Better Than the Sons of Kings: Boys and Monks in the Early Middle Ages* (Peter Lang, 1989).

Quispel, Gilles, *Gnostica, Judaica, Catholica: Collected Essays of Gilles Quispel,* Johannes van Ort, ed., (Brill, 2008).

Rabelais, Francois, *Gargantua and Pantagruel*, transl. M.A. Screech (Penguin, 2006).

Raftery, Mary, *Suffer the Little Children* (Continuum International Publishing Group, 2002.)

Ragacs, Ursula, "Reconstructing Medieval Jewish-Christian Disputations," in *Medieval Exegesis and Religious Difference* (Fordham University, 2015).

Ratzinger, Joseph, *Introduction to Christianity* (Herder & Herder, 1971).

Raven, Maarten, *Egyptian Magic* (The American University in Cairo, 2012).

Ray-Mermet, Théodule, *Moral Choices: The Moral Theology of Saint Alphonsus Liguori* (Liguori Publications, 1998).

Raz-Krakotzkin, Amnon, *The Censor, the Editor, and the Text: The Catholic Church and the Shaping of the Jewish Canon in the Sixteenth Century* (University of Pennsylvania, 2007).

Reeves, Marjorie, *Prophetic Rome in the High Renaissance* (Oxford University, 1992).

Reichert, Klaus. "Pico della Mirandola and the Beginnings of Christian Kabbala," in *Mysticism, Magic and Kabbalah in Ashkenazi Judaism* (Walter de Gruyter, 1995).

Reitbergen, Peter, *Power and Religion in Baroque Rome* (Brill, 2006).

Reuchlin, Joahnnes, *On the Art of the Kabbalah,* transl. Martin and Sarah Goodman (University of Nebraska, 1983).

Rice, Eugene F. (ed.), *The Prefatory Epistles of Jacques Lefévre D'Etaples and Related Texts By Jacques Lefèvre d'Étaples* (Columbia University, 1972).

Ridolfi, R., *The Life of Giloramo Savonarola* (Routledge & Kegan Paul, 1959).

Riley, Lawrence J., *The History, Nature and Use of Epikeia in Moral Theology* (Catholic University of America, 1948).

Riordan, William, *Divine Light: The Theology of Denys the Areopagite* (Ignatius Press, 2008).

Rocke, Michael, *Forbidden Friendships: Homosexuality and Male Culture in Renaissance Florence* (Oxford University, 1996).

Rohde, Erwin, *Psyche: The Cult of Souls and Belief in Immortality Among the Greeks* (1925).

Roob, Alexander, *The Hermetic Museum: Alchemy and Mysticism* (Tashchen, 2015).

Rosenthal, Judah, "Anti-Christian Polemics in the Biblical Commentaries of Rashi," in *Studies and Texts in Jewish History* (Jerusalem, 1967).

Rössner, Philipp Robinson, introduction to Luther's *On Commerce and Usury* (Anthem Press, 2015).

Roulier, Fernand, *Jean Pic de la Mirandole (1463–1494): Humaniste, philosophe et théologien* (Éditions Slatkine, 1989).

Routledge, Warren B., *Holocaust High Priest* (Castle Hill, 2015).

Rowland, Ingrid D., *The Culture of the High Renaissance: Ancients and Moderns in Sixteenth Century Rome* (Cambridge University, 1998).

Ruderman, David B., *Preachers of the Italian Ghetto* (University of California, 1992).

Rudolph, Kurt, *Gnosis: The Nature & History of Gnosticism* (Harper & Row, 1987).

Rummel, Erika, *The Case Against Johann Reuchlin* (University of Toronto, 2002).

Rustow, Marina, *Heresy and the Politics of Community: The Jews of the Fatamid Caliphate* (Cornell University, 2008).

Saebo, Magne, [ed.], *Hebrew Bible Old Testament: The History of Its Interpretation from the Renaissance to the Enlightenment* (Göttingen, 2008).

Sagi, Avi, "Both are the Words of the Living God: A Typological Analysis of Halakhic Pluralism," in *Hebrew Union College Annual* no. 65 (1995).

Salza, John and Siscoe, Robert, *True or False Pope?* (St. Thomas Aquinas Seminary, 2015).

Santi, Bruno, *The Marble Pavement of the Cathedral of Siena* (Scala Firenze, 1993).

Savonarola, Girolamo, *Prediche sopra Aggeo con il Trattato circa il reggimento e governo della città Firenze,* Luigi Firpo, ed., (Rome, 1965).

Schäfer, Peter, *The Origins of Jewish Mysticism* (Princeton University, 2011).

Scheck, Thomas P., "Pelagius's Interpretation of Romans," in *A Companion to St. Paul in the Middle Ages* (Brill, 2013).

Schlegel, Ursula, "On the Picture Program of the Arena Chapel," in *Giotto: The Arena Chapel Frescoes* (W.W. Norton, 1995).

Schmidt-Biggemann, Wilhelm, *Philosophia Perennis: Historical Outlines of Western Spirituality in Ancient, Medieval and Early Modern Thought* (Springer, 2004).

Schmitt, Charles B., *Gianfrancesco Pico della Mirandola (1469-1533) and His Critique of Aristotle* (Martinus Nijhoff, 1967).

Schwartz, Howard , *Tree of Souls* (Oxford University Press, 2004).

Schwartz, Yossef, "On Rabbinic Atheism: Caramuel's Critique of Cabala," in *Juan Caramuel Lobowitz: The Last Scholastic Polymath* (Prague: Institute of Philosophy, 2008).

Scotti, Dom Paschal, "English Catholicism and the Dublin Review" in *Out of Due Time: Wilfrid Ward and the Dublin Review* (Catholic University of America, 2006).

Secret, Francois, *Les Kabbalistes Chrétiens de la Renaissance* (Dunod, 1964).

Secret, Francois, *Guillaume Postel, Le Thresor des Proheties de l'Univers* (The Hague, 1969).

Sedgwick, Mark, *Against the Modern World: Traditionalism and the Secret Intellectual History of the Twentieth Century* (Oxford University, 2004).

Setton, Kenneth M., *The Papacy and the Levant* (1204-1571), vol. 3 (American Philosophical Society, 1984).

Seznec, Jean, *The Survival of the Pagan Gods: The Mythological Tradition and Its Place in Renaissance Humanism and Art* (Princeton University, 1995).

Siegmund, Stefanie, *The Medici State and the Ghetto of Florence* (Stanford University, 2005).

Siniossoglou, Niketas, *Radical Platonism in Byzantium: Illumination and Utopia in Gemistos Plethon* (Cambridge University, 2011).

Shapin, Steven A., *Social History of Truth* (University of Chicago, 1995).

Shapira, Yitzhak, *Torat Ha'Melech* (Jerusalem, 2009).

Shaw, Gregory, *Theurgy and the Soul: The Neoplatonism of Iamblichus* (2014).

Shaw, Ian, and Nicholson, Paul, *The Dictionary of Ancient Egypt* (Abrams, 1995).

Shear, Adam, "Judah Moscato's Scholarly Self Image and the Question of Jewish Humanism," in *Cultural Intermediaries: Jewish Intellectuals in Early Modern Italy* (University of Pennsylvania, 2004).

Shear, Adam, "Judah Moscato's Sources and Hebrew Printing in the Sixteenth Century," in *Rabbi Judah Moscato and the Jewish Intellectual World of Mantua* (Brill, 2012).

Shrimplin-Evangelidis, Valerie, "Sun-Symbolism and Cosmology in Michelangelo's Last Judgment," in *Sixteenth Century Journal* (no. 4, 1990).

Shumaker, Wayne, *Renaissance Curiosa: John Dee's Conversations with Angels, Girolamo Cardano's Horoscope of Christ, Johannes Trithemius and Cryptography, George Dalgarno's Universal Language* (Center for Medieval & Early Renaissance Studies, 1982).

Simonsohn, Shlomo, "A Contract for Publishing Hebrew Books in Cremona," in *Shlomo Umberto Nachon* (Shlomo Meir Institute [Jerusalem], 1978).

Slater, Thomas, S.J., *A Short History Of Moral Theology,* (Benziger Brothers, 1909).

Slavenburg, Jacob, *The Hermetic Link: From Secret Tradition to Modern Thought* (Ibis Press, 2012).

Slights, Camille, *The Casuistical Tradition in Shakespeare, Donne, Herbert and Milton* (Princeton University, 1981).

Sommerville, Johann P., *Conscience and Casuistry* (Cambridge University, 2002).

Spector, Sheila A., *Francis Mercury van Helmont's Sketch of Christian Kabbalism* (Brill, 2012).

Spitz, Lewis W., *Reuchlin's Philosophy: Pythagoras and Cabala for Christ,* in *Archiv fur Reformationsgeschichte*, XLVII (1956).

Steinmetz, Greg, *The Richest Man Who Ever Lived: The Life and Times of Jacob Fugger* (Simon & Schuster, 2015).

Steinsaltz, Adin, The Koren Talmud Bavli, 28 vols. (Jerusalem: Koren Publishers, 2012-2017).

Steinsaltz, Adin, *The Talmud: The Steinsaltz Edition,* 21 vols. (Random House, 1991).

Stern, David, *The Hebrew Book in Early Modern Italy*, Joseph R. Hacker and Adam Shear, eds., (University of Pennsylvania, 2011).

Stinger, Charles L., *The Renaissance in Rome* (Indiana University Press, 1998).

Stoltzenberg, Daniel, *Egyptian Oedipus: Athanasius Kircher and the Secrets of Antiquity* (University of Chicago, 2013).

Stow, Kenneth R., *Catholic Thought and Papal Jewry, 1555-1593* (Jewish Theological Seminary of America, 1976).

Stuckrad, Kocku von, *Location of Knowledge in Medieval and Early Modern Europe: Esoteric Discourse and Western Identities* (Brill, 2010).

Suarez, Francisco, S.J., *Tractatus Quintus de Juramento et Adjuratione* in *Opera Omnia*, 24 vols. (Paris, 1859), vol. 14.

Sullivan, Henry W., "Jews of Prague & Jews of Spain: Juan Caramuel's Account of Medieval Sephardic Writings," in *Juan Caramuel Lobowitz: The Last Scholastic Polymath* (Institute of Philosophy, 2008).

Sullivan, Scott M., "In Defense Of The Falsiloquium," University of St. Thomas (http://scottmsullivan.com/articles/Falsiloquium.pdf)

Sweeny, Jon M., *The Pope Who Quit* (Image Books, 2012).

Swetnam-Burland, Molly, *Egypt in Italy: Visions of Egypt in Roman Imperial Culture* (Cambridge University, 2015).

Symonds, John Addington, *The Life of Michelangelo Buonarroti,* vol. II (Scribner's, 1899).

Szonyi, Gyorgy, *John Dee's Occultism: Magical Exaltation through Powerful Signs* (State University of New York, 2004).

Tavuzzi, Michael M., *Renaissance Inquisitors* (Brill, 2007).

Taylor, Jeremy, *Doctor Dubitantium, or the Rule of Conscience in All Her General Measures,* in: *Whole Works* (London, 1847-1854), 10 vols.

Taylor, Thomas, *Iamblichus' Life of Pythagoras* (Inner Traditions, 1986).

Terpstra, Nicholas, *Lost Girls: Sex and Death in Renaissance Florence* (Johns Hopkins University, 2010).

Thomas, Hugh M., *The Secular Clergy in England, 1066– 1216* (Oxford University, 2014).

Thorndike, Lynn, *The Place of Magic in the Intellectual History of Europe* (Columbia University, 1905).

Thornton, Bruce S., *Eros: The Myth of Greek Sexuality* (Westview Press, 1997).

Tietze-Conrat, Erica, "Neglected Contemporary Sources Related to Michelangelo," in *Art Bulletin*, June 1943.

Tishby, Isaiah, *The Wisdom of the Zohar,* transl. David Goldstein, 3 vols. (Littman Library, 2002).

Toor, Kiran, Kiran, *Coleridge's Chrysopoetics* (2011).

Travers, P.L. *What the Bee Knows* (Penguin Books, 1993).

Trexler, Richard C., *Public Life in Renaissance Florence* (Cornell University, 1980).

Trinkaus, Charles, *In Our Image and Likeness: Humanity and Divinity in Italian Humanist Thought*, 2 vols. (University of Chicago, 1970).

Trinkaus, Charles, *Renaissance Transformations of Late Medieval Thought* (Ashgate, 1999).

Toussaint, Stéphane. "Giovanni Pico della Mirandola (1463–1494): The Synthetic Reconciliation of All Philosophies," in *Philosophers of the Renaissance* (Catholic University of America, 2010).

Turner, Patricia, and Coulter, Charles Russell, *Dictionary of Ancient Deities* (Oxford University, 2000).

Tutino, Stefania, *Shadows of Doubt: Language and Truth in Post-Reformation Catholic Culture* (Oxford University, 2014).

Tyrrell, Peter, *Founded on Fear: The Hidden History of a Childhood with the Christian Brothers*, Diarmuid Whelan, ed. (Irish Academic Press, 2006).

Unger, Miles J., Magnifico: *The Brilliant Life and Violent Times of Lorenzo de' Medici* (JR Books, 2008).

Unterman, Alan, *The Kabbalistic Tradition* (Penguin, 2008).

Uzdavinys, Algis, *Orpheus and the Roots of Platonism* (2011).

Valcke, Louis, "Jean Pic de la Mirandole" in *Dialogue* (no. 34; 1995).

Vanhaelen, Maude, "Ficino's Commentary," in *The Rebirth of Platonic Theology* (Harvard University Center for Italian Studies, 2013).

Varchi, Benedetto, *Storia fiorentina di Benedetto Varchi*, Lelio Arbib, ed., (Florence, 1843-1844), 3 volumes.

Vaughan, Herbert M., *The Medici Popes: Leo X and Clement VII* (G.P. Putnam's Son, 1908).

Vickers, Brian, *Occult and Scientific Mentalities in the Renaissance* (Cambridge University, 1984).

Vittorio, Gabrieli, "Giovanni Pico and Thomas More," *Moreana*, November, 1967.

Voderholzer, *Meet Henri de Lubac: His Life and Work* (Ignatius Press, 2008).

Voragine, de Jacobus, *Sermones quadragesimales: Edizione critica* (Edizioni del Galluzzo, 2005).

Voss, Angela., *Marsilio Ficino* (North Atlantic Books, 2006).

Wachter, Johann Georg, *Der Spinozismus im Jüdenthumb oder die von dem heutigen Jüdenthum und dessen Geheimen Kabbalah vergötterte Welt* (New Print Stuttgart-Bad Cannstatt, 1994).

Waite, A.E., *The Holy Kabbalah* (University Books, 1971).

Walker, D. P. *Spiritual and Demonic Magic from Ficino to Campanella* (Pennsylvania State University, 2000).

Wallis, Richard T., *Neoplatonism and Gnosticism* (State University of NY, 1992.

Ward, Wilfrid, "Introduction," in *Newman's Apologia Pro Vita Sua: The Two Versions of 1864 & 1865 Preceded by Newman's and Kingsley's Pamphlets* (Oxford University, 1913).

Watts, Pauline Moffit, "Pseudo-Dionysius the Areopagite and Three Renaissance Neoplatonists: Cusanus, Ficino and Pico" in *Supplementum Festivum* (Medieval Rensaissance Texts & Studies, 1987).

Weed, Thurlow, and Weed, Harriet A., *Autobiography of Thurlow Weed* (Houghton, Mifflin, 1884).

West, John Anthony, *Serpent in the Sky: The High Wisdom of Ancient Egypt* (Quest Books, 2014).

Weinstein, Donald, *Savonarola: The Rise and Fall of a Renaissance Prophet* (Yale University 2011).

Weir, Anthony, Jerman, James, *Images of Lust: Sexual Carvings on Medieval Churches* (Routledge, 1999).

Westcott, Brooke F., *Essays in the History of Religious Thought in the West* (Macmillan, 1891).

Wicks, Jared, *Cajetan Responds: A Reader in Reformation Controversy* (Catholic University of America, 1978).

Wilberforce, Samuel, "Dr. Newman's Apologia," *Quarterly Review*, October 1864.

Wilkinson, Richard H., *The Complete Temples of Ancient Egypt* (Thames and Hudson, 2000).

Wilkinson, Robert J,.*The Kabbalistic Scholars of the Antwerp Polyglot Bible* (Brill, 2007).

Wilkinson, Robert J., *Orientalism, Aramaic and Kabbalah in the Catholic Reformation* (Brill, 2007).

Wilkinson, Robert J., *Tetragrammaton: Western Christians and the Hebrew Name of God* (Brill, 2015).

Williams, George L., *Papal Genealogy: The Families and Descendants of the Popes* (McFarland, 1998).

Wilson, Douglas, *A Study Guide to Calvin's Institutes* (Canon Press, 2011).

Wilson, Douglas, *Papa Don't Pope: Why I'm Not a Roman Catholic* (Canon Press, 2015).

Wilson, Peter H., *Heart of Europe: A History of the Holy Roman Empire* (Harvard University, 2016).

Wind, Edgar, *Pagan Mysteries in the Renaissance* (Norton and Co., 1968).

Winroth, Anders, *The Making of Gratian's Decretum* (Cambridge University, 2004).

Witcomb, Christopher L.C.E., *Copyright in the Renaissance: Prints and Privilegio in Sixteenth Century Venice and Rome* (Brill, 2004).

Wolfson, Ellliot, "Messianism in the Christian Kabbalah," in *Jewish Messianism in the Early Modern World* (Springer, 2001).

Wood, Thomas, *English Casuistical Divinity during the Seventeenth Century with Special Reference to Jeremy Taylor* (London, 1952).

Wright, N.T., *The Resurrection of the Son of God* (Fortress Press, 2003).

Yates, Frances A., *Astraea: The Imperial Theme in the Sixteenth Century* (Routledge, 1975).

Yates, Frances A., *Giordano Bruno and the Hermetic Tradition* (University of Chicago Press, 1991).

Yates, Frances A., *The Occult Philosophy in the Elizabethan Age* (Routledge & Kegan Paul, 1979).

Yates, Frances A., *The Rosicrucian Enlightenment* (Routledge and Kegan Paul, 1986).

Zambelli, Paola, *White Magic, Black Magic in the European Renaissance* (2007).

Zeldes, Nadia, "Sicilian Converts in the Contemporary Mediterranean Context (1400-1492)," in *Guglielmo Raimondo Moncada alias Flavio Mitridate: Un ebreo converso siciliano* (Officina di Studi Medievali, 2008).

Zimmerman, Jens, *Re-Envisioning Christian Humanism* (Oxford University, 2016).

General Index

Scripture Index

USURY IN CHRISTENDOM
The Mortal Sin that Was and Now Is Not

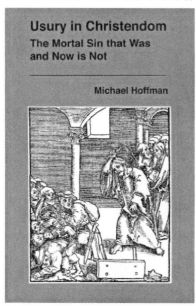

Usury in Christendom
The Mortal Sin that Was and Now is Not

Michael Hoffman

In *Usury in Christendom* Michael Hoffman focuses on the suppressed biblical, patristic and medieval Catholic dogma on profit on loans, and provides new information on the record of early Protestant resistance to the usury revolution.

Western civilization was profoundly disfigured by the exculpation of the charging of interest on debt. The result has been a pursuit of usurious profit unconstrained by the Word of God, the dogma of His true Church, or the *consensus patrum* of fifteen centuries.

Partial List of Contents: Double-Talking Encyclical. King Edward's Act Against Usury. Critical Distinction Between *Ger* and *Nokri*. Christ's Parable of the Talents and the Mammon of Unrighteousness. Leviticus Jubilee. Root and Branch of the Money Power. Escape Clause for Mortal Sin. Usury and the Fathers of the Early Church. Unanimous Medieval Struggle Against Interest on Money. The Dogmatic Third Lateran Council. Council of Lyons II. Council of Vienne. Usury in Medieval Canon Law. Magna Carta's Bishop. Confessors' Manuals Classifies Usury as Mortal Sin. Christian Economics of Thomas Aquinas, Dante Aligheri, Ezra Pound, Wendell Berry, Arthur Penty, Vincent McNabb, John Ruskin. The Unholy Trinity of Florence. The Usurer's Dilemma. The Usurer's Fire. The Usurer's Indulgence.

The Ciompi Insurrection. Manifest and Occult Usury. Mortal Sin for a Worthy Cause. The Den of Thieves Returns to the House of God. Papist Origins of Usury Legalization. Usury Unites With Simony. The Papist Roots of Protestant Capitalism. Casuistry and Usury. Early Years of the Protestant Campaign Against Usury. Biting and Profitable usury.

Some Myths of Max Weber. Early Puritan Resistance to Economic Secularization. Permission for Usury in Late Stage Puritanism.

A Capitalist Summa: Ludwig Von Mises and Ayn Rand. Misdirection from the Right. Primacy of Gentile Usury. Breeding of Money. 1917 and 1983 Codes of Canon Law.

416 pages. Illustrated. Softcover.

For current prices visit us online:

http://www.revisionisthistory.org/page7/page7.html

E-mail: rarebooks14@mac.com

Independent History & Research
Coeur d'Alene, Idaho 83816-0849